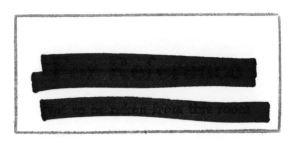

HEALTH CARE ETHICS

CRITICAL ISSUES

John F. Monagle, PhD
President, American Institute of Medical Ethics
Davis, California
Adjunct Professor of Bioethics
College of Professional Studies
University of San Francisco
San Francisco, California

David C. Thomasma, PhD
The Fr. Michael I. English SJ Professor of Medical Ethics
Director, Medical Humanities Program
Loyola University Chicago Medical Center
Maywood, Illinois
Director, International Bioethics Institute
Tiburon, California

AN ASPEN PUBLICATION®
Aspen Publishers, Inc.
Gaithersburg, Maryland
1994

Library of Congress Cataloging-in-Publication Data

Health care ethics : critical issues / [edited by] John F. Monagle,
David C. Thomasma.
p.   cm.
Contains original and previously published articles.
Includes bibliographical references and index.
ISBN 0-8342-0505-X
1. Medical ethics.   I. Monagle, John F.   II. Thomasma, David C.,
1939–   .
[DNLM: 1. Ethics, Medical.   2. Ethics, Institutional.   W 50 H4344
1994]
R724.H344   1994
174'.2—dc20
DNLM/DLC
for Library of Congress   93-34320
CIP

Editorial Resources: Jane Colilla

Library of Congress Catalog Card Number: 93-34320
ISBN: 0-8342-0505-X

Printed in the United States of America

1 2 3 4 5

Love is the superabundance of the highest form of true friendship toward another.

Aristotle, *Nicomachean Ethics*

We dedicate this book to
Marjorie Monagle and Doris Thomasma,
whose love and support
we prize and cherish.

Table of Contents

Contributors

William L. Allen, J.D.
The Medical Humanities Program
Department of Community Health and Family Medicine
University of Florida College of Medicine
Gainesville, Florida

John D. Arras, Ph.D.
Division of Bioethics
Department of Epidemiology and Social Medicine
Albert Einstein College of Medicine
Montefiore Medical Center
Bronx, New York

Margaret P. Battin, Ph.D.
Professor of Philosophy
Adjunct Professor of Internal Medicine
University of Utah
Salt Lake City, Utah

Diane Beeson, Ph.D.
Associate Professor of Sociology
California State University, Hayward
Hayward, California

Clarice Bell, M.D.
Department of Family Practice
Tallahassee Memorial Regional Medical Center
Tallahassee, Florida

Patricia Benner, R.N., Ph.D., F.A.A.N.
Professor, Department of Physiological Nursing
University of California, San Francisco
School of Nursing
San Francisco, California

Jurrit Bergsma, Ph.D.
Professor, Social Sciences and Medicine
Medical Psychologist and Registered Psychotherapist
IMPC, Odijk, The Netherlands
Permanent Visiting Professor, Medical Humanities
    Program
Loyola University Chicago Medical Center
Maywood, Illinois

Robert H. Binstock, Ph.D.
Professor of Aging, Health, and Society
Professor of Biomedical Ethics
Case Western Reserve University
School of Medicine
Cleveland, Ohio

Susan S. Braithwaite, M.D.
Clinical Professor of Medicine
Medical Humanities Program
Ambulatory Care Staff Physician
Hines VA Hospital
Maywood, Illinois

James F. Bresnahan, S.J., J.D., LL.M., Ph.D.
Co-Director, Ethics and Human Values
Northwestern University Medical School
Chicago, Illinois

Allan S. Brett, M.D.
New England Deaconess Hospital
Harvard Medical School
Boston, Massachusetts

Dan W. Brock, Ph.D.
Department of Philosophy
Center for Biomedical Ethics
Brown University
Providence, Rhode Island

Rev. Dennis Brodeur, Ph.D.
SSM Health Care System
St. Louis, Missouri

Laurel A. Burton, Th.D., F.C.O.C.
Bishop Anderson Professor of Religion and Medicine
Department of Psychology and Social Sciences
Rush-Presbyterian, St. Luke's Medical Center
Chicago, Illinois

Christine K. Cassel, M.D.
Chief, Section of Internal Medicine
Department of Medicine
The University of Chicago
Chicago, Illinois

Josepha Cheong, M.D.
Department of Psychiatry
College of Medicine
University of Florida Medical Center
Gainesville, Florida

Larry R. Churchill, Ph.D.
Professor of Social Medicine
UNC School of Medicine
Chapel Hill, North Carolina

David B. Clarke, J.D., M.P.H.
Director, Massachusetts Health Decisions
Chair, Massachusetts Health Care Proxy Task Force
Sharon, Massachusetts

Jeffrey L. Crabtree, O.T.R., F.A.O.T.A.
President, ElderServe
Suisun City, California

John W. Douard, Ph.D.
Assistant Professor of Philosophy and Health Policy
Institute for the Medical Humanities
University of Texas Medical Branch
Galveston, Texas

Charles J. Dougherty, Ph.D.
Director of the Center of Health Policy and Ethics
Creighton University
Omaha, Nebraska

Paul T. Durbin, Ph.D.
Professor of Philosophy
University of Delaware
Newark, Delaware

Ellen H. Elpern, R.N., M.S.N.
Clinical Nurse Specialist
Pulmonary Medicine/Medical Nursing
Rush-Presbyterian, St. Luke's Medical Center
Chicago, Illinois

Mark I. Evans, M.D.
Professor and Vice Chief of Obstetrics and Gynecology
Professor of Molecular Biology and Genetics
Professor of Pathology
Director, Division of Reproductive Genetics
Director, Center for Fetal Diagnosis and Therapy
Hutzel Hospital/Wayne State University
Detroit, Michigan

John C. Fletcher, Ph.D.
University of Virginia School of Medicine
Center for Biomedical Ethics
Charlottesville, Virginia

Joel E. Frader, M.D.
Associate Professor of Pediatrics
Associate Professor of Anesthesiology/Critical Care
    Medicine
Associate Director, Center for Medical Ethics
University of Pittsburgh
Children's Hospital of Pittsburgh
Pittsburgh, Pennsylvania

Cory Franklin, M.D.
Professor of Medicine/Medical Ethics
University of Health Sciences/The Chicago Medical School
Director, MICU/Wd 15
Cook County Hospital
Chicago, Illinois

Thomas D. Geracioti, Jr., M.D.
Associate Professor of Psychiatry
University of Cincinnati Medical Center
Chief, Psychiatry Service
Veterans Affairs Medical Center
Cincinnati, Ohio

Glenn C. Graber, Ph.D.
Department of Philosophy
University of Tennessee
Knoxville, Tennessee

Arlene Gruber, M.S.W., M.A.
Rainbow Hospice
Park Ridge, Illinois
Teaching Associate, Medical Humanities
Stritch School of Medicine
Loyola University Medical Center
Maywood, Illinois

Mary Harward, M.D.
Department of Medicine
University of Florida College of Medicine
Gainesville, Florida

T. Patrick Hill, M.A.
Director of Education, Choice In Dying, Inc.
New York, New York

Kenneth V. Iserson, M.D., M.B.A., F.A.C.E.P.
Director, Arizona Bioethics Program
University of Arizona Health Sciences Center
Professor of Surgery
University of Arizona College of Medicine
Tucson, Arizona

Eric T. Juengst, Ph.D.
Chief, Legal and Social Implications Branch
National Center for Human Genome Research
National Institutes of Health
Bethesda, Maryland

Jeffrey P. Kahn, Ph.D., M.P.H.
Center for the Study of Bioethics
Medical College of Wisconsin
Milwaukee, Wisconsin

Loretta M. Kopelman, Ph.D.
Professor and Chair
Department of Medical Humanities
East Carolina University School of Medicine
Greenville, North Carolina

Erich H. Loewy, M.D.
Professor of Medicine (Ethics)
Director, Clinical Ethics
University of Illinois School of Medicine at Peoria
Department of Medicine
Peoria, Illinois

Roberta Springer Loewy, R.N., M.A., Ph.D. Candidate
Loyola University Chicago
Peoria, Illinois

Patricia Marshall, Ph.D.
Assistant Professor and Assistant Director, Medical Humanities Program
Loyola University Chicago Medical Center
Maywood, Illinois

Richard A. McCormick, S.J., Ph.D.
Notre Dame University
Department of Theology
Notre Dame, Indiana

S. Van McCrary, Ph.D., J.D., M.P.H.
Assistant Professor
Medical Humanities Program
Department of Community Health and Family Medicine
University of Florida College of Medicine
Gainesville, Florida

Diane E. Meier, M.D.
Associate Professor of Geriatrics and Internal Medicine
Mount Sinai School of Medicine
New York, New York

Steven H. Miles, M.D.
University of Minnesota
Hennepin County Medical Center
Minneapolis, Minnesota

John F. Monagle, Ph.D.
President, American Institute of Medical Ethics
Davis, California
Adjunct Professor of Bioethics
College of Professional Studies
University of San Francisco
San Francisco, California

Ray Moseley, Ph.D.
Director, Medical Humanities
University of Florida Medical Center
Department of Community Health
Gainesville, Florida

George B. Palermo, M.D.
Clinical Professor of Psychiatry and Neurology
Director of Criminological Psychiatry
Medical College of Wisconsin
Milwaukee, Wisconsin

Edmund D. Pellegrino, M.D.
John Carroll Professor of Medicine and Medical Ethics
Georgetown University
Washington, D.C.

Stephen G. Post, Ph.D.
The Center for Biomedical Ethics
CWRU, School of Medicine
Cleveland, Ohio

Timothy E. Quill, M.D.
Associate Chief of Medicine
The Genesee Hospital
Rochester, New York

Michael A. Rie, M.D.
Director, Trauma Intensive Care Service
Associate Professor of Anesthesiology and Surgery
University of Kentucky School of Medicine
Lexington, Kentucky

Myles N. Sheehan, S.J., M.D.
Division on Aging
Harvard Medical School
Department of Medicine
Division of Gerontology
Beth Israel Hospital
Boston, Massachusetts

David C. Thomasma, Ph.D.
The Fr. Michael I. English S.J. Professor of Medical Ethics
Director, Medical Humanities Program
Loyola University Chicago Medical Center
Maywood, Illinois
Director, International Bioethics Institute
Tiburon, California

Robert D. Truog, M.D.
Associate Professor of Anaesthesia (Pediatrics)
Harvard Medical School
Associate Director, MICU
Boston Children's Hospital
Boston, Massachusetts

James D. Watson, Ph.D.
Director, Cold Spring Harbor Laboratory
Cold Spring Harbor, New York

Patricia H. Werhane, Ph.D.
Peter and Adeline Ruffin Professor of Business Ethics
Darden School of Business Administration
University of Virginia
Charlottesville, Virginia

Bruce David White, D.O., J.D.
Clinical Ethics Center
Saint Thomas Hospital
Nashville, Tennessee

William J. Winslade, Ph.D., J.D.
James Wade Rockwell Professor of Philosophy in
   Medicine
Institute for Medical Humanities
University of Texas Medical Branch
Galveston, Texas

Suzanne B. Yellen, Ph.D.
Assistant Professor of Psychology
Rush-Presbyterian, St. Luke's Medical Center
Chicago, Illinois

Introduction

This book is a response to requests from health care professionals and educational institutions. Many individuals and schools have been using an earlier publication of ours, *Medical Ethics: A Guide for Health Professionals*, in which important ethical issues for health professionals were examined. Health care ethics as conceptualized in that book includes both clinical and public policy ethics. Since the field of health care ethics changes so rapidly, other critical issues soon began to emerge that were examined in that book only peripherally or not at all. It now seems time to bring out a complementary volume that focuses on biothical issues that have newly arisen.

We are happy to be able to include articles on the genome project, reproductive rights, frozen embryos, HIV, autonomy in long-term care settings, withholding and withdrawing fluids and nutrition, euthanasia, and physician-assisted suicide (or medicide); articles on national issues such as the allocation of health care resources, institutional missions and obligations, competition and entrepreneurship in health care, and rationing; and articles on new methodologies in bioethics. Many of us are struggling with the need for a new method of examining issues in health care ethics beyond appeal to principles. A concluding chapter by John Monagle is devoted to bioethical decision making based on friend-ship. The above are just a few of the newer issues in the bioethical field that readers will find challenging and stimulating.

Special thanks from us must go to our editors at Aspen, Sandy Cannon, Jane Colilla, Amy Martin, and Barbara Priest, who encouraged us to bring out this volume, and to Irene Zaura and Heather Unluata, secretaries of the Medical Humanities Program at Loyola University of Chicago Stritch School of Medicine, for their tireless efforts in communicating with authors and organizing the many details required by the project. Without their help it would have been impossible to publish this book. David Clarke helped us a great deal in reviewing and organizing manuscripts for inclusion in various sections of this volume. His help was invaluable. Our authors, also, deserve our gratitude, since they so graciously labored under a very difficult deadline. Finally, one of us, David C. Thomasma, is grateful to Loyola University of Chicago for allowing him a sabbatical, during which some of the work on this book was carried out.

John F. Monagle
Davis, California
February 19, 1994

David C. Thomasma
Chicago, Illinois
February 19, 1994

Part I

Genetics, Reproduction, and Neonatology

Chapter 1

Human Genome Research and the Responsible Use of New Genetic Knowledge

Eric T. Juengst and James D. Watson

On October 1, 1990, the 15-year clock for the U.S. portion of the "human genome project" officially started at the National Institutes of Health and the Department of Energy. Starting with the project, and within it, is something new for federally supported programs of scientific research, concurrent funding for work aimed at anticipating the social consequences of the project's research and developing policies to guide the use of the knowledge it will produce. As a result, the National Center for Human Genome Research at NIH will quickly become the vehicle for the largest U.S. investment in biomedical ethical, legal, and social analysis to date.

The U.S. National Center for Human Genome Research (NCHGR) was established to pursue, along with other scientific organizations, the international effort to characterize the form and content of the human genome. The information that will be obtained from this research—high-resolution genetic linkage and physical maps of all human chromosomes and human DNA sequence data—will be a resource for studies of gene structure and function that will increase our understanding of the genetic aspects of human health and disease manyfold.

It has been clear since the conception of the human genome project, however, that the process of uncovering this knowledge will require professional and public deliberations over an important set of social policy questions: questions about the responsible use of genetic information. The most immediate consequence of genome research will be the development of new diagnostic and predictive tests well in advance of corresponding therapeutic or curative advances. The implications of acquiring and using that knowledge about individuals raise policy questions at multiple levels within society. The primary purpose of the Ethical, Legal and Social Implications Program at the NCHGR is to anticipate and address these questions early in the life of the scientific project, to help optimize the benefits to human welfare and opportunity that its new knowledge can provide, and to guard against its misuses.

The program's agenda of issues has been drawn broadly, since it extends beyond the conduct of the genome project to its applications (and implications) as well. Thus, the agenda includes basic questions about our understanding of health and normal variation and the definitions of terms like "disability" and "genetic disease" as well as the many practical problems that

Source: Reprinted from *International Journal of Bioethics*, Vol. 2, No. 2, pp. 99–102, with permission of Eric T. Juengst and James D. Watson © 1991.

turn on those interpretations. These problems range from designing responsible protocols for conducting genetic research with large families to extending legal employment and insurance discrimination protections to people who simply carry single (but detectable) copies of genes that, in double dose, cause diseases like sickle cell anemia or cystic fibrosis.

Three major sets of questions have been identified by the program as particularly important to pursue as the genome initiative proceeds.

1. *Issues involved in the integration of new genetic tests into health care.* Human genome research is expected to greatly increase the number of gene-based diagnostic and prognostic tests available to health professionals. The social policy problems involved in integrating those tests effectively into medical practice include developing standards for a number of dimensions of health care. These include standards for (1) ensuring the accuracy and quality control of genetic tests, (2) defining the indications for testing and the design of testing protocol, (3) establishing the credentials of clinicians who perform tests, (4) protecting the confidentiality of information obtained from testing, (5) controlling access to and use of test results by third parties like health insurers, and (6) providing reimbursement for testing and test-related counseling. In the United States, concerns about these questions are discussed against the background of previous national experiences with other widespread screening programs for genetic conditions (such as phenylketonuria, sickle cell disease, and spina bifida) that were put into place by public policy in advance of careful clinical assessments of these services.

The current focus of much of the discussion of these issues is a test for the DNA mutations involved in cystic fibrosis, which now makes widespread testing for CF carrier status conceivable. Be-

cause the U.S. population at risk for CF is relatively large, the professional practices and policies developed with respect to CF carrier testing are expected to establish important precedents for the development of subsequent tests, like the genetic predictors of breast and colon cancer risk now on the horizon. As a result, the center is sponsoring an NIH initiative to evaluate and establish sound policies before the test for CF carrier status becomes diffused into practice.

2. *Issues involved in educating and counseling individuals about genetic test results.* The primary risk that the diffusion of genetic tests poses is the misinterpretation of their findings and the resulting potential for psychological trauma, stigmatization, and discrimination against those availing themselves of the tests. Because the evaluative assumptions we tend to make about genetic explanations of health problems (i.e., that they imply immutable, inheritable problems that intrinsically implicate the bearer's identity), individuals and social institutions sometimes stigmatize genetic disorders and treat those with them unfairly. This risk broadens as the genetic elements of more health problems are uncovered and gene-based tests for susceptibilities and carrier states are developed.

To protect against these risks, NCHGR is soliciting and supporting projects aimed at improving professional and public understanding of these tests and their implications. For example, a philosopher is leading an interdisciplinary team of geneticists and physicians in a scholarly effort to clarify concepts of genetic susceptibility and draw out the social meaning of their different interpretations. In another study, a historian is examining how the language of public health movements, including notions of quarantine and hygiene, has influenced public perceptions and policies regarding human genetics. Other projects involve social scientific studies of contemporary genetic risk perceptions, stigmatization, and discrimination. The conclusions of these studies, and the continuing involvement of those at risk for genetic stigmatization in the program's projects, will help inform the professional deliberations of the medical community and give substance to educational projects seeking to improve public understanding.

3. *Issues of access to and use of genetic test results by third parties, including insurance providers, researchers, and employers.* One way to combat the unfair use of genetic information is to protect its privacy. Because genetic information pertains to the most personal aspects of individuals' lives—their health problems and reproductive plans—most wish to ensure its confidentiality. But genetic information almost always has implications for other people's welfare as well: spouses, children, and extended family members. The interests of insurers, employers, and biomedical researchers can also be affected. As a result, the ethical and legal bases (and limits) of such protections are still unclear. Thus the program is supporting research projects on the legal status of genetic information, the professional ethical issues involved in maintaining confidentiality within families, and the social policy questions involved in the use of genetic information by employers and insurers. Meanwhile, the program is also working directly with the states and federal agencies that regulate U.S. insurance industry and commercial hiring practices to help them develop responsible policies regarding the use of genetic testing.

These issues will all continue to attend new advances in human genetics, quite apart from the human genome initiative. Fortunately, they are also issues for which there are some precedents, at both professional and public levels. This background allowed both of the early science policy evaluations of the genome project, by the U.S. National Academy of Sciences and the U.S. Congress's Office of Technology Assessment, to highlight the ethical and social implications of the project. As their reports point out, however, the human genome initiative will dramatically extend the range of health problems, health care professionals, and patients who become involved in the issues. It is primarily the complexity of that broadened context that gives these issues their urgency as social-policy-making problems.

The NCHGR's ethical and social implications program has attracted a great deal of scholarly, congressional, and media attention as an innovation in U.S. science funding. It has also prompted new attention to these issues by other scientific organizations and international programs devoted to genome research. From a broader perspective, however, these efforts can be interpreted as a natural development for NIH and the other scientific groups who are becoming involved in this kind of inquiry. As the biomedical sciences mature, biomedical scientists' social responsibilities also grow. Scientists work increasingly with policy-makers, health care providers, and the public to anticipate the human implications of the knowledge they provide. Over the past twenty years, professional and public discussions of these implications—under the banners of bioethics, technology assessment, and science policy—have become an integral part of the biomedical research process. Over the next 20 years, advances in human genetics, accelerated by the human genome project, will feature prominently in these discussions. By pursuing the study of the ethical, legal, and social implications of genome research in concert with its scientific initiatives, the human genome research community simply takes up its responsibility to help make those discussions as timely, well informed, and productive as possible.

Chapter 2

The Human Genome Initiative and Primary Care

S. Van McCrary and William L. Allen

During the next 15 years, scientists funded by the Human Genome Initiative (HGI) of the National Institutes of Health (NIH) will attempt to map and sequence each of the estimated 100,000 genes in the human cell.[1] The information acquired as a result of this project will enable physicians to diagnose a significantly greater number of diseases (and predispositions to disease in asymptomatic persons) than permitted by current technology.[2] It will also likely raise the visibility of preventive measures and health promotion as components of standard medical practice.

Some may speculate that the information generated from the HGI will not have a great impact on the daily practice of medicine because genetic testing will be too complex or expensive or because the proportion of diseases having a genetic component will be limited. On the contrary, it appears likely that the foreseeable genetic testing technologies may soon be both cost-effective and available for an array of diseases with high incidence rates in the U.S. population. Such a development could dramatically alter the routine practice of primary care physicians.

Little has been written in the United States regarding genetic testing as it relates to primary care.[3] However, the issue has been explored to a limited degree in the United Kingdom and European countries.[4] This article addresses the following questions: What is the current state of genetic testing practice in primary care? What is the likely course of development of HGI-derived predictive testing? What are the implications of such expanded genetic screening for patients seeking insurance coverage and employment? What moral and practical issues must primary care physicians confront as a result of this emerging technology?

CURRENT PRACTICE

Currently, genetic testing is not a routine component of the practice of primary care physicians. However, many physicians already use the most basic method of genetic analysis, that is, taking case histories and recording them in a family genogram. Case histories currently provide much useful information regarding poten-

Many thanks to Harry Ostrer, Ray Moseley, Lee Crandall, and R. Whit Curry for their helpful comments regarding earlier versions of the manuscript. This work was supported by a grant from the U.S. Public Health Service, National Institutes of Health, No. HG00402.

tial susceptibilities of individuals to diseases with genetic components. For example, primary care physicians commonly use family genograms to estimate an individual's risk of coronary artery disease. Except for single-gene diseases such as Huntington's disease or hemophilia, however, the information gathered from case histories is merely suggestive. In contrast, it is likely that tests based on HGI technology will be much more precise than case histories. At this time, genetic testing generally occurs in primary care settings only in the following circumstances: (1) when there is obvious underlying disease, (2) when particular family histories are remarkable for rare Mendelian conditions with grave implications for morbidity and mortality, (3) when developmental delay or abnormality in children raises suspicions of disease with unidentified etiology, and (4) as part of limited screening among practitioners who engage in prenatal and obstetrical care. However, even these uses of genetic tests are not uniformly applied due to variations among individual clinicians and practice settings. Furthermore, many primary care physicians are untrained in techniques of genetic counseling. Thus systematic genetic screening is not yet prevalent in primary care settings.

FUTURE GENETIC TESTING TECHNOLOGY

Genetic factors probably play a substantial role in common syndromes such as cancer, cardiovascular disease, and neurodegenerative disorders, which affect 30, 40, and 20 percent of the U.S. population respectively.[5] In addition, genetic influence also plays a role in Mendelian disorders, each individually rare, that affect 1 percent of the population cumulatively.[6] At present, genetic testing technologies exist for cystic fibrosis and fragile X syndrome through carrier testing and prenatal diagnostic tools. The widely publicized screening for Huntington's disease uses familial tracing of genetic characteristics rather than actual DNA analysis. Other tests that are available at present include tests for

Duchenne type muscular dystrophy, hemophilia A, sickle cell anemia, and the thalassemias. Tests that are due very soon include those for predisposition to various types of cancers, including colorectal and breast cancer, melanoma, and some leukemias.[7] Germline mutation analysis will be the tracing technology for some of the cancers to be identified. Testing expected in the longer term will likely identify genetic components of various multifactorial diseases, including heart disease, schizophrenia, and neurodegenerative diseases such as Alzheimer's and Parkinson's.[8] Thus, the trend in the development of genetic-testing technology is from tests for rare diseases toward screening for diseases with high incidence, including the more frequent causes of death in the United States.

As new testing technologies become cost-effective and readily available for use in primary care settings, the primary care physician of the near future will have at his or her disposal a vast array of screening services for use in health promotion and prevention. However, the current shortage of trained genetic counselors is unlikely to be alleviated in the near future. This will place the burden on primary care physicians to perform personally many services now associated with specialists in genetic counseling. Thus, the primary care physician of the future may need to be trained in risk assessment and genetic counseling as a routine part of his or her practice.

Issues of predictive value become critically important when considering the expanding class of genetic-testing technologies. For particular tests to be professionally and morally acceptable, it will be necessary to establish minimum levels of sensitivity and specificity. The extreme emotional connotations of false positives, combined with the potential adverse health effects of false negatives, make professional standardization of predictive value in genetic-screening tools a moral imperative. Issues of incomplete penetrance and variable expressivity must also be considered. Common diseases are multifactorial in etiology, requiring numerous adverse genetic and environmental events to occur for frank disease to be expressed (penetrant).[9] The timing and severity of these events accounts for marked variability in age of onset and severity of manifested disease. Primary care physicians must take into account, first, that some persons who test positive for a genetic disease will never manifest symptoms, and second, that even if symptoms arise in particular individuals, their severity is subject to substantial variability. Thus, the predictive value of a positive genetic test result may be limited for purposes of determining the age of onset, severity, or absolute likelihood of disease.[10]

INSURANCE AND EMPLOYMENT: IMPLICATIONS FOR PATIENTS

Physicians engaged in primary care should be aware that the likely proliferation of genetic information regarding their patients has potential to harm their patients' ability to obtain employment and insurance, including health, life, and disability income coverage. Critical components of these issues are use, and potential for negligent handling and abuse, of medical records containing genetic test results. Although insurers currently use genetic information in the form of family histories, the new understandings generated by the HGI are likely to increase both the amount and precision of such information. Since information of this type, under current practice, will be included in the medical record, insurers will seek access to data regarding genetic tests performed on particular patients applying for insurance. Once in the hands of insurers, such genetic information could be used to deny coverage, charge higher rates, or establish exclusions from coverage for particular diseases. Such genetic information will also be included in medical information databases, which share information acquired and to which other insurers and potential employers have access.[11] The type of genetic information most useful to insurers will depend to a great extent on two kinds of factors. Factors of the first type include whether the disease identified is chronic or acute, the probable life expectancy of the patient, and the likely

severity of symptoms—indicators of the amount of medical treatment that could be required and the time period for delivering it. Factors of the second type are used to assess the degree of certainty of developing frank disease (depending heavily on whether the patient is homozygous or heterozygous for the genetic condition) and concern issues of penetrance and variable expressivity—indicators of the likelihood of claims and the dollar amounts involved. Insurer interest in genetic data will also depend on the type of insurance, and face value of the policy, that the patient is seeking to buy.

Adverse consequences could also ensue regarding the effect of genetic information on employment. Many persons in the United States currently receive their health insurance from self-insured employers and employer groups. These groups are not subject to regulation by state insurance law but are loosely regulated under federal law.[12] Genetic test results indicating that prospective employees may develop health problems at some indefinite time in the future could be used to deny employment in favor of persons with "clean" genetic profiles. Courts have recently upheld the ability of self-insured groups to reduce, retroactively, benefits payable for identified disorders.[13] When combined with the ability to predict claims, this practice may have devastating effects on employees' access to health care.

The ethical, legal, and social implications of the potential effects of genetic information on insurance consumers and providers are yet to be determined, but it is probable that the impact will be significant and that changes in both insurance practice and regulation will ensue. The issues are exceedingly complex and are likely not amenable to a simple solution. However, one point is clear—some of the problems for health insurance generated by expanding genetic technologies (e.g., access to health care) would likely be ameliorated by adoption of legislation providing universal coverage with mandatory community rating (i.e., establishing uniform rates for geographic communities based on the aggregate risk experience and extending coverage without regard to individual variation). However, the problems raised by widespread genetic testing persist. Access to employment and life and disability insurance will likely remain a problem for persons whose medical records may lead third parties to perceive them as genetically defective.

INFORMED CONSENT AND CONFIDENTIALITY IN GENETIC SCREENING

Informed consent and confidentiality are two key elements of the patient-physician relationship. How physicians treat information—both in disclosing it to patients and protecting it from those without right of access—is one determining characteristic of whether doctors respect their patients as persons with moral claims. Ethicists have long recognized the three basic elements of informed consent as disclosure of appropriate information, competence, and voluntariness.[14] For purposes of the HGI, disclosure is a critical element of informed consent because the implications of genetic tests that patients might choose to undergo will probably not be obvious to the average person. Increased frequency of genetic testing in routine practice will also highlight the need for improved physician counseling skills. Thus, primary care physicians have a moral obligation to counsel their patients about the practical implications of the new genetic tests in addition to appropriate medical issues. Three general areas of moral and practical concern for primary care providers will now be addressed.

Insurance and Employment

We believe that the possible adverse impacts of unfavorable genetic test results on the ability of patients and their families to acquire insurance and employment are risks that every reasonable person would want to know. Issues that should be taken into account when genetic testing is considered include the following: (1)

whether the test results will be available to a current or potential employer, whether an employee will be considered by the company likely to make costly claims on the self-insurance plan and thus not be hired or promoted; (2) whether a company will refuse to hire a person because of perceived susceptibilities to workplace environmental hazards instead of eliminating them; (3) whether a positive genetic test result will be considered a "pre-existing condition" that could make a person ineligible for certain types of coverage; and (4) whether a company will, for all employees, retroactively reduce the benefits payable for specific diseases to a very small amount, as it is currently allowed to do under U.S. law. One additional important issue is that genetic test results may also apply to lineal descendants, who may then share the same problems of access to insurance and employment that their parents did. Each of these issues clearly has potential to affect patients' lives in highly significant ways and should thus be part of the disclosure process in seeking informed consent for testing.

Emotional Impact

External factors affecting a moral analysis of disclosure also include the potential psychological effects of disclosure on patients' lives. Even if less than certain, knowledge of one's possible long-term future course of health may be especially threatening information that requires particular sensitivity by the disclosing health professional. Some patients may not wish to know such information, and others who initially think they desire such knowledge may change their minds upon careful consideration of the consequences. Thus, a threshold issue in disclosure is a predisclosure discussion of ways that genetic information may affect patients' lives psychologically and socially as well as economically. Such discussions are a routine component of genetic counseling as currently practiced. As noted above, however, primary care physicians may not have access to genetic counselors and may thus have to develop the requisite skills and knowledge to assist their patients in dealing with all aspects of the decision to undergo genetic testing.

To force persons to be tested who are strongly opposed to finding out information about their genetic status would be a clear breach of their moral claims to self-determination. Nonetheless, primary care screening for genetic disorders furthers legitimate health promotion goals. An appropriate method of pursuing such goals seems to be to provide general screening programs in primary care settings (when such screening becomes the standard of care) that offer an option for patients who simply "don't want to know" to refuse testing. Such an approach would preserve health promotion goals without compromising the moral interests of patients with conscientious objections to acquiring genetic information.

Handling Genetic Information in Primary Care Practice

Physician-patient confidentiality prohibits disclosure of medical information, including genetic information, to those not authorized by the patient or by law. The sensitive nature of genetic information may require clinicians to adopt a higher standard of protection for such information than that provided for the standard medical chart. Thus primary care physicians should use particular caution when disclosing genetic information regarding their patients. An appropriate level of protection for such information may require special educational programs as well as stringent recordkeeping and disclosure policies and practices by primary care physicians and their staffs.

Primary care practices should adopt formal office policies for handling records of genetic tests, combined with staff educational programs explaining the reasons for added security of genetic records. An excellent first step toward dealing with genetic information in medical offices is for each practice to adopt a special genetic information training program for all support staff, including nurses, office administrators, and secretaries, to make sufficiently clear the sensitive nature of confidential genetic information and the potential adverse implications of inappropriate disclosure to patients or third parties. In addition to educational programs, office policies and practices might also include (1) limiting the number or type of staff members who have access to genetic test results (and, if office medical records are computerized, establishment of access control mechanisms for genetic information, including passwords); (2) segregating genetic test results from other medical records, if feasible; and (3) personal verification by the physician of a patient's written permission to release information regarding genetic test results. Such office practices and policies will protect patients' interests and will demonstrate physicians' and staff members' respect for confidentiality of medical records and commitment to a legitimate process of informed consent.

CONCLUSION

In summary, the HGI presents dramatic new challenges for both health professionals and policy makers. Practitioners of primary care will soon have large numbers of new preventive tools that may improve the health of patients and raise the usual standard of care. Accompanying this expanding genetic technology, however, will be increased problems of confidentiality of records and informed consent for testing. Providers of primary care should be prepared to deal with these ethical issues within their own practices and should take the lead in developing new practical solutions to these emerging dilemmas.

NOTES

1. Council on Ethical and Judicial Affairs, American Medical Association, Use of Genetic Testing by Employers, *JAMA* 266 (1991):1827–1830.

2. E.T. Juengst, The Human Genome Project and Bioethics, *Kennedy Institute of Ethics Journal*, March 1991, 71–74.

3. J.C. Rogers and M. Rohrbaugh, The SAGE-PAGE Trial: Do Family Genograms Make a Difference? *Journal of the American Board of Family Practice* 4 (1991):319–326; L.A. Whittaker, The Implications of the Human Genome Project for Family Practice, *Journal of Family Practice* 35 (1992):294–301.

4. J.S. Fitzsimmons, Genetic Counseling and the General Practitioner, *The Practitioner* 225 (1981):328–338; D. Siggers, How General Practitioners Can Contribute to Genetic Services, *The Practitioner* 230 (1986):729–733.; D. Shickle and A. May, Knowledge and Perceptions of Haemoglobinopathy Carrier Screening among General Practitioners in Cardiff, *Journal of Medical Genetics* 26 (1989):109–112; E.K. Watson et al., Screening for Carriers of Cystic Fibrosis through Primary Care Services, *British Medical Journal* 303 (1991):504–507; B. Mattsson and E.W. Almquist, Attitudes towards Predictive Testing in Huntington's Disease: A Deep Interview Study in Sweden, *Family Practice* 8 (1991):23–27.

5. R. Moseley et al., *The Ethical, Legal, and Social Implications of Predictive Genetic Testing for Health Insurance: Policy Analysis and Recommendations* (Gainesville, Florida: The Human Genome Insurance Project, 1993).

6. Ibid.

7. H. Ostrer et al., Insurance and Genetic Testing: Where Are We Now? *American Journal of Human Genetics*, 52 (1993):565–577..

8. Ibid.

9. Moseley et al., Ethical, Legal, and Social Implications of the Human Genome Initiative.

10. Ibid.

11. J. Kratka, *For Their Eyes Only: The Insurance Industry and Consumer Privacy* (Boston: Massachusetts Public Interest Research Group, 1990).

12. Ibid.

13. McGann v. H & H Music, 946 F.2nd 401 (5th Cir., 1991), cert. denied, 61 U.S.L.W. 3352 (1992).

14. A.R. Jonsen et al., *Clinical Ethics,* 2nd ed. (New York: Macmillan Publishing Co., 1986).

Chapter 3

Genetics and the Problem of Harm

Jeffrey P. Kahn

From the short history of bioethics we ought to realize that moral issues in biomedicine tend to arise in part as a function of advances in knowledge, skill, and technology. This has been the case in the areas of withholding and withdrawing treatment, decisions to forgo resuscitation, organ transplantation, and the use of fetal tissue, to name only a few.

One of the latest sets of issues to arise due to scientific advance surrounds the broad area of genetics. New and substantial financial commitment to the scientific study of the human genome is a reflection of the importance placed on genomic research and of advances recently achieved. Along with these advances have and will continue to come profound changes in the way health and disease are viewed. For example, as genetic bases for diseases and susceptibility to them are uncovered and tests for them developed, life-style choices and their impact on health will either be (1) unimportant, in that one's genome has been "preprogrammed" to prevent these diseases; or (2) vitally important, in that one's genetically preprogrammed susceptibility may be influenced by certain behaviors and environmental or workplace exposures. With our advancing knowledge of the role genetics plays in health and disease and our in-

creasing ability to change genetic makeup, the connection between our genome and whatever shortcomings we experience will be difficult to avoid. However, this connection is philosophically problematic, since it implies that individuals are somehow harmed by their genetic makeup. The defensibility of this position, along with its philosophical implications, will be examined in the remainder of this chapter. If we view alteration of genetic disposition as morally praiseworthy, or at least acceptable in some circumstances, the "force" of the moral approval depends in large part on the justification for making the alteration. It is sometimes argued that genetic alteration benefits the individual and the gene pool as a whole by removing deleterious genes and thereby their potential negative effects on individuals and populations.[1] The moral mandate to act to provide some benefit is generally weaker than the mandate to avoid harm. If genetic alteration can be justified on the grounds that it avoids harm, then the case becomes the more compelling one based upon

Source: Portions reprinted from Jeffrey P. Kahn, Genetic Harm: Bitten by the Body That Keeps You? *Bioethics*, Vol. 5, No. 4, pp. 289–308, with permission of Basil Blackwell Ltd., © 1991.

views regarding the moral imperative to avoid causing harm, views expressed in the political writings of John Stuart Mill concerning the limits of personal liberty.[2] This is not to say that beneficent genetic alteration is morally indefensible. On the contrary, beneficent acts are morally laudable albeit lacking all the normative force that comes in calling for nonmaleficence. To see this, consider the different conclusions about similar scenarios involving harmful situations: In the first case, an individual strolling down a country road comes upon a swimming hole in which a child is clearly struggling to stay afloat. The decision whether to rescue the child is basically a decision whether to act to remove the child from a presently harmful condition. The passer-by has no role in causing the harm and arrives at such time that he is only in a position to enact its removal. In choosing not to rescue the drowning child, the passer-by fails in some moral duty of beneficence, since only in the case of actions involving the actual infliction of harm can prohibitions against maleficence be invoked, except in arguably overbroad analyses of what counts as causing harm.[3] This is an important difference in need of clarification because the strength of the moral conclusions we draw about required and proscribed action will be dependent on it.

A failure to rescue, as in the above example, appears qualitatively different from the same example changed in the following way. Instead of coming upon a child already in the pond, the passer-by sneaks up behind the child frolicking on a dock and pushes her into the deep water below. In the altered example, the passer-by has actively caused harm to the child by pushing her into the water. Even if we maintain that there are compelling moral arguments for both rescuing the child and refraining from pushing her into the water, it seems that pushing her is somehow morally "worse" than merely holding back from rescuing her. In either case the child is harmed, but one way to explain the difference between cases is by distinguishing between the failure to benefit (the first example) and the failure to avoid harming (the second example). If we were

to modify the example yet again and replace the pond with some genetic malady, then we could productively ask both whether the genetic predisposition can sensibly be said to harm and whether a failure to "correct" the genetic disposition causing the malady would more correctly be characterized as a failure to benefit or a failure to avoid harming. How the analysis ends up on this point will impact the basis for and the extent to which conclusions about the uses of genetic testing, screening, and manipulation can be defended.

THE VIEW THAT GENES CAUSE HARM

The conceptual fuzziness of claiming that a person's genetic makeup can be said to harm him or her arises for two reasons. First, harm is a contextual concept requiring some unharmed status with which to compare the harmed state. Purported harms that are a function of our genetic disposition and thus our very existence offer no real basis for this comparison, since the only status in which the individual is not harmed is one in which he or she does not exist.

Second, *what* we are and *that* we are we owe to our genetic constitution, at least in some sense. Whatever harms we might realize as a product of our genetic makeup is what has elsewhere been called a harm "constitutive of [our] very identities."[4] One conclusion of what I will call this "constitutive view" is, as Derek Parfit explains it in a somewhat different context, that certain choices (e.g., reproductive choices) will result in future people being "badly off," but if we had not made those same choices, the people in question would never have existed. Thus these choices cannot be *worse* for the future people.[5] Parfit further claims that this counterintuitive conclusion derives from relying upon appeal to individual interests and rights to support claims regarding what makes us worse off. We must then attempt to explain how, if ever, our existence may harm us. To address this and the other questions raised, I propose to examine what constitutes harm and whether it makes sense to say that our genetic makeup may harm us.

To do this I will describe three approaches to the problem of describing the status of negative effects our genes have upon us, which I have named the technical harm view, the constitutive view, and the harmful conditions view. On the technical harm view, the standard definitions of harm are applied to genetic disposition in an attempt to couch genetic defects or flaws in terms of harming. The constitutive view rejects applying the concept of harm to genetic disposition on the grounds that it is impossible to separate genetic disposition from individual identity. Lastly, the harmful conditions view, which I conclude is the most successful of the three, focuses on the tendency of certain genetic dispositions to cause harm in the future and thus avoids what I will argue are the "context" shortcomings of the other two approaches.

Harm always occurs relative to some state of being that existed before or that would have been the case had the harming act not occurred. Keeping this relativity in mind, what are we to make of the claim that our genetic material harms us? Is the proper comparison state the way we would have been had the harming genetic material not been harmful? This comparison is difficult to defend, since the act that at least begins the chain of events leading to the genetic defect is the same act that causes us to *be* at all. Further, if we construe the proper comparison state to be the genetically unharmed one, then we must all consider ourselves harmed, since each of us carries around some not insignificant number of genetic defects. More troubling still for accepting an unharmed genome as the appropriate comparison state is the question of whether personal identity persists through changes in the genome, since for the purpose of assessing harm it certainly cannot be correct to compare the state we are in to the state of our being someone else altogether.

But how different would we really be? How much of our identity is determined by a particular combination of genes? For example, it is defensible to argue that the well-known "boy in the bubble" would still be the same boy out of the bubble should the genetic defect leading to his lack of immune function be repaired. On the other hand, a child with Lesch-Nyhan syndrome is arguably not the same child should the enzyme deficiency causing the syndrome be corrected. But defense of such a statement requires analysis of personal identity outside the scope of this chapter.[6] Suffice it to say that the issues that arise from analyzing harms in terms of the very things that make us who we are are troublesome, thorny, and untidy. Some of these issues will be addressed in a later section of this chapter.

EXAMINING THE COMPETING VIEWS

New or expanding areas of genetic technologies—mapping the human genome, recombinant techniques, gene probes, and even gene therapy—bring with them new ways of looking at ourselves. One byproduct of genetic knowledge is that the levels at which causes for illness, disease, and susceptibility can be detected become increasingly more basic. Consequently, as information about disease- and susceptibility-conferring traits is uncovered, we may begin to see our most basic raw material, our genes, as being subpar, defective, and even harmful. Depending on the status our genetic makeup and thus the life that follows from it is accorded, different moral conclusions can be drawn. If the technical harm position can be supported (i.e., that the negative effects of genetic disposition satisfy the definition of harming), conclusions about the moral obligations of parents to offspring based on obligations to avoid harming can be defended. If the technical harm position is shown to be fatally flawed, conclusions of a weaker nature can be drawn based upon parental obligations to positively benefit and to respect rights to positive provision (if these obligations can be claimed to exist). The conclusions drawn from this discussion will thus affect the context in which certain moral obligations are viewed and discussed.

The Technical Harm View

What Does It Mean To Harm?

The term *harm* usually refers to two general categories of states that make an individual in some way worse off than some comparative state. Without discussing the complicating factor of responsibility for harming, the two categories can be roughly divided into harming as setback to some pre-existing or deserved interests and harming as wronging or violation of individual rights.

As a basic definition, we can turn to the "setback to interests" standard, as explained by Joel Feinberg: "One person harms another . . . by invading, and thereby thwarting or setting back, his interest. The test, in turn, . . . of whether such an invasion has in fact set back an interest is whether that interest is in a worse condition than it would otherwise have been in had the invasion not occurred at all."[7]

Some have argued that this understanding of harm is insufficient for explaining why certain situations that intuitively appear to be harms ought not be committed, the contention being that definitions like this one depend on event-harms—harms caused by a change in a situation marked by an event—and fail to include situations that we might want to call harms but where the interests in question are not per se set back or where there is no event on which the act of harming can be pinned.[8] Any basic definition of harm must be construed to include not only event-harms but the harms caused by the status quo as well. An example helps illustrate this point.

Imagine a people kept as veritable slaves by the despot ruling the country in which they are unfortunate enough to live. For all of their lives under this ruler, many of the people's interests have been set back by the restriction of their liberty, their being forced to do backbreaking labor, and so on. This ruler clearly harms his people by acting in ways that set back their interests. But imagine further that this despot is overthrown in a bloodless coup and that the new ruler realizes the economic opportunity offered by an enslaved population and so continues the status quo. The new ruler makes no positive act to harm his people (by setting back interests), and in fact his decision makes the people neither better nor worse off than they had been prior to his reign. Certainly we would like to call this a case in which maintaining the status quo itself harms,

with the proper context for comparison being the state preceding the status quo even if it is generations in the past. In this way, even children born into slavery would be harmed though the comparative state predates their existence. As will be discussed below, the example of status quo harms is instructive for the concept of genetic harm.

The second category of harm is embodied in the notion of "wronging." A wrong is committed by one person against another "when his indefensible (unjustifiable and inexcusable) conduct violates the other's right, and, in all but certain very special cases, such conduct will also invade the other's interest and thus be harmful."[9] This understanding of harm focuses not on the worsened state of the affected interests but on the unjust violation of *rights*. Thus, this understanding of harm is dependent on the identification and articulation of individual rights. If rights exist, harm has been done if one or more of these rights have been unjustly violated. The key determination after the identification and articulation of rights then becomes whether their violation is just. This determination depends largely on the priority given to the violated rights; a violation of one individual's right in the interest of protecting a right of higher priority held by another individual may well be considered a just violation and therefore not a harm in the sense of a wrong.

For nonharmful wronging then, the issue at stake revolves not around questions of harm but around questions of rights. For instance, we may argue that there exist certain rights that individuals enjoy as "birthrights." If a so-called birthright is unjustly violated, the individual has been wronged and therefore would have grounds for a moral complaint. The difficulty is in determining what sorts of rights count as birthrights and on what grounds the existence and inviolability of these rights can be defended. Without a satisfactory account of such rights—for instance, the right of individuals to be born genetically unharmed—a moral case would be difficult if not impossible to make for individuals who would fall into the category of those genetically harmed if it were to be based on the argument that they should be morally protected from acts that wrong them. But since any such argument would presuppose that we understand what constitutes a genetically harm-free state, any effort to define genetic harm as wronging effectively begs the "can we be harmed by our genes?" question. Therefore, nonharmful wronging does not offer much in the search for the proper description of the status of the negative effects of our genes.

How Genes Can Harm

Given the above discussion of harm, how might our understanding of genetics be construed such that an individual's genes can cause him or her harm? The problem raised will hopefully be clear by now: The most widely accepted and intuitively satisfying definition of harm, the setback to interest standard, is difficult to apply in cases where the context of comparison is nonexistence—a state with questionable ontological significance. For if a genetically harmed individual were not to have been conceived—say her parents knew that conception at a particular time would likely result in such an "affected" offspring—and conception was postponed until the risk subsided, the resulting offspring would be a different individual.[10] This question may thus reduce to whether an individual is better off never having existed than existing in the genetically harmed state. If the genetically harmed state cannot be compared to a prior, unharmed condition of the particular individual, a more productive tack might be to compare the harmed state with a genetically nondefective state— some sort of standard of genetic comparison. In fact, unless we have a standard of genetic "normalcy," likely based on phenotypic products of genes, then it makes no sense to speak of genetic defects or flaws. Against what standards or baseline would such comparisons be made?

If we rely on some standard of comparison, what range of phenotypes or levels of functioning are we then to regard as nondefective? We are now told that we all carry some number of genetic defects and recessive genes for lethal disorders.[11] If the standard were to be genetic "perfection,"

we would all qualify as genetically harmed, effectively rendering the concept meaningless.

How Our Genetics Fit or Fail To Fit Definitions of Harm

Given the definitions of harm examined, individuals suffering from genetically caused disease or illness cannot legitimately be said to be (technically) harmed. As has been shown, this is because of the unique situation arising in cases where what causes harm is constitutive of the individual's very identity. The determination of whether a harm has been committed is made by measuring the status of previously existing personal interests. When the question of harm focuses on part of our makeup that is a result of what occurs at the time of conception, it is difficult to attach any meaning to a comparison state that is prior to the harm, since that state would necessarily predate existence. Thus, if a technical harm view is to make sense, it would require some standard of genetic normalcy in which we would have some set of interests prior to our existence. The shorthand claim in such an argument is that we are conceived harmed. A way of rehabilitating the concept and incorporating genetic defects into a description of how genes harm will be examined below. First, however, the view opposite the technical harm view must be considered: What about accepting our genetic lot as the mantle we must wear as a function of our identity?

The Constitutive View

In this view, when analyzing genetic disposition in terms of harm, it just makes no sense to speak of setbacks to interest or the continuation of the status quo as harms because the pre-status-quo state "caused" by conception is nonexistence. Put another way, whatever harms we realize due to our genetic makeup are themselves constitutive of our very identity. If we did not experience those particular harms, then we would not be who we are.

Even if an individual's interests can be shown to be set back by his or her genetics, a troubling ontological problem persists. Given that harm is constituted by the setting back of interests, how can we say that the very thing that determines our interests, our genetic material, also sets back our interests? Interests are a highly individual thing, specific at least in part to the genetic disposition of the individual. Thus, is it more correct to say that genetic disposition sets back interests or that it in fact *defines* interests? If the latter is the case, and it appears to explain at least part of the story, then it must just be wrong to attribute harmfulness to our genetic makeup. In an effort to understand how genetic disposition affects identity, consider an example mentioned above, the well-known boy in the bubble. The case was well publicized, with magazine articles, newspaper stories, and even a television movie telling the boy's story. The boy had a rare genetically caused congenital immunodeficiency (severe combined immunodeficiency, or SCID), which is marked by the absence of both humoral and cellular immunity (i.e., there is no defense against any infection).[12] To prevent almost sure death from infection, the boy was required to live in a sterile environment, first in a totally enclosed room and later in a semiportable "bubble." As the accounts of his life show, the disease had a profound effect on the boy's identity. In his case, the immune deficiency caused by some genetic flaw severely limited activities, experiences, and interactions in which he could participate. Surely many of the boy's interests were set back by his disease, yet the disease was just as surely an important factor in making him who he was. So how could something so important to making the boy who he was also be said to harm him?

Clearly certain interests are set back in the boy's case, and while the setbacks are undoubtedly severe, the setbacks are part of what makes the boy who he is. In the end, the constitutive view concludes that individuals can be harmed neither by what they are *not* (it may be more correct to say that they are not benefited) nor by what they *are*, because *what* they are makes them *who* they are, and it makes no sense to claim your very identity harms you.[13]

For this same reason, the constitutive view is inadequate for explaining which and whether genetic dispositions cause harm, because its answer must always be that our (genetic) lot in life is just that and to postulate any other is to postulate a life that belongs to someone else. But such a view fails to capture a critical notion—the idea that while the setting back or dooming of interests may be a fact of many lives, that fact does not imply the individuals who continue to experience those lives do not experience harm. This critical notion is the basis for the next section.

Rehabilitating Genetic Harm: The Harmful Conditions View

The discussion of whether individuals conceived with genetic defects are harmed has up to this point focused on conception as the act that purportedly (and without conceptual success) causes the individual harm. The misdirected focus on conception beats a path into ontological quicksand and in the process causes us to overlook the more important and appropriate focus on continued (affected) existence as a cause of harm. This appreciation of the dynamic nature of the effects of genetic disposition is not captured by views that use as their point of reference the time at which genetic disposition is set. While our genomes must be "set" at conception, the effects of our genetic dispositions are never realized at the point of conception but often occur long after birth and into later life. A measure of harmfulness that appreciates the dynamic nature of these effects is the notion of a harmful condition.

Being Harmed versus Harmful Conditions

In analyzing genetic harms, the distinction between being harmed and being placed in a harmful condition is important because identifying conception as the act creating harm cannot satisfy the requirements of harming. I want to argue instead that any analysis focusing on conception as the act that purportedly harms is in fact misled; the harm that befalls some individuals because of their genetic disposition is not due to their conception but to the fact that their genetic disposition has adverse effects on their interests throughout their lives.

The distinction between *harming* conditions and *harmful* conditions is as follows. Harming conditions are the outcomes of acts of harming, acts that in some way worsen or violate our interests or rights. Harmful conditions, on the other hand, are the outcomes of acts that place us in situations such that our interests tend to be impaired, defeated, thwarted, and so on, but are not actually made worse off by the acts. The key is that in occupying a harmful condition, an individual is much more likely to experience harm than if he or she were not in such a condition.[14] The importance of this distinction is that harming conditions can only be caused by harmful acts whereas harmful conditions can be the outcome either of harmful acts or nonharmful acts. Certain experiences like short-term torture with no lasting effects count as harming conditions but not harmful conditions because the setback to interests is experienced only during the period of torture, with no tendency for the condition to generate further harm. On the other hand, the existence of a time bomb in a hotel lobby cannot be called a harming condition, at least before the bomb explodes, because during the pre-explosion interval it sets back no one's interests. But it should count as a harmful condition because, so long as the bomb remains planted and ticking, it will surely generate harm sometime in the future.

The parallelism between certain genetic dispositions and ticking time bombs should require no explanation, but since the distinction between harming states and harmful conditions is key for analysis of genetic harms, it requires careful attention. One way of making the connection between technical harms and harmful conditions is to view harmful conditions as harms due to the status quo. In status quo harms, the reference state is the present and the harms occur in the future. This switch in reference states or contexts allows the discussion of harm to move from the realm of technical harms into the realm of harmful conditions. It is in this way that status quo harms (as in the above example of the enslaved population) can be covered by conceptual notions of harm.

Harmful Conditions As Conditions of Future Harming

As another way of viewing harmful conditions, it may help to distinguish between the future and present harms some lives hold. Rather than presently satisfying the criteria for harming, in harmful conditions situations exist that, while not setting back interests immediately, ensure or at least make very likely the occurrence of future harms. An example of the type of life that holds future rather than present harms would be living with the gene for Huntington's disease. We can conclude that this life probably will cause harm in the future—many if not all of the individual's future basic interests are likely to be set back since there is a high probability that the disease will manifest itself sometime in the future. But even assuming for the sake of argument that such individuals will certainly experience blocked basic interests sometime in the future, the intervening years in which the individual lives a potentially healthy and fulfilling life argue that this case is different from one in which the setbacks to interests are concurrent with the beginning of life. Thus, I propose to categorize those harms of life that are not realized concurrent with the beginning of life but are "programmed" to occur sometime in the future by the genetic condition into which the individual is born as the harmful conditions of genetic disposition. Once the future harms are realized, harmful conditions turn into harming conditions, with the reference condition switching to the prior harmful condition.

Consider an example that elucidates the distinction between harming and harmful conditions. Mr. and Mrs. Lowry conceive a child. Since Mrs. Lowry is over 40 years old, her physician recommends that she undergo amniocentesis, and after some private discussion, Mr. and Mrs. Lowry agree. At the appropriate time in the pregnancy, Mrs. Lowry undergoes the procedure, and the analysis of the amniotic fluid reveals a fetus with serious medical problems.

Chromosomal analysis reveals a fetus suffering from Lesch-Nyhan syndrome; a genetic disorder in which an enzyme necessary for normal development is not produced, thereby leading to severe mental retardation, spastic cerebral palsy, and self-mutilation of fingers and lips by uncontrolled biting.

Assuming for this case that the predictions made by amniocentesis are 100 percent accurate, the certain prognosis and debilitating nature of the abnormality affecting their future offspring lead Mr. and Mrs. Lowry to wrestle with the question of aborting the pregnancy. If the child is born, does his genetic disposition harm him, and if so, in what way? The Lowrys, by dint of a decision to allow the life that will result in Baby X to continue, would decide to allow an individual to be born into a life holding future harms. Baby X's interests in self-locomotion, bodily integrity, interaction with others, and more are all jeopardized by the physical and mental states that are manifestations of the identified enzyme deficiency. But Baby X does not experience harms immediately upon conception into a life with Lesch-Nyhan syndrome or one of a number of similarly severe maladies manifesting themselves sometime after birth, because while at conception or sometime during development the wheels have been set in motion for the harms due to the disease to be realized sometime later in life, the individual's immediate outlook appears to be that of a developmentally normal infant. By virtue of the fact that many of Baby X's basic personal interests are sure to be set back in the future due to his affliction with Lesch-Nyhan syndrome, his birth with the genetic defect and the syndrome it causes place him into a life that holds future harms (i.e., a life that is essentially a harmful condition).

Contrast the case of Baby X and his future harming condition with the case of a child with trisomy 13 or trisomy 18 or any child who experiences a present harming condition from birth. The obvious difference between the two cases is that the child with trisomy 18 suffers the harms caused by that condition from the beginning of his or her life; any setbacks to interests such a child realizes by dint of the condition begin with

the flaw in the distribution of chromosomes shortly after conception.[15] Unlike Baby X, the child with trisomy 18 will enjoy no years of "normal" life but realizes the consequences of his or her affliction concurrently with his or her life.

Genetic Disposition As a Harmful Condition

The key defective or faulty act that sets back individual interests in a case of genetic harm is then not the fertilization of the egg by the sperm but rather the allowance of the individual to exist in a state that tends to set back his or her interests, that is, in a harmful condition. What is the condition that harms the individual? It cannot be conception, since that merely begins the process of development. Besides, the likelihood of the condition that will result in a compromised life being present at conception is no greater than the likelihood that that condition will occur sometime during the early or later stages of fetal development. In fact, in the case of many genetic defects, the process responsible for the abnormality takes place during some part of the cellular divisions that occur postconception.

For instance, suppose that the failure in enzyme production that results in Lesch-Nyhan syndrome occurs because of a genetic "misfiring" not at conception but at a point eight or nine weeks into development. The fact that the genetic flaw occurred some time after conception makes no difference in terms of whether the fetus could be said to be harmed. Further, it is not the genetic flaw that is the act harming the infant but living in the condition resulting from that flaw. Therefore, the harm at issue is that of a future harm, whether the state be genetic, environmental, or induced otherwise, and the act that leads to the future harm is the act of allowing birth and subsequent continuation of what amounts to a harmful (if not presently harming) condition.

The approach of viewing genetic disposition as harming whether by allowing to live or by mere conception is not without its critics. The legal world has been quick to discount similar claims, focusing on cases of "wrongful life" for numerous reasons, among them that it is logically impossible to be harmed by one's life (that the state of one's personal interests cannot be made worse off by life):[16] "No comparison [between the harmed and the unharmed state] is possible since were it not for the act of birth the infant would not exist. By his cause of action, the plaintiff cuts from under himself the ground upon which he needs to rely in order to prove his damage."[17] In this quote Gidion Tedeschi, like others, contends that, in cases of wrongful life, if the act (allowing life to continue) had not taken place, it makes no sense to ask if the individual would be better off because the individual would not *be*. But this contention seems to be due to an unnecessary metaphysical entanglement. If the harms of living (setbacks to interests) outweigh its benefits, then it would in fact be better not to live. This is not to say that nonexistence is some odd state of being, but only that if the harms of one's life outweighs its benefits, then life may not be worth living and the only way to make the situation better is through some preharm condition, that is, nonexistence. If the future status of an individual's life is known in advance to be on balance harmful, deciding whether life in the known state or nonexistence would make the individual better off could rationally and defensibly be answered in favor of nonexistence. Defense of this position goes a long way toward defense of the theoretically similar view of genetic disposition as a harmful condition.

In his later work, Joel Feinberg recast his analysis of wrongful life from focusing on conception as harmful to instead saying that such individuals are harmed if, because of a breach of duty by another, they "come into existence in a condition such that it *would be rational to prefer nonexistence to that condition*."[18] Thus he rephrased the nature of the argument from being one about conception to being one about living and continued life in order to better fit definitions of harming. This change in focus is an important move in accounting for claims of wrongful life as well as explaining how genetic disposition may harm.

The phrase *harms of conception* for the harms befalling individuals in cases of genetic harm is better replaced with *harms of continued existence*. Clearly, the condition of one's life can set back one's interests. In cases of wrongful life, what is not so clear is whether those setbacks to interests due to life are worse than nonexistence since they are on balance harmful. For Feinberg, the answer lies in whether it would be rational to *prefer* nonexistence over life with those setbacks to interests. I have argued elsewhere that such an approach has its own difficulties and that instead certain more objective criteria must be fulfilled if a harming life is to be outweighed by the prospect of nonexistence.[19] If it can be determined which harms in a life are severe enough to make it not worth living, the high probability or certainty of similar levels of harms growing out of a harming life would argue that those harming lives require an obligation to avoid harming's gaining concreteness through the avoidance of their conception or continued life. If the fulfilled and potentially fulfilled interests in one's continued life are counted as the benefits and future benefits of life, blockage of the fulfillment of all such interests would be tantamount to the transformation of life's benefits into harms.

For an individual who lives in a state of sufficient cognitive and affective incapacity, the realization of any basic life interests, in such things as human interaction, communication, meaningful sensory perception, and some level of independence, is made impossible. If by definition (present or future) harms are setbacks to interests, then total blockage of interests can also be termed harms. Further, if every interest in one's life has been irreparably and permanently blocked, and the fulfillment or potential fulfillment of one's interests are seen as the benefits of one's life, then a life so affected would properly be said to contain only harms and to be devoid of benefits.

As a general criterion, a life objectively consisting only of harms and lacking any benefits must qualify as satisfying a range of theoretical reasons to opt for nonexistence, such as the following: It would clearly be rationally required to avoid the life of such individuals;[20] the harms entailed by such a life certainly outweigh its benefits, since there are no benefits;[21] no individual would consent to being brought into life only to experience harms;[22] and no one would prefer to live under such conditions over the option of the continuation of their life being avoided.[23] When this general criterion is satisfied by a given life, I contend that there can be little doubt that the life is not worth living and that nonexistence is therefore better. Put a different way, if nonexistence holds a neutral value, then lives satisfying the above general criterion could arguably be said to have negative value—they are on balance harmful. If that is the case, then such lives can be called worse than nonexistence.

The preceding digression aside, wrongful life is a topic whose detailed examination is better left for another discussion. For now it can be said that while your genes may cause harm by placing you in a harmful condition, it is left unresolved whether the harm is great enough to warrant preventing them by preventing life itself. What this analysis does point out is that if and when techniques become available, we may have a moral obligation to rectify genetic harms through the manipulation of genetic material. A critical question necessarily left unresolved in this discussion is which harmful genetic dispositions deserve redress and which are acceptable as necessary variability. I will propose an initial answer to this question in the section addressing the implications of the harmful conditions view, but these and questions like them await further careful attention and analysis.

In describing how genetic disposition harms, the harmful conditions view better captures the fact that genetic disposition can set back interests not as a function of conception or identity but as a function of what the future holds. Like the time bomb silently ticking away before it explodes, genetic disposition harms not because it satisfies the technical definition of harm but because of what it holds in store in terms of future harming. The harmful conditions view thus offers a description of the harming effects of genetic disposition without the reference problem of the technical harm view and does so in a way more true to events than does the constitutive view.

THE IMPLICATIONS OF ACCEPTING A HARMFUL CONDITIONS VIEW OF GENETICS

Since harmful conditions (or conditions of future harming) increase the risk of harm, and since there is the prima facie moral obligation to avoid the risk of harming, then if a harmful conditions view is defensible, there exists a prima facie obligation to avoid some harmful conditions caused by genetic disposition. Of course much work needs to be done to determine how much risk of harm warrants avoidance, what the benefits of the harmful condition might be, and so on. But acceptance of the harmful conditions view opens the door to viewing our genetic disposition as harmful and thus morally deserving of rectification or avoidance.

To draw once more upon the example of the drowning child, consider a third scenario in which the bystander happens upon a child who is in a harmful condition. Suppose that the child is playing on a rickety pier extending out into the pond and that the bystander knows that both the planks and the pylons of the pier are in such an advanced stage of rot that its collapse is imminent. While we would not say that the child was being harmed at the time, we would say that harm was very likely to befall him imminently. Thus he was in a harmful condition, although the time before the actual harm will be caused is admittedly short. This case is somewhat different from that of happening upon an already drowning child, since the bystander's action will avoid harm rather than remove it. This distinction is important in that to fail to act in the case of the drowning child is to fail to act after the harming has occurred rather than before. A sped-up version of the same distinction is the difference between failing to aid the victims of a bomb blast and failing to defuse a timed explosive before it detonates. Both are important actions and moral arguments can be made for each, but they nonetheless seem qualitatively different based on whether a harm has already occurred. The important perspective is that strong moral arguments can be made for action in either case and that they are based on rectification of harm—the understanding of the type of harm that comes with genetic disposition is what will distinguish which form the obligation takes.

HOW ACCEPTING THE NOTION OF GENETIC HARM MAY IMPACT PRACTICE

One practical application of the concept of genetic harm is that viewing genetic disposition as in some way harming helps distinguish between therapeutic gene therapy and gene therapy for enhancement. By therapeutic gene therapy I mean gene therapy intended to undo or "repair" some genetic flaw, while by gene therapy for enhancement I mean gene therapy undertaken with the goal of improving an existing trait.[24] The view of some genetic dispositions as harmful conditions lends support to this distinction, since it offers a means of distinguishing gene therapy for the purpose of removing a harmful condition from gene therapy for the purpose of enhancing some characteristic or functioning, in the following way. Drawing from the above discussion of wrongful life, life in particular states are worse than nonexistence when the setbacks to interests those lives hold are *on balance harmful*. If genetic disposition adversely affects interests such that the state is on balance harmful, gene therapy could be justified as a way of avoiding the future harms genetic disposition holds, with reference to obligations to avoid harmful conditions. If the determination is that genetic disposition adversely affects interests but that the state is not on balance harmful, gene therapy would only be justifiable based on the more tenuous moral arguments in support of obligations of positive beneficence.[25]

As examples, compare gene therapy for the purpose of repairing the gene responsible for production of the enzyme adenosine deaminase (the lack of this enzyme leads to SCID and near-certain death within the first few years of life)[26] with gene therapy to increase an individual's height from that within the normal range for the general population to that within the range for professional basketball players. Repairing the

enzyme deficiency avoids the dooming of all interests by death and thus removes an on-balance harmful condition. Increasing height through gene therapy, on the other hand, may avoid the harmful condition of a future inability to see from the back of large crowds, stand in deep water, or play professional basketball, but gene therapy for this purpose addresses a condition that is *not* on balance harmful. While this is not the place to do it, this rough distinction itself deserves a far more sophisticated treatment. When fleshed out, this conceptual step should aid defense of therapeutic gene therapy without necessarily accepting similar conclusions for genetic enhancement. This would not be the case if the constitutive view were adopted, since on that view any genetic manipulation would necessarily be viewed as either enhancement or altering identity.

Viewing some genetic dispositions as harmful conditions also holds important ramifications for genetic counseling and reproductive decision making. Since it can be shown that genetic disposition can place individuals in harmful conditions from birth, if it can be further shown that there exist obligations to avoid or prevent certain harmful lives, say if the harms promoted by the condition outweighed the benefits of continued existence, then duties to seek out genetic information of offspring along with duties to act on this information could be defended. This task I leave for another discussion.

CONCLUSION

My aim in this discussion has been to show that the use of the language and concept of harming when speaking of genetic disposition is appropriate and defensible, and in fact provides a meaningful way of describing the negative effects of our genes and a way to view some genetic variations as deserving rectification. I have called this approach the harmful conditions view of genetic disposition and with it defended the concept of genetic harm. Further, I have offered a short argument for obligations to avoid certain genetically harmful lives and also offered some thoughts on how accepting the concept of genetic harm may impact practice, including offering a rough distinction between gene therapy for therapeutic purposes and gene therapy for enhancement purposes.

The brief conclusion of this discussion is that of the three views examined, the harmful condition view wins out by best explaining what we mean when we say that our genes harm us. From this initial discussion, a good deal more stands to be done in order to flesh out this approach and the ramifications it holds for genetic research, genetic counseling, gene therapy, and reproductive decision making.

NOTES

1. See Gene Therapy, *Briefings in Medical Ethics*, no. 7, December 1990; W.F. Anderson, Human Gene Therapy: Scientific and Ethical Considerations, *Journal of Medicine and Philosophy* 10 (1985):275–291; L. Walters, The Ethics of Human Gene Therapy, *Nature* 320 (1986):225–227; J. Glover, *What Sort of People Should There Be?* (Middlesex, England: Penguin Books, 1984), 25–52.

2. J.S. Mill, *On Liberty*, 1859.

3. J. Feinberg, *Harm to Others* (New York: Oxford University Press, 1984), 171ff.

4. M. Hanser, Harming Future People, *Philosophy and Public Affairs* 19, no. 1 (1990):47–70.

5. See D. Parfit, *Reasons and Persons* (Oxford: Oxford University Press, 1984), 351–379; for responses to some critiques of these views, see Comments, *Ethics* 96 (July 1986):854ff.

6. For a more detailed analysis of personal identity and genetic alteration, see R. Elliot, Identity and the Ethics of Gene Therapy, *Bioethics* 7, no. 1 (1993):27–40.

7. Feinberg, *Harm to Others*, 34.

8. See, for example, D. Mathieu, Respecting Liberty and Preventing Harm: Limits of State Intervention in Prenatal Choice, *Harvard Journal of Law and Public Policy* 8, no. 1 (1985):19–55; E. H. Morreim, Conception and the Concept of Harm, *Journal of Medicine and Philosophy* 8 (1983):137–157.

9. Feinberg, *Harm to Others*, 34.

10. Parfit outlines various forms of this example in *Reasons and Persons*, 351–379.

11. See K. Nolan and S. Swenson, New Tools, New Dilemmas: Genetic Frontiers, *Hastings Center Report* 18 (October-November 1988):40–46.

12. *Stedman's Medical Dictionary*, 24th ed. s.v. "severe combined immunodeficiency."(Baltimore: Williams & Wilkins, 1982), 695.

13. For a stronger version of this argument, see N.J. Zohar, Prospects for "Genetic Therapy"—Can a Person Benefit from Being Altered? *Bioethics* 5, no. 4 (1991):289–308.

14. Feinberg, *Harm to Others*, 31.

15. R. Weir, *Selective Nontreatment of Handicapped Newborns* (New York: Oxford University Press, 1984), 45.

16. Aside from the philosophical qualms that legal scholars have aired as regards wrongful life cases, they have also cited difficulties in measuring damages, social policy objections to allowing children to sue their parents, and public policy obstacles standing in the way of deciding that certain lives are not worth living.

17. G. Tedeschi, On Tort Liability for Wrongful Life, *Israeli Law Review* 1 (1966):529.

18. J. Feinberg, Wrongful Life and the Counterfactual Element in Harming, *Social Philosophy and Policy* 4, no. 1 (1986):161.

19. I analyzed this problem in greater detail in my doctoral dissertation, *The Principle of Nonmaleficence and the Problems of Reproductive Decision Making* (Ann Arbor, Mich.: University Microfilms International, 1989), esp. chap. 3.

20. See Feinberg, Wrongful Life and the Counterfactual Element in Harming, 164. This general position is also put forward without elaboration in his book *Harm to Others*. See also Comment: Wrongful Conception and the Right Not to Be Harmed, *Harvard Journal of Law and Public Policy* 8, no. 1 (1985):57–77.

21. Parfit, *Reasons and Persons*, 487–490.

22. H.T. Engelhardt, *The Foundations of Bioethics* (New York: Oxford University Press, 1986), 221–223; H.T. Engelhardt, Ethical Issues in Aiding the Death of Young Children, in *Beneficent Euthanasia,* edited by M. Kohl (Buffalo, N.Y.: Prometheus Books, 1975), 180–192.

23. Parfit, *Reasons and Persons*, 487–490.

24. For fuller explanations along similar lines, see Anderson, Human Gene Therapy; Walters, The Ethics of Human Gene Therapy; Glover, *What Sort of People Should There Be?*

25. For a detailed discussion of the arguments supporting obligations growing out of the principles of nonmaleficence and beneficence, see T.L. Beauchamp and J.F. Childress, *Principles of Biomedical Ethics*, 3rd ed. (New York: Oxford University Press, 1989), chaps. 4 and 5.

26. *Stedman's Medical Dictionary*, 24th ed., s.v. "severe combined immunodeficiency." 695; Walters, The Ethics of Human Gene Therapy.

Chapter 4

Ethics in Reproductive Genetics

John C. Fletcher and Mark I. Evans

Analogies are often crucial in ethical debate. For example, to what can we compare the magnitude of new knowledge and techniques in reproductive genetics and their potential for benefit or harm? We often see or hear an analogy to the discovery of atomic energy and the use of the atom bomb, but are both parts of the analogy acceptable?

The discoveries of atomic energy and the molecular basis of genetics are alike in magnitude. However, two reasons seem to weigh against using the bomb as an analogy for the potential benefit or harm expected from reproductive genetics. One is that the atom bomb was made in military secrecy. There was no public debate. Debate about genetic knowledge, especially in fetal diagnosis and therapy—the main subjects of this chapter—has been anything but secret. Second, the atomic bomb was used in the context of a world war. This fact gave rise to an indelible and problematic association of atomic energy with war and weapons. However, the context for the development of human genetic knowledge has been mainly medical. Is war or battle an appropriate analogy for medicine's interest in fetal diagnosis and therapy? Some try to portray prenatal diagnosis as part of a war be-

tween a consumer society and persons with disabilities or as a "search-and-destroy" mission against the fetus. Is war a good analogy for the medical uses of genetics?

The answer depends on how much coercion, open and hidden, we see in society's pressures on women, their mates, and families to use genetic knowledge to avoid disorders and serious disabilities. Previous coercive uses of genetic knowledge must not be forgotten or minimized. A strong eugenics movement, associated with coercive measures, arose during this century. Proponents believed that many poor, immigrant, and other vulnerable populations were genetically "inferior." The United States and other nations mandated coercive policies on immigration. Several states forced sterilization on those considered to be "feeble-minded." The scientific knowledge base for this eugenics movement was largely fictitious. Today, there are signs of overt coercion in genetic practices in some nations[1] and a potential for a renewed eugenics move-

Source: Reprinted from *Clinical Obstetrics and Gynecology*, Vol. 35, No. 4, pp. 1–20, with permission of J.B. Lippincott, © 1992.

The authors thank Maureen A. Berkner for her help in editing this manuscript.

ment in many nations. However, on the basis of the practices explored in this article, the analogy of war is not appropriate in post–World War II human genetics. These two activities are dissimilar in terms of coercion.

An analogy other than war or battle is needed to portray the potential for good or evil of reproductive genetics. We propose that a better analogy is that these developments are like an "experiment in living"[2] that provides data for ethics. This term also was used in the field of ethics.[3] How should women and their mates (and those who are asked to help them with genetic issues in pregnancy) live and choose? We view the last two decades of work in prenatal diagnosis and the birth of in utero fetal treatment as a social experiment (underway in many nations) in living and making choices at the beginning of human life. At times, these choices are between life and death. The experiment yields data for ethics. Data needs to be recorded and debated with public participation.

The experiment began in the late 1960s with amniocentesis. A major shift occurred in cultural and moral evolution. Parents, physicians, and society could learn during the second trimester of pregnancy, not at birth or later, if the fetus had a hereditary disorder. We all faced a new ethical problem. What should be done with this knowledge? By whom should it be done, how, and why? Should society's interests[4] in preventing harm play a strong role in approaches to these questions? Before amniocentesis, the options in pregnancies with high genetic risks were to abort them or prepare for a delivery that entailed a further decision to institutionalize or place the infant for adoption. Prenatal diagnosis reduced abortions in at-risk couples[5] and offered a new option of selective abortion. This option can be chosen as a result of several motives, e.g., preventing burdens and suffering of an affected child, hope for an opportunity to replace that lost child, and desire not to add genetic or economic burdens to society. Prenatal diagnosis also opened the door of opportunity for fetal therapy. In some cases, treatment in utero is possible but not often advisable. We hope fetal treatment will

continue and advance. However, concern about risks to women, their future pregnancies, and their infants who are subjected to "halfway technologies" should remain high until the fetal-therapy dimension of this experiment in living has been developed.

OVERVIEW OF ETHICS IN REPRODUCTIVE GENETICS

Ethics as a systematic human pursuit has two main goals: knowledge and guidance. Descriptive ethics is the study of moral behavior and beliefs to increase knowledge. Normative ethics is the search for and commendation of guidance in ethical problems. Accordingly, our tasks are twofold: (1) to describe approaches that can be taken currently by physicians and other counselors with patients in the clinical setting[6] of reproductive genetics and (2) to outline some resources for evaluating the adequacy of these approaches as ethical guidance. Exhibit 4–1 lists the major problems, and the text of the chapter follows this outline.

We take an ethical position that tries to join (1) claims of basic ethical principles in clinical practice and research (defined briefly in Exhibit 4–2) with (2) claims of caring in particular situa-

---

Exhibit 4–1 Ethical Problems in Reproductive Genetics

Before prenatal diagnosis
  Genetic counseling and informed consent
  Controversial indications
  Research and informed consent
After prenatal diagnosis
  Abortion choices
  Disclosure dilemmas
  Confidentiality and third-party interests
  Twin, multifetal, and third-trimester dilemmas
Before experimental fetal therapy
  Prior group review
  Case selection
  Informed consent
  Twin pregnancies
  Refusal of proven therapy
Research in fetal diagnosis and therapy
  The consequences of no federal support

Exhibit 4–2 Ethical Principles for Practice and Research

Respect for Persons: The duty to respect the self-determination and choices of autonomous persons, as well as to protect persons with diminished autonomy, e.g., young children, mentally retarded persons, and those with other mental impairments.

Beneficence: The obligation to secure the well-being of persons by acting positively on their behalf and, moreover, to maximize the benefits that can be attained.

Nonmaleficence: The obligation to minimize harm to persons and, wherever possible, to remove the causes of harm altogether.

Proportionality: The duty, when taking actions involving risks of harm, to so balance risks and benefits that actions have the greatest chance to result in the least harm and the most benefit to persons directly involved.

Justice: The obligation to distribute benefits and burdens fairly, to treat equals equally, and to give reasons for differential treatment based on widely accepted criteria for just ways to distribute benefits and burdens.

Adapted from the Belmont Report[7] and Beauchamp and Childress.[8]

tions. Claims of caring are a corrective for the generality of principles. To care means to identify with the feelings and needs of others and to nurture their most important relationships, such as those formed in families or between clinicians and patients.

Controversy surrounds fetal research and experimental fetal therapy. Ethical controversies have been difficult to resolve in contemporary societies because no one vision of the moral life can unify the vast differences among the many moral traditions that coexist. Ethical claims based on theism exclude those who cannot assent to a theistic faith. Ethical claims that appeal to reason alone or to an enlightenment that science and secularity supposedly confer have not prevailed, even in technologically developed societies. How should the task of normative ethics be pursued in such a pluralistic cultural context?

Our views are partly in sympathy with a two-tiered approach to ethics,[9] which is similar to a two-level analysis.[10] The many particular moral traditions that compete for loyalty in daily life are on one level. These traditions function well enough for many human tasks, but when faced with the most controversial issues, no one tradition provides guidance for an entire society and its multiple moral communities. When a need arises for ethical guidance in controversial problems—as in fetal diagnosis and therapy—the best way to proceed initially in a secular society is to search for better approaches to ethical problems in partnership with persons having the greatest experience with such problems. Study and evaluation of these approaches can yield grounds for ethical agreement. However, these agreements will not be fixed or unchanging, a result that would not satisfy those who desire shared agreement about the "foundations" for ethical guidance.

A search for ethical guidance does not have to be unprincipled or undisciplined. The following commitments are required for a "secular bioethics." First, there is a baseline of respect for prevailing approaches ("experiments in living and choosing") to ethical problems among different communities, families, and health care professionals. Second, we evaluate these approaches over time by studying the consequences (the benefit or harm) associated with following them. Third, we renounce coercion or the force of law in conflicts generated by ethical problems, at least until the facts indicate a problem of such magnitude that the law is required to correct it. We consult with colleagues and patients in several nations[11] in long-term evaluations of the major approaches to ethical problems in human genetics.

ETHICAL PROBLEMS BEFORE PRENATAL DIAGNOSIS

Genetic Counseling and Informed Consent

Genetic counseling is indicated ethically before any use of prenatal diagnosis. The goal is to educate patients and prepare them for the choices they must make during the informed consent process of prenatal diagnosis. Informed consent and genetic counseling are interdependent and yet separate in terms of process and goals.

Nowhere has the traditional paternalism in medicine and in early human genetics[12] been more transformed than in the practices of informed consent and nondirective genetic counseling.[13] In these practices, a standard of adequate and accurate information to patients must prevail. All subsequent information provided to the patient and family, including prognosis, treatment, recurrence risks, and reproductive options, must be based on the accuracy of the primary diagnosis. Genetic counseling itself has been defined as follows:

> a communication process which deals with the human problems associated with the occurrence, or the risk of occurrence, of a genetic disorder in a family.[14]

Ethically laden options frequently are seen during the counseling process.[15] Patients almost always ask, "What would you do in my situation?" An international survey[16] answered by 682 of 1,098 surveyed medical geneticists (64 percent) in 19 nations[17] gave five ethical options in counseling:

1. Suggest that while you will not make decisions for patients you will support any they make.
2. Tell patients that decisions, especially reproductive ones, are theirs alone and refuse to make any for them.
3. Inform patients what most other people in their situation have done.
4. Inform patients what you would do if you were in their situation.
5. Advise patients what they ought to do.[18]

These choices reflect the competing claims between the ethical principles of respect for persons and their autonomous decisions and the desire to prevent or avoid harm. Respect for patient autonomy was favored. A strong consensus was given to positions 1 (94 percent) and 2 (92 percent). Except for Turkey, position 1 had the strongest consensus in all except two nations,

France and Hungary, which placed position 2 first. Only one nation (Turkey) had a strong consensus for position 4.

The approach of nondirective counseling and respect for patient autonomy must not be absolutized. Physician or counselor refusal to respond to patients' appeals to discuss ethical problems is a form of ethical absolutism. A rigid refusal to respond is unfair, uncaring, and blind to the claims of other principles. Patients' appeals can be addressed best by explaining that most persons do not know what they "might do" unless they were placed in a difficult situation and then inviting the patients to discuss their moral concerns.

The following reasons support counselor responsiveness when asked moral questions. First, genetic counselors themselves have ethical views. Frankness was advised if counselors held strong views.[19] However, the counselor needs to reassure the patient that agreement is not required. Also, patients often want to know how others in their situation have resolved moral dilemmas, and they can benefit from this information. Moreover, some patients are incapacitated, e.g., persons with severe mental retardation or those who may be immature and dependent. Some are self-destructive and harm the fetus by behavior such as substance abuse. Rigid nondirectiveness may lead to more harm.[20]

The incidence of ineffective counseling, due to lack of evaluation, is probably far greater than the incidence of directive counseling.[21] Wide gaps and defects were found in communication, language, and empathy between counselors and their patients.[22] It was found that women in New York were not offered the help of a support group of other women with similar experience. The goal of counseling is to respect persons, and this cannot be realized without a practical form of caring.

Controversial Indications for Prenatal Diagnosis

When amniocentesis was still in a research phase and a scarce resource, advance refusal of abortion was seen by many to be a controversial indication. Some advised not providing services to such patients.[23] Some centers required a prior commitment to abortion with a signed consent form.[24] There were attacks on this position as unfair and an absolutizing of the option of abortion.[25]

How do geneticists see this issue now? A case was posed in the international survey.[26]

Case 1

"A woman 42 years old requests prenatal diagnosis for Down syndrome. She and her husband are already the parents of a Down syndrome child. She tells you that they are opposed to abortion and that she will carry the fetus to term even if it is diagnosed as having Down syndrome. They would like to have prenatal diagnosis, however, to give themselves additional time to prepare for the birth of another affected child. What would you do?"[27]

Eighty-five percent of respondents said that they would do the prenatal diagnosis in this case as a matter of justice. A mixed response was given where prenatal diagnosis was a scarce resource (Brazil, Greece, India, and Turkey). Currently, clinicians in developed nations do not withhold prenatal diagnosis from such couples.[28]

Maternal anxiety and sex selection are two requests for prenatal diagnosis sometimes considered controversial. These two cases were also posed on the survey.

Case 2

"A woman age 25 years with no family history of genetic disorders and no personal history of exposure to toxic substances requests prenatal diagnosis. Nevertheless, she appears very anxious about the normalcy of the fetus and persists in her demands for prenatal diagnosis even after being informed that in her case the potential medical risks for the fetus, in terms of miscarriage, may outweigh the likelihood of diagnosing an abnormality. Assume that your clinic has no regulations that would prevent you from doing prenatal diagnosis for her. What would you do, as a professional?"[29]

Case 3

"A couple requests prenatal diagnosis to select the sex of the child. They already have four girls and are desperate for a boy. They say that if the fetus is a girl, they will abort it and will keep trying until they conceive a boy. They also tell you that if you refuse to do prenatal diagnosis for sex selection, they will abort the fetus rather than risk having another girl. The clinic for which you work has *no* regulations prohibiting use of prenatal diagnosis for sex selection. What would you do?"[30]

For the maternal-anxiety case, 73 percent would do either prenatal diagnosis for maternal anxiety or refer the patient (10 percent). There was a strong consensus against this in the five nations where prenatal diagnosis is scarce (Brazil, the former German Democratic Republic [GDR], Hungary, Japan, and Turkey). Aside from considerations of fairness in access, no ethical reason excludes anxiety alone as an indication for prenatal diagnosis. These cases can be clustered into three types: (1) cases of "informed" maternal concern that also may involve anxiety based on knowledge of chromosomal risks and/or exclusion from access to diagnosis because of existing policy on maternal age, (2) cases of "unfounded" maternal anxiety based on unproven risks of genetic harm, and (3) cases of "morbid anxiety" related to pre-existing mental illness or emotional problems developing during pregnancy. Different approaches to each type are required. However, there is no ethical problem with prenatal diagnosis in the maternal-anxiety case provided that counseling and informed consent are adequate.

The sex-selection case placed respondents in the greatest ethical conflict. Twenty-five percent would do prenatal diagnosis for sex selection, and 17 percent would refer the couple elsewhere for this procedure. Their major reasons were based on respect for patient autonomy. Strong consensus against it was found in Australia, Brazil, Denmark, the former Federal Republic of Germany, France, GDR, Israel, Italy, Japan,

Norway, Switzerland, Turkey, and the United Kingdom. Their reasons were to protect a presumably normal fetus and not to waste resources. Nations with the largest percentages who would do prenatal diagnosis were Hungary (60 percent), India (37 percent), the United States (34 percent), Canada (30 percent), Greece (29 percent), and Sweden (28 percent). When referrals were added, however, a majority in the United States (62 percent), Hungary (60 percent), and India (52 percent) would either do a prenatal diagnosis in this case or refer the patient.

The respondents tended not to view sex selection as a serious ethical problem. They ranked it last on a list of ten issues that "ought to be of primary concern to medical geneticists in the near future." Nonetheless, in India, the problem is so serious that the central government has proposed a law against sex selection in the federal district and government hospitals. The state of Maharashtra has passed a law fining physicians who participate in such actions.[31]

Several reasons support excluding sex selection alone as an indication for prenatal diagnosis. First, gender is not a genetic disorder. Second, a President's Commission noted that sex selection violates the principle of equality between the genders.[32] Third, sex selection is a precedent for "genetic tinkering," at parental request, with traits that are unrelated to any disease. Cooperation with a desire for sex selection recalls the old eugenics[33] and is a precedent for a new eugenics. Fourth, in addition to the President's Commission, several working parties or international groups have discouraged[34] or omitted sex selection from medical indications in prenatal diagnosis.[35] It was argued that, under Britain's Abortion Act of 1967, sex selection is illegal.[36]

For these reasons, sex selection in the kind of case given on the survey is not an acceptable practice.[37] However, physicians' responses to this request should be caring and not condemning. They should include informing patients about sources of help with this request. We cannot recommend a position that only condemns

the desire in patients for help with a problem, i.e., a new pregnancy after several children of the same gender. It is inconsistent for physicians opposed to being "gagged" in their discussions of options for abortion[38] to be silent in these cases. The case in the survey is different circumstantially from two other types, i.e., families at risk for sex-linked disorders when a diagnosis cannot be made by DNA methods and families from cultures with a strong male preference.[39] Prenatal diagnosis would be justified for sex-linked disorders. In requests that reflect strong cultural pressures for a male child, we recommend noncooperation but willingness to refer, as in the case cited.[40]

Research and Informed Consent

When a procedure in prenatal diagnosis is in a research stage of development or being offered in the context of research, special efforts to obtain informed consent ethically are required. Patients should know which procedures are proved or unproved and the risks and benefits of each to the fetus and to themselves. There is an ethical problem of unfair constraints on research in prenatal diagnosis in the federal sector of science that far outweighs the magnitude of ethical problems of informed consent. The last section of the chapter will discuss these problems in relation to fetal therapy.

ETHICAL PROBLEMS AFTER PRENATAL DIAGNOSIS

Abortion Choices

Abortion choices are influenced strongly by pre-existing beliefs and prior discussions with family and physicians. However, in this context, a choice cannot be made until after prenatal diagnosis. Abortion choices have been the most controversial problem in this field (as measured by public debate and discussion in the literature). However, far fewer persons are affected adversely by selective abortion than are harmed by poor access to prenatal care combined with genetic services. The statistical incidence of positive findings after prenatal diagnosis does not exceed 4 percent of all cases.[41] Most couples in this situation choose abortion. Factors that affect all elective abortions also affect genetic abortions, such as socioeconomic causes, failed contraception, or personal reasons. Also, not all parents choose abortion after they receive the "bad news," e.g., in disorders like cystic fibrosis.[42] Genetic abortion choices are perplexing and a special source of suffering for the reasons shown in Exhibit 4–3.

The most complex abortion choices after prenatal diagnosis involve weighing the severity and treatability of particular genetic disorders[43] and the quality of life of an affected child in a particular family. The claims of the principle of proportionality are foremost because any choice leads to harm. How great is the harm? Can it be minimized? Who should decide what is proportionate? What economic and social resources are available? A public policy was advocated to allow abortion only for "fetal deformity of such magnitude that life-supporting efforts would not be considered obligatory after birth."[44] This proposal agrees with the federal law on decisions for selective nontreatment of handicapped newborns.[45]

This position is more open to the claims of several ethical principles and the claim of caring than the almost absolute ban on selective abortion found in Roman Catholic teaching.[46] However, this stand[47] still contrasts sharply with the prevailing practice, which is to respect parental decisions after counseling on the disease, its course, and issues in caring for the child.

We predict that abortion debate will soon include legislation proposals to adopt a similar position.[48] The social choice will be to support the present practice of respect for parental choice within limits or to authorize a list of approved untreatable and fatal disorders for abortion. Any such list making raises questions about who is to make the list and what counts as severity and treatability. At any rate, three types of harmful consequences are foreseeable in states that adopt this approach. Any one or all of them also will tend to restrict voluntary genetic services. First, many women would be forced to continue preg-

Exhibit 4–3 Why Are Genetic Abortion Choices So Difficult?

1. Most are wanted pregnancies.
2. Belief that the fetus at mid-trimester has a high moral status.
3. Wide spectrum of severity in some chromosomal and genetic disorders.
4. Treatability of some disorders and a longer lifespan of affected children.
5. Concern that abortion will harm the mental health of a prior affected child who is still living.
6. Concern to avoid neglect of persons with genetic disorders who survive or to avoid a precedent for pediatric euthanasia.
7. Concern that environment-based contributions to some genetic disorders will be underestimated and obscured.
8. Many parents will have already viewed the fetus on ultrasound and bonded.

nancies against their wishes or to go to states without legal restrictions on genetic abortions. Second, some parents would be forced to assume costs for marginal treatments unless society assumed all costs. Third, parents who objected to genetic abortion of a "listed" condition might be stigmatized.

Respect for parental choice has resulted in more beneficial than harmful consequences. Currently, there are fewer abortions of unaffected fetuses for genetic reasons than in the past. More wanted infants are being born to couples at higher genetic risk than in the past. Also, because practitioners respect the moral views of patients, this fact opens decision making to influence from different moral traditions. These would include a view that any abortion is immoral, a conservative but more moderate view,[49] or "graded" view giving lower moral status to previable fetuses.[50]

Disclosure Dilemmas

Respect for parental choice was supported in responses to three cases on the international survey that also had disclosure dilemmas included with abortion choices.[51]

Case 1

"Prenatal diagnosis has revealed an abnormal fetus. The prospective parents come to see you in a genetics clinic. In this question you are asked how you would react to two different fetal conditions—Turner syndrome (X0) and XYY—in your professional capacity."[52]

Case 2

"Maternal serum alpha-fetoprotein has been elevated in your patient on two occasions, but level II ultrasound shows no abnormality, despite careful examination of the fetal head, spine, abdomen, and kidneys. The fetal karyotype is normal. Amniotic alpha-fetoprotein is elevated, and acetylcholinesterase is borderline. Results raise the possibility of a small neural tube defect. What do you tell the parents?"[53]

Case 3

"Lab analysis of amniotic fluid cells suggest that the fetus may be a trisomy 13 mosaic. Medical geneticists responsible for the analysis disagree as to whether the lab results are artifacts of culture—i.e., false positives. Results of repeat tests are unavailable until after 24 wk gestational age. You were not responsible for the lab work in this case and have not taken one side or the other. You are, however, the medical geneticist who will meet and counsel the pregnant woman. What do you do? Would you disclose colleague disagreements?"[54]

The study found strong consensus in each case for nondirective counseling and for respecting the choices of parents. Eighty-four percent of respondents would be nondirective for XYY and 88 percent for X0. There were exceptions, based on cultural differences in interpreting the severity of these disorders. Exceptions to strong consensus were France, Hungary, and the former GDR, where 65 percent, 60 percent, and 43 percent, respectively, would advise carrying an XYY fetus to term or give optimistically slanted information. In India, Hungary, Turkey, and Norway, 46 percent, 40 percent, 40 percent, and 33 percent, respectively, would advise aborting an X0 (Turner) fetus or give pessimistic information. In India, geneticists cited poor chances for marriage of an infertile girl and a resultant economic burden on the family. Women

geneticists were 5.63-fold more likely than men to be nondirective for X0 and 3.45-fold more likely than men to be nondirective for XYY.

In the maternal serum alpha-fetoprotein case, 98 percent (> 93 percent in each nation) would tell the couple that there might be a small neural tube defect; 87 percent would then counsel nondirectively, 5 percent would advise carrying to term, and 8 percent would advise abortion. In the case of ambiguous results, 97 percent would tell the patient that there might be an abnormality, but fewer (66 percent) would disclose that colleagues disagreed about the interpretation.

Confidentiality and Third-Party Interests

Case Report

You are evaluating a child with an autosomal recessive disorder, for which carrier testing is possible and accurate. In the process of testing relatives for genetic counseling, you discover that the mother and half the siblings are carriers, but the husband is not. The husband believes that he is the child's biologic father.

Cases involving a discovery of false paternity can occur in these circumstances and also in the context of prenatal diagnosis. Should you approach the couple together? If so, the options are to tell them (1) what the laboratory tests reveal about the child's parentage, (2) that they are both genetically responsible, (3) that the origin of the child's disorder is not genetic, (4) that you have not been able to discover which of them is genetically responsible, or (5) the facts about the child's parentage and ask for the name of the child's biologic father so he can be informed that he is a carrier. Another approach involves telling the mother alone, without her husband being present, and letting her decide, perhaps with additional help, what to tell her husband.

This case presents a dilemma between a duty to tell the truth and the duty to prevent harm to the family and to the already vulnerable child who has the disorder. In a similar case on the international survey, 96 percent of respondents believed that protection of the mother's confidentiality overrode disclosure of true paternity; for this reason they chose to tell the mother alone. The major ethical problem with this way of resolving the case is that the biologic father may not be informed of his carrier status, and the husband may continue to believe that he is a carrier. In our view, we should also ask the mother if she wants expert help in informing her husband of the true situation (based on the hypothesis that it is highly likely that it will be discovered). The major strength of this approach is in its caring and respect for the privacy of the woman.

In cases with potent family secrets like false paternity, most geneticists would act caringly to protect the woman's privacy and confidentiality. They would communicate their concern to her that her husband falsely believed that he was a carrier and that another man may not know that he carries a recessive trait. They would offer to obtain additional psychologic or counseling help for her to deal with the issue of disclosure, but they would not undertake this sensitive task themselves.

Twin, Multifetal, and Third-Trimester Dilemmas

A survey of 737 geneticists and obstetricians and ethicists and clergy with known involvement in biomedical ethics compared their views of abortion for social reasons, for anomalies in singleton and twin pregnancies, for sex selection, and in cases of multifetal pregnancies.[55] Choices of selective abortion (emptying the uterus) became choices of selective termination in twin and multifetal cases when parents want to continue the pregnancy. The questionnaires were given to members of the American Society of Human Genetics, International Fetal Medicine and Surgery Society, Society of Perinatal Obstetricians, members of the Society of Christian Ethics, and Protestant, Catholic, and Jewish clergy involved in bioethics.

The responses showed acceptability of abortion in singleton pregnancies that increased with the severity of the anomalies involved and decreased with advancing gestation. The same trend was observed in twins, although the acceptability of selective termination of the affected twin in the second and third trimester was lower than for singleton pregnancies. Overall, acceptance of selective termination was associated strongly with the trimester of pregnancy, indication for selective termination, and fetal number. Medical specialty was the only independent variable affecting acceptance of selective termination in relation to indication, trimester, and number of fetuses. The highest acceptance was among geneticists, and the lowest was among nonmedical professionals.

At the time of the first cases of selective abortion in twin cases, first-trimester prenatal diagnosis was not feasible. Currently, prenatal diagnosis and selective termination can be done by 10–11 weeks of pregnancy or earlier. However, the ethical arguments for the procedure are the same in the second trimester as in the first trimester, and most respondents (physicians and nonphysicians alike) approved of selective termination in both trimesters. The same moral argument that supports selective termination in a singleton pregnancy—preventing the birth of a seriously affected infant to reduce suffering—supports the selective termination of an affected twin. The difference between the two cases is that, in the latter instance, we save the life of a normal twin that would have been aborted. To terminate in twin cases, the center in which the procedure is to be done must be able to deal with the added risks to the mother from the procedure.

In multifetal pregnancies (greater than three), if the woman wants to continue the pregnancy, there is little ethical controversy among those surveyed over reducing the number to two. There is more controversy on whether to reduce triplet gestations at all and even more on whether to reduce from two to one. The ethics of selective termination in multiple gestations was discussed extensively previously.[56] Currently, we are re-evaluating a position opposed to termination of all but one fetus. This position is permissive toward selective termination in presumably normal twin pregnancies. More data are needed on the relative risks of twin pregnancies compared with singleton pregnancies and the risks of intervention.

Others describe two situations in which third-trimester prenatal diagnosis is indicated:[57] (1) clinical findings of fetal growth retardation and polyhydramnios, suggestive of trisomy 18, and (2) when fetal therapy is considered, e.g., before a shunt to drain an intracranial sonolucent area to exclude a chromosomal or genetic disorder. They also note that as third-trimester prenatal diagnosis becomes more common using ultrasonography, nonfatal disorders (45,X; 47,XYY) also will be discovered. What should the approach be to managing disorders in the third trimester?

Three decision paths were described for advise by the physician: (1) When nothing can be done to benefit the fetus, the choice is between termination of pregnancy or withholding all treatment except comfort care at birth; (2) when only minimal benefits can be offered to the fetus, the choice is between treatment and only comfort care; and (3) if more than minimal benefits can be obtained for the fetus, only treatment should be recommended.[58] In each of these three decisions, however, the pregnant woman is the key decision maker. Treatment includes measures like fetal surveillance, tocolysis, Caesarean section, or delivery in a tertiary-care center. These authors reported 72 cases in which only two third-trimester abortions were done. One was for fetal anencephaly at 26 weeks and the other, for fetal triploidy at 26 weeks.

This approach differs in some respects from an earlier argument by these authors that third-trimester abortions were justified if, when delivered, the infant's death would be imminent or the infant would be neurologically devastated.[59] The more recent discussion leaves room for third-trimester abortions "when there are no beneficence-based obligations to the fetus."[60] These authors did not specify what these terms mean, but they could be interpreted to apply in cases of late diagnosis of severe and untreatable disorders with which infants live rather than die at birth. However, the terminations reported were done only in cases when the infant's death

after delivery was certain. The moral line that has been drawn between fetal viability and nonviability is elastic and technology dependent. For this reason, the role of viability in abortion policy will lessen. It is likely that more legal restrictions on abortions in the third trimester will occur. We also predict that there will be strong efforts to restrict elective abortions to the first trimester, except for diagnosed genetic disorders, and that the concept of "brain life" will play a larger role in public policy on abortion and embryo research.[61] This emphasis will stress the benefits of earlier prenatal diagnosis and earlier abortion, if indicated.

Before Experimental Fetal Therapy

This section addresses the following question. What are the major ethical problems in experimental fetal therapy and the most widely shared approaches to these problems?

Investigators in many nations have advanced fetal therapy since the pioneering work.[62] We were involved in the first (and only) fetal therapy experiment at the Clinical Center of the National Institutes of Health to prevent recurrence of 21-hydroxylase deficiency in a fetus of a woman whose previous female child needed surgery after birth to correct masculinized genitalia.[63] This sad event deeply influenced both parents to prevent the birth of another affected infant by abortion. They were informed about the untested concept of fetal therapy with dexamethasone suppression of the fetal adrenal gland. They were somewhat uninterested in the experiment until they viewed the fetus by ultrasonography. The experiment was done, and a female infant was delivered at 39 weeks who was a carrier, like her mother, but was not affected seriously. The mother volunteered that, even after many talks with physicians, she really did not understand that the disease was a genetic disorder. She said, "I thought that it was my fault because of something I had done." The experiment showed that suppression of the fetal adrenal was possible, and subsequent fetal diagnosis and drug therapy of this type was successful, especially in France.[64]

The first international fetal therapy meeting, sponsored by the Kroc Foundation in 1982,[65] led to the International Fetal Medicine and Surgery Society. In this annual meeting, ethical problems in experimental fetal therapy are debated and reconsidered. The records of these meetings chronicle the ethical problems in experimental fetal therapy and approaches to their resolution. The major ethical problems of experimental fetal therapy, listed in terms of their chronologic evolution, are shown in Exhibit 4–4.

Prior Group Review

Do the risks and benefits of experimental fetal therapy require ethical consideration by prior group review? There is a line between innovative treatment—a previously untried maneuver done in the reasonable but unproven expectation that it may provide medical benefit, usually in a desperate situation—and research with its systematic approach to selection of subjects and strategies to reduce bias. In a strict sense, fetal therapy during the last decade has been innovative treatment and not research. There have been no controlled trials in fetal therapy. Investigators in the United States and Europe could have proceeded without prior group review. The possible ethical problem with this choice would have been less-than-optimal consideration of the risks and benefits. However, physicians in the United States and in Europe have submitted their protocols to institutional review boards (United States) and ethics committees (United Kingdom and Europe) and continue to do so.

Case Selection

How should cases for experimental fetal therapy be selected? This is the most frequent and difficult ethical problem because of the lack of knowledge that usually is gained by controlled trials. Which cases will benefit? The worst result of a poor selection is that a prena-

Exhibit 4-4   Ethical Problems in Experimental Fetal Therapy

1. Risk/benefit assessment: research or innovative treatment?
2. Selection of cases for treatment.
3. Optimizing informed consent.
4. Twin pregnancies.
5. Refusal of proven fetal therapy.

tally treated child who would have died survives but with persisting defects from "half-corrected" problems. Guidelines for selection have been proposed yearly using experience gained since 1982, studies of the natural history of fetal disorders, and information from a registry. These guidelines are imperfect and always subject to revision. Recent reviews of medical[66] and surgical[67] approaches of fetal therapy show slow but steady progress on a number of fronts, but the knowledge base is narrow as a result of lack of controlled trials and other research.

Informed Consent

What is the optimal informed consent process for fetal therapy? This topic was discussed in the first conference and developed thereafter. Precautions are needed because of the vulnerability of pregnant women (and their abundance of kin altruism!) and the enthusiasm for treatment that can occur. The precautions shown in Exhibit 4–5 were recommended.

Twin Pregnancies

Should experimental fetal surgery be attempted in twin pregnancies? The ethical problem is risk to the presumably healthy fetus imposed by an unproven treatment. After three years of restraint on this issue, the 1985 meeting of the International Fetal Medicine and Surgery Society approved, in principle, doing surgery for congenital hydronephrosis on one twin when the other was assumed to be normal. However, we are not aware of any twin cases in which such surgery has been done.

Refusal of Proven Fetal Therapy

How should physicians respond if a pregnant women refuses proven fetal therapy in a context where the risk to her appears balanced and acceptable? The ethical problems are that (1) preventable and lasting harm to the fetus may occur and (2) the procedure violates the woman's bodily integrity and autonomy. A significant literature has developed on the potential for this problem.[68] Because most fetal therapies are unproved, women may refuse them, and no ethical problem is posed. In the context of proven fetal therapy, only one case of a refusal of treatment of fetal erythroblastosis by a pregnant woman who was afraid of the risks of acquired immune deficiency syndrome after transfusion was brought to our attention.[69]

Refusal of physician-recommended Caesarean section has been a different story. This issue should be seen against the background of the high operative rate in the United States. A period of collective self-examination followed an important study of court-ordered Caesarean sections[70] showing that cases were limited mainly to minority and non-English-speaking patients. Currently, many emphasize restraint in going to court in the first place.[71] Also needed are social programs to provide better access to prenatal care, prevention of low birth weights, education for young persons about reproduction, and expanded genetic services, especially to those who cannot afford them. As fetal therapy grows, refusals may occur more frequently (as seen in other medical areas). Public policy and legal considerations are important aspects of this topic because society's interests are strong in protecting the choices of pregnant women and enhancing the well-being of fetuses and children.

Workers in fetal therapy see other ethical problems that are more controversial, e.g., issues of organ retrieval and brain death in anencephalic infants, requests for third-trimester abortions, and requests for reduction in multiple pregnancies and normal twin pregnancies. Each is a mine field of conflict and an arena in which either the issues of personhood or the moral status

Exhibit 4–5 Informed Consent Process in Fetal Therapy

1. An impartial physician to "speak for" the fetus.
2. The mother's own physician, at least by phone, to help her understand the risks.
3. Involvement of family, especially the father.
4. Ethics consultation, by request.
5. Psychiatric consultation, on physician request.

of the fetus are of paramount importance. However, the five problems we listed are the most frequent and often the most difficult in the field. Each fetal-therapy team must prepare protocols to respond to these problems.

RESEARCH IN FETAL DIAGNOSIS AND THERAPY

The Consequences of No Federal Support

In this final section, we examine ethical and public policy issues surrounding the lack of federal support for research in fetal diagnosis (including preimplantation embryo diagnosis) and fetal therapy.[72] In our view, this situation is the most serious ethical problem confronting clinicians. Our aim is to encourage restoration of support, beginning with fetal gene therapy.

Progress in fetal diagnosis and therapy, including human fetal gene therapy, is weighed down by a great contradiction. On the one hand, any research that involves the embryo or the fetus in the context of elective abortion or obtaining fetal tissue for transplantation after elective abortion cannot be federally supported or even National Institutes of Health peer reviewed because of social controversy about abortion or research-induced embryo loss. On the other hand, a revolution in knowledge about human genetics is underway with federal support of the Human Genome Project.[73] Currently, what was once unattainable can be attained, i.e., a natural history of a genetic disorder, including some cancers, from the earliest stages of fertilization to the end of human life. This possibility realizes the insight of Samuel Taylor Coleridge: "The history of man for the nine months preceding his birth would, probably, be far more interesting and contain events of greater moment than all the threescore and ten years that follow it."[74]

The Human Genome Project is the most important scientific effort bearing on fetal diagnosis and therapy, but a great contradiction confronts this project. From the same fund that supports basic research, the nation is being asked to spend approximately $3 billion by the year 2005 to gain genetic knowledge, but biomedical and clinical research is restrained, even closed, to the following research activities, each of which affects the future of fetal therapy:

1. Experimental somatic cell gene therapy in diagnosed and affected fetuses to be delivered.[75]

2. Fetal tissue transplant research with tissue or cells from early induced or spontaneous abortions[76] for treatment of diseases with genetic causes in liveborn affected individuals (Parkinson disease, diabetes mellitus—Type I, diGeorge syndrome, and diseases that destroy normal hemoglobin or produce inadequate immune systems) and possibly in fetuses for such or similar conditions.[77]

3. Basic DNA research involving fetal tissues or embryonic cells after early induced abortion to understand gene expression and understand the natural history of genetic diseases, including some familial cancers. Such research could facilitate development of gene therapy by recombinant DNA or by drugs.

4. Research on diagnosis of genetic disease in the human preimplantation embryo to learn if embryo selection can prevent genetic disease, avoid selective abortion, and perhaps open a way to germ-line gene therapy.[78]

There is no legal or constitutional question about the authority of the federal government to deny funds or National Institutes of Health sci-entific peer review to these activities. There is no constitutional "right" for any research to be funded. The Supreme Court has ruled that the government may choose to promote one or more interests above a constitutionally protected activity, such as, in this case, the protection of the interests of fetuses and embryos above the freedom of research understood as free speech.[79] We do not raise legal questions. Rather, we question the ethical or public policy wisdom of erecting a growing wall of separation, similar to the wall that exists between organized religion and the state, between public and private support of the kinds of research listed. Religion and government should be separated, but research and government should not. Many health benefits have been lost, as documented by the Institute of Medicine,[80] and the consequences have been extremely serious to the quality and quantity of biomedical research in fetal diagnosis, maternal-fetal medicine, reproductive genetics, and cancer in the United States.

In opposition to this wall of separation in research, we stress that there is a moral obligation to learn whether these paths of research—and we place fetal gene therapy first—will lead to forms of therapy for fetuses and liveborn persons that will relieve and prevent suffering and premature death. The morality of research does not arise from its source of funding but from its goals and the ethical principles that structure and pattern research activities.

SOURCES OF A MORAL OBLIGATION TO LEARN

What are the sources of a moral obligation to learn? To advance this argument we refer to and modify the content of the Belmont Report,[81] an early consensus document on the ethics of biomedical research in the United States. It proposed three major ethical principles to guide research with human subjects, including the human fetus: respect for persons, beneficence, and justice.

A more complex set of five ethical principles (Exhibit 4–2) is required to guide the scope and practice of biomedical research. This earlier report interpreted beneficence to contain within it the imperatives to avoid and prevent harm. The principle of nonmaleficence, which is especially prominent in the history of biomedical ethics,[82] is relevant to ethical issues in research. Also, the Belmont Report used the beneficence principle as the source for "application" of assessments of risks and benefits to human subjects and society. The principle of proportionality provides more direct and cogent guidance for risk-benefit assessments, one of the most difficult tasks in research ethics, especially when the fetus is involved.

In a prior review of research with human subjects, there is an obligation to ask, "Should this research be done at all?" To examine this question fully requires four principles: respect for a person's autonomy, beneficence, nonmaleficence, and justice. After good reasons for a "yes" response appear, the risk-benefit issues can be treated more fully in the context of proportionality.

The ethics of biomedical research should be shaped by the five principles defined in Exhibit 4–2. These principles also require five tasks of biomedical researchers and institutional review boards: selection of goals for research, informed consent, risk-benefit assessments, selection of subjects, and protection of the freedom to pursue important biomedical knowledge. We discuss here the first and last tasks in the case of fetal gene therapy and other fetal and embryo research. These two tasks are additions to the topics in the Belmont Report.

Goals for biomedical research should be set primarily to cure and prevent the greatest sources of human suffering and premature death and to relieve the pain and suffering caused by these disorders. Most Americans support goals of research that are aimed at treating and preventing genetic diseases and cancer, beginning with the fetus, as long as such research is conducted within the constraints of ethics and law.

Human gene therapy, beginning with the fetus, is a symbol of hope in a sea of human suffering caused by heredity, including that which occurs with abortion of a genetically affected fetus.[83] The extent of such suffering is enormous. Approximately 22 percent of newborn deaths in developed nations are caused by congenital malformations or genetic disorders.[84] Approximately one-third of children admitted to pediatric units in Western nations need treatment for the complications of genetic disorders, congenital defects, or mental retardation.[85] Cancer is now best understood as a genetic disease.[86]

Also, couples who want children have an added burden of high loss of abnormal human embryos after implantation; these losses increase with maternal age.[87] As more women seek higher education, enter the work force, and postpone earlier child bearing, the trend toward later pregnancies and their higher chromosomal risks will increase.

The punishing weight and anxieties of these burdens of heredity explain why most Americans support human genetic therapy to treat particular children. Also most approve of therapy to correct a gene "that would carry the disease to future generations."[88]

If these reasons are persuasive, it is because they acknowledge a moral obligation to learn whether fetal gene therapy—and other measures—are feasible and safe to attempt for the first time. This obligation falls on all of us, whether we are in the government or not. The criterion for such experiments must be that all efforts be directed toward correcting and preventing transmissible genetic disorders, including some cancers. All efforts, in short, must be directed toward treatment, not enhancement of traits that have little or nothing to do with disease.

We ranked the four restrained biomedical and clinical reasearch activities in the order of their clinical relevance to fetuses and also to live-born persons with genetic or other diseases to optimize the development of human genetic therapy. Each activity, considered in the light of the ethical principles discussed, must be placed within the social context of priorities of other goals for biomedical research.[89]

NOTES

1. Probably the only mandatory practices of prenatal diagnosis occur in the People's Republic of China. Dr. Nianhu Sun of Beijung Union College Hospital ("Bioethics in Medical Genetics in China," presented at the Japan Society of Human Genetics Meeting, Fukui, Japan, August 3, 1990) stated that prenatal diagnosis is mandatory for women who have given birth to one child with a birth defect and who wish to have a second child. The permit to have a second child only will be issued if she agrees to have prenatal diagnosis. If the fetus has a defect, abortion is not legally mandatory, but a woman who decides to carry such a fetus to term will be so "laughed at for her silliness" that she cannot persist against the weight of community opinion. If this report is true, the People's Republic of China is unique in mandating prenatal diagnosis for second pregnancy.

It is likely that the only mandatory genetic screening that occurs under religious and state auspices is in Cyprus. On the authority of the Greek Orthodox Archbishop, no couple has the cooperation of an Orthodox priest to marry without proof of carrier screening for thalassemia. It was reported that there have been no new cases of thalassemia in Cyprus as a result of prenatal diagnosis and selective abortion of affected fetuses [A.M. Kuliev, Human Genetic Information: Science, Law, and Ethics, *Ciba Foundation Symposium* 29 (1990):163]. Others reported a 90 percent prevention rate in Sardinia, based on an intense educational program in community meetings and information to physicians, schools, social workers, and mass media [A. Cao, Antenatal Diagnosis of Beta-Thalassemia in Sardinia, in *Genetics, Ethics, and Human Values,* edited by Z. Bankowski and A. M. Capron (Geneva: World Health Organization, CIOMS, 1991), 72]. The incidence of thalassemia major has dropped from 1:250 to 1:1,000 live births. Only five of 715 (0.7 percent) pregnant women with diagnosed fetal thalassemia chose to continue the pregnancy. In addition to these cases, there were four affected infants born as a result of false paternity and 15 as a result of the parents' ignorance of thalassemia because they had "no information" or counseling before pregnancy.

2. A. MacBeath, *Experiments in Living* (London: MacMillan, 1952), 70.

3. J. Ladd, *Ethical Relativism* (Belmont, Calif.: Wadsworth, 1973), 121.

4. S. Elias and G.J. Annas, *Reproductive Genetics and the Law* (Chicago: Yearbook Medical, 1987), 48; J.C. Fletcher, What Are Society's Interests in Human Genetics and Reproductive Technologies? *Law, Medicine, and Health Care* 16 (1988):131.

5. Danish Council of Ethics, *Fetal Diagnosis and Ethics: A Report* (Copenhagen: Clausen Offset, 1991), 58.

6. A. Cao, Antenatal Diagnosis of Beta-Thalassemia in Sardinia, in *Genetics, Ethics, and Human Values*, edited by Z. Bankowski and A.M. Capron (Geneva: World Health Organization, CIOMS, 1991), 72.

7. National Commission for the Protection of Human Subjects of Biomedical and Behavioral Research, *The Belmont Report* (Washington, D.C.: U.S. Government Printing Office, 1983).

8. T.L. Beauchamp and J.F. Childress, *Principle of Biomedical Ethics* (New York: Oxford University Press, 1989), 21.

9. H.T. Engelhardt, *The Foundations of Bioethics* (New York: Oxford University Press, 1986).

10. R.M. Hare, *Moral Thinking* (Oxford: Clarendon Press, 1981).

11. D.C. Wertz and J.C. Fletcher, *Ethics and Human Genetics: A Cross-cultural Perspective* (Heidelberg: Springer-Verlag, 1989).

12. D.J. Kevles, *In the Name of Genetics* (New York: Knopf, 1985), 258.

13. F.C. Fraser, Genetic Counseling, *American Journal of Human Genetics* 26 (1974):636; F. Vogel and A.G. Motulsky, *Human Genetics: Problems and Approaches* (Heidelberg: Springer-Verlag, 1986), 15.

14. Ad Hoc Committee on Genetic Counseling, Genetic Counseling, *American Journal of Human Genetics* 27 (1975):240.

15. J.C. Fletcher et al., Ethical Aspects of Medical Genetics, *Clinical Genetics* 27 (1985):199.

16. Wertz and Fletcher, *Ethics and Human Genetics*.

17. On answers to 14 clinical cases in the survey, strong consensus was defined as more than 75 percent of respondents in more than 75 percent of nations. A moderate consensus was more than 67 percent of respondents in more than 67 percent of nations.

18. Wertz and Fletcher, *Ethics and Human Genetics*, 34–35.

19. Y.E. Hsia, The Genetic Counselor as Information Giver, in *Genetic Counseling: Facts, Values and Norms*, edited by A.M. Capron et al. (New York: Alan R. Liss, 1979), 184.

20. J.C. Fletcher, Genetic Screening, Prenatal Diagnosis, and Counseling, in *Ethical Issues at the Outset of Life*, edited by W.B. Weil and M. Benjamin (Boston: Blackwell Scientific Publications, 1987), 87.

21. D.C. Wertz et al., Communication in Health Professional-Lay Encounters: How Often Does Each Party Know What the Other Wants to Discuss? in *Information and Behavior*, vol. 2, edited by B.D. Ruben (New Brunswick, N.J.: Transaction Books, 1988), 329.

22. R. Rapp, Chromosomes and Communication: The Discourse of Genetic Counseling, *Medical Anthropology Quarterly* 2 (1988):143; R. Rapp, Communication about the New Reproductive Technologies: Cultural, Interpersonal, and Linguistic Determinants of Understanding, in *Women and New Reproductive Technologies: Medical, Psychosocial, Legal, and Ethical Dilemmas*, edited by J. Rodin and A. Collins (Hillsdale, N.J.: Lawrence Erlbaum Associates, 1991), 135.

23. F. Fuchs, Amniocentesis: Techniques and Complications, in *Early Diagnosis of Human Genetic Defects: Scientific and Ethical Considerations*, edited by M. Harris, DHEW Publication no. (NIH) 72-25 (Bethesda, Md.: Fogarty International Center, 1971), 11; M.N. MacIntyre, Discussion: Risks in Amniocentesis, in Harris, *Early Diagnosis of Human Genetic Defects*, 143.

24. J.W. Littlefield, The Pregnancy at Risk for a Genetic Disorder, *New England Journal of Medicine* 282 (1970):627.

25. MacIntyre, Discussion: Risks in Amniocentesis.

26. Wertz and Fletcher, *Ethics and Human Genetics*.

27. Ibid., 21–23.

28. S.L. Clark and G.R. Devore, Prenatal Diagnosis for Couple Who Would Not Consider Abortion, *Obstetrics and Gynecology* 73 (1989):1035.

29. Wertz and Fletcher, *Ethics and Human Genetics*, 23.

30. Ibid.

31. D.T. Joseph, Amniocentesis and Fetal Feticide in Bombay, in report presented to the government of Maharashtra, 1986; J.C. Verma and B. Singh, Ethics and Medical Genetics in India, in Wertz and Fletcher, *Ethics and Human Genetics*, 267.

32. President's Commission for the Study of Ethical Problems in Medicine and Biomedical and Behavioral Research, *Screening and Counseling for Genetic Conditions* (Washington, D.C.: U.S. Government Printing Office, 1983), 57.

33. Kevles, *In the Name of Genetics*.

34. T.M. Powledge and J.C. Fletcher, Guidelines for the Ethical, Social, and Legal Issues in Prenatal Diagnosis, *New England Journal of Medicine* 300 (1979):168; J.L. Hamerton et al., Chromosome Disease, in Prenatal Diagnosis: Past, Present, and Future (special issue), *Prenatal Diagnosis* (1980):11; Report of the Working Group on Genetic Screening and Testing, Proceedings of the XXIVth CIOMS Round Table Conference, in Bankowski and Capron, *Genetics, Ethics, and Human Values*, 184; Empfehlung der Ethikkommission der Gesellschaft fur Anthropologie und Humangenetik, Against the Disclosure of Fetal Sex before the 14th Week of Gestation, in *Prenatale Diagnostik und Therapie*, edited by J. Murken (Stuttgart: Ferdinand Enke Verlag, 1987), 321.

35. National Institute of Child Health and Human Development, *Antenatal Diagnosis: Report of a Consensus Development Conference*, DHEW Publication no. (NIH) 79-173 (Washington, D.C.: U.S. Department of Health, Education, and Welfare, 1979).

36. M.A. Crawford, Ethical and Legal Problems of Early Prenatal Diagnosis, *British Medical Bulletin* 39 (1983):310.

37. D.C. Wertz and J.C. Fletcher, Fatal Knowledge? Prenatal Diagnosis and Sex Selection, *Hastings Center Report* 19, no. 3 (1989):21.

38. Rust v. Sullivan, 111 S.Ct. 1759 (1991).

39. H.H. Kazazian, Prenatal Diagnosis for Sex Choice: A Medical View, *Hastings Center Report* 10, no. 1 (1980):17.

40. Another situation meriting more discussion as a controversial indication is request for fetal information related to the compatibility of the fetus as a future marrow or organ donor. A case report [R.D. Clark et al., Conceiving a Fetus for Bone Marrow Donation: An Ethical Problem in Prenatal Diagnosis, *Prenatal Diagnosis* 9 (1989):329] raised these questions and prompted response [N. Fost, Guiding Principles for Prenatal Diagnosis, *Prenatal Diagnosis* 9 (1989):335]. In the report of this case, it mistakenly was alleged that the parents were "willing to abort as many fetuses as necessary prior to conceiving one which met these specifications." The mistake was corrected in a retraction [R.D. Clark et al., Letter of Retraction, *Prenatal Diagnosis* 9 (1989):549], and the rest of the case report is accurate in every respect.

41. National Institute of Child Health and Human Development, *Antenatal Diagnosis*.

42. D.C. Wertz et al., Attitudes toward Abortion among Parents of Children with Cystic Fibrosis, *American Journal of Public Health* 81 (1991):992.

43. E.T. Juengst, Prenatal Diagnosis and the Ethics of Uncertainty, in *Medical Ethics: A Guide for Health Professionals*, edited by J.F. Monagle and D.C. Thomasma (Gaithersburg, Md.: Aspen Publishers, 1988), 12.

44. R.A. McCormick, *How Brave a Brave New World? Dilemmas in Bioethics* (Washington, D.C.: Georgetown University Press, 1981), 200.

45. Public Law 98-457, amending 42 USC 510(a), 1984; L.H. Glantz, Allowing Babies to Die: Legal Issues, in *Fetal Diagnosis and Therapy*, edited by M.I. Evans et al. (Philadelphia: J.B. Lippincott, 1989), 488.

46. G.M. Atkinson and A.S. Moraczewski, eds., *Genetic Counseling, the Church and the Law: Pope John XXIII Medical-Moral Research and Education Center* (Chicago: Franciscan Herald Press, 1980), 122.

47. McCormick, *How Brave a Brave New World?*

48. Ibid.

49. Ibid.

50. G.R. Dunstan, The Moral Status of the Human Embryo: A Tradition Recalled, *Journal of Medical Ethics* 1 (1984):38.

51. Wertz and Fletcher, *Ethics and Human Genetics*.

52. Ibid.

53. Ibid.

54. Ibid.

55. M.I. Evans et al., Attitudes on the Ethics of Abortion, Sex Selection, and Selective Termination among Health Care Professionals, Ethicists, and Clergy Likely to Encounter Such Situations, *American Journal of Obstetrics and Gynecology* 164 (1991):1092.

56. M.I. Evans et al., First Trimester Selective Termination in Octuplet and Quadruplet Pregnancy, *Obstetrics and Gynecology* 71 (1988):289.

57. J.W. Larsen and M.D. MacMillin, Second and Third Trimester Prenatal Diagnosis, in *Fetal Diagnosis and Therapy,* edited by M.I. Fletcher et al. (Philadelphia: J.B. Lippincott, 1988), 36.

58. F.A. Chervenak and L.B. McCullough, An Ethically Justified, Clinically Comprehensive Management Strategy for Third-Trimester Pregnancies Complicated by Fetal Anomalies, *Obstetrics and Gynecology* 75 (1990):311.

59. F.A. Chervenak et al., When Is Termination of Pregnancy during the Third Trimester Morally Justifiable? *New England Journal of Medicine* 310 (1984):501.

60. Ibid., 503.

61. H.M. Sass, Brain Life and Brain Death: A Proposal for a Normative Agreement, *Journal of Medicine and Philosophy* 14 (1989):45.

62. A.W. Liley, Intrauterine Transfusion of Foetus in Haemolytic Disease, *British Medical Journal* 2 (1963):1107.

63. M.I. Evans et al., Pharmacologic Suppression of the Fetal Adrenal Gland in Utero, *JAMA* 253 (1985):1015.

64. E. Mornet et al., First Trimester Diagnosis of 21-Hydroxylase Deficiency by Linkage Analysis to HLA-DNA Probes and by 17-Hydroxyprogesterone Determination, *Human Genetics* 73 (1986):358; M. David and M.G. Forest, Prenatal Treatment of Congenital Adrenal Hyperplasia Resulting from 21-Hydroxylase Deficiency, *Journal of Pediatrics* 105 (1984):799; M.G. Forest et al., Prenatal Treatment in Congenital Adrenal Hyperplasia due to 21-Hydroxylase Deficiency: Update 88 of the French Multicentric Study, *Endocrine Research* 15 (1989):277.

65. M.R. Harrison et al., Fetal Treatment, *New England Journal of Medicine* 307 (1982):1051.

66. M.I. Evans et al., Pharmacologic and Gene Therapy, in *Reproductive Risks and Prenatal Diagnosis*, edited by M.I. Evans (Norwalk, Conn.: Appleton and Lange, 1992), 321.

67. R.W. Jennings et al., Fetal Surgery, in Evans, *Reproductive Risks and Prenatal Diagnosis,* 311.

68. G.J. Annas, Protecting the Liberty of Pregnant Patients, *New England Journal of Medicine* 316 (1987):1213; J.A. Robertson and J.D. Schulman, Pregnancy and Prenatal Harm to Offspring: The Case of Mothers with PKU, *Hastings Center Report,* 17, no. 4 (1987):13; D. Johnson, A New Threat to Pregnant Women's Autonomy, *Hastings Center Report* 17, no. 4 (1987):33; L.J. Nelson and N. Milliken, Compelled Treatment of Pregnant Women, *JAMA* 259 (1988):1060; N.K. Rhoden, Informed Consent in Obstetrics: Some Special Problems, *Western New England Law Review* 9 (1987):67; T.H. Murray, Moral Obligations to the Not-Yet-Born: The Fetus as Patient, *Clinics in Perinatalogy* 14 (1987):329; W.J. Curran, Court-ordered Cesarean Sections Receive Judicial Defeat, *New England Journal of Medicine* 316 (1987):1192; J.A. Robertson, Legal Considerations in Fetal Treatment, in *The Unborn Patient,* 2nd ed., edited by M.R. Harrison et al. (Philadelphia: W.B. Saunders, 1990), 14; J.C. Fletcher and A.R. Jonsen, Ethical Considerations in Fetal Treatment, in Harrison et al., *The Unborn Patient.*

69. Frank J. Craparo, MD, informed us of such a case that occurred at Pennsylvania Hospital in 1991 and plans to prepare a report for publication.

70. V.E. Kolder, Court-ordered Obstetrical Interventions, *New England Journal of Medicine* 316 (1987):1192; N. Rhoden, The Judge in the Delivery Room: The Emergence of Court-ordered Cesareans, *California Law Review* 74 (1987):1951.

71. American College of Obstetricians and Gynecologists, Patient Choice: Maternal-Fetal Conflict, technical bulletin 55, 1987.

72. The National Institute of Child Health and Human Development recently decided to fund a study of efficacy in fetal surgery for diaphragmatic hernia. This is the first clinical research project in fetal therapy that the National Institutes of Health has funded.

73. U.S. Department of Health and Human Services, *Understanding Our Genetic Inheritance: The U.S. Human Genome Project: The First Five Years FY 1991–1995* (Washington, D.C.: U.S. Government Printing Office, 1990).

74. S.T. Coleridge, *Miscellanies, Aesthetic and Literary* (1803).

75. We see this activity as "hampered" and the remaining three as "blocked." It is uncertain whether fetal gene therapy experiments can be approved by the Human Gene Therapy Subcommittee and the Recombinant Advisory Committee alone. Will a recommendation also be

necessary from an Ethics Advisory Board (EAB) required by federal regulation but unchartered since 1980? There is precedent for review of federally supported fetal research by an EAB. Technically, a fetal gene therapy project would not require any use of the "waiver of minimal risk" so problematic in investigative fetal research in the context of elective abortion. Fetal gene therapy is therapeutic in intent, designed to "meet the health needs of . . . the particular fetus" [45 *Code of Federal Regulations* 46, 206]. However, the Secretary of Health and Human Services can request advice from the EAB about ethical issues raised by individual applications or proposals [46.204 (b)]. Reinstating an EAB is controversial because of links with fetal research.

76. Federally funded therapeutic research with fetal cells after spontaneous abortion would not be precluded by the current moratorium. However, there have been no proposals submitted to the National Institutes of Health. Why? The answer may lie in the rate of infection and chromosomal abnormalities in spontaneous abortions. Another reason may be the absence of an EAB to which to refer proposals. We must presume that there is a strong perception of an obstacle in the minds of investigators even though no obstacle exists.

77. J.L. Touraine, In Utero Transplantation of Hemopoietic Stem Cells in Humans, *Transplantation Proceedings* 23 (1991):1706.

78. J.C. Fletcher and W.F. Anderson, Human Gene Therapy: A New Stage of Debate, *Law, Medicine, and Health Care*, in press.

79. J.A. Robertson, The Scientist's Right to Research: A Constitutional Analysis, *Southern California Law Review* 51 (1978):1203.

80. Institute of Medicine, *Science and Babies: Private Decisions, Public Dilemmas* (Washington, D.C.: National Academy Press, 1990), 147.

81. The Belmont Report discussed three tasks in the protection of human subjects: informed consent, risk-benefit assessment, and selection of subjects. We add two more tasks: selection of goals for research and protection of the freedom of the pursuit of important biomedical knowledge by research. The Belmont Report focused primarily on protection of human subjects and its drafters assumed that freedom of research was not a major issue. We believe that the byproducts of the conflict on abortion, especially in the federal sector, include policies, practices, and moratoria that unfairly restrict the freedom to pursue important biomedical knowledge.

82. T.L. Beauchamp and J.F. Childress, *Principles of Biomedical Ethics*, 3rd ed. (New York: Oxford University Press, 1989), 120.

83. There is much evidence that genetic abortions cause serious emotional trauma to both parents. More research

freedom will increase a trend in earlier prenatal diagnosis that has already reduced (1) complications of second-trimester abortion to the pregnant woman and (2) the emotional harm of midtrimester genetic abortion [B.D. Blumber et al., The Psychological Sequelae of Abortion Performed for a Genetic Indication, *American Journal of Obstetrics and Gynecology* 122 (1975):799; P. Donnai et al., Attitudes of Patients after "Genetic" Termination of Pregnancy, *British Medical Journal* 282 (1981):621; N.J. Leschot et al., Therapeutic Abortion on Genetic Indications: A Detailed Follow-up Study of 20 Patients, in *On Prenatal Diagnosis,* edited by M. Verjaal and J.H. Leschot (Amsterdam: Rodopi, 1982), 85; O.W. Jones et al., Parental Response to Mid-trimester Therapeutic Abortion Following Amniocentesis, *Prenatal Diagnosis* 4 (1984):249; T.M. Marteau et al., The Impact of Prenatal Screening and Diagnostic Testing upon the Cognitions, Emotions, and Behavior of Pregnant Women, *Journal of Psychosomatic Research* 33 (1989):7]. One study documented a need for support and caring after abortion or pregnancy loss after first-trimester chorionic villus sampling [R.B. Black, A 1 and 6 Month Follow-up of Prenatal Diagnosis Patients Who Lost Pregnancies, *Prenatal Diagnosis* 9 (1989):795]. In prenatal diagnosis, women who lose their fetuses at any time would benefit from intervention and supportive care by clinicians [M.C.A. White-Van Mourik et al., Patient Care before and after Termination of Pregnancy for Neural Tube Defects, *Prenatal Diagnosis* 10 (1990):497; S.H. Elder and K.M. Laurence, The Impact of Supportive Intervention after Second Trimester Termination of Pregnancy for Fetal Abnormality, *Prenatal Diagnosis* 11 (1991):47] and companionship of persons close to them.

84. J. Galjaard, Early Diagnosis and Prevention of Genetic Disease, in *Aspects of Genetic Disease*, edited by H. Galjaard (Basel, Switzerland: Karger, 1984), 1.

85. R.L. Brent, The Magnitude of the Problem of Congenital Malformations, in *Prevention of Physical and Mental Congenital Defects* (New York: Alan R. Liss, 1985), 55.

86. J.M. Hall et al., Linkage of Early-onset Familial Breast Cancer to Chromosome 17q21, *Science* 250 (1990):1684; J. Marx, Genetic Defect Identified in Rare Cancer Syndrome, *Science* 250 (1990):1209; D. Malkin et al., Germ Line p53 Mutations in a Familial Syndrome of Breast Cancer, Sarcomas, and Other Neoplasms, *Science* 250 (1990):1233.

87. D. Warbarton, Reproductive Loss: How Much Is Preventable? *New England Journal of Medicine* 316 (1987):158; S. Harlap et al., A Life Table of Spontaneous Abortions and the Effects of Age, Parity, and Other Variables, in *Embryonic and Fetal Death*, edited by I.H. Porter and E.B. Hook (New York: Academic Press, 1980), 148.

88. U.S. Congress, Office of Technology Assessment, *New Developments in Biotechnology: Public Perceptions of Biotechnology*, Publication no. (OTA) BP-BA-45 (Washington, D.C.: U.S. Government Printing Office, 1987), 73.

89. The ethical, scientific, and political aspects of these issues are discussed more fully in J.C. Fletcher, Controversies in Research Ethics Affecting the Future of Human Gene Therapy, *Human Gene Therapy* 1 (1990):307; J.C. Fletcher, Fetal Tissue Transplantation Research and Federal Policy: A Growing Wall of Separation, *Fetal Diagnosis and Therapy* 5 (1990):211.

Chapter 5

Reproductive Freedom: Its Nature, Bases, and Limits

Dan W. Brock

What moral right do people have to reproductive freedom? What is the content of reproductive freedom? What are the moral bases of any such right? What are the moral limits to the right to reproductive freedom? New reproductive technologies represent fertility aids to the otherwise infertile, while various means, new and old, of contraception represent means of limiting fertility to prevent procreation, and so I shall employ each as paradigmatic means, though of course not the only means, for testing the content and limits of the right to reproductive freedom.[1] One important respect in which my discussion will be incomplete is that I will not address the special moral issues surrounding abortion; though abortion is an important component of reproductive freedom, taking up the special moral issues it raises would divert my focus from characterizing the right to reproductive freedom more generally. Throughout, except where I indicate to the contrary, I shall be concerned with moral, not legal, rights, claims, and judgments. These are the issues I shall address in this chapter. Since the territory and issues are wide ranging and complex, I cannot hope to fully explore any of the issues. Instead, my hope is to provide a moral framework or geography of the issues that may be helpful in providing some order and structure to the debates and facilitate exploring particular issues in greater detail and depth.

WHAT IS REPRODUCTIVE FREEDOM?

John Robertson characterizes "procreative liberty," which I take here to be effectively equivalent to reproductive freedom, as "freedom in activities and choices related to procreation," but notes that "the term does not tell us what activities fall within its scope."[2] Moreover, if reproductive freedom is defined in the service of defending a moral claim to its protection, for example, in defense of a moral right to reproductive freedom, then its characterization will be morally controversial. My account of the nature, bases, and limits of the moral right to reproductive freedom will comprise the body of this chapter. Nevertheless, a preliminary account of the content of reproductive freedom can be offered at the outset.

Source: This chapter was originally prepared as a paper for a conference on "Women, Equality, and Reproductive Technology," part of a larger project on the capabilities approach in economic development of the World Institute for Development Economics Research, the United Nations University, Helsinki, Finland, whose financial support of, and permission to reprint, the author's work is gratefully acknowledged.

A common distinction in moral and political philosophy is between negative and positive rights. Negative rights require that others *not* act in particular ways that would violate the right—for example, your right not to be killed morally requires that others not perform any action that would kill you. Positive rights require others *to* act in ways required by the right—for example, if you have a right not to be allowed to die from starvation, then some others are morally required to provide you with food when that is necessary to prevent you from starving. Rights used in moral and political discourse are often complex combinations of both negative and positive rights—for example, the right to life is often understood to include both the negative right not to be killed and some positive right to aid necessary for life. The right to reproductive freedom that I shall be exploring in this chapter should be understood as containing both positive and negative components—for example, as forbidding the state to prevent access to means of contraception,[3] but also requiring that it be provided to women who would otherwise not have access to it. It should not be assumed, however, that any negative component of the right to reproductive freedom must have a positive correlate as well. For example, it may be morally wrong to interfere with a woman's use of some very expensive new reproductive technology that she has secured with her own funds, but not morally required, because of its great cost, to make that same reproductive technology available at public expense to anyone who needs and wants it. A particularly controversial part of the right to reproductive freedom is the scope and extent of its positive components—what actions, services, positive aid, and circumstances it requires others to secure for individuals as part of their right and whom it requires to do so.

It is common to think of reproductive freedom as a freedom of women, with men's role historically having been one of largely limiting or infringing it. Without denying the historical claim, I want to leave open that both women and men may have significant moral claims to reproductive freedom, claims that sometimes mutually support each other and that in other cases come into conflict. In either the typical case of coital reproduction or in cases making use of one or another new form of noncoital reproductive technology, men play a necessary causal role in the reproductive process, either by engaging in sexual intercourse with women or by furnishing their sperm. Moreover, some of the interests or values that I shall argue form the basis for a moral right to reproductive freedom apply to men as well as women. Thus, while the principal issues bear on women's reproductive freedom, we do well at the outset not to focus exclusively on them.

The Choice of Whether To Procreate, with Whom, and by What Means

Reproductive freedom involves, first, uncoerced choice about whether to procreate at all, or more precisely whether to participate in procreative activity with a willing partner. I have already noted that there are activities and choices intended to *lead to* reproduction and other activities and choices designed to *prevent* reproduction. Both are part of reproductive freedom. When the decision about procreation is positive, reproductive freedom includes the choice of whether to reproduce by coital or noncoital means. In the case of coital means, it includes with whom to engage in intercourse in order to reproduce. In the case of noncoital methods, it can include which method and which other persons may be involved in furnishing sperm, ova, or uterus or involved in some other way. (These might be thought of as the technical means of reproduction if that did not have an overly antiseptic connotation.) Reproductive freedom thus includes at least some access to new reproductive techniques, though as I shall argue later not unlimited access without regard for the costs of those reproductive services.[4]

The Choice of the Social Context in Which Reproduction Takes Place

Reproductive freedom also should include some control over and choices about the social context in which reproduction will take place, for example, in or out of marriage, in heterosexual or homosexual relationships, as a sole parent or with another who will share parenting, and so forth. In an interpretation I shall defend later, reproductive freedom should be understood to require as well a wide range of background social and legal practices that affect and facilitate the practices of having and raising children. These include policies of maternal and paternal leave in the workplace; availability of adequate child care for working parents; legal policies that forbid various forms of discrimination related to childbearing and parenting; practices that provide reasonable opportunities for mating, whether in or out of marriage, with or without an expectation or obligation to reproduce; and so forth. More generally, reproductive freedom may be appropriately understood to require that reproduction not have to take place in circumstances in which it results in unjust deprivations or has other unjust impacts on those who choose to reproduce; of course, this means that it will often be morally controversial whether a particular impact of a choice to reproduce (or not to reproduce) is an unjust impact.

The Choice of When To Reproduce

The advent of modern methods of contraception and procreation make the choice of when to reproduce an increasingly important component of reproductive freedom. Contraception gives control over when one will not reproduce, while new reproductive techniques make it possible for women to reproduce at times when it would have been either unlikely or impossible for them to do so in the past. Control over the timing of reproduction is important, for example, on the one hand to enable women to avoid pregnancy at a time when they are too young to want or be able to assume the usual responsibilities of parenthood and, on the other hand, to enable women, and sometimes men as well, to work or pursue careers before they begin families and thereby reduce or eliminate the career disadvantage they commonly suffer in the workplace from time spent in having and raising children. The general point is that the timing of reproduction within a person's life can have myriad complex and important impacts on that life over which reproductive freedom should provide some control.

The Choice of How Many Children To Have

Reproductive freedom is understood in many, but not all, societies to include control over the decision about how many children to have. An important violation of many women's reproductive freedom is coercion to have more children than they want to have, for example, in order to provide increased economic security to the family or to produce a child of the desired (usually male) gender. Many population control policies, on the other hand, are designed to limit the number of children that people have. Such policies range along a spectrum in the means they employ, including educational programs and rational persuasion at one end and economic incentives to have fewer children, economic penalties for having more than the desired number of children, and forced sterilization or abortion after a specified number of children at the other end. It is problematic whether a moral right to reproductive freedom should include a right to have an unlimited number of children, as opposed to a right to have some limited number of children; whether it should depends in part, I believe, on social conditions such as the degree of need to control population growth. There is an important difference between the right to be a parent and the right to have an unlimited number of children, for at least two reasons. First, some of the interests that support the former, for example, the desire to have the psychologically and emotionally deep experience of parenthood, do not support the latter. Second, significant portions of the costs of having children are in many societies externalized, that is, borne by others besides the parents (or children), and so those others may reasonably have some say or control in the costs imposed on them.

The Choice of What Kind of Children To Have

Perhaps one of the most controversial possible components of reproductive freedom is the freedom to choose what kind of children to have. Demographic statistics that indicate there are many millions of "missing women" in the world support other evidence that male infants are commonly favored, especially in conditions of severe deprivation, in ways that lead to disproportionate female infant and early childhood deaths or that female infants are often allowed to die or actively killed.[5] In these respects, parents or others are choosing, whether freely or under coercion, what sex their children will have. The choice of a mate is sometimes in part an attempt of individuals, albeit by crude and imperfect means, to control the nature of their offspring. The enormous increase in knowledge of human genetics that has taken place in recent years, together with techniques of prenatal genetic screening of potential offspring, has already produced substantial abilities to control the nature of one's children. This now takes largely a negative form by parents employing genetic testing that can determine that a fetus has, or has an increased risk of having, a genetically based disease or disability, with the parents then having the choice to abort an affected fetus. When the condition can be treated in utero, the pregnant woman, in most countries where such treatment is available, has the authority to decide, through the law of informed consent, whether to seek treatment of the fetus.[6]

The Human Genome Project now underway and scheduled to be completed within the next 15 years is intended to map and sequence the entire human genome.[7] This project holds out the prospect of vastly increasing our ability to detect genetic diseases and disadvantages and either to treat them in utero or to abort the fetus when that is not possible or wanted. When genetic diseases or disabilities could be treated during pregnancy, a pregnant woman's right to decide about such treatment for her fetus might be based on her own right either to bodily integrity or to decide about her own health care, for example, if the treatment involves surgical invasion of her own body, or on her right as the potential infant's mother to decide for it. When her decision is to treat such a disease, her decision will usually be in the interests of her future child and so supported both by any right she has to decide, either based in her right to reproductive freedom or her right to give informed consent to medically invasive treatment, and by her future child's interests. Failure to proceed with treatment in cases where there is little if any risk to her and substantial harm to her future child to be prevented I take up later under limits to the right to reproductive freedom.

Looking further into the future, the Human Genome Project, together with other medical advances, is likely to make possible "genetic engineering" that will enable manipulation of the genetic traits of offspring, not just to eliminate genetically based diseases and disabilities, but to affect or produce genetically based positive traits desired by the parents or others.[8] It is much more difficult to determine the extent to which such control should be understood as a part of reproductive freedom, and I can say only a little about the issue here. In many, if not most, societies, parents are accorded significant discretion and control in the raising of their children, including decisions about their children's education, religious exposure and training, and more generally the values that will be passed on to the children. Some significant discretion of this sort is necessary for whoever is assigned primary responsibility for the rearing of children, which again in most societies is the parents. This parental autonomy is not unlimited, however, either in morality or the law. The fundamental interests of the child place moral limits on this parental autonomy, as reflected in typical child abuse and neglect statutes in the law. Thus, the interests of the person the child will become are one source of moral limits on this parental autonomy.[9]

The more difficult issue is the extent to which the broader society can legitimately claim a role in such decision. Individual decisions of this form of positive eugenics by parents could potentially have a substantial impact on the nature of the overall society of which they are members. Moreover, the decisions do not solely, or even principally, affect the parents—their primary impact is on the nature of the persons created through this positive eugenics, who will be the future members of the society. Thus, the pregnant woman's or parent's interest in self-determination, understood as in part the making of significant decisions about one's own life, does not decisively establish that such positive eugenics decisions should be the pregnant woman's or parent's. These decisions do, of course, significantly affect parents' lives. However, the self-determination interest of individuals grounds resting the authority with them to make particular decisions only when those decisions either do not significantly affect others or have effects on others that are disproportionately small in comparison with their effects on the individuals in question. There is thus some case for the employment of collective societal decision making, for example, through use of democratic decision procedures, to determine at least the broad parameters within which eugenic choices might be made as a part of reproductive freedom.

We have then a very preliminary sketch of what reproductive freedom includes, and even such a sketch makes clear that the common understanding of reproductive freedom as essentially concerned with preventing pregnancy by contraception, or procreation by abortion, is far too narrow. Even the broader understanding, which includes access to means of enhancing or creating fertility by new reproductive techniques, is too narrow as well, because it too ignores many important effects on women's, and to a lesser extent men's, lives that reproductive choices have and that are plausibly thought a part of reproductive freedom. Of course, the extent to which a moral right to reproductive freedom ought to secure an individual's control over many of these aspects of reproductive freedom is morally controversial. I shall begin to address those issues in the next section of this chapter, which takes up the possible moral bases of a right to reproductive freedom. It is worth adding

that which of these aspects of reproductive freedom should be secured by law, and in what ways, is a separate issue that is not my main concern here—the law may be an inept means for securing some aspects of this moral right.

THE INTERESTS AND VALUES THAT GROUND A MORAL RIGHT TO REPRODUCTIVE FREEDOM

Which of the components discussed in the last section should be part of a moral right to reproductive freedom, and what its more detailed specification should be, will depend on what interests or values ground the right or, put differently, what moral arguments serve as the defense of the right. I will sketch three alternative accounts or bases of such a right—they will only be sketched because to develop them fully would take us into issues of moral and political philosophy that cannot be pursued here. The first argument, which is perhaps the most common argument for a right to reproductive freedom, derives that right from a broader right or interest of individuals in self-determination. The second argument, most natural within, though not exclusive to, utilitarian or general consequentialist moral views, derives the right from the important contribution reproductive freedom typically makes to individuals' good or welfare. The third argument grounds the right in a principle of equality, in the version I sketch here, specifically equality of expectations and opportunity between genders. I emphasize that I do not take these different arguments in defense of a moral right to reproductive freedom to be mutually exclusive, forcing us to choose among them (or others). Instead, I believe each captures something important about reproductive freedom, so that a full account of a moral right to reproductive freedom must incorporate all three.

Self-Determination

In a sentence, by our interest in self-determination I mean our interest in making significant decisions about our own lives for ourselves, according to our own values or conception of a good life, and having those decisions respected by others. John Rawls has characterized this interest as based in our capacity to form, revise over time, and pursue a plan of life.[10] Of course, reference to a plan of life should not be taken too literally, as implying that people sit down at any point in time and work out a fully detailed plan for the rest of their lives. Instead, the idea is that because persons have conceptions of themselves as beings who persist over time, with both a past and a future as well as a present, they have the capacity to form more or less long term plans and intentions for their lives. Other things equal, the further into the future, the less detailed and fixed these plans will typically be.

In addition, persons have the capacity to form what Harry Frankfurt has called second-order desires, desires that take other desires, not first-order activities and experiences, as their object.[11] I would prefer to put this point in terms of our capacity to value having particular desires or motivations. We share with other animals a capacity for goal-directed behavior, and so a capacity in some sense for intentional behavior. Unlike other animals, however, we have the capacity to engage in second-order reflection about our aims and ends and to affirm or deny them as our own and as defining not just who we happen to be but as well who, what kind of person, we wish to be. It is this capacity that makes it sensible to say that, unlike other animals, persons have a conception of the good, which is more than simply having desires and motivations, a feature we share with other animals. When, as happens to all of us to a greater or lesser extent, our desires are not as we want them to be, we can, within limits, take steps to change them to bring our actual motivational structure into closer conformity with the character that we value or want to have.

It is by this second-order reflection about what we value having and being that we are able to form and then to act on a conception of our good rather than simply being guided by instinct and environmental stimuli. Of course, none of this is to deny that our social and natural environment deeply affects our values and conception of good. By having our choices about the life we want for ourselves respected by others, in the sense at least of not being interfered with even if they disagree with the choices we make, we are able to take some control and responsibility for our lives and for the kinds of persons we become.

Rawls has characterized our autonomy interest as a highest-order interest, meaning, at least in part, that it is of a higher order or importance than the particular aims and values that give content to our conception of the good or plan of life at any point in time.[12] These aims and values, we know from our own and others' experience, can and will change over time in both predictable and unpredictable ways. For most of us most of the time, the objects of our aims and desires have value because we desire them, and should we cease to desire them, they will cease to have value for us. Our interest in self-determination, on the other hand, is our interest in being valuing agents, able to guide our own lives in this way. Self-determination is a central condition of personhood.

I initially characterized self-determination as making significant decisions about our own lives for ourselves and according to our own aims and values, and these two components are distinct. Most people value making important decisions about their lives for themselves rather than having the decisions made for them by others, even if others might make better decisions as evaluated by those individuals' own values. In this respect, self-determination is part of a moral ideal of the person, not simply valuable in maximizing the satisfaction of our other desires. In turn, the value of making decisions concerning reproduction lies not solely in individuals being able to make the best or wisest decisions, but also in this exercise of self-determination being part of an attractive moral ideal of the person.

A second necessary point about the value of self-determination is that its exercise can be more or less important or valuable on different occasions and in different decisions. One of the most important factors determining this differential importance or value is the nature of the decision in question. Deciding what you will have for breakfast tomorrow is of vastly less significance to your life than deciding what career you will pursue, whom you will marry, or whether you will have children. Other things being equal, the more central and far-reaching the impact a particular decision will have on our lives, the more substantial our self-determination interest in making it. This is why self-determination is so important in most of the decisions or choices that I have suggested comprise reproductive freedom—specifically, choices about whether to procreate, with whom to do so, by what means to do so, and when and how often to do so. Few decisions that people make are more personal than these, in the sense that what is the best choice depends on people's own personal aims and values, or more far-reaching in their impact on people's lives. (On the other hand, the claim to control the choice of what kind of children to have, whether the sex selection now to some extent possible or the much broader powers likely available in the future, is less plausibly a central aspect of individual self-determination. This choice is less a matter of individual self-determination than of determination of another, and while self-determination supports parents shaping their children to some extent during childrearing, the moral claim to determine what another is like is substantially weaker than the moral claim to self-determination.) The claim of a moral right to self-determination encompassing these reproductive choices can thus be based on the premise that individuals' interest in self-determination concerning these choices is of sufficient moral importance that decision-making authority over them should in nearly all cases be left with those individuals. (I say "in nearly all cases" because I do not believe such a right is plausibly taken to be absolute and never overridden by other moral considerations. I spell out the main sorts of overriding considerations

below in "Moral Limits of Reproductive Freedom.") The self-determination defense of reproductive freedom seeks to place reproductive choices within the broader moral context of individual self-determination in order to help explain and justify the importance of those choices to individuals.

What I have called here the moral interest or right of self-determination is often called in the law the interest or right of *privacy*, as the courts in the United States have constructed that right, or alternatively a constitutionally protected *liberty interest*.

Individual Good or Welfare

A second line of argument in defense of reproductive freedom appeals to the contribution it makes to individuals' welfare, well-being, or good (hereafter, I shall usually use only the notion of individual good, though these concepts are not interchangeable in all contexts). The precise form this argument takes will depend in part on the account of individual good employed. It is common in the philosophical literature to distinguish three main types of theory of the good for persons. Each is a theory of what is intrinsically good or valuable, that is, roughly, good independent of its consequences and relations to other things; many other things are instrumentally good because they lead to what is intrinsically good.

Conscious experience theories hold that people's good comprises certain kinds of positive conscious experiences, often characterized as pleasure or happiness (though on many theories of happiness, it is not fully reducible to any kind of conscious experience) and the absence of pain or unhappiness. Preference or desire satisfaction theories of the good for persons hold that what is good is the satisfaction of people's desires or preferences. Satisfying people's desires is to be distinguished from the satisfaction people normally experience from having their desires satisfied. Satisfaction of desire occurs when the object of a desire obtains; for example, my desire to be in Boston tomorrow is satisfied just in case I am in Boston tomorrow, independent of any conscious experience of satisfaction or enjoyment I may or may not experience when I am there. Finally, what can be called objective good theories deny that a person's good consists only of positive conscious experiences or desire satisfaction, but hold that some things are good for people even if they do not want them and will not obtain pleasure or happiness from them.[13] Objective good theories differ as to what is held to be objectively good for persons, but typical views appeal to the possession of certain virtues, for example, courage or trustworthiness, or ideals, for example, being autonomous or self-determined.

Many difficult and complex issues are involved in attempting to give a full and precise account of any of these alternative kinds of theory of the good for persons, and those issues often have important substantive implications for a defense of reproductive freedom as promoting individuals' good. Just to illustrate this point, desire satisfaction theories of the good for persons do not equate an individual's good with the satisfaction of that individual's actual desires at any point in time. Rather, it is only the satisfaction of people's desires that have been corrected or "laundered" in a variety of ways that is plausibly held to be good for people.[14] People's actual desires are often for what will be bad for them due to misinformation about the objects of their desires (a 13-year-old girl has false beliefs about what it will be like to become a mother at that age), due to socialization that has shaped their desires in irrational ways (a woman chooses to try to satisfy her husband's desire for more children whom she does not want because she has been taught that she should defer to his desire to have a male child), and due to many other respects in which people's desires can be defective and not a reliable measure of their good.

When reproductive freedom is defended as promoting people's good, what choices and conditions will constitute a right of reproductive freedom will depend importantly on the details of the account of the good for persons to which appeal is made. Nevertheless, it is clear that there is at least a broad connection between people's good and securing reproductive freedom for them on each of the main accounts of that good. Securing and respecting the various components of reproductive freedom that I singled out in the first section usually contributes to the happiness of all affected. Likewise, it usually will promote general desire satisfaction. And finally, it usually will promote typical objective components of the good, for example, individual self-determination. But it is important to this line of defense of reproductive freedom that each of the above empirical claims is only plausible with the qualification "usually" that I have given it. Defending a right to reproductive freedom by its promotion of individuals' good comes up against the general problem of defending moral rights in this way.[15]

A distinctive feature of typical claims of a moral right to reproductive freedom is that the rights' possessor is morally entitled to make his or her own reproductive choices even when those choices do not maximize the good for all affected or do not best promote his or her own good when only it is significantly affected. It is notoriously difficult to defend moral rights with this nonutilitarian or nonconsequentialist feature, as opposed to social or legal rights, within a general utilitarian or consequentialist moral framework of maximizing the good. The point is not that a consequentialist moral framework fails to make a right to reproductive freedom absolute, in the sense that it is never overridden by other conflicting moral considerations. I do not believe that the right to reproductive freedom is absolute in that sense. Instead, the point is that a moral right to reproductive freedom that is nonabsolute but nevertheless nonconsequentialist in its strength is at the least difficult ultimately to defend by this appeal to the good consequences of respecting reproductive freedom. With that said, however, I should add that respecting most of the aspects of reproductive freedom singled out in the first section does usually promote individuals' good, and in those cases this is one significant part of the overall moral case for doing so.

Equality of Expectations and Opportunity

The third line of defense of reproductive freedom, specifically of a moral right to reproductive freedom, is based on a moral principle of equality. The equality defense best illuminates why some of the components of reproductive freedom discussed in the first section, but less commonly understood as such, are important components of reproductive freedom. On the other hand, we will see that other components of reproductive freedom discussed in the first section seem not to be supported by the equality defense, and so their support must come from elsewhere.

The first part of the equality defense is the premise that gender, whether one is male or female, is a morally irrelevant property of persons, in the sense that it morally ought not affect people's social and economic expectations in life and their opportunity to attain desired positions and benefits.[16] In this respect, it is like race, and the premise about its moral irrelevance should be as morally uncontroversial as the analogous premise regarding race.

This premise is not a denial of natural difference between the genders, since it is a banal truism that, at the least, only women get pregnant. This is a natural fact of biology that it is not now possible to change and by itself represents no unjust inequality between the genders. What are unjust are forms of straightforward gender discrimination that disadvantage women and systematic social and economic impediments related, in ways subject to social change and control, to natural gender differences, such as the fact that only women get pregnant. And, of course, in most of the world today both of these kinds of gender discrimination are common. Reproductive freedom then serves equality in two important ways: First, it can help mitigate gender disadvantages that women suffer that are specifically tied to reproduction; second, it can mitigate the effects of other gender discrimina-

tion against women that is not tied specifically to reproduction.

To illustrate this relation between reproductive freedom and equality, consider the components of reproductive freedom of women having the choices of whether to procreate, when to do so, and how many children to have. Even with the best social supports and accommodations to pregnancy and childbearing, they typically have deep and far-reaching effects on women's lives. The effects include not just the often transforming and deeply meaningful experiences of childbearing and parenting themselves, of course, but other less desirable impacts such as reduced economic independence and disadvantages in the pursuit of careers. The effective choice and control over whether to procreate gives women the opportunity to decide whether the expected benefits of having children outweigh the other disruptions and burdens it will impose on them, at least to the extent these factors can be understood and weighed before having children. Control over the timing of procreation and the number of children she will have gives a woman additional control over the nature and timing of the impact of reproduction on her life.

In many, if not most, countries, childbearing and childrearing take place in social settings in which additional major, though preventable, disadvantages in opportunities and expectations attend these roles. The aspects of reproductive freedom that include choosing whether, when, how often, and with whom to procreate then take on commensurably greater moral importance. That moral importance becomes in part their role in permitting women to mitigate the effects of these unjust gender-based inequalities on their lives.

The equality defense of reproductive freedom, like the self-determination defense, supports some aspects of reproductive freedom more clearly and persuasively than others. I have already noted, at least in a very general way, the relation between gender-based inequalities and control over whether, when, and how often to procreate; the decision about whom to procreate with can have substantial implications for the inequalities that will attend childbearing and childrearing as well. Choices about what kind of children to have, on the other hand, are for the most part neither inextricably nor in fact linked to reducing or compensating for gender-based inequalities; this aspect of reproductive freedom appears not to be significantly supported by the equality defense. The equality defense of reproductive freedom is most essential, however, in making clear why a variety of social and legal circumstances and practices, such as maternity leave and child care, which form the social and legal background within which reproduction takes place, are properly considered a part of reproductive freedom. A central purpose of these circumstances and practices is either to prevent or to compensate for gender-based inequalities in expectations and opportunities that would otherwise attend reproduction.

SOME IMPLICATIONS OF THE DIFFERENT GROUNDS OF REPRODUCTIVE FREEDOM

Reproductive Freedom for Men

I noted earlier that I did not want to assume at the outset that reproductive freedom applies only to women. Having examined briefly the distinct interests and values that underlie and support reproductive freedom, we can now see why reproductive freedom applies, though in a substantially more restricted way, to men as well. Probably all three lines of support for reproductive freedom, but certainly the first two, lend some support to reproductive freedom for men. I believe we can see a recognition of this reflected in the fact that in well-functioning and relatively egalitarian relationships, most of these choices which are part of reproductive freedom are made in a mutual way, as joint decisions of the two parties. (This is true not only in heterosexual relationships but in homosexual relationships as well, though I shall focus on the more common heterosexual case in considering the reproductive rights of men.) This reflects both the nature of those relationships and the recognition

by each partner that these decisions will have a major impact on both parties' individual lives and lives together.

Different aspects of reproductive decisions and choices will have more or less impact on the male partner in the relationship, and so there is a case for a commensurately greater or lesser role for men in different reproductive decisions. In decisions that bear most directly on the woman and her life, such as decisions concerning the impact of the pregnancy itself, the woman's wishes ought morally to be generally determinative; in extreme cases, such as when the woman's health or life may be seriously threatened by the pregnancy, entirely so. When the decisions bear more equally on both partners' lives, such as whether to have children at all, the decisions ought morally to be more mutual and joint, seeking compromise in the case of conflict and with neither party imposing an unacceptable choice on the other.

Interestingly, the more gender-egalitarian the relationship with regard to childbearing and, more importantly, childrearing roles and responsibilities, the stronger is the moral case for the male partner's role in the decisions. Likewise, the more the social and legal setting within which childbearing and childrearing will take place minimizes the disadvantages and burdens in expectations and opportunities that fall on women, the stronger the moral case for men having substantial roles in the decisions. Thus, by relinquishing unjust gender-based advantages, men gain a greater moral claim to share in reproductive decisions.

Is More Reproductive Choice Always Better Than Less?[17]

New means of contraception or abortion and new reproductive techniques each may appear to unqualifiedly increase the reproductive freedom of women, at least when access to these services is made available to them. New means of contraception or abortion provide additional choice and so extend women's control over child bearing—pregnancies can be more easily, effectively, and safely prevented or terminated than was possible before their development. New reproductive techniques even more clearly seem only to provide the option of having children to women who did not have that option before because of fertility problems. If new methods of contraception and reproduction give women choices they lacked before, without affecting the choices and alternatives they already had, then they appear to unqualifiedly increase freedom. What is mistaken in this line of reasoning is the assumption that these new methods always leave all of women's previous alternatives in place without alteration—they often do not. But if so, then whether the new means of contraception or reproduction are on balance a benefit to women is more complex than it at first appears. Even whether these new techniques represent a gain on balance in reproductive freedom, or more precisely in the overall value of reproductive freedom, is not so straightforward and must be assessed in terms of their effects on the different underlying interests and values promoted by reproductive freedom.

There is not space here to try to assess all the significant effects on women's reproductive freedom of new means of contraception, abortion, and reproduction. I do, however, at least want to provide examples of how these new means of contraception, abortion, and reproduction can diminish instead of enhance each of the three alternative underlying moral values that support reproductive freedom. They cannot be judged enhancements of reproductive freedom in the abstract, but instead must be evaluated for all of their effects in the actual social contexts in which they will be introduced.

First, consider individual self-determination—is it always enhanced by the introduction of new contraceptive or reproductive alternatives? To answer, we need in part to know whether the new alternatives are considered of any value by those persons offered them. The value of self-determination to a person is not increased by obtaining an alternative in which the person has and will have no interest. But assume, since it is usually true, that the new con-

traceptive and reproductive alternatives are desired by many women. We can still only infer from this that women's self-determination is enhanced if the introduction of the new alternatives has no effects on the nature or desirability of any of their other alternatives and choices. And there often are such effects, particularly in settings of pervasive gender discrimination and inequality. New choices that did not exist before can often lead to coercive pressure from others to pursue unwanted alternatives. Here are some examples: Use of new reproductive techniques often carries substantial psychological, economic, and other burdens for women who can be pressured to pursue these techniques by spouses or others even though they find them unduly burdensome; in societies where it is important for economic or other reasons to have a male heir, women can be pressured to abort a female fetus or to continue to try to have a male child when the woman wants no more children; coercive population policies limiting the number of children women can have can be enforced by new methods of compulsory contraception or abortion; with new forms of prenatal diagnosis of genetically transmitted diseases such as Down's syndrome, together with the availability of abortion if the fetus is found to have the disease, women who oppose abortion in such cases can be pressured to obtain it.

This last example illustrates a more subtle impact on a woman's self-determination that has been noted by Gerald Dworkin.[18] Before the advent of genetic screening, if a woman had a child with a genetically transmitted disease like Down's syndrome, this was typically viewed by her and others as a natural misfortune for which she was not morally responsible. If a woman now chooses not to perform genetic screening of her fetus, or learns that her fetus has Down's syndrome and then chooses not to abort it, she is now responsible for having chosen to bear a child with Down's syndrome. Even if she had not wanted the new choice of performing genetic screening with the subsequent option of abortion, once that screening is widely available, it may be rational for her to exercise the choice and to abort an afflicted fetus. This is because the existence of the new alternative of screening for genetic defects and aborting if they are found has changed the previous nature of child-bearing—before one had no choice but to take one's chances in the genetic lottery, whereas now it is by choice that one does so. If she does not avail herself of genetic screening and abortion of a handicapped fetus, others may now consider that she chose to have such a child and so is undeserving of special help needed to care for her child; she is responsible for coping with consequences she knowingly and freely brought on herself. Knowing that others will feel and act this way can make it rational for her to choose genetic screening and to abort a handicapped fetus, though she would have preferred not to have had this choice available to her.

I should not be misunderstood as claiming that new methods of contraception, abortion, and reproduction on balance reduce women's self-determination—there is no reason to believe that. Instead, the point is that these new choices, whose availability typically increases the self-determination of women who want them, cannot be assumed to increase self-determination in all cases because of the effects they can have on other alternatives and choices. In particular instances their overall effect on a woman's self-determination may be negative. But the more important lesson for social policy is that the introduction of these new choices should be accompanied by attention to how they may affect other alternatives of women and make women vulnerable to new forms of coercion. A concern for enhancing women's self-determination requires policy and legal measures to minimize any negative effects on their self-determination.

The second ground of reproductive freedom was its role in promoting the good or welfare of women. Here too, while new means of contraception, abortion, and reproduction almost certainly on balance have a positive effect on the welfare of women as a class, their impact is not uniform. Both the coercion just discussed to ac-

cept new alternatives that are otherwise unwanted, as well as the effects of those alternatives themselves, such as pursuit of psychologically and economically burdensome fertility treatments, are harms and welfare reductions. An example not employing new reproductive techniques illustrates how new alternatives can lead to a loss in welfare for a woman even in the absence of any coercion. New practices of international adoption, where the children of poor families from underdeveloped countries are made available to economically privileged persons in the developed world, can lead to the poor parents giving up a child for the sake of the child's future opportunities and welfare, though they otherwise do not wish to do so and experience a great loss from doing so. Particular social, cultural, and legal settings may make some of these welfare reductions particularly likely or prevalent and in turn make steps to prevent these welfare reductions particularly important.

Finally, gender equality in expectations and opportunities is not always enhanced by increasing reproductive choices in the areas of contraception and fertility. This is most obvious in the case of fertility treatments that enable otherwise infertile couples to reproduce by such means as in vitro fertilization. The treatments necessary to produce a successful pregnancy are often extremely expensive, mounting into many thousands of dollars. Where these treatments are either not covered by a national health insurance program or national health service or are covered only by private insurance not available to all of a country's citizens, they must be financed by individuals. In such circumstances, their high cost will mean that many, if not most, people who need the services in order to reproduce will be unable to afford them. Childrearing and parenting have enormous importance in the lives of many people. Leaving whether otherwise infertile couples can bear children to whether they can afford very expensive fertility and reproductive services creates a particularly problematic inequality. If a similar inequality was introduced among fertile couples by a straightforward legal prohibition of poor persons procreating, there would be little disagreement that the policy was morally indefensible. The analogy is not complete or perfect, but it is close enough to make clear the problematic moral inequality in expectations and opportunities created by differential access to fertility services among rich and poor. Of course, similar concerns can be raised about differential access among rich and poor that remains widespread in many countries today, including the United States, to contraception and abortion services, despite their much lower cost in comparison with relatively exotic fertility treatments.

Some other moral concerns raised by the availability of new methods of contraception, abortion, and reproduction raise more subtle issues about equality. Here is one example. Many people have moral objections to practices of surrogate motherhood in which a woman is paid to bear a child who is to be given up at birth to those who engaged her services and will rear the child as its parents. Friends of the voluntary nature of markets and market transactions often defend such arrangements on the grounds that, so long as the choice of each party to enter into it is fully free, each considers him- or herself to be made better off by the arrangement. The defender of surrogacy then sees objections to the practice as misplaced moralism or paternalism. Sometimes this is the nature of the objections, but not always.

Critics of surrogacy sometimes raise the specter of a class of women who are the "baby makers" for the more privileged classes who do not wish their careers and other pleasures to be interrupted by the demands of pregnancy. Often this is a concern about the exploitation of women who are unjustly deprived of a normal range of opportunities and for whom the role of surrogate is their best opportunity. Surrogacy is seen as an exploitative purchase of what critics believe should not and would not otherwise be for sale (another's body), analogous in its moral character to the rich buying kidneys or other organs for transplant from the poor. I have put this objec-

tion to surrogacy in terms of exploitation, for this is the form it commonly takes, but the objection can be put in terms of equality as well. For some to have their bodies used in this way simply for the convenience of others seems to many people to introduce an unnecessary and objectionable inequality between rich and poor. My point is not that surrogacy arrangements are on balance morally objectionable—I am not convinced of that—but rather that they illustrate subtle worries about equality, and not just about gender inequality.

MORAL LIMITS OF REPRODUCTIVE FREEDOM

I have not sought here to specify a right to reproductive freedom in any detail, but only to suggest its main components together with the different moral grounds that can be offered in support of it. However, even at this level of generality, it is clear that the right is not unlimited. Some reproductive choices are morally impermissible, though whether they should also be proscribed by law is a separate issue that I will not take up here. In thinking about the moral limits of reproductive freedom, it is helpful to distinguish reproductive choices not to conceive or procreate from choices to reproduce.

Moral Limits on Choices Not To Reproduce

First, consider choices not to conceive or procreate. These will be primarily choices to employ one or another method of contraception or of abortion. While abortion is to many people the most contentious and important moral issue of reproductive freedom, that issue is sufficiently complex in its own right that I have had to set it aside here. My own view is that a human fetus has no serious moral right not to be killed, or put differently, it is not wronged by being killed, but I will not argue for that view here.[19] Instead, supposing that abortion is not morally wrong simply because it kills the fetus, what other moral limits are there on a woman's moral right to use contraceptives so as not to conceive or to have an abortion so as to terminate a pregnancy? The burdens on a woman of an unwanted pregnancy and of having to rear an unwanted child (when the alternative of giving the infant to a willing other to rear is not feasible) are in nearly all cases sufficiently great that there is no competing moral consideration of sufficient importance to override her right to choose not to reproduce.[20] This is clearest with regard to the negative component of her right—her moral claim against others that they not interfere with or prevent her using contraception or abortion services otherwise available to her. But the cost of those services is sufficiently low, and the interests grounding this aspect of her right to reproductive freedom is sufficiently weighty, that those services should be socially provided to women unable to secure them or pay for them on their own. If properly considered health care services, they should be included as part of a right to health care, but in any event they are properly part of a right to reproductive freedom.[21] I believe this conclusion applies not just in relatively wealthy developed countries, but in poorer underdeveloped countries as well. Although in the poorer countries the cost of providing the services is a relatively greater social burden, the burdens there on women of unwanted pregnancies and children are also commonly greater.

Moral Limits on Choices To Reproduce Grounded in Potential Harms to the Child

When a woman's choice is to, rather than not to, reproduce, the effects, specifically the harms and burdens, on others of her decision can be sufficiently weighty to place significant limits on her moral right to reproduce. It will be helpful to distinguish cases where harms and burdens are to the child she will bear as opposed to other persons. Many of the most contentious issues concerning limits on reproductive freedom concern harms to the child a pregnant woman will bear, and I will address these first.

It might be thought that if abortion of any nonviable fetus is held to be morally permissible,

then surely less serious harms to the fetus than taking its life must be permissible as well, but this would be a mistake. Serious harm caused by a woman to her fetus, for example, by excessive alcohol use during pregnancy, is a moral wrong to the child that fetus will later become. At a later time her child will unquestionably be a person deserving of the moral protections due persons generally. These protections include that actions not have been performed at an earlier time that result in serious harm to it now. Since my concern now is with cases in which a woman intends to bring her fetus to term, my defense of these moral protections does not depend on any particular assumptions or positions about the moral status of the fetus. The claim that a child can be wronged by prenatal harms done to it by its mother or others is compatible with holding that it would have been morally permissible for its mother to abort it before it was born.

A second mistake to be avoided concerns how serious harms to the fetus must be to wrong the child the fetus will later become. Here, it is important to distinguish whether it is procreating itself, that is, bringing the child into existence, that wrongs it or instead other actions that result in harms to the fetus and later child. Reproductive freedom is often used loosely by commentators to include both sorts of actions. First, consider the case where procreation itself results in the harm. Procreation itself is plausibly held to be a wrong to the child brought into existence only if the child's existence is so burdensome and without compensating benefits to it that its life is reasonably held to be, from its standpoint, worse than no life at all. Some few genetically transmitted diseases, for example, trisomy 18 syndrome, do generally create such existences. But the vast majority of genetically transmitted diseases and handicaps, such as the more common cases of Down's syndrome or spina bifida, do not generally make the lives of those who have them so bad as to be worse than no life at all. Since the alternative for the child with a handicap that still leaves it with a life worth living is not to have existed at all, either by not having been conceived or by having been aborted, it is not harmed and so not wronged by being brought to term by a mother who knows it has this handicap.

Derek Parfit has questioned this link between harming and wronging with a case similar to the following.[22] Suppose a woman learns that if she conceives now, her child will have a moderate handicap, say paralysis in its legs, though still a life clearly worth living, but if she delays conception by two months, she will have a normal child. If she goes ahead and conceives now because to delay two months would interfere with her vacation plans, most people would hold she acts wrongly. However, as Parfit points out, by doing so she does not harm her child or make it worse off because the only alternative for it to being conceived with this handicap is not to have been conceived at all. If she had waited two months, she would have had a different child, not the same child without the handicap. I believe no moral right to reproductive freedom should be taken to morally justify her action in a case like this. If so, then for a woman to act wrongly in conceiving and bringing a child to term, it cannot be necessary that the child be harmed simply by being brought into existence. We should either reject the requirement that an individual be harmed in order to be wronged or reject that someone must be wronged for a persons to have acted wrongly. Whichever choice we make, such a case does delineate an additional limit on reproductive freedom. As knowledge of human genetics increases in the future, together with capacities to prevent genetically transmitted diseases, similar cases will arise more often in practice. Parfit correctly notes that cases of this sort are common now when young girls decide to become pregnant knowing that if they waited several years to do so they could give their child a significantly better life.

The actions, apart from procreation itself, that are harmful to the child who has been conceived but has not yet been born are more varied and common. They include failure to obtain adequate prenatal care or to maintain an adequate diet, as well as positive actions such as smoking, drug and alcohol abuse, and other behaviors and exposures potentially harmful to the fetus. Of course, the vast majority of women will make every reasonable effort not to harm their fetus. But in the cases of those who do not, are their actions nevertheless not wrong because they fall within a right to reproductive freedom?[23] I will argue that beyond some threshold of harm, such actions are not justified by the right to reproductive freedom, but are instead morally wrong.

Consider the case of born children. Parents who have freely assumed the roles and responsibilities of parenthood are not morally or legally obliged always to act in ways that will minimize harms or maximize benefits to their children. Quite apart from worries about enforcement, that is too high a moral standard to impose on them; it fails to give adequate recognition to the parents' own interests and self-determination. On the other hand, a variety of actions harmful to a child are prohibited by law in many countries under child abuse and neglect statutes and are widely agreed to be morally wrong. Whether an action constitutes a morally or legally permissible or impermissible harm or failure to benefit depends on a number of factors, including the probability, severity, and irreversibility of the harm to the child, as well as the burdens to the parents of avoiding the risky or harmful action. Precisely where the threshold should be placed beyond which the actions are wrong is morally controversial. However, so long as the pregnant woman intends to bring the child to term, the standard should not be different for harms to fetuses than for harms to children; the harm to the fetus is just as wrong as the harm to the child it will become.

What will often, or even usually, be different is the avoidability of, or the burden of avoiding, the harm by the pregnant woman as opposed to a parent of a born child; when a woman is pregnant, many actions that would otherwise significantly affect only her now unavoidably affect the fetus she is carrying. This means that some risks or harms caused by a parent to a born child that would be wrong because easily avoidable would not be wrong in the case of a pregnant woman and her fetus.

Public policy in this area is politically and ideologically charged because the actions harmful to the fetus are largely done only by women, since only they become pregnant (though in fact actions of men sometimes are comparably risky or harmful to a fetus and so should be subject to the same scrutiny), and because coercive policies or laws designed to prevent risks or harms to a fetus can be deeply invasive of the pregnant woman's privacy, liberty, and self-determination. The moral evaluation of legal and other policy interventions to prevent these harms raises a variety of additional considerations that I will not pursue here. My concern has been with whether a woman's actions can become sufficiently harmful to her fetus when she intends to bring that fetus to term that they exceed the limits of her right to reproductive freedom. I have argued that they can. Indeed, I believe that it is more than a little misleading even to frame issues about the morality of most such actions under the concept of reproductive freedom; as I have already indicated, they are probably better understood and evaluated by analogy with other parent-child relations and responsibilities.

Onora O'Neill has proposed a somewhat broader limit on the right to reproductive freedom. She argues that the right to procreate of either women or men is contingent upon their "having or making some feasible plan for the child to be adequately reared by themselves or by willing others."[24] Here, the focus is specifically on the act of procreation, not other actions that affect an already conceived fetus. There are two possible defenses of this limit on the right to reproduce. The first is no different than that just considered above—prevention of potential harm to the fetus and the child the fetus will become, in this case from procreating without adequate means available for rearing the child. The second possible defense of this limitation on reproductive freedom is that procreating without a feasible plan for rearing the child is irresponsible to the other persons who will have to step in and assume the burdens of rearing the child. Thus, the defense of this limitation on the right to reproductive freedom may appeal to the interests

of the potential child or to the interests of other members of the society.

There are many issues in working out the details of this limitation that I shall not pursue, such as what counts as a "feasible plan for the child to be adequately reared," what obligations others or the state may have to provide services or other help to enable would-be parents to have such a feasible plan, and so forth. But the plausibility of such a limit can perhaps be best seen in cases where it is widely agreed that individuals do not have a moral right to reproduce because of their inability to rear children—where the individuals are so cognitively impaired as to be clearly incapable of adequately rearing children. In such cases, it is common to sterilize individuals with their guardians' consent when that is necessary to prevent their procreating.

This limit on reproductive freedom has substantial policy implications, as O'Neill notes, for such issues as whether policies designed to limit population growth violate individuals' right to reproductive freedom. Such policies are often applied in countries and circumstances in which many would-be parents lack any feasible plan for adequately rearing their children. An obvious moral worry about this limit is that it would fall disproportionately on the economically and socially disadvantaged as well as disproportionately on underdeveloped countries. This does not mean that this limit is mistaken, but rather provides an additional moral reason to remedy the unjust economic and social disadvantages.

Moral Limits on Choices To Reproduce Grounded in Potential Harms or Burdens to Others Besides the Child

There are several significant kinds of cases where individuals' choices to reproduce create serious enough harms to others besides the child to ground moral limits on those individuals' right to reproduce. First, sometimes individuals who are unable to conceive coitally are likely to be able to conceive only with very expensive fertility treatments and services. The legitimate moral claims of individuals to social resources, for example, government funding, for those treatments and services are not unlimited. What that limit should be is highly controversial and dependent in part on a particular society's level of wealth, but if arrived at by fair procedures, not clearly violative of plausible standards of justice and fairly applied to individuals, such a limit is morally defensible.

A second case is also an instance of potentially excessive and unjust economic burdens on others from individuals' choices to reproduce. This is a generalization of the second defense noted above of O'Neill's proposed limit on the right to reproductive freedom. I noted earlier that in many societies the costs of individuals having and raising children is to some extent externalized, that is, imposed on other members of society. For example, when parents lack sufficient economic resources to raise their children, the costs of meeting the children's basic needs for food, shelter, health care, and education, as well as other less visible costs, fall in a host of ways on others. I believe it is clear that on both the self-determination and individual good or welfare defenses of reproductive freedom, the more an individual's reproductive choice has an unwanted, adverse impact on the self-determination or welfare of other individuals, the weaker the individual's moral claim to make that reproductive choice. More specifically, the others affected have some moral claim to influence the choice and to have the impact on them considered in the choice. When the impact on others is spread widely across the rest of the society, then it is plausible that the society, through social or governmental decision processes, could impose some limits on the reproductive choices in question.

Assessing the moral import of externalization of the costs of having and rearing children is complicated by two points. First, the degree to which parents externalize the costs of children often varies with the economic means of the parents; other things being equal, the least well off parents will externalize proportionately more of these costs, while the best-off parents may exter-

nalize little or none of the costs. Second, the distribution of income, specifically the extent of economic inequality, in many countries is itself unjust by most standards of distributive justice. Consequently, some externalization of worst-off individuals is only a result of their unjust disadvantages. The first point implies that this limitation on reproductive freedom would fall disproportionately on the poor, while the second point tends to undercut this effect to the extent that the greater externalization of costs by the poor is only a result of their unjust circumstances. Working out the overall impact for reproductive freedom of the fact of externalization would require substantial, complex economic data, but, even with these data, their moral import is likely to remain highly controversial.

Finally, the cumulative impact of reproductive choices in a society will have a substantial impact on population growth in that society, which in turn will affect the quality of life of its members in myriad ways. Here too, there is a plausible moral case that the society is entitled to take steps to limit population growth in order to preserve or enhance the quality of life of its members.[25] As noted earlier, those steps can range along a broad continuum in the degree, if any, of their coerciveness. Noncoercive measures, such as educational programs, providing economic incentives to limit the number of children individuals have, and raising the standard of living in the society, can limit population growth without interfering with reproductive freedom.[26] Other coercive measures will vary in the degree of their coerciveness, and, other things equal, less coercive measures are, of course, to be preferred to more.

CONCLUSION

In order to sketch a moral framework for thinking about reproductive freedom, I have had to cover a great deal of ground in this chapter. I have not discussed new methods of contraception and fertility in any detail, but have used them as paradigms of measures to enable individuals to limit or to enhance reproduction. The issues that I have raised are difficult and complex, and in order to try to attain some degree of comprehensiveness, I have forgone pursuing any of them fully here. Because of this and because of the issues that I have no doubt overlooked, it is accuracy, not modesty, that requires calling this only a sketch of a moral framework concerning reproductive freedom. I have taken that moral framework to include three main questions. First, what are the components, or different behaviors and social conditions, that should be considered to constitute reproductive freedom? Second, what are the moral grounds of reproductive freedom, the main lines of moral argument in defense of a moral right to reproductive freedom? Third, what are the main moral limits to individuals' moral right to reproductive freedom? The answers I have provided to these questions themselves raise many more unexplored questions and issues.

NOTES

1. A good general treatment of the relation of reproductive freedom to the new reproductive technologies is the report of the Ethics Committee of the American Fertility Society, Ethical Considerations of the New Reproductive Technologies, *Fertility and Sterility* 46, no. 3, suppl. 1 (1986):1–94. See also R. T. Hull, ed., *Ethical Issues in the New Reproductive Technologies* (Belmont, Calif.: Wadsworth, 1990).

2. J. Robertson, Embryos, Families, and Procreative Liberty: The Legal Structure of the New Reproduction, *Southern California Law Review* 59 (1986):955.

3. Griswold v. Connecticut, 381 US 479 (1965).

4. I use "new reproductive techniques" instead of the more common "new reproductive technologies," since, as Daniel Wikler's discussion of turkey-baster babies illustrates, many new methods of reproduction hardly qualify as technology.

5. A. Sen, Women's Survival as a Development Problem, *Bulletin of the Academy of Arts and Sciences* (November 1989).

6. A comprehensive treatment of informed consent can be found in R. Faden and T.L. Beauchamp, *A History and Theory of Informed Consent* (New York: Oxford University Press, 1986).

7. See, for example, V. McKusick, Mapping and Sequencing the Human Genome, *New England Journal of Medicine* 320 (1990):910–915. A useful bibliography of the ethical, social, legal, and scientific aspects of the project is in the special issue on the Human Genome Initiative, *Jurimetrics: Journal of Law, Science, and Technology* 32 (1992).

8. J. Glover, *What Sort of People Should There Be*? (New York: Penguin Books, 1984).

9. See, for example, the United Nations Declaration of the Rights of the Child, United Nations, General Assembly Resolution 1386 (XIV), November 20, 1959, published in the Official Records of the General Assembly, Fourteenth Session, Supplement No. 16, 1960, p. 19.

10. J. Rawls, *A Theory of Justice* (Cambridge, Mass.: Harvard University Press, 1971).

11. H. Frankfurt, Freedom of the Will and the Concept of a Person, *Journal of Philosophy* 68 (January 1971): 5–20.

12. J. Rawls, Kantian Constructivism in Moral Theory, *Journal of Philosophy* 77 (1980):515–572.

13. I have discussed all three of these theories at much greater length in Quality of Life Measures in Health Care and Medical Ethics, in *The Quality of Life*, edited by A. Sen and M. Nussbaum (Oxford: Oxford University Press, 1992); there I called objective good theories "ideal theories" because they typically posit some ideal of the person as what is objectively good. One of the best recent treatments of these alterative theories is J. Griffin, *Well-Being* (Oxford: Oxford University Press, 1986).

14. See R. Goodin, Laundering Preferences, in *Foundations of Social Choice Theory*, edited by J. Elster and A. Hylland (Cambridge: Cambridge University Press, 1986).

15. Much of the very large literature on this problem is within the framework of giving a utilitarian or general consequentialist account of moral rights. See, for example, T. Scanlon, Rights, Goals, and Fairness, in *Public and Private Morality*, edited by S. Hampshire (Cambridge: Cambridge University Press, 1978); R. Frey, ed., *Utility and Rights* (Minneapolis: University of Minnesota Press, 1984).

16. There is a substantial debate about what should be the object of egalitarians' concern. The principal alternative positions include equality of welfare, of resources, of opportunities, and of capabilities and functionings. My appeal here to "expectations" in the equality defense of reproductive freedom aims to be neutral between these different positions, though of course a full equality defense of reproductive freedom would have to spell out the specific conception of equality employed.

17. This title is borrowed, with minor change, from G. Dworkin, Is More Choice Better Than Less? in *The*

Theory and Practice of Autonomy (Cambridge: Cambridge University Press, 1988); the substance of this section owes much to Dworkin's paper as well.

18. Ibid., 67–68.

19. But see M. Tooley, *Abortion and Infanticide* (Oxford: Oxford University Press, 1984), for the most developed version of what I believe is largely the correct account of the morality of abortion.

20. I say "nearly all" cases because I believe we can at least imagine a few particular cases where a woman's reasons for not continuing a pregnancy to term, or at least to viability, may be of sufficiently limited importance, for example, it interferes with a planned vacation, and her responsibility to others such as her spouse to bring the fetus to term sufficiently great, that it would be morally wrong to terminate the pregnancy. However, these cases are sufficiently rare that I believe they have little import for policy and law.

21. N. Daniels, *Just Health Care* (Cambridge: Cambridge University Press, 1985).

22. D. Parfit, *Reasons and Persons* (Oxford: Oxford University Press, 1986), chap. 16.

23. Some philosophers defend an account of moral rights according to which there is a right to do wrong; cf., for example, J. Waldron, A Right to Do Wrong, *Ethics* 92 (1981):21–39. In this view the harming might be permitted by the right to reproductive freedom, but nevertheless not be morally justified. For reasons there is not space to pursue here, I interpret the right to reproductive freedom, as I would interpret other moral rights, as not making actions (all things considered) morally permissible that are also (all things considered) morally unjustified or wrong.

24. O. O'Neill, Begetting, Bearing, and Rearing, in *Having Children: Philosophical and Legal Reflections of Parenthood*, edited by O. O'Neill and W. Ruddick (New York: Oxford University Press, 1979).

25. M. Bayles defends such population control measures and argues that many do not violate or infringe a right to procreate in Limits to a Right to Procreate, in *Ethics and Population*, edited by M. Bayles (Cambridge, Mass.: Schenkman, 1976).

26. Though some have argued that not all offers, for example, of the sort contained in economic incentives, are noncoercive. See, for example, J. Feinberg, *Harm to Self* (Oxford and New York: Oxford University Press, 1986); D. Zimmerman, Coercive Wage Offers, *Philosophy and Public Affairs* 10 (1981):121–145.

Chapter 6

Frozen Embryos and Questions of Implantation

Glenn C. Graber

I am convinced that the most fruitful way to discuss complex issues such as the many questions about whether and when to implant frozen embryos is to begin with a specific case example. Only through the richness (not to mention the messiness) of concrete life-situations can the full dimensions of the moral issues be appreciated. Since I was in a position to follow closely a concrete case involving frozen embryos,[1] I will orient this essay around it. The conclusions reached in analyzing this case will be relevant to other cases, even if they are not directly generalizable into universal rules.

DAVIS v. DAVIS

In an ironic coincidence, I was working through Jonsen and Toulmin's *Abuse of Casuistry*[2] one afternoon in February 1989 in preparation for a graduate seminar when the telephone rang and a local reporter informed me that, a few miles away from where I sat, a young man named Junior Davis had just filed a petition for divorce and that the petition included the request that his wife Mary Sue be restrained from implanting any of the seven "preembryos" which the couple had previously placed in frozen storage. Suddenly the enterprise of casuistry took on

a less antiquarian significance. Here was a case with precisely the feature that originally prompted the development of casuistical thinking—that is, it does not fit comfortably under any familiar principle, although several different principles or sets of principles seem germane to it to some degree. Thus, a straightforward deduction from ethical principles[3] does not appear to be tenable as a way of arriving at an ethical conclusion in this case. At the very least, it would seem that there must be preliminary reasoning about *which* set of (partially relevant) principles to apply and/or about how to *think* about the case. Again and again, as I described the Davises' situation to colleagues, students, and friends, the listener would respond with the casuistical prompt, "Well, what you say about this case depends on how you think about these entities, doesn't it?"

At least five constructions suggest themselves:

1. We can view this as like a *natural pregnancy* (with the difference that it is taking place outside the woman's body).

2. We can think of it as like a *child custody dispute* (with the difference that the organism is not yet a child; indeed, it is

highly unlikely that all seven of the organisms will become children, and in fact there is a considerable likelihood that none would survive to birth even if all seven were serially implanted).

3. The divorce petition portrayed this as a *property dispute* (with the difference being the unusual nature of the property in question).

4. We could focus on the *processual* nature of the in vitro fertilization procedure and compare it to a surgical procedure that the patient seeks to stop in the middle (say, after having been sliced open but before being sewn back up).

5. One commentator compared the situation to *rape* ("an odd technological rape of the male's reproductive powers").

Each conceptualization invokes specific principles of action, but each also has difficulties if applied to the case at hand. I propose to discuss them in reverse order.

Rape

One of my colleagues suggested in a newspaper interview that to implant the pre-embryos against Mr. Davis's wishes would be "an odd technological rape of the male's reproductive powers" (an image that Junior himself invoked later, in his testimony at the court hearing). This construction would invoke the strongest possible argument against implantation. Rape is unquestionably morally wrong. However, this analogy seems to me utterly inappropriate. What is most troublesome ethically about rape is that it involves forced, intrusive intimacy, but nothing of this sort is a feature of the case at hand. At this point, the sperm is already outside the man's body. The intimate episode (i.e., the harvesting of his sperm) is now past, and Junior Davis acknowledges that he consented to and cooperated willingly with that procedure. Implantation and gestation would involve no further intimacy involving him, so it could hardly be characterized as rape.

Process

This seems too weak an analogy to be decisive in this case. The notion of a process is neutral with regard to the "matter" of the process, whereas the thorniness of our case is precisely due to the fact that human reproductive material is involved. This is, in crucial ways, *unlike* an appendectomy or other surgical procedure. There is something involved which, even if we do not regard it at present as a baby, could become a baby.

Further, the analogy to a continuous or ongoing process is weakened by the fact that these embryos had been stored frozen for several months at the time Mr. Davis raised the issue, and they could probably be safely stored for at least two years more. This analogy might be more compelling if Mr. Davis had filed his petition between the time he donated sperm one morning and their planned implantation a few hours or days later.

Property

The attorney for Junior Davis argued that the pre-embryos are "property held jointly." Here the obvious equitable settlement would be an equal division of the property. Some states have explicit community property standards for divorce cases; most other states would apply an equality standard in the case of property that was clearly jointly "produced." This analogy would be more compelling if Mr. Davis were seeking possession of the property (although we would still have to find grounds for distinguishing it from the child custody analogy). However, Mr. Davis insisted, instead, that he be given at least copossession of all seven embryos in order to prevent any of them from being used to make him a father against his wishes. By this argument, he acknowledges that these items have a significance quite different from the usual property involved in a divorce settlement.

We should not exaggerate the disanalogy, however. There are probably situations in other divorce actions in which one spouse demands destruction of some item (e.g., his or her love letters to the other, or photographs of them together, or the hooked rug they created as a joint project).

Child Custody

In some ways the situation is analogous to a child custody dispute, but Mary Sue Davis's attorney admitted in his brief that he could find no basis in state or federal law for assigning such a status to life at this stage of development. This analogy, too, is weakened in the present case by the fact that the father is seeking destruction of the embryos, not custody of them. Even if he sought custody, however, we would have to decide whether conceptuses are to be treated like children for these purposes. Suppose he sought custody for purposes of their gestation in a surrogate mother. Would the genetic mother merit visitation rights?

Pregnancy

The situation might be compared to an extracorporeal pregnancy. Two key differences raise questions about this as the best analogy: (1) the fact that this process takes place outside the woman's body (resulting in the paradoxical situation in which there is a pregnancy but no one who is pregnant), and (2) the fact that, in a natural pregnancy, a progression from fertilization to implantation is a process that will continue on its own unless some action is taken to interrupt it, whereas, in the present case, some action will have to be taken to move on to the implantation stage. The first of these differences "spoils" the analogy of pregnancy in terms of giving guidance for the present situation. Our society gives the legal right of decision about continuing or terminating a pregnancy wholly to the woman, but surely this is primarily because the ordinary pregnancy takes place within her body and intervention to alter its course would be invasive. In short, the feature that forms the basis of this policy is precisely what is lacking in the case at hand.

THE CIRCUIT COURT RULING

Judge W. Dale Young, who heard the case of Junior and Mary Sue Davis, saw himself in a quandary similar to that I have just described. He pointed out that Tennessee divorce law contains provisions for (1) property settlements and (2) child custody arrangements and thus that he had to decide which to apply here or else find (3) some common-law basis for a decision. Further, as he explained in a 13-page appendix on the role of a judge, he faced the added restrictions that (1) he had to base his findings of fact entirely on the testimony he had heard in the courtroom plus information that could be considered common knowledge and (2) his findings of law must be linked decisively to Tennessee statutes, case law, or common law that has been recognized in the state.

The result was a curious argument indeed. Judge Young concluded that the entities in question are children because (1) they are *not* property, (2) the Davises' *intent* was to produce children, and (3) distinctions between this stage of prenatal development and others (prior to and including birth) cannot be defended.

The last of these strains of argument is especially problematic. Judge Young rejected the testimony of several expert witnesses that these entities are "preembryos" on the grounds that these witnesses all draw this term from a technical report of the Ethics Committee of the American Fertility Society[4] and the term is not found in available dictionaries or encyclopedias (and thus it does not qualify as "common knowledge" of which he could take judicial notice). Yet, in the next stage of his argument, he gave considerable weight to expert testimony drawn from scientific reports about gene mapping, which can hardly be considered common knowledge. (The difference perhaps was that the expert, Jerome Lejeune, was present to testify and claimed expert, first-hand knowledge of this information.)

Furthermore, there is a classic fallacy of equivocation in this stage of the judicial argument. Some expert witnesses maintained that these entities are not yet embryos on the ground that cell differentiation is not yet manifest. By "differentiation," they referred to heterogeneity *among* the cells of the same entity (i.e., internal differences between the cells that form bone, cells that compose the tissue of various organs, and even cells that will be part, not of the baby, but of the placenta). Yet this claim was regarded as rebutted by testimony from the French geneticist that these entities are genetically unique at fertilization and thus "differentiated" from cells of any *other* embryo. (Even this claim is not scientifically accurate. Twinning might occur after this stage of development, yielding two genetically identical fetuses.)

The bombshell finding (which received widespread publicity) that "human life begins at conception" was thus arrived at by default—no evidence of which the court could take judicial notice supports drawing the distinction anywhere else in the developmental process. Statutory and judicial suggestions that legally protected life begins at viability or at birth were dismissed by insisting that they apply only to the issue of abortion and thus are not applicable to divorce actions such as the present case.[5] The philosophical, theological, and political debate currently raging in our society about when protected human life begins was sidestepped on procedural grounds: The French geneticist testified that scientific findings establish that human life begins at conception; this testimony was not rebutted in the trial record; the external debate on this matter did not qualify for judicial notice in this ruling.

There was a curious mixture of subjective and objective perspectives in the course of the argument from this premise to the conclusions about disposition of the (pre)embryos. Beginning with a claim about the couple's intent, the argument moved on to an "objective" analysis of the status of the embryos, and then, on the strength of that, Judge Young invoked an objective best-interests-of-the-child standard. On the basis of this standard, it was concluded that it would be in the best interests of the embryos (he called them "children in vitro") to be implanted and given an opportunity to develop. But then, in deciding

whether to allow Mrs. Davis to bear them or to donate them to another couple, no consideration at all was given to the obvious question of whether a single-parent environment might serve the best interests of the child less well than a two-parent home. Instead, Judge Young returned at this point in the argument to the intent of the father and pointed out that he had said in testimony that he would prefer to have his ex-wife bear them rather than turning them over to strangers. But surely this subjective element is not the decisive consideration if the question at hand is the best interests of the child!

Given the judicial restrictions, as Judge Young explained them, the testimony in the case, as he summarized it, and the limited options available to him under Tennessee law, one can comprehend why Judge Young reached the decision he did. However, I find myself wishing he had been less of a legalist and had borrowed some tricks from the casuists. Perhaps the result would not have been as true to the letter of the law, but it might have been much more appropriate from an ethical perspective. As it is, we were left with an argument so riddled with limitations and puzzles that it can only add further confusion to an already thorny societal debate.

THE TENNESSEE SUPREME COURT RULING

Fortunately, this is not the end of the matter. The Court of Appeals overruled the Blount County Circuit Court and the Tennessee Supreme Court upheld the Court of Appeals decision, with some additional reasoning of its own. To begin, the Supreme Court returns to the American Fertility Society's way of characterizing these entities:

> We conclude that preembryos are not, strictly speaking, either "persons" or "property," but occupy an interim category that entitles them to special respect because of their potential for human life.[6]

Second, Justice Martha Craig Daughtrey, who wrote the court's opinion, stressed that the right of procreational autonomy stemming from the right of individual privacy "is composed of two rights of equal significance—the right to procreate and the right to avoid procreation."[7] This leads to the following set of conclusions.

> In summary, we hold that disputes involving the disposition of preembryos produced by *in vitro* fertilization should be resolved,
>
> [1] first, by looking to the preferences of the progenitors.
> [2] If their wishes cannot be ascertained, or if there is dispute, then their prior agreement concerning disposition should be carried out.
> [3] If no prior agreement exists, then the relative interests of the parties in using or not using the preembryos must be weighed.
>> [3a] Ordinarily, the party wishing to avoid procreation should prevail, assuming that the other party has a reasonable possibility of achieving parenthood by means other than use of the preembryos in question.
>> [3b] If no other reasonable alternatives exist, then the argument in favor of using the preembryos to achieve pregnancy should be considered.
>> [3c] However, if the party seeking control of the preembryos intends merely to donate them to another couple, the objecting party obviously has the greater interest and should prevail.[8]

This clearly makes the interests of "the progenitors" supreme. No consideration is given to the pre-embryos in and of themselves. (Indeed, it is difficult to see any measure at all of "special respect" being shown for them in these conclusions.) Nor is there consideration of the interests of a couple whose only opportunity for pregnancy might lie in receiving donated pre-embryos—the intent "merely" to donate them to another couple is viewed as diminishing the strength of one's claim to control the pre-embryos.

This glorification of genetic linkages matches the outcome of the court case involving Anna Johnson, who was paid to serve as gestational hostess to an embryo composed of egg and sperm from the couple who planned to raise the child.[9] When she sought to retain custody of the child after its birth, the judge awarded custody to the couple, declaring of the "gestational carrier" that "she and the child are genetic hereditary strangers."

I would argue that it remains an open question whether genetic relationship is more important than gestational nurturance. Because the separation of these has become possible only through recently developed technology, we have not been prodded to consider the comparative value of these roles. They are remarkably different: Genetic contribution is made in an instant but it clearly remains forever; nurturance takes longer and the residual traces of it are less obvious.

The judge in the Anna Johnson case compared her to a foster parent "providing care, protection, and nurture during the period of time that the natural mother was unable to care for the child." But we all know of cases in which children feel much closer to their foster parents than to their genetic parents—especially if the genetic parents are neglectful or abusive. In this situation, as well, courts are inclined to return children to their genetic parents if the parents make a convincing case that they are capable of providing for the child (sometimes against the protests of both the child and foster parents, who claim they have established a deep bond), so genetics seem to be the primary consideration in these cases, too. However, there was a dramatic departure from this trend in a Florida case recently when an eleven-year-old boy was allowed to "divorce" his natural mother and be adopted by foster parents who had provided care for him for years, with only infrequent visits or attempts at communication by his natural mother.

Furthermore, it is significant that the outcome in the Tennessee ruling is not that the frozen pre-embryos are relegated to foster care but that they are not brought to life at all. I would maintain that donation to an infertile couple would be an appropriate expression of "special respect" for the nature of these entities, as well as a beneficent concern for the plight of the infertile couple. The Supreme Court opinion describes at some length[10] the reasons Junior Davis cites for not wanting his genetic material to be born and raised in a foster-care setting, but I think the case for giving him the final say in this matter is not sufficiently supported. All that is said is that "decisional authority rests in the gamete-providers alone."[11]

I would not maintain that the pre-embryos have an independent right to life. I am convinced that this strident and atomistic approach to constructing this case is not justifiable. To think in terms of rights here is to import an adversarial tone to a deliberative process that ought to be focused on more constructive moral notions like best interests and respect. Furthermore, it requires stressing the separateness of the parties when it is more apropos to recognize their connectedness—both the connectedness of the progenitors to each other and to the pre-embryo and the potential connectedness of the pre-embryo with its gestational mother and within the family in which she or he would be reared.

I think it is equally divisive and strident to vest all authority in the gamete providers without recognizing the interests and welfare of others, including the possibilities of life for the fetus and what the fetus could mean to an infertile couple.

Ironically, I would base my case for donation of the pre-embryos to an infertile couple partly on the *improbability* of successful pregnancy. The gamete providers' concerns can be addressed in part by pointing out to them that there is less than 1 chance in 20 that any one embryo will survive implantation. Even if all seven of the embryos in this case are donated, there is less than a 50 percent chance that any of them would be born. This is significantly different from the mother who gives her baby up for adoption after birth and may continue to wonder about the

baby's life situation; the pre-embryo becomes, at most, the abstract possibility of a baby—and an improbable possibility at that. This feature could be made use of in counseling the gamete providers to assuage their concerns about the future.

If we focus less on notions of rights (which seems to be an integral element of the property construction) and construe this case more in terms of notions of benefit, harm, and respect, I think we will be led to the conclusion that the appropriate outcome of this case would have been the donation of the unused embryos to an infertile couple who are incapable of contributing gametes of their own.

This seems to me the appropriate policy of in vitro fertilization clinics in general. Some now give the gamete providers absolute authority over the disposition of any unused pre-embryos, but this is too much an invocation of the property construction. Any measure of special regard for these entities in themselves suggests pursuing measures that offer them the possibility (however remote) of developing into children.

The gamete providers emphatically do not continue to have child support responsibilities. To suggest this would be to invoke the child custody model. Similarly, it is inappropriate to think of this (as some gamete providers might be inclined to do) as tantamount to giving a baby up for adoption. The altruistic elements of organ donation are more appropriate parallels here.

In sum, I would argue that we need to emphasize constructions of this sort of case that maximize the benefits to all whom we count in our moral community while not violating the special respect due the pre-embryos. In the method of casuistry, the process of (1) repeated construction of the case in terms of analogous situations and (2) critically analyzing the moral implications of these analogies may lead to an understanding of the case of frozen pre-embryos that transcends any categories now available to us without abandoning the moral wisdom of the past. This is the path to sound moral progress.

NOTES

1. Davis v. Davis, Circuit Court for Blount County, Tennessee at Maryville, Equity Division (Division I), No. E-14496 (September 21, 1989); reversed and remanded in the Court of Appeals of Tennessee, Eastern Section, C/A No. 180 (September 13, 1990); affirmed in the Supreme Court of Tennessee at Knoxville, No. 34 (June 1, 1992).

2. Albert R. Jonsen and Stephen Toulmin, *The Abuse of Casuistry* (Berkeley: University of California Press, 1988).

3. What a colleague and I have elsewhere called an "application model" of ethical reasoning; see Glenn C. Graber and David C. Thomasma, *Theory and Practice in Medical Ethics* (New York: Continuum, 1989), especially pp. 21ff.

4. The Ethics Committee of the American Fertility Society, Ethical Considerations of the New Reproductive Technologies, *Fertility and Sterility* 46, no. 3, suppl. 1 (1986): vii, 26S–31S; revised edition, *Fertility and Sterility* 53, no. 6, suppl. 2 (1990):vii, 31S–36S.

5. This partitioning of divorce actions off from abortion law had the curious implication that, although Mary Sue Davis had an obligation to implant these embryos, she retained the legal right to abort the pregnancy if she wished.

6. Davis v. Davis, Tennessee Supreme Court, at 20–21.

7. Ibid., at 31–32.

8. Ibid., at 39.

9. For a discussion of this case, see George J. Annas, Crazy Making: Embryos and Gestational Mothers, *Hastings Center Report* 21, no. 1 (1991):35–38.

10. Davis v. Davis, Tennessee Supreme Court, at 36–38.

11. Ibid., at 33.

Chapter 7

Abortion: The Unexplored Middle Ground

Richard A. McCormick

During the Republican National Convention in August 1988, I listened to an interview with fundamentalist minister Jerry Falwell and Faye Wattleton, president of Planned Parenthood, on the subject of abortion. Falwell kept insisting that unborn babies were the last disenfranchised minority—voiceless, voteless, and unprotected in the most basic of civil liberties. Wattleton's statements all returned to the concept of privacy and the woman's right to decide whether she would or would not bear a child. It was a tired old stalemate. Nether party budged an inch. The moderator identified their only common ground as the fact that this is a great country in which people are free to disagree.

Unfortunately, the Falwell-Wattleton exchange is an example of the way discussions on abortion are often conducted. One point is picked as central and then is all but absolutized. The discussion accomplishes nothing except perhaps to raise everyone's blood pressure. All remarks return to the single absolutized starting point and are interpreted in light of it. Thus Falwell sees nonviolent demonstrations at abortion clinics as signs of hope for a transformation of consciousness and a growing rejection of abortion. Wattleton sees them as unconstitutional and violent disturbances of a woman's exercise of her prerogative to make her own choice.

Are we doomed forever to this kind of dialogue of the deaf? Perhaps, especially if the central principles identified by both sides are indeed central. An important difference in these "central issues" should be noted here. Falwell and those who share his view are speaking primarily of the *morality* of abortion and only secondarily about public policy or the civil rights of the unborn. Wattleton says little about morality (though she implies much) but puts all her emphasis on what is now constitutional *public policy*. On his level, I believe Falwell is right. On her level, Wattleton is right (in the sense that *Roe v. Wade* does give women a constitutional right). Two planes passing in the night at different altitudes.

What rarely gets discussed in such heated standoffs is what public policy *ought to be*, especially in light of *which morality*. The linkage of these two in a consistent, rationally defensible, humanly sensitive way almost always falls vic-

Source: Reprinted from *Second Opinion*, Vol. 10, pp. 41–50, with permission of Richard McCormick, © 1989.

tim to gavel-pounding. It never gets discussed. Unless this linkage is made more satisfactorily in the public consciousness than it has been, any public policy on abortion will lack supportive consensus and will continue to be seriously disruptive of social life. The terms *prochoice* and *prolife* will continue to mislead, label, and divide our citizenry.

Can we enlarge the public conversation so that a minimally acceptable consensus might have the chance to develop? I am probably naive to think so. But I have seen more unexpected and startling things happen—Vatican II, for example. Falwell and Wattleton could agree on a few things beyond the edifying puff that this is a great country because people are free to disagree. I call my proposed area of conversation "the unexplored middle ground." If we talked more about this middle ground, we could perhaps establish a public conversational atmosphere with a better chance at achieving a peaceable public policy. I say perhaps because I am not at all optimistic. Still, it is worth a shot.

Before listing possible elements for this unexplored middle ground, I want to make three introductory points. First, diverting attention to the middle ground is not an invitation to compromise. To attempt to discover what we might agree on is not to forfeit our disagreements. It is only to shift the conversational focus. It is to discuss one's convictions with a different purpose, with different people, in a different way.

Second, my own *moral* position is abundantly clear from previous writings.[1] So is my conviction that the policy set in *Roe v. Wade* does not adequately reflect the position of a majority of Americans. Although that conviction should in no way hinder the search for a middle ground, it does warn the reader that the "middle ground" I propose is influenced by these postures. The consensus I would like to see develop and be reflected in policy is not unrelated to my own beliefs. It will undoubtedly shape my identification and wording of the "unexplored middle ground." Indeed, some—from both sides—will undoubtedly see my middle ground as a poorly disguised presentation of only one point of view, hardly in

the middle. I acknowledge the possibility in advance, but forge ahead nonetheless.

Third, when I speak of a common ground I do not mean that all or many now agree on these points. But I believe there is solid hope that they can be brought to agreement.

ELEMENTS OF A MIDDLE GROUND

1. *There is a presumption against the moral permissibility of taking human life.* This means that any individual or society sanctioning this or that act of intentional killing bears the burden of proof. Life, as the condition of all other experiences and achievements, is a basic good, indeed the most basic of all goods. If it may be taken without public accountability, we have returned to moral savagery. For this reason all civilized societies have rules about homicide, though we might disagree with their particulars.

I take the presumption stated above to be the substance of the Christian tradition. The strength of this presumption varies with times and cultures. Cardinal Joseph Bernardin has noted that the presumption has been strengthened in our time.[2] By that he means that in the past capital punishment was viewed as a legitimate act of public protection. Furthermore war, in which killing was foreseen, was justified on three grounds: national self-defense, the recovery of property, and the redressing of injury. Now, however, many people (including several recent popes) reject capital punishment and view only national self-defense as justifying violent resistance. While such applications remain controversial, they are not the point here. The key principle is the presumption against taking human life.

2. *Abortion is a killing act.* So many discussions of abortion gloss over the intervention as "the procedure" or "emptying the uterus" or "terminating the pregnancy." In saying that abortion is a killing act, I do not mean to imply that it cannot be justified at times; the statement does not raise that issue. I mean only that the one certain and unavoidable outcome of the intervention is the death of the fetus. That is true of

any abortion, whether it is descriptively and intentionally direct or indirect. If the death of the fetus is not the ineluctable result, we should speak of premature delivery. To fudge on this issue is to shade our imagination from the shape of our conduct and amounts to an anesthetizing self-deception. All of us should be able to agree on this description, whether we consider this or that abortion justified or not.

(A final gloss. I here pass over—with no intention of ignoring it—a key issue: At what point does interruption of the reproductive process merit the name *abortion*? That is a legitimate question. Plausible reasons exist for saying that only interruption of an *implanted*, fertilized ovum deserves this name. Here, however, I wish not to distract from the main assertion—one that applies to the 1.3 to 1.5 million abortions done per year in this country.)

3. *Abortion to save the life of the mother is morally acceptable.* Readers may wonder why I bother to mention this point. I do so because those who are morally opposed to abortion frequently see their position caricatured into unrecognizability. Such a caricature only intensifies opposition and polarization.

Let me cite a recent instance. The *New York Times* is hardly celebrated for its serene objectivity in this realm (it has supported *Roe v. Wade* from the beginning). In an editorial on George Bush's supposed gender gap it reported the Republican platform as follows: " 'That the unborn child has a fundamental individual right to life which cannot be infringed.' In other words, given a choice between saving the fetus or the mother, the mother must die" (August 19, 1988).

The interpretation of a "fundamental individual right to life" is so distorted that it comes as close to editorial hucksterism as can be imagined. Those who formulate their convictions in terms of a "fundamental right to life" by no stretch of the imagination deny a similar right to the mother. Nor does such a general statement about fetal rights even address situations of conflict. The language is meant to restate for the abortion context the presumption mentioned in my first point.

Presumptions can at times be overcome. Here it would be useful to recall the statement of J. Stimpfle, bishop of Augsburg: "He who performs abortion, *except to save the life of the mother*, sins gravely and burdens his conscience with the killing of human life."[3] The Belgian bishops made a similar statement.[4]

Agreement on this point may seem a marginal gain at best. But in the abortion discussion, *any* agreement can be regarded as a gain, especially when it puts caricatures to rest.

4. *Judgment about the morality of abortion is not simply a matter of a woman's determination and choice.* Prochoice advocates often present their position as though the woman's choice were the sole criterion in the judgment of abortion. But I believe that very few if any really mean this, at least in its full implications. It is simplistic and unsustainable. Taken literally, it means that *any* abortion, at *any* time, for *any* reason, even the most frivolous, is morally justified if only the woman freely chooses it. That is incompatible even with the admittedly minimal restrictions of *Roe v. Wade*. I know of no official church body and no reputable philosopher or theologian who would endorse the sprawling and totally unlimited acceptance of abortion implied in that criterion. It straightforwardly forfeits any and all moral presumptions protective of the unborn. In this formulation, the fetus becomes a mere blob of matter.

Conversation about the fourth point will not, I am sure, bring overall agreement on the abortion issue. But it might lead to a more nuanced formulation on the part of those identified with the prochoice position. It might also lead to a greater sensitivity on the part of some prolife advocates to the substantial feminist concerns struggling for expression and attention in the prochoice perspective.

5. *Abortion for mere convenience is morally wrong.* This only makes explicit the above point. Once again, agreement on this point may seem to represent precious little gain. And even agreement might be fugitive because of the problem in defining the phrase "mere convenience." One person's inconvenience is another's tragedy, and

so on. Yet for those not hopelessly imprisoned in their absolutisms. I think agreement is possible if discussion is restrained.

Furthermore, such discussion could be remarkably fruitful. Those who agree with the statement—and that would include some, perhaps many prochoice advocates—eventually would have to say *why* such abortion is morally wrong. Such a discussion could go in one direction only: straight to the whys and wherefores of the claims of nascent life upon us.

6. *The conditions that lead to abortion should be abolished insofar as is possible.* I refer to poverty, lack of education, and lack of recreational alternatives to sexual promiscuity among teenagers. Nearly everyone agrees with these prescriptions, but they should be emphasized much more. In other words, we have tended to approach abortion too exclusively as a problem of *individual choice*. Left at that, it tends to divide people. Were it also approached as a *social problem*, it could easily bring together those in opposition at the level of individual choice.

7. *Abortion is a tragic experience to be avoided if at all possible.* Regardless of one's moral assessment of abortion, I believe most people could agree that it is not a desirable experience in any way. It can be dangerous, psychologically traumatic, generative of guilt feelings, and divisive of families. And, of course, it is invariably lethal to fetuses. No amount of verbal redescription or soothing and consoling counseling can disguise the fact that people would prefer to achieve their purposes without going through the abortion procedure. It is and always will be tragic.

8. *There should be alternatives to abortion.* This is a corollary to the preceding point. Its urgency is in direct proportion to the depth of our perception of abortion as a tragic experience. It seems to me that the need for alternatives should appeal above all to those who base their approach on a woman's freedom of choice. If reproductive choice is truly to be free, then alternatives to abortion should be available. By alternatives I mean all the supports—social,

psychological, medical, financial, and religious—that would allow a woman to carry her pregnancy to full term should she choose to do so. Expanding the options is expanding freedom.

9. *Abortion is not a purely private affair. Roe v. Wade* appealed to the so-called right of privacy to justify its invalidation of restrictive state abortion laws. In public debate assertions about a woman's "control over her own body" often surface. Such appeals either create or reinforce the idea that abortion is a purely private affair. It is not—at least not in the sense that it has no impact on people other than the woman involved. It affects husbands, families, nurses, physicians, politicians, and society in general. We ought to be able to agree on these documentable facts.

I am proposing that the term *privacy* is a misleading term used to underline the primacy of the woman's interest in abortion decisions. Communal admission of this point—which is scarcely controversial—would clear the air a bit and purify the public conversation.

10. Roe v. Wade *offends many people. So did previous prohibitive laws.* On these matters those who acknowledge facts must agree. But to place these facts together invites people out of their defensive trenches. In other words, it compels them to examine perspectives foreign to their own.

11. *Unenforceable laws are bad laws.* Unenforceability may stem from any number of factors. For instance, a public willingness to enforce the law may be lacking. Or the prohibited activity may be such that proof of violation will always be insufficient. Or attempts to enforce might infringe other dearly treasured values. Whatever the source of the unenforceability, most people agree that unenforceable laws undermine the integrity of the legal system and the fabric of social life.

Our own American experience with prohibition should provide sufficient historical education on this point. Its unenforceability stemmed from all the factors mentioned above and more. It spawned social evils of all kinds. In this respect Democratic Senator Patrick J. Leahy of

Vermont once remarked that amendments should be used not to create a consensus but to enshrine one that exists. He added:

> The amendments that have embodied a consensus have endured and are a living part of the Constitution. But where we amended the Constitution without a national meeting of minds, we were forced to retract the amendment, and only after devastating effects on the society.[5]

This is an obvious reference to the Eighteenth Amendment.

12. *An absolutely prohibitive law on abortion is not enforceable.* By "absolutely prohibitive" I mean two things. First, such a law would prohibit all abortions, even in cases of rape and incest and in cases where the life of the mother is at stake. Second, by "abortion" would be meant destruction of the human being *from the moment of conception.* The latter was the intent of the Human Life Statute (S.158) introduced by Jesse Helms on January 19, 1981. It sought by a simple majority of both houses to declare the fetus a human being from the moment of conception. Thus in effect it sought to redefine the terms *person* and *life* to bring them under the protective clauses of the Fourteenth Amendment.

I say that such an absolutely prohibitive law is unenforceable. First, it has no consensus of support, as poll after poll over the years has established. Even religious groups with strong convictions against abortion have noted its unenforceability. For example, the Conference of German Bishops (Catholic) and the Council of the Evangelical Church (Protestant) issued a remarkable joint statement on abortion some years ago.[6] After rejecting simple legalization of first-trimester abortions (*Fristenregelung*), they stated that the task of the lawmaker is to identify those conflict situations in which interruption of pregnancy will not be punished (*straflos lassen*). I mention the German example because of the apparently ineradicable American tendency to identify moral conviction with public policy ("There oughta be a law!"). This penchant is vis-

ible in the refusal of some prolife advocates to admit any toleration into public policy.

The second reason an absolutely prohibitive law would not work concerns specification of legal protection *from the moment of conception.* If this were enshrined in the penal code and attempts made to enforce it, we would be embroiled in conspiracy law (the *intent* to abort). Why? Because in the preimplantation period there is no evidence of pregnancy. Lacking such evidence, one could not prosecute another for having performed an abortion, but only for having *intended* to do so. That is just not feasible.

13. *There should be some public policy restrictions on abortion.* This point may seem to lack bite: after all, those most polarized could agree on this "middle ground," and even *Roe v. Wade* admitted "some" control. This tiny island of agreement is not important in itself. By focusing on it, however, discussants will be forced to face these two questions: What kind of control? and Why?

I admit that discussing these questions could take us right back to square one. But it could also lead to a more nuanced and sophisticated notion of public policy in a pluralistic society.

14. *Witness is the most effective leaven and the most persuasive educator concerning abortion.* I do not mean to discredit the place of rational discourse. We abandon such discourse at our own risk, and very often the result is war. I mean only that genuine education is eye-opening. The most effective way of opening eyes is often the practical way of witness. We come to understand and appreciate heroism much more by seeing heroic activity than by hearing or reading a lecture on it. Are we not more selfless when surrounded by people who are concerned for others? Are we not more fearlessly honest when friends we deeply admire exhibit such honesty?

Those with deep convictions about freedom of choice for women or, on the other hand, about the sanctity of fetal life would be considerably more persuasive if they emphasized what they are for rather than what they are against, and did so *in action*. Prolife advocates (whether individuals, organizations, or institutions such as dioceses) should put resources into preventing problem pregnancies; when those pregnancies occur, they should support them in every way. Paradoxically, the same is true of those who assert the primacy of free choice. For if the choice is to be truly free, genuine alternatives must exist. In summary, putting one's money where one's mouth is can be done at least as effectively (and far more so, I believe) through means other than picketing.

15. *Abortion is frequently a subtly coerced decision.* Ethicist Daniel Callahan pointed out 15 years ago that "a change in abortion laws, from restrictive to permissive, appears—from *all data* and in *every country*—to bring forward a whole class of women who would otherwise not have wanted an abortion or felt the need for one."[7] The most plausible interpretation of this phenomenon, according to Callahan, is that the "free" abortion choice is a myth. He states,

> A poor or disturbed pregnant woman whose only choice is an abortion under permissive laws is hardly making a "free" choice, which implies the possibility of choosing among equally viable alternatives, one of which is to have the child. She is being offered an out and a help. Nor can a woman be called free where the local mores dictate abortion as the conventional wisdom in cases of unmarried pregnancies, thwarted plans, and psychological fears.[8]

Interestingly, agreement that many abortion decisions are coerced might result in cooperation between prochoice and prolife advocates. The concern of prochoicers for true freedom would lead them to attempt to reduce or abolish coercive forces by offering genuine alternatives. The prolife faction should rejoice at this provision of alternate options because it would reduce the felt need for abortion and thus the number of abortions.

16. *The availability of contraception does not reduce the number of abortions.* I include this element because I have been exposed to discussions of abortion soured by the introduction of statements like the following: "The Catholic Church, being so staunchly opposed to abortion, should be in the forefront of those backing contraception to prevent it. By condemning contraception the church adds to the number of abortions." Someone making such a remark supposes that support for contraception will reduce the number of abortions performed.

One of a group of "minor" truths listed by Daniel Callahan in 1973 was the following: "There is no evidence yet from any country that, with enough time and [the] availability of effective contraceptives, the number of abortions declines."[9] Clearly the availability of effective means of contraception is one thing; official approval of their use is quite another. But as witnessed by the number of Catholics who depart from official church teaching on contraception, official disapproval does not seem to make much difference. Callahan's assertion should therefore serve as a rebuttal to the above statement about Catholic inconsistency. I do not attach much conciliatory significance to this rebuttal except that it clears the air of distracting and one-sided statements.

17. *Permissive laws forfeit the notion of "sanctity of life" for the unborn.* This is a hard saying, but that does not make it less true. Here Daniel Callahan is at his best—and most tortured. He grants a woman the right not to have a child she does not want. But he is unflinchingly honest about what this means. "Under permissive laws," he notes, "any talk whatever of the 'sanctity of life' of the unborn becomes a legal fiction. By giving women the full and total right to determine whether such a sanctity exists, the fetus is, in fact, given no legal or socially established standing whatever."[10] Callahan does not like being backed into this corner. But he is utterly honest. His legal position does not allow for any pious doublethink. The law "forces a nasty either-or choice, devoid of saving ethical ambiguity." I wish that all discussants, on both sides, were so honest.

18. *Hospitals that do abortions but have no policy on them should develop one.* I introduce

this as a contribution to the unexplored middle ground because non-Catholic health care facilities have approached the problem almost exclusively in terms of patient autonomy. I know that some hospitals have grown nervous about this posture because it amounts to simple capitulation to patient preferences. They have begun to see that theirs is not a carefully reasoned moral stance on abortion but an abdication of the responsibility to develop one.

The counsel to develop a policy is relatively nonthreatening because it does not dictate what that policy ought to be. It is promising because it suggests that ethical complexity and ambiguity might become more explicit, which would represent an advance in the dialogue.

19. *The "consistent ethic of life" should be taken seriously.* I happily borrow the term *consistent ethic of life* from Cardinal Joseph Bernardin. Many have observed that the most vociferous about fetal rights are among our most hawkish fellow citizens. Something is amiss here. Abortions should be viewed within the larger context of other life-and-death issues, such as capital punishment and warmaking.

20. *Whenever a discussion becomes heated, it should cease.* This is the final piece of middle ground I propose. I am not suggesting that abortion is so trivial a concern that heat is inappropriate. Rather I know from long experience that shouting sessions on abortion only alienate and divide the shouters. Nothing is illumined, not because the offerings are not illuminating but because nobody is either listening or being heard.

The idea of an unexplored middle ground and the invitation to explore it will please few. Yet the abortion problem is so serious that we must grasp at any straw. A nation that prides itself on its tradition of dignity and equality for all and the civil rights to protect that equality cannot tolerate a situation in which 1.3 to 1.5 million human fetuses are being denied this equality and these rights. We must at least continue to discuss the problem openly. Quite simply, the soul of the nation is at stake. Abortion's pervasiveness represents a horrendous racism of the adult world. When it is justified in terms of rights, all of our rights are endangered because their foundations have been eroded by arbitrary and capricious application.

For this reason (and for many others) I think it important that abortion continue to occupy a prime place in public consciousness and conversation, even though we are bone-weary of the subject. If we settle for the status quo, we may be presiding unwittingly at the obsequies of some of our own most basic, most treasured freedoms. That possibility means that any strategy—even the modest one of keeping a genuine conversation alive by suggesting a middle ground as its subject—has something to recommend it.

NOTES

1. See, for example, R.A. McCormick, Public Policy on Abortion, in *How Brave a New World?* (Washington, D.C.: Georgetown University Press, 1981).

2. J. Bernardin, *Origins* 13 (1983–1984):491–495; *Origins* 14 (1984–1985):707–709.

3. F. Scholz, Durch ethische Grenzsituationen aufgeworfene Normen probleme, *Theologish-praktische Quartalschrift* 123 (1975):342.

4. Les évêques belges, Déclaration des évêques belges sur l'avortement, *Documentation Catholique* 70 (1973):432–438.

5. Cited in M.C. Segers, Can Congress Settle the Abortion Issue? *Hastings Center Report* 12 (June 1982):20–28.

6. Conference of German Bishops and the Council of the Evangelical Church, "Fristenregelung" entschieden abgelehnt, *Ruhrwort*, December 8, 1973, 6.

7. D. Callahan, Abortion: Thinking and Experiencing, *Christianity and Crisis*, January 8, 1973, 296.

8. Ibid.

9. Ibid., 297.

10. Ibid.

Chapter 8

Social and Ethical Issues in the Prenatal Diagnosis of Fetal Disorders

Diane Beeson

Prenatal diagnosis is bringing the revolution in molecular biology to human reproduction. Originally introduced for "high-risk" pregnancies, fetal diagnostic procedures are increasingly becoming part of the health care routines of normal pregnancy. Both the nature and the speed of these developments raise a vast array of social and ethical concerns.

This chapter examines some of the social and ethical issues of particular relevance for health care providers debated in an extensive and rapidly growing literature on prenatal diagnosis. It begins with a description of the expanding power and promise of these technologies. This is followed by a discussion of concerns about prenatal testing. These concerns are organized into three general areas: (1) those focused on its purpose, (2) those related to clinical practice, and (3) concerns about consequences. The conclusion summarizes the issues and suggests constructive responses for providers.

DIAGNOSTIC TECHNIQUES

An increasing number of techniques provide information about the developing fetus. Amniocentesis was the first procedure to become well established as a method of detecting fetal disorders in high-risk pregnancies. In the 1970s, the possibility of removing amniotic fluid during the second trimester gained utility with the discovery that the fetal cells it contained could be cultured and karyotyped.[1] U.S. Supreme Court decisions in 1973 loosening restrictions on abortion coincided with technical developments to bring second-trimester amniocentesis into widespread use.[2] Research efforts are now underway to assess the feasibility of conducting this procedure in the first trimester of pregnancy.[3]

Amniocentesis has been made safer and easier to use by virtue of ultrasound guidance. This technology is used to determine fetal age and detect certain malformations. Recently developed vaginal probes using ultrasound permit an even earlier and closer look at the developing fetus. Perceptions of ultrasound as noninvasive and the absence of evidence of fetal harm have led to its increasing importance as a diagnostic tool. Routine ultrasonography for every pregnant patient is becoming increasingly common.[4]

A newer procedure, chorionic villus sampling (CVS), came into use in the 1980s. This technique permits first-trimester prenatal diagnosis

I would like to thank Rene Anspach, Paul Billings, Troy Duster, and Abby Lippman for helpful comments on an earlier draft of this chapter.

of fetal cells extracted by catheter from the villi of the placental chorion. While amniocentesis can be done without ultrasound guidance, CVS absolutely requires it to maneuver the catheter into the placenta.[5] The earlier diagnosis made possible through CVS has been regarded as preferable to amniocentesis because it permits earlier abortion when disorders are detected. In addition to more favorable timing for the procedure itself, CVS enables more rapid completion of most biochemical and molecular diagnoses than the 10–30 days usually required after amniocentesis.[6] This potential for producing earlier results has led to the rapid and widespread proliferation of CVS in spite of the fact that, according to some studies, it may have a slightly higher risk of procedural failure and fetal loss than amniocentesis.[7] By 1992, more than one hundred thousand such procedures had been conducted as part of continuing efforts to assess safety and accuracy.[8]

The least invasive and most promising approach to prenatal diagnosis is maternal serum screening. With this procedure, information about the fetus is obtained simply by studying components of maternal blood. One widely studied component is alpha-fetoprotein, which is present at elevated levels when the fetus has a neural tube defect. Measurement of this protein has also become a routine practice and in many areas, a mass screening test. An estimated 50 percent of all pregnancies in the U.S. are screened for neural tube defects using this method.[9]

Maternal serum screening is being refined as a screening test for Down's syndrome. If these efforts are successful, a blood test early in pregnancy may soon replace maternal age as the basis for deciding whether amniocentesis or other tests are indicated.[10]

THE PROMISE OF PRENATAL DIAGNOSIS

The information revealed as a result of prenatal diagnosis can provide reassurance or invite intervention. Those who offer or seek prenatal diagnosis view it as increasing the options of prospective parents. Many prospective parents perceive certain genetic disorders as tragic and as entailing suffering for the affected child, other family members, and themselves. They prefer abortion to continuing the pregnancy when fetal anomalies are detected. From this perspective, these tests provide a means of "enhancing the opportunities for the individual to obtain information about . . . child-bearing risks and to make autonomous and noncoerced choices based on that information."[11]

A recent national survey indicates that two-thirds of respondents would want to undergo prenatal diagnostic tests themselves (or would want their partners to do so) and that they believe such tests will do more good than harm. This positive attitude toward prenatal testing is strongest among those who are young and educated and who follow news about science and health.[12] This approval of fetal testing appears to be unrelated to attitudes toward abortion, suggesting that many see value in the information it provides even when they do not consider abortion an option.[13]

Information about the health of the fetus can be useful to prospective parents in preparing for the birth, facilitating early therapy, or otherwise arranging support for the expected infant.[14] Beyond this, many believe that as fetal therapy becomes safer and more effective, it will eliminate the major ethical objections to prenatal diagnosis.

Advocates of prenatal diagnosis admit that it is accompanied by some formidable challenges. However, they take the position that even if some problems are created by these technologies, they can be substantially reduced as we learn to make earlier diagnoses with less invasive procedures. For example, research is underway to retrieve fetal cells from the blood of women during the first trimester of pregnancy. Many hope this will lead to a noninvasive method for prenatal diagnosis of the entire fetal genome.[15]

Until fetal therapy is more effective, genetic testing done at the preimplantation stage can be combined with in vitro fertilization to avoid abortion entirely. For those who find manipulation and selection of gametes more acceptable than the manipulation of embryos, preconception diagnosis prior to in vitro fertilization is a possibility.[16]

In spite of the paucity of effective prenatal therapies developed to date, the availability of prenatal diagnosis has made pregnancy an option for some couples who would not otherwise risk bearing a child with a genetic disease. For others who, without the reassurance prenatal testing can provide, would never allow any pregnancy to go to term, abortion can be averted. Clinicians report that many women urgently, and even desperately, seek out these technologies. While research on the use of these technologies from the perspective of pregnant women is sparse, it appears that the majority of those who have chosen prenatal diagnosis view it as enhancing their reproductive freedom.

PROBLEMS AND CHALLENGES

New technologies inspire fear as well as hope. They often require adjustments in our personal lives, reorganization of our social institutions, and redistribution of resources. They have the potential for unanticipated negative consequences as well as benefits. The next section considers concerns along these lines.

Purpose

The most fundamental challenge to prenatal diagnosis is the questioning of its purpose. Ideally, prenatal diagnosis would permit treatment of the fetus. In spite of promising developments, in the overwhelming majority of cases of fetal abnormality, virtually the only significant medical intervention is abortion. Deciding if and/or when this is appropriate is a major challenge for both providers and patients.

Many oppose prenatal diagnosis because they oppose abortion categorically. This includes certain ecclesiastical hierarchies. The Catholic church, for example, has taken the position that "a human fetus may not be directly aborted even for the highest motives such as wanting to free the infant from a lifelong burden of pain and suffering."[17] In 1980 the Surgeon General of the United States took a similar position.[18]

The debate cannot, however, be reduced to pro-life and pro-choice positions. Many pro-choice analysts are uncomfortable with abortion as a systematic response to fetal defects. For example, Nancy Press and Carol Browner concluded in their study of California's maternal serum alpha-fetoprotein (AFP) program that both providers and women who use prenatal diagnostic services wish to avoid discussion of pregnancy termination. They describe the presentation of AFP screening as a routine part of prenatal care as contributing to a "collective fiction" that obscures the centrality of abortion decision making and the eugenic implications of the practice. They question whether this is an appropriate way to create policy and action.[19]

Abortions following second-trimester amniocentesis are particularly problematic because the fetus is approaching viability and because their timing makes them particularly physically and emotionally traumatic for the pregnant woman.[20] There is controversy over the type of abortion that is preferable under these circumstances, and the decision about the kind of abortion may pose an ethical dilemma for the practitioner. Dilation and evacuation under general anesthesia may be preferred by patients, but, depending on the skill of the physician, it may not be the safest method. In addition, this form of abortion may be particularly repugnant from the perspective of clinicians. The alternative, however, carries with it the possibility that the intended abortion can result in a live birth. Even if patients are given a choice, their decision will necessarily be strongly influenced by the information and judgments communicated by the care provider.[21]

Not only is the timing of abortion and the choice of technique often difficult for both the prospective parents and clinicians, but opinion varies widely as to the level of severity of conditions for which abortion is appropriate. Some approve abortion only for diseases such as Tay-Sachs or anencephaly that are fatal to young children but oppose it for more treatable disorders, such as PKU or even cystic fibrosis.

As we learn more about genetics, we are discovering that many diseases may have a genetic component. Is increased susceptibility to cancer or heart disease an appropriate indication for abortion? What about late-onset diseases? How many years of good health should one expect for one's children? If we learn that Alzheimer's disease has a genetic component that can be detected in utero, should we make prenatal diagnosis available to prevent it?

Some believe that abortions on the basis of prenatal diagnosis are immoral and reflect a "eugenic mentality that welcomes only 'premium babies.'"[22] Saxton proposes that the highest quality of our lives and the deepest experiences of our humanness are not achieved by destroying imperfect fetuses. She believes that physicians by the very nature of their work develop a distorted picture of disability. Appropriate counseling from her perspective would involve asking the client the following:

> Was she satisfied that she had sufficient knowledge about disability, and awareness of her own feelings about it so that she could make a rational choice? Did she personally know any disabled adults or children? What was she taught about disability by adults when she was young? Was she aware of the distorted picture of the lives of disabled people presented by the posters, telethons, and stereotyped characters in the literature and media? I would ask her to consider the opportunities for herself in taking on the fears and prejudice, the expectations and pressures of her family and friends.[23]

Disease and disability are not the only potential targets of selective abortion. Sex detection is one consequence of most forms of prenatal diagnosis. With ultrasound alone this information can be obtained in the first trimester and thus may become the basis of a decision to abort. While most university-based clinics in North America refuse to provide diagnostic services for sex preselection, many private clinics and companies do provide this service. Interest in

sex selection is not as intense in North America as in some other parts of the world, but some obstetricians and gynecologists are contributing to normalization of the practice by euphemistically referring to it as "family completion."[24]

At the same time, opposition to the practice of using prenatal diagnosis for sex preselection may be mounting. Wertz and Fletcher note that the state of Pennsylvania prohibits abortion for certain purposes, including sex choice. They warn that laws limiting abortion choices are worse than the abuses they intend to prevent, and they advocate "moral suasian" to encourage geneticists and other appropriate health workers to withhold this information or to refuse to abort on the basis of fetal sex.[25]

One attempt to resolve the ethics of using abortion to prevent the birth of fetuses with genetic disorders was made by a group of bioethicists from the Hastings Institute of Society, Ethics, and the Life Sciences. They agreed that the purpose of prenatal diagnosis should be to allow for treatment and eventual cure of disease in the fetus or infant. Since this is possible only in a small fraction of cases, they concluded that abortion "can be morally justified for the relief of suffering and burden to family and society." They advocated protection of individual choice and the autonomy of parents, "even when we disagree with their courses of action."[26]

Ethicists and clinicians continue to struggle with the often conflicting principles of the medical injunction to do no harm, respect for patient autonomy, and the professional ethic of nondirective counseling, as Ruth Cowan has noted. She suggests that feminist ethics might provide a path out of this dilemma. The basic principle from this perspective is that nurturance assumes the highest priority. That is, nurturance is the basis as well as the goal of all human relationships. When individuals cannot, for whatever reasons, make decisions for themselves, the persons who have the right to make the decision are those who are nurturing the individual in question. This places the decision to abort entirely in the hands of the pregnant woman. It requires physicians and others to abide by her decision "even if made by a calculus, even a eugenic calculus with which the provider did not agree—unless the provider was willing to take over the continuing nurturance of the fetus."[27]

The abortion issue is thus resolved by placing a high value on parental autonomy or control. This position remains the dominant one among medical geneticists in the United States and has been shown to be widespread cross-nationally as well.[28]

Practice

There are many aspects of the practice of prenatal diagnosis that have received the attention of ethicists, health care providers, and researchers. This section focuses on those related to communicating with or counseling prospective parents about the procedures and related issues.

The necessity for accurate and appropriate information about the risks and benefits of the various procedures and diagnostic findings has fueled the development of the genetic counseling profession. The goal of genetic counseling is to help people understand and, if possible, adjust to genetic information and to assist them, when necessary, in making decisions about what course to follow.[29] Because genetic advances are taking place far more rapidly than counselors can be trained, counseling related to prenatal diagnosis is increasingly provided by health providers untrained in genetic counseling. Whatever one's training, the communication with prospective parents regarding prenatal diagnosis poses a variety of ethical challenges.

There is widespread agreement that decision-making autonomy of the person counseled is paramount and that information should be provided with a "nondirective" strategy on the part of the counselor.[30] This policy has been advocated to protect against control by the medical profession and genetic counselors as well as against remnants of eugenicist proclivities of the past. It is currently the dominant policy despite the fact that total nondirectiveness is probably impossible to achieve[31] and that providers as well as clients have reported difficulty accepting the policy.[32] Some procedures, such as maternal serum screening, may be accompanied by little

or no counseling as they become increasingly routine. This may work for those whose test results are normal, but it can increase the shock of abnormal results. Where counseling is provided, there is often a very fine line between education and manipulation.[33] The ethical challenges of prenatal diagnosis counseling are similar to those of neonatal intensive care, where Anspach has noted that the dependence of parents on experts may lead not to informed consent but to the production of assent.[34] This is partly due to the fact that providers have great power to arouse or diminish the fears of pregnant women and their partners. As an early report from the National Academy of Sciences pointed out, "It is generally agreed that some amount of fear arousal increases the likelihood that people will act, but specifying (and inducing) the optimum amount is extremely difficult."[35]

The choice of information selected is an important issue. Genetic counseling is described by anthropologist Rayna Rapp as "resolutely statistical," reinforcing a medical rather than a social definition of the problems of childhood disability. She points out that today's urban patients, many of whom are multilingual, may find clinical and epidemiological discourse alien and irrelevant or unresponsive to their actual concerns. This often results in a "discourse in which multicultural clients and science-based health professionals communicate and miscommunicate."[36]

Prospective parents, as Abby Lippman has shown, often seek information on the consequences of life with a disabled child for themselves, the child, and other loved ones. They may not find the emphasis on probabilities helpful, since their predominant perception is that a particular outcome is actually binary. They must be prepared for the fact that it will or will not happen.[37] Lippman found that what prospective parents often seek is to explore various scenarios. This enables them to choose the option that can most effectively minimize losses.[38] Genetic counseling rarely, if ever, helps families explore the social consequences of various alternatives, such as how other families have been affected by the birth of disabled children, or the social services and resources available to them as parents.[39]

In a study of how Down's syndrome is presented in medical texts, Lippman and Brunger illustrated that Western biomedicine is not objective and value free but depicts Down's syndrome in terms grounded in the practitioner's own medical subculture. Medical descriptions of Down's syndrome—rather than revealing the variability of the condition—selectively represent the condition in uniform, distancing, negative, ungendered, and static terms. Lippman and Brunger suggest that this perception tells us more about the culture of biomedicine than about Down's syndrome. Their critique is particularly relevant to prenatal diagnosis because the " 'normative' view of this condition . . . has become generally accepted in North America as a privileged reason for abortion."[40]

Lippman and Wilfond have observed further that, in the case of Down's syndrome and cystic fibrosis, the information provided to parents with either healthy children or no children in genetic counseling sessions "differs strikingly from that provided to those who have a child with one of these conditions."[41] The differences observed include the fact that information provided before birth is largely negative while information provided after birth tends to be more positive. The before-birth information focuses on technical matters and potential medical complications. Only after the birth of a child with one of these conditions is a more hopeful approach taken, with attention given to the "compensating aspects of the condition" or to the availability of medical and social resources. This suggests that all practitioners have a responsibility to reflect carefully on the information they provide on the meaning of diagnostic findings.

Consequences

Prenatal diagnosis, like all technologies, often has consequences beyond those directly intended. Two related areas in which its consequences have been critically examined are the psychosocial dimension and the implications for reproductive control.

Psychosocial Consequences

Early in its evolution, it became apparent that prenatal diagnosis evokes intense emotional responses in pregnant women. This is not surprising since pregnancy—independent of such interventions—has been recognized as a life crisis[42] or major life transition.[43] In this age of prenatal diagnosis, the psychosocial stages of pregnancy increasingly are organized around the diagnostic technologies rather than emerging in response to biological changes.[44]

Studies of psychosocial responses to amniocentesis indicate that it engenders anxiety in fathers as well as mothers. This anxiety has two peaks: one prior to amniocentesis and the second prior to receiving results. Among women it tends to be highest among those who have previously given birth to children with disabilities.[45] One common strategem for coping with high levels of anxiety prior to receiving test results is "suspension of commitment to pregnancy,"[46] resulting in what Rothman calls "the tentative pregnancy."[47] In addition to creating an emotional barrier between mother and fetus by establishing a set of interactions based on the possibility of severe genetic disorder and subsequent miscarriage or abortion, prenatal diagnosis often temporarily reduces the mother's confidence in the pregnancy and therefore may weaken her capacity to adjust her own living habits to provide optimal nurturance to the developing fetus during the period before test results are available.[48]

Heightened anxiety has been studied in women with false positive elevations of maternal serum AFP; anxiety persists throughout the period of testing until normal results are ultimately obtained. This anxiety appears to be unrelieved even when extensive counseling is provided, but anxiety does subside to relief with the notification of normal test results.[49]

Psychological studies of responses to CVS suggest that, as might be expected, CVS results in earlier reduction in anxiety levels, greater attachment during the second trimester, and less procedure-related discomfort. The earlier diagnosis is preferred when risk levels are perceived as comparable to amniocentesis.[50]

All forms of prenatal diagnosis fuel Rothman's concern about our tendency to reduce very complex social relationships to biological processes. She suggests that attachment between mother and child is an interaction that begins long before birth. She asks us to consider not only the fetus but also the mother, as well as the effects of reconstructing pregnancy. In the past, women have always experienced the process of pregnancy as "part of ourselves very gradually becoming someone else." Now, with prenatal diagnosis, it is transformed into a production process that starts from separation and only later comes to intimacy. Rothman suggests it is a grave error to recognize that the relationship between mother and fetus has significance only when it can be viewed through the professional's eyes.

The idea that science can reduce our understanding of human complexity has also been noted by the medical historian S.J. Reiser. He has extensively analyzed the trend in medicine to disregard the patient's sensory perceptions and judgments. Interestingly, Reiser points out that, not only are the patient's perceptions devalued, but the sensory perceptions of the physician or health care provider and the quality of verbal communication between the provider and the client are eroded by this process as well.[51] This suggests that special attention is required on the part of practitioners to maintain sensitivity to the patient's experience and concerns when using high-tech diagnostic tools.

Ultrasound is a good example of this. Its potential for intensifying the reality of the pregnancy was recognized very early, yet we still know very little about its effects on the patient's experience of pregnancy. It seems to have the potential for hastening development of maternal-fetal attachment. In a study of women who lost their pregnancies through miscarriage or elective terminations, Rita Beck Black found that nearly two-thirds of the women reported that the visual image produced by ultrasound made them feel closer to the fetus. It tended to reduce the emotional distance some women tried to maintain from their high-risk pregnancy. Following the loss of the pregnancy, the heightened

reality provided by the ultrasound was perceived by some as a gift and by others as an unwarranted added burden. Black suggests that the intensity of feelings the ultrasound evokes may facilitate the bereavement process.[52]

In pregnancies that go to term, ultrasound can also engender anxiety, depression, and hostility when providers are insensitive in verbalizing their observations. Patients appear to need reassurances of normality as providers study the visual images. If reassurance of normality is not provided, the patients may have negative responses even in the absence of an unequivocal diagnosis of impairment. Furthermore, slips of the tongue, incorrect diagnosis, and identification of structures that cannot be deciphered are not uncommon. These constitute what Lumley calls "diagnostic toxicity." She believes ultrasound is so widely used that it is too late to investigate whether it affects maternal bonding, but she argues that the case for investigating the procedure's diagnostic toxicity is urgent.[53]

When prenatal diagnosis reveals the sex of the fetus, it often has significant consequences. Some parents report more intense feelings of attachment, but knowledge of the sex of the fetus may also result in parental disappointment and even emotional disengagement from the pregnancy. Once the sex of the fetus is known, a name is often given. This naming symbolizes a new relationship and arouses new expectations in family members. It can change the dynamics between the parents and their feelings about the pregnancy in both negative and positive directions. Many centers now ask clients to think carefully about whether or not they want this information before giving birth.[54]

The impact of prenatal testing is most dramatic when a fetal defect is revealed. When parents choose to have a second-trimester abortion, feelings of guilt, depression, and grief are often intense in both parents. Even though most couples report they would make the same decisions again, these feelings have been found to be more intense than in cases of elective abortion for nongenetic reasons or in cases of natural fetal death.[55] The work of Rita Beck Black and others suggests that most women who undergo prenatal diagnosis, even those who learn of fetal defects and opt to terminate the pregnancy, cope well with the experience.[56] Nevertheless, it is clear that prenatal genetic testing is a major psychological event for women, particularly when the testing reveals a serious defect in the baby. Black recommends the development of minimum service standards for these women, including follow-up with assessment. This would make it possible to identify those who most need clinical support. She, like many other researchers, calls for ongoing inquiry into the reactions of mothers and fathers to prenatal testing and pregnancy loss.[57]

Control of Reproduction

Observers from several disciplines have noted that use of reproductive technologies in general represents the male appropriation of women's reproductive power. From the introduction of forceps to in vitro fertilization, professional dominance of the reproductive process has caused growing concern.[58] This increasing use of reproductive technologies has been described by Wajcman as reinforcing the Cartesian model of the body as a machine and pregnancy as a technical problem to be fixed by medical tinkering.[59] Not only is the body viewed as a machine but as "an inherently defective machine," according to Davis-Floyd, while pregnancy is defined as "dangerous and dependent on (mostly) male managers and scientists for its success."[60] Viewed from this perspective, prenatal diagnosis can be seen as intensifying women's fear and mistrust of the pregnancy process and subverting both the appreciation of and the capacity for nurturance.

The control issue has been intensified by the advent of fetal therapy. Prenatal diagnosis has created the potential for physicians to define themselves as advocates of the fetus over the objections of the pregnant woman. Once the possibility of abortion has been ruled out, medical opinion can result in intervention against the wishes of the pregnant women—and at considerable cost to her health. Court-ordered obstetrical interventions are becoming increasingly common. They have been obtained for Caesarean sections, hospital detentions, and intrauterine transfusions. The majority of women involved have been members of a minority group, and disproportionately large numbers of them were unmarried and did not speak English. These cases suggest that loss of reproductive control during pregnancy is a more pressing issue for some segments of the population than for others.[61]

This concern is supported by Charles Bosk's study of genetic counseling. He found that the championing of individual autonomy was limited to outpatient services. He noted that the pursuit of cure placed decision making in the hands of physicians. He warns that, given the increasing ability to intervene with gene therapy, support of even outpatient autonomy may not continue.[62]

The most immediate threat to reproductive control may be restrictions on abortion, which can be legal or economic. Most states do not permit their medical assistance funds to be used for abortion, many permit private insurers to exclude coverage for most abortions unless the life of the woman is threatened, and none requires insurers to pay for abortions for genetic disorders.[63] On the other hand, insurers have a long-term economic interest in reducing the costs of medical care and for this reason may encourage or even pressure parents in the direction of abortion for genetic indications.[64]

Given the increasing control of others over the reproductive process once prenatal diagnosis is begun, it is not surprising that conflicts arise over what constitutes appropriate uses of prenatal diagnosis. Actions of individual litigants, often those who have given birth to a child affected with a genetic disorder, are a major force driving the use of these technologies, according to Ellen Wright Clayton.[65] Other women undergo the process very reluctantly or refuse prenatal diagnosis entirely as a way of taking control, as Robin Gregg found in a recent study of pregnancy. In this way they avoid the ramifications and risks of both positive and inaccurate test results.[66] Such choices are increasingly likely to be defined as irresponsible as prenatal testing becomes more widely used.

CONCLUSION

Prenatal diagnosis is a powerful collection of technologies. It is well established and here to stay. Like other technological developments, it has the potential for misuse, but it carries with it the promise of continued improvement and effective fetal therapy. In the meantime, many prospective parents value the increased options and reassurance it affords.

Dedication to the development of the technical aspects of the procedures has not been matched by attention to the consequences of these procedures in the lives of pregnant women and their families. The psychosocial consequences for individuals are no more clearly understood than are the consequences for our culture and society in general.

One responsibility of health care providers is to pay attention to the social context in which these technologies are offered and applied. Specialization must not encourage us to ignore approaches to health care and disability that could make larger, faster, and cheaper contributions to the reduction of human suffering. The narrow focus on prenatal genetic testing has been labeled "geneticization,"[67] and it could, in the absence of vigilance, provide a "backdoor to eugenics," as suggested by Duster.[68]

Developing sensitivity to the social context has benefits for client-provider interaction as well. It increases sensitivity to diversity among clients, a major concern of a recent conference on "Reproductive Genetic Testing: Impact on Women." The final report made it clear that differences among women must be recognized. The report emphasizes that efforts to evaluate prenatal diagnosis must go beyond mechanistic issues of biological safety and technical efficacy. Women's race, ethnicity, class, education, religious beliefs, exposure to and experience of disability, values, resources, health, reproductive histories, and support systems (or lack thereof) are only a few of the variables that influence the meaning of prenatal diagnosis in their lives.

Until we have given as much attention to the social impact of these procedures as we do to their technical aspects, the interests of pregnant women and their families will be best served by providers who refuse to make assumptions about what is best for their clients. The differences among women must now be addressed through a willingness to listen to the women and their family members and to pay heed to their thoughts and feelings about prenatal diagnostic services. Health care professionals must attend to the consequences of prenatal diagnosis for the relationship between mother and fetus, between family members, and between the pregnant woman and her community as well as the consequences for society in general. Beyond this, practitioners can promote client-centered evaluation processes in their own professional organizations and institutions.

NOTES

1. J.C. Hobbins, Amniocentesis, in *The Unborn Patient: Prenatal Diagnosis and Treatment*, edited by M. Harrison et al. (Philadelphia: W.B. Saunders, 1991), 60.

2. J.W. Larsen et al., Second and Third Trimester Prenatal Diagnosis, in *Fetal Diagnosis and Therapy: Science, Ethics and the Law*, edited by M.I. Evans et al. (Philadelphia: J.B. Lippincott, 1989), 37.

3. Hobbins, Amniocentesis; M.I. Evans et al., Early Genetic Amniocentesis or Chorionic Villus Sampling: Expanding the Opportunities for Early Prenatal Diagnosis, *Journal of Reproductive Medicine* 3 (1988):450.

4. M.I. Evans et al., Report of the Council on Scientific Affairs of the American Medical Association: Ultrasound Evaluation of the Fetus, *Fetal Diagnosis and Therapy* 6 (1991):132–147.

5. Ibid.

6. W.A. Hogge, Chorionic Villus Sampling, in *The Unborn Patient*.

7. G.G. Rhoads et al., The Safety and Efficacy of Chorionic Villus Sampling for Early Prenatal Diagnosis of Cytogenetic Abnormalities, *New England Journal of Medicine* 320 (1989):609–617; A. Lippman et al., Canadian Multicentre Randomized Clinical Trial of Chorion Villus Sampling and Amniocentesis, *Prenatal Diagnosis* 12 (1992):385–476.

8. L. Jackson and R. Wapner, Chorionic Villus Sampling:

10 Years Experience, oral presentation at the Sixth International Conference on Early Prenatal Diagnosis of Genetic Disease, Milan, Italy, May 18–20, 1992.

9. F.J. Meaney et al., Providers and Consumers of Prenatal Genetic Testing Services: What Do the National Data Tell Us? *Fetal Diagnosis and Therapy*, in press.

10. J.E. Haddow et al., Prenatal Screening for Down's Syndrome with Use of Maternal Serum Markers, *New England Journal of Medicine* 327 (1992):588–593.

11. President's Commision for the Study of Ethical Problems in Medical and Biomedical and Behavioral Research, *Screening and Counseling for Genetic Conditions: The Ethical, Social, and Legal Implications of Genetic Screening, Counseling, and Education Programs* (Washington, D.C.: U.S. Government Printing Office, 1983), 55.

12. E. Singer, Public Attitudes toward Genetic Testing, *Population Research and Policy Review* 10 (1991):235–255.

13. Ibid.

14. E. Thomson et al., "National Institutes of Health Workshop Statement—Reproductive Genetic Testing: Impact on Women, *American Journal of Human Genetics* 51 (1992):1161–1163.

15. J.O. Price et al., Prenatal Diagnosis with Fetal Cells Isolated from Maternal Blood by Multiparameter Flow Cytometry, *American Journal of Obstetrics and Gynecology* 165 (1991):1731–1737.

16. Y. Verlinsky et al., Preconception and Preimplantation Genetic Diagnosis of Genetic Diseases, *Journal of In Vitro Fertilization and Embryo Transfer* (1(1990):1–5.

17. G.M. Atkinson and A.S. Maraczyewski, *Genetic Counseling, The Church, and The Law: A Task Force Report of the Pope John Center.* (St. Louis, Mo.: Pope John XXIII, 1980).

18. M. Sun, Amniocentesis: Be prepared. *Science 2* (1980):1253.

19. N. Press and C.H. Browner, "Collective Fictions": Similarities in Reasons for Accepting MSAFP Screening Among Women of Diverse Ethnic and Social Class Backgrounds, *Fetal Diagnosis and Therapy*, in press.

20. M.C.A. White-Van Mourik et al., The Psychosocial Sequelae of a Second-Trimester Termination of Pregnancy for Fetal Abnormality, *Prenatal Diagnosis* 12 (1992): 189–204.

21. Larson, Jr. and MacMillin, Second and Third Trimester Prenatal Diagnosis, 36–43.

22. M.B. Mahowald, Is There Life after Roe v. Wade? *Hastings Center Report* July/August (1989):22–27; R. Hubbard, Eugenics: New Tools, Old Ideas in *Embryos, Ethics and Women's Rights: Exploring the New Reproductive Technologies*, edited by E.H. Baruch et al. (1988): 225–235.

23. M. Saxton, Prenatal Screening and Discriminatory Attitudes About Disability in *Embryos, Ethics and Women's Rights: Exploring the New Reproductive Technologies*, edited by E.H. Baruch et al. (1988)217–224.

24. A. Lippman, Dept. of Epidemiology and Biostatistics, McGill University, Montreal, Quebec, Personal Communication, January 1993.

25. D.C. Wertz & J.C. Fletcher, Sex Selection Through Prenatal Diagnosis: A Feminist Critique in *Feminist Perspectives in Medical Ethics*, edited by H.B. Holmes and L. Purdy (Bloomington: Indiana University Press, 1992): 240–253.

26. T.M. Powledge and J. Fletcher, Guidelines for the Ethical, Social, and Legal Issues in Prenatal Diagnosis, *New England Journal of Medicine* 300 (1979):168–72.

27. R.S. Cowan, Genetic Technology and Reproductive Choice: An Ethics for Autonomy in *The Code of Codes: Scientific and Social Issues in the Human Genome Project*, edited by D.J. Kevles and L. Hood (Cambridge, Mass.: Harvard University Press, 1992), 244–264.

28. D.C. Wertz and J.C. Fletcher, Attitudes of Genetic Counselors: A Multinational Survey, *American Journal of Human Genetics* 42 (1988):592–600.

29. President's Commission for the Study of Ethical Problems in Medicine and Biomedical and Behavioral Research, *Screening and Counseling for Genetic Conditions* (1983), 4.

30. Ibid., 37.

31. Ibid., 56.

32. L.E. Karp, The Terrible Question, *American Journal of Medical Genetics* 14 (1983):1–3; Rothman, *The Tentative Pregnancy: Prenatal Diagnosis and the Future of Motherhood* (New York: Viking, 1986), 40–48.

33. M.J. Goodman and L.E. Goodman, The Overselling of Genetic Anxiety, *Hastings Center Report*, October 1982, 2–27.

34. R.R. Anspach, From Principles to Practice: Life-and-Death Decisions in the Intensive-Care Nursery, in *New Approaches to Human Reproduction: Social and Ethical Dimensions*, edited by L.M. Whiteford and M.L. Poland (Boulder, Colo.: Westview Press, 1989).

35. National Research Council, Assembly of Life Sciences, Division of Medical Sciences, Committee for the Study of Inborn Errors of Metabolism, *Genetic Screening Programs, Principles, and Research* (Washington, D.C.: National Academy of Sciences, 1975), 246; cf. p. 171.

36. R. Rapp, Chromosomes and Communication: The Discourse of Genetic Counseling, *Medical Anthropology Quarterly* 2, no.2:143–147.

37. A. Lippman-Hand and F.C. Fraser, Genetic Counseling: Parents' Responses to Uncertainty, *Birth Defects* (original article series) 15 (1979):325–339.

38. A. Lippman-Hand and F.C. Fraser, Genetic Counseling: The Postcounseling Period. I. Parents' Perception of

Uncertainty, *American Journal of Medical Genetics* 3 (1979):113–127.

39. D. Beeson and M.S. Golbus, Decision Making: Whether or Not to Have Prenatal Diagnosis and Abortion for X-Linked Conditions, *American Journal of Medical Genetics* 20 (1985):107.

40. A. Lippman and F. Brunger, Constructing Down Syndrome: Texts as Informants, *Sante Culture Health*, in press.

41. A. Lippman and B.S. Wilfond, Twice-Told Tales: Stories about Genetic Disorders, *American Journal of Human Genetics* 51 (1992):936–937.

42. See G.L. Bibring et al., Study of the Psychological Processes in Pregnancy and of the Earliest Mother-Child Relationship, parts 1 and 2, *Psychoanalytic Study of the Child* 16 (1961):9–72.

43. A. Rossi, A Transition to Parenthood, *Journal of Marriage and Family* 30 (1968):26–39.

44. D. Beeson, Technological Rhythms in Pregnancy: The Case of Prenatal Diagnosis by Amniocentesis, in *Cultural Perspectives on Biological Knowledge*, edited by T. Duster and K. Garrett (Norwood, N.J.: Ablex, 1984), 145–181.

45. This pattern of anxiety is noted in a review of studies of the impact of amniocentesis by E. Adler et al., Psychological Issues in New Reproductive Technologies: Pregnancy-Inducing Technology and Diagnostic Screening, in *Women and New Reproductive Technologies: Medical, Psychosocial, Legal and Ethical Dilemmas*, edited by J. Rodin and A. Collins (Hillsdale, N.J.: L. Erlbaum, 1991),111–133.

46. D. Beeson and M.S. Golbus, Anxiety Engendered by Amniocentesis, *Birth Defects* (original article series) 15 (1979):191–197.

47. B.K. Rothman, *The Tentative Pregnancy: Prenatal Diagnosis and the Future of Motherhood* (New York: Viking, 1986), 101–115.

48. Beeson and Golbus, Anxiety Engendered by Amniocentesis.

49. B.K. Burton and R.G. Dillard, The Psychological Impact of False Positive Elevations of Maternal Serum Alpha-Fetoprotein, *American Journal of Obstetrics and Gynecology* 151 (1985):77–82.

50. A. Lippman et al., Chorionic Villi Sampling: Women's Attitudes, *American Journal of Medical Genetics* 22 (1985):395–401. For a review of studies of mood states in pregnancy, with particular emphasis on women having prenatal diagnosis, see S.L. Tunis and M.S. Golbus, Assessing Mood States in Pregnancy: Survey of the Literature, *Obstetrical and Gynecology Survey* 46 (1991):340–346.

51. S.J. Reiser, *Medicine and the Reign of Technology* (Cambridge: Cambridge University Press, 1978), 227.

52. R.B. Black, Seeing the Baby: The Impact of Ultrasound Technology, *Journal of Genetic Counseling* 1 (1992):45–54.

53. J. Lumley, Through a Glass Darkly: Ultrasound and Prenatal Bonding, *Birth* 17 (1990):214–217.

54. Beeson, Technological Rhythms in Pregnancy.

55. B.D. Blumberg et al., The Psychological Sequelae of Abortion Performed for a Genetic Indication, *American Journal of Obstetrics and Gynecology* 122 (1975):179.

56. R.B. Black, A One- and Six-Month Follow-up of Prenatal Diagnosis Patients Who Lost Pregnancies, *Prenatal Diagnosis* 9 (1989):795–804.

57. R.B. Black, Women's Voices after Pregnancy Loss: Couples' Patterns of Communication and Support, *Social Work in Health Care* 16 (1991):19–36.

58. A. Oakley, From Walking Wombs to Test-tube Babies, in *Reproductive Technologies: Gender Motherhood and Medicine*, edited by M. Stanworth (Minneapolis, Minn.: University of Minnesota Press, 1987).

59. J. Wajcman, *Feminism Confronts Technology* (University Park, Pa.: Pennsylvania State University Press, 1991), 67.

60. R.E. Davis-Floyd, *Birth as an American Rite of Passage* (Berkeley: University of California Press, 1992), 72.

61. V.E.B. Kolder et al., Court Ordered Obstetrical Interventions, *New England Journal of Medicine* 316 (1987):1192–1196.

62. C.L. Bosk, *All God's Mistakes: Genetic Counseling in a Pediatric Hospital* (Chicago: University of Chicago Press, 1992), 150.

63. E.W. Clayton, Reproductive Genetic Testing: Regulatory and Liability Issues, *Fetal Diagnosis and Therapy*, in press.

64. P.R. Billings et al., Discrimination as a Consequence of Genetic Testing, *American Journal of Human Genetics* 50 (1992):476–482.

65. Clayton, Reproductive Genetic Testing.

66. R. Gregg, *Pregnancy in a High Tech Age: Paradoxes of Choice* (New York: Paragon House, in press).

67. A. Lippman, Prenatal Genetic Testing and Screening: Constructing Needs and Reinforcing Inequities, *American Journal of Law and Medicine* 18 (1991):15–50.

68. T. Duster, *Backdoor to Eugenics* (New York: Routledge, 1990).

Chapter 9

Prenatal Screening for Maternal Drug Use

Ray Moseley, Josepha Cheong, and Clarice Bell

Toxicology screening of pregnant women for illicit drug use raises several difficult ethical and policy issues for the health care provider. Often the testing was completed without informed consent, based on suspicion by these women's physicians and nurse practitioners.[1] Those that test positive for the presence of illicit drugs were then reported to authorities.[2] Consequently, several of these women were charged with child abuse and/or other crimes.[3]

Several rationales exist for prenatal illicit drug testing without consent and for requiring the reporting to legal authorities of the results of those tests.[4] The first is that testing will identify and prevent harm to the fetus.[5] Second, testing will identify and prevent harm to the mother. Also related is the argument that the potential harm to the fetus and mother resulting from drug use is so serious that it justifies overriding both informed consent requirements and health care provider–patient confidentiality with regard to reporting test results.[6] Finally, reporting of the test results to the appropriate legal authorities is argued to be in the best interest of both medical and societal concerns.

These arguments and conclusions are based on several assumptions. The first assumption is that illicit drug use clearly and seriously harms the fetus and mother. Second, these arguments assume that this potential harm can be prevented if the health care provider reports the positive test results to the appropriate legal authorities. Third, they assume that illicit drugs pose a significantly greater source of harm than do prescription drugs to both the fetus and the mother. In addition, they assume that the consequences of prenatal testing produce more good than harm. Finally, these arguments assume that the goals of preventing harm to the fetus and mother cannot be met in an alternative manner that violates fewer rights.

We believe that all of these assumptions have been overstated by proponents of prenatal drug testing. When these assumptions are carefully evaluated, they do not justify a general policy of prenatal testing without consent based solely on the "suspicion" by the health care provider or the reporting of test results to legal authorities. (The exception that we envision is where other evidence points to the likelihood of child abuse, and release of the results of the screen for illegal drugs, with a proper court order, would serve to confirm the child abuse charge.)

Despite the very strong negative emotional impact on the pregnant woman using illicit drugs, it is far from clear that prenatal toxicology screening, for either illicit or prescription drugs, will prevent any harm to the fetus, and it may, in fact, cause greater harm to the fetus and the mother. In reviewing the extensive literature on the prenatal maternal use of cocaine and other illicit drugs, one can conclude that in some cases a degree of harm to the fetus does occur. With the prenatal use of cocaine, investigators have found the following associated complications: placental abruption, premature rupture of membranes, unexplained fetal death, liver failure, and "jittery babies."[7] In many if not most of these cases, the harmful effects seen are the result of the combined or synergistic effects of cocaine and other factors, such as alcohol, poor nutrition, and lack of prenatal care.[8] In many cases, however, only mild harmful effects or none at all are evident in the fetus.[9] It should also be noted that these conditions are also present in some cases where no drugs were involved. It is impossible to say in any particular case whether illicit or prescription drug use or some other unknown factor is the cause of the baby's condition.

One might respond that using a criterion of "clear harm to a fetus" is much too stringent a standard. However, the use of a more liberal criterion of "possible harm to the fetus" as the proposed justification for violating the mother's right to informed consent(and as an indicator of child abuse) leads to serious consistency problems and slippery-slope ramifications.

One line that might be drawn to prevent that slide down the slippery slope is based on whether drug use is legal or illegal. However, such a line invites severe criticism, since that distinction is based on no clear and consistent rationale. For example, much harm clearly occurs to fetuses through the mothers' use of legal drugs such as alcohol and cigarettes and as a result of their life styles (e.g., poor diets resulting in poor nutrition).[10] The effects of compromised life styles and/or the prenatal use of these legal drugs are in many cases at least as harmful as—and sometimes more harmful than—the prenatal use of illicit drugs.[11] If harm to the fetus is the major reason that the use of illicit drugs would justify violation of the mother's rights, then these above-mentioned legal though potentially harmful activities of the mother should also be considered adequate justification. The obvious problem with this approach is that there seems to be no stopping the slide down the slippery slope.[12] For example, what would happen if research discovered that women who "use" caffeinated beverages have a higher incidence of harm to the fetus?[13] Should the physician then test prenatally, without informed consent, for the presence of caffeine and intervene, possibly by reporting for child abuse the pregnant woman who is caught drinking a cup of coffee? Such intrusions into the private lives of pregnant women would seem grossly unwarranted and could lead to a restrictive list of acceptable and unacceptable activities for pregnant women.

Even if prenatal use of illicit drugs is established as harmful to the fetus, toxicology screening of pregnant women will probably have minimal effect on the medical condition of the newborn. Drug testing does not always reveal the substance abused; nor does it reveal the extent of the drug use or when during the pregnancy the drugs were used. Even if the time of exposure to illegal drugs is known, the current state of knowledge does not clearly indicate when during the pregnancy or at what dosages harm to the fetus occurs.[14]

Even when drug testing occurs very early in the pregnancy and effective intervention is implemented to stop further drug use, there is no guarantee that harm to the fetus will be prevented.[15] In addition, this highly optimistic scenario of early screening and intervention is unlikely because early screening is rare. Most pregnant women who use illicit drugs usually seek prenatal care relatively late in their pregnancy if at all. Furthermore, the assumption that these patients will get effective treatment is highly questionable, since current access to drug treatment programs is severely limited and successful treatment rates are low.

Another problem is the possibility of serious long-range consequences of prenatal drug testing on both the health of the pregnant woman and the fetus. Not surprisingly, much anecdotal evidence reports that pregnant women may fail to seek any prenatal care if they feel that they may be at risk for being charged with child abuse, being incarcerated, or losing their child. In fact, lack of prenatal care is apparently a bigger factor in the overall health of the fetus than is the use of illicit drugs.[16] We simply do not have available the empirical evidence to know if prenatal drug screening will help or harm the fetus and/or the mother.

Additionally, several other problems are raised by a policy of assuming that the suspicion of prenatal drug use justifies violating the mother's rights. These problems include the handling of false positive test results, funding the potentially tremendous increase in the caseload of child abuse investigations, and determining the follow-up for pregnant women with positive test results. Prenatal screening also raises the ever-controversial issue of whether a fetus is a child and therefore should have the rights of a child.

One might object to prenatal drug testing for *all* patients as too intrusive or too costly but favor testing those women whom health care providers "suspect" of illicit drug use. This approach, however, is open to the possibility of abuse and mistakes. How would a health care provider decide to test *this particular* pregnant woman for illicit drug use? Recent studies have indicated that the high proportion of prenatal drug use reported among poor black women is due partly to the fact that poor black women are subject to a highly disproportionate number of drug tests although much illicit drug use occurs among middle class whites.[17] Clearly, stereotypes influence even a health care provider's practices.

In contrast, a more strictly medical rationale exists for prenatal screening for a wide variety of drug use (including illicit drugs). Knowledge of prenatal drug use provides important diagnostic information that the physician may use to determine the risk category for the infant. This information would also be useful in identifying possible postnatal complications. With this knowledge, prenatal interventions could be implemented to aid the expectant mother in discontinuing drug use, thus reducing the possible harm to the fetus and benefiting the mother by treating her drug dependency. Following delivery, the infant could be immediately examined for drug-induced complications or dependency, and possible social work interventions could be initiated to determine the adequacy of the home environment. If pregnant women are made aware that they and their fetuses will be helped and not penalized by drug screening, they may be more likely to seek prenatal care and to maintain a trusting relationship with their health care providers.

Even if one feels that drug screening is a useful diagnostic tool in preparing for the birth, this conviction does not automatically justify testing the mother without her permission.[18] In other words, does the danger posed by the prenatal use of illicit or prescription drugs constitute an exception to the recognized legal and ethical rights of patients to be informed about the consequences of a procedure and to give consent prior to the procedure? Legitimate exceptions to informed consent requirements must meet strict conditions. In the case of a legitimate exception, the consequences of following informed consent must cause both serious and likely harm to the patient or third parties, and *not* asking for informed consent would allow the serious harm to be avoided. Even in the case of prenatal drug screening, there is no definitive evidence that most pregnant women would refuse to be tested, especially if the results remain confidential and are used only for diagnostic purposes. Before a policy allowing drug testing without informed consent can be accepted, additional empirical data must be gathered to demonstrate that these expectant mothers will not consent and/or give accurate information about their drug use once they have understood that the test results will be used to help them.

In conclusion, the ethical and legal issues regarding prenatal drug screening are indeed difficult and complex ones. The arguments for and against such testing are equally persuasive. Yet despite these arguments, further research and data are required before a policy of testing without informed consent may be established.

NOTES

1. I.J. Chasnoff, Drug Use and Women: Establishing a Standard of Care, *Annals of the New York Academy of Science* 562 (1989):208–210.

2. C. Mahan, Deputy Secretary for Health and State Health Officer, memo on reporting substance abuse newborns to the abuse registry, July 31, 1989.

3. This case (When Courts Take Charge of the Unborn, *New York Times*, January 9, 1989, A1, A11) is but one of several cases that have been widely reported, including cases in Florida; Washington, D.C.; Connecticut; and Wyoming.

4. K. Jost, Mother versus Child, *American Bar Association Journal*, April 1989, 84–88; R. Sherman, Keeping the Baby Safe from Mom, *National Law Journal* 11, no. 4 (1988):1, 24–25; J. Levin and M. Li, Will All Addicted Pregnant Women Have Their Babies Taken into Care? *Lancet*, January 24, 1990, 230; J. Carvel, Fetus as Ward of Court? *Lancet*, February 13, 1988, 369.

5. D.A. Frank et al., Cocaine Use during Pregnancy: Prevalence and Correlates, *Pediatrics* 82 (1988):888–895.

6. Sherman, Keeping the Baby Safe from Mom; Levin and Li, Will All Addicted Pregnant Women Have Their Babies Taken into Care; Carvel, Fetus as Ward of Court?; F.A. Chervenak and L.B. McCullough, Perinatal Ethics: A Practical Method of Analysis of Obligations to Mother and Fetus, *Obstetrics and Gynecology* 66 (1985):442–446.

7. I.J. Chasnoff et al., Cocaine Use in Pregnancy, *New England Journal of Medicine* 313 (1985):666–669; R. Cherukuri et al., A Cohort Study of Alkaloidal Cocaine ("Crack") in Pregnancy, *Obstetrics and Gynecology* 72 (1988):147–151; L.P. Finnegan, Effects of Maternal Opiate Abuse on the Newborn, *Drug Toxicity in the Newborn Federation Proceedings* 44 (1985):2314–2317; J. Smith, The Dangers of Prenatal Cocaine Use, *American Journal of Maternal Child Nursing* 13 (1988):174–179; S.N. MacGregor et al., Cocaine Use during Pregnancy: Adverse Perinatal Outcome, *American Journal of Obstetrics and Gynecology* 157 (1987):686–690.

8. Cherukuri et al., A Cohort Study of Alkaloidal Cocaine ("Crack") in Pregnancy.

9. Ibid.; Finnegan, Effects of Maternal Opiate Abuse on the Newborn; Smith, The Dangers of Prenatal Cocaine Abuse.

10. Cherukuri et al., A Cohort Study of Alkaloidal Cocaine ("Crack") in Pregnancy; A.P. Streissguth et al., Natural History of the Fetal Alcohol Syndrome: A 10-year Follow-up of Eleven Patients, *Lancet* July 13, 1985, 85–91; J. Wright, Fetal Alcohol Syndrome, *Nursing Times,* March 26, 1986, 34–35; J. Waterson, Alcohol and Pregnancy, *Nursing Times,* August 28, 1985, 38–40; M.S. Scher et al., The Effects of Prenatal Alcohol and Marijuana Exposure: Disturbances in Neonatal Sleep Cycling and Arousal, *Pediatric Research* 24, no. 1 (1988):101–105; R. Lincoln, Smoking and Reproduction, *Family Planning Perspectives* 18, no. 2 (1986):79–84; J.C. Kleinman et al., The Effects of Maternal Smoking on Fetal and Infant Mortality, *American Journal of Epidemiology* 127 (1988):274–282; T.R. Martin and M.B. Bracken, The Association between Low Birth Weight and Caffeine Consumption during Pregnancy, *American Journal of Epidemiology* 126 (1987):813–821; E.R. McAnarney, Young Maternal Age and Adverse Neonatal Outcome, *American Journal of Diseases of Children* 141 (1987):1053–1059.

11. Cherukuri et al., A Cohort Study of Alkaloidal Cocaine ("Crack") in Pregnancy.

12. One slippery slope possibility is that reporting of the results of a screen for illegal drugs will encourage the pregnant woman, because of the fear of a child abuse charge, to seek an abortion.

13. Martin and Bracken, The Association between Low Birth Weight and Caffeine Consumption during Pregnancy.

14. I.J. Chasnoff et al., Temporal Patterns of Cocaine Use in Pregnancy: Perinatal Outcome, *JAMA* 261 (1989):1741–1744.

15. Ibid.; Cherukuri et al., A Cohort Study of Alkaloidal Cocaine ("Crack") in Pregnancy.

16. Jost, Mother versus Child.

17. Frank, Cocaine Use during Pregnancy; Smith, The Dangers of Prenatal Cocaine Use; I.J. Chasnoff et al., The Prevalence of Illicit Drug and Alcohol Use during Pregnancy and Discrepancies in Mandatory Reporting in Pinellas County, Florida, *New England Journal of Medicine* (1990):1202–1206; National Institute on Drug Abuse, *Cocaine Use in America,* DHHS Pub. No. ADM 85-1414 (Washington, D.C.: GPO# HE 20.8216:61, 1986).

18. E.T. Juengst, Prenatal Diagnosis and the Ethics of Uncertainty, in *Medical Ethics: A Guide for Health Professionals,* edited by J.F. Monagle and D.C. Thomasma (Gaithersburg, Md.: Aspen Publishers, 1988).

Part II

Issues in Adult Medicine

Chapter 10

The Patient Self-Determination Act

David B. Clarke

The federal Patient Self-Determination Act (PSDA) became effective on December 1, 1991—more than 15 years after California became the first state to pass its Natural Death Act and more than 22 years after Louis Kutner coined the term "living will" in a law journal proposal.[1] Planning for and implementation of the PSDA began in 1990, shortly after the law was passed as part of the Omnibus Budget Reconciliation Act (OBRA) and continued throughout 1991. At the time of preparation of this manuscript (January 1994), it is assumed that state agencies and health care providers affected by the legislation will have initiated programs and protocols designed to meet its basic requirements.

It is also presumed that programs initiated to meet PSDA requirements, either by states or institutions, will not be static. The PSDA is a dynamic process, intended to foster communication between health care providers and consumers and between persons and their chosen health care decision-making surrogates. While the core requirements of the PSDA can be implemented at a superficial level, the long-term benefits will only be realized through significant and fundamental changes in institutional policy, public and professional education, and social awareness.

The PSDA requires Medicare and Medicaid institutional providers to

1) provide written information to in-patients upon admission (or upon enrollment or initial entry into service) about:

    a. the person's rights under law to make health care decisions, including the right to accept or refuse treatment and the right to complete state-allowed advance directives, and

    b. the provider's written policies concerning implementation of those rights;

2) document in the person's medical record whether or not the person has completed an advance directive;

3) not discriminate or condition care based on whether or not the person has completed an advance directive;

4) ensure compliance with state laws concerning advance directives;

5) provide education for staff and the community on issues concerning advance directives.

In addition, each state (acting through a state agency, association, or other private nonprofit entity) must develop a written description of the law of the state—whether in statute or case law—concerning advance directives and distribute the document to local health care providers (see 1a above).

The PSDA, then, is a call to states and health care providers to educate professionals and the public about local laws concerning health care decision-making rights and advance directives. As such, it is a federal law necessitating broad agreement among legal and health care professionals on current rights and obligations in the health care arena and massive and persistent education efforts directed variously at medical professionals, administrators, social service providers, and the lay public.

The PSDA is *not* a law providing a universally accepted advance directive, though many would argue that that would certainly facilitate the process of public information and awareness. It is *not* a law to force health care professionals to talk more candidly with patients nor, in itself, to prompt consumers to initiate discussions with their providers. The PSDA will not resolve the issues arising from the provision of care to persons who have neither completed an advance directive nor expressed to others their wishes about treatment preferences or desired quality of life.[2] Nor does the PSDA deal directly with the developing issues of physician-assisted suicide and euthanasia. However, both supporters and critics of the PSDA believe that the new law will raise public awareness of these and related issues as health care decision making generally becomes more focused.

Since the PSDA relies on state law for the content of implementation efforts, the process of satisfying the PSDA will inevitably change in the months and years ahead. Legislation and court decisions at state and national levels will prompt states to revise and redistribute the "statement of state law" on health care decision-making rights and advance directives. As laws and institutional policies change, health care facilities will modify and reprint materials included in preadmission packets and provided to patients on admission. And professionals charged with patient and community education may develop effective teaching skills they never dreamed of using.

This article intends to address each of the major sections of the PSDA in light of the comments above. Attention will also be given to issues that have already arisen during this initial implementation period and to problems that are only tangentially related to the PSDA and its implementation.

BACKGROUND

Advance Directives

All states now have at least one kind of advance directive.[3] *Advance directive* is the general term for a variety of documents designed to enable competent adults to make health care decision-making plans in advance of future incapacity, including terminal illness. At present, advance directives are prescribed exclusively by individual state law. There is no federal legislation that allows for a uniform directive to be honored in all states, nor requires states to honor directives signed in other states. Efforts are underway, however, on both fronts.[4]

Advance directives are generally of two types: instructional and proxy. An instructional directive (most often called a living will or terminal care document) allows a competent adult to specify treatment wishes in advance of a terminal illness or condition during which the person is not capable of making sound health care decisions. Most living will laws specify a written form patterned loosely on the original document circulated widely by what is now the New York–based organization Choice in Dying. Whether called a natural death act, a rights of the terminally ill declaration, or a declaration of a desire for a natural death, most instructional directives share common features. They are written statements, to be signed by a competent adult, witnessed and perhaps notarized, that affirm that, in the event of terminal illness, the person wishes to forgo treatments that would serve only to prolong the dying process and would not effect a cure or recovery.

A proxy directive is very different. Patterned after a well-established legal document called a durable power of attorney, a health care proxy (or durable power of attorney for health care) allows a competent adult to choose another person to make health care decisions for him or her, according to his or her wishes, if—at any time and for any reason—the person becomes unable to make his or her own health care decisions. The chosen health care agent (or attorney-in-fact, in the case of a health care power of attorney) can make any health care decision that the person could him- or herself, except where the law or the person sets limits on the agent's authority to make certain kinds of decisions.

Some states have both directives, and in fact both might be needed in certain states to ensure that certain treatments are selected or avoided. No two states have the same laws, and no one form is accepted in each of the 50 states. The PSDA simply requires states and providers to give information about what is legally permitted in that state.

Researchers continue to express concern about the efficacy of advance directives, both instructional and proxy.[5] Typical was a letter to the *New England Journal of Medicine* in December 1991 signed by 16 physicians, nurses, lawyers, and ethicists.[6] The authors listed reservations about both forms of directive, including assertions that patients prefer to avoid discussions of future incapacity and death, patients cannot predict accurately their future preferences, patients may change their minds, an appointed agent might turn out to be a poor choice as a surrogate decision maker, and the documents or agents may specify treatments that the provider has sincere conscientious objections to using.

In many states, implementation of the PSDA has followed close on the heels of new or recently modified advance directive legislation. It is understandable that both providers and con-

sumers will have to "feel their way" for the foreseeable future in assessing the value of both the PSDA and any state-specific advance directive legislation. And perhaps more than in the case of other kinds of legislation, the development of advance directives has been characterized by a high degree of modification and compromise. Concerted efforts of interest groups such as the professional medical community, institutional and agency providers, senior advocates, and religious associations have combined to produce legislation that may be virtually immune from legislative modification, at least in the near term. Those who favor extended trial implementation periods often get their wish, and more. Those who favor legislative "fine-tuning" of the law may have to be unusually patient. Answers to some questions will not come quickly, nor will they come as succinctly as advocates and critics might hope.

Almost everything known about the effect of advance directives—on professional practice, public opinion, patient preferences, courts, and consumer tendencies—is based on studies done *prior* to the PSDA. Advance directives have been in legal use since 1977. However, the PSDA has given the concept a "bump start" by requiring facilities to provide education to staff, patients, and the community. The professional literature has been disappointingly slow to indicate whether research studies were conducted before or after the wave of public and professional education on advance directives and the PSDA during 1991 and early 1992. It was encouraging in early 1993 to see articles emphasizing the need for empirical research in this complex field since passage of the PSDA.[7]

Patient Self-Determination Act

The PSDA was introduced in the United States Senate by John C. Danforth (R-Missouri) and Daniel Patrick Moynihan (D-New York) in October 1989, shortly before the case of Nancy Cruzan was first heard in a Missouri district probate court. Six months later, Representative Sander M. Levin (D-Michigan) sponsored a significantly revised version of the bill in the House. Many of the original provisions proposed by Danforth, Moynihan, and Levin were ultimately deleted from the "ambitious" legislation, including requirements that

- states need to have advance directive legislation (at the time, six did not)
- agencies "document the treatment wishes of such patient, and periodically review such wishes with the patient"[8]
- agencies "implement an institutional ethics committee which would initiate educational programs for staff, patients, residents and the community on ethical issues in health care, advise on particular cases, and serve as a forum on such issues."[9]

The PSDA was signed by President Bush in December 1990 as part of the Omnibus Budget Reconciliation Act of 1990, and it became effective December 1, 1991. In retrospect, political caution and expediency prevailed, though many of the excised provisions came to pass regardless. Passage of the PSDA itself prompted several states to enact advance directive legislation. Many providers willingly document patients' treatment wishes. And the education component was retained, though not as part of a specific obligation to establish an ethics committee.

As passed, the PSDA required the Secretary of Health and Human Services to "develop and implement a national campaign to inform the public of the option to execute advance directives and of a patient's right to participate and direct health care decisions," develop or approve nationwide informational materials, and assist state agencies to develop state-specific documents. To date, the federal government has provided little help to the states or health care facilities in this regard. There has been no coordinated "national campaign," and the offer of the Health Care Financing Administration (HCFA) to give assistance to states was sent out four months after the 1991 PSDA effective date. HCFA issued final interim regulations regarding the PSDA in early March 1992.[10]

The case of Nancy Cruzan brought national attention to the need for widespread education about the use of advance directives. Nancy Cruzan, a 23-year-old Missouri woman, was left in a persistent vegetative state as a result of a single car accident. After her parents accepted the fact that their daughter would never regain either consciousness or any level of meaningful existence, they petitioned a Missouri court for permission to have her removed from artificial nutrition and hydration. Nancy Cruzan had never completed an advance directive of any kind, had left no written evidence of her treatment preferences in case of future incapacity, nor had she legally appointed a surrogate decision maker for her health care. A local probate judge, accepting oral testimony from her parents and personal friends that Nancy would not have wanted her life to be sustained under such conditions, granted her parents permission to have her removed from life supports. The attorney general of Missouri appealed the matter to the Supreme Court of Missouri, and the case was eventually heard by the U.S. Supreme Court.

The only question put before the U.S. Supreme Court—the first time that court had considered the issue of the "right to die"—was: Can the state of Missouri require "clear and convincing evidence" of Nancy's own wishes in deciding whether to grant permission to Nancy's parents. "Clear and convincing" is one of the highest levels of evidentiary proof required by the law in order to prove as true a statement or event. In a criminal trial, for example, a person can be found guilty only if a judge or jury finds him culpable "beyond a reasonable doubt"—the highest standard required in a court of law. "Clear and convincing," a slightly lower standard, is often taken to mean written evidence, such as could be shown by an advance directive, letter, diary, or other document written by the person him- or herself.[11] The Supreme Court ruled that while such a high level of proof is not required in such cases, states are indeed permitted to set the standard at that level.

The case was returned to the trial court, where additional witnesses testified that Nancy herself had told them that she would not want to live in a condition she now was in. Finding that this new evidence met the clear and convincing standard, the judge ruled in favor of Nancy Cruzan's parents on December 14, 1990. No further appeal was filed. Nancy Cruzan died several days after her health care providers agreed to withdraw artificially supplied food and water.

In an important side note to the Cruzan case, Supreme Court Justice Sandra Day O'Connor wrote in her concurring opinion,

> Few individuals provide explicit oral or written instructions regarding their intent to refuse medical treatment should they become incompetent. States which decline to consider any evidence other than such instructions may frequently fail to honor a patient's intent. Such failures might be avoided if the State considered an equally probative source of evidence: the patient's appointment of a proxy to make health care decisions on her behalf. . . . These procedures for surrogate decisionmaking, which appear to be rapidly gaining in acceptance, may be a valuable additional safeguard of the patient's interest in directing his medical care.[12]

STATEMENT OF STATE LAW

The PSDA requires that states develop written statements of local law concerning advance directives that would be distributed by covered providers or organizations to patients, residents, members, or clients. Efforts to meet this requirement have varied considerably. In a recent evaluation of each state's response, researchers sought to identify the process used to comply, the difficulties encountered, and the effects of the PSDA on the effort itself.[13]

Most states read the language of the statute narrowly: The drafting effort was led by a state agency in 33 states and by a hospital or legal association in another 12. Massachusetts Health Decisions, a nonprofit health education and public opinion organization, was the sole consumer group taking a lead role by convening a state-

wide task force of 16 professional, provider, and education associations and state agencies. Most states worked collaboratively with a variety of concerned groups and organizations. Typical representation came from professional associations (hospital, medicine, nursing, hospice, long-term care, social work, chaplaincy, and law), interested state agencies (health and human services, attorney general, elder affairs), and, to a lesser extent, consumer organizations (illness support, aging, health promotion). It is interesting to note that only 1 state had a minority group involved, though 19 states had plans to translate the state law description.

While the statute requires only a description of advance directive law, most states included related information about informed consent, decision making in the absence of an advance directive, and competency (to complete a directive) and capacity (to make one's own health care decisions). Most also addressed the role of health providers in counseling patients' decisions to forgo or withdraw life-sustaining treatments, and the kind of information generally needed to make health care decisions.

In the survey, 40 states reported problems or concerns with their own state law. These fell into five categories: (1) concerns about living will laws, (2) concerns about durable power of attorney legislation, (3) decision making absent advance directives, (4) nutrition and hydration, and (5) witnessing procedures. Ten states introduced new legislation to remedy the problems or clarify ambiguities. Fifteen simply noted the uncertainty in their public description of the law (e.g., "If you have no family, or if there is disagreement about what treatment you would want, a court *may* be asked to appoint a guardian to make those decisions for you"). Other states did nothing or sought clarification from their attorney general.

Since all states now have a written statement, was the required process a total success? No, but all states will have the opportunity to modify their statement and must inevitably do so as federal and state laws change. For instance, only ten states included information about updating the directive. Just over half advised discussion with family or friends. Only six described the process for determining incapacity (in order to invoke the advance directive). Less than half addressed the issue of having the directive honored in other states.

From a lay person's point of view, these omissions may be critical. Many, if not most, people will first learn about advance directives on admission, just as envisioned by the PSDA. Easy access and quick comprehensibility may determine whether the concept is worth a second thought—then or at a later time. Since health facilities are not required to distribute advance directives, the statement of state law may be the only introduction to advance directives offered by a facility to new patients. It is important, then, that the document convey not only the letter of the law but its spirit. The intent of the PSDA is to educate and foster communication. If the initial exposure to information does not promote those goals, then subsequent efforts may prove starkly ineffective.

Collaborative efforts to refine and improve the statement of state law may also point out inconsistencies and vague areas in the law. Rose Gasner, former legal director at Choice in Dying, points out that the law regarding treatment refusal has "developed very haphazardly in many states, as the legislatures and the courts have responded to the fast-paced development of the issue. . . . Coalition work can create opportunities for law reform and bring together those interested groups that need to be involved in the political process to ensure passage of amending or substitute legislation.[14]

"ON ADMISSION . . . "

Providers must give inpatients, on admission, written information about a person's health care decision-making rights, including the right to complete an advance directive. Presumably this statement will be taken verbatim or adapted from the statement of state law, also required by the PSDA and discussed above.

Providers must also give to inpatients, on admission, written information about the pro-

vider's policies respecting the implementation of patients' health care decision-making rights. In most cases, this has not required a burst of administrative development by institutions. Facilities have routinely added policies concerning informed consent protocols, advance directives, and decision making in the absence of family or advance planning documents. Where this has not yet been done at all, or has not been modified to reflect current law or practices, many professional associations and private organizations have excellent resources for developing policies.[15]

It is essential that policies reflect both the reality of professional interaction in the facility and the moral philosophy guiding the provision of care (conscientious objection to advance directives is covered in a later section). For example, most proxy laws require a determination of capacity to be made by an attending physician before the patient's named health care agent is legally authorized to act. If frequent or lengthy visits by an attending physician are not the general rule, as is often the case in long-term care facilities and hospice and home care, then policies should clearly indicate how the facility will honor advance directives completed by patients, residents, or clients.

Providers must document in the patient's medical record whether or not the patient has executed an advance directive. For most facilities, this also means filing a copy of the advance directive itself in the patient's medical record, according to state law. The PSDA is silent, as are most state laws, on the extent of the provider's responsibility to secure a copy of the directive once a patient says he or she has completed one. Providers should be encouraged to use reasonable efforts to emphasize the importance of having a copy of the directive in the medical record where the person is or is planning to be a patient or resident. Yet consumers have the final responsibility of making sure that their completed directive is filed and has been discussed with their provider, surrogate, and any other person who may have an interest in their health care.

For supporters and critics alike, the three required items above are the "heart and soul" of the PSDA. Without them, the act is all gums and no teeth. But it has become abundantly clear that providers will comply with the law in a variety of ways, from the marginally legal and painfully superficial to the exemplary. Anecdotal evidence has some providers handing out photocopies of articles about advance directives from the popular press. And that's all. Other providers have given directives and decision-making rights top billing in comprehensive preadmission packets, complete with state law, instructions, and blank forms plus a referral number for more information.

Facility staff should be encouraged to develop presentation skills that both meet the letter of the law and promote the kind of careful consideration needed to make advance directives work as intended. For example, nursing intake personnel at the University of Minnesota Hospital asked patients on admission the following questions:

1. Have you discussed your current medical condition with a family member or close friend?
2. Has a family member or close friend been told what medical treatment you want or do not want if you are unable to speak for yourself?
3. Have you told your doctor what medical treatment you want or do not want?
4. Have you written a living will? If yes, have you discussed it with your doctor?[16]

Who will present the required information is an important concern in many facilities and organizations. Typically, information is included in preadmission packets for people voluntarily admitted into service. This is especially true of HMOs, nursing homes, and hospice and home care agencies. It is important to note that every Medicare and Medicaid provider has the obligation to query patients and provide information, even though many patients will have been exposed to the information from a previous provider.

In large institutions, however, the task has proven more difficult. Admissions clerks are often the first employees to give out information, with information or counseling backup provided variously by social service staff, chaplains, patient care representatives, or nurses. Unless patients are already familiar with the facility and its staff, they may find it very difficult to make the necessary connection between printed information received as a small part of a typical admissions packet and an identified staff resource. Both printed information and initial information providers should point to further sources of information and conversation.

Whoever provides required information and asks patients if they have completed an advance directive should stress that completing an advance directive is a voluntary act by patients. It is too easy for advance directives to be included in a stack of forms to sign, and most experts agree that admission is an inappropriate place to complete advance directives. Admission personnel must also be familiar with

- the process for completing advance directives under state law
- institutional policy on having employees witness advance directives as well as other legal documents
- the general elements of a valid advance directive under state law
- institutional policy on honoring or dishonoring advance directives
- the answers to the most commonly asked questions or the name and phone number of the person identified as a primary resource on advance directives (see also "Staff Education" below)

ENSURING COMPLIANCE

The PSDA requires that covered providers will ensure compliance with state laws on advance directives. Compliance will be a logical extension of efforts to educate thoroughly the medical and professional staff involved with implementing advance directives in any facility. Rose Gasner believes that "this section of the PSDA may serve as a basis for a new federal legal argument placing responsibility on the facility for knowledge of the law, as well as holding facilities responsible for the actions of staff."[17]

She cites the example of a physician who refuses to comply with the decision of an authorized agent. In this case, many state statutes require the physician to transfer the patient to another physician who *is* willing to honor the request. Gasner argues that the PSDA compliance section may put the burden on the facility as well as the physician to ensure the prompt transfer of the patient.

OBJECTION ON THE BASIS OF CONSCIENCE

The PSDA, as it was passed as part of OBRA 1990, does not "prohibit the application of a State law which allows for an objection on the basis of conscience for any health care provider . . . which, as a matter of conscience, cannot implement an advance directive." Most state directives do, in fact, include provisions for conscientious objection on religious, moral, or professional ethical grounds.

The interim final regulation issued by HCFA in March 1992 tries to clarify the provider's obligation to alert patients on admission of any conscientious objection—as a matter of written policy—by the facility. It states that the provider must inform the person in writing of state laws regarding advance directives and of the policies of the provider regarding the implementation of advance directives, including a *clear and precise* explanation of the provider's conscientious objection to implementing an advance directive.

Charles Sabatino, assistant director of the American Bar Association's Commission on Legal Problems of the Elderly, points out that providers and consumer advocates have very different views of the "clear and precise" requirement. Providers contend that it is better to adopt general, flexible policies so that objections can be handled on a case-by-case basis and that the standard itself is unrealistic. A facility's policies rarely take into account the personal values of each member of the professional staff. Consumers, on the other hand, feel that the requirement doesn't go far enough: The too-general

language can be used to thwart any treatment option raised by a patient or agent that the facility objects to—whether or not as a matter of conscience.

The Commission suggests that provider policies

1. clarify any differences between institution-wide conscience objections and those that may be raised by individual physicians
2. explain the basis for any facility objection (e.g., religious, moral, professional)
3. identify the state legal authority permitting the objection
4. describe the range of medical conditions or procedures affected by conscience objections
5. describe what steps will be taken to transfer or otherwise accommodate people whose wishes are impeded by the institution's policy[18]

NONDISCRIMINATION

Under the PSDA, providers may not condition care or otherwise discriminate against a person based on whether or not he has completed an advance directive. Indeed, many state statutes and statements of state law have already made note of this requirement. The Massachusetts statement, for example, reads, "You are not required to complete a Health Care Proxy on admission or at any other time in order to receive medical care from any health care providers. You have the right to receive the same type and quality of health care whether or not you complete a Health Care Proxy."[19]

Providers are cautioned that this provision may inadvertently be violated if admissions staff give the impression that an advance directive, included as just one of a number of required forms to be completed at or before admission, is part of the regular admissions routine. Staff must alert patients that advance directives are voluntary documents that require significant prior thought and conversation to be truly effective.

Some providers have the mistaken impression that the requirements of the PSDA apply only to Medicare or Medicaid patients rather than to all admitted inpatients in facilities that accept Medicare or Medicaid payments.

Some people will never sign an advance directive, and that right must be respected. Patients may have family constellations upon whom they depend utterly and may have confidence in the family's efforts to make appropriate decisions. Some may come from cultures where naming as an agent someone other than a family leader would be an unforgivable affront. And still others may be resigned to live and die fatalistically, either unwilling or unable to choose a surrogate. These are strictly personal choices for the patient, however frustrating or burdensome they may be for ultimate decision makers.

It is altogether appropriate, however, to let patients know that if they don't make choices about their future health care and health care decision makers, the choices may still have to be made. But they may be made by total strangers.

EMERGENCY ADMISSIONS

Nonvoluntary admissions may require special consideration in the development of facility policy, professional practice, staff education, and statewide protocols. Emergency admissions are addressed in the HCFA final regulations, but only with regard to the timing of informing patients of decision-making rights:

> If a patient is incapacitated at the time of admission . . . , then the facility should give advance directive information to the patient's family or surrogate to the extent that it issues other materials about policies and procedures. . . . This does not, however, relieve the facility of its obligation to provide this information to the patient once he or she is no longer incapacitated or unable to receive such information.[20]

Anecdotal evidence indicates that institutional emergency departments will not honor an advance directive unless it is absolutely clear that the incapacitated patient's preference would have been to refuse emergency care. Some emergency departments have begun keeping card files or other records of advance directives, though this is practical only in smaller facilities. Most difficult are emergency admissions where an appointed health care agent has accompanied the now-incapacitated patient to the facility and demands that his authority be honored in directing treatment on behalf of the patient. Many emergency medical staff believe that the emergency room is not the time or place to make a critical judgment call: Either spend time making a written determination of patient incapacity, validate the integrity of the written advance directive, verify the identity of the authorized agent, and engage in the required informed consent procedures with the agent *or* treat the patient. Supporters of this view argue that they would opt to treat the patient under typical implied consent protocols, at least to the point of stabilization, and then follow advance directive procedures—even if that meant withdrawing life-sustaining treatment.

Some consumer groups, as well as providers, have already begun efforts to educate consumers about the appropriate use of emergency services. Most laypersons are unaware of the legal requirements to "activate" a health care agent's decision-making authority, assuming that simply being a holder of a validly signed document is sufficient to direct treatment decisions. In addition, most laypersons are unaware of state laws that require emergency medical service staff to provide life support at the scene. Hospice home care presents a typical situation. A person cares for a dying spouse at home, supported by hospice services. Though counseled about the actual events of dying and death, the caregiver and appointed health care agent (who is, however, not yet authorized by a physician's determination of incapacity) panics at the onset of a terminal seizure and calls emergency services. Emergency personnel arrive and begin treatment despite the caregiver's protests that the dying patient wanted no heroic measures.

In response to frequent episodes like the one above, several states have taken the lead in establishing preadmission DNR procedures, either through legislation, regulation, or statewide adoption of protocols.[21] While the situations covered by "do not resuscitate" orders are far fewer than usually addressed in advance directives, emergency service personnel nevertheless believe the new guidelines help to recognize patient autonomy in treatment preferences. Several states now employ a dated DNR bracelet as a way of notifying emergency service staff. It is hoped that these tentative steps will encourage wider observance of more comprehensive advance directives among emergency services and institutional emergency departments.

PSYCHIATRIC ADMISSIONS

At admission, some patients are not capable of receiving or comprehending information, nor of completing advance directives. Many, as described above, are emergency admissions and can receive the required information at a later time. Other people, however, are neither emergency admissions nor adjudicated legally incompetent. Such cases are common in long-term care facilities, where up to one-half of all admissions may be persons who are mentally and functionally incompetent but who have not been declared so by a court and do not have a legal guardian. Since the law assumes that all persons are competent to conduct their own affairs until a court determines otherwise, and since many advance directive laws presume the validity of signed directives, facilities with significant admissions of "questionably competent" persons will need to get good counsel in developing effective but legally sound policies.

It is useful to remember that, as a general rule, competency is something determined by a judge in an impartial court hearing. The law presumes competence until proven otherwise. Capacity to make health care decisions is frequently determined (as allowed and required by law) by an attending physician in following an advance directive state statute. Indeed, the two concepts may be quite separate and distinct: A person involuntarily committed to a psychiatric facility may still be legally capable of making his or her

own health care decisions—so long as he or she can participate meaningfully in the traditional informed consent or refusal process.[22] To the extent that any person can engage in significant discussion about his or her own health care, treatment preferences, quality of life, or personal values, he or she can not only help shape future options but also help providers become aware of his or her wishes.

Most proxy and durable power of attorney statutes do not specify a time period during which an attending physician must determine that a person has either lost or regained decision-making capacity. The danger exists that the act of determining capacity can be misused as a management tool. For example, if a physician is uncomfortable with treatment preferences being expressed by a still competent patient, or if dealing with the designated agent seems to be easier or more consistent with his or her own values, then the physician has the option—albeit unprofessional, illegal, and unethical—to determine the patient incapacitated for the purpose of seeking consents or refusals from the agent. Conversely, if the physician believes that the designated agent will make treatment choices inconsistent either with his or her professional values or the known wishes of the patient, already incapacitated, the physician may postpone making a determination of incapacity and rely temporarily on other vehicles for securing treatment consents or refusals.

To be sure, these are gross abuses of professional authority and would open the physician to substantial liability. Yet in the often hazy area of capacity determination, where hesitation, caution, and prudence are more the rule than the exception, the law provides little direction for physicians, who may be guided at a practical level by their good professional instincts and their desire to take "the long view." In becoming familiar with advance directives, many physicians are still uncomfortable dealing with designated agents, who are often strangers to them but who hold the authority of consent and refusal no less certainly than their competent patients. The obligation of a physician to get to know an agent should be shared by both the physician and the patient. The agent deserves to be brought into conversations between doctor and patient well before the agent may be required to consult with the doctor in making choices on behalf of the patient. Should misuses of capacity determination as a management tool become anything more than isolated incidents, legislatures might consider modifying statutes to require that patient assessments and reassessments be made within specified time periods.

STAFF EDUCATION

Throughout 1991 and early 1992, health care facilities, education and training organizations, lawyers, bioethicists, and others held thousands of seminars, conferences, video-linked teleconferences, and in-service sessions concentrated on advance directives and the PSDA. By late 1992, however, the bloom was clearly off the rose. Staff development personnel typically reported, "We did that last year. All our staff know about the living will; we had an in-service and put a sample will in everyone's mailbox."

Regular and periodic education should be provided to all health care staff with direct patient contact, including physicians, nurses, social service professionals, patient care representatives, chaplains, admissions clerks, and others who may be in a position to talk with inpatients about directives. Even if their obligation is only to refer the patient to a more knowledgeable resource, staff should be aware of the basics. Because of staff turnover, especially among physicians, nurses, and nursing aides, facilities should include information on advance directives and policy in the basic orientation process.

Passage of the PSDA has prompted a deluge of clinical articles and educational information on advance directives as well as on the law itself. Much of this material is generic and not specific to any one state's law. Health care professionals are obliged to have not just a general knowledge of advance directives but a solid understanding of their own state's law and their facility's policies to implement it. Educational materials for staff and the public should contain information specific to the state and facility.

Many physicians have been reluctant to honor advance directives for fear of liability. Some simply ignore directives entirely.[23] Even the advantage of having an identified decision maker was not enough to persuade them to accept a surrogate, legally appointed or not. Because most education efforts have been aimed at consumers, not providers, some physicians are still unaware that state statutes offer full immunity from criminal or civil prosecution if the physician follows the wishes of a validly appointed health care agent in good faith. While this does not totally insulate providers, it does give some assurance that a physician's reasonable efforts to secure informed consent through conversations with an agent will not lead to the devastating consequences of a successful suit for malpractice or, worse, wrongful death.

Admissions and records staff should be aware of basic form requirements as specified or allowed by state law. Many providers believe that the only advance directives submitted to them will be the ones they themselves distribute to patients and the public. This certainly is not so and will become less true as time passes. People will be introduced to directives from a variety of sources: lawyers, doctors, financial planners, insurance agents, senior organizations, illness support groups, religious organizations, and libraries, to name a few. In states with a prescribed form, nonconforming documents may be less of a problem than in states with either no form or only suggested language. Gatekeepers of the medical record ought to be able to spot a faulty document before it is filed and flag it without referring the document to the legal department or administration.

Patients will naturally assume that if they complete a document in good faith and submit it to the facility for filing, they can depend on the terms of the document being honored. While the PSDA does not address the issue of filing the form itself, many state statutes do. I believe that facilities that do not object to honoring advance directives (by conscience and as an explicitly stated policy) have a moral obligation to tell patients whether the form submitted will be honored in the event of future incapacity. There can be no guarantees, understandably. But of what use to a patient is a directive dismissed as non-conforming or defective when pulled from a medical record just at the time it might be of use—that is, after the patient has become incapacitated and is unable to redo the directive?

Should facility staff help patients complete advance directives? This may depend, in part, on whether the facility has formal policies that support conscientious objection to advance directives. In general, however, facilities should be encouraged to provide the means for a patient to complete an advance directive while in the facility. The facility should have an adequate supply not only of the required materials to provide at admission but additional information to be considered at a later time, appropriate and state-specific forms, a personal resource person, and at least several people who can serve as witnesses to signing (if allowed by local law).

PUBLIC EDUCATION

Long-term health education campaigns, like those on smoking cessation, substance abuse, HIV prevention, nutrition, and women's health, have taught us a valuable lesson. We know that education works . . . but it takes a long time. The legal requirements of the PSDA will certainly result in many people being given information on their rights to accept or refuse recommended treatment and on advance directives. But the real change occurs when completing a living will or health care proxy comes to be perceived, quite simply, as the right thing to do, like giving up smoking or cutting back on prime rib and pizza in favor of grilled chicken and pasta salad. Systemic changes cannot be forced. They can be facilitated by persuasion, perhaps eased by suggestion. But transformations happen when all participants in the system begin to operate as if the change had already taken place. In the case of PSDA, the 15–20 percent advance directive completion rate will jump to 50–60 percent when both providers and consumers of health care agree that having a directive makes life easier and more certain for everyone.

The PSDA requires health care facilities to provide information to patients, residents, clients, or members on admission. Real change will occur when physicians in private practice routinely ask their 18-year-old patients, "Say, now that you can vote and you have your own place, did you ever give any thought to who would make health care decisions for you if you got in a skiing accident and were unconscious for a few weeks?" Real change will occur when lawyers give out free copies of advance directives to clients, perhaps as part of an overall estate planning discussion. Real change will occur when colleges and universities include advance directives in admission packets sent to incoming frosh. "Dear Frosh Parent: We look forward to welcoming Carmen to our beautiful campus in early Fall. During these summer months, we hope you and your daughter will give some thought to what it means for a young person to make the transition into adulthood. Moving away from home into a new environment is certainly part of that change. But making one's own choices, especially about matters as personal as health care, is also a matter for adults. We have enclosed a pamphlet on the Massachusetts Health Care Proxy . . . "

Physicians can be the best primary source of information. Written materials for the professional office are now available in every state from a variety of sources. Virtually every professional health care association in the country has some kind of PSDA or advance directive publication for general use. There are videos on advance directives, health care power of attorney forms available in Braille, large type, and dozens of non-English languages, and books sold in shopping mall bookstores on all facets of health care decision making for the lay as well as professional reader.[24] Trained medical office staff can be good sources of information and responsive to patient questions. But nothing will substitute for the sincere suggestion from a trusted doctor to consider the issue. Physicians must reclaim their roles as teacher and counselor in this regard.

Any public education program must emphasize the importance of talking with one's chosen health care agent and family members. Most advance directive forms are easy to complete and take little time. The discussions needed to give substance to those forms are not. But there are good resources here as well. The values history—an in-depth assessment of personal values, activities, goals, and preferences—has become a useful teaching tool as well as personal supplement to any kind of advance directive.[25] Initiating a discussion with family members is perfect for role play exercises, and especially useful in settings where family members are actually present. The American Hospital Association, American Medical Association, American Association of Retired Persons, and most of the community Health Decisions programs have suggested guidelines for holding conversations with one's family, chosen agent, or physician.[26]

Any print materials distributed by your facility should be in a language, format, and style appropriate to your community.[27] If you have the chance to develop your own materials, make sure the drafting committee represents a cross section of interested people. Members might include a physician, a nurse, a lawyer, an ethicist, a clergy person, a records administrator, the lay community, and maybe even a visiting English or humanities professor. Before you go to press, test a draft with your own staff, patients, and community members.

In the past two years, many providers have discovered that inviting the public into a health care facility to hear a talk about advance directives rarely attracts an overflow crowd. Following are suggestions for fulfilling the PSDA community education requirement.

1. If you invite the public, do whatever you need to ensure your facility is known to be the sponsor—but unless you have a well-established reputation for holding lively, community-based meetings and events at your facility, hold the event somewhere else.

2. Work with other health care or social service providers in your area to present programs. If you work for a long-term care facility, join with staff from other nursing homes, a local hospital and hospice, or the local town nurse. A shared program will attract more people, reduce the staff burden on each facility, and provide economies of scale for print materials. It also reassures laypeople that this is not a competition for new clients: If several institutions and agencies are working together, with common materials, it *must* be okay.

3. Develop a linguistic or cultural minority outreach program in collaboration with other neighborhood organizations.

4. Work with local secondary schools, junior and community colleges, and universities to present programs to the 18- to 24-year-old crowd. Remember, many of the major cases of health care decision making and incapacity involved young people, not elders (Karen Ann Quinlan, Nancy Cruzan, Paul Brophy, and Elizabeth Bouvia). Teachers in civics, health, health care administration, social work, and even government would appreciate your willingness to help with an occasional class.

5. Offer your help to classes of entering students in local medical schools, nursing schools, and schools of the allied health professions.

6. Adopt the "train the trainers" model of education. Develop a program to train office staff of physicians in your area. And make sure the physicians are invited too.

7. Develop a program to train local parish clergy on the use of advance directives.

8. Develop a program to train a group of your best facility volunteers—the people who make you feel guilty because you never seem to have enough challenging tasks for them. Many facilities are using their volunteers rather than paid staff to provide community education.

9. Offer an intergenerational program, or one for your patients and their families, or for family members only. Offer a program for patients and their chosen agents.

10. Offer a program for employee assistance professionals in your area. How about benefits managers or staff in human resources?

11. Develop a program that provides "brown bag" seminars for employees in local corporations. (California and Massachusetts Health Decisions both have active programs for corporate employees. Almost without exception, employees are grateful to have the opportunity to con-

sider the topic when they are healthy and making other kinds of future plans.)

12. If your facility does not have its own video production studio, do a program for your local community access cable station. Six months later, you can sponsor a repeat showing.

13. Invite your board president, mayor, governor, or one of your legislators to sign an advance directive at a public event.

14. At every public event, make sure two items are given out without fail: free copies of an advance directive and a simple 3- or 4-question evaluation to be returned anonymously. If you do not know what went wrong, you will never get it just right.

The Patient Self-Determination Act is one of those rare pieces of legislation that gives us a good sense of things as we know they ought to be in the best of all worlds but few specifics on how to construct that world. No health care facility runs quite like another, and no two health care professionals share identical values. In a health care system strained by legislation and public opinion from all sides, the requirements of the PSDA remind us that the enduring value of good health care comes not from legislated procedures but from the quality of human relationships born and nurtured in the system. The PSDA encourages health care providers and consumers to talk candidly with each other about matters of consequence: Will I get well? How will you treat me? What do you do here? Who will speak for me? Can I trust you? In a perfect world, all such questions merit straight and honest answers. Let us hope that the PSDA succeeds in encouraging both providers and consumers to ask the right questions and answer honestly.

NOTES

1. L. Kutner, Due Process of Euthanasia: The Living Will, A Proposal, *Indiana Law Journal* 44 (1969):537–554; Omnibus Budget Reconciliation Act of 1990, Sections 4206 and 4751, Public Law 101-508, signed by President Bush on November 5, 1990, and effective December 1, 1991.

2. However, as of June 1992, 30 states had passed "family consent" statutes that give a priority by which certain family members (e.g., one's spouse, adult children, etc.) are authorized to act for the incapacitated person. Only four states—Arizona, Florida, Illinois, and New York—include "close friend" in the list of permissible surrogates. Traditional guardianships and protective service proceedings are available, though courts are reluctant to become involved in large numbers of health care decisions. For a complete listing, see C.P. Sabatino, Surrogate Decision-making in Health Care, in *Health Care Decision-Making in the '90s: The Surrogate and Advance Directives at the Bedside* (Chicago: American Bar Association Section of Real Property, Probate and Trust Law, 1992). For full discussion of the issues, see New York State Task Force on Life and the Law, *When Others Must Choose: Deciding for Patients Without Capacity*, 1992; 304 pp. Order from Health Education Services, PO Box 7126, Albany, NY 12224.

3. Choice in Dying, *Refusal of Treatment Legislation: A State by State Compilation of Enacted and Model Statutes* (New York: Choice in Dying, 1991; with annual updates).

4. See, for example, the draft "Health-Care Decisions Act" proposed by the National Conference of Commissioners on Uniform State Laws, 676 North St. Clair Street, Suite 1700, Chicago, IL 60611. See also T.A. Eaton and E.J. Larson, Experimenting with the 'Right to Die' in the Laboratory of the States, *Georgia Law Review* 25 (1991):1253–1326.

5. In "the battle of the forms," a number of articles have appeared in which authors not only urge the use of a particular kind of advance directive over another, but also question the effectiveness of the PSDA in achieving its goals by means of promoting advance directives. For a sampling, see G.J. Annas, The Health Care Proxy and the Living Will, *New England Journal of Medicine* 324 (1991):1210–1213; A.S. Brett, Limitations of Listing Specific Medical Interventions in Advance Directives, *JAMA* 226 (1991):825–828; L. Emanuel and E. Emanuel, The Medical Directive: A New Comprehensive Advance Care Document, *JAMA* 261 (1989):3288–3293; R.S. Olick, Approximating Informed Consent and Fostering Communication, *Journal of Clinical Ethics* 2, no. 3 (1991):181–195.

6. S.M. Wolf et al., Sources of Concern about the Patient Self-Determination Act, *New England Journal of Medicine* 325 (1991):1666–1671.

7. J. Lynn and J. Teno, After the Patient Self-Determination Act: The Need for Empirical Research on Formal Advance Directives, *Hastings Center Report* 23, no. 1 (1991):20–24.

8. M.M. Handelsman, Federal Policy Regarding End of Life Decisions, in *Euthanasia: The Good of the Patient, the Good of Society,* edited by R. Misbin, (Frederick, Md: University Publishing Group, in press).

9. Ibid.

10. Department of Health and Human Services, Health Care Financing Administration, Medicare and Medicaid Programs; Advance Directives, 42CFR Parts 417, 431, 434, 484, 489, 498.

11. The "clear and convincing" standard, adopted by Missouri and New York, has prompted concern that relatives or caregivers of persons in persistent vegetative states might never be able to have treatment withdrawn, no matter how futile the present or proposed treatment.

12. Cruzan v. Director, Missouri Department of Health, 110 S.Ct. 2841 (1990), concurring opinion.

13. J.M. Teno et al. (Center for Evaluative Clinical Science, Dartmouth Medical School; and American Bar Association, Commission on the Legal Problems of the Elderly), Evaluation of the Impact of the Patient Self-Determination Act: State Response to Write Description of State Law, presented at Choices and Conversations, national PSDA conference sponsored by the Pacific Center for Health Policy and Ethics, University of Southern California Law Center, Pasedena, California, January 8–9, 1993.

14. M.R. Gasner, The PSDA: A Next Logical Step, *Journal of Clinical Ethics* 2, no. 3 (1991):173–177.

15. See, for example, American Association of Homes for the Aging, Patient Self-Determination Act of 1990: Implementation Issues (Washington, D.C.: American Association of Homes for the Aging, 1991); California Consortium on Patient Self-Determination, *The PSDA Handbook,* hospital edition (Los Angeles: Pacific Center for Health Policy and Ethics, University of Southern California Law Center, 1991);J.F. Monagle and D.C. Thomasma, *Medical Ethics: Policies, Protocols, Guidelines and Programs* (Gaithersburg, Md.: Aspen Publishers, 1992).

16. R. Jackson and A. Carlos, Getting Ready for the PSDA: What Are Hospitals and Nursing Homes Doing? *Journal of Clinical Ethics* 2, no. 3 (1991):177–181.

17. Gasner, The PSDA.

18. C.P. Sabatino, Surely the Wizard Will Help Us, Toto? Implementing the Patient Self-Determination Act, *Hastings Center Report* 23, no. 1 (1993):12–16.

19. Massachusetts Health Care Proxy Task Force, Consensus Report (Sharon, Mass.: Massachusetts Health Decisions, 1992).

20. Department of Health and Human Services, Health Care Financing Administration, Medicare and Medicaid Programs; Advance Directives, 42CFR Parts 417, 431, 434, 484, 489, 498.

21. Examples of programs designed to recognize pre-admission DNR orders include Connecticut (Emergency Medical Services), Virginia (EMS-initiated legislation), North Carolina (county-by-county adoption of EMS guidelines), California (EMS; guidelines adopted county by county; legislation introduced), New York (State Department of Health; 1992 legislation), and Montana (legislation). Also, MedicAlert® (2323 Colorado Avenue, Turlock, CA 05380) has initiated a national preadmission DNR project.

22. For a model policy for implementing living wills and medical durable powers of attorney for the Virginia Department of Mental Health, Mental Retardation and Substance Abuse Services, see K.H. Swisher, Implementing the PSDA for Psychiatric Patients: A Commonsense Approach; *Journal of Clinical Ethics* 2, no.3 (1991):199–205. See also New York Task Force on Life and the Law, *When Others Must Choose: Deciding for Patients without Capacity* (New York: New York Task Force on Life and the Law, 1992; order from Health Education Services, P.O. Box 7126, Albany, NY 12224). On the nature of competency in general, see especially B. Chell, Competency: What It Is, What It Isn't, and Why It Matters, in *Medical Ethics: A Guide for Health Professionals,* edited by J. Monagle and D. Thomasma (Gaithersburg, Md.: Aspen Publishers, 1988).

23. M.Z. Solomon et al., Decisions Near the End of Life: Professional Views on Life-sustaining Treatment, *American Journal of Public Health* 83, no. 1 (1993):14–23.

24. In my experience, three of the best are G.J. Annas, *The Rights of Patients: The Basic ACLU Guide to Patient Rights, 2nd Edition* (Carbondale, Ill.: Southern Illinois University Press, 1989); N. Dubler and D. Nimmons, *Ethics on Call* (New York: Harmony Books/Crown Publishers, 1992); and T. Scully and C. Scully, *Making Medical Decisions* (New York, Fireside Books/Simon & Schuster, 1989).

25. P. Lambert et al., The Values History: An Innovation in Surrogate Medical Decision-Making, *Law, Medicine and Health Care* 18 (1990):202–212. The values history is published without copyright and may be reproduced and adapted as necessary.

26. See, for example, B. Mishkin, *A Matter of Choice: Planning Ahead for Health Care Decisions* (Washington D.C.: American Association of Retired Persons, 1986); American Hospital Association, *Put It in Writing: A Guide to Promoting Advance Directives* (Chicago: American Hospital Association, 1991).

27. T.C. Davis et al., The Gap between Patient Reading Comprehension and the Readability of Patient Education Materials, *Journal of Family Practice* 31 (1990):533–538; J. Klessig, The Effect of Values and Culture on Life-Support Decisions, *Western Journal of Medicine* 157 (1992):316–322.

ADDITIONAL RESOURCES

American Bar Association, Commission on Legal Problems of the Elderly. *Patient Self-Determination Act State Law Guide,* Washington, D.C.: Commission on Legal Problems of the Elderly, 1991.

Brunetti, L.L., et al. Physicians' Attitudes toward Living Wills and Cardiopulmonary Resuscitation. *Journal of General Internal Medicine* 6 (1991):323–329.

Danis, M.M., et al. A Prospective Study of Advance Directives for Life-sustaining Care. *New England Journal of Medicine* 324 (1991):882–888.

Gieszl, H.C., and Velasco, P.A. The *Cruzan* Legacy: Legislative and Judicial Responses and Insights for the Future. *Arizona State Law Journal* 24 (1992):719–799.

Meisel, A. Legal Myths about Terminating Life Support. *Archives of Internal Medicine* 151 (1991):1497–1502.

Menikoff, J.A., et al. Beyond Advance Directives: Health Care Surrogate Laws. *New England Journal of Medicine* 327 (1992):1165–1169.

National Health Lawyers Association. *The Patient Self-Determination Directory and Resource Guide.* Washington, D.C.: National Health Lawyers Association, 1991.

New York State Task Force on Life and the Law. *Life-Sustaining Treatment: Making Decisions and Appointing a Health Care Agent.* New York: New York State Task Force on Life and the Law, 1987.

Orentlicher, D. The Illusion of Patient Choice in End-of-Life Decisions. *JAMA* 267 (1992):2101–2104.

President's Commission for the Study of Ethical Problems in Medicine and Biomedical and Behavioral Research. *Deciding to Forego Life-Sustaining Treatment: Ethical, Medical and Legal Issues in Treatment Decisions.* Washington, D.C.: U.S. Government Printing Office, 1983.

———. *Making Health Care Decisions: The Ethical and Legal Implications of Informed Consent in the Patient-Practitioner Relationship.* Washington, D.C.: U.S. Government Printing Office, 1982.

Seckler, A.B., et al. Substituted Judgment: How Accurate Are Proxy Predictions? *Annals of Internal Medicine* 115 (1991):92–98.

Uhlmann, R.F., et al. Physicians' and Spouses' Prediction of Elderly Patients' Resuscitation Preferences. *Journal of Gerontology* 43 (1988):M115–121.

Wanzer, S.H., et al. The Physician's Responsibility toward Hopelessly Ill Patients. *New England Journal of Medicine* 310 (1984):955–959.

Wanzer, S.H, et al. The Physician's Responsibility toward Hopelessly Ill Patients: A Second Look. *New England Journal of Medicine* 320 (1989):844–849.

Zweibel, N.R., and Cassel, C.K. Treatment Choices at the End of Life: A Comparison of Decisions by Older Patients and Their Physician-selected Proxies. *Gerontologist* 29 (1989):615–621.

Chapter 11

Patient Concerns about Advance Directives

Suzanne B. Yellen, Ellen H. Elpern, and Laurel A. Burton

This chapter addresses patient concerns about advance directives. It is based largely on an empirical study of patient opinions and behaviors about advance directives for medical care[1] that predated implementation of the Patient Self-Determination Act (PSDA) and how (and if) preferences for aggressive treatment in end-of-life decisions are communicated to members of the medical treatment team.[2] In October 1990, the PSDA was enacted by Congress to increase public awareness of options, including advance directives for making health care choices.[3] This act, which became effective in December 1991, requires health care institutions receiving government funds to inform clients of their rights under state law to make decisions regarding medical care, including the right to refuse medical or surgical treatment and the right to formulate advance directives. Specifically, health care providers were mandated to develop and maintain written policies regarding advance directives, provide written information to patients explaining state law and institutional policies regarding advance directives, document in the medical record whether the patient had completed an advance directive, and educate staff and the community about advance directives.

The PSDA focuses on personal autonomy, making it clear that patients have a right to make decisions about their medical care. However, questions about the PSDA remain, including the extent to which patients truly desire autonomy and self-determination, whether autonomy has possible deleterious effects, and whether there are limitations to how literally advanced directives should be followed. For example, it has been suggested that patients vary in terms of how much they want various factors to be considered when making decisions and that literal adherence to advance directives may not truly reflect patient preferences.[4]

CASE ILLUSTRATIONS

The above questions are reflected in the following scenarios and suggest how difficult it can be to determine (1) how the delivery of information can affect patient well-being, (2) whether the completion of an advance directive ensures that patient self-determination will be maintained, and (3) whether the delivery of information about advance directives promotes or detracts from patient autonomy. In our first scenario, an 18-year-old boy is preparing for a day-surgery procedure that, he has been assured, is routine. Prior to admission, he receives a packet of materials, including information about advance directives. The boy and his parents become concerned that the procedure is far more life threatening than has been explained to them and feel obligated to execute these documents prior to admission. At the hospital, they present the documents and express anger at their doctor because the advance directive information clearly signaled to them that the procedure was anything but routine. Was this young man empowered toward self-determination by receiving a packet of materials without the opportunity for discussion?

The second example involves a 70-year-old female with progressive chronic renal failure who had previously consented to implantation of a fistula in preparation for hemodialysis. After implantation of the fistula but prior to initiation of dialysis, she was hospitalized with respiratory failure, a gangrenous leg, and sepsis. The patient lacked decisional capacity. Her family presented the medical treatment team with a living will signed four years previously stating that in the event of terminal illness she did not want dialysis or other aggressive care and requested that she be removed from the respirator. Prior to the execution of her living will, however, the patient had given her informed consent to many of the same treatments that her living will specified she should not receive (e.g., the fistula placement, intravenous therapies, and brief nasal gastric tube feedings). Did her written wishes express autonomy and direction with respect to the nature and aggressiveness of treatment or did they instead cause confusion among medical treatment team members and disagreement between the treatment team and family? Did the patient's later actions indicate revocation of the earlier? Were her actions, in fact, contradictory? Had the attending physician been aware of her living will prior to its presentation by the family?

In our third scenario, a 67-year-old woman with a history of metastatic breast cancer enters the hospital through the admitting department. The admissions clerk—often the person charged with completing the procedures that comply with the PSDA—hands the woman a packet of materials along with a form for the patient to sign, saying, "Here, read this and sign the form." Did this delivery of information help the woman recognize that there were sensitive issues that might warrant consideration? Was she helped to exercise her freedom in an informed way and in accordance with her own values?

The point of these three scenarios is that people in the health care professions often have little understanding of patient concerns about advance directives or about the impact on patient well-being of receiving this information. Some may view receipt of this information as helpful and informative, whereas others may become frightened. Some patients may truly want this information and view it as a means of enhancing self-determination, whereas others may not want to receive information and view its receipt as an infringement on their right to privacy. In our study, we were concerned about two questions. First, how do patients prefer to hear about advance directives and will the manner in which this information is presented have implications for their well-being? Second, with whom are patients discussing treatment preferences and is execution of an advance directive associated with ongoing doctor-patient communication and clarification of wishes as the treatment for medical conditions changes? In addressing these questions, we used a sample comprising inpatients at a large tertiary care center, outpatients in physician offices, and people in the community who were not under treatment for any medical condition.

WHAT IMPACT DOES KNOWLEDGE ABOUT ADVANCE DIRECTIVES HAVE ON IMPLEMENTATION BY PATIENTS?

Prior to the advent of the PSDA, popularization of advance directives in the general press and magazines may have led medical treatment team members to mistakenly assume (1) that people correctly understand the purpose of an advance directive and (2) that knowledge of advance directives is associated with execution of one. These assumptions are not necessarily valid. A large majority of people in our sample (77 percent) had heard of the term *living will* and some (25 percent) had heard of the term *durable power of attorney for health care*. However, being familiar with the terms was not necessarily associated with understanding the purpose of these documents. While 77 percent had heard of a living will, only 52 percent could correctly describe its purpose. Common misconceptions about living wills included the belief that they were a means of designating the disposition of property after death, related to organ or body donation, or that they were intended to prolong life. On the other hand, most people who had heard of a durable power of attorney for health care could correctly identify its use.

Further, only 29 percent of those who were familiar with either living wills or durable power of attorney for health care had actually executed one. Factors that influenced the tendency to execute one included being older and in poorer health, having a friend or relative who had formulated an advance directive, reading about or witnessing a terminal illness where the dying process was prolonged, and the fear of becoming a burden (especially financial) on the family.

It is clear from our research data that many people are familiar with advance directives but relatively few tend to formalize their wishes using these documents. Our study used both closed and open-ended questions to determine barriers to completing advance directives. Common reasons given for not completing an advance directive were procrastination and lack of information (96 percent and 78 percent respectively). Some subjects actually had the document in their possession but had not completed it. Other open-ended responses for not completing an advance directive included not believing it was necessary, reluctance to deal with mortality, concerns about causing distress to family members, worry over what would happen if the person changed his or her mind, and an expression of trust that family members would "do what's right."

Procrastination and lack of information were also primary reasons for not completing an advance directive in our forced-choice questions as well. We asked our subjects to indicate agreement or disagreement with a series of attitude statements about why people (in general) may not have executed an advance directive. The reasons for not completing an advance directive and percentage of subjects expressing agreement are listed in Table 11–1. As can be seen in this table, 44 percent of our sample endorsed the belief that thinking about living wills is depressing and related to thoughts about dying, and 23 percent agreed that people may think that living wills are not a good idea. However, despite agreement with statements that living wills make people think about dying and may not be a good idea, only a tiny percentage of our sample (3 percent) did not want to receive information about advance directives.

What factors might intervene between the predisposition toward use of an advance directive and the action to execute one? One possible explanation is ambivalence about facing end-of-life issues. Many people demonstrate an "illu-

Table 11–1 Possible Reasons for Not Signing an Advance Directive

Statement	Agreement
Never got around to making one	96%
Never heard of one	78%
Prefer not to sign legal documents	58%
Hard to decide in advance of critical illness	56%
Want the doctor to raise the issue first	46%
Depressing to think about dying	44%
Would rather have someone else decide	31%
Legal language too hard to understand	29%
Unnecessary as long as you have people you can trust around you	27%
Don't think they're a good idea	23%
Mostly for the old and sick	21%

Source: Reprinted from E. H. Elpern, E.H. et al., Opinions and Behaviors Regarding Advance Directives for Medical Care, *American Journal of Critical Care*, Vol. 2, No. 2, pp. 161–167, with permission of the American Association of Critical Care Nurses, © 1992.

sion of invulnerability" that protects them from the belief that bad things can happen to them.[5] Extending this illusion to the medical domain, patients may prefer to believe that advancing illness or death is something that happens to other people rather than to them. This belief thus helps them to maintain a positive outlook until serious illness and impending mortality undermines this perception. Only then may patients be ready to consider what actions, if any, should be taken to extend life and to formalize them in an advance directive.

Another explanation suggested by our data is a reluctance to sign "legal" documents. Many of our respondents believed that execution of an advance directive required the assistance of a lawyer. For these people, the time and expense anticipated in visits to a lawyer may have served as a deterrent to executing an advance directive. Discomfort in making anticipatory decisions about life-supportive care was also a concern for a number of our subjects. Some may have perceived an advance directive as a rigid and unalterable declaration about the use of life support and worried about loss of control and flexibility during critical illness. Indeed, while our study did not uncover this issue, each of the authors has personal clinical evidence of this concern.

Does discussion about advance directives have a deleterious impact on patient psychological well-being? This question was addressed by Schneiderman et al. as part of a larger investigation of the effects of offering advance directives on medical treatment and cost.[6] Their results suggest that being given information about advance directives has no significant positive or negative effect on patient health status, medical therapies, or patient psychological well-being as measured by patient satisfaction with physicians, psychological well-being, and health-related quality of life. In our study, and in our clinical experience, patients are not distressed by broaching the topic of advance directives. Many commented that they had thought about how they would wish to be treated if terminally ill with no hope for recovery, had discussed it with family or friends, but had not thought to discuss

it with their physician. Following completion of their participation in the study, so many subjects requested further information about living wills and durable power of attorney for health care that data collectors began to keep copies of the forms with them to give to patients.

WITH WHOM DO PATIENTS DISCUSS TREATMENT WISHES?

Our data indicated that irrespective of completing of advance directives, a significant number of patients (65 percent) are talking about how they would wish to be treated if they were critically ill. However, there is no particular pattern as to with whom these "communicators" are discussing wishes. Some discuss them with family members (55 percent), whereas others discuss them instead with friends (18 percent) or physicians (14 percent). Many who indicated that they had spoken about their treatment preferences characterized the discussions as "general, vague, or casual." Even if patients had completed an advance directive, there was no guarantee that the medical treatment team would be aware of its existence. Specifically, 29 percent of our sample had either a living will or a durable power of attorney for health care or both. However, less than half of this group (46 percent) had informed their physicians of its existence, and only 25 percent of respondents with advance directives had specifically discussed their treatment preferences with their physician.

Our data suggested that discussions about end-of-life care are being held but are usually nonspecific and restricted to family members and friends. Failure on the part of patients to initiate this type of discussion with health care professionals should not be interpreted to mean that they wish to avoid the topic. To the contrary, most of our subjects indicated that the topic was important to them, they had thought about what they would want if critically ill, and they would feel comfortable speaking about their wishes with doctors, nurses, chaplains, psychologists, and social workers. Why, then, is there such an apparent reluctance on the part of health care professionals to initiate discussions about advance directives? One reason may be a fear that if they raise end-of-life issues, it may take away hope.[7] Data from our study indicate that this concern is largely unfounded and most patients would not be distressed by talking about advance directives, although they are equally divided about who (physician or patient) should initiate the discussion. As can be seen by these data, members of the health care team cannot assume that patients are discussing their wishes with them.

They also cannot assume that patients are discussing their wishes with family members or that family members will even honor the wishes of their loved ones when it comes to treatment decisions. Family members may not be the most appropriate surrogates to turn to when patients lack decisional capacity and treatment decisions must be made. The following case illustrates this concern. Several years ago, one of the authors was involved in the care of a 32-year-old single man who was dying from advanced liver cancer. His greatest concern and source of psychological distress was that he might be kept alive on machines by parents who were unable to "let go." He fully discussed treatment limitations with his attending physicians, who were aware of his wishes but concerned about the ramifications of an angry and overinvolved family when the patient was no longer able to speak on his own behalf. He was also well aware that he could not accurately predict all future treatment decisions that might need to be made. To protect his end-of-life wishes, this young man completed a durable power of attorney for health care, appointed his best friend as his agent, and was able to die in the manner he wished.

PROVIDING INFORMATION ABOUT ADVANCE DIRECTIVES

According to the PSDA, institutions must provide written information to patients about advance directives. The specifics of how this information is communicated have been, to a large extent, left in the hands of individual institutions

in accordance with state law. Because we were uncertain of the impact of the PSDA on patients, and because we were hopeful that information about its impact could help shape hospital policy, questions of how, when, and by whom to best render information about advance directives and by whom were addressed by our study prior to implementation of the act. Specifically, we assessed (1) when patients wished to receive this information, (2) what is the preferable form of delivery for information about advance directives, (3) how comfortable patients would be in discussing it with a hospital representative, and (4) the degree of comfort felt by patients in discussing advance directives with different hospital personnel (e.g., the attending physician, nurse, chaplain, psychologist, etc.).

Most respondents preferred to be given information about advance directives either before (51 percent) or at the time (32 percent) of admission to the hospital. Few believed that it should be given after discharge, and only 3 percent preferred that the hospital not provide the information to them. The method of information provision most preferred was face-to-face discussion (41 percent). Written information alone was preferred by 32 percent of those interviewed, while written information with the opportunity for face-to-face discussion was favored by 17 percent.

The majority of subjects in our study anticipated a moderate or high degree of comfort in discussing advance directives. Specifically, 52 percent indicated they would be very comfortable and 30 percent indicated comfort, accounting for 82 percent of the entire sample. A qualitative sampling of anticipated reactions to a discussion about advance directives yielded predominantly positive descriptors, such as "curious, receptive, and appreciative." Negative responses were anticipated by fewer subjects and included descriptors such as "frightened, alarmed, and depressed." Most subjects (94 percent) indicated they would be comfortable discussing advance directives with their attending physicians. Seventy-eight percent of respondents reported they would be comfortable discussing advance directives with a nurse. Comfort with other hospital personnel was more variable (see Table 11–2). Interestingly, in light of the fact that these discussions are most often carried out in admitting departments, most (61 percent) were uncomfortable with the prospect of discussing advance directives with admitting clerks.

As can be seen from these data, patients are more than willing to discuss potentially sensitive issues such as end-of-life issues. While some acknowledge that it may be depressing and related to thoughts about dying, rarely would they prefer *not* to receive this information. Patients prefer to receive this information prior to admission to the hospital and favor some opportunity for face-to-face discussion. Our data strongly suggest that patients are most comfortable discussing these issues with their primary physician but also feel some degree of comfort in discussing them with nurses and other hospital personnel. Physicians, nurses, and other care providers need not fear patient responses to inquiries about advance directives. We urge health care institutions and providers to be proactive rather than reactive in addressing end-of-life considerations, including advance directives. This should be done early in the doctor-patient relationship and often thereafter. Indeed, it has been suggested that physicians routinely introduce exploration of values about end-of-life decisions by making the question, "Have you signed an advance directive?" a part of every patient history.[8]

DO ADVANCE DIRECTIVES PROMOTE PATIENT AUTONOMY?

Much of the confusion regarding self-determination may stem from a shift in the power dynamics of the doctor-patient relationship from paternalism to an autonomy in medical decision making. Thirty years ago, the prime decision maker was the physician, whom everyone believed would use his or her power to do what was right and in the patient's best interests. Now, patient rights rather than physician responsibility are paramount. The power has shifted from the profession of medicine to the personhood of the patient. That is why we place an emphasis on self-determination. However, our research and clinical experiences suggest that people want an interactive and collaborative process rather than one in which either the patient or physician has total power. One must also be sensitive to the fact that the degree to which people desire an interactive versus a directive process may vary tremendously, and health care providers may need to ask patients directly how involved they wish to be in treatment decisions. Handing a packet of information to a patient at the time of admission may be interpreted as coercive by some or just another set of papers to sign by others. In the scenarios cited earlier, the older woman with breast cancer may have regarded the advance directive material as relatively unimportant while the young man and his parents regarded it as threatening. In neither case was autonomy promoted.

Table 11–2 Comfort in Discussing Advance Directives

Treatment Team Member	Very Comfortable	Somewhat Comfortable	Not at All Comfortable
Attending MD	91 (69.47%)	32 (24.43%)	8 (61.1%)
Psychologist	48 (36.64%)	45 (34.35%)	38 (29.01%)
Nurse	59 (45.04%)	46 (35.11%)	26 (19.85%)
Chaplain	72 (54.96%)	22 (16.79%)	37 (28.24%)
Admit Clerk	15 (11.45%)	40 (30.53%)	75 (57.25%)
Social Worker	48 (36.64%)	49 (37.40%)	34 (25.95%)
Lawyer	36 (27.48%)	34 (25.95%)	61 (46.56%)

Source: Reprinted from *Cambridge Quarterly of Healthcare Ethics,* Vol. 1, No. 4, p. 382, with permission of Cambridge University Press, © 1992.

The spirit of the PSDA encouraged ongoing dialogue and review of patients' personal rights and choices with respect to medical care. Unfortunately, implementation has been directed more toward literal interpretation of the law, which means that information is typically disseminated in the easiest way possible, usually in the admissions department. Providing patients with printed information is not enough, nor is accepting patient preferences for treatment at one time as the basis for all future preferences. Both our clinical experience and ongoing research with cancer patients suggest that patients' preferences for treatment may shift as a function of where they are on the illness trajectory, and previously unacceptable treatments sometimes become desirable in the face of progressive illness. The scenario describing the patient with progressive renal disease exemplifies the need to engage patients and family members in communication—*while they are healthy*. Questions should include personal values, whether they have formulated advance directives, and what their treatment preferences might be in the face of progressive disease. Dialogue about these issues must be held at reasonable intervals. Avoiding these discussions inevitably leads to confusion and anger, particularly if the decisions of family surrogates are inconsistent with those demonstrated behaviorally in the past by the patient.

CONCLUSION

Discussion of end-of-life wishes and advance directives is not something to be feared by health care professionals. In most instances, patients have thought about how they would wish to be treated in the face of terminal illness and may have even formalized their treatment preferences in an advance directive. However, there is no guarantee that members of the health care team will be aware of patients' advance directives unless they actively seek this information from patients under their care. They need not fear distressing patients with information or questions about advance directives. Results from our study and others do not demonstrate that being given information about or discussing advance directives has a negative impact on patient psychological well-being. Patients actually prefer that decision making be collaborative. They are comfortable in having face-to-face discussions with members of the health care team and prefer to be actively involved in decisions affecting their medical care. Finally, the time to initiate these discussions is early in the doctor-patient relationship. Treatment preferences should then be reviewed on a regular and ongoing basis. We believe that health care providers have a responsibility to initiate, in a compassionate way, conversations about advance directives. This results overall in both better health care and better patient–treatment team relationships.

NOTES

1. E.H. Elpern et al., Opinions and Behaviors Regarding Advance Directives for Medical Care, *American Journal of Critical Care* 2, no. 2:161–167.

2. S.B. Yellen et al., Communication about Advance Directives: Are Patients Sharing Information with Physicians, *Cambridge Quarterly of Healthcare Ethics* 1 (1992):377–387.

3. Omnibus Reconciliation Act 1990, Public Law 101-508.

4. A. Sehgal et al., How Strictly Do Dialysis Patients Want Their Advance Directives Followed? *JAMA* 267 (1992):59–63.

5. L. Perloff, Perceptions of Vulnerability to Victimization, *Journal of Social Issues* 39 (1983):41–61.

6. L.J. Schneiderman et al., Effects of Offering Advance Directives on Medical Treatment and Costs, *Annals of Internal Medicine* 117 (1992):599–606.

7. J.C. Holland, Stage-specific Psychological Issues: Clinical Course of Cancer, in *Handbook of Psychooncology*, edited by J.C. Holland and J.F. Rolland (New York: Oxford University Press, 1989).

8. W.B. Ventres and S.S. Spencer, Doctor-Patient Communication about Resuscitation: 'Have You Signed an Advance Directive?' *Journal of Family Practice* 33, no. 1 (1991):21–23.

Chapter 12

Advance Directives: Panacea for Safeguarding Patient Autonomy or a Convenient Way of Avoiding Responsibility?

Erich H. Loewy

An advance directive allows the making of health care decisions that will come into effect if and when one becomes incapacitated, especially but not only critical decisions that may influence one's chances for recovery. It has found much favor among ethicists, physicians, and hospital administrators, although the reasons for this enthusiasm differ: Ethicists see in advance directives a reaffirmation of patient autonomy, physicians are relieved to have the clearly expressed wishes of their patients ahead of time and feel that such wishes may make their job easier and also lessen the likelihood of malpractice suits, and administrators see in such directives a way of minimizing their hospital's legal liability. Although laypersons have shown considerable enthusiasm for the idea of advanced directives, this enthusiasm has not been translated into widespread use of such instruments. Most persons, in fact, have not executed an advance directive.

Not only has the concept of advance directives been greeted with enthusiasm, but in the United States advance directives have been the subject of both state and federal law. At the federal level, the Patient Self-Determination Act (PSDA) became effective in December 1991. It,

in turn, has spawned a rash of legislation in several states. Legislation at the state level has been aimed not only at supporting the PSDA but also at extending it. Illinois, among other states, passed a surrogate act that determines the general hierarchy of surrogates for patients who become incompetent or unconscious and who have not executed an advance directive. In an effort to comply with the PSDA as well as with state acts, hospitals have rather hurriedly begun to assess ways and means of implementing the use of such instruments.

Most see few reasons to quibble with such an attempt: All of us want to exercise control over our own destiny and want to have a chance to finish our own "work of art" in our own way. Our particular way of living, valuing, and envisioning our destiny and our own style of life is unique to each one of us. We are, as Cassell pointed out some time ago, the artists of our own lives.[1] As good a composer as Mahler may have been, Mahler would have found it difficult to complete Schubert's "Unfinished" in Schubert's own way, just as van Gogh would have had difficulty completing a Rembrandt self-portrait in a way Rembrandt would have been pleased with.

Implementing the federal and state acts regarding patient self-determination was aimed at giving patients legitimate choices when it comes to their own end-of-life decisions. The passage of the PSDA and the attempts in several states to bolster and extend it should be expected, therefore, to be embraced with open arms. On the whole, advance directives and acts such as the Illinois surrogate act, by producing some order in a legally chaotic situation, give some legal protection to physicians and hospitals. Giving such protection, if the shield of protection is used wisely and responsibly, may be an ethically good thing.

However, I am somewhat skeptical about these instruments for a number of reasons. First, I have some hesitation about the ability of people to predict what "they would want" under circumstances few can truly foresee or imagine. It is hard to judge in a competent way what one would want were one incompetent: None of us can truly put ourselves into the shoes of a confused, demented, and hopelessly ill patient. We might readily believe that we might, if demented, confused, or hopelessly ill, want one thing, only to find when we get there that "things" had changed. Demented, confused, and hopelessly ill patients, however, still have "interests." It is, on the other hand, no more reasonable to speak of the "wishes" or "interests" of the permanently comatose or vegetative than to speak of the "interests" or "wishes" of anything else that lacks the necessary substrate for having wishes or interests. Here and for that very reason, advance directives make more sense: The confused, demented, and hopelessly ill patient still has interests (although such interests are a matter of conjecture), while the permanently vegetative or comatose lacks the capacity for having interests. My interest in what happens to me should I become permanently vegetative or comatose is my current interest in what happens to me in a future when interests, because there are none, can no longer change. Such reservations can easily be countered by pointing out the obvious: Someone will have to make choices at a time when I am demented, confused, and hope-lessly ill and that someone will necessarily either be myself (ahead of time) or someone else to whom my values and wishes are even more opaque at the time than they are to me in advance. On the whole, one may assume that properly executed instruments, while far from ideal, will be most helpful: All things considered, I still have a better chance of predicting how I would feel in a given situation than does someone else. Moreover, my interest now in what happens to me once I am permanently unconscious is a legitimate interest and is analogous to my legitimate interest in what happens to persons and ideals I now treasure once I am dead.

My other hesitations about these instruments are not as easily countered. They concern not the concept of advance directives but their application. I fear that such instruments (1) can easily be misinterpreted and lead physicians to undertreat rather than overtreat patients, (2) may be executed by patients haphazardly and unthinkingly (yet another form to be filled out on admission to the hospital or in the physician's office) and without careful interaction with and guidance by physicians, (3) have the potential of adding another technical layer of decision making to an already overtechnicalized process, (4) are apt to decrease physicians' and institutions' sense of responsibility for very difficult and troubling decisions, and (5) could easily allow physicians to concern themselves less and less with the properly agonizing ethical questions of patient care.

Nevertheless, I do not question the desirability of having the clearly expressed wishes of patients as a guide for physicians, and I certainly do not quibble with having patients select surrogates for themselves. Physicians have all too long chosen the means of getting to a mutually agreed goal and have also pre-empted their patients' right to choose their goals for themselves. Physicians historically have ignored and still tend to forget that a patient's "biomedical good" is not necessarily the ultimate good in the patient's hierarchy of values.[2] If used properly, advance directives could be a great help to patients, families, and those concerned with, in more than the merely technical sense, properly caring for them. However, I fear that mindless enthusiasm and application may introduce yet another technical and blindly followed layer of medical decision making. Rather than being helped to make responsible and ethically appropriate choices, physicians and hospitals may no longer agonize over difficult decisions but substitute a legalistic following of such instruments. Advance directives may serve to encourage physicians to communicate with their patients in an ongoing manner and guide the choices their patients make; on the other hand, such instruments may be used by institutions and physicians to distance themselves all too easily from an individual patient's particular situation by taking refuge in a general rule. The concept of patient autonomy would not be well served if medicine were to throw out the baby of genuine, ethical, and caring decision making with the bath water of physician paternalism.[3]

Furthermore, and especially when it comes to the "living will," I fear that caregivers, institutions, and sometimes patients and families are apt to grossly misinterpret such instruments and to jump to the conclusion that the existence of such a document is tantamount to a patient's desire not to be vigorously or aggressively treated come what may. In fact, this is exactly what has happened in many of our institutions. Patients who have a living will are apt to be treated far less vigorously than those without such an instrument in situations in which a treatment exists that has a good chance of returning the patient to what the patient would consider to be acceptable function. I have often heard caregivers question the advisability of potentially useful aggressive therapy in the case of a patient who was known to have executed a living will. Caregivers all too frequently forget that most living wills request physicians not to prolong their life beyond hope for a return to what they would accept as meaningful function. Deciding not to treat the treatable under the false assumption that an instrument requesting physicians "not to be ridiculous" is actually requesting them not to be aggressive does not serve the patient's interest or welfare.

Historically, physicians have, at least in theory, always been concerned about their patients' welfare and have strived to serve it. Although always (at least in theory) concerned to serve the "good" of their patients, the former and current way of determining what that good is differ substantially. Likewise, the nature of the obligation of physicians (and lately that of institutions) has been viewed differently from place to place over time. In ancient times and up to the era of Newton, the obligation to save life was not conceived to be a medical obligation. Rather, the three obligations of ameliorating suffering, helping nature restore function or health, and refraining from treating those "hopelessly overcome by illness" were accepted.[4] As medicine increased in effectiveness, the obligation to save life became an accepted medical obligation—and even, in recent times, almost a medical obsession. Medicine also used to be a predominantly paternalistic profession in which pursuing as well as defining a patient's good was accepted by all as the profession's task. Physicians defined what was proper and chose what to do; patients "complied." The emphasis on patient autonomy is a modern one. It has several roots: Although medicine has become more complex, the general education of patients has improved so that they are more capable of sharing in decision making. The complexity and technical nature of medicine, furthermore, has made it possible to sustain biological existence far beyond the time when a patient would, in the natural course of things, have died. In today's hospitals, few patients die unless a conscious decision to do no more is made: It is almost always possible to prolong life another few minutes, hours, days, and even weeks, months, and years by utilizing yet another technical modality.[5] A patient's biological functioning can be prolonged far beyond the time when all notions of having a life are appropriate.[6] Medicine's capacity to prolong life has not been seen as an unalloyed blessing by patients, relatives, or even the medical profession itself, which often but wrongly assumes that prolonging life under all circumstances is a professional ethical obligation.

Furthermore, especially in this century in the United States, where a capitalist philosophy prevails according to which autonomy is the highest good and beneficence only a questionable general obligation, physicians more and more frequently regard themselves and have more and more frequently been seen as entrepreneurs. Patients have been transformed into consumers and physicians into "bureaucrats of health."[7] Indeed, the physician as entrepreneur and the "medical-industrial complex" (a term coined but a concept hardly thought appropriate by Relman)[8] interested in pursuing profit has been touted as the proper basis of medical morality.[9] Market forces and competition would see to it that the best possible care at the lowest possible cost would be supplied to alert and freely contracting consumers. Physicians seek to satisfy their patients desire to be healed (and at the lowest possible cost) not as much to benefit patients as to attract more customers to themselves.[10] A market philosophy, of course, rests on the assumption that patients and physicians are truly "equal contractors." If patients and physicians are, indeed, equal contractors and patients employ their physicians for a specific self-chosen act of healing, adhering blindly and in lock step fashion to advance directives makes sense: Following specific rules without much regard to particular situations is, after all, what bureaucrats (at least bureaucrats in the narrow sense of the word) are expected to do.

I want to be clearly understood: I do not want to return the profession to a time when crass paternalism was the order of the day. There is still too much paternalism abroad. But neither do I want to see the profession surrendering (and surrendering gladly) its basic and ultimate responsibility—a responsibility we have come to accept as transcending the technical. The concept of physicians as "bureaucrats of health" who (no matter how well) perform a technical task does not foster true autonomy. True autonomy, which

implies freedom of choice, is possible only when patients and physicians act jointly. Advance directives can help bring about situations in which a dialogue between physician and patient is improved or they can bring about a situation in which physicians and health care institutions abrogate their responsibility and justify this abrogation by a mere obeisance to the concept of autonomy.[11]

Advance directives, when properly used to foster true patient autonomy, have much to recommend them. Among other things, they can (1) stimulate patients to think about such issues; (2) allow patients to speak about their preferences with their physician, relatives, and friends; (3) allow patients either to express their wishes or to select a trusted other who can make choices for them; and (4) help resolve some of patients' fears of entrapment in and by the medical system. All of these advantages, however, imply leadership by health professionals who must carefully inform, discuss, listen to, and ultimately counsel patients and their families. When done properly, this process should (at first but perhaps not ultimately) take more rather than less time.

Stimulated by the PSDA, hospitals have often gone beyond the law, which only requires hospitals to ask about the existence of advance directives but does not require or suggest that patients be asked to execute such documents at the time of admission. Many hospitals have developed various ways of having patients who lack such instruments at the time of admission execute them at that time. Supposedly, in the name of serving patient autonomy, a form that can be signed at the time of admission is made available: another sheet, together with many others, that is mindlessly signed. At other times, a clerk or nurse, variably trained and a stranger to the patient, will discuss such an instrument with the patient and obtain a signature.

Such a process does not result in true patient autonomy. An autonomous decision must be based on adequate information and sufficient deliberation as well as being noncoerced. Having patients execute an advance directive as part of the hospital admitting process or a bit later on the ward but still while hurried, fearful, and ill (and, in that sense coerced) makes a sham of the document's value or intent. Executing an advance directive in such a perfunctory or hasty fashion allows the health care team, the hospital administration, and perhaps even society at large to "cop out," to abandon a patient to his or her autonomy and then to wash their hands of the whole problem, as bureaucrats of health might be encouraged to do.[12]

To ensure that the process and the decision can have meaning and truly serve the patients self-selected interests, adequate discussion with caregivers, family members, and friends is essential. Moreover, the decision made must be authentic (i.e., consistent with the patient's world-view). Although authentic decisions can seem inauthentic, a decision that seems inauthentic should raise questions regarding whether the individual had proper knowledge and sufficient time for deliberation and whether coercion may have occurred. Institutions and their health care professionals can only know if a decision is or is not authentic by having some idea about the patient's values, hopes, fears, and biography. When a patient at the time of admission is confronted with a slip of paper to sign or asked to make such a decision at that time (a decision that can have momentous consequences and that requires thorough discussion and careful thought), autonomy, rather than being fostered, is merely being paid lip service.

I fear that advance directives are often obtained and used in this way. Ideally, advance directives stimulate dialogue between caregivers and their patients so that the patients can truly become partners (I deplore the word *contractor;* physicians are, after all, not plumbers). When patients execute advance directives without extensive discussion with trusted health care providers, they often will make choices motivated by unrealistic fears. Patients handed forms in physician's offices and merely asked to fill them out are, in a sense, abandoned. Without careful

and ongoing dialogue between caregiver and patient, executing an advance directive is barely an improvement over not executing one. When done properly (that is, when done in conjunction with an ongoing dialogue between the patient, family, and caregiver), the physician's office (rather than the attorney's) is probably the best place to achieve the avowed aim of fostering autonomy. The value of this process lies not so much in the instrument executed as in the dialogue between physician and patient, in which the patient gains vital information and in which each individual gets to know and appreciate the other's values.

Patients' understanding of what is done (What is CPR? Why are ventilators used?) is often quite meager when they sign such directives, and it is properly the physicians' task to see that this is not the case. When, for example, a patient insists that he or she "would never want to be on a ventilator," it is the physician's task to explain what a ventilator entails: Ventilators, after all, can be used temporarily (as in anesthesia or to get a patient through a bout of severe pneumonia), permanently (as when a patient with chronic lung disease finally becomes entirely and permanently ventilator dependent), or as a comfort measure. When patients decline CPR or intubation, careful explanations are similarly in order. Such explanations must delve into some of the details of what is proposed, be attentive to the patients' understanding or misunderstanding of what is involved, and deal with the patients' impressions and fears. The media, instead of helping clarify these situations and striving to supply perspective and context, have muddled the waters even more and created unrealistic panic in many laypersons. A terrible and often lurid picture of the indignity and suffering endured during resuscitation or by patients on a ventilator is often painted. Many patients who adamantly refuse resuscitation or ventilator usage (in situations where such procedures would not only sustain life but may well serve to restore meaningful function) do so because they have been ill informed. Because no careful explanation of what is done has been given, they cannot and do not understand what resuscitation, ventilator usage, or other forms of therapy entail.

Patients often believe (and, regrettably, so do physicians) that once a procedure or a course of therapy is started, it cannot be stopped. Patients often not so much oppose being on a ventilator, being intubated, or having CPR as fear that if the consequences are not what is hoped for, therapy must, come what may, be continued. Patients do not want to commit themselves to being permanently ventilator-bound or to living on in a severely mentally reduced fashion, and given the alternatives as they see them, they are simply not willing to "give it a shot." Alleviating such fears can often be done through discussion preparatory to executing an advance directive. A blanket statement that "I would never want a ventilator used" (or be resuscitated or intubated) is hardly one that ought to be accepted without careful and repeated explanation. Unfortunately, physicians often share the belief that once therapy is started, it cannot (morally or legally) be withdrawn. This belief (which is factually untrue, there is no real ethical difference between not starting and withdrawing therapy)[13] has frequently led to a hesitation to initiate CPR and other measures. Rather than erring on the side of sustaining life when the prognosis is yet unclear, many physicians have become hesitant and refrain from the attempt.

Patients' fears and their frequent misunderstanding of medical facts point out the fallacy in the doctrine of "equal contractors." When one party to a bargain is fearful and when his or her technical information and understanding are sketchy or distorted, while the other party has no fear and has information and understanding that are more accurate, equality does not truly exist. This calls the very basis of entrepreneurialism in medicine into question—the claim that physician and patient meet as equal contractors to make and carry out choices. Looking at patients as equal partners runs the danger of exaggerating inequality by bypassing explanation and dialogue. Instead of fostering autonomy, it very

well may do the opposite: Patients will be free to make choices but will not truly understand the implication of the choices they make. The inequality of patient and physician, while it cannot be entirely eliminated, can be attenuated and individually addressed. Physicians who truly subscribe to meaningful patient autonomy will be ethically compelled to do all they can to lessen this difference and to restore their patients' autonomy.[14]

Patients have become increasingly more distrustful of the entire medical establishment, albeit somewhat less so of their own particular physician (this is somewhat akin to polls showing that citizens mistrust Congress but tend to trust their own representatives). Advance directives are, in part, an expression and outcome of such distrust. This distrust is not entirely unjustified. When physicians see themselves as entrepreneurs whose chief interest (and whose chief legitimate interest according to some) is in accumulating as much material wealth as possible; when they own and are known to own laboratories, free-standing surgical, or x-ray clinics; or when they are known to derive excessive profit from a practice whose conditions only they themselves can control, trust is not apt to be greatly enhanced. This is especially true since laypersons (1) know perfectly well that they have little chance of truly understanding what is and what is not needed and (2) suspect (often with good reason) that physicians are apt to profit greatly from the suggestions (or the lack of suggestions) made. Patients fear exploitation by an establishment for its own financial purposes (not unreasonably, if entrepreneurialism is indeed a proper basis for medical morality). Further, in our system of medical care, in which insurance is often either nonexistent or totally inadequate when it is needed most, patients fear pauperization by a basically entrepreneurial system only too eager to treat them until their last penny is gone.

In some states (Illinois is an example), new acts prescribe a hierarchy of surrogates starting with spouses, to be used when no advance directives exist. In these states, surrogates have acceptable legal standing in making decisions. The theory on which laws are based is laudable: The person most apt to understand the patient's life style and attitudes is to make the decision. A decision based on such knowledge, even if by proxy, would foster the patient's ultimate autonomy and permit the patient to end his or her life in a fitting manner. There is a severe fallacy in such a law: Regrettably, a person's spouse is not in all circumstances the individual closest to that person (a man estranged from his wife for five years and living with his devoted girlfriend is unlikely to appreciate having his wife-in-name-only chosen). Families do not, in reality, come in the neat packages envisioned by these laws.

Physicians and hospitals have expressed considerable enthusiasm for surrogate acts. They would allow them to receive direction from a legally stipulated person. If the rules were followed, the chance of malpractice suits would, in theory, be remote. Furthermore, it is hoped by some physicians that the time spent in talking with or arbitrating among many family members could be greatly reduced. In my view, however, it remains the physician's responsibility to ascertain that the legally stipulated surrogate is, indeed, ethically acceptable—that he or she is the person most apt to make the choices the patient would have made. This means far more than following lock step a convenient hierarchical list. It implies becoming familiar with a patient's biography as well as with the nexus of relationships in which the patient was and is enmeshed. To attempt to superimpose a given vision of how families "ought to be" upon the way a given family in fact is is to negate personal as well as family autonomy. Discussing possible surrogates with patients and noting the particular personal relations and arrangements and documenting them in the medical record may promote the patient's good and may foster a more meaningful autonomy. Choosing the proper surrogate is not materially different from choosing the proper antibiotic: Textbooks may indicate that my strep throat should be treated with penicillin, but doing so without inquiring into allergies would be considered to be malpractice. Likewise, choosing a surrogate merely because he or she is the "textbook surrogate" is unacceptable. Neither in ethical nor in technical questions can physicians who claim to serve their patients best interests turn their judgment over to a neat algorithm and feel that their job is done.

Decisions from surrogates (whether picked by reference to a legally established list or in somewhat more responsible ways) still require, if they are to be accepted as true choices by the surrogates, substantial explanation and dialogue. Informing surrogates and engaging in dialogue with them, just as informing and engaging in dialogue with patients when executing advance directives, ultimately remains the physician's responsibility.

Decisions can only be made with proper knowledge and understanding of the medical facts, of prognostic realities, and of possible goals and options. Decisions are not likely to be properly made on the spur of the moment or under the stress of acute illness, fear, or pain. Having patients execute an advance directive or surrogates make decisions under such conditions (or having patients execute such a document without careful deliberation or adequate discussion with those closest to them) may be legally acceptable, but it is, at the very least, ethically problematic.

Last but not least, advance directives are executed and choices are made in a community. The interests of family and community are not irrelevant to the decision made. We are not, as some would have it, "moral strangers" who share no ethical framework and have no common interests or values except the desire to be left alone to pursue our own autonomous choices.[15] Such a minimalist vision of community or of medical practice ruptures the main tradition in medicine, which, though paternalistic, recognized the existence of beneficent obligations. The vision of community as composed of moral strangers is as impoverished as it is false. We are all (whether American, European, or Fijian) united by certain inescapable common conditions and interests and therefore possess certain basic values and basic moral frameworks. We share (thanks to what Kant calls our "common structure of the mind")[16] a common sense of logic as well as basic biological needs. Beyond this, however, we are at the very least united by a desire to avoid suffering (even when what causes suffering may be different); to pursue our own interests and goals; and, as social animals, to realize ourselves in the embrace of others.[17] That may not get us very far toward being moral intimates, but it means we are far from being moral strangers. While perhaps not moral intimates or even friends, persons are at least moral acquaintances.[18] As moral acquaintances, we make decisions knowing quite a few basic things about each other; we respect the basic features that unite us as well as the uniqueness of each of us.

Persons are social beings who for that reason have obligations toward each other. Autonomy does not exist in a vacuum but is developed, enunciated, and ultimately exercised in our common life together. To deny the social nexus of autonomy is threatening both to the social nexus and to autonomy. Persons cannot truly be persons outside their social nexus or outside their community, and the community cannot exist, develop, thrive, and grow without the unique contributions of the individuals within it.[19] When it comes to making decisions for oneself (whether decisions made for the here and now or for the distant or not-so-distant future), one must be mindful of this interdependence. To require families (or communities) to make such decisions totally setting aside any self-interest or to allow such decisions to be made entirely unmindful of the needs and interests of the family or community in which such decisions are to be made is to rip such decisions from the soil that spawned them.[20]

The enthusiasm for advance directives among professionals, institutions, and the population at large must be tempered. A variety of ways of increasing the usefulness of directives have been developed.[21] For example, some instruments go beyond a simple wish "not to be resuscitated or not to have life prolonged" and plumb the patient's actual values when it comes to such decisions. The development of these instruments and their incorporation into more traditional directives may help address many problems. However, the basic problem remains the same, and these more specific directives must be executed with the help and advice of physicians who attempt to get to know their patients and after proper discussion of the relevant issues with family and friends over time. If they are used as a check sheet and blindly followed, they run the danger of adding a virtually meaningless layer to an already overbureaucratized and overmedicalized process.

As with all else, the way advance directives and laws appointing a hierarchy of surrogates are used will determine their merit. Medicine has been guilty of crass paternalism, to which such legal acts and instruments are seen as a remedy. Paternalism (even if the intent is beneficent) is an unjustifiable form of control. But replacing a paternalistic system with an entrepreneurial system in which consumers freely contract with "bureaucrats" and bureaucrats feel no responsibility for caring about patients but merely adhere to their client's previously expressed wish will not improve matters. Our worship of autonomy and our neglect of beneficence has led to the devastating social conditions in this country, where 20 percent of the populace have little if any access to timely medical care. Beneficence implies respect for autonomy: One cannot be truly beneficent without respecting the goals and wishes of others.[22] But having respect for autonomy means more than leaving persons alone to their own freely chosen fate. Autonomy without social justice is a cynical mockery (freedom of speech is of little use to a homeless or hungry person).

Medically, respect for patient autonomy implies more rather than less physician involvement: It implies that physicians genuinely seek to remain in dialogue with their patients and take great care in selecting proper surrogates. It is a form of focused physician beneficence—focused on promoting a patient's individual choice and integrating it into the structure of the patient's family and community. Beyond this, having respect for autonomy implies a respect for the community, without which autonomy is moot. Patients, just as physicians, have responsibilities, responsibilities that transcend cooperating with their physician only to further their own personal ends. Patients and physicians are not moral strangers but are fellow travelers on a perilous journey. In making decisions for patients, the goals, values, and interests of all are legitimate considerations. Advance directives can, if used properly, function as vehicles through which a dialogue can be started and continued. If used improperly, they can foil the opportunity for dialogue and make a mockery of what they were intended to do: allow an expression of autonomy in the context of the general community.

NOTES

1. E.J. Cassel, Life as a Work of Art, *Hastings Center Report* 14, no. 5 (1984):35–37.

2. E.D. Pellegrino and D.C. Thomasma, *For the Patient's Good: The Restoration of Beneficence in Health Care* (New York: Oxford University Press, 1988).

3. E.H. Loewy, Advance Directives: A Question of Patient Autonomy, *Cambridge Quarterly*, in press.

4. D.W. Amundsen, The Physician's Obligation to Prolong Life: A Medical Duty without Classical Roots, *Journal of the History of Medicine* 32 (1977):403–421.

5. E.H. Loewy and R.W. Carlson, Futility and Its Wider Implications: A Concept in Need of Further Examination, *Archives Internal Medicine* 153 (1993): 429–431.

6. T. Kushner, Having a Life versus Being Alive, *Journal of Medical Ethics* 1 (1984):5–8.

7. H.T. Engelhardt, *The Foundations of Bioethics* (New York: Oxford University Press, 1986); H.T. Engelhardt, Morality for the Medical Industrial Complex: A Code of Ethics for Mass Marketing of Health Care, *New England Journal of Medicine* 319 (1988):1086–1089.

8. A.S. Relman, The New Medical-Industrial Complex, *New England Journal of Medicine* 303 (1980):963–970.

9. Engelhardt, Morality for the Medical Industrial Complex.

10. Engelhardt, *Foundations of Bioethics*.

11. E.H. Loewy, Advance Directives and Surrogate Laws: Ethical Instruments or Moral Cop-out, *Archives of Internal Medicine* 152 (1992):1973–1976.

12. Engelhardt, *Foundations of Bioethics*.

13. A. Meisel, Legal Myths about Terminating Life Support, *Archives of Internal Medicine* 151 (1991):1497–1502.

14. E.J. Cassell, The Function of Medicine, *Hastings Center Report* 7, no. 6 (1977):16–19.

15. H.T. Engelhardt, *Bioethics and Secular Humanism* (Philadelphia: Trinity Press International, 1991).

16. I. Kant, *Kritik der Reinen Vernunft* (Frankfurt: Suhrkamp, 1984).

17. E.H. Loewy, The Role of Suffering and Community in Clinical Ethics, *Journal of Clinical Ethics* 2 (1991):83–89; E.H. Loewy, *Suffering and the Beneficent Community: Beyond Libertarianism* (Albany, N.Y.: SUNY Press, 1991).

18. E.H. Loewy, Freedom and Community: The Ethics of Interdependence (Albany, N.Y.: Suny Press, 1993).

19. Ibid.

20. J. Hartwig, What about the Family? *Hastings Center Report* 20, no. 2:5–10; E.H. Loewy, Families, Communities and Making Medical Decisions, *Journal of Clinical Ethics* 2 (1991):150–153.

21. H.M. Sass and R. Kielstein, *Die Wertanamnese* (Bochum, Germany: Zentrum für Medizinische Ethik, 1992); E.J. Emanuel and L.L. Emanuel, Living Wills: Past Present and Future, *Journal of Clinical Ethics* 1 (1991):9–19.

22. Pellegrino and Thomasma, *For the Patient's Good*.

Chapter 13

Ethics and Brain Chemistry

Thomas D. Geracioti, Jr.

In this chapter, the influence of central nervous system chemical processes on personal values and decision-making capacity will be briefly addressed, and ethical issues observed or anticipated in the clinical or haphazard alteration of brain chemistry will be enumerated.

BRAIN CHEMISTRY, VALUES, AND DECISIONAL CAPACITY

If consciousness itself is predicated upon brain function, and all value judgments and decisions are acts of consciousness, then brain function is necessarily involved in ethics. Even a pantheistic notion of consciousness, according to which a plant or even a stone may be considered to have a type of self-consciousness, must allow for the importance of the central nervous system (CNS) in subserving human thought. It is indisputable that the destruction of various portions of the cerebral cortices or limbic areas in humans, whether through trauma, tumor, stroke, toxin, hypoxia, or infection, may have an impact on intellectual capacity and moral competence.

Alterations in brain chemistry, then, may greatly affect the capacity of an individual to make ethical choices. This topic has been discussed at length in other contexts, but mainly with reference to grave or incapacitating mental disabilities, coercive treatments and involuntary commitment, and medicolegal considerations of insanity or mental impairment and criminal or civil responsibility.

Abnormalities in brain chemistry, however, are a matter of degree. Punctate cerebral infarctions, chronic cerebral hypoxia related to atherosclerosis or chronic obstructive pulmonary disease, or low-grade thyroid dysfunction are all common and can all invisibly influence the human character. Moreover, brain function and consciousness are normatively influenced by a variety of factors, including diet, pharmaceutical preparations, massage, music, caffeine, sunlight, color, and stressful or elating life circumstances. Mood influences values. An elevated mood engenders optimism while a depressed mood is associated with pessimism. At either extreme, judgment is impaired, although it must be mentioned that individuals with abnormally pronounced mood swings, such as people with bipolar affective syndromes, are sometimes among the most creative and productive members of society.[1] At any rate, values held by an individual can be state dependent and might change based on the configuration of the individual's CNS.

Ultimately, the view that there is a strict boundary between the capacity and incapacity to make moral decisions is naive. In general, we must allow that mild to moderate fluctuations in values and decisional capacity are normative. Thus, a belief or choice adhered to over a long period of time usually, but not always, carries more personal imperative than one that is intense but fleeting. Unfortunately, the issue of choice or belief is complicated by the fact that important beliefs, wishes, or values can remain unconscious or available to consciousness only in a distorted form or in a fleeting manner. In fact, since Freud we recognize that motivations and wishes that are not accessible to consciousness exist in all of us and influence our behavior and morals.

While CNS configurations and the conscious and unconscious meanings they subserve influence individual value systems, the value systems themselves can be neither explained nor endorsed solely by reference to neurobiological processes. Scientific advances do not resolve moral problems; rather, scientific advances, by extending the realm of the possible, tend to create ever more complex ethical dilemmas.

ETHICAL ISSUES IN THE CLINICAL MODULATION OF BRAIN CHEMISTRY

Psychopharmacology of Everyday Life

Rapid progress in psychiatry and neuroscience has placed us on the threshold of an era where neurochemical processes underlying specific components of thought and behavior are subject to clinical manipulation. At present, to be sure, preclinical understanding of brain neurochemistry, derived from in vitro and in vivo studies of rats and other experimental animals, far outstrips our knowledge of human brain function. Yet, designer pharmacology is converging with advances in the understanding of neuronal pathways subserving behavior and consciousness. Appetite, memory, sexuality,

mood, aggression, energy level, anxiety level, and sensory perception can even now be clinically or experimentally modulated to varying degrees. Hallucinations, paranoid states, and even transcendental states can be generated pharmacologically. New intoxicants can be developed. More progress in this area is to be expected. As a thought exercise, one might imagine the mental equivalent of a Michael Jackson–like surgical makeover or pharmaceuticals with neuron-sprouting or -modulating effects analogous to the effects of the anabolic steroids on muscle development. Someday citizens may find specific alterations in mental function to be as available as cosmetic surgery. "The real problem in the field of psychopharmaceuticals is not so much the creation of any of the classes of drugs . . . but determining who should make the decisions as to when they should be used, on whom and by whom."[2] For example, would it be desirable to develop a drug that could reliably and robustly increase sexual desire, and, if so, under what conditions? An enhanced sex drive might increase sex crimes, disrupt some families, or siphon off time and energies needed to address complex cognitive problems. Or what about the use of neurochemical suppression of aggressive thoughts in violent criminals?

Moral considerations have thus far limited the search for safe, short-acting intoxicants without addictive potential, although, given the present state of technology, it is likely that such agents could be rapidly developed if desired.[3] Small doses of alcohol, perhaps mixed with tannin, may be safe, but large doses or chronic use is associated with significant morbidity, including axial subcortical neurodegeneration. Moreover, intoxication with alcohol is associated with impairment in many cognitive spheres. Cannabis, too, appears to be associated with significant morbidity after chronic use and can acutely disrupt memory. While controlled clinical experimentation with existing hallucinogenic agents such as cannabis and lysergic acid diethylamide has ground to a virtual standstill, the recent characterization and localization of the cannabinoid receptor in the brain should lead to renewed scientific interest in the unique and important actions of cannabinoid compounds in the human CNS.[4]

Current Issues in Clinical Psychopharmacology: Serotonin-Uptake Inhibitors

The development of potent new mood-enhancing agents that have specific neurochemical targets and few apparent side effects, such as the serotonin-uptake inhibitors fluoxetine hydrochloride and sertraline, has opened a new era in antidepressant psychopharmacology. Unlike the older antidepressant agents, these drugs are almost never lethal in overdosage, have no known adverse effects on cardiac function or blood pressure, and are without troublesome anticholinergic activity. Given their relative safety and the paucity of side effects, it is to be expected that the serotonin-uptake inhibitors will be administered to people for whom use of a mood-elevating drug would not have been previously considered. Both experimental[5] and anecdotal evidence supports the notion that the serotonin-uptake inhibitors might have activating, anxiolytic, or mood-elevating effects in already healthy people.

Randolph Nesse of the University of Michigan encountered a young, healthy woman without a personal or family history of major depression or dysthymia who had been prescribed fluoxetine for weight loss.[6] She requested continuation of the fluoxetine, relating that, while taking the drug, she felt more decisive, confident, and energetic:

> I used to be uncomfortable with strangers at parties, but now I can go up to anyone and say anything I want to . . . I don't feel nervous or worried about what people think of me. Also, I am more decisive, and people say I am more attractive. I'm usually even eager to get out of bed in the morning. Everything is just—well, better. I hardly ever feel bad anymore.[7]

Our ability to clinically eradicate the experience of anxiety, with either antidepressant medication or benzodiazepines, raises the ethical issue of whether or not it is prudent to do so. Nesse, writing from an evolutionary perspective, points out that the ability to experience anxiety, like other types of psychic pain or suffering, can have beneficial consequences, such as alerting one to danger.

Preliminary experience with fluoxetine suggests that for many normal people it can enhance a sense of peacefulness and well-being, increase tolerance to stress, reduce anxiety, and increase energy. Although insomnia is a frequent side effect of fluoxetine, some ambitious individuals even welcome the ability to work longer hours resulting from the reduction in their need for sleep. While these effects may appear desirable, potential dangers may exist in altering normal brain function. For example, it is possible that use of mood-elevating agents might provoke hypomanic or frankly euphoric states in vulnerable individuals, or even induce rapid mood cycling, which can subsequently be difficult to treat.[8]

Marshall Ginsburg, at the University of Cincinnati College of Medicine, consulted with a 50-year-old man who had recently been displaced from his job as a corporate chief executive officer (CEO). Mr. C., as he shall be called, sought help working through his indecision about whether to accept his demotion and remain with his current company or to accept the offer of another CEO position with a new corporation in a distant city. Although Mr. C. did not show clinical evidence of major depression, nor did he have a personal or family history of depression, he was dysphoric. After discussing the alternatives for working through the patient's concern, Dr. Ginsburg prescribed fluoxetine hydrochloride, 20 mg daily. Within a few weeks, Mr. C.'s dysphoria was eradicated, and instead he said he felt as good as he ever had in his life. He decided to remain in the city at his now low-responsibility job and to devote time to hobbies and to traveling with his wife. Mr. C. claimed that he was now able to enjoy extensive leisure for the first time in his life (M. Ginsburg, personal communication).

It is possible that fluoxetine influenced this patient's decision to accept a demotion that he would not otherwise have endured or that it was involved in the reorganization of his priorities vis-à-vis work and leisure. That is, fluoxetine administration may have influenced Mr. C's values.

Drugs in Childhood: Psychopharmacology by Proxy

An 18-month-old child in a rural area was brought to a local child psychiatrist because, unlike her older sister, she was "wild" and her mother had trouble handling her. As a toddler, the child was "jokingly" taught to call herself "the bad one." She did not sleep through the night. She repeatedly pulled all the tissues out of the tissue box and emptied cereal boxes onto the floor. Her mother, who is now a chronic pain patient, was fed up with this behavior, and a psychiatrist prescribed the psychostimulant methamphetamine for the child, which has a paradoxical calming effect in her age group. Her mother called the methamphetamine her "sweet pill." A physician who was a friend of the family said, "The only thing wrong with this child are her parents." She took methamphetamine until the age of nine. She was an excellent student, skipped a grade in high school, and successfully completed college and graduate school. She neither drank alcohol nor experimented with drugs. She had one lifetime sexual partner, but, after the breakup of this relationship, she presented for treatment of depression and anxiety. She regretted having had sexual relations and felt as if she were a "slut." Although attractive, intelligent, and highly effective in the workplace, she had persistently low self-esteem and low self-confidence.

It is difficult or impossible to implicate the pharmacologic agent retrospectively as a contributing factor to this patient's sense of inferiority. However, this case hints of one potential ethical danger in this type of pharmacology by proxy: Children may frequently be "treated" for the benefit of the parents. A child might be used by a parent as an extension of his or her own sense of self, and the problems of the parent may be played out through the child. It is possible

that the impact of having been given a "sweet pill" throughout this individual's early childhood imparted a deeply rooted sense of defectiveness during years when the consolidation of her self-esteem should have occurred. Additionally, it is possible that chronic amphetamine use generated a biochemical vulnerability for anxiety and depression, perhaps by stimulating subconvulsive electrical instability or "kindling" her central nervous system. On the other hand, other factors, such as poor parental empathy, might have been more important in the failure of the patient to consolidate her sense of self-esteem.

The details of the present case aside, it is unequivocally the case that behaviors of children that are not abnormal to begin with are sometimes targeted pharmacologically for the sake of the parents. As more information regarding the development of the human brain accrues and our armamentarium of substances with which to alter neuronal development grows, more attention will need to be focused on the ethical issues involved in modulation of brain function in childhood. It is conceivable that parents may one day have the opportunity to influence brain growth or to selectively alter a child's memory, stress responsiveness, or personality by pharmacologic means. Eventually it may be considered acceptable or even advantageous to administer specific modulators of brain neurochemistry to children. However, bioethical protocols and policies need to be developed relative to brain modulators for children.

CLINICAL PSYCHOPHARMACOLOGY AND PSYCHOTHERAPY

It should not be forgotten that the human psyche is capable of self-generating a tremendous range of altered and transcendental states or that psychotherapy can be a powerful clinical tool. Often, prescription of a psychoactive drug is given in place of psychotherapy. There exist a multiplicity of reasons for this type of situation: the inability of the patient to afford the 50 or 100 or 200 psychotherapy sessions needed to address the problem; the patient's resistance to psychotherapy; belief on the part of either the physician or the patient that psychotherapy does not work, that it will not treat a "chemical imbalance" (this language unfortunately implies that some disturbances of the mind are chemically based or "organic" while others are somehow nonchemical or, I suppose, inorganic. In fact, every movement of consciousness in every person entails some "chemical" and neuroelectric activity of brain neurons. There is no doubt that meaning can influence brain chemistry. For example, most people would show a prompt release of norepinephrine if confronted suddenly in their workplace with a pack of starving, rabid wolves), the physician's time pressures, and the patient's desire to go away with a feeling that something has been done, among others.

Prescribing medication, instead of psychotherapy, reinforces the patient's unwillingness or inability to look at him- or herself and confront his or her inner and interpersonal struggles. Many physicians and patients are content to treat the symptoms of a problem (e.g., anxiety) without addressing the underlying problem itself. Commonly, patients are maintained on benzodiazepines for years without ever achieving or even attempting, psychological insight. Yet their anxiety is ameliorated. Because of the cost-effective nature of most psychopharmacologic interventions compared with psychotherapeutic ones, many patients and physicians in specific circumstances choose to attempt treatment with medication alone to see if the symptoms remit before moving on to psychotherapy. This has the added benefit of clarifying the effects of the medication on the patient as compared with the more typical situation of concurrent use of psychopharmacology and psychotherapy. If a patient gets better with combined psychotherapy-psychopharmacology, it is very difficult to know the relative contributions of the treatment modalities to the cure. Thus, many patients undoubtedly remain on medication for some time without knowing whether or not it is helping. This is a problem for many agents whose side effects are bothersome or potentially dangerous or for which problems of dependence or cross-tolerance exist.

THE FUTURE OF CLINICAL NEUROCHEMISTRY: SELECTED TOPICS

Neuropeptides

Neuropeptides, endogenous neurotransmitter substances synthesized intracellularly and coded directly from genetic material, are presently the objects of intense interest among psychobiologists and have been so for over two decades.[9] These substances appear to be potent and specific neuromodulators, with brain molar concentrations typically two or three orders of magnitude lower than those seen for the "classical" neurotransmitters (those formed from dietary precursors via enzymatic action), such as the catecholamines, the indolamines, acetylcholine, and the steroids. Several dozen neuropeptides have already been discovered, although their specific functional brain system or cognitive or behavioral correlates remain to be elucidated. As progress is made in the identification of the neurobehavioral pathways subserved by peptides, it is to be expected that novel peptide therapeutics will be generated; the development of specific neuropeptide receptor agonists and antagonists will also be of great importance in this regard. Ultimately, it is likely that modulation of gene expression will provide the most power to manipulate the production and actions of proteins and neuropeptides.

Peptide Delivery into the Brain

A limiting factor to date in the clinical application of peptides as neuropharmaceuticals is the existence of a blood-brain barrier that largely prevents circulating peptides, which are water soluble, from gaining access to the CNS. Advances in techniques that permit introduction of these substances into the brain will be of major importance. The intracerebroventricular method of administering neuroactive substances has the inherent drawback of requiring penetration of brain tissue in order to gain access to the cerebral ventricles. At present, invasive methods of delivering peptides into the CNS are not in general use, although the introducing of nerve-growth factor into the cerebral ventricles of patients with Alzheimer's-type dementia syndrome has been attempted.[10]

The development of "noninvasive" techniques (techniques that do not require instrumentation of the brain or its covering), such as methods for disguising peptides in biolabile, lipophilic molecular environments that permit them to permeate the blood-brain barrier,[11] should eventually make it possible for a variety of neurochemicals to gain access to the CNS after peripheral administration. Intranasal application of certain neuroactive substances, which may allow access to the CNS directly via the cribiform plate, may find increasing uses. Pheromones, odorant molecules given off by one organism that can engender physiologic changes in another organism, may exist endogenously, or be developed, in humans. It should also be emphasized that the modulation of CNS neurochemistry does not necessarily require entry of the neuromodulator into the central compartment. Agents that remain in the periphery may induce central effects by stimulation of CNS afferents that synapse in brainstem areas on their way to higher brain centers.

Neural Implants

CNS ablation surgery such as prefrontal leukotomy, once quite popular in this country, is no longer considered either an effective or ethical treatment for mental illness. However, in contrast to surgeries that remove brain tissue, techniques involving the transplantation of functional brain tissue may hold promise for future clinical utility. Neural implants have already been performed in many patients with Parkinson's disease, using both autografts and fetal tissue,[12] with some limited success and much ethical debate to date. It must be noted that an adequate supply of fetal tissue for use in clinical research and practice will require utilization of tissue obtained from electively aborted fetuses.[13] The ethics of the clinical use of fetal brain tissue will thus be inextricably tied to the ethics of induced abortion.

BRAIN CHEMISTRY AND THE FUTURE OF PUBLIC HEALTH

As Isaiah Berlin pointed out, human liberty is inherently bipolar.[14] At one pole, liberty constitutes the freedom to do as we wish; at the other, liberty constitutes the right to avoid being impinged upon by others who are doing as they wish. Increasingly, human actions, either individual or collective, will have repercussions on the brain neurochemistry of others.

Mounting evidence indicates that various environmental exposures play a role in the modulation of CNS function. Pollution of the air and water by various forms of toxic waste, combustion products, and ionizing radiation and by the widespread adoption of synthetic, nonbiodegradable materials in everyday life is now occurring. The risk of neurotoxicity is not restricted to selected occupations[15] but is rather a public health problem.[16]

While the potential dangers of bodily entry of radioactive particles, mercury, lead, volatile solvents, organophosphates, benzene, carbon monoxide, and many other compounds are well known, the neurochemical effects of a dizzying array of compounds generated as manufacturing products or byproducts remain unknown or unstudied. Even electromagnetic fields, such as those generated by power lines, appear to have the capacity to alter brain function, although little is known about this.[17] If the manners and mechanisms of electromagnetic influence of CNS function become known, it is likely that therapeutic uses of electromagnetic fields will be found.

Importantly, it is often exceedingly difficult to detect alterations in brain chemistry, even by those afflicted; the organ afflicted is in fact that used to assess itself. Every psychiatrist is familiar with people whose brains support unshakably delusional beliefs about themselves and the world. An organ that is quite capable of denying to itself even evidence of severe self-fragmentation may even more facilely adapt to mild alterations in its own function. Furthermore, family members, friends, and coworkers of individuals who develop subtle brain dysfunction are rarely aware of the problem. Psychiatrists or neuro-psychologists frequently are not able to reach definite conclusions regarding the presence or absence of acquired abnormalities in cognitive function because sufficient baseline neuro-psychological information is often not available.

The assessment and alteration of processes harmful to the human central nervous system are restricted, however, by many factors that reduce the interest of the common working citizen in these matters. Prominent factors include habit, ease and convenience of current practices, lack of education and knowledge, short-term economic preoccupation or frank greed, and the psychological defense of denial (a primitive means of protecting one's self from experiencing pain).

To a very large extent, man-made environment modulators of brain chemistry can be controlled. Knowledge of the neurochemical correlates of scientific advances will provide important guidance in formulating ethical applications of emerging technologies. As Archbishop Angelini states, "It is necessary that the develop-

ment of science and technology induce confidence and not fear in Man, hope and the prospect of real progress and not a threatening nightmare."[18]

CONCLUSION

The issues raised in this chapter are nascent. More questions than answers are engendered by the examination of neurochemical correlates of ethical capacity and of an ethical approach to advances in psychopharmacology and the neurosciences. I have attempted to show that the consideration of brain chemistry is of general relevance to ethical capacity. However, elucidation of the relationship of specific central nervous system configurations, and modulations thereof, to specific value choices in healthy people has yet to be attempted. Finally, I have tried to introduce emerging ethical concerns related to our dramatically increasing ability to alter brain chemistry, in both controlled and haphazard manners, in the clinical situation and in everyday life.

NOTES

1. F.K. Goodwin and K.R. Jamison, *Manic-Depressive Illness* (New York: Oxford University Press, 1990).

2. N.S. Kline, Manipulation of Life Patterns with Drugs, in *Psychotropic Drugs in the Year 2000: Use by Normal Humans*, edited by W.O. Evans and N.S. Kline (Springfield, Ill.: Charles C Thomas, 1971).

3. Ibid.; M.M. Katz, The Need for New Intoxicants, in *Psychotropic Drugs in the Year 2000: Use by Normal Humans*, edited by W.O. Evans and N.S. Kline (Springfield, Ill.: Charles C Thomas, 1971).

4. A.C. Howlett et al., The Cannabinoid Receptor: Biochemical, Anatomical and Behavioral Characterization. *Trends in Neuroscience* 13 (1990):420–423.

5. I. Hindmarch and J.Z. Bhatti, Psychopharmacological Effects of Sertraline in Normal, Healthy Volunteers, *European Journal of Pharmacology* 35 (1988):221–223.

6. R.M. Nesse, What Good Is Feeling Bad? The Evolutionary Benefits of Psychic Pain, *The Sciences* (New York Academy of Sciences), November-December 1991, 30–37.

7. Ibid.

8. Goodwin and Jamison, *Manic-Depressive Illness.*

9. A.J. Prange et al., Peptides: Application to Research in Mental Disorders, in *New Frontiers of Psychotropic Drug Research*, edited by S. Fielding (Mt. Kisco, N.Y.: Futura Publishing, 1979).

10. B.N. Saffron, Should Intracerebroventricular Nerve Growth Factor Be Used to Treat Alzheimer's Disease? *Perspectives in Biology and Medicine* 35 (1992):471–486.

11. N. Bodor et al., A Strategy for Delivering Peptides into the Central Nervous System by Sequential Metabolism, *Science* (1992):1698–1700.

12. N.P. Quinn, The Clinical Application of Cell Grafting Techniques in Patients with Parkinson's Disease, in *Progress in Brain Research*, vol. 82, edited by S.B. Dunnett and S-J Richards (Amsterdam: Elsevier Science Publishers, 1990).

13. J. Kline et al., Fetal Tissue Supply, *Science* 257 (1992):1189–1190.

14. I. Berlin, Two Concepts of Liberty, in *Four Essays on Liberty* (New York: Oxford University Press, 1969).

15. P.J. Landrigan and D.B. Baker, The Recognition and

Control of Occupational Disease, *JAMA* 266 (1991):679–680.

16. Conservation Foundation, *State of the Environment: A View toward the Nineties* (Washington, D.C.: Conservation Foundation, 1987); A. Leaf, Potential Health Effects of Global Climatic and Environmental Changes, *New England Journal of Medicine* 321 (1989):1577–1583.

17. U.S. Congress, Office of Technology Assessment, *Biological Effects of Power Frequency Electrical and Magnetic Fields*, OTA-BP-E-53 (Washington, D.C.: U.S. Government Printing Office, 1989).

18. F. Angelini, Technology, Development, Stewardship and Ethical Considerations, *Annals of the New York Academy of Science* 534 (1988):858–862.

Chapter 14

The Plight of the Deinstitutionalized Chronic Schizophrenic: Ethical Considerations

George B. Palermo

Deinstitutionalization and noninstitutionalization of the mentally ill are complex issues from both a practical and an ethical point of view. Deinstitutionalization was suggested by and implemented with the unanimous support of the antipsychiatry movement of the 1960s and of those citizens who were primarily interested in civil liberties. The opinions of the recipients of this new revolutionary reform in the field of psychiatry, the patients and their families, were not researched prior to its application. During the past three decades, the implementation of the programs has taken place so rapidly that the goals originally proposed have been only partially achieved. Their ethics have come under frequent scrutiny as their failures are increasingly becoming more apparent. Because of this, confusion and ambivalent feelings have been experienced by professionals involved in the care of the mentally ill, the patients themselves, and the families of the patients.

At the basis of this drastic reform of the mental health care system in the United States and abroad was a longstanding controversial issue regarding the nature of mental illness—whether its main cause is organic (or hereditary) or environmental. The so-called nature-versus-nurture issue has existed for centuries in the medical psychiatric field. Over the years, great psychiatrists and humanistic scholars who held diverse and at times opposite theoretical views tilted the balance toward one explanation of mental illness or another. Nonetheless, both approaches have, alternately, greatly benefited the mentally ill by promoting better understanding of the psychodynamics and pharmacotherapy of mental disorders.

The popularity of each side of the controversy has waxed and waned depending on changes in the social, historical, and political context. In order to better understand the strong impetus that deinstitutionalization had during the 1950s and 1960s and the early 1970s and its trickle-down effect, which still continues, one needs to analyze many of the factors involved. It should not be difficult to recognize that after the defeat of some of the European totalitarian regimes at the end of World War I, a new wave of commitment to freedom spread throughout Europe and the United States. Assuming that the sociopolitical context of any nation usually has a substantial influence on important social issues and decisions, it is easy to understand why human and civil rights were viewed the world over as essential and inalienable and why the concept of human dignity was acclaimed as the most important value to be taken into account in decision making. A new sensitivity and a humanitarian approach to social problems came to prominence. Self-criticism paved the way to new solutions to social problems.

The decision to deinstitutionalize the mentally ill was influenced by the fact that the hospitals housing them were generally antiquated and the conditions were often extremely poor. The leaders of society became attentive to the problems, and they decided, helped by chain discoveries of major antipsychotic and antidepressant drugs and by a concomitant shift of the financial burden from the states to the federal government, to tear down the old asylums and rapidly discharge the chronic patients to their families or to halfway houses and homes for the elderly.[1] Gradually, even the acutely ill were directed to outpatient care in mental health centers or in fragmented outposts called catchment areas. The above decision to deinstitutionalize, theoretically interesting even though utopian, lacked a holistic, objective appreciation of the diseases affecting the mentally ill—diseases whose treatment has baffled people for centuries. However, overenthusiasm, which usually diminishes sound reflection, took over.

The mentally ill have long been the object of societal attention. They are people affected by a disease of the mind, usually schizophrenia and manic-depressive illness, that is thought to impair their wholesome social functioning, making them helpless and unable to make decisions for themselves, prey to perceptual distortion in how they view the surrounding world, fearful of being in the midst of crowds, deeply tortured by unusual unconscionable thoughts, at times paranoid, and occasionally dangerous to themselves and others. Hospitalization is frequently an essential step in the case of patients who have a severe mental illness—the psychotic ones or those who are depressed and dangerous to themselves or others—and care and treatment often cannot be delivered with conscience and expertise in any alternative setting.

Utilitarian and deontological theories have supported different practical approaches to the plight of the mentally ill and the ethics involved in the search for the solution to their problems. However, no solution has yet been found. The patient, in the meantime, continues to be a suffering being, a victim of frequent rejection, poor experimentation, and lack of humane concern. Recently, the Alliance for the Mentally Ill, which addresses the patients' humane needs, their civil rights, and the needs and rights of their families, has become vociferous in its support of their welfare. It is interesting to note that a loud cry for a more humanitarian approach to the welfare of the mentally ill comes from their families. They obviously speak from both their hearts and from their minds.

The patients, for their part, often seem to apathetically disregard the rejection of the present–day system of care and its frequent and dehumanizing delivery. They become noncompliant with their treatments and reject attempts to help them. They have apparently lost trust in the professionals caring for them. They may feel that they were pushed out of their old places of refuge, or they may feel abandoned and resent the new therapeutic dispositions. They feel unwanted and occupy the streets, open spaces in buildings, and the waiting rooms of bus or train stations, testimony to their unintended victimization. One wonders, at times, whether they, the sick and the weak, are showing an attitude of passive aggression.

In trying to apply the Hobbesian view of contractarian social morality to the plight of the mentally ill, one realizes that it may allow some form of exploitation of the weak. It would be better to see people as self-originating sources of valid claims and implicitly consider them as moral persons. John Stuart Mill stated that civil libertarians "conceive liberty to be so important a value to society that it transcends other values."[2] "Everyday morality, however, tells us that mutual beneficial activities must first respect the rights of others including the rights of those too weak to defend their interests."[3] Only then does morality equate with impartiality. Ethically, there is no doubt that the autonomy of any individual and his or her right to make a free choice should always be upheld, but one may question whether the majority of the mentally ill, especially those who roam the streets, still retain their capacity to decide on their own behalf. Many psychotic people have a great deal of difficulty in making serious decisions and in preserving their human dignity.

The principle of beneficence applies not only to interpersonal encounters, such as between a doctor and patient, but also within any normal intrapsychic-intrapersonal system. A healthy person possessing a moral and autonomous self should be able to function in such a way that any decision made by him or her, especially relating to his or her physical and mental health, will ultimately be beneficial and will not lead to a worsening of his or her condition. If the mentally ill are unable to decide about their welfare, should it not be up to an ethically interested social group, beyond partisanship, to decide what is good for them? Optimally, such a group should be formed by the representatives of the families of the mentally ill, the recovered mentally ill, mental health professionals, and political legislators. Freedom from hospitalization and treatment is not always the expression of one's right to freedom of choice. At times, it even prevents freedom of choice.

HISTORICAL SKETCH

It is reasonable to assume that mental illness and/or insanity have been present in the world since shortly after the appearance of *homo sapiens*. Since our ancient progenitors had not yet reached the stage of mind-body development of present-day humans, and since the development of society was at its beginning, it can safely be argued that the manifestations of mental illness or insanity were different than those confronting us now. Without doubt, early humans must have reacted in a primitive way to the particular psychosocial factors of their rudimentary community. It is also reasonable to think that humans gradually began to define, through progressive

refinement of their knowledge and understanding of their biological and psychological nature, the significance, the boundaries, and the manifested behavior of what later came to be called mental illness and/or insanity. Throughout the centuries, humans slowly jettisoned (1) naive, magical, and superstitious thinking due to ignorance or misunderstanding of natural phenomena and (2) unconscious projections (primitive attempts to understand inner feelings and emotions) unto a mythological cosmos, where the forces of nature were soon supplanted by anthropomorphic gods. As human insight into the human psyche grew through the centuries, humans began to appraise the feelings and behavior of the people around them and slowly defined and redefined their significance and described behaviors as well as the difference between the unusual and the common. Humans eventually grouped together the unusual, the strange, and the abnormal on one side and the common and normal on the other. That applied to feelings and behavior as well, as the dichotomies between good and bad, evil and holy, mad and sane saw their beginning.

Indeed, as humans became more inquisitive and more rational as well as more observant of human behavior, a clear dichotomy in the description of human conduct appeared on the social horizon, and soon the concepts of mad and sane became commonplace. The concept of madness carried and unfortunately still often carries the connotation of unusual, evil, irrational, aggressive, violent, and disruptive. The terms *mens sana* or *mens insana* were coined, and *insanity* usually referred to psychosis and/or schizophrenia or mania.

Through the centuries, society approached the unusual and disruptive mad and their madness in different ways. The emotions of fury, revenge, and grief were well described in Homer's *Iliad* and *Odyssey*. The heroes appeared to be at the mercy of the good- and bad-natured gods of Olympus or of the furies or fate itself. It was only with the Greek philosophers and playwrights that both men and mythological heroes began to possess a psyche of their own. The madness and despair of Oedipus, described by Sophocles, is perhaps the best-known example. It ushered in a period during which reason was used to try to understand nature, society, and human behavior.[4] Plato and his followers thought of madness as irrational and as the antipode of human dignity, and irrational madness was seen as a menace that reason should combat.[5] Even though the Hippocratic tradition denied that madness was due to supernatural visitations but held that is was essentially due to physical and natural causes, including heart, brain, blood, and humor dysfunctions, madness continued to remain, through the centuries, an inexplicable and feared manifestation. Later, Augustinian philosophy reflected upon the spiritual disharmony as the basis of humans' emotional ills, especially in their relationship to God, a thought that psychotherapists should be reminded of today.

The Roman Empire categorized the manifestations of the major mental illnesses as *furiosus, insania, amentia, and dementia.* During the reign of Justinian (483–565 A.D.), understanding and a humane attitude were shown toward the mentally ill. They were admitted to institutions for the poor and the infirm, perhaps as a result of the influence of Christianity. The mad were viewed as children—and were treated with compassion.[6]

In the early medieval period, a small number of homes for the insane were built, and a few monasteries sheltered a couple of lunatics each.[7] However, the majority of the mentally ill lived with their families, were kept under continuous scrutiny by the villagers, or were left to themselves as forgotten people. (This kind of treatment still exists in present-day society, although it is rare). Leprosy, a deadly and disfiguring illness, became pandemic in Europe during the medieval period, and from the high middle ages to the end of the twelfth century, leprosariums and lazarets multiplied at a rapid pace. As leprosy gradually declined, the physical structures that had been used for the care of the lepers were used to house vagabonds, criminals, and people who were different and thought to be mad. The psychotics were even denied basic human and spiritual support. "Access to churches was denied to madmen, although ecclesiastical law did not deny them the use of the sacraments."[8] The mad were mistreated, mocked, expelled from towns, or forced to live at the periphery of cities. The rejection of the mad became so comprehensive that they were eventually confined on ships that would deliver them to different lands where they would be partially and for an undetermined period of time protected by their anonymity. "Water and navigation certainly play a role [in this rejection]. Confined on the ship, from which there is no escape, the madman is delivered to the river with its thousand arms, the sea with its thousand roads, to that great uncertainty . . . prisoner in the midst of what is the freest."[9] Brant's *Narrenschiff,* Bosch's *Ship of Fools,* and other works had served to immortalize that curious historical period during which human folly was seen as sinful and as something to be rejected. A few people, however, thought that the voice of folly might be a medium for the voice of God or have some recondite benefit (e.g., Erasmus's *Praise of Folly*).

Eventually, an attempt to care for the insane was made. The Hôpital Général in France and the first houses of correction in Germany and England became the forerunners of future asylums.[10] However, the plight of the schizophrenic and the manic continued. "One-tenth of all the arrests made in Paris for the Hôpital Général concern the insane, demented men, individuals of wandering mind and persons who have become completely mad."[11]

Later, during the eighteenth and nineteenth centuries, Europe was inundated by the establishment of a great number of schools, prisons, houses of correction, workhouses, and madhouses that dealt with the insane, who were felt to be a social threat. An attempt was made to confine and shut away the different, the weird, the peculiar, and the mad. It continued for many years, during which time the mad were housed in antiquated hospital structures. Tuke had already reported on the sad condition of the insane at Bethlehem Hospital. The Salpêtrière was no different. There, the mad (schizophrenic or manic) were chained to their cell doors and to the walls, like beasts, living in filth. At times they even had iron rings around their necks. Eventually, the mad were freed from real chains by the humane approach of people like Chiarugi, Pinel, Tuke, and Dix, and the birth of the asylum took place. The mad were no longer subjected to restraints, segregation, unusual diets, and even opium (to calm their agitation and soften their physical constitution). Eventually, Kraeplin, Pinel, Esquirol, Bleuler, and others better appraised the schizophrenias and freed the mad from the aura of evilness. The revolutionary ideas of Freud further assisted the sane in their attempt to properly address the problem of the mad by stressing that madness is the outcome of inner psychological conflicts and that any possible resolution comes from the intensive application of the old Socratic dictum—know thyself.

The above historical sketch indicates the vicissitudes of the mad through the centuries, their plight and the defensive mass hysteria of the sane during various periods of social change. More recently there has been a focus on the potential powers of humans and their ability to be both artists and masters of their destiny. Thus, the mad began to be viewed as humans in search of themselves or of a new self, and the sane were finally willing to help and to understand their plight in a compassionate way.

LIFE, LIBERTY, AND THE PURSUIT OF HAPPINESS

One of our constitutional axioms is that each individual has an inalienable right to life, liberty, and the pursuit of happiness. Even though the interpretation of the concepts of life and liberty may vary from one individual to another, it is unquestionable that the range of interpretation has definite boundaries. In other words, there are certain basic features that are common to any reasonable interpretation of the concepts. Life, in a social context, is not a mere vegetative state or a bizarre, disorganized type of existence. Optimally, life is the expression of the rational and reasonable behavior of an individual who has

sufficient mental capacity to care for him- or herself, to be alone or with others in a way neither injurious to self or to others, and to be productive and beneficial to self and others. It is a state where free choice, autonomy, self-interest, and willpower exist in a state of social communion, not in a vacuum, and where the same basic principles of reasonable ethical thinking and behavior are accepted by the majority of people involved.

Autonomy and liberty are similar concepts, and both encompass one of the most important human rights; the right to freely decide in matters that only involve oneself. It is a right that should be exercised by all citizens in a responsible way; the right, not to license, but to liberty usually goes hand in hand with responsibility. Responsibility is a state of "moral, legal, or mental accountability," and being responsible is being "able to choose for oneself between right and wrong, . . . able to answer for one's conduct and obligations."[12] All too often the acute and chronic mentally ill exercise the right to choose in a way that is harmful to them, physically or mentally, and therefore in an irresponsible way. They have often lost their discriminative capacity, and they may not be aware of the moral consequences of their decisions.

The essence of what is called mental illness is not changed by social, economic, or political theorizing. Indeed, mental illness, regardless of the philosophical approach to it, will continue to be a condition of the mind that manifests itself as confusion of thinking, inability to appreciate the surrounding reality, fluctuation of mood, lack of interest, poor judgment, and occasionally delusional or hallucinatory thinking and behavior. Based on the above, it is hard to accept that acute and chronic states of mental illness do not interfere with ethical choice making and the mental capacity to freely choose as well as moral accountability and responsibility toward self and others. The mentally ill cannot be expected to exercise their inalienable right to liberty when their state of mind does not allow them to do so. Consequently, it is unethical to permit the aimless vagabondage of homeless schizophrenics and to force a nonhospitalization law upon sick persons incapacitated by a disorganizing mental condition and in need of treatment in a supervised asylum. The frequent and insistent demands of the families of the mentally ill that their sick relatives be hospitalized for appropriate treatment and possibly custodial care instead of being left in the streets in their psychotic and disruptive state are objective, humane, and moral. Can a self-appointed group of guardians, upholding libertarian or utilitarian views, make decisions for the mentally ill and exclude from a decisional forum their voices and those of their families? Can they refrain from taking action when viewing how the homeless chronic mentally ill live?

Lastly, in considering the last prong of the constitutional axiom—the pursuit of happiness—one must recognize that it too does not seem to be reflected by the way of life of the homeless mentally ill. The deranged homeless schizophrenics, whose rational thinking is highly disrupted, are obviously pursuing, if anything at all, a state of socioethical abasement, an outcome of their mental confusion. The exercise of civil rights or liberties should not call for personal, self-injurious consequences. Can the behavior of the mentally ill be seen as the dramatization of their need for adequate care—their cry for help? If the behavior of the homeless mentally ill is accepted as their right to self-expression and free choice, it must be noted that it certainly contrasts with the rights of the majority, who consider it offensive to human dignity and contrary to the welfare of the mentally ill.

In conclusion, the old constitutional axiom does not seem consistent with the life of the homeless mentally ill. This realization makes it even more evident that the well-intended reform of our mental health system has not achieved its goals. Libertarian philosophy, stressing freedom from hospitalization and freedom from treatment for the mentally ill at any cost, has created social confusion and raised ethical and legal issues that need to be confronted. "The most conspicuous misdirection of psychiatric practice—the precipitate dismissal of patients with severe, chronic mental disorders such as schizophrenia from psychiatric hospitals—certainly required a vastly oversimplified view of mental illness . . . as though it were not their illnesses but society that deprived them of freedom in the first place."[13]

SOCIOETHICAL CONSIDERATIONS

The primary objective of the President's Commission on Mental Health consisted of "maintaining the greatest degree of freedom, self-determination, autonomy, dignity, and integrity of body, mind, and spirit for the individual while he or she participates in treatment or receives services."[14] The therapeutic programs were to be carried out in the least restrictive environment. Bachrach, in a sound analysis of the problem of deinstitutionalization, aptly stated that the quality of restrictiveness per se does not greatly contribute to better patient care. It is, indeed important to focus the attention on the quality of the program within the chosen setting, whether it be "essentially therapeutic, maintaining or custodial."[15] The idea of the least restrictive environment lacked the necessary foreseeability and flexibility that would have made it patient specific. However, the focus should not be only on adequate programs but also on dealing with people in a humane way. The mentally ill were placed in a situation that was not conducive to mental healing when deinstitutionalization at any cost was set into motion. And the cost was paid by many of the patients, occasional guests of our jails and permanent guests of our streets. "The argument that being inside the hospital is necessarily worse than anything on the outside simply does not hold. There are cases where patients . . . would be better off inside if those conditions cannot be met," stated Bachrach.[16] The proof that deinstitutionalization, born out of a humanitarian philosophy, economic juggling, and therapeutic frustration, was utopian and impractical lies in the presence of thousands of schizophrenics on our streets or in our jails, often chained and crying out, as at the time of Pinel and Dorothea Dix.

At present, it is very difficult for a mentally ill person to be admitted or readmitted to an institution because of the belief that only a limited number of patients should be kept in a psychiatric ward to avoid overcrowding and provide better quality care. This phenomenon of "treating the census" in order to ensure the quality of care has added a new dimension to the problem of caring for the mentally ill. What of those refused admission? Is it not immoral to maintain proper care for a few at the price of depriving a large group of the mentally ill, especially the chronic mentally ill, of almost any care? For example, many patients are discharged from psychiatric hospital units prematurely. It is unethical to discharge a mentally ill patient prior to the complete stabilization of his or her mental illness. It is also nontherapeutic and often leads to decompensation and irrational behavior at home or on the street. The ethical responsibility to dispense care to the "consumer-patient" is put to the test, and the professional dispensers of that care are pulled apart by having to be loyal both to the patient and to the system. In addition, the provision of care is often fragmented and the professional is bound to lose touch with the total patient. Patients often are seen but not admitted to mental hospitals. It would be worthwhile to find out how they feel about being denied admission, especially whether they find satisfactory the alternative sources of care to which they are referred, assuming that they follow through with the referrals, and also whether the rejection they may feel causes antisocial behavior. Research should delve into "whether use of community resources (coupled with other available social supports) is sufficient to stabilize their problems and deter further applications for hospital admission."[17]

Our moral problems seem to increase with the passing of time. Together with deinstitutionalization, a policy of noninstitutionalization has also been implemented. "While many patients are discharged from psychiatric hospitals into supportive settings, and the illnesses of other patients are resolved to the point that little support is needed, thousands of other patients have been discharged into inadequate settings or into the streets."[18] A great many of them live on sidewalks or in cardboard shelters. They often are sent to jail for simple misdemeanors, and from jail they are sent to outpatient psychiatric and social services and then sometimes to poorly supervised halfway houses, where their noncompliance with treatment brings them back to the streets.[19] This transinstitutionalization has compounded the problem of city management and created new moral issues. Is it more ethical for a schizophrenic to be in jail than in an asylum? The average citizen looks stupefied as one more wall of the edifice of social morality comes down—the abandonment of and lack of adequate psychiatric care for the many mentally ill living in our streets and in our jails.

The issue of the futility of treatment for chronic schizophrenics is raised at times. Indeed, in spite of the advent of new psychotropic medication, currently 25 percent of all schizophrenics will probably not recover from their mental illness or even improve. Nonetheless, one should assume that illness in general, and mental illness in particular, is basically treatable, and chronic mental patients should not be abandoned or discarded like unusable objects. Some illnesses, in comparison with half a century ago, now have specific and successful treatment modalities. Others can be made more tolerable while intensive research is pursued in the search for a definitive cure. At the same time, mental health professionals should concern themselves more with the ethics of their profession, become more attentive to the welfare of their patients, and not allow uncalled-for interference in the delivery of appropriate care.

It is to be hoped that moral virtues and ethical standards will be upheld in all aspects of psychiatric practice. It is increasingly evident that the legal focus on liberty clashes with the treatment needs of the patients. The paternalistic attitude of psychiatry has been questioned. One could argue that the psychiatrist, like other physicians, clings to "that priestly role which since the dawn of history has been so important a component of the identity of the physician."[20] The professional attitude of any psychiatrist should include not only benevolence but also practicality and objectivity. The view that freedom from hospitalization and treatment should be supported at any cost, on the contrary, is founded on utopian ideas mixed with a great deal of emotionalism. Nevertheless, in order to help the schizophrenics who are roaming the streets of the cities, a certain balance between the paternalistic and the libertarian must eventually be reached.

STATISTICAL DATA

The advent of psychopharmacology in the 1960s was marked by one of those surges of optimism characteristic of psychiatry during the past two centuries,[21] and old institutional structures and traditional psychiatric practices were soon viewed as detrimental to patients. Some European countries, notably Finland, Norway, Germany, and Great Britain, had already pioneered social and hospital reforms even prior to the development of the antidepressants and psychotropic drugs.[22] The schizophrenics, who constitute the predominant population in mental hospitals, responded positively to the new medications. Chlorpromazine was treated as a panacea, as were other psychotropics and antidepressants that followed later. Chronic schizophrenics seemed to return to life—to become self-sufficient, cooperative, and more friendly—and were again able to engage in a moderate degree of interpersonal life. Acute schizophrenics also responded rapidly to treatment. Patients were discharged to those families willing to accept them back home. Halfway houses or community living quarters with minimal supervision were organized. In some cases, discharged patients were allowed to live alone. Deinstitutionalization and noninstitutionalization were well under way.

In the United States, for humanitarian as well as for socioeconomic reasons, this movement took place rapidly. In 1963, the Congress, acting on recommendations by the Joint Commission on Mental Illness and Health, passed the Mental Retardation Facilities Act and the Community Mental Health Centers Act. Patients were soon transferred from the snake pits to neighborhoods.[23]

There is no doubt that well-coordinated and humanitarian programs for the mentally ill were long overdue and that a new and more dynamic approach was necessary to combat the chronicity of their illness and to replace antiquated and poorly run institutions. However, as previously stated, the implemented programs were largely a failure. "Often the ideals of deinstitutionalization amount in practice to little more than the shifting of people from one institutional setting to another—from the lunatic asylum to the nursing home, boarding house, or private hospital."[24] The reality is even more bleak. Indeed, many schizophrenics, as above stated, do not comply with their treatments, resist the supervision of social agencies, and are averse to hospitalization, and these individuals often land in the streets and sometimes end up in the jails.[25] According to the National Coalition for Jail Reform (USA), up to one million of those filing through the jails each year (roughly 20 percent) are mentally ill or developmentally disabled.[26] Most of the mentally ill in the jail system are chronic schizophrenics or manic-depressives who have often been charged with petty crimes or misdemeanors committed because they are mentally confused.[27] They should be called pseudo-offenders to differentiate them from real criminals. Nevertheless, they are housed in jails or prisons, and both they and their jailers deny their mental illness. They, the patients, prefer criminalization to psychiatrization, to hospitalization, and to treatment, confident that an overwhelmed and often lenient judicial system will quickly return them to the liberty of their homeless way of life.[28] "Of those offenders assessed mentally ill only 23% claimed to be receiving treatment at the time of arrest or incarceration . . . [and] the asylum-like function of the jail makes the job of maintaining incarcerated persons most difficult. . . . An emotionally distraught person may be stripped naked and chained to the floor to prevent a suicide attempt."[29] What a sad cyclical return of the past.

It is, indeed, ironic that in our so-called progressive society, centuries after the emancipatory vision and the efforts of Pinel, Chairugi, Tuke, and Dix, for whom the asylum was to become a place where the mad would be treated humanely, the jails and the streets have become repositories of the mentally ill. Comparative statistics show that in 1955 the census in U.S. mental hospitals was 634,000, whereas U.S. jails housed 185,780 inmates.[30] In 1988, the jail census had risen to 603,928 and the mental hospital census had declined to less than 160,862.[31] The nation's 3,493 local jails have become a dumping ground for the mentally ill in our communities.

Many of those not in jail are cluttering the streets of our cities. As early as 1970, Goldfarb, through thorough evaluation of the homeless individuals who were admitted to the Manhattan Bowery Project in New York, had established that 33 percent of them were primarily suffering from schizophrenia and had a secondary diagnosis of alcoholism.[32] The typical chronically homeless person in a Philadelphia study emerged as a white individual, over age 40, with a diagnosis of schizophrenia, substance abuse, or both.[33] A study in Baltimore of 298 men and 230 women randomly selected from missions, shelters, and jails found that 91 percent of the men and 80 percent of the women suffered from some form of psychiatric illness. Schizophrenia was diagnosed in 12 percent of the men and 17 percent of the women.[34] Schizophrenia, substance abuse, and personality disorders are the most common psychiatric diagnoses among the homeless. Except in a few cases, the homelessness of the mentally ill is the result of the way deinstitutionalization has been implemented and not of deinstitutionalization per se.[35]

> Deinstitutionalization meant granting asylum in the community to a large marginal population, many of whom can cope to only a limited extent with the ordinary demands of life, have strong dependency needs, and are unable to live independently . . . and can survive and have their basic needs met outside of the state hospital only if they have a sufficiently structured community facility or other mechanism that provides support and controls.[36]

About 40 percent of the homeless suffer from a major mental illness. Orr reported that the percentage of the mentally ill offenders in jail ranged from 10 to 50 percent.[37] Briar stated that about 20 percent of the jail population was composed of former or new patients of mental institutions.[38] They are the social misfits mentioned by Reusch and the pseudo-offenders described by Snow. Adler reported an increase in the arrest rate for the mentally ill that was substantially higher than that of the general population.[39] As causes of this rate of increase, she cited improper pharmacotherapeutic management, abuse of or noncompliance with medication, the natural progression of mental illness, and the new social phenomenological approach to mental illness. She also stated that her previous estimate that 10.9 percent of inmates were psychiatrically ill was greatly underestimated. Statistics gathered by Petrick revealed that 35 percent of the prisoners in the King County Jail (Washington State) were psychotic.[40] Out of 102 prisoners referred for psychiatric evaluation in the Los Angeles jail system in 1982, 75 percent were diagnosed as schizophrenic, 22 percent as having major affective disorders, and only 2 percent as having organic brain syndromes and adjustment disorders.[41] Lastly, in a recent analysis of a sample of 272 inmates in a county jail examined for competency to stand trial, the number of schizophrenics was estimated at 103 (37.87 percent of the total sample). Of the offenses, 83.5 percent were misdemeanors and 16.5 percent were felonies, and only 57.28 percent of all the inmates were found to be competent to stand trial.[42]

IN DEFENSE OF PROVIDING A NEW TYPE OF ASYLUM

Daily observation and statistical studies affirm the fact that many of the mentally ill live on the street. It seems clear that we need to provide asylum for people whose disadvantages include "social isolation, vocational inadequacy, and exaggerated dependency needs . . . [and the inability] to withstand pressure."[43] "While many chronic patients eventually attain high levels of social and vocational functioning, many cannot meet simple demands of living, even with long term rehabilitative help."[44] They need an asylum, "an inviolable place of refuge" and "a place of retreat and security."[45] There the homeless mentally ill who presently live on the street should find "the network of inter-related programs that meet the varied needs of a very heterogenous population."[46]

The concept of an asylum is still a valid one, despite previous problems in implementing a system of refuge. "Institutional care has historically included a complex and extensive set of functions in the service of psychiatric patients."[47] The patients were receiving substandard care in antiquated institutions, but the therapeutic efforts, even though inadequate, addressed each patient in his or her totality. At present, the fragmentation of care for the mentally ill has created a never-ending carousel they are unable to escape from.

One reason for the failure of deinstitutionalization is that it is based on the assumption that mental illness is either sociogenic or even nonexistent. Bachrach stated, "Among the many problems plaguing society today is the failure to recognize that a portion of chronic psychiatric patients still require asylum and a failure to offer that asylum even when the need for it is recognized."[48] In England, the 1982 health legislation promoting the idea of entitlement to mental health services has been highly criticized as "an empty promise, if it is not accompanied by places in the form of secure accommodations suitable for that patient. The problem may be exacerbated for offender-patients for whom the only alternative may be prison. . . . There is a serious lack of resources for detained mentally disordered patients who need secure conditions."[49] In Italy, laws have recently been passed to reform the reform—Mental Health Law 180.[50] In the United States and other Anglo-Saxon countries, the general feeling is also that the earlier changes have to be amended.

In 1989, Mosher and Burti, in support of deinstitutionalization, provided "practical, common sense, flexible, good enough administrative and clinical guidelines to allow the development and implementation of effective psychosocially oriented community mental health systems."[51] Their guidelines, put forth decades after the implementation of the reform of 1958 in the United States, indicate that even they recognize deinstitutionalization has been less than a total success.

CONCLUSION

Assuming that the role of medical ethics is primarily to sensitize people to the moral issues that arise in caring for the sick, one should try, as objectively as possible, to focus attention on the application of those rules that tend to harmonize the goals and desires of all participants in the care process. It is essential not to forget that medical ethicists should be driven, not by passionate feeling, but by the intention of pursuing an objective moral analysis of the issues at hand through a process of a detailed assessment of the principles and concepts involved. Ethics is more a process than a pronouncement. Ultimately, any decision, as in the case of deinstitutionalization, rests with the leaders of society. It must be remembered, however, that the consequences are experienced by society at large. Because of that, no major ethical decision affecting the welfare of others should be made solely on sociopolitical grounds.

McHugh, in his essay "Psychiatric Misadventures," points out that, at the basis of occasional misdirected efforts in the field of psychiatry, one usually may find "oversimplification . . . misplaced emphasis . . . [or] pure invention."[52] In acknowledging the vulnerability of the psychiatric field to error, he reported a comment made by Szasz, an important leader of the antipsychiatry movement. According to Szasz, psychiatry creates schizophrenia, since an individual is identified as schizophrenic on the basis of an existing system of psychiatry. Szasz's reasoning is worthy of a sophist, but when the well-being of people is at stake, one should be wary of sophistry. People expect and deserve an objective appraisal of what concerns them. Social theories are certainly important tools in the assessment of the human condition, but social factors per se seem to be only contributing factors in the genesis of schizophrenia and manic-depressive disorders, the most common mental illnesses among the homeless mentally ill.

Although one can be sympathetic with Szasz's motive, which is to do away with unnecessary restrictions, it is unethical to avoid treating people who are genuinely ill. The mental health professionals who accept Szasz's sociological approach to mental illness "abandon the role of protecting patients from their symptoms and become little more than technicians working on behalf of a cultural force."[53]

The idea that institutions were essentially oppressive was part of the cultural baggage of the 1960s. The vision of the alternative life that the chronic schizophrenics supposedly wanted to live was dreamed up by enthusiastic but wrongheaded reformers. "It is now obvious to every citizen of our cities that these patients have impaired capacity to comprehend the world and that they need protective and serious active treatment."[54]

Bachrach aptly stated that "the public policy initiative, which has for several decades dominated service planning for chronic psychiatric patients, may be viewed as a precipitous effort to change an entrenched and established system of care."[55] The absence of asylums has greatly limited the effectiveness of community-based services for many chronically ill psychiatric patients. Asylums should be places where people may reside and be provided with up-to-date care, where the mentally ill may find temporary comfortable surroundings and humane attention,

where freedom from sickness is a main goal, along with restoration of autonomy, decisional capacity, self-respect, and human dignity.

Serious devastating illnesses such as schizophrenia should be of central concern in a moral society. The plight of the mentally ill in our streets and jails is certainly a reflection of the ongoing moral decay of our society. Bachrach nicely summarizes one of the social and moral problems confronting us today:

> Although the original motivation for deinstitutionalization was humane and well intentioned, its consequences have, at times, been unexpected and harmful to the chronically ill.... Chronically ill psychiatric patients are ... severely disabled and disenfranchised populations with few resources ... economically deprived... [and] require help in arranging for life's basic necessities, including food, shelter, medical care and social support.[56]

And the following statement indicates why we need to attempt a solution:

> People with mental problems are our neighbors. They are members of our congregations, members of our families; they are everywhere in this country. If we ignore their cries for help we will be continuing to participate in the anguish from which those cries for help come. A problem of this magnitude will not go away. Because it will not go away, and because of our spiritual commitments, we are compelled to take action.[57]

The action must be taken by dedicated humanistic professionals who treat their patients-clients, not as objects, but as human beings and who are willing to join in a communal attempt to aid the mentally ill regain their mental health, their autonomy, their self-respect, and their humanity.

NOTES

1. H.C. Solomon, The American Psychiatric Association in Relation to American Psychiatry—Presidential Address, *American Journal of Psychiatry* 115 (158):1–9.

2. P. Chodoff, Involuntary Hospitalization of the Mentally Ill as a Moral Issue, *American Journal of Psychiatry* 141 (1984):385.

3. W. Kymlicka, The Social Contract Tradition, in *Companion to Ethics,* edited by P. Singer (Cambridge, Mass: Blackwell Reference, 1991), 190.

4. M. Foucault, *Madness and Civilization,* trans. R. Howard (New York: Vintage Books, 1988); R. Porter, *A Social History of Madness* (New York: E.P. Dutton, 1989).

5. M.M. Mackenzie, *Plato on Punishment* (Berkeley and Los Angeles: University of California Press, 1981).

6. G. Zilboorg and G.W. Henry, *A History of Medical Psychology* (New York: Norton, 1941).

7. Porter, *Social History of Madness.*

8. Foucault, *Madness and Civilization,* 10.

9. Ibid., 11.

10. Porter, *Social History of Madness.*

11. Foucault, *Madness and Civilization,* 65.

12. *Webster's Ninth New Collegiate Dictionary,* s.v. "responsibility" and "responsible."

13. P.R. McHugh, Psychiatric Misadventures, *American Scholar,* Autumn 1992, 498.

14. L.L. Bachrach, Is the Least Restrictive Environment Always the Best? Sociological and Semantic Implications, *Hospital and Community Psychiatry* 31 (1980):97.

15. Ibid., 101.

16. Ibid., 99.

17. J.R. Morrissey et al., Being "Seen but Not Admitted." A Note on Some Neglected Aspects of State Hospital Deinstitutionalization, *American Journal of Orthopsychiatry* 49 (1979):155.

18. R. Peele, The Ethics of Deinstitutionalization, in *Psychiatric Ethics,* edited by S. Bloch and P. Chodoff (Oxford, New York, and Melbourne: Oxford University Press, 1991), 303.

19. G.B. Palermo et al., Escape from Psychiatrization: A Statistical Analysis of Referrals to a Forensic Unit, *International Journal of Offender Therapy and Comparative Criminology* 36 (1992):89–102.

20. Chodoff, Involuntary Hospitalization of the Mentally Ill as a Moral Issue, 387.

21. A. Scull, Deinstitutionalization and the Rights of the Deviant, *Journal of Social Issues* 37 (1981):6–20.

22. L. Klerman, The Psychiatric Patient's Right to Effective Treatment: Implications of Asheroff vs. Chestnut Lodge, *American Journal of Psychiatry* 147 (1990):409–418.

23. R. Sommer and A. Osmond, The Mentally Ill in the Eighties, *Journal of Orthomolecular Psychiatry* 10 (1981):193–201.

24. K. Jones et al., The Current Literature: The 1978 Italian Mental Health Law—A Personal Evaluation: A Review, *British Journal of Psychiatry* 159 (1991):560.

25. G.B. Palermo et al., Jails versus Mental Hospitals: A Social Dilemma, *International Journal of Offender Therapy and Comparative Criminology* 35 (1991):97–104.

26. K.H. Briar, Jails: Neglected Asylums, *Social Casework* 64 (1983):388.

27. P.J. Hilts, Survey Finds Many Jails Holding Mentally Sick on Minor Charges, *New York Times,* September 10, 1992, A12.

28. Palermo et al., Escape from Pscyhiatrization, 89–102.

29. Briar, Jails, 389.

30. U.S. Bureau of Census, *Historical Statistics of the United States* (Washington, D.C.: U.S. Bureau of Census, 1960).

31. U.S. Bureau of Census, *Statistical Abstracts of the United States* (Washington, D.C.: U.S. Bureau of Census, 1990).

32. C. Goldfarb, Patients Nobody Wants: Skid Row Alcoholics, *Diseases of Nervous System* 31 (1970):274–281.

33. A.A. Arce and M.J. Vergare, Identifying and Characterizing the Mentally Ill among the Homeless," in *The Homeless Mentally Ill: A Task Force Report of the APA,* edited by H.R. Lamb (Washington, D.C.: American Psychiatric Association, 1984), 75–89.

34. F. Kass, Mental Illness and Homelessness: Majority of Homeless People Found to be Mentally Ill, *Psychiatric News* 24 (1989):14.

35. C.L.M. Caton, *Homeless in America* (New York and Oxford: Oxford University Press, 1990).

36. H.R. Lamb, Deinstitutionalization and the Homeless Mentally Ill, in *The Homeless Mentally Ill: A Task Force Report of the APA,* edited by H.R. Lamb (Washington, D.C.: American Psychiatric Association, 1984), 58.

37. J.H. Orr, The Imprisonment of Mentally Disordered Offenders, *British Journal of Psychiatry* 133 (1978):194–199.

38. Briar, Jails, 387–393.

39. F. Adler, Jails as Repository for Former Mental Patients, *International Journal of Offender Therapy and Comparative Criminology* 30 (1986):225–236.

40. J. Petrick, Rate of Psychiatric Morbidity in a Metropolitan County Jail Population, *American Journal of Psychiatry* 133 (1976):1439–1444.

41. H.R. Lamb and R. Peele, The Need for Continuing Asylum and Sanctuary, *Hospital and Community Psychiatry* 35 (1984):798–802.

42. Palermo et al., Escape from Psychiatrization, 89–102.

43. Lamb and Peele, Need for Continuing Asylum and Sanctuary, 798.

44. Ibid.

45. *Webster's Ninth New Collegiate Dictionary,* s.v. "asylum."

46. L.L. Bachrach, Asylum and Chronically Ill Psychiatric Patients, *American Journal of Psychiatry* 141 (1984):977.

47. Ibid., 975.

48. Bachrach, Is the Least Restrictive Environment Always the Best? 977.

49. J. Shapland and T. Williams, Legalism Revived: New Mental Health Legislation in England, *International Journal of Law Psychiatry* 6 (1983):366.

50. La Riforma della Legge 180: Nuove Norme sulla Tutela della Salute Mentale, *Psichiatra and Medicina: Attualità in Neuroscienze, Psicogeriatria e Psicologia Medica,* September 1991, 8–11.

51. L.R. Mosher and L. Burti, *Community Mental Health: Principals and Practice* (New York and London: W.W. Norton, 1989), 381.

52. McHugh, Psychiatric Misadventures, 504.

53. Ibid.

54. Ibid., 501.

55. Bachrach, Asylum and Chronically Ill Psychiatric Patients, 975.

56. Ibid., 976.

57. R. Carter, A Voice for the Voiceless: The Church and the Mentally Ill, *Second Opinion* 13 (1990):47.

Chapter 15

Bioethical Dilemmas in Emergency Medicine and Prehospital Care

Kenneth V. Iserson

Emergency medicine is at once the oldest and the newest of medical specialties. Stemming from the aid given to injured comrades from time immemorial, the modern domain of emergency medicine encompasses care in hospital emergency departments (EDs) and urgent care centers and prehospital care (care provided by ambulance crews and medically trained flight crews). Emergency medical practitioners confront many of the traditional ethical dilemmas of physicians. However, there are also new ethical dilemmas that stem from their added responsibilities in the health treatment system and radical alterations of the available emergency treatments.

The U.S. health treatment system increasingly fails to meet the needs of the medically indigent. EDs have attempted to take up the slack but often lack the resources to care for the indigent and their primary task of treating the acutely ill and injured. Four key ethical dilemmas face emergency medical practitioners: how to continue to supply care for the critically ill and injured while providing care for the medically indigent, who often can get medical treatment nowhere else; how to aggressively treat critical patients and yet not be paternalistic toward those who can par-

ticipate in their own health care decisions; how to respect both the living and the dead and yet keep current in necessary life-saving skills; and how to perform research ethically to advance the entire field of emergency care while safeguarding patients. Each of these will be discussed in more detail below.

SAFETY NET

The U.S. health treatment system is in shambles, and EDs have been described as the system's *safety net*.[1] Medically indigent patients who cannot access the U.S. health treatment system in any other way do so through EDs. EDs have taken up the slack but they often lack adequate resources to do everything demanded of them. This poses a significant dilemma: whether to skimp on their primary duty of providing emergency medicine or to refuse to be a major source of care for the medically indigent.

In the main, EDs are still trying to do both. However, at the edge of the profession and gaining ground quickly are advocates of the position that EDs should turn away those patients who seem to have minor complaints.[2] While triage (sorting and prioritizing the treatment of patients by the seriousness of their illness) is a common practice, EDs have traditionally never refused treatment to people who come seeking their help. Yet, as is clear to anyone who has gone to an ED on a Friday or Saturday night, the wait for care for a nonemergent condition may be lengthy. In some instances, to speed the process and save resources, patients with minor complaints are seen in adjacent clinics rather than in the ED. Yet all patients are eventually seen.

Recently, however, a new trend is taking hold—refusal of treatment. Some EDs now deny treatment to patients who present with what are considered minor problems. Rather than being sent to adjacent clinics, they are simply given phone numbers for clinics where they can try to make appointments to be seen. Researchers have shown that most of these patients will never see a health care provider for their problem. Many of these problems, however, are self-resolving or so minimal that any delay in care is not deleterious. What then is the dilemma?

Emergency medicine, in all of its manifestations, has been held out to the American public over the past two decades as an unfailing source of medical treatment at any time and for any problem. Practitioners are reneging on this promise.[3] The EDs refusing care are not those in the posh suburbs but those in the crowded inner cities, where the greatest percentage of medically indigent people reside.

The choice is between supplying EDs with enough resources to both act as a "safety net" and continue to treat the acutely ill or injured and refusing medical treatment to those who seek care at EDs as a last resort.

PATERNALISM

The major resource in emergency medical care is time. The time that an ED's limited personnel allocate to any patient is a lost resource. The split-second decisions they make are often immutable. The pressure to make critical decisions is nowhere as intense or as constant as in emergency medicine. This constant pressure to use time and resources efficiently, combined

with patients who are often critically ill or injured and lack decision-making capacity, tends to make emergency medical practice paternalistic. As a consequence, the practitioners' values and their patients' desire to exercise autonomy sometimes are in direct conflict.

Emergency medicine occurs in its most basic form during wars and disasters, and in these situations practitioners often make immediate decisions about who gets treatment and who is allowed to die. In the usual hospital and prehospital scenario, the inclination of practitioners is similarly to make immediate unilateral decisions about how to save life and limb. These interventions are generally beneficial, and patients do want and expect aggressive and immediate action by emergency medical teams. Too easily, however, especially given medicine's (and nursing's) traditional attitudes, aggressive action becomes transformed into paternalism. ED and prehospital patients commonly complain that "things are done to them" without prior discussion or acquiescence. Significantly, these "things" often commit patients to large expenses for tests or procedures. In cases where patients lack decision-making capacity and there is an expectation of patient benefit from the medical team's actions, aggressive intervention is not only reasonable, it is essential. Engaging in this type of behavior with patients who maintain decision-making capacity is what causes problems.

Paternalism can also occur in cases of "futility." In emergency medicine and prehospital care, what constitutes futility for the emergency patient and when to withhold or withdraw life-sustaining measures are closely linked issues. The development of advanced cardiopulmonary life support and newer techniques in trauma resuscitation increase practitioners' capacity to extend biological life, although the benefits to patients remain uncertain. Yet there are few guidelines other than lack of success in a "reasonable" amount of time to aid prehospital or ED practitioners in deciding when to abandon therapeutic interventions. Aside from the still rare prehospital advance directive order, few patient guidelines exist either. The clinicians are then forced to make unilateral decisions about further care—often paternalistically providing unwanted treatments.

USING THE NEWLY DEAD FOR PRACTICE AND TEACHING

The public demands and expects that all emergency practitioners will be skilled in critical life-saving skills and teach those skills to new practitioners. The most efficient and practical way for them to remain proficient in little-used skills is for them to practice on the newly dead.

For many years, physicians learned technical skills such as intubation and central line placement by practicing on patients who had recently died. Recently, however, it has been suggested that post-mortem procedures are only permissible if prior consent is obtained from relatives. This position, though, ignores the nature of informed consent, contravenes patient altruism, and disregards society's interest in having an optimal number of medical care providers experienced in lifesaving techniques.

The general requirement that informed consent be obtained is based on the concept of patient autonomy. In theory, the consent process increases communication between the physician and patient prior to dangerous, disfiguring, or seriously invasive procedures. Requiring that prior consent be obtained by emergency medical personnel in order to practice lifesaving procedures on the newly dead is a misapplication of informed consent and misrepresents the concept of patient autonomy.

The dead, of course, have no claim to autonomy. Autonomy, based on the principles of freedom and liberty, is a function of personhood. But the dead are no longer persons, although by societal consent, a living person can express a wish for the disposition of his or her body through an advance directive or a legal will, neither of which are normally available in the ED. Nevertheless, the wishes of a person should be respected after that person has died, which often means respecting the person's altruistic decision to offer his or her body to medicine despite the relatives' reluctance.[4] The relatives' "quasi-property rights" to a corpse are strictly limited and do not give the relatives either moral or legal authority to counteract stronger competing claims.

Society also has a substantial interest. That interest is to maintain an optimal number of ED and emergency medical system personnel proficient in lifesaving procedures. The medical professions recognize that both primary instruction and continued practice are necessary for proficiency in lifesaving skills. This instruction and practice are best done using fresh cadavers, since the available alternatives are not adequate. But while there is a recognition that unreasonable barriers should not be placed in the way of training, some limits should exist.

Alternatives to the use of fresh cadavers are inadequate. Although models, animals, and donated, embalmed cadavers are useful for learning or practicing some aspects of critical care, they are generally poor imitations of the critical patient. The use of animals, aside from being logistically ever more difficult, is itself ethically problematic. Donated, preserved cadavers are less realistic, are expensive, and have limited availability. Models have been shown to have even less utility.[5]

If a legal or ethical requirement existed for consent prior to post-mortem ED instruction, it would decrease the number of clinical personnel trained in lifesaving procedures. The need to request this permission from distraught relatives would raise significant emotional barriers for clinicians to overcome in order to practice and teach the procedures. In a survey of medical personnel involved in organ harvesting, a dislike of "adding to relatives' distress by asking permission for donation" was the single biggest barrier to organ procurement.[6] This barrier is unlikely to be breached, especially for the seemingly more trivial request to use cadavers for practice and teaching. Any impediment is further compounded by the stringent time limitations imposed by the onset of rigor mortis, by the rapid transport of the body to the morgue, and by the press of other duties once ED staff have completed a resuscitation attempt.

In summary, informed consent has an appropriate and vital role to play in keeping modern medicine from infringing on the rights of individuals. But extending the range of appropriateness to include consent requirement for ED post-mortem practice and teaching cannot be justified. The concept of autonomy would not be advanced, and future patients, the medical profession, and society would be harmed.[7]

RESEARCH UNDER UNUSUAL CIRCUMSTANCES

Emergency medicine cannot remain static. If it is to progress, research on the treatment of critical patients in prehospital situations and EDs is necessary. The outcome of this research will be beneficial to society. Yet societal strictures on informed consent prohibit much of this work.

Research in "acute care" is a troubling area for Institutional Review Board (IRB) approval and informed consent. Confusion about ethical and legal requirements has hampered research efforts and reduced subsequent patient benefits. Critical acute care patients seen in EDs and prehospital situations have typically suffered unexpected events that carry a high probability of mortality or severe morbidity unless immediate medical intervention is provided. Owing to the lack of substantive research on their medical and surgical problems and the difficulty in implementing research protocols, thousands of individuals receive untested and even inappropriate care each day in the United States. They deserve better. Acute care research can be implemented more widely and still satisfy both bureaucratic mandates and the ethical requirements to protect patients and research subjects.

It has been previously argued that acute care research is justified if the usual ethical requirements for research are modified to reflect the uniqueness of the situation. The recommenda-tions are not to (1) use an explicit definition of acute care as distinct from other modes of critical care, (2) eliminate the requirement for informed consent (as usually understood), and (3) require stringent IRB oversight regarding the unique ethical problems raised by this research. It has been further suggested that IRB oversight include review of the protocol by a panel of individuals who represent possible enrollees in the proposed study.[8]

OTHER TROUBLESOME AREAS

Although the dilemmas discussed above represent the kind of ethical issues that arise in emergency medical care, many other serious conflicts exist. Emergency medicine practitioners daily face the question of whether to override patient autonomy based on doubts regarding a patient's decision-making capacity. Not only must decisions be founded on meager information, in prehospital situations they must be made by physician extenders with variable amounts of education and experience and under the worst possible conditions.

In the ED, the basic beneficent value of alleviating pain runs up against two other values—to the detriment of patients. The physicians' stricture against doing harm keeps adequate analgesia from many patients who are suspected of "drug-seeking" behavior. This includes many patients with migraines and back pain and some with kidney stones (all classic complaints of drug seekers). Of course, the majority of patients with these complaints are only seeking relief for an acute problem. Similarly treated, but for different reasons, are patients who need pain relief before they are taken to the operating or procedure room. Many physicians want patients to be coherent rather than comfortable when they sign an operative permit. Therefore, many of these same patients wait hours without adequate analgesia, especially those with fractures and abdominal catastrophes requiring surgery, due to the legal necessity of getting the patients' signatures on operative permits.

One other dilemma commonly faced by emergency physicians does not seem to have an adequate solution. A patient's decision-making capacity is usually easy to determine in most clinical practice. If there are doubts, the patient's understanding can be tested.[9] In emergency care, on the other hand, the patient is under the severe stress of an acute and unexpected illness and is newly arrived in strange surroundings. The concept of patient autonomy governs much of modern U.S. biomedical ethics. It is unclear, however, how to determine whether a patient is acting autonomously in a crisis. The patient gasping for breath who refuses intubation, the AIDS patient who at the last moment verbally changes a well-thought-out advance directive, or the patient agreeing to take a risky medication or undergo a major operative procedure under these circumstances may be exhibiting panic behavior rather than autonomy in any accepted sense.

Clearly, many ethical issues in emergency care still need to be explicated, discussed, and resolved.

NOTES

1. American College of Emergency Physicians, Emergency Care Guidelines, *Annals of Emergency Medicine* 20 (1991):1381–1395.

2. R.W. Derlet et al., Triage of Patients out of the Emergency Department: Three-Year Experience, *American Journal of Emergency Medicine* 10 (1992):195–199.

3. K.V. Iserson, Assessing Values: Rationing Emergency Department Care, *American Journal of Emergency Medicine* 10 (1992):263–264.

4. R.M. Oswalt, A Review of Blood Donor Motivation and Recruitment, *Transfusion* 17 (1977):123–135; A. Spital and M. Spital, Living Donation: Attitudes outside the Transplant Center, *Archives of Internal Medicine* 148 (1988):1077–1080.

5. R.D. Stewart et al., Effect of Varied Training Techniques on Field Endotracheal Intubation Success Rates, *Annals of Emergency Medicine* 13 (1984):1032–1036.

6. R.E. Wakeford and R. Stepney, Obstacles to Organ Donation, *British Journal of Surgery* 76 (1989):435–439.

7. K.V. Iserson, Requiring Consent to Practice and Teach Using the Recently Dead, *Journal of Emergency Medicine* 9 (1991):509–510.

8. K.V. Iserson and M. Mahowald, Acute Care Research: Is It Ethical? *Critical Care Medicine* 20 (1992):1032–1037.

9. A.E. Buchanan, The Question of Competence, in *Ethics in Emergency Medicine*, edited by K.V. Iserson et al. (Baltimore: Williams and Wilkins, 1986).

Chapter 16

Social Systems and Professional Responsibility

Arlene Gruber

Suggestions have been made that new models of autonomy and bioethics are needed because the acute care model is too limited in scope to address the issues in home care and chronic illness.[1] Since acute care bioethics addresses issues within a narrow physician–individual patient framework, it is believed that issues involving broader systems—the family, the community, and the general society—are poorly served. Talk of "models" implies the existence of discrete systems of patient care. Such systems do not exist. Although acute care illness and chronic illness differ in some of their characteristics, the individuals experiencing these illnesses share the need for a response to their specific personal and social challenges, whether they are short or long term.

One of the professions involved in home care—and indeed one that since its inception has been involved in working with clients in community settings—is social work. Among its core values are client self-determination, maximum realization of each individual's potential within the context of social responsibility, and a strong social welfare system (defined as the organized norms and institutions by which we care for one another). Since these values are also the issues

any "new ethics model" should deal with, this chapter draws upon the social work framework used in addressing professional responsibility. This is not an ethical decision-making framework but a mindset of the profession in its relationships with individual clients and with society. Another way of stating this is that the mindset is the profession's lived understanding of its societal job assignment and core values. Since a profession's framework or mindset determines the material chosen to be used in the ethical decision-making process (e.g., the facts of the case, the values of all parties involved etc.), the understanding professionals have of their profession's framework is crucial to their ability to make sense of the dilemmas they face. Instead of a call for new models of autonomy and bioethics, the call should be for health care professionals to gain a clearer understanding of the complexity of their relationships with and responsibilities to patients, families, and society.

A NEW MODEL OF AUTONOMY?

For a number of years in the recent past, medical literature, which has included serious discussions of health care ethics, focused on the patient's right to be included in the medical decision-making process. This attention to autonomy was, to a great degree, a reaction to medicine's commitment to physician beneficence, which unfortunately evolved from acting in the patient's best interest to paternalistically intervening without knowledge and consideration of the patient's values, goals, and wishes.

Originally, autonomy was defined as the freedom to choose among available options and act upon the choices made.[2] *Autonomy* was treated as synonymous with *self-determination* by some authors[3] and by the social work profession. In the acute care model, the physician-patient relationship is understood to be a time-limited contractual relationship entered into by rational, self-interested individuals; the contract outlines the rights and responsibilities of each party. Autonomy, as a condition in the contract, ensures that the patient is made an active participant in the medical decision-making process, is given the necessary information to make crucial medical decisions, and is not coerced into making decisions based more on the physician's values than his or her own. There is concern that this contractual model of the professional-patient relationship could limit the responsibilities of the professional if he or she accepts as morally obligatory only those responsibilities mutually agreed upon. "It elevates isolation and separation as the necessary starting point of human commitment"[4] with the extreme possibility that professional responsibility would end when patient autonomy was proclaimed.

The contractual model, it is argued, may be functional in the acute care setting, where patients need to protect themselves from professionals who have superior knowledge, power, and authority and whose values and goals may differ from those of the patients. However, since professionals caring for the elderly and chronically ill must address social and not just medical issues, and since they are likely to be confronted with numerous autonomous individuals and community agencies, the call is for an "accommodating" or "negotiating" autonomy that can mediate competing interests and varied responsibilities.[5] The concern seems to be that an empowering and rights-enhancing patient-centered ethic of autonomy blocks the possibility of allowing patients to think and act as communal, interdependent people.

Because of these concerns about the emphasis on individualism and its seeming inapplicability to the needs of systems, autonomy has been redefined as a "cluster of notions including self determination, freedom, independence, liberty of choice and action";[6] an "internally problematic concept having several polarities";[7] "a goal toward which people strive, which never really exists";[8] an ideal that must be "reconceptualized in terms that are relevant to the world of long-term care";[9] and the "responsible use of freedom [which is] diminished whenever one ignores, evades, or slights one's responsibilities."[10]

Additionally, there is particular concern that even families have begun framing their moral dilemmas as conflicts between the competing values of caring and autonomy rather than interpreting them as difficulties that arise in family relationships.[11] Since the demand for equal consideration by family members is perceived to be a legitimate one, it has been suggested that it may be morally correct "for a physician to sacrifice the interests of her patient to those of nonpatients"; the patient must realize that, as a member of a family, he or she is "morally required to make decisions on the basis of thinking about what is best for all concerned," not only what is good for him or her. It is no longer considered acceptable to advocate that "the interests of family members should be irrelevant or should take a backseat to the interests of the patient."[12]

THE SOCIAL WORK PERSPECTIVE

The difficulty experienced by professionals in weighing autonomy and beneficence; the difficulty of determining whether or not it is appropriate to persuade, cajole, or act paternalistically when a patient's decision is considered to be unwise or appears to go against previously stated values; the guilt or sadness felt when a patient's choice has been overridden—all of these factors led people to question the validity of autonomy or the possibility that it can be honored. Hence also the modified definitions, the "linguistic contortions,"[13] believed necessary to maintain the viability of the concept.

Self-determination—determination of oneself by oneself—is rejected by some as a legitimate goal, because they cannot make sense of the notion that they should be asked to accept socially unacceptable decisions or behaviors. But this is precisely why autonomy is so perplexing, why it is given so much attention. There is no problem accepting the *acceptable,* but reminders are necessary regarding the protection, if not the acceptance, of that which deviates from social norms.

It is feared that to accept self-determination in its literal meaning would jeopardize its status as a professional value. If a client chooses to behave illegally or immorally, the professional must either allow the unacceptable act or prevent it. It is possible for the professional to mistakenly believe that adherence to self-determination as an important value requires him or her to act complicitly—to support or at least refrain from preventing the illegal or immoral behavior.

Another example of linguistic contortion is Bart Collopy's six polarities of autonomy: decisional versus executional autonomy, direct versus delegated autonomy, competent versus incapacitated autonomy, authentic versus inauthentic autonomy, immediate versus long-range autonomy, and negative versus positive autonomy.[14] These are not, however, all sets of contrary qualities: A person can exercise decisional and executional autonomy, address immediate and long-range issues, and have his or her negative right and positive right to freedom recognized. The cases Collopy uses to illustrate the polarities merely show that at times decisional autonomy can be present when executional autonomy is not, that care should be taken not to give automatic priority to either immediate or long-range considerations, and that honoring negative freedom without attempting to enhance that freedom through positive intervention can result in neglect.

The points Collopy makes are important, but the language used in making them is unfortunate: Autonomy is not authentic; authenticity is a characteristic of an autonomous choice or of an autonomous person. Autonomy is not competent; a certain type of competence is required for autonomous decision making. Autonomy is not immediate or long range; consequences are immediate or long range. Collopy mistakes criteria for determining whether or not a person can or should be allowed to exercise his or her right as modifiers of the right. Aspects *external* to the right or value or principle of autonomy are presented as if they were *internal* to it.

It is important, therefore, that self-determination or autonomy be understood and accepted as a qualified particular right that certain persons possess under certain conditions. It is a particular, not a universal, right because it is possessed by a limited class of persons (e.g., decisionally incapacitated persons are excluded). It is a qualified, not an absolute, right because it may justifiably be suspended in certain situations (e.g., when the interests of others are adversely affected to an unacceptable degree). Qualified particular rights are the most troublesome for professionals because the decision regarding who will qualify for the right and the decision as to whether or not the right will be suspended are more often than not judgment calls.[15] But once health care professionals accept the fact that they are dealing with a qualified particular right, the problems that are inevitably experienced with autonomy can be put in the proper perspective. They are *accompanying*, not inherent, problems. They are problems that exist because of the complexity of human relationships, not because of the complexity of the concept.

If professional ethics is viewed in the context of the individual professional and his or her clients (as has been suggested of medicine in the ethics literature), the social context of autonomous choice can easily be overlooked. The social worker, however, treats the client-in-situation. This means that the client is never viewed as an isolated individual; whatever problem the client brings to the professional for resolution exists in his or her relationships with family members, the health care team, the immediate community, and society as a whole. The treatment (be it psychotherapy, a discharge plan from the hospital, or long-term home care) involves working with the client as a member of various social systems all of whom have rights.

> A live and struggling client is vividly before us, and we feel keenly our responsibility to his concerns and to his self-determination. But the fact that he is our client does not place him in a preferred ethical realm, with a higher order of claim . . . the thoughtful worker is alert to the others who will be affected by whatever the immediate business may be. . . . It is a test of professional maturity for a social worker to show his genuine concern for a client while making clear that he does not identify with the client's partisanship.[16]

In this context, the responsibility of the professional does not end when the patient declares his or her autonomy in the acute or long-term setting, for autonomy or self-determination is not a condition of contract. It is, rather, part of the human condition. It is too important to be misunderstood. Having open discussions about the difficulties professionals have with autonomy is not a mistake; leaving people with the impression that social factors somehow dilute autonomy is. Care must be taken to ensure that self-determination is not "defined out of existence."[17]

A NEW BIOETHICS

The call for a new bioethics is in part a call for a better understanding of the human and social significance of chronic illness. In the acute care model, the physician attempts to protect the patient's interests by keeping the patient free from sickness and disease; the physician's intervention is predominantly focused on the patient's illness. In chronic care, the physician helps the patient to integrate the illness and its effects into his or her life. One of the physician's

roles is to protect the integrity of self while changes take place.

> The primary obligation of chronic care medicine, then, is not to protect the person's interests in the sense of keeping them from being affected by illness . . . but rather to assist the person in keeping the transformative power of illness under control, to integrate new subjective interests (wants) and new objective interests (needs) into a coherent and satisfying life.[18]

Achieving a satisfying life is dependent to a great degree upon maintaining good relationships with family members, professional caregivers, and society. The family provides, at the very least, love and emotional support; the professional caregivers provide available community resources; and society provides recognition and acceptance of the needs of the chronically ill and the elderly through social policy and funding.

In reality, the ability of a disabled or elderly individual to continue to live according to his or her needs and values is often challenged by the needs and values of others. In the first section of this chapter, the weighing of competing choices was addressed. In this section, the issue is the provision of additional options the lack of which diminishes the quality of the individual's life. Jennings states that it is "not whether public and community services should be provided to supplement family care, but what goals these family assistance programs should serve and what moral aspects of family relationships we want to preserve and strengthen as we publicly assist families with their caregiving responsibilities."[19]

Some believe that "for children living in a modern system of social welfare, the consequences of failing in one's filial duties are usually less dramatic, and the strength of the duties is correspondingly weaker."[20] This is not the case. Since in home care a higher priority is still placed on the "medical" issues than on the social issues, the gap between need and available community-funded resources (home health aides, homemaking services) is great.

Therefore, two concerns for professionals are (1) the making of decisions regarding the fair distribution of health care resources while at the same time acting as a patient advocate, and (2) the necessity of intervening in family systems. How these concerns are addressed will depend upon whether the physician views the patient as an isolated individual to whom allegiance is owed or as a member of numerous social systems, each of which has legitimate demands.

A more appropriate way of phrasing this is that how these issues are addressed will depend upon the physician's view of him- or herself in relationship to his or her patients. As in the discussion of autonomy, the suggestion is that, rather than a new bioethics, what is needed is an accurate understanding of professional responsibility.

The Moral Universe of Professions

Professions are occupations that have been granted a special status in and by society. They address societal needs whose importance is recognized not only by those individuals who are experiencing those needs but by society as a whole. The suggestion has been made that no matter what the societal job assignment (the specific need addressed), each profession focuses only on a limited aspect of the total well-being of its clients.[21] The job assignment or aspect of well-being determines one of the profession's central values. (For example, medicine's job assignment is health; a central or core value, the job assignment value it shares with society, is also health.) And because they are a part of the social arrangement that provides individuals with goods, services, and opportunities necessary to lead full and productive lives, professions and their members are moral instrumentalities of society.[22]

Professional morality is a type of role morality that narrows the "moral universe"[23] of each profession, allowing its members to give greater or lesser weight to some values than is usually given in private morality. "The complexity of the moral world is thereby reduced and made manageable . . . by parcelling out responses to given situations in such a way that no profession is sensitive to *all* situations or has available to it a full range of responses."[24]

For example, when treating a patient, the physician in the acute care model (if this model is understood correctly) focuses primarily, if not exclusively, on illness. The physician might recognize that a patient has an illness-related social issue and that another profession (social work) with another societal job assignment should be consulted to address that issue, but the physician's involvement is still with "health" or "illness." The physician's moral universe includes only those factors necessary for the physician and the patient to make medical decisions.

The Social Work Perspective

The societal job assignment of social work is the mediation of the person's need to be a full and productive member of the relevant social systems and the ability of those systems to provide the means for integrating its members and enriching their social contribution. This is done in settings (hospitals, schools, mental health agencies, the community) that are designed to harmonize individual needs and social resources. One of social work's responsibilities is to develop and strengthen the social welfare system (which includes health care).

Therefore the social worker who receives a referral from a physician will address not only the specific problem for which the consult was called but will recommend that all needs discussed during the psychosocial assessment process be addressed either by that social worker or by professionals in other agencies. The social worker's mediating function results in a focus on the client's *general* well-being (e.g., the client's physical and mental health, the client's finances, possible legal issues and family problems, etc.).

As a consequence, the social worker's moral universe is not a narrow one. Rather, the social worker's professional relationship draws him or her into the life of the client as a person with conflicting roles, complex obligations, and value dilemmas.[25]

The social worker must assist clients in acknowledging their responsibilities to individuals and social systems that exist outside of the professional-client relationship. The client's responsibilities to others are grounded in his or her membership as a moral agent in various social systems; the professional's responsibilities are grounded in his or her profession's relationship to society and its individual members through its function or job assignment and its core values.

Professional commitments must not be perceived as being

> made only to a select few clients, to the professionals' contract partners. They can be met only by professions and professionals who understand that their commitment as professionals is also a commitment to the total society and who will therefore involve themselves actively . . . even aggressively in such matters as . . . the just distribution of medical . . . services, and access to health . . . care on the basis of need.[26]

If, as Jennings suggests, the physician is to become involved in helping patients integrate new wants and needs into a coherent and satisfying life, the physician's moral universe must expand to include not just issues relating to discrete decisions regarding illness but those that relate to the patient as whole person. Inherent in the suggestion that decisions must be made regarding the extent of family assistance programs and the moral aspects of family relationships is the suggestion that individuals will make those decisions. The physician, in choosing to be among those individuals, must recognize and accept the necessity of intervening in family and societal systems.

The question is not *whether* professionals, including physicians, have the moral authority to intervene in the family system and the family's style of caregiving but *how* they should exercise that moral authority. The question is not whether professionals, including physicians, should detach the ethical concerns about the distribution of resources from the ethics of individual patient care but how they should weigh two competing but legitimate responsibilities. Here again it is possible to mistakenly assume that because carrying out the responsibilities is difficult, the responsibilities do not really exist.

CONCLUSION

An examination of the reasons given for believing that new models of autonomy and bioethics need to be developed suggests that instead health care professionals need a better understanding of their responsibilities to clients in the context of social roles and social systems. Certain dilemmas that appear to be new are in fact just easier to avoid in acute care than in home care. It is, for example, much easier to focus on the decisions and social needs of a single individual than it is to weigh the needs of the family, the community, and the general society.

It is also much easier to demand that decisions be made by someone other than the practitioner (e.g., let society decide whether or not homemaking services should be provided for individuals over the age of 80, or let another profession be solely responsible for family issues). This allows the professional to, with clear conscience, act according to specific policies without having to give any thought to the rules of common morality upon which the policies are grounded. In some cases, it also allows the professional *not* to act because of supposed boundaries between professions erected on the misperceived notion that there exist discrete sets of professional responsibilities. A narrow moral universe can be very attractive because it limits the range of necessary interventions; it does not, however, serve the best interests of the patients or society.

NOTES

1. B. Collopy et al., The Ethics of Home Care: Autonomy and Accommodation, *Hastings Center Report* 20, no. 2, suppl. (1990); B. Jennings et al., Ethical Challenges of Chronic Illness, *Hastings Center Report* 18, no. 1, suppl. (1991).

2. S. Gadow, Medicine, Ethics, and the Elderly, *Gerontologist* 20 (1980):683.

3. T.L. Beauchamp and L.B. McCullough, *Medical Ethics: The Moral Responsibilities of Physicians* (Englewood Cliffs, N.J.: Prentice-Hall, 1984), 42.

4. D. Callahan, Autonomy: A Moral Good, Nor a Moral Obsession, *Hastings Center Report* 14, no. 5 (1984):41.

5. Collopy et al., The Ethics of Home Care; H.R. Moody, From Informed Consent to Negotiated Consent, *Gerontologist* 28, suppl. (1988):65–70.

6. B.J. Collopy, Autonomy in Long Term Care: Some Crucial Distinctions, *Gerontologist* 28, suppl. (1988):10.

7. Ibid., 11.

8. E. Cassell, Life as a Work of Art, *Hastings Center Report* 14, no. 5 (1984):36.

9. Moody, From Informed Consent to Negotiated Consent, 64.

10. J. Hardwig, What about the Family? *Hastings Center Report* 20, no. 2 (1990):8.

11. P.G. Clark, Ethical Dimensions of Quality of Life in Aging: Autonomy vs. Collectivism in the United States and Canada, *Gerontologist* 31 (1991):633.

12. Hardwig, What about the Family? 5, 6.

13. F.E. McDermott, Against the Persuasive Definition of Client Self Determination, in *Self Determination in Social Work*, edited by F.E. McDermott (London: Routledge and Kegan Paul, 1975), 131.

14. Collopy, Autonomy in Long Term Care.

15. C.L. Clark and S. Asquith, *Social Work and Social Philosophy: A Guide for Practice* (London: Routledge and Kegan Paul, 1985).

16. S. Bernstein, Conflict, Self-Determination, and Social Work, in *Values in Social Work: A Re-examination,* Monograph 9 (New York: National Association of Social Workers, 1967), 73.

17. McDermott, Against the Persuasive Definition of Client Self Determination, 136.

18. Jennings et al., Ethical Challenges of Chronic Illness, 11.

19. Ibid., 14.

20. S. Selig, et al., Ethical Dimensions of Intergenerational Reciprocity: Implications for Practice, *Gerontologist* 31 (1991):626.

21. D. Ozar, "Professions and Their Ethics: The Foundations of Professional Obligation" (Unpublished manuscript).

22. P.F. Camenisch, *Grounding Professional Ethics in a Pluralistic Society* (New York: Haven Publications, 1983), 54.

23. G.J. Postema, Moral Responsibility in Professional Ethics, in *Profits and Professions: Essays in Business and Professional Ethics,* edited by W.L. Robison et al. (Clifton, N.J.: Humana Press, 1983), 39.

24. D. Luban, *Lawyers and Justice: An Ethical Study* (Princeton, N.J.: Princeton University Press, 1988), 127.

25. R.T. Constable, Relations and Membership: Foundations for Ethical Thinking in Social Work, *Social Thought* 15, no. 3–4 (1989): 63.

26. P.F. Camenisch, On Being a Professional, Morally Speaking, in *Professional Ideals,* edited by A. Flores. (Belmont, Calif.: Wadsworth, 1984), 25.

Chapter 17

Long-Term Care for Older People: Moral and Political Challenges of Access

Robert H. Binstock

As the twentieth century approaches its end, the goal of improving access to humane and appropriate long-term care services is becoming widely shared in the United States. Opinion polls indicate that a substantial majority of Americans in all adult age groups fear the financial, familial, psychological, and social consequences of dependence on long-term care and favor the general principle of expanding government insurance for long-term care as the principal means of expanding access to it.[1] A number of bills to provide public long-term care insurance have been introduced in Congress in the past few years, with estimated annual price tags ranging up to $50 billion, and President Clinton's plan for health care reform contains a long-term care initiative.

Why has long-term care begun to emerge from the shadows cast by the more dramatic treatments and cures offered by acute care medicine?

One major element is the enormous growth of our older population (those aged 65 and over), which doubled from 16 million in 1960 to 32 million in 1990 and is expected to more than double again by the middle of the next century.[2] Persons in this age category presently constitute 12 percent of our population and are expected to constitute 20 percent as early as the year 2030.

Also important in the evolution of demands for reforming long-term care has been a growing constituency of adult children of elderly patients who perceive the importance of long-term care services because of their direct involvement in the provision of care for their parents, who are typically afflicted by any one or more of a wide variety of disabilities and diseases. Over 13 million adults in the United States who have disabled elderly parents or spouses are potential providers of long-term care, financial assistance, and emotional support; 4.2 million of them provide direct care in the home setting.[3]

Disabled children and younger disabled adults and their families are additional constituencies likely to support greater access to long-term care. Leaders of the American Coalition of Citizens with Disabilities, representing 8 million disabled persons, have expressed the hope that it might form a powerful political alliance with organizations representing 32 million older people to pursue this issue of mutual concern.[4]

Despite the underlying needs and expectations of these constituencies, enactment of a government program to substantially expand access to long-term care in the immediate future is problematic because of the considerable funds that would be required. The need to "reduce the federal deficit" is a rhetorical mainstay of contemporary politics. Spiraling health care costs are widely considered to be one of the major problems of our society.

Among those who espouse the goal of increased public funding for long-term care, there is substantial disagreement regarding the most appropriate and effective strategies to secure the necessary money. One point of view, advocated by biomedical ethicist Daniel Callahan, among others, is that adequate public financing can be obtained by setting limits to acute care for older persons. He envisions an ample expansion of access to long-term care produced from a direct reallocation of funds saved by categorically denying life-extending care to persons in their late 70s or older.[5] Putting aside the ethical and moral issues raised by this proposal, such a perspective is not validated by economic or political analysis. The funds that could be saved through implementation of Callahan's rationing proposal would yield only about 5 percent of what would be needed to provide adequate access to long-term care, and the complex realities of the politics of public resource allocation would work against any such direct transfer from one category of health care expenditure to another.[6] Indeed, framing policy issues from this perspective may retard rather than accelerate a substantial expansion of access to long-term care because a policy of old age–based rationing would tend to debase the moral value of frail and disabled elderly people.

Improved access to long-term care is more likely to be realized through a direct and explicit national policy that specifies new tax revenues to expand substantially the public resources available for that purpose. But such a policy raises some fundamental moral and political issues regarding the just use of government power. This chapter delineates those issues and suggests the contexts in which they will need to be faced if an enduring and effective policy of increased access to long-term care is to be enacted.

THE NEED FOR LONG-TERM CARE

An individual's need for long-term care is indicated by functional status rather than by specific illness or disability. A person with arthritis, for example, may or may not be dependent upon supportive care from others.

A fundamental and widely accepted measure of functional status and need for long-term supportive care is a person's ability to perform five specific activities of daily living (ADLs) without help from someone else. These ADLs are bathing, transferring from a bed or a chair, dressing, toileting, and eating.

At present, about 5.1 million Americans aged 65 and over need assistance with at least one ADL. Some 1.5 million of them are in nursing homes.[7] The remaining 3.6 million are in their own homes or some other type of residential facility, such as a congregate living community, an adult foster home, or a board and care facility.[8]

A supplementary measure of functional status is limitations in instrumental activities of daily living (IADLs), such as being able to prepare meals, manage money, use the telephone, or do light housework. Some 4.9 million older people who live outside nursing homes are unable to perform at least one IADL; about 5.5 million have at least one ADL or IADL limitation.[9]

A large number of services are useful for long-term care patients, whether they are in nursing homes or home care settings. The U.S. Office of Technology Assessment has identified 40 different types, ranging from traditionally defined health care services through homemaking, shopping, transportation, meal, and chore services to education, counseling support groups, and respite for family caregivers.[10]

Most older persons and their families have a distinct preference for receiving such services as "home care" rather than as care in a nursing home.[11] About 3 million elderly people were provided home care in 1990.[12] Yet about 40 percent of those who are not in nursing homes and experience limitations in ADLs and/or IADLs do not receive all of the help they need.[13]

It is estimated that some 80–85 percent of the home care received by older persons are provided on an informal, unpaid basis by their spouses, siblings, and adult children and by broader kin networks.[14] About 74 percent of dependent community-based older persons receive all their care from family members or other unpaid sources; about 21 percent receive both formal and informal services; and only about 5 percent use just formal, paid services.[15]

Formal services provided by home health agencies will play an increasingly larger role in the years ahead. The changing demographics of family structure, as well as steadily increasing labor force participation by middle-aged women (who have done a major share of the informal caregiving in their roles as daughters and daughters-in-law), suggest that the percentage of informal home care will decline and that the amount of formal services will grow.[16] There has already been a substantial increase in formal services in recent years. Between the early 1970s and 1986, the number of Medicare-certified home health care agencies tripled, from 2,000 to 6,000.[17]

The overall need for long-term care for older people is likely to grow dramatically in the future because of the combined effects of demographic population aging and age-specific morbidity rates. The number of Americans reaching older old-age categories is increasing rapidly, and the prevalence of disabling diseases and conditions rises markedly among persons in their mid-70s and older.

In 1990, there were 3.3 million persons aged 85 and older, constituting 10 percent of the population aged 65 and older; in the year 2000, there will be 4.6 million (13 percent of the older population); and by 2040 there will be 12.3 million (18 percent).[18] Similarly, there were 13.2 million persons aged 75 and older in 1990, comprising 42 percent of the older population; in 2000, there will be 16.6 million (48 percent); and by 2040 there will be 37 million (55 percent).[19]

The potential implications of this aging of the older population for long-term care can be appreciated by considering the substantial differences among different old age groups with respect to their use of care and their degree of functional disability. About 1 percent of Americans aged 65–74 years are in nursing homes; this compares with 6 percent of persons 75–84 years of age and 22 percent of persons aged 85 and older.[20] The greater number of persons who will be in the older old-age categories is a major factor in projections that the current nursing home population of 1.5 million persons will increase to 2.1 million by the year 2000 and will reach 2.6 million in 2020.[21]

The same pattern holds true for persons outside nursing homes. The percentage of older persons residing in the community who need help with ADLs increases dramatically by five-year age intervals. The proportion needing help rises from 7.7 percent in the 65- to 69-year-old category to 26.6 percent in the aged 85 and over group, with the largest proportional increase occurring between the 70- to 74-year-old category and the 75- to 79-year old category.[22]

The combined effects of high morbidity rates at older ages and the growing numbers and proportions of older people aged in their late 70s and 80s have generated considerable anxiety about the fiscal implications of an aging population. One projection suggests, for example, that Medicare costs for persons aged 85 and older may increase sixfold by the year 2040 (estimated in constant, inflation-adjusted dollars).[23]

ISSUES OF ACCESS

Whether a long-term care patient is in a nursing home, living at home, or in another type of residential setting, services in an ideal system would be amply available, of high quality, provided by well-trained personnel, easily located and arranged for, and well funded through public and private resources. The present system, however, is far from ideal.

The supply of services is insufficient; service providers lack education and training, and the quality of many services is poor.[24] Moreover, the system is so fragmented that even when high-quality services are sufficiently available, many patients and families do not know about them and require help in defining their service needs and in arranging for services to be provided.[25]

Underlying each of these problems, in turn, is the issue of financing. As is the case with most aspects of the U.S. health care delivery system, the characteristics of long-term care services are substantially shaped by the nature and extent of policies for funding them.[26]

More than 80 federal programs and a plethora of state and local public and private agencies are sources of funding for long-term care services.[27] But each source regulates the availability of funds with rules as to eligibility and breadth of service coverage and changes its rules frequently, and patients are often ruled ineligible for funding through Medicare, Medicaid, and other programs.[28] Thus, despite the many sources of funding, specific patients and caregivers may find themselves ineligible for financial help and unable to pay out of pocket for needed services. In one study, about 75 percent of the informal caregivers for dementia patients reported that they did not use formal services because they were unable to pay for them.[29]

The Medicare health insurance program does not reimburse patients for long-term care, either in nursing homes or at home. Private long-term care insurance, which is in an early stage of product development, is very expensive for the majority of persons, and its benefits are limited in scope and duration. Only 3 percent of older persons have any private long-term care insurance, and only about 1 percent of nursing home costs are paid for by private insurance.[30] Even when the product matures, it is unlikely to be a panacea. A Brookings Institution study suggested that by the year 2018, when all the "bugs" are worked out, some 25–45 percent of elderly people would be able to afford private long-term care insurance premiums and that private insurance benefit payments would only account for 7–12 percent of all nursing home benefits.[31]

Paying the costs of long-term care can be a catastrophic financial experience for patients and their families. The annual cost of a year's care in a nursing home averages $30,000 and ranges as high as $80,000. Equivalent care provided in a home setting is just as expensive when the informal services provided by family and friends are included as expenses. Although nursing homes originally developed as an alternative to home care, their financial costs have redirected attention during the past two decades to home care as a possible cheaper alternative. But numerous demonstrations and studies have concluded that home care is not cheaper for patients who would otherwise be appropriately placed in a nursing home.[32]

Patients and their families paid over $29.5 billion out of pocket for long-term care services in 1992. The total national expenditure for long-term care was an estimated $85 billion. Expenditures on nursing homes totaled $65 billion. Home health care services provided by agencies participating in Medicare and Medicaid accounted for expenditures of $8.5 billion. Payments for related non-health-home-care services to other home care service providers accounted for an estimated $7.5 billion in additional spending.[33] Out-of-pocket payments accounted for 44 percent of nursing home expenditures and 11 percent of home care expenditures.[34]

Medicaid, the federal-state insurance program available to persons of all ages who qualify as economically poor, does pay for long-term care in nursing homes (accounting for nearly 50 percent of total national nursing home expenditures). But Medicaid does not pay for the full range of home care services that will be needed in most cases. Most state Medicaid programs provide reimbursement only for the most "medicalized" services that are necessary to maintain a long-term care patient in a home environment; rarely reimbursed are essential supports such as chore services, assistance with food shopping and meal preparation, transportation, companionship, periodic monitoring, and respite programs for family and other unpaid caregivers.

Medicaid does include a special waiver program authorized by the federal government in 1981 that allows states to offer a wider range of nonmedical home care services if limited to those patients who otherwise would require Medicaid-financed institutional care. Although 48 states participate, relatively few aged and disabled patients are served. In 1991, about one-third of state funds spent on home care through this waiver program (about $550 million) were for dependent elderly people and younger disabled adults; nearly two-thirds was spent on persons with mental retardation or related conditions.[35] The National Governors Association estimated that only 59,000 elderly persons were served by the waiver program in 1987.

FORCES FOR IMPROVING ACCESS

Substantial public recognition of a need to improve access to long-term care is relatively recent. The major initial impetus for this increased awareness has been successful advocacy efforts on behalf of older people, particularly the efforts undertaken by a political coalition concerned about Alzheimer's disease (AD) that began to form in the mid 1970s.[36] Advocates for victims of Alzheimer's formally coalesced in 1988 with the broader constituency concerned about chronically ill and disabled older persons. The Alzheimer's Association, the American Association for Retired Persons (AARP), and the Families U.S.A. Foundation (a small organization originally established to improve the plight of poor older people) allied during the presidential campaign to undertake a lobbying effort organized under the name Long-Term Care '88.[37]

The next year an explicit link was forged between advocates for the disabled and the elderly when Representative Claude Pepper introduced a bill to provide comprehensive long-term home care insurance coverage for disabled persons of any age who are dependent in at least two ADLs.[38] Although this bill was not voted on by Congress, it was a milestone in that it was the first major legislative response to the fact that the number of functionally disabled adults aged 18–64 years who live outside institutions is more than twice the total of all comparably disabled persons aged 65 and older.[39]

Since then, several dozen long-term care bills have been introduced in Congress, and President Clinton has also proposed federal action. The lobbying efforts for long-term care that were launched in the 1988 presidential campaign have broadened to encompass the needs of disabled people and have been carried forward by a coalition named the Long-Term Care Campaign. This Washington-based interest group claims to represent nearly 140 national organizations (with more than 60 million members), including religious denominations; organized labor and business groups; nurse, veteran, youth, and women groups; consumer organizations; and racial and ethnic groups, as well as older and disabled persons.[40]

Ironically, just when the principle of expanding government long-term care insurance is gaining public recognition and is favored by many leaders in Congress, the economic costs of doing so appear to be politically prohibitive. Any substantial public initiative in long-term care is expected to cost tens of billions of dollars a year. Major long-term care bills introduced in Congress since the 1989 Pepper bill have ranged from $21 billion to $50 billion in projected expenditures for the first year, depending upon their varied details regarding specific populations eligible for coverage and technical provisions regarding the timing, nature, and extent of insurance coverage.[41]

Because of such cost estimates, most analysts of Congressional health policies and politics do not expect a major long-term care bill to be enacted within the next few years. Moreover, the enactment of the Medicare Catastrophic Coverage Act (MCCA) in 1988 and its repeal in 1989 because of constituent complaints about the new taxes needed to finance it have made some members of Congress particularly wary of undertaking a major expansion of health care benefits that centrally involve older persons.[42] There are some lessons from the rapid demise of the MCCA, however, that can be applied constructively by advocates who seek the enactment of a comprehensive policy to improve access to long-term care.

LESSONS TO BE LEARNED FROM THE "CATASTROPHIC" CATASTROPHE

The MCCA, developed through the initiatives of public officials in the White House, the Congress, and the federal bureaucracy,[43] was the first major expansion of benefits to older persons in 16 years. It provided insurance coverage for economically catastrophic hospital and physician bills, outpatient prescription drugs, and some elements of long-term care. About one-third of these new benefits were to be financed through increased premiums paid by all Medicare Part B enrollees, and two-thirds through a progressive, sharply escalating surtax levied on middle and higher income Medicare enrollees—about 40 percent of program participants.

During the period of nearly two years between the introduction of the bill and its enactment as law, neither Congress nor the aging advocacy groups (such as the 33-million-member AARP) floated "trial balloons" to enable older Americans to understand what sorts of benefits they would receive through the MCCA and who would pay for them. Consequently, when the proposal finally did become law, there was no popular constituency supporting it. But there was distinct opposition to it from those older persons who had to pay the most new taxes and who perceived that they already had private insurance coverage for the benefits provided through the new law.[44] They constituted a small minority, yet they were dispersed throughout every Congressional district. When they protested vociferously against the act, Congress received no evidence of countervailing popular support for the new law (despite the fact that it was endorsed by AARP lobbyists).

What political lessons can be learned from the MCCA catastrophe? How might they be applied by advocates for elderly people and disabled people in a campaign to expand public long-term care insurance through federal legislation?

One lesson may be that, in the contemporary political context, the traditional elitist top-down approach to social legislation, exemplified in the MCCA, needs to be inverted. If a major program of public long-term care insurance is to be enacted and endure, then it will probably require bottom-up political support. The policy will need to be genuinely sought by those at the grass-roots level, with their desires and demands

articulated actively in virtually every Congressional district. A second lesson is that the nature of what is demanded (its details and consequences) should be fairly well worked out and comprehended at the grass-roots level so that constituents, as well as Congress and federal bureaucrats, understand the legislation's implications.

APPLYING THE LESSONS TO LONG-TERM CARE POLITICS

Although favorable sentiment has crystallized around the general principle of public long-term care insurance, the principle masks many basic value issues that have just begun to surface in public discussion. Widespread debate on these issues will be required for a substantial proportion of Americans to understand and support the implications of any proposed law. Otherwise, even if the proposed law is enacted, it could be as quickly repealed as the poorly understood MCCA.

From the perspective of older persons, the need for long-term care is typically seen as a need uniquely their own, and the predominant, though not exclusive, element of interest in additional public insurance has been generated by an economic concern. That concern is the possibility of becoming poor through "spending down," that is, depleting one's assets to pay for long-term care and then becoming dependent on a welfare program, Medicaid, to pay nursing home bills. There is a distinct middle-class fear of using savings and selling a home to finance one's own health care. This anxiety reflects a desire to protect one's estate as well as the psychological intertwining of personal self-esteem with one's material worth and independence.

The political weight of this type of concern, however, is not substantial in today's public policy climate. The political era in which categorical old age entitlement programs were created and sustained with relative ease appears to have ended in the late 1970s. The aged have become scapegoats for a variety of America's problems, and many domestic policy concerns have been framed as issues of intergenerational equity.[45]

If expanded public long-term care insurance is to be enacted as an old age entitlement, to serve older persons as a buffer against spending down, there are some fundamental moral and political issues that the American public will need to confront and resolve. These issues include the following: Assuming that we can improve laws for protecting spouses of long-term care patients from impoverishment, why shouldn't older people spend their assets and income on their health care? Why should government foot the bill? Why should it be government's responsibility to preserve estates? So they can be inherited? Should government take a more active role than at present in preserving economic status inequalities from generation to generation? On what basis should some persons be taxed to preserve the inheritances of others? Should the taxing power of government be used to preserve the psychological sense of self-esteem that for so many persons is bound up in their lifetime accumulation of assets—their material worth?

Widespread public debate on such issues may very well fail to resolve them in a fashion that supports a major initiative in long-term care to protect older persons from paying for their care. Indeed, research findings are even beginning to show that the incidence and prevalence of the spenddown phenomenon may be grossly exaggerated by advocates for long-term care.[46] Moreover, it appears that many nursing home patients who are paid for by Medicaid become eligible for that program by sheltering and transferring their financial assets rather than by spending down until they are poor.[47] Many nursing home patients have apparently been adept at preserving their estates—and perhaps passing them on as legacies—while having government pay for their long-term care through Medicaid, a program intended for the poor.

In contrast to older persons, younger disabled persons do not perceive long-term care insurance as basically an issue of whether the government or the individual patient and/or family pays

for the care. At least as important to them is the issue of basic access to services, technologies, and environments that will make it feasible to carry forward an active life. They argue that they should have assistance to do much of what they would be able to do if they were not disabled.

The Americans with Disabilities Act of 1990, achieved through vigorous advocacy efforts, will help to eliminate discriminatory as well as physical barriers to the participation of people with disabilities in employment, public services, public accommodations and transportation, and telecommunications. But it will not provide the elements of long-term care desired by disabled younger adults, such as paid assistance in the home and for getting in and out of the home, peer counseling, semi-independent modes of transportation, and client control or management of services.

Although the disabled have advocated for long-term care services, they have rejected a "medical model" that emphasizes long-term care as an essential component of health services. This is understandable given their strong desire for autonomy, independence, and as much "normalization" of daily life as possible. By the same token, disabled people have traditionally eschewed symbolic and political identification with elderly people because of traditional stereotypes of older people as frail, chronically ill, declining, and "marginal" to society.

The efforts of disabled people to advocate on their terms for government long-term care initiatives, however, have made little progress. Rather, progress in getting long-term care insurance on the national policy agenda—for persons of all ages—has been due largely to advocates for the elderly and to broader concerns about the projected health care needs generated by an increasingly larger and older population of elderly people.

LONG-TERM CARE AND UNIVERSAL HEALTH INSURANCE

The most promising strategy for elderly people and disabled people to further their mutual interests in long-term care may lie in a coalition for grass-roots advocacy that focuses on such care as an essential part of a full continuum of covered services that constitute an adequate national health insurance program. The Pepper Commission laid the foundation for this approach in 1990 by proposing a $43-billion package of benefits for the long-term care of all disabled persons as an integral component of its sweeping proposals for reforming American health care.[48]

To be sure, a commitment to this perspective would require advocates for the disabled to tone down their traditional rejection of the medical model. And advocates for the elderly would need to moderate their emphasis on concerns about spending down assets. But in the climate of fiscal austerity and social policy retrenchment that has characterized American domestic policy for more than a decade, those traditional advocacy approaches for seeking costly public initiatives have little political appeal.

Even though health care cost containment seems to have become an end in itself, new legislation that would make health care universally available would likely receive widespread support. A grass-roots campaign focused on obtaining adequate health care for all, with extensive discussion of the issues, might help most Americans understand that long-term care, traditionally overshadowed by the drama of high-tech and quick-fix acute care, is an important part of our contemporary health care scene (it presently accounts for about 10 percent of annual health care expenditures).[49]

In a campaign for national health insurance, disabled people and elderly people might be joined not only by advocates for other groups interested in access to affordable long-term care, such as victims of AIDs, but also by other broad constituencies, and by the elements of organized labor, big business, the health insurance industry, and health care professionals that have already declared their general support for the principle of national health insurance or one or another form of it.

In addition, public discussion of the fundamental value issues that underlie proposals for universal health insurance may lead us to broader ethical and moral perspectives. Perhaps we will see that there are no inherent reasons for making distinctions between age groups, for isolating and ignoring the disabled, for separating the relatively poor from the relatively wealthy, or for treating long-term care as any less important than acute care.

Political philosopher Michael Walzer has observed that notions of justice throughout history have varied not only among cultures and political systems but also among distinct spheres of activities and relationships within any given culture or political system.[50] Nothing requires us to devise or accept separate spheres of justice within health care. Widespread and thoughtful consideration of the fundamental issues that underlie long-term care reform may well lead us, finally, to delineate the health care arena as a sphere of justice within which no distinctions are made among Americans on the basis of their demographic, economic, and social characteristics or their limitations in activities of daily living.

NOTES

1. S. McConnell, Who Cares about Long-Term Care? *Generations* 14, no. 2 (1990):15–18.

2. C. Taeuber, Diversity: The Dramatic Reality, in *Diversity in Aging: Challenges Facing Planners and Policymakers in the 1990s,* edited by S. Bass et al. (Glenview, Ill.: Scott, Foresman, 1990), 3.

3. R. Stone and P. Kemper, Spouses and Children of Disabled Elders: How Large a Constituency for Long-Term Care Reform? *Milbank Quarterly* 67 (1989):485–506.

4. P. Rubenfeld, Ageism and Disabilityism: Double Jeopardy, in *Aging and Rehabilitation: Advances in the State of the Art,* edited by S.J. Brody and G.E. Ruff (New York: Springer, 1986), 323–328.

5. D. Callahan, Dementia and Appropriate Care: Allocating Scarce Resources, *Dementia and Aging: Ethics, Values, and Policy Choices,* edited by R.H. Binstock et al. (Baltimore: Johns Hopkins University Press, 1992), 141–152.

6. See R.H. Binstock and S.G. Post, eds., *Too Old for Health Care?: Controversies in Medicine, Law, Economics, and Ethics* (Baltimore: Johns Hopkins University Press, 1991).

7. Senate Special Committee on Aging, *Developments in Aging: 1991,* vol. 1 (Washington, D.C.: U.S. Government Printing Office, 1992), 204.

8. J. Leon and T. Lair, *Functional Status of the Noninstitutionalized Elderly: Estimates of ADL and IADL Difficulties,* DHHS Pub. No. (PHS) 90-3462, National Medical Expenditure Survey Research Findings no. 4 (Rockville, Md: Public Health Service, Agency for Health Care Policy and Research, 1990).

9. Ibid.

10. U.S. Congress, Office of Technology Assessment, *Confused Minds, Burdened Families: Finding Help for People with Alzheimer's and Other Dementias* (Washington, D.C.: U.S. Government Printing Office, 1990), 16.

11. Commonwealth Fund, *Proceedings of the Commonwealth Fund Commission on Elderly People Living Alone: Long-Term Care Workshop,* Background Paper Series no. 11 (Baltimore: Commonwealth Fund, 1988).

12. M. Haug, Foreword, in *Home Care for Older People: Health and Supportive Services,* edited by M.G. Ory and A.P. Duncker (Newbury Park, Calif: Sage, 1992), vii–viii.

13. R. Stone et al., Caregivers of the Frail Elderly: A National Profile, *Gerontologist* 27 (1987):616–626.

14. Senate Special Committee on Aging, *Aging America: Trends and Projections* (Washington, D.C.: U.S. Government Printing Office, 1989).

15. K. Liu et al., Home Care Expenses for the Disabled Elderly, *Health Care Financing Review* 7, no. 2 (1985):52.

16. E.M. Brody, *Women in the Middle: Their Parent Care Years* (New York: Springer, 1990).

17. P.H. Feldman, *Who Cares for Them? Workers in the Home Care Industry* (Westport, Conn.: Greenwood Press, 1990), 7.

18. Taeuber, Diversity.

19. Ibid.

20. E. Hing, *Use of Nursing Homes by the Elderly: Preliminary Data from the 1985 National Nursing Home Survey,* Advance Data no. 135 (Hyattsville, Md: U.S. Department of Health and Human Services, National Center for Health Statistics, 1987).

21. Senate Special Committee on Aging, *Aging America.*

22. M.J. Gornick et al., Twenty Years of Medicare and Medicaid: Covered Populations, Use of Benefits, and Program Expenditures, *Health Care Financing Review* 22, annual suppl. (1985).

23. E.L. Schneider and J.M. Guralnik, The Aging of America: Impact on Health Care Costs, *JAMA* 263 (1990):2335–2340.

24. U.S. Congress, Office of Technology Assessment, *Losing a Million Minds: Confronting the Tragedy of Alzheimer's Disease and Other Dementias* (Washington, D.C.: U.S. Government Printing Office, 1987).

25. U.S. Congress, Office of Technology Assessment, *Confused Minds, Burdened Families.*

26. R.L. Kane and R.A. Kane, Health Care for Older People: Organizational and Policy Issues, in *Handbook of Aging and the Social Sciences,* 3rd ed., edited by R.H. Binstock and L.K. George (San Diego: Academic Press, 1990), 415–437.

27. U.S. Congress, Library of Congress, Congressional Research Service, *Financing and Delivery of Long-Term Care Services for the Elderly* (Washington, D.C.: U.S. Government Printing Office, 1988).

28. U.S. Congress, Office of Technology Assessment, *Losing a Million Minds.*

29. S.K. Eckert and K. Smyth, *A Case Study of Methods of Locating and Arranging Health and Long-Term Care for Persons with Dementia* (Washington, D.C.: U.S. Congress, Office of Technology Assessment, 1988).

30. J.M. Wiener, Which Way for Long-Term Care Financing? *Generations* 14, no. 2 (1990):4–9.

31. A.M. Rivlin and J.M Wiener, *Caring for the Disabled Elderly: Who Will Pay?* (Washington, D.C.: Brookings Institution, 1988).

32. W.G. Weissert, Strategies for Reducing Home Care Expenditures, *Generations* 14, no. 2 (1990):42–44.

33. This estimate is calculated by assuming that nursing home payments were 80 percent of the national total of long-term care expenditures, as reported by the U.S. General Accounting Office, Long-Term Care for the Elderly: *Issues of Need, Access, and Cost* GAO-HRD-89-4, (Washington, D.C.: U.S. Government Printing Office, 1989).

34. S.T. Sonnefeld et al., Projections of National Health Expenditures through the Year 2000, *Health Care Financing Review* 13, no. 1 (1991):17.

35. N.A. Miller, Medicaid 2176 Home and Community-based Care Waivers: The First Ten Years, *Health Affairs* 11, no. 4 (1992):162–171.

36. P. Fox, From Senility to Alzheimer's Disease: The Rise of the Alzheimer's Disease Movement, *Milbank Quarterly* 67 (1989):58–102.

37. McConnell, Who Cares about Long-Term Care?

38. U.S. House of Representatives, *Long-Term Care Act of 1989,* H.R. 2263, 101st Cong., 1st sess., 1989.

39. Gornick et al., Twenty Years of Medicare and Medicaid.

40. Long Term Care Campaign, Pepper Commission Recommendations Released March 2nd, *Insiders' Update,* January-February 1990, 1.

41. Senate Special Committee on Aging, *Developments in Aging: 1990,* vol. 1 (Washington, D.C.: U.S. Government Printing Office, 1991).

42. G.L. Atkins, The Politics of Financing Long-Term Care, *Generations* 19, no. 2 (1990):19–22.

43. J.K. Iglehart, Medicare's New Benefits: Catastrophic Health Insurance, *New England Journal of Medicine* 320 (1989):329–336.

44. M. Holstein and M. Minkler, The Short Life and Painful Death of the Medicare Catastrophic Coverage Act, in *Critical Perspectives on Aging: The Political and Moral Economy of Growing Old*, edited by M. Minkler and C. Estes (Amityville, N.Y.: Baywood Publishing Co., 1991), 189–208.

45. Binstock and Post, *Too Old for Health Care?*

46. K. Liu et al., Medicaid Spenddown in Nursing Homes, *Gerontologist* 30 (1990):7–15.

47. S.A. Moses, The Fallacy of Impoverishment, *Gerontologist* 30 (1990):21–25.

48. U.S. Bipartisan Commission on Comprehensive Health Care, *A Call for Action: Final Report,* Senate Print #101-114, (Washington, D.C.: U.S. Government Printing Office, 1990).

49. Sonnefeld et al., Projections of National Health Expenditures through the Year 2000.

50. M. Walzer, *Spheres of Justice* (New York: Basic Books, 1983).

Chapter 18

Treating Senility and Dementia: Ethical Challenges and Quality-of-Life Judgments

Stephen G. Post

This chapter focuses on the patient with a progressive dementia, most often of the Alzheimer's type. Although the discussion centers on the elderly, it should be kept in mind that dementia, the loss of mental function from a previous state, can occur in all ages. If Alzheimer's disease is the dementia of the elderly, increasingly AIDS dementia is the dementia of those who are young. Not every issue related to ethics and dementia can be covered here. Instead, I attempt to provide an introduction to some of the concerns that might be considered most pressing.

DIAGNOSTIC DISCLOSURE

Should patients with Alzheimer's disease be told their diagnosis? An article with this question as its title points out that new diagnostic knowledge about Alzheimer's disease is "likely to swing the pendulum even more decisively in favor of truth-telling."[1] Authors Drickamer and Lachs refer to new clinical biologic markers that may increase diagnostic accuracy. So long as clinical diagnosis of Alzheimer's disease is uncertain, some clinicians regard it as ethical to withhold information about diagnosis and prognosis from patients, even those able to comprehend. If diagnosis becomes certain rather than probable, this position will no longer be tenable.

It is remarkable how truth telling in cases of dementia is much rarer than truth telling in cases of cancer and most other disease diagnoses. Some physicians suggest that with cancer they can at least offer some therapeutic hope to the patient, but progressive dementia is currently incurable. Yet the principles of veracity and patient self-determination require in nearly all cases that the truth is told to dementia patients as early as a reasonably certain diagnosis is possible. Patients have a clear legal and ethical right to decide, while still competent, for or against the use of technologies should they become incompetent. They should know the general course of the disease from mild to profound.

Drickamer and Lachs, however, reject this extension of patient autonomy through advance directives because (1) the new self with severe dementia is arguably no longer the old self, and (2) the old self may have overly grim views of progressive dementia that fail to appreciate the unanticipated "contentment" of some patients in the severe stages of decline. Do these authors mean that progressive dementia is ordinarily benign? Contrary to Drickamer and Lachs, in the final analysis the patient does hold the right to make anticipatory choices for the demented self. Respect for autonomy is the moral principle honoring freedom under conditions of competence.

There are some physicians and other health care workers, as well as many family members, who fear that telling the truth will cause distress to the patient, that he or she will feel stigmatized, become depressed even to the point of despair, and become more difficult to manage. So it is suggested by some that the best interests of patients dictates nondisclosure of progressive dementia. However, most health professionals who work closely with demented patients believe that such concerns are unwarranted, that telling the patient the diagnosis only rarely elicits an adverse reaction. Rather, disclosing the diagnosis to the patient allows him or her to participate as far as possible in the development of a plan of action for the future.

There are important reasons to err on the side of disclosing probable diagnosis. Many patients already suspect that they have Alzheimer's disease even if family members want to "protect" them from knowing. There are patients who want to know their diagnosis so that friends and neighbors will understand that they are not being unpleasant or purposefully forgetting names. Foley describes a case in which the patient was relieved to find out his diagnosis and his prognosis; the revelation obviated embarrassment and annoyance at his forgetfulness.[2] Experienced health care professionals have all known situations where the family agonized over whether to tell the patient about a diagnosis, only to have the patient say, "That's what I've thought all along." In a case with which the author is familiar, Murray C. convinced his wife to bring him into the ElderHealth Center after he read an article about Alzheimer's disease in the newspaper. Once diagnosed, he went to his neighbors and old friends to explain that his forgetfulness was beyond his control and that he meant no offense. There is no reason for a conspiracy of silence regarding progressive dementia.

AUTONOMY

Patients are often denied autonomy once the diagnosis of dementia has been made. This approach, less frequent now than in the past, ignores the variability of the clinical state. In the early stages of progressive dementia, or in a mild case, normal exercise of autonomy is possible. Varying degrees of tactful supervision are necessary. When the dementia is more severe, the exercise of autonomy may have to be restricted, but only in the severe and profound stages should it be denied completely. Here advance directives come into play.

When a decision is to be made about a course to be pursued, autonomy may have to be restricted because the person is psychotic or amnesic or because planning ability and judgment are damaged. Such restrictions should be made only after a detailed history has been obtained and the person has been closely observed over a period of time.[3] The capacity to make decisions does not require that all mental functions be working optimally. Patients who have memory disorders or other kinds of disturbed neurological function are not necessarily incapable of understanding ethical import. There may be periods of clarity or of impairment. Even a severely impaired patient may be able to exercise autonomy for certain matters that seem inconsequential to the caregiver but that have acquired great importance for the demented person.

Obviously, all the wishes of the patient with dementia cannot be gratified. The amnesic patient with bad eyesight should not be driving an automobile; the frail, insulin-dependent, diabetic old woman with cardiac failure cannot live alone; the intractably incontinent and unruly patient without a family or friends must have institutional care. Yet even in exceptional cases, patients have the right to have their problems explained in a way they can understand, not just once but as often as necessary.

Advance directives, generally in the form of a living will, are justified as an extension of autonomy. It is too much to expect that people in any numbers will compose advance directives about how they wish to be managed when or if they become demented. Only a small minority of people, generally less than 20 percent, compose advance directives expressing their wishes in regard to dying and death. Yet ideally the patient with dementia should have a living will and a durable power of attorney for health care. In the case of a progressive dementia, arrangements should be made early in the course of the disease, when the patient is still capable of understanding and deciding.

Early after diagnosis is the time to arrive at decisions about cardiopulmonary resuscitation and about levels of treatment to be undertaken when severe illness occurs, when swallowing fails, or when death is imminent. Many patients are incapable of putting together a specific plan, even with help, but patients with moderate dementia are often able to identify people they trust to make later decisions for them. Usually the person chosen will be the next of kin, but there should always be an alternate if for some reason the first nominee becomes unable to act.

QUALITY OF LIFE AND JUST TREATMENT LIMITATIONS

There is much reason to respect the autonomy of the patient who, in knowing his or her diagnosis, is still able to indicate treatment preferences through advance directives relevant to the later stages of dementia when the patient becomes incompetent. While many, if not most, patients will not request lifesaving treatment, there are some who will. This raises the complicated question of how much health care a just society owes those who become severely demented. For patients in the advanced stages of progressive and eventually fatal dementia, the use of life-prolonging medical technologies for reasons other than palliation remains a matter of medical, moral, and societal debate.

The obvious moral basis for treatment limitation is quality of life. But there are valid cautions about appeals to quality of life, because a reliable qualitative measure of a patient's experi-ence is impossible and because the idea of quality of life can be conveniently misused to rid society of unproductive lives. Also, quality of life is at least partly contingent on the extent to which a supportive environment is created to enhance patient well-being. Even with these cautions in mind, however, quality of life can be objectively assessed to a considerable degree. Were quality of life to be given no moral consideration, then it would be necessary to keep every patient alive to the last minute through the use of every technology available. The essential publication in this area is *The Concept and Measurement of Quality of Life in the Frail Elderly.*[4]

A desirable instrument for assessing the complexities of the severity of dementia is the Washington University Clinical Dementia Rating (CDR), which considers memory, orientation, judgment and problem solving, community affairs, home and hobbies, and personal care. In effect, this is a partial quality-of-life indicator that can be used to identify mild, moderate, severe, profound, and terminal phases of progressive dementia. What it does not do is identify the ethically appropriate limits, if any, on the use of lifesaving interventions along this CDR continuum. For this is an ethical problem rather than an empirical one.

At what point in the progression of dementia is prolongation of life ethically unacceptable? There are times when provision of comfort care has the side effect of prolonging life, creating difficult decisions for physicians and family. Should an airway be placed when dyspnea is causing severe distress or should narcotic and sedative medication be used instead? Should a gastrostomy be placed when aspiration follows dysphagia, or should spoon-feeding or withdrawal of food and fluids be the approach? Should acute appendicitis or acute diverticulitis be treated surgically or with antibiotics or analgesics and sedatives? There are no easy answers for individual cases, and the many considerations that must be taken into account include the stage of the disease, the severity of dementia, the suffering of the patient, the ability of the patient to cooperate with things like surgery or endoscopic examination, and the emotional state of the family.

A degenerative disease such as Alzheimer's, if it is the primary diagnosis, can justifiably be looked on as an extended terminal illness. As early as 1976, Robert Katzman wrote, "In focusing attention on the mortality associated with Alzheimer disease, our goal is not to find a way to prolong the life of severely demented persons."[5] However, as was pointed out in 1985, within the medical community and in society as a whole "consensus breaks down when the attempt is made to determine the nature of the therapeutic obligation to the demented patient, particularly with respect to life-sustaining treatment."[6] Perhaps consensus is now more possible. Discussions about the moral justification for medical interventions with respect to quality and quantity of life and about the importance of avoiding "futile" treatment are now more common.[7] Presumably no physician wishes to provide interventions that will be of no value to the patient.

In an international empirical study of physician attitudes toward aggressive treatment interventions in the case of elderly people with advanced dementia, considerable disagreement was evident both across and within countries.[8] The authors were interested in finding out the decisions physicians would make when confronted with a critically ill, demented elderly man. They presented the case of an 82-year-old man brought to an emergency room with life-threatening gastrointestinal bleeding and blood pressure of 70/40. Three years earlier, the man was diagnosed by a neurologist as suffering from probable Alzheimer's disease. He cannot answer a simple question coherently but seems to understand some simple commands. His behavior is agitated; he wanders, does not recognize his daughter, and has urinary incontinence.

Between March 1987 and April 1989, 897 physicians in academic medical centers at family practice, medical, and geriatric rounds were questioned. Countries included Australia, Bra-

zil, Canada, Scotland, Sweden, the United States, and Wales. Physicians were asked to select from among the following four options (assuming there was no directive from patient or family):

(1) MICU [medical intensive care unit] (removal to medical intensive care unit if needed, mechanical ventilation if needed, insertion of a central venous catheter)
(2) MAX [maximum therapeutic effort] (no transfer to medical intensive care unit, no mechanical ventilation except for surgery if needed)
(3) LIM [limited therapeutic effort] (no transfer to medical intensive care unit, no invasive procedures, limited use of antibiotics, intravenous therapy if needed, radiography and blood tests if medically indicated)
(4) SUPP [supportive care only] (comfort and palliation, intravenous fluid only if it improves comfort, no radiography, no blood tests, no antibiotics)

The authors conclude that there is wide variation of opinion both within and between countries, that physicians over 40 years of age and those in family medicine are more likely to decide against aggressive interventions, and that Brazilian and American physicians are the most technologically aggressive while Australians are the least aggressive. For example, only 6 percent of Australian physicians chose MICU, whereas 32 percent of U.S. physicians did so. Conversely, 21 percent of Australian physicians chose supportive care compared to only 3 percent of U.S. physicians.

The variation that this study demonstrated is difficult to interpret. No information is provided regarding the reasons for the differences of opinion. For example, the study does not indicate how strong a factor physicians' fear of legal suit for undertreatment might be. Further, level of training was not the same across physicians recruited from various countries, and availability of technology was not taken into account. Two significant factors may be the number of hospices available and the extent to which hospice access for dementia patients who are not approaching death is limited. As an advocate for a hospice approach to treatment of patients with advanced progressive dementia points out, hospices find dementia difficult to handle because it usually involves a more prolonged dying period than, for example, terminal cancer.[9] But whatever the reasons physicians may have for their approach, this study indicates that a consensus on ethical treatment levels still eludes us.

A less relational view of quality of life might assign a higher value to the inner experiences of the self despite the fact of relational loss or suggest that more self-identity may be present in the patient than meets the eye. Patients with severe dementia do demonstrate underlying affective responses, and they may have occasional windows of clarity when some self-identity surfaces, but in the profound and terminal stages, there is no discernible self-identity remaining. It is very unlikely that self-identity is maintained; the appearances of loss cannot be explained as a deterioration in communicative abilities alone.

David C. Thomasma rightly states that we must be circumspect in judging the quality of life for any patient, since there is ultimately a subjective aspect to all qualitative assessments.[10] There is no absolute certainty about how or when deterioration in communication and short-term memory gives way to a loss of internal sense of self-identity. However, as Aristotle argued, some degree of uncertainty is an aspect of most good practical reasoning. When a person is unaware of his or her environment; is mute, bedridden, and incontinent of bladder and bowel; demonstrates no measurable intellectual functions; and faces inevitable death, comfort care is all that medicine should offer. Comfort care means palliation only, that is, it excludes artificial nutrition and hydration, dialysis, antibiotics, and all other medical interventions unless necessary for the control of pain and discomfort.

There is philosophical literature to support this suggestion, although we need not agree with it in all respects. Dan W. Brock asks an essential question: How much health care does justice require for the elderly with severe dementia?[11] Brock concentrates on the effects of dementia such as the erosion of memory and other cognitive functions that "ultimately destroy personal identity."[12] He notes the crucial role played by "memory and other forms of psychological continuity in maintaining the identity of a person through time."[13] Finally, the person is destroyed by dementia. Experience becomes disconnected, disjointed, and incoherent. The patients are "cut off from the self-conscious psychological continuity with their past and future that is the basis for the sense of personal identity through time and which is a necessary condition of personhood."[14] Brock makes a claim that is uncontroversial: Once a person has died, health care is inappropriate. He also argues that patients in the persistent vegetative state (PVS) have no right to health care since they are no longer the subjects of conscious experience. The patient with severe dementia, however, remains the subject of such experience and is capable of suffering pain and enjoying sensuous pleasures. Nevertheless, both memory and self-identity have been ravaged, the links between past and present are broken, and the "temporal glue" of the self is undermined. This loss implies, for Brock, that the severely demented have "claims to palliative, but not life-sustaining" healthcare.[15] They retain, however, an interest in care and comfort, so that a painful tumor might be removed for palliative reasons. As for patients who still have memory function to a substantial degree, Brock argues that life-saving care should not be denied them if they desire it.

Daniel Callahan constructs a somewhat similar comparison, pointing out that for the patient who is brain dead, no further care of any kind is called for. The patient in the persistent vegetative state retains an interest in "minimal nursing care only," not inclusive of artificial nutrition and hydration. Of the patient who is severely demented, Callahan writes, "On the one hand, he has lost his capacity for reason and usually—but not always—human interaction. On the other hand, there will be no clear ground for believing that the capacity to experience emotions has been lost."[16] Callahan recommends nursing care only, including artificial nutrition and hydration. Whether or not one agrees with this position on nutrition and hydration, Callahan's main point is that death "need not be resisted."[17] Such treatment limitations are based on the quality of life and the underlying disease condition rather than on old age–based cutoffs.[18]

LONG-TERM CARE

Caring is solicitude. It is present to the extent that anxiety is felt about the well-being of another. Modern rescue medicine has often neglected this aspect of care provision. Caregiving as a vocation has been devalued in our society. The tasks of long-term caring are readily viewed as demeaning. Partial or constant dependence on others is interpreted as an unreasonable and burdensome imposition. Caring is a basic human need that reminds us of a fundamental reality: We are human beings who share social interdependence. In our age of emphasis on autonomy, rights, and freedoms, it is essential to recognize our inherent dependence on others and the reality of human fragility. At the same time, caring often compels advocacy for the autonomy and rights of dependent people.

The lack of support for caregiving is a measure of its devaluation. To do for others what they cannot do for themselves requires, in addition to compassion, great commitment and expenditure of time and resources. But is has been noted that "as a society, we have created a situation in which we place a higher value on the act of flipping a hamburger than on the act of caring for chronically disabled individuals."[19] Given this reality, some people who are attracted to the vocation of caring are unable to sustain a minimally decent standard of living for themselves and frequently elect to pursue other career paths. Family caregivers in need of training, encouragement, and assistance must frequently go to unusual lengths to locate people in the community who are willing to devote their time and energies to assist with daily caregiver tasks. We neither adequately train nor adequately compensate caregivers; this remarkable omission can blight the lives of vulnerable citizens.

Complicating this devaluation is the dramatic rise in the need for long-term care in all age groups, a rise partly caused by medical progress. Lifesaving interventions allow people to survive but may leave them in need of extended or even lifelong care. Premature infants may be saved through neonatal intensive care and go on to live reasonably independent lives, but some are permanently impaired and become dependent on family members in ways that are frequently unanticipated and that family members are ill-equipped to deal with. As the human life span increased from approximately 50 years at the turn of the century to nearly 80 years now, periods of dependence on caregivers extend far beyond what was usual a few generations ago.

Daughters and daughters-in-law are the ones typically called on to provide emotional support and assistance for those needing long-term care. Over the last few years, national attention has been focused on "women in the middle"— women sandwiched between job and family responsibilities. The extension of the human life span means that "contemporary adult children provide more care and more difficult care to more parents and parents-in-law over much longer periods of time than ever has been the case before."[20] Studies indicate that daughters or daughters-in-law are more than three times as likely as sons to assist an elderly caregiver with a disabled spouse, and women outnumber men as the caregivers for severely disabled parents by a ratio of 4:1.[21] Although results vary somewhat from study to study, about half of these women caregivers experience stress in the form of depression, sleeplessness, anger, and emotional exhaustion.[22]

While women caregivers must be appreciated for all that they do, we are concerned that significant numbers of women are harmed by the social expectation that they embrace caregiving as their exclusive duty in life no matter how severe the threat to their own well-being. In response to this harm, we propose that policy makers, researchers, and male family members give systematic attention to it. Of course, men provide some direct caring and emotional support, but the bulk of the burden falls on women. Caregiving may require a correction of gender inequities and a revision of gender roles in the family such that men do more direct caring.[23]

There is a vital need to support family caregivers. Remarkably, despite the often unanticipated and unplanned for burdens of caregiving, more than 80 percent of elderly persons with disabilities are cared for at home. The family is a crucial caring resource. At present, social policy often does little more than cheer the family on. Parents of severely disabled children will sometimes succeed against the odds, but there are many who complain about "extending a child's dependence beyond a parent's natural strength."[24] As one mother writes, "All I see is a sleepy life of never-ending diaper changing for us."[25]

First and foremost, society should *never* assume that caregiving obligations, capabilities, and capacities within the family are unlimited. There are instances of caregivers who have sacrificed themselves radically out of love for a family member and genuinely feel that they discovered themselves in the process.[26] But more generally, extremes of self-denial ultimately take a severe toll on caregivers, and they place the recipients of care at risk for neglect and abuse.

Society must recognize limits to caregiving for most people. Before the point of caregiver burnout is reached, it becomes the responsibility of society to provide aid. Family caregiving is a precious moral resource, and for this very reason it merits careful protection. The surest way to weaken and destroy this resource is to overwhelm it.

Precise limits will depend on individual circumstances. But there is no need to argue about or wait for the precise point at which the burden of caring becomes unsustainable. Rather, we must recognize the proportions of the problem and create programs to deal with it. If many intact families provide care that is uniquely beneficial to the recipient, then it is ethically unsound and poor public policy to press them to the point where they will surrender their parent, spouse, or child to an institution in desperation. Everyone loses.

At present, long-term care is underfinanced, especially as compared to available acute care medical services.[27] Respite care, day care, in-home services, and a broad array of community-based programs could make the burden of caregiving more tolerable, but they do not get adequate attention in our society. We must establish a proper balance between preventive, acute, transitory, and long-term care services and facilities. Priority should be placed on developing a full spectrum of care lest caregivers slide beyond the breaking point. We must be satisfied that simply caring for the dying is appropriate, and certainly severe progressive dementia is a terminal condition. The art of dying should involve caring, and dying should in many cases be allowed to occur, as it once did, in the home. It is not so much death as the absence of caring and the denial of reality that may be the enemy.

Those in need of long-term care are often physically dependent. But this dependence on others does not mean that respect for autonomy and integrity should be denied. Recent reforms stress the development and updating of individualized care plans in which nursing home residents participate and give consent to treatment recommendations. It is easy to overlook the importance of choice in the context of routine, everyday matters. Recipients of long-term care are actually most concerned about everyday matters, including meals, sleep schedules, and bathing time. All reasonable choices of residents should be respected.[28]

Access to personal property, telephone use, and visits by friends and relatives are all important. The use of chemical and physical restraints should be kept to the least restrictive level possible and should be regularly reviewed. Use of restraints should always be discussed with residents and their families. Medical treatments and medications can be legitimately refused. Living wills and other advance directives should be encouraged. These and many other choices are appropriate in the nursing home or in the person's own home.

The basic dignity of the recipient of care should also be respected. This includes allowing choices but goes far beyond it, encompassing a respectful attitude on the part of the caregiver. Basic care and comfort in a clean environment is critical to well-being. Respect for privacy, full participation in care planning, giving or withholding consent to treatment, and all other "civil" rights should be routine expectations for all residents of long-term care. Conflicts inevitably arise about the times of rising and retiring, the necessity of getting dressed and undressed, and what to eat and whom to eat with. Interpersonal problems with personnel or with other patients appear. Intimate relations between patients, even sexual activity, are often seen. Restraints, either physical or chemical, are often used as a solution to problems like wandering or noisiness or falling. Most nursing homes are understaffed, and the pressure of work makes one-on-one relationships between staff and patients very difficult. It is easy for patients under such circumstances to lose all autonomy and to be denied all their rights. Patients with dementia are not able to make quick decisions, and their delay results in the decisions being made by institutional caregivers.

All these factors make for conflict of values. The autonomy of the patients in ordinary aspects of daily living is in conflict with the needs of the staff to dress, bathe, toilet, transport, keep order, and record. Patients must get up, get dressed, eat, sit, walk, and retire on an inflexible schedule determined by others.

BEHAVIOR CONTROL

Family caregivers sometimes put tremendous pressure on the psychiatrist to "do something" quickly about behaviors that are offensive or frightening and result in emotional strain. Our society has come to expect prompt control of such behaviors, often through chemical means. The caregivers might already be women in the middle, and an aging parent in a delusional or agitated state can be the straw that breaks the camel's back. For these and other reasons, some of them economic, it is difficult to sustain the commitment to methods that are not destructive of whatever ability to reason the patient with dementia still possesses. Interventions that do not affect the personal identity of patients (insofar as it still exists), are physically less intrusive with respect to the brain, and require active patient participation both cognitively and affectively are certainly costly.[29] In some cases, the respect owed to the mind of an elderly person becomes grist in the mill of medical efficiency.

While there are no absolute guidelines in this area, it is clear that technological shortcuts can make the demented elderly passive recipients rather than active agents. Families know that the human brain is the center of mentation, emotion, and personality and that, ideally speaking, this ultimate perimeter of personhood should not be invaded except as a matter of last resort after less invasive measures have been exhausted. But this ideal forms a dialectic with the realities of cost containment and family caregiver stress. There is reason to worry about excessive use of drugs and ECT in geriatric psychiatry, for our society lives by the quick fix and can easily make scapegoats of the elderly.

Elderly persons, in their inevitable decline, eventually withdraw from some of the interests and pleasures of youth. Whether elderly persons feel more isolated than other age groups is a matter of some debate.[30] However, there are often selected cases in which an elderly person struggles with what Emil Durkheim first called anomie and what sociologists define as "the homelessness of modernity." Isolation, poor communication, removal from the preferred environment, and loss of mobility are problems that can frequently be solved through social rather than chemical means. Yet the basic forms of assistance that such solutions require take resources and willingness to care in the most basic sense of the term. It is unfortunate that chemical custodianship is sometimes the only timely response.

It is valid and beneficent to treat depression and other psychiatric ailments with drugs. But as Salzman emphasizes, not all unhappiness or sense of uselessness in geriatric patients "represents true depression that requires pharmacotherapy."[31] There are many instances in which social isolation or loss of meaning are the root of the problem, and these factors can be mitigated socially or religiously. Salzman recommends ECT only for those patients who do not respond to antidepressant treatment, whose medical condition does not indicate the use of antidepressants, or whose depression is life threatening and/or delusional.

With specific reference to Alzheimer's disease and associated dementias, Martin and Whitehouse argue that "behavioral interventions (i.e., making modifications in the environment) are generally preferable to medications for the treatment of most behavioral problems."[32] These authors point out that use of medication is important in cases of depression, psychosis, anxiety, and sleep disturbances. But they urge a cautious use of psychoactive drugs, offering two basic guidelines: (1) Treatment should be purposeful, with the target symptom well defined, and (2) "employ as few drugs as possible, start with low doses, increase dosages slowly, and monitor carefully for side effects."[33] Polypharmacy and overmedication are particular problems in this patient population.

Mace suggests caution in using drugs to reduce disturbed behaviors (wandering, restlessness, irritability) "at dosages that interfere with remaining cognitive function and at which side effects occur."[34] She also stresses the importance of changing the physical or psychosocial environment first, prior to use of drugs. Spar and La Rue recommend supportive therapy in the early stages of dementia and individual psychotherapy so long as the patient's capacity for insight is preserved. Family intervention is useful at all stages of illness, as are environmental interventions generally (physical and social). Various drugs can be beneficial but ought not to be the first recourse.[35]

Ours is an overmedicated society. In the ethics literature, two general value orientations with respect to drugs and mental health are often alluded to: pharmacological Calvinism and psychotropic hedonism. Psychiatrist Gerald Klerman originally drew this distinction. The first view is one of general distrust of all drugs but especially those that are not clearly therapeutic. It favors verbal insights and self-determination. Psychotropic hedonists, on the other hand, see drugs as the first response to life's unpleasantries.[36] Those holding the first view might deal with a depressed early-onset victim of dementia through psychotherapeutic measures if possible. Effort is made to engage the patient as an active agent of change—as reasonably cognitively intact and capable of basic insights. Drugs are treated as a secondary means, less valued than insight and self-determination and not to be resorted to prematurely. By contrast, the psychotropic hedonist is more likely to resort to drugs immediately, since they are a valuable technology.

No doubt, behavioral problems such as hyperactivity, restlessness, resistiveness, and assaultiveness can be symptomatically managed by modification of the patient's environment, gentle persuasion, and exercise, but in most cases, sooner or later, the patient will require a psychotropic medication. The question is, will recourse to drugs be sooner or later?

There is tremendous pressure to make it sooner. Patients sometimes need to be controlled in less-than-ideal surroundings and with inadequate personal care. Concern for pressures on caregivers (e.g., adult daughters or daughters-in-law) is valid to a degree. Music therapy, art therapy, and group activities may be inaccessible. It will never be possible to create a state-of-the-art Alzheimer's unit in every nursing home. Unfortunately, the pressure to use drugs for custodial rather than therapeutic reasons, so-called chemical straitjacketing, will remain. Drug use for custodial reasons is a serious problem in long-term care facilities for the elderly, particularly in cases of understaffing or other institutional inadequacies.

Long-term care ombudsmen continue to struggle for the full implementation of resident rights: "You have the right to be free from physical and chemical restraint except to the minimum extent necessary to protect you from injury to yourself, to others, or to property."[37] As much as possible, chemical restraints are to be avoided, not just because of what they do to the mental state of the resident but because of their damaging side effects. Antipsychotics can lead to dry mouth and lethargy, and long-term use can lead to tardive dyskinesia; antimanics can lead to nausea, vomiting, and diarrhea. In home care, the possible need to control outbursts that can terrify a caregiver is predicated on the importance of keeping the care system intact, but major tranquilizers can also have negative consequences. It is important to appreciate the variable effects of disease and to understand that surprisingly small doses are often very effective.

OTHER ISSUES

The decision to withhold food and fluids is very difficult but even more difficult is the decision to withdraw them when they have been administered by artificial means over a period of time. The futility of the effort becomes more convincing with the passage of months and even years. Some who accept the morality of with-holding life support are unable to accept the morality of withdrawing it once started. Although most ethicists point out that there is no significant moral difference between withholding and withdrawing, some clinicians are unable to regard them as morally equivalent.

Some neurological disorders that produce dementia may impair swallowing very severely at a time when the patient's dementia has not progressed very far. In such instances, gastrostomy would seem indicated. When the dementia has progressed to a more severe stage, with loss of communication and marked reduction in consciousness, the removal of the gastrostomy tube and cessation of food and fluids is regarded by most physicians as a valid moral option. If the decision to withdraw food and fluids is made, it must be with the approval of the family. If the family is in conflict, it is generally better to delay withdrawal until the conflict can be resolved.

Keeping patients with advanced dementia comfortable requires neither causing death by human hand nor striving for prolongation. The author does not advocate active euthanasia (i.e., mercy killing), chiefly because of the possibilities for abuse. Also, many physicians, probably a substantial majority, regard it as a moral imperative that they not actively kill another human being.[38] Four Austrian nursing aides, after all, did kill 49 elderly demented residents in a long-term care setting five years ago.[39] One aide was quoted by police as saying, "The ones who got on my nerves were dispatched directly to a free bed with the Lord."

NOTES

1. M.A. Drickamer and M.S. Lachs, Should Patients with Alzheimer's Disease Be Told Their Diagnosis? *New England Journal of Medicine* 326 (1992):948.

2. J.M. Foley, The Experience of Being Demented, in *Dementia and Aging: Ethics, Values, and Policy Choices,* edited by B.H. Binstock et al. (Baltimore: Johns Hopkins University Press, 1992), 31–43.

3. M.P. Alexander, Clinical Determination of Mental Competence: A Theory and Retrospective Study, *Archives of Neurology* 45 (1988):23–26.

4. J.E. Birren et al., eds., *The Concept and Measurement of the Quality of Life in the Frail Elderly* (New York: Academic Press, 1991).

5. R. Katzman, The Prevalence and Malignancy of Alzheimer Disease, *Archives of Neurology* 33 (1976):217–218.

6. N. Rango, The Nursing Home Resident with Dementia: Clinical Care, Ethics, and Policy Considerations, *Annals of Internal Medicine* 102 (1985):835–841.

7. R.D. Truog et al., The Problem with Futility, *New England Journal of Medicine* 326 (1992):1560–5640.

8. E. Alemayehu et al., Variability in Physicians' Decisions on Caring for Chronically Ill Elderly Patients: An International Study, *Canadian Medical Association Journal* 144 (1991):1133–1138.

9. L. Volicer, Need for Hospice Approach to Treatment of Patients with Advanced Progressive Dementia, *Journal of the American Geriatrics Society* 34 (1986):655–658.

10. D.C. Thomasma, Ethical Judgments of Quality of Life in the Care of the Aged, *Journal of the American Geriatrics Society* 32 (1984):525–527.

11. D.W. Brock, Justice and the Severely Demented Elderly, *Journal of Medicine and Philosophy* 13 (1988):73–99.

12. Ibid., 74.

13. Ibid., 86.

14. Ibid., 88.

15. Ibid., 73.

16. D. Callahan, *Setting Limits: Medical Goals in an Aging Society* (New York: Simon and Schuster, 1987), 183.

17. Ibid., 183.

18. R.H. Binstock and S.G. Post, eds., *Too Old for Health Care? Controversies in Medicine, Laws, Economics, and Ethics* (Baltimore: Johns Hopkins University Press, 1991).

19. R. Applebaum and P. Phillips, Assuring the Quality of In-Home Care: The "Other" Challenge for Long-Term Care, *Gerontologist* 30 (1990):444–448.

20. E.M. Brody, *Women in the Middle: Their Parent-Care Years* (New York: Springer, 1990):13.

21. Ibid., 35.

22. Ibid., 42.

23. S.M. Okin, *Justice, Gender, and the Family* (New York: Basic Books, 1989).

24. H. Featherstone, *A Difference in the Family* (New York: Basic Books, 1980).

25. Ibid., 35.

26. R. Darling, *Families against Society* (Beverley Hills, Calif.: Sage Library of Social Research, 1979).

27. Brody, Women in the Middle, 260.

28. R.B. Rust, *Understanding Your Rights: A Guide to Ohio's Bill of Rights for Residents of Nursing Homes and Rest Homes* (Cleveland: Long Term Care Ombudsman, 1990), 17.

29. G. Dworkin, Autonomy and Behavior Control, *Hastings Center Report* 6, (1976):23–28.

30. B. Silverstone and S. Miller, Isolation in the Aged: Individual Dynamics, Community, and Family Involvement, *Journal of Geriatric Psychiatry* 13 (1980):27–47.

31. C. Salzman, Clinical Guideline for the Use of Antidepressant Drugs in Geriatric Patients, *Clinical Psychiatry* 46 (1985):38–43.

32. R.J. Martin and P.J. Whitehouse, The Clinical Care of Patients with Dementia, in *Dementia Care: Patient, Family, and Community,* edited by N.L. Mace (Baltimore: Johns Hopkins University Press, 1990), 25.

33. Ibid., 25.

34. N.L. Mace, The Management of Problem Behaviors, in *Dementia Care: Patient, Family, and Community,* edited by N.L. Mace (Baltimore: Johns Hopkins University Press, 1990), 95.

35. J.E. Spar and A. La Rue, *Geriatric Psychiatry* (Washington, D.C.: American Psychiatric Association Press, 1990), 118–121.

36. G. Klerman, Behavior Control and the Limits of Reform: The Use of New Technologies in Total Institutions, *Hastings Center Report* 5, no. 4 (1975):40–45.

37. Rust, *Understanding Your Rights,* 12.

38. L. Kass, *Toward a More Natural Science: Biology and Human Affairs* (New York: The Free Press, 1985).

39. F. Protzman, Killing of 49 Elderly Patients by Nurse Aids Stuns Austria, *New York Times,* April 18, 1989, 1A.

Chapter 19

Autonomy of the Elderly Living in Nursing Homes

Jeffrey L. Crabtree

Ethicists and others have begun to differentiate between the ethical dilemmas of acute and chronic medical care[1] and explore the unique ethical issues facing older adults and their caregivers.[2] While much work has been done to uncover the special needs of older and chronically disabled adults, there still remains the challenge of better understanding how to foster and uphold the autonomy of nursing home residents.

This seems true in large measure because the nursing home setting has inherited a conception of autonomy from acute health care that can mislead caregivers and residents alike.[3] This conception is based on the etymological roots of the term *autonomy*, which means political self-rule, although the conception is then extended to include "self-governance by the individual: personal rule of the self while remaining free from both controlling interferences by others and personal limitations . . . that prevent meaningful choice."[4]

This conception of autonomy appears so far removed from the daily experiences of those residing in nursing homes that we are intellectually and morally forced either to look for ways to reconcile this formal conception of autonomy with the real world of dependence on others and

interference from the nursing home staff and governing body or, as Agich has said, to develop a conception of autonomy that "acknowledges the essential social nature of human development and recognizes dependence as a nonaccidental feature of the human condition."[5]

This chapter proposes that neither the aging process nor dependence on others is solely responsible for pre-empting the personal autonomy of older adults residing in nursing homes. It asserts that nursing home governance, the nursing home physical (built) environment, and the response of well-meaning caregivers to dependence, taken together, do seriously challenge the nursing home residents' autonomy. And, finally, it discusses the implications of these assertions for the autonomy of nursing home residents.

NURSING HOME GOVERNANCE

Governance is basic to the issue of promoting autonomy in nursing homes. Foldes states that "one responsibility of the management must be to create opportunities among the residents and staff to explore and find common ground, to define and articulate their shared interests."[6] He further suggests that even in the awkward setting of the nursing home, the residents must have authority over the affairs of daily life.

To understand how governance relates to resident autonomy requires an exploration of the current models of governance and the examination of rights and obligations of caregivers and residents alike. According to Kari and Michels, there are two likely models of governance operating in nursing homes: the medical model and the service model (see Table 19-1).[7] The medical model of governance closely resembles the traditional medical model of health care, in which the patient is essentially passive and obedient to medical authorities.[8] Under the medical model, only the professional staff are empowered to make decisions. They are responsible for the care and well-being of passive and obedient nursing home residents. This model is hierarchical in nature. The nursing home residents and nurses aides share the lowest rungs of the hierarchy.

The service model of governance is essentially the same as the medical model in terms of the position of the nursing home residents in the hierarchy and their role as passive recipients of care. In both models, the critical elements of governance that could support and nurture individual autonomous actions are missing. Nursing homes operating under these models are not likely to include residents in decisions about nursing home policies or daily routines, to encourage the residents to explore roles other than that of recipient of care, or to encourage independence. Under these forms of governance, simple decisions regarding bathing times or menus are made by the nursing home staff.

One example of how nursing home governance interferes with the autonomy of residents can be seen in the typical ways of dealing with the issue of mechanical restraints. Most investigators agree that mechanical restraints are often used for inappropriate reasons, and they question whether "restraints are safe or effective and whether their benefits outweigh their risks in clinical care."[9] The typical reaction to the controversy, however, is to focus on methods for altering the staff's behavior. Responses include guidelines for restraint use, information about the dangers of using restraints, or "teaching staff members how to identify and analyze behavior and to use this analysis in the identification of alternative actions."[10] Seldom is there an attempt to hold residents accountable for their own or their fellow residents' behaviors or to explore forms of governance that would empower residents and staff alike to seek specific solutions to individual cases.

The community model of governance, as discussed by Kari and Michels,[11] combines the concepts of social support theory[12] with the concepts of citizen politics[13] to yield a view of governance that is collaborative rather than hierarchical. Under this form of governance, residents can have influence on the daily routines of the nursing home and on individual options and choices through a process of democratic decision making and policy making.

Governance defines the limits of the rights and obligations of those working or living in a nursing home. Even resident rights such as those mandated by the Omnibus Budget Reconciliation Act of 1987 can be restricted in application by the day-to-day process of operating a nursing home. Furthermore, from a resident's point of view, these legal rights may be incidental to the day-to-day process of living in a nursing home. The resident may have infrequent opportunities to exercise many of the rights guaranteed by this law (e.g., the right to choose his or her own attending physician, the right to refuse a transfer to another room within the facility, and the right not to be subjected to corporal punishment or involuntary seclusion).

Despite the guarantee of certain legal rights, the resident's right to make mundane choices, because of the governance of the nursing home, could be violated hourly. The resident might be unable to change an item of clothing because the laundry is not open to residents, be unable to eat a snack because no one is available to get into the kitchen, be unable to stay up to watch a movie because the nurse's aides must see to it

Table 19–1 *Models of Organizational Governance*

Medical Model	Therapeutic Model	Community Model
Focuses on acute care, disease, and disability.	Focuses on the provision of a variety of services.	Focuses on capabilities and the ability to contribute.
Facilitates dependency on staff.	Facilitates dependency on staff.	Encourages interdependency among all members.
Information and knowledge are seen as technical expertise.	Information and knowledge are compartmentalized and perceived as serving the client.	Information and knowledge are perceived as wisdom gained from experience.
Uses specialized language, which creates dependency.	Uses specialized language, which creates dependency.	Uses a common language accessible to all.
Focuses on patients' rights.	Focuses on clients' consumer needs.	Focuses on contribution and reciprocity among staff and resident members.
Uses a reductionistic, scientific approach.	Uses a programmatic approach that tends to fragment spiritual, physical, and social well-being.	Uses a holistic approach that addresses physical, social, and spiritual well-being.
Creates a social structure based on a hierarchy.	Creates a social structure based on a hierarchy.	Creates a democratic, egalitarian social structure.
Is staff intensive.	Is staff intensive.	Includes nonprofessional and mutual caregiving.
Activities geared toward improved physical functioning.	Activities geared toward personal development and contentment.	Opportunities for public decision making and contribution.
Holds staff responsible.	Holds staff responsible.	Holds all accountable.
Empowers staff.	Empowers staff.	Encourages relational empowerment.

Source: Copyright 1989 by the Lazarus Project. Reprinted by permission.

that all residents are in bed by a certain hour, be unable to get out of a wheelchair because the staff are afraid he or she might fall, be unable to complain about rough treatment from an employee for fear of possible retaliation, or not be taken seriously because of the all too frequent infantilizing of residents by staff.

To further understand the relation of governance to resident autonomy, it is useful to explore the concept of rights. Hare suggests there are three senses of a right.[14] In the first sense, "I have a right to do something if I have no obligation not to do it"; in the second sense, I have a right if others have obligations not to stop me; and in the third sense, "I have a right if others . . . have obligations positively to see to it that I can do or have that to which I have the right."[15]

To clarify, let us consider the situation of an older man who is recuperating from a fractured

hip. Assume his physician has recommended he walk whenever he can but use a walker for the next two weeks until he is stronger and the pain in his hip subsides. In his own home, this gentleman would have the right (in Hare's first sense) to get out of bed in the middle of the night to go to the bathroom unassisted if he had no obligation not to do it. Since his physician recommends he walk whenever he can, he has no obligation not to do it. He has the right in the second sense because members of his family want him to get stronger and have an obligation not to stop him.

The same gentleman in a nursing home may not have the right to get out of bed to go to the bathroom unassisted because the nursing home staff have been instructed to assist all post-hip-fracture patients to the bathroom to prevent a fall. As Waymack and Taler suggest, "residents may well have to accept a subservient and obedient role, in essence abrogating some of their personal autonomy and dignity in exchange for attentive and kind treatment on the part of the staff."[16]

The nursing home management operating under the medical model of governance are likely to consider themselves to have an obligation to ensure residents' safety. Because of the litigious nature of our society, the nursing home could be sued or receive serious citations from Medicare if it allowed individuals to fall. Yet this obligation clearly takes away a right of a resident. From the point of view of the community model of governance, the older man would have had the opportunity to express his wishes to be as independent as possible to the members of the community, including the director of nursing and the administrator. He might have been able to show he would be safe and would thus have maintained his right to move about the nursing home unassisted.

On the other hand, during such discussions, other members of the community could have shown him why he should modify his wishes, perhaps because he is unfamiliar with the surroundings and could become confused and fall. But at least he would have had the opportunity to participate in the decision-making process and would know he could initiate a discussion at a later date to change that decision. Throughout the process he would maintain some control in defining appropriate limits to his behavior.

THE PHYSICAL ENVIRONMENT OF NURSING HOMES

The total nursing home environment is too complicated to deal with given the scope of this chapter. However, it will be useful to examine the physical environment to gain some understanding of what impact it can have on a resident's autonomy.

Of the approximately 19,000 nursing homes in America, only about 20 percent are nonprofit and 5 percent are government operated.[17] Nursing homes are designed with profit and econo-

mies of scale in mind. Decisions regarding the number of rooms in a facility, the configuration of the rooms, the number of beds per room, and the design of the equipment are driven by the perceived demand for services in the community, projections of reimbursement mix (ratios of private insurance to Medicare and Medicaid income), and ease of medical and administrative management.

The resulting buildings tend to be uniform structures designed for a homogenous population—people thought to be incapable of caring for themselves. But what about the nursing home residents who must call it their home? This is typically a heterogeneous group of people. Some are legally competent and some are not. Some may have an acute illness, such as pneumonia, and some may suffer from decreased functioning of the heart and lungs. Some may have Parkinson's disease or another neurological disease, and some may have severe sensory losses. Some undoubtedly will have a combination of problems.

Within this context of diverse diseases and impairments is a wide variance in what individual residents are able to do for themselves. Individuals recover from pneumonia or hip fractures at different rates and with different degrees of ultimate capability. Some residents with cardiopulmonary disease dress themselves, bathe independently, and take short leaves of absence from the nursing home. Others are bedridden and require total care. Nursing home residents are as heterogeneous in terms of capability and independence as they are in terms of their diseases and impairments.

The typical nursing home physical environment comes closest to meeting the needs of the most ill, most dependent, and least competent residents. Hallways that radiate out from the nurse's station allow quick access to each room and let the nursing staff see when a call light has been activated. Assigning two or three residents to a room makes changing bed linen or bathing the ill or comatose residents more efficient. Raised beds on wheels make cleaning floors and caring for bedridden residents easier and reduce the risk of back injuries. Small night stands containing water and a bed pan save time and energy.

However, this uniform environment, with its emphasis on efficiency, often encourages learned helplessness[18] and is incongruent with the needs and desires of residents who may be dependent upon others for only some activities of daily living (ADLs) or instrumental activities for daily living (IADLs) and capable of choosing what help they need, when they want that help, and whom they want to provide the help. And perhaps the most significant restriction on autonomy occurs in cases where residents are precluded from making the changes in the environment that would make it fit their own abilities and capacities better (changes they would likely make in their own homes).

THE WELL-MEANING RESPONSE TO DEPENDENCE

Chronic disability has been found to be closely correlated with growing old. As Scanlon indicates, of the population 65 to 69 years of age, 13 percent need some kind of long-term care.[19] Even more significant, of the population 85 years of age or over, 55 percent require some form of assistance. The number of older adults with deficits in ADLs and IADLs appears to be increasing rapidly and at rates that will make the provision of quality social and health care for those with chronic needs a difficult challenge.[20]

The aging process alone, however, does not limit older people's autonomy nor create special ethical dilemmas for caregivers. Rather, it is the accumulated effect of deficits and the response of caregivers (both professional and informal caregivers) to these deficits that leads to dependence of older people upon others. For example, if an elderly woman falls when transferring into the bath tub, family members can respond in ways that foster or reinforce dependence (perhaps by bathing her or hiring someone to bathe her) or that help her to maintain her independence (by purchasing a bath bench, a handheld shower, and other equipment that make bathing safer). The woman may continue to show signs of inability to perform activities of daily living, and on each occasion the family and other caregivers have the opportunity to intervene in ways that support her right and ability to choose the kind of help she wants. If the caregivers take over an activity in the name of helping, they remove the woman's control of when, where, or how the activity is performed. The accumulation of deficits and increased intervention can reduce the expectations others place upon the woman as well as the confidence she has in her ability to lead an independent life.

The opportunities for helping (or interfering) with the residents' ADLs and other significant choices within the nursing home are legion. Twenty-four hours a day, nursing home staff are present and available to help those who request it or actively impose their will on the residents, depending upon their personal views and values.

Older adults enter nursing homes for a variety of reasons; some require total care whereas others need short-term rehabilitative services. Regardless of the reason for admission or the level of ability of the resident, the nursing staff is likely to perform any number of ADLs for the person. This help is offered in the name of safety or caring, but all too often there is no consideration of whether it will foster dependence or independence.

For example, suppose an older gentleman is transferred to a nursing home from an acute care hospital where he was treated for pneumonia. He is weak but is expected to recover and be able to return to his residential care facility, where he has lived for three years. There he only required help with bathing, otherwise he was independent and active. He has a history of hypertension and reliably took his oral medications. Once admitted to the nursing home, however, his hypertensive medications are administered by the staff, and he is bathed, shaved, and dressed by the staff as well. Meals are brought to his bedside. Under this regimen, he becomes less active and weaker and thus grows dependent upon the staff.

During a case conference on this resident, the staff might easily conclude that the man is too weak and dependent to be able to return to his residential care home. This illustrates the paradox of helping. It shows how mild deficits and inappropriate or aggressive intervention can reduce an older adult's level of activity, reduce the expectations others place upon that person, and also reduce the confidence the person has in being able to lead an independent life.

IMPLICATIONS FOR THE AUTONOMY OF NURSING HOME RESIDENTS

There are likely to be few circumstances more challenging to traditional definitions of autonomy, let alone the personal autonomy of older adults, than the combination of being dependent on others and living in a nursing home that, through its environment and its governance, inhibits or denies the right to make simple daily choices, such as what to wear or what to eat for breakfast. Even recognizing that freedoms and choices generally associated with autonomy "are always curtailed by the broader context of social duties on the one hand, and physical limitations on the other"[21] does not alleviate the moral pain of observing firsthand or experiencing this assault on personal autonomy.

Direct suggestions of what can be done to maintain or improve nursing home residents' autonomy are outside the scope of this chapter. However, it is hoped that an examination of various facets and conceptions of autonomy will help caregivers and older adults become a part of the solution rather than perpetuators of the problem.

Thomasma has suggested there are five distinct but overlapping freedoms associated with autonomy.[22] While he used this analysis to help explain his "rule of dependency," it is helpful here as a means to gain an appreciation of a conception of autonomy applicable to older adults residing in nursing homes. Thomasma's first

freedom is the *freedom from* obstacles to carrying out one's desires.[23] This is the freedom from direct and indirect interference. He suggests that loss of health constitutes direct interference in one's freedom from obstacles. Prejudice or propaganda that limit one's options exemplifies the indirect loss of the freedom from obstacles.

His second freedom, the *freedom to know* one's options,[24] includes freedom of speech, freedom of assembly, and other freedoms that support political freedom. On a more personal level, this freedom is supported by policies of informed consent.

The third freedom is the *freedom to choose* goals and relate means to goals.[25] This freedom, according to Thomasma, is the foundation of social responsibility and personal character.

The *freedom to act* is Thomasma's fourth freedom. He suggests this freedom, in the political realm, is exercised at the ballot box. On a personal level, this is the freedom to commit to one's values. It "guarantees that not only are one's wishes one's own . . . but that one's actions are also one's own."[26]

The fifth freedom is the *freedom to create* new options. This is the freedom to give meaning to one's existence no matter how harsh or limited it may be.

Many might argue that the loss of some of these freedoms is the natural consequence of aging, of illness, or of being dependent upon others. Others might argue that these freedoms are unnecessarily taken from nursing home residents. In order to sort through these conflicting views and understand the implications of nursing home governance and environmental characteristics and the response of caregivers to the needs of residents, it will be useful to apply Hare's analysis of rights to Thomasma's five overlapping freedoms of autonomy.

There is a distinction between recognizing that one ought to do a thing and that one is obliged to do that thing. Hare asserts that the idea of "a right" is tied to the sense of obligation. He maintains there are three distinct senses of a right: First, individuals have a right if they have no obligation not to exercise that right. Second, individuals have a right to do something if others have obligations not to stop them. In the third sense, individuals have a right if others have obligations to see to it that they can exercise that right.

Does a competent nursing home resident have a right to be free from *direct* obstacles to carrying out his or her wishes? As Thomasma and others have noted, limitations of strength and endurance and blindness, hearing loss, and other physical deficits often directly interfere with a person's ability to carry out a desire. The first and second senses of a right do not seem to apply in such situations. In fact, it is common for people to adapt and adjust their desires to the realities of their capacity without feeling their personal autonomy is being seriously eroded.[27]

Does a competent nursing home resident have a right to be free from *indirect* obstacles, such as limited opportunities for socialization because of nursing homes rules and regulations or limited opportunities to perform self-care tasks because of nursing staff routines or attitudes? A nursing home resident would not necessarily have an obligation to impose such limits on him- or herself (Hare's first sense of right). The resident might, however, choose to accept limits on choices when the cost of choosing certain options was greater than he or she was willing to pay. As Dworkin explains, "the assessment of whether one's welfare is improved by having a wider range of choices is often dependent upon an assessment of the costs involved in having to make these choices."[28]

An elderly woman resident may be used to bathing and shampooing her hair daily. In the nursing home, she might have only two scheduled showers a week. The effort required of her to remove the obstacles to more frequent baths, the responsibility she would have to accept, and the social pressure from the staff associated with "special treatment" may be disproportionate to the benefits gained by having freedom from those obstacles.

Does a competent nursing home resident have a right to the freedom to know his or her options? This freedom relates to the widely accepted in-formed consent doctrine. A competent male resident, for example, has the right to know his options because, according to Hare's analysis, he has a right if others have a positive obligation to see to it that he has the right. As in the case of freedom from indirect obstacles, however, the resident might prefer to not know alternatives to a particular treatment because the cost of choosing a different treatment might be greater than he wants to pay. He has that right if he has no obligation not to know his options and if others have an obligation not to stop him from knowing his options. He simply chooses not to exercise this right.

In addition, the resident has the right (both because he has no obligation not to exercise that right and because others have an obligation not to stop him) to know the likely consequences of each option. In many ways, this freedom is critical, in that exercising it may help the resident to better understand which options are the most beneficial or meaningful. For example, the resident may not be aware of the debilitating consequences of prolonged bed rest and of the benefit for regaining strength by performing as much of his own ADLs as possible. Believing he has all of the information needed to make a reasonable decision, he succumbs to the staff's lower expectations and allows them to perform most of his personal care tasks, thereby exacerbating his weakened condition.

Does a competent nursing home resident have a right to the freedom to choose goals and relate means to goals? In both the first and second sense of a right, the resident has the right to choose goals and marshal the means necessary to achieve them. One goal might be to go on a brief shopping trip. However, if the nursing home management denies that it has an obligation to see to it that the resident can reach that goal (by ensuring, for example, that the resident has sufficient resources), for all practical purposes he or she will likely be unable to exercise that freedom.

Does the competent nursing home resident have a right to act? Again, in both the first and second senses of a right, the resident has the right to act. The actions in question may be as mundane as shaving and dressing or as spiritual as committing one's self to a particular form of worship. The nursing home management may accept the obligation to see to it that the resident can worship in the manner desired but ignore its obligation to see to it that the resident can perform normal daily tasks.

Does a competent nursing home resident have a right to the freedom to create new options? This freedom may in some ways be the most personal and the one that is not enlightened by Hare's senses of a right. But as Dworkin has suggested, by exercising this freedom, "persons define their nature, give meaning and coherence to their lives, and take responsibility for the kind of person they are."[29]

CONCLUSION

Collopy, Dubler, and Zuckerman have pointed out how caregivers may disregard a person's capacity to choose when they see that person as unable to act.[30] This exemplifies a common inability to see the trees of discrete freedoms for the forest of abstract autonomy.

Perhaps there will always be differing points of view among philosophers over where the line should be drawn between beneficence and paternalism in the nursing home setting. There will likely always be conflicts between the rights of individual residents. However, whether or not capable nursing home residents are able to make day-to-day choices has more to do with issues such as nursing home governance, the physical environment of the nursing home, and the caregivers' responses to the dependence of residents than with abstract conceptions of autonomy. Nursing home residents' freedom of choice, no matter how seemingly small or mundane, can be protected by appropriate democratic governance, facilitated by a better understanding of residents' rights and freedoms, and fostered in a supportive environment.

NOTES

1. B. Jennings et al., Ethical Challenges of Chronic Illness, *Hastings Center Report* 18(1) (suppl.) (1988):1–16.

2. G.J. Agich, Reassessing Autonomy in Long-Term Care, *Hastings Center Report* 20(6) (1990):12–17; B. Collopy et al., New Directions in Nursing Home Ethics, *Hastings Center Report* 21(2) (suppl.) (1991):1–16; R.A. Kane and A.L. Caplan, eds., *Everyday Ethics: Resolving Dilemmas in Nursing Home Life* (New York: Springer, 1990); M.H. Waymack and G.A. Taler, *Medical Ethics and the Elderly: A Case Book* (Chicago: Pluribus Press, 1988).

3. Collopy et al., New Directions in Nursing Home Ethics.

4. T.L. Beauchamp and J.F. Childress, *Principles of Biomedical Ethics,* 3rd ed. (New York: Oxford University Press, 1989), 68.

5. Agich, Reassessing Autonomy in Long-Term Care, 12.

6. S.S. Foldes, Life in an Institution: A Sociological and Anthropological View, in Kane and Caplan, *Everyday Ethics,* 35.

7. N. Kari and P. Michels, The Lazarus Project: The Politics of Empowerment, *American Journal of Occupational Therapy* 45 (1991):719–725.

8. Jennings et al., Ethical Challenges of Chronic Illness.

9. R.J. Moss and J. LaPuma, The Ethics of Mechanical Restraints, *Hastings Center Report* 21(2) (1991):22–25.

10. L. Varone et al., To Restrain or Not to Restrain? The Decision-making Dilemma for Nursing Staff, *Geriatric Nursing,* September-October 1992, 272.

11. Kari and Michels, The Lazarus Project.

12. M. Minkler, Applications of Social Support Theory to Health Education: Implications for Work with the Elderly, *Health Education Quarterly* 8, (1981):147–165; M. Minkler et al., Social Support Theory and Social Action Organizing in a "Grey Ghetto": The Tenderloin Experience, *International Quarterly of Community Health Education* 3 (1992):3–15.

13. H. Boyte and F. Lappe, The Language of Citizen Democracy, *National Civic Review* 79 (1990):417–425.

14. R.M. Hare, *Moral Thinking* (New York: Oxford University Press, 1981).

15. Ibid., 149–150.

16. Waymack and Taler, *Medical Ethics and the Elderly,* 190.

17. Collopy et al., New Directions in Nursing Home Ethics.

18. S.S. Foy and M.M. Mitchell, Factors Contributing to Learned Helplessness in the Institutionalized Aged: A

Literature Review, *Physical and Occupational Therapy in Geriatrics* 9, no. 2 (1990):1–23.

19. W.J. Scanlon, A Perspective on Long-Term Care for the Elderly, *Health Care Financing Review* (December suppl.) (1988):7–25.

20. S.R. Kunkel and R.A. Applebaum, Estimating the Prevalence of Long-Term Disability for an Aging Society, *Journal of Gerontology: Social Sciences* 47, no. 5 (1992):S253–260.

21. D.C. Thomasma, Freedom, Dependency, and the Care of the Very Old, *Journal of the American Geriatrics Society* 32 (1984):911.

22. Ibid.

23. Ibid., 908.

24. Ibid.

25. Ibid.

26. Ibid.

27. R.L. Rubenstein et al., *Elders Living Alone: Frailty and the Perception of Choice* (New York, Aldine De Gruyter, 1992).

28. G. Dworkin, *The Theory and Practice of Autonomy* (Cambridge: Cambridge University Press, 1988), 66.

29. Ibid., 20.

30. B. Collopy et al., The Ethics of Home Care: Autonomy and Accommodation, *Hastings Center Report* 20(2) (suppl.) (1990):1–16.

Chapter 20

Ethical Pitfalls and Benefits of Disclosure of HIV-Positive Status

David C. Thomasma and Patricia Marshall

Since the beginning of the acquired immuno-deficiency syndrome (AIDS) pandemic, disclosure of a positive status for human immunodeficiency virus (HIV) infection has been a major ethical issue. At first, the focus was on the ethical obligation of individuals who tested positive to reveal their status to sexual partners. Almost everyone agrees that within the context of an intimate sexual relationship, it is a duty of the highest importance to reveal one's HIV-positive status to a lover and to mutually decide to take proper precautions. This disclosure, however, is one of many voluntary ones that occur within human relationships.

Today, however, the public dimension of the disease has begun to preoccupy us. Most importantly, disclosure is now urged in medical relationships and may possibly be required. What was once an intimate matter has now become an issue of public concern and regulation. An example of public concern was demonstrated in a poll of teenagers who were asked about specific dimensions of the AIDS epidemic. The poll revealed a high level of fear. Forty-nine percent of seniors polled by National Scholastic Surveys thought that all students should undergo mandatory testing. Fifty-five percent of the students

thought that teachers with AIDS should be identified. Fifty-one percent of the students thought that famous people with AIDS should disclose this fact.[1]

Rather than redoubling efforts at education, public response to these concerns seems instead to focus on public regulation. The case of Jeffrey Hanlon in New York provides a good example. This case involved politics at the highest level. No less a figure than Governor Cuomo of New York announced that Hanlon would be extradited to Michigan to face charges that he did not tell his sexual partner, Kevin Leiffers, that he was infected with an AIDS-related HIV virus. Michigan is one of 20 states with an AIDS disclosure law.[2]

Spillover from these efforts to protect individuals from the harm of contracting the HIV virus will continue. A number of scenarios have emerged about the proper response to disclosure by physicians and patients of their HIV-positive status. We will examine each of these for their strengths and weaknesses and propose a compromise that builds on the ethical principles that arise in the separate scenarios. Given the fear and rejection that any epidemic induces, public discussion of ethical issues in this arena is clouded by high emotions. The stigma associated with HIV infection further exacerbates ethical resolutions of public policy issues in the health care arena. Therefore our effort will take into account the emotional overlay that accompanies public debate about the issue of disclosure of HIV status.

THE PROBLEM

Recently, ethical concerns in the AIDS crisis have shifted to the problem of disclosure on the part of health care professionals. Is it really wise to establish a policy requiring health care professionals to tell patients that they have tested positive for HIV? Fears in the community have been heightened by reports of patients being exposed to AIDS by a dentist in Florida.[3] Since the risk of contracting AIDS from health care professionals is so small, it seems unreasonable for patients to carry this fear with them into their doctor's or dentist's office, especially when universal precautions are used. It also seems unreasonable to base either our ethics or our public policy (e.g., proposing mandatory testing of all patients and health care professionals) on such a remote possibility of contracting AIDS from a health care professional.

Yet studies have shown that patients are concerned about transmission of the virus in medical and dental settings.[4] Moreover, the uncertainty in the scientific community about how AIDS was transferred in the dental case may be sufficient cause for a reasonable person to consider the threat of contracting AIDS from a health professional a "real" risk. It is no wonder that the AIDS crisis has created a Pandora's box of good and bad responses from the general public, health care professionals, institutions, and politicians. The contagious nature of human immunodeficiency virus and the certainty of death both contribute to the tension and confusion surrounding the public policy and ethical debates regarding AIDS. This leads directly to the primary clash between public fears and the rights of individuals and groups to privacy. Public fears

are rendered all the more poignant by reports that Dr. David Acer, the dentist who infected at least three patients, did not use gloves, reused equipment, and otherwise kept his condition private in order not to jeopardize the sale of his practice.[5] The desire of individuals for privacy in this matter is understandable in light of the serious repercussions of disclosure of HIV-positive status in almost every area of a person's life. Further, the politicization of the issue, from the responses of mayors to the laboratories of the NIH, exacerbates it and contributes to public anxiety.[6]

SCENARIO 1: BUSINESS AS USUAL

In a politically correct society, individuals with AIDS and those who test positive for the infection would be treated no differently than the uninfected population. In fact, disclosure in such a society would likely mean that affected individuals would be treated with increased compassion, respect for privacy, and extra measures of social justice to right the imbalance of illness.

Most often this is what we expect from others in society, and especially from health care providers when someone becomes ill. As a society, we regroup around the sick person, show support for that person and his or her family, and maintain the person's job until the person can return, even if intermittently. In the case of serious and terminal illness, help may be offered to the individual who is suffering not only by close companions, coworkers, and health care professionals but by society at large. Hospice care is an example of this expected response to illness.

Thus, disclosing that one has AIDS would have no bearing on how one is treated by others; it would not be a threat to one's employment, nor would there be long-term negative effects on the care that is given. Physicians and other health care providers would be able to disclose their positive status without worrying that they might have to close down their practice. Patients would not turn away from that practice out of fear they might contract the disease. Health care professionals would take proper precautions and treat all patients in need of care rather than refusing to treat HIV-positive patients because of an exaggerated fear of contagion.

Most Americans expect, too, that health care professionals will assume the risks of dying to care for persons with AIDS, just as they did in the yellow fever epidemic that hit river cities such as New Orleans and Memphis following the Civil War. Opinions on the duty to treat, however, remain divided, and examples of less-than-heroic behavior by practitioners are well publicized.[7] A Wisconsin surgeon bluntly refused to treat patients with AIDS, arguing that altruism is not an essential requirement in a modern form of health care delivery and that there is no obligation to place oneself at risk operating on individuals who will die anyway. Conversely, in an experimental study intended to gauge the willingness of dentists to treat individuals suspected of being HIV infected, an actor, playing the part of a patient, assumed the roles of a heterosexual, a homosexual, and an IV drug user.[8] Only 1 dentist in the study group of 102 refused to treat the "homosexual"; another dentist refused to care for the "IV drug user." Other research on health care professional attitudes regarding the treatment of persons with AIDS also indicates the prevalence of altruism.[9]

Strong arguments have been made by medical ethicists, dentists, and physicians in support of the role-specific duty to care for the ill, one that does not allow for withdrawal because of danger to self. Professional organizations such as the American Dental Association (ADA) and the American Medical Association (AMA) have published explicit recommendations concerning the obligation of their members to treat persons with AIDS. In these recommendations, altruism is seen as an essential component of a commitment to care for others.[10]

Professional concerns regarding a duty to treat cannot be separated from the actual or perceived risk of contracting HIV infection from a patient. After emphasizing the low risk assumed by health care workers in caring for people with AIDS,[11] in June 1987 the Centers for Disease Control (CDC) reported three cases of AIDS

contracted by health care workers from occupational exposure to blood.[12] By 1991, 24 documented cases of health care professionals' contracting AIDS from patients had been reported.[13] There appears to be less risk of a health care professional transmitting the AIDS virus to a patient during dental and medical procedures. Retrospective studies of three HIV-infected surgeons found that no patients were infected during surgical operations.[14]

The publication of new guidelines for universal precautions and the development of improved protective procedures, such as boots and waterproof gowns, have lessened the risk of exposure to HIV. Moreover, recent studies have demonstrated that compliance with universal precautions reduces occupational exposure to patients' bodily fluids.[15] Although the AMA, the ADA, and the American Nursing Association have issued statements on the HIV-infected health care worker, it is unlikely that there will be consensus in the health care community on policy issues in the near future. In January 1991, both the ADA and the AMA published statements recommending that HIV-infected health care professionals refrain from performing invasive procedures or obtain informed consent from patients.[16] Subsequently, the AMA offered in specific cases to help retrain physicians who might represent a risk to patients if they contracted AIDS. Discrepancies between the recommendations of the AMA, other professional associations, and the CDC underscore continued anxiety regarding health care workers infected with the AIDS virus, also underscored by the recent controversy over whether HIV-positive dentists and physicians should inform patients of their HIV status.

The CDC guidelines of July 15, 1991, recommended that physicians who deal with blood and bodily fluids be tested for HIV and that if they prove positive, they should refrain from invasive procedures unless a special panel approves their actions.[17] The CDC suggests that state and local health departments create review panels to advise HIV-positive health care professionals on whether or not they should perform invasive procedures that pose a significant risk of HIV exposure to patients. Mandatory testing for HIV or hepatitis B infection is not recommended, and the need for training in appropriate infection control precautions is emphasized. No official statement regarding disclosure to patients is made. In this respect, the draft guidelines of the CDC are less restrictive than the current recommendations of the AMA.

The original CDC recommendations were sharply criticized by many health professionals, economists, and health policy experts.[18] Opponents point to the grave consequences of disclosure for the health care worker's personal and professional well-being and financial security. A second problem lies in the lack of an adequate understanding of what constitutes an invasive procedure. Moreover, critics say that the extremely low risk of HIV transmission from professional to patient does not warrant restrictions on practice or other exclusionary measures. Generally, those who argue against constraints on practice and against the need for disclosure tend to play down the seriousness of HIV infection in their discussion of the magnitude of the risk. Critics of the CDC guidelines also argue that they do not go far enough in providing assistance to health care institutions that employ HIV-infected dentists and physicians.[19]

Opponents of the AMA recommendations point to a lack of scientific data that would allow categorization of procedures as safe or hazardous and as requiring or not requiring disclosure. Landesman cautions against the implications of a policy that would prevent infected physicians and dentists from practicing, arguing that the first derivative policy would be testing of health care workers and students.[20] The second derivative policy would be testing of patients. Finally, Landesman foresees the possibility of alterations in the concept of *significant risk.*

SCENARIO 2: OPTIONAL DISCLOSURE

When individuals disclose an illness that threatens other persons in society, they risk being ostracized by society. This is certainly true whether one is a patient or a health care professional with AIDS.[21] The confusion, fear, and misunderstandings surrounding the problem of HIV transmission are not limited to health care settings.

Thomas Duane, a candidate for the city council in New York in 1991, disclosed that he was HIV positive. He was running in a district with a high homosexual population against a candidate, Liz Abzug, who had previously announced that she was a lesbian. In making this disclosure, Duane said, "In one sense, it's nobody's business. But I am a candidate for public office and I believe in being candid."[22] His announcement may even have gained him sympathy. Contrast this openness with the recent past, when negative public reactions in some communities first isolated and finally drove out children with AIDS from school. Despite efforts to increase public knowledge concerning transmission of the AIDS virus, many Americans continue to be afraid of contracting AIDS from casual contact on the job.[23]

It takes courage to run even a very small risk of getting a disease that is invariably terminal. It takes even more fortitude to disclose the fact that one has AIDS to patients. It may mean that one's practice will be curtailed or even closed down, as happened to Dr. Neal Rzepkowski, a physician, who volunteered information about his HIV-positive status to both administrators and selected patients.[24] Although he voluntarily informed his superiors and in many cases his patients that he had AIDS, none ever protested until increasing pressure to make a disclosure arose pursuant to Dr. Acer's revelations in Florida. Even though there is no evidence that physicians have ever infected patients with AIDS, the president of Brooks Memorial Hospital in upstate New York announced Rzepkowski's forced resignation on the basis of such fears. It ended his career at the age of 39. He was the first health care worker forced to resign since the draft CDC guidelines recommended that physicians with the virus tell patients and refrain from invasive procedures.[25] These losses of both professional work and personal status are real possibilities.

They have to be faced along with the fear of death from the HIV infection.

The risk of transmitting AIDS to patients must be measured against the risk of real harms experienced by those who will be mandated to curtail their practice and disclose their HIV status, such as the loss of privacy and the loss of patients and even livelihood. Studies have repeatedly demonstrated that the public fear of AIDS is so great that patients will avoid contact with a dentist or physician who is believed or known to have AIDS.[26] One survey reports that 56 percent of more than 2,000 Americans contacted in a nationwide survey said they would change physicians if they learned their physician was HIV infected; 25 percent said they would change physicians if they learned their doctor was treating AIDS patients.[27] In a similar study on patient attitudes toward dentists with AIDS, two-thirds of the respondents said they would switch dentists if they learned their dentist was HIV infected.[28] At the present time, health care workers who test positive for HIV are unlikely to escape discriminatory behavior toward persons with AIDS.

Loss of confidentiality is only one of the dangers of disclosure. Society's inability to protect from harm practitioners who choose to disclose does not inspire confidence. Moreover, professional organizations have yet to demonstrate adequate means of protection and compensation for HIV-infected members. Wariness about any kind of public disclosure without extensive protections in place seems very prudent.

Voluntary testing for health care workers, voluntary restriction of procedures that pose a risk of transmission if a health care worker tests positive for HIV, voluntary disclosure to patients through informed consent—these appear to be reasonable policies given the epidemiological reality of the AIDS crisis. Moreover, the voluntary nature of each supports and reinforces the integrity of both HIV-infected individuals and the communities in which they live and work.

Voluntary testing, however, does not address the potential harm that may result if HIV-infected patients or HIV-infected health care workers choose to forgo testing and either knowingly or inadvertently place someone at risk for contracting the AIDS virus. Nor does voluntary testing take into account the problem of accidental exposure to HIV infection. Requiring HIV testing following an injury sustained during the course of a dental or medical procedure would safeguard individuals who later seroconvert. A negative baseline test would support claims that the HIV infection was directly linked to the documented incident.

SCENARIO 3: MANDATORY DISCLOSURE

About 40 percent of those at high risk for contracting AIDS have not been tested for infection. A survey of 14,000 people in a study reported at the annual meeting of the American Psychological Association revealed that 38 percent of homosexuals had not been tested in the last five years, and neither had 47 percent of those who used IV drugs during the past year nor 60 percent of those who reported having multiple sex partners.[29] It is not only the general population that is not being tested. Health care workers themselves may hide their HIV-positive status because they are afraid (and rightly so) that revealing it may cause them to lose their jobs. Many, it appears, are even forgoing medical care to keep their condition secret. The fear is very extensive, according to a survey of infected health workers recently released.[30] This means that patients are being exposed to physicians with AIDS without their knowledge, and physicians are clearly being exposed to patients with AIDS without their knowledge.

These considerations lead to pressure to require disclosure in all health care relationships. Perhaps one reason for the public's deep-seated fear is the seriousness of the consequence.[31] Fear of the stigma attached to AIDS is another reason for public aversion. In the United States, the stigma surrounding HIV infection is heightened by the association of the illness with the already stigmatized populations of homosexuals and IV drug users.[32] Finally, fear of AIDS persists, in part, because physicians and other health professionals hedge their scientific bets.[33] Their assurances that one cannot contract HIV through casual contact are often accompanied by a scientific caveat suggesting that, as yet, we do not know everything there is to know about the disease. Mistakes and accidents happen. Science cannot prevent mishaps that occur in an apparently safe relationship such as that between a doctor and a patient. Furthermore, although transmission of HIV through accidental exposure is rare, once contracted, the disease will inevitably be fatal. Thus, the fears that patients and professionals profess about contracting AIDS are not irrational. Normally a one in a million risk is considered insignificant. But is it insignificant when the final outcome is death? In light of this third scenario, protections that would not normally be required are therefore needed.

Some examples of mishaps are almost bizarre. Blood and urine samples to be tested for AIDS and hepatitis fell from a cargo plane flying over the city of Cape Coral, Florida. A cooler containing bags of the samples broke when it landed on a road in a sparsely population area of the city. The investigating police officer identifying the samples touched the materials and was tested for possible infection.[34]

Recent reports of accidental exposure to HIV contribute to fears. Trust in common protective procedures, such as testing of donated blood for HIV, has been eroded with the announcement that, despite testing, HIV-tainted blood may have accidentally been distributed by a Portland, Oregon, Red Cross blood collection center.[35] At a hospital in Chicago, cotton swabs that had been used on an HIV-infected patient were re-used on a woman during a routine pelvic exam.[36] Three individuals who were recipients of organs donated in 1985 from a man unknowingly infected with HIV have died of AIDS, and up to 59 recipients of various organs or tissue grafts from the same donor may be infected.[37] People feel betrayed when considering the repercussions of what they perceive as careless accidents made by medical practitioners.

Police officers, especially, seem lately to be the victims of aggressive behavior toward them by persons suspected or known to have AIDS. A police officer covering the AMA convention in March 1991 was bitten by someone demonstrating against mandatory testing and disclosure. The biter was from New York and had AIDS. The officer required testing. The act itself had a murderous intent. In another incident, police officers participated in the arrest of a previously convicted felon and known IV drug user. The felon was bleeding and spat blood on the officers during his arrest. In court the head state's attorney notified the officers that they could not ask the judge for HIV or hepatitis tests. Nonetheless, one officer asked the judge in court for such tests, and the judge ordered them. Apparently, police officers are not able to know if they have been exposed. The state's attorney notified the officers that the results would be confidential. As one officer put it, "How ridiculous! How can O'Malley [the state's attorney] justify putting a police officer through numerous blood tests and a series of shots for hepatitis resistance, when an offender has protected rights? This is a gross waste of taxpayer's money. . . . Results should be made available immediately to police departments whenever this situation occurs."[38]

Not only do the police demand mandatory disclosure, so do prisoners. After a dentist at a federal jail in Chicago voluntarily disclosed that he had AIDS, six mob suspects sought immediate release on the grounds, as their lawyer put it, that the Metropolitan Correctional Center was a "warehouse of death." An attorney for the dentist charged that the Federal Bureau of Prisons "invited this kind of panic" by notifying far more patients about the dentist's infection than recommended by the CDC. Apparently the CDC suggested only a handful of patients who were at risk be notified. Instead the bureau notified all 900 patients seen by the dentist over the eight years he worked there. In the motion filed on behalf of the mob suspects, the attorney, Allan Ackerman, asked, "Can the CDC and the MCC guarantee that the dentist never sprayed saliva when he spoke? Never coughed, sneezed, guffawed?"[39] Quite properly, an attorney of the ACLU AIDS and Civil Liberties Task Force retorted that it was irresponsible for anyone to argue that AIDS can be contracted by sneezing or guffawing.

The dentist, in turn, became the first health care professional to sue to prevent disclosure of his AIDS status, fearing that he will be in danger from the inmates (rightly, we think) and that he will be discriminated against and ostracized because of such disclosure. The suit on his behalf, filed by the ACLU, would require that his AIDS status not be revealed to anyone except in medically justified cases.[40] As noted above, the AMA rejected a proposal for mandatory testing. Yet the Illinois General Assembly passed on July 15, 1991, and sent to the governor for signing, a bill to require that notification be sent to patients treated by health care workers who have told the state that they had AIDS.

While discussion continues in the health care arena, state and local jurisdictions are taking steps to regulate disclosure and limit the activities of HIV-infected health care professionals. In New Jersey, Judge Phillip S. Carchman ruled that a surgeon with AIDS must inform patients before operating.[41] This controversial ruling is the first attempt by the courts to balance the risk of a patient's right to know against a professional's right to privacy. In Florida, former Governor Lawton Chiles pushed for a law, the first of its kind in any state, to require HIV-infected health care professionals to report this fact to a medical board.[42] It is not clear whether or how this information might be made public.

Concerns about such a law focus on the problems of mandatory reporting, mandatory testing, loss of confidentiality, and loss of income and professional livelihood. As Carisa Cunningham of the AIDS Action Council noted, "People with HIV will be driven out of the health professions."[43]

In an attempt to equate HIV infection with other public health problems for which testing is readily performed, many public health experts and practitioners have called for screening so that the AIDS epidemic can be contained.[44] Mandatory testing in hospitals and on the job have been proposed.[45] Although mandatory testing may alleviate certain problems surrounding HIV transmission in dental or medical settings, it does not guarantee a compassionate community response to the HIV-infected patient or practitioner.

THE ACT OF DISCLOSURE

We generally find abhorrent any suggestion that there be mandatory reporting of HIV-positive status, either on the part of patients or on the part of caregivers, unless there is a need to know. With respect to patients, this requirement would only become operative if the caregiver would need to know the nature of the disease the patient suffered in order to treat the patient with the best possible therapy, not for the presumed "protection" of the caregiver (unless there was exposure). Similarly, caregivers do need to let their superiors know of their status, if known, so that the harmful effects of the disease on the caregiver's performance can be monitored.

Mandatory disclosure can be justified if there has been exposure. If an individual has exposed a caregiver to infected blood, for example, either by an action (e.g., biting) or inadvertently, through a needlestick, or if a caregiver, for example, a surgeon, bleeds into the open cavity of a patient upon whom he or she is operating, then there is an obligation to disclose because of the minimal but nonetheless increased risk that this exposure has created.

Let us look more carefully at the act of disclosing information. As we noted at the outset, such an act normally occurs in intimate relationships. It may occur slowly, as part of a gradual process of personal revelation within the context of love. Indeed, it may be related to what Heidegger called the revelation of being within the existence of an individual, an unveiling of the potentialities and challenges of overcoming the nonexistence that is our death.

Far removed from this intimate act is the kind of disclosure demanded by public policy. Usually disclosure in the public arena, such as the revealing of a conflict of interest, is required if and only if one chooses to run for office, for example. The efforts of society ought to be directed toward maintaining relationships within the context of disclosure between patients and providers. This can only happen when the *mutual* interests, rights, and obligations of both individuals *and* community are recognized and respected.[46]

An English Institute of Medical Ethics working party proposal argues that a desirable relationship of mutual empowerment between a patient and a physician is more likely to be achieved if the patient is made aware of explicit ground rules of confidentiality and can expect them to be adhered to. Medical confidentiality is not an absolute value but is couched within the context of the doctor-patient relationship and the need for medical discretion. This creates ambivalence today on the part of both physicians and patients about disclosing HIV-positive status to one another or to agents of society. The working party argues that the primary values in a healing relationship can only be the doctor's duty to each patient and the patient's need to exercise informed choices within the relationship. Other concerns must take a back seat to these two fundamental principles.[47]

Social contracts that articulate and act upon reciprocal responsibilities encourage the expression of a beneficent morality. We must move beyond the cognitive, behavioral, and affective walls that force an artificial separation between the personal autonomy of patients and health providers. If HIV-positive health care workers must obtain informed consent from patients before doing an invasive procedure, HIV-positive patients should be required to inform all health care professionals of their status as well. Policy aimed at minimizing the transmission of HIV in health care settings should emphasize the collective responsibility of both groups to refrain from placing others at risk and, when a risk is present or unavoidable, to disclose their HIV status.

A significant deterrent to disclosure for both patients and health care workers who are HIV positive is the very real threat of discrimination. Currently, neither society nor our professional organizations have demonstrated a willingness to give support to HIV-infected individuals for responsibly disclosing their HIV status. Quite the contrary, persons who test positive for HIV and or have AIDS face loss of employment, loss of self-esteem, and in some cases loss of friends and family. Until health care workers are properly rewarded for disclosure, it is unlikely that their resistance to disclosure will lessen.

In this regard, Jonsen calls attention to the obligations of organized professions to support and compensate, rather than punish and sanction, health care workers who become HIV-infected.[48] In addition to educating the public about HIV transmission, there should be organizational support in the form of concrete advice on adjustments in practice and some type of financial assistance for loss of income as a result of disclosure of HIV-positive status. Sharing the burden of responsibility with the HIV-infected provider would enhance the credibility of the profession in the public's eye.[49] Jonsen pointedly asks the question, "Is individual responsibility a sufficient basis for public confidence?" His answer is a resounding no!

> The conscientious judgment of individuals about how they should assure their patients' safety is the indispensable and essential element of responsibility. But that responsibility requires in addition the external sanction and support that communal and social responsibility provides. The HIV-positive providers must be responsible persons in responsible communities; they must know that their colleagues will support their responsibility in tangible ways.[50]

No physician ought to be required to close down a practice on the basis of the disclosure itself. It seems to us, however, that such disclosure will lead to a loss of patients. In order to minimize patient loss based on irrational fears, society itself might be persuaded that disclosure by both patients and health care professionals is in the best interests of both parties and might support disclosure by offering incentives to disclose and instituting penalties for those who unjustly discriminate against individuals who have the courage to place another's interest above their own.

To reinforce the importance of mutual respect and the social obligations of both health care

workers and patients, we summarize recommendations in the literature and our own as follows:

1. Educational strategies aimed at informing
   health care workers of the importance of
   universal precautions should be developed and rigorously applied. Concurrently, possible strategies to reinforce
   compliance with universal precautions
   should be explored.

2. Invasive dental and medical procedures
   that might place individuals at risk for
   contracting the AIDS virus should be
   documented, investigated, and categorized. Since none has yet been proven to
   place patients at risk, there is no need for
   proposals to limit the ability of physicians
   to perform any procedures.[51]

3. Strict enforcement of antidiscrimination
   laws and regulations designed to protect
   persons with AIDS is necessary.

4. An effective means of financing the
   health-related costs of HIV infection for
   all individuals who test positive for the
   AIDS virus and for institutions that treat
   AIDS patients should be developed and
   implemented. Angell suggests instituting
   a nationally funded program for treatment
   of HIV-infected individuals similar to the
   program for end-stage renal disease.[52]
   Hospitals who carry the burden of treating persons with AIDS should not be expected to shoulder the added expenses
   alone.[53] Creative approaches to ensure the
   financial solvency of hospitals must be
   explored.

5. Financial reimbursement mechanisms
   should be developed and implemented by
   professional organizations to compensate
   for the loss of income incurred by HIV-
   positive health care workers who must or
   voluntarily do end their practice. In addition, alternative forms of insurance that
   might be purchased by HIV-positive
   health care providers to protect their
   families should loss of income result
   from the AIDS infection should be developed.

6. Expert panels should decide on a case-by-
   case basis whether to restrict or curtail an
   individual's practice.

CONCLUSION

We support the principle of social obligation
implied by the CDC's recommendations that
HIV-infected professionals curtail invasive procedures or obtain informed consent from patients. This should hold true of all health care
professionals. Compliance with universal precautions will provide protection, but as the epidemic continues, the number of patients who
contract HIV in the course of medical or surgical
procedures will surely increase. The majority of
health care workers would prefer to be informed
if they are treating a patient infected with the
AIDS virus. Conversely, patients have consis-
tently expressed a desire to know if their physician is HIV positive. Public policy, however,
should be driven by the need to protect community welfare and safety, not by uninformed opinions as to what should be done.

Most likely market economics will bring
about the middle course we recommend. In order to feel safe about putting one's family in the
hands of a doctor, patients like Paul Vanden-
Dolder will increasingly demand a written guarantee from prospective family health care providers that they do not have AIDS nor are
infected with HIV.[54] Criticism from physicians
and dentists suggested that the provider's affir-
mation that he was not infected was "unseemly"
and "essentially meaningless." It was unseemly
because the risk of contamination is so small. It
was meaningless because persons can be infected for months without testing positive. Yet
dentists and physicians are starting to post in
their offices or publicly attest in other ways to
their negative status with regard to HIV.[55]

Guidelines that support changes in practice by
a health care professional who tests positive (and
disclosure when informed consent is necessary)
reinforce rather than diminish the public's trust
in the ability of health care professionals to provide care in a "risk free" environment. Everything possible should be done to minimize po-

tential risks to both professionals and patients and to emphasize the importance of the healing relationship. The recommendations we have outlined are steps in this direction.

NOTES

1. K.S. Peterson, Teen Poll Reveals AIDS Fear, *USA Today*, April 24, 1992, 1D.

2. S. Sanchez, AIDS Extradition OK'd, *USA Today*, September 11, 1991, 1A.

3. D.L. Breo, Meet Kimberly Bergalis—The Patient in the Dental AIDS Case, *JAMA* 264 (1991):2018–2019.

4. B. Gerbert et al., Patients' Attitudes toward Dentistry and AIDS, *Journal of the American Dental Association*, November 1989, suppl., 16–20; B. Gerbert and B. Maguire, Public Acceptance of the Surgeon General's Pamphlet on AIDS, *Public Health Reports* 104 (1989): 13; P. Marshall et al., Patients' Fear of Contracting the Acquired Immunodeficiency Syndrome from Physicians, *Archives of Internal Medicine* 150 (1990):1501–1506; P. Marshall et al., Touch and Contamination: Patients' Fear of AIDS, *Medical Anthropology Quarterly* 4 (1990):129–144.

5. A. Quindlen, When Principle Collides with Personal Fears, *Chicago Tribune*, July 9, 1991, sec. 1, p. 15.

6. M. Cimons, U.S. to Expand AIDS Definition, Increasing Cases, *Chicago Sun-Times*, August 9, 1991, 10; F. Spielman, No-show Daley out as Honorary AIDS Walk Head, *Chicago Sun-Times*, August 9, 1991, 26; G. Holbert, PBS Drops Film on Catholic Church, AIDS, *Chicago Sun-Times*, August 13, 1991, 38; J. Crewdson, Probe Finds Fraud in AIDS Studies, *Chicago Tribune*, August 11, 1991, sec. 1, p. 1.

7. R.M. Ratzan and H. Schneiderman, AIDS, Autopsies, and Abandonment, *JAMA* 260 (1988):3466–3469; D.M. Laskin, Treatment of Patients with AIDS: A Matter of Professional Ethics, *Virginia Dental Journal* 66 (1989):7–8; A. Zuger and S.H. Miles, Physicians, AIDS and Occupational Risk: Historic Traditions and Ethical Obligations, *JAMA* 258 (1989):1924–1928; D. Ozar, AIDS, Risk and the Obligations of Health Professionals, in *AIDS and Ethics: Biomedical Ethics Reviews*, edited by J.M. Humber and R.F. Almeder (Clifton, N.J.: Humana Press, 1989); J.F. Lundberg, Legal and Ethical Aspects of the AIDS Crisis, *Journal of Dental Education* 53 (1989):515–517; K.F. Marshall, Surgeons Fear Threat of AIDS in the Air, *British Dental Journal* 169 (1990):276; M. Houpt, To Treat of Not to Treat, *Journal of the American Dental Association* 120 (1990):378, 380.

8. H.M. Hazelkorn, The Reaction of Dentists to Members of Groups at Risk of AIDS, *Journal of the American Dental Association* 119 (1989):611–619.

9. B. Gerbert, The Impact of AIDS on Dental Practice: Update 1989, *Journal of Dental Education* 9 (1989):529–530; B. Gerbert, AIDS and Infection Control in Dental Practice: Dentists' Knowledge, Attitudes, and Behaviors, *Journal of the American Dental Association* 114 (1987):311–314.

10. E.D. Pellegrino and D.C. Thomasma, *For the Patient's Good: Restoration of Beneficence in Health Care* (New York: Oxford University Press, 1988).

11. M.A. Sande, The Transmission of AIDS: The Case against Casual Contagion, *New England Journal of Medicine* 324 (1986):380–382; J.M. Mann et al., HIV Seroprevalence among Hospital Workers in Kinshasa, Zaire: Lack of Association with Occupational Exposure, *JAMA* 256 (1986):3099–3112; D.K. Henderson, HIV-1 in the Health-Care Setting, in *Principles and Practice of Infectious Diseases*, 3rd ed., edited by G.L. Mandell et al. (New York: Churchill Livingstone, 1990).

12. Cf. *Newsweek*, June 1, 1987, 55. See also What Are Your Odds for Getting AIDS from Patients, *Emergency Medicine*, September 30, 1987, 69–73; Loopholes in AIDS Risk Data, *Emergency Medicine*, September 30, 1987, 3–4.

13. U.S. Public Health Service, Centers for Disease Control, Estimates of the Risk of Endemic Transmission of Hepatitis B Virus and Human Immunodeficiency Virus to Patients by the Percutaneous Route during Invasive Surgical and Dental Procedures (Centers for Disease Control, Atlanta, January 30, 1991, draft).

14. B. Mischu et al., A Surgeon with AIDS: Lack of Evidence of Transmission to Patients, *JAMA* 264 (1990):467–470; F.P. Armstrong et al., Investigation of a Health Care Worker with Symptomatic Human Immunodeficiency Virus Infection: An Epidemiological Approach, *Military Medicine* 153 (1987)414–418; J.J. Sachs, AIDS in a Surgeon, *New England Journal of Medicine* 313 (1986):1017–1018.

15. B.J. Fahey et al., Frequency of Nonparenteral Occupational Exposures to Blood and Body Fluids before and after Universal Precautions Training, *American Journal of Medicine* 90 (1991):145; E.S. Wong et al., Are Universal Precautions Effective in Reducing the Number of Occupational Exposures among Health Care Workers? A Prospective Study of Physicians on a Medical Service, *JAMA* 265 (1991):1123–1128.

16. American Dental Association, Interim Policy on HIV-infected Dentists (American Dental Association, Chicago, January 16, 1991); American Medical Association, AMA Statement on HIV Infected Physicians (American Medical Association, Chicago, January 17, 1991).

17. American Health Consultants, CDC Draft Calls for Local Panels to Manage Infected Workers, *AIDS Alert* 6 (1991):81–85.

18. L. Gostin, The HIV-infected Health Care Professional, *Archives of Internal Medicine* 151 (1991):663–665; D. Price, What Should We Do about HIV-Positive Health Professionals? *Archives of Internal Medicine* 151 (1991):658–659; S. Landesman, The HIV-Positive Health Professional: Policy Options for Individuals, Institutions, and States, *Archives of Internal Medicine* 151 (1991):655–657.

19. Landesman, The HIV-Positive Health Professional.

20. Ibid.

21. R.J. Blendon and K. Donelan, Discrimination against People with AIDS: The Public's Perspective, *New England Journal of Medicine* 319 (1988):1022–1026; L. Gostin, The AIDS Litigation Project: A National Review of Court and Human Rights Commission Decisions, Parts 1, 2, *JAMA* 263 (1990): 1961–1970, 2085–2093; G.M. Herek and E.K. Glunt, An Epidemic of Stigma: Public Reactions to AIDS, *American Psychologist* 43 (1988):886–891.

22. D. Cox, Manhatten Politician Says He Has AIDS Virus, *Chicago Sun-Times*, August 9, 1991, 23.

23. Survey Shows AIDS Fear High in Workplace, *Chicago Tribune,* February 14, 1988, sec. 7, p. 13A.

24. Doctor with AIDS Virus Forced Out, *Chicago Tribune*, July 28, 1991, sec. 1, p. 18.

25. Ibid.

26. Marshall et al., Patients Fear of Contracting the Acquired Immunodeficiency Syndrome from Physicians; Gerbert et al., Patients' Attitudes toward Dentistry and AIDS.

27. B. Gerbert et al., Physicians and Acquired Immunodeficiency Virus: What Patients Think about Human Immunodeficiency Virus in Medical Practice, *JAMA* 262 (1989):1969–1972.

28. Ibid.; Gerbert et al., Patients' Attitudes toward Dentistry and AIDS.

29. AIDS Study: Many at Risk Not Tested, *Chicago Tribune,* August 20, 1991, sec. 1, p. 10.

30. K. Painter, Health Workers Hide AIDS to Protect Jobs, *USA Today,* September 10, 1991, D1.

31. It should be noted, however, that many persons exposed to the virus never contract AIDS.

32. P. Conrad, The Social Meaning of AIDS, *Social Policy,* Summer 1986, 51–56.

33. B. Gerbert et al., Why Fear Persists: Health Professionals and AIDS, *JAMA* 269 (1988):3481–3483.

34. Blood Samples Fall from Florida Plane, *Chicago Tribune,* August 26, 1991, sec. 1, p. 14.

35. J. Kleinhuizen, Oregon Fear: Tainted Blood, *USA Today,* April 18, 1991, 1A.

36. J. Thorton and C. Mount, AIDS Error Confirmed by Hospital, *Chicago Tribune,* April 26, 1991, sec. 2, p. 2.

37. P. Gorner and M.L. Millenson, Organ Transplant Doctors Try to Calm Fears on AIDS, *Chicago Tribune*, May 18, 1991, sec. 1, pp. 1, 4.

38. T. Lally, Police Rights (letter to the editor), *Chicago Sun-Times,* August 12, 1991, 22.

39. R. Rossi, Six Mob Suspects Want out after Jail AIDS Disclosure, *Chicago Sun-Times*, August 13, 1991, 3.

40. M. O'Connor and J. Crimmins, Prison Dentist Sues to Hide AIDS, *Chicago Sun-Times*, August 10, 1991, 3.

41. J.F. Sullivan, Judge Rules Surgeon Infected with AIDS Must Tell Patients, *New York Times,* April 26, 1991, 13.

42. Ibid.

43. Ibid.

44. S. Staver, Wider AIDS Virus Testing Urged: Mandatory Testing Strongly Opposed, *American Medical News,* March 13, 1987, 9–11; M.D. Hagen et al., Routine Preoperative Screening for HIV: Does the Risk to the Surgeon Outweigh the Risk to the Patient? *JAMA* 259 (1988):1357–1359; A.M. Fournier and R. Zeppa, Preoperative Screening for HIV Infection: A Balanced View for the Practicing Surgeon, *Archives of Surgery* 124 (1989):1038–1040.

45. Cf. *Newsweek,* February 16, 1987, 22.

46. E.H. Loewy, AIDS and the Human Community, *Social Science and Medicine* 27 (1988):297–303; E.H. Loewy, Ethical and Communal Issues in AIDS: An Introduction, *Theoretical Medicine* 11 (1991):173–183.

47. K.M. Boyd, HIV Infection and AIDS: The Ethics of Medical Confidentiality, *Journal of Medical Ethics* 18 (1992):173–179.

48. A.R. Jonsen, Is Individual Responsibility a Sufficient Basis for Public Confidence? *Archives of Internal Medicine* 151 (1991):660–662.

49. Ibid.

50. Ibid., 662.

51. R. Bayer, Public Health Policy and the AIDS Epidemic: An End to HIV Exceptionalism? *New England Journal of Medicine* 324 (1991):1500–1504.

52. M. Angell, A Dual Approach to the AIDS Epidemic, *New England Journal of Medicine* 324 (1991):1498–1499.

53. T.A. Brennan, Transmission of the Human Immunodeficiency Virus in the Health Care Setting—Time for Action, *New England Journal of Medicine* 324 (1991):1504–1509.

54. J. Kirby, AIDS Fears Shaping Health-Care Choices, *Chicago Tribune,* August 19, 1991, sec. 1, p. 1.

55. Ibid.

Chapter 21

How AIDS Activists Are Changing Research

Loretta M. Kopelman

The views of activists and investigators sometimes seem to be on a collision course over who should control the testing and use of promising new treatments for those with human immunodeficiency virus (HIV) infection and acquired immunodeficiency syndrome (AIDS). AIDS activists believe that people's interests are sometimes needlessly sacrificed to rigid and overdemanding research procedures. For example, they decried the slow pace of testing by the Food and Drug Administration (FDA) and its tight control over who can receive untested or experimental therapies. Typically, only those enrolled in clinical trials (CTs) of investigational new drugs can receive them; women, children, and those with serious complications are often excluded from these studies. Activists find such rules misguided since they prevent many people from receiving a desired treatment for a rapidly progressing fatal illness. They want access to promising new drugs (whether or not they are being tested) as well as to preliminary information about the efficacy and safety of those drugs currently being tested. Patients should have more choice about whether they are willing to undergo risky, experimental, or even untested therapies, they argue.

In contrast, investigators fear changes that could undermine proven research methods. Modifications in the testing and availability of new treatments might help a few, investigators argue, but will harm many in the long run if untested or poorly tested therapies become widely available. They argue the government has a duty to protect the public from dangerous and ineffective "therapies." They also point to the remarkable gains that have been made in many diseases in a relatively short time because new treatments were systematically evaluated. The best way to improve treatments and protect the public, some argue, is to give investigators the freedom to set the goals, priorities, and methods for testing promising new treatments.[1]

The activists, however, reject such protection and seek a more active role in setting priorities and in saying how studies are conducted. They have drawn attention to the evaluative and ethical nature of many issues regarding the testing and use of promising new treatments. These evaluative and ethical judgments concern decisions about the initiation of trials, the use of placebos, randomization, the selection of subjects, the ending of trials, and how to best protect the general public with respect to promising new treatments. These are not matters that can be settled entirely by science, and activists want a say in resolving them.

To resolve this conflict, research needs to be seen as a cooperative venture where investigators accommodate patients' views of what is in their interests, and patients accommodate proven research methods. Cooperation through representation in the review and development of new treatments would build patient trust and enhance patients' sense of control over their lives. Research can be a cooperative venture, however, only if people without technical knowledge can understand enough to be partners. After discussing how research methods are beginning to change, I will examine critics' charges that patients do not know enough about research regulations and design to be regarded as partners in a cooperative venture and therefore need to be protected. There is a line between what constitutes too much and too little protection of the public. The dispute between AIDS activists and many investigators concerns where to draw that line and who should draw it.

PROTECTING THE PUBLIC OR UNJUSTIFIED PATERNALISM?

Over the years, investigators have devised techniques to protect the public from untested and dangerous drugs. These methods usually involve several different stages of testing and "hard" endpoints to evaluate the effectiveness of treatments. In AIDS research, these hard endpoints are usually death or opportunistic infections.

The FDA has a fourfold classification of drug studies, and traditionally one phase is completed before the next begins. *Phase I* studies focus upon the safety of the investigational new drugs and are usually done with small numbers of people. The subjects, often normal volunteers or selected patients, are typically not randomized. *Phase II* testing usually continues with a small number of patients, carefully monitored to determine the efficacy as well as the safety of the new

treatment. *Phase III* clinical trials are often expanded so that efficacy and safety can be studied in many patients. Investigators prefer Phase III studies to be double-blind (neither doctors nor their patients know which treatment they receive) and randomized (the assignment to treatment arms is made by a chance mechanism). If there is a drug currently being used, they will test it against the new treatment. If there is not, they prefer to test the investigational new drug against a placebo (an inert preparation such as a sugar pill or saline injection). Hundreds and sometimes thousands of patients participate to allow well-grounded comparison between the experimental treatment and the standard treatment if there is one or a placebo if there is no standard treatment.

To be enrolled in Phase III trials, patients may have to meet strict eligibility requirements. This offers more assurance that the results reflect differences among the treatments studied. Often women, children, and those with severe complications are excluded. While such restrictions enhance the trial's internal validity, they raise problems about generalization. If the therapies are only tested on adult men, for example, one does not know how the therapies affect women or children. Results of studies are not usually made public until Phase III trials have been completed and published.

Phase IV studies are used to collect additional information after the new therapy has been released for marketing. Once a drug has been marketed, it is important to continue to collect information since physicians may use it in ways other than those for which it has been tested or may find rare reactions. In this way, investigators gather data about new uses or previously excluded populations such as children, women, and individuals with complications.

Activists were dissatisfied with this way of conducting clinical trials. Often taking many years to complete, these preset rigid phases of testing kept promising new drugs away from the public. Activists also charged the strict eligibility criteria were unfair to those excluded.[2] In addition, when testing takes so long, newer studies show that the ongoing protocol no longer provides optimal care for all its patient-subjects. Hence, activists demanded more flexibility.

There have been some changes in response to these criticisms.[3] Surrogate or "soft" endpoints sometimes replace hard endpoints in ending trials. For example, soft endpoints were used in approving dideoxyinosine (DDI) for marketing. Investigators did not know how DDI affected the hard endpoints of death or opportunistic infections, but they did know it increased lymphocyte levels. The use of soft or surrogate endpoints to end trials satisfied those who wanted to speed up trials but brought criticism from those who questioned whether we understood enough about the relationship between the hard and soft endpoints.[4]

In addition, in an attempt to defuse some of these problems, the Public Health Service (PHS) expanded the availability of investigational new drugs by means of a parallel track.[5] Patients with HIV-related diseases can obtain experimental drugs even though they are not enrolled as subjects in the clinical trials of the drug. These regulations require that there are no therapeutic alternatives, the drugs are being tested, there is some evidence of their efficacy, there are no unreasonable risks for the patient, and the patient cannot participate in the clinical trials.

Byar et al. favor this and other ways of modifying the traditional ways of doing trials.[6] Many more doctors could include their patients in trials if investigators streamlined data sets by asking fewer but more pertinent questions. In addition, investigators can sometimes speed up testing by using factorial designs that compare two or more drugs simultaneously. The use of more flexible entry criteria and streamlining of data sets also encourages more collaboration with physicians around the country. This would have the consequence of enabling more patients to enroll, making results more generalizable. It would also make treatments available to more patients and minimize the use of parallel treatment tracks.

Byar et al. do, however, spell out a proposal for parallel track of uncontrolled Phase III trials that meet the following requirements.

(1) There must be no other treatment *appropriate* to use as a control; (2) there must be sufficient experience to ensure that the patients not receiving therapy will have a uniformly poor prognosis; (3) the therapy must not be expected to have substantial side effects that would compromise the potential *benefit* to the patient; (4) there must be a *justifiable expectation* that the potential *benefit* to the patient will be sufficiently large to make interpretation of the results of a nonrandomized trial unambiguous; and (5) the scientific rationale of the treatment must be sufficiently strong that a positive result would be widely *accepted*.[7] [emphasis added].

I have stressed certain words in this quotation because they are highly evaluative: "appropriate," "a justifiable expectation," "benefit," and "accepted." Appropriate for what? Expected by whom? Acceptable or beneficial in what way? Answering these questions involves more than scientific judgments. Careful answers to them also require evaluative and moral judgments about risks and benefits in relation to some goal.

Patients' perspectives on these issues are often different from investigators' perspectives. Investigators are interested in improving care for future patients. Patients may be more interested in how the treatment will affect them personally. For example, an investigator's primary interest may be assessing differences in group survival over five years, while a patient may be more interested in such quality-of-life aspects as potential cost, hospital stays, nausea, confusion, or dementia.

Even with this move to greater flexibility, then, the conception of a clinical trial as a cooperative venture could be undermined by having investigators determine when flexibility is acceptable, a justifiable expectation, or appropriate. For example, why should this proposal be limited to life-threatening diseases? How poor must the prognosis be to qualify? These are not questions that science alone can answer. AIDS activists want to help make key judgments about what sort of testing and priorities *are appropriate*.

In May 1992, a promising new antiviral agent, D4T (Stavudine), began Phase II and III testing. This testing illustrates the changes we have just discussed. First, Phase II testing was not completed before Phase III began. Second, D4T is being compared to AZT and physicians can obtain D4T for their HIV patients on a parallel track free from the manufacturer; children under 13 years of age and women who are pregnant or breast-feeding infants are excluded.[8] The same manufacturer distributed DDI (trade name didanosine) to over 23,000 patients on expanded-access programs.

Not everyone is happy about these changes. Some believe they reduce public safety by undercutting proven methods and scientific standards. The general public may not understand that drugs available on a parallel track are largely untested or why insurance companies refuse to pay for untested therapies. Moreover, members of the public may not participate in clinical trials once they realize the promising new drug is available outside the study.

CAN RESEARCH BE A COOPERATIVE VENTURE?

Critics argue that viewing research as a cooperative venture where patient-subjects are seen as partners in the clinical trials rests upon a "shaky foundation."[9] They doubt whether so-called informed consent is really informed or whether patients can understand enough about risks or benefits of alternative treatments, randomization, interim data, probabilities, or the scientifically rigorous methodology used in testing to make them anything like partners.[10] Some assert that the problem is that patients, families, and their advocates tend to rely upon anecdotal information and so-called common sense.[11] These critics agree that research cannot be a cooperative venture, but they fall into two distinct groups when it comes to the question whether to defend the traditional clinical trial methodologies.

Defenders of Traditional Clinical Trial Methods

One group of critics believes that we must defend investigators' freedom to design what they regard as the best studies, and to do this they want to restrict patients' "rights." These critics argue that patients have a right to optimal treatment but not to pick their treatment.[12] The current understanding of patients' rights is unreasonable, they hold, and disrupts clinical trials. If investigators give up more control, they claim, we would further slow medical progress and muddy the waters with even worse methodology. These critics conclude that we should support investigators' freedom to design the best clinical trials and modify patients' rights for the sake of public utility.

It seems unlikely, however, that AIDS activists would be satisfied with *fewer* rights and less control, even given these critics' assurances that future patients will benefit from better clinical trials. These activists do not agree that investigators are making choices that are most socially useful. Giving investigators the "right" to design trials without interference is ineffective, moreover, if patients will not enroll in them or follow directions if they do participate.

Critics of Traditional Clinical Trial Methods

Another group of critics also denies that research can be a cooperative venture with patient-subjects because patients do not understand enough to be partners. But they reach a different conclusion about what policy to adopt. These critics maintain that investigators do not explain, and most patients do not understand, that at some point in the trial it may become apparent that some groups are getting suboptimal care.[13] Without informed consent, traditional methods put medical advances ahead of patients' rights and welfare. The patient should come first, and doctors should not enroll their patients in studies where they do not come first. Traditional research methods, they hold, typically violate physicians' duties to their patients.[14] These critics understand the physicians' duty, or what some call the *therapeutic obligation,* as the duty to provide patients with what their doctors believe is the best available care. These critics view traditional clinical trial methodology as entailing that some patients will receive suboptimal care, and they conclude that such methods are incompatible with the traditional duties of health care professionals.

This statement of the therapeutic obligation, however, presumes that there is a best treatment and that it is up to physicians to determine what is the best treatment for their patients. Both assumptions are often false. First, many times it is uncertain which of two treatments is best. A moral requirement for justifying clinical trials is that the arms must be in clinical equipoise. This is usually understood to mean that the community of investigators and physicians are uncertain about which treatment being tested is best, so there is no known therapeutic advantage to a patient's assignment to any one of the various treatment arms.[15] If physicians must provide what they believe is the best treatment available for their patients, then we must assume they believe there is a best treatment. Yet, this is incompatible with the assumption underlying clinical trials—that the best treatment is recognized to be unknown. It is not surprising, therefore, that these critics reject traditional methods of testing. They assume treatments cannot be in clinical equipoise.

Second, this formulation of the therapeutic obligation (that physicians must provide patients with what they believe is the best available care) is paternalistic because it assumes that physicians know what is best for patients. Yet AIDS activists have demonstrated they are unwilling to let others decide what is best for them. Many patients want to consider treatments in light of their goals, values, and principles to determine how alternative treatments affect the quality of their lives. If patients do not think the treatment arms of the trial are in equipoise from their perspective, they will refuse to participate. This led

Lo to conclude, "Thus, the concept of equipoise should include the potential volunteers of the clinical trial, as well as the community of investigators."[16]

Both kinds of critics of research as a cooperative venture agree that patients cannot understand enough to be genuine partners and that as a result we have to make some hard choices between investigators' freedom to design what they consider the best trials and patients' rights or welfare. In what follows, I want to question their common assumption that patient-subjects cannot participate as partners because they lack technical knowledge or fail to appreciate that they may be in a group that does not do as well as others.

KNOWLEDGE OR CONTROL?

If the difficulties about viewing research as a cooperative venture centered around the patients' lack of understanding, as some critics believe, then these disagreements would evaporate where there exists a competent and informed subject population. Quite the reverse has happened with the AIDS epidemic, even though many of the patients are highly educated and informed. While individual patients are sometimes ignorant and uncertain, as a group these patients and their families or advocates grow increasingly more informed and more vocal. There are a large number of newsletters, media, and governmental reports about HIV infections (and other chronic diseases) that many patients, families, and advocates carefully follow.

It is also doubtful that the primary problem is just an information gap. Consider how investigators and clinicians react when results seem counterintuitive or when they or their family members are sick. In the January 1991 issue of the *Journal of Clinical Oncology,* an article by Belanger et al. shows that physicians and nurses may accept the results of large randomized trials theoretically but reject them in practice when the results are inconsistent with their own intuitions.[17] In addition, they found that oncologists and oncology nurses were reluctant to agree to participate in clinical investigations when they viewed themselves as the patients. In an editorial in the same issue, Hayes writes, "First, we must be certain that our recommendations to patients are no different than those we would make for ourselves or our families. . . . Moreover, when possible, we should base our treatment recommendations on properly generated data. To do so requires that we not be quick to accept results of studies that support our biases."[18]

When oncologists and oncology nurses are faced with insufficient data, they ought to conclude that this is an ideal time to conduct and enroll as patients in a clinical trial. But when making decisions for themselves or their families, they tended to break the tie with hunches or intuitions. The explanation for their reaction cannot be an information gap. It is possible that some oncologists recommend clinical trials for others but not for themselves or that they are suspicious of how clinical trials are conducted.

Another important explanation, I believe, is that when the decision is *personal* and *risky,* we are reluctant to admit there is genuine uncertainty. When patients enroll in a randomized controlled double-blind clinical trial, they do not control their treatment options. When the stakes are high, clinical trials and randomization force us to confront uncertainty and our lack of power. We have to admit that we may do well or badly depending upon a chance assignment. Our uncertainty may give rise to images of alternative ways our lives may go, and it makes most of us very uncomfortable.

The problem with clinical trials and randomization when the stakes are high is that, not only do we have no control, but we have no defenses against the fact that we have no control. Like the oncologists in the Belanger survey or patients who demand greater access, we prefer to think our intuitions are reliable. I believe that this has less to do with a knowledge gap and more to do with a very human response to uncertainty, risk, and loss of control, especially when the stakes are high.

Critics, however, could say this shows why investigators should be in charge. The tendency to operate by intuitions when we are personally involved shows why research should not be a cooperative venture, they might respond. Yet denying patient-subjects a say in the design of studies ignores their power to defeat trials they dislike. Achievement of the freedom to design and execute studies as investigators believe best, without interference from patients, families, or advocates, will be an empty victory if few patients will participate in them or cooperate if they do enroll.

Critics argue that potential subjects do not know enough to be partners in the testing and use of promising new treatments. Yet these people know enough to defeat trials if they do not perceive them as being in their interest. If a study does not seem to be in their interest (assuming that they are properly informed of the risks and benefits), they will not enroll—or if they do enroll, they may refuse to follow the investigators' directions. Thus, one practical reason for agreeing that patients should be regarded as partners is that they have the power to undercut trials.

Patients can defeat trials by not following the investigators' instructions. For example, Merigan, in a recent issue of the *New England Journal of Medicine*, revealed that the clinical trial of zidovudine (AZT) against a placebo was jeopardized by the fact that 9 percent of the patients who were given a placebo were taking AZT on their own. As Merigan writes, "If these irregularities had been more widespread, the useful effects of the drug could have been obscured in the trial, to the detriment of future patients infected with human immunodeficiency virus (HIV). Specifically, the early initiation of zidovudine therapy in asymptomatic patients would not have become standard practice."[19]

Patients can also defeat trials by refusing to enroll in them. For example, the National Surgical Adjuvant Project for breast and bowel cancers set out to conduct randomized clinical trials on the survival rates of women with breast cancer. Women were asked to give consent before randomization to lumpectomy versus simple mastectomy with or without radiation. Women were asked to go into surgery not knowing if they had cancer, and if they had it, not knowing which treatments they would receive. Because of this uncertainty, many physicians were reluctant to ask their patients to participate in these studies; doctors who agreed to ask them found many women unwilling to accept such conditions.[20] In response to the slow accrual rate, investigators switched to a prerandomized schema. Subjects were informed of their proposed group assignment, treatment options, and the nature and purpose of the study at the time consent was sought. The accrual rate increased sixfold. Several authors found this suspicious and questioned if physicians, perhaps unconsciously, were enthusiastic about whatever assignment the women got since they knew the assigned treatment in advance of seeking consent.[21]

These critics of prerandomization discount what I believe could be an important explanation. Patients may find prerandomization design more acceptable because they know what treatment they will receive. It is not that they cannot understand randomization. Randomization is no harder to understand than the flip of a coin. The problem with randomization is related, I believe, to how we react to uncertainty when we are very apprehensive. When there is great potential loss or gain, agreeing to randomization forces us to confront uncertainty. We cannot rationalize that we have control or that there is some reasonable way to break the tie. The issue is not merely about information but also involves our difficulty in admitting that we have little control. Randomization forces us to admit we have no defenses against uncertainty, risk, and loss of control.

MORAL AND VALUE JUDGMENTS IN RESEARCH

AIDS activists have drawn attention to longstanding debates over how new therapies should be tested and used. Many of these are evaluative and ethical and not just scientific disputes, and informed people of good will can legitimately disagree about the issues involved.

Beginning Trials

AIDS activists were eager to have compound Q tested because of some evidence from laboratory tests that it could combat the HIV virus. Compound Q is derived from Chinese cucumber roots. Frustrated by what they took to be a slow reaction to a promising new drug, members of Project Inform organized trials on their own. They obtained compound Q illegally. Their trial had no institutional review and no independent data safety monitoring committee; some subjects suffered serious complications and death. Critics argue that people rushed to conduct a trial before safe dosages had been established.[22] Compound Q is now being systematically tested. The lack of agreement and cooperation about when to begin a trial, however, sadly led to some deaths.

Using Placebos

There are many methodological advantages to using placebos. A placebo control trial can show a treatment's efficacy uncontaminated by the patient's expectations (the placebo effect) and can also unequivocally establish one drug as a standard therapy. This happened for AZT and aerosol pentamidine for treatment of HIV and opportunistic infections. Such conclusive tests have important consequences. If insurance companies are shown these therapies work, they will pay for them.

To use a placebo in clinical trials, however, it should be uncertain when the trial begins whether the patients are better off with the placebo or the experimental treatment. If a reasonable and informed person would want the promising treatment, it may be wrong to use a placebo.[23] Moreover, the subjects in clinical trials are patients, and their health care professionals have a duty to provide optimal treatment for all their patients. If the placebo arm is not offering good care, the health care professionals are not fulfilling their moral commitment to their patients. Yet we may disagree over what we really know or what the reasonable person would want. For example, when AZT was first being tested, some objected that it was wrong to use a placebo. They maintained that under the circumstances, a reasonable person would want AZT because the drug *might* help them. They knew that the placebo would not help them. Other argued that until the testing was completed, we would not really know if the treatment is better or worse than a placebo.

Selecting Subjects

Restricting eligibility criteria for the sake of the internal validity of a study has, as we have seen, raised problems about fairness and generalizability. Restrictions were imposed to make studies more internally valid and allegedly designed to protect vulnerable research subjects. Critics, however, see them as unfair. For example, Pizzo argued that a variety of regulatory obstacles keep children with AIDS from getting the only drugs that could help them.[24] Federal and state rules then restricted the use of untested drugs such as AZT on children.

Women also claimed that rules allegedly designed to protect them from untested drugs really harmed them. One reason that women were excluded was that they might become pregnant and the fetus could be harmed by an experimental drug. Barring women from participating in trials just because they are or might become pregnant denies them the same access to new and promising therapies as men. It assumes that there will be a conflict of interest between the needs of the mother and fetus, and that the welfare of the fetus should come first as a matter of policy. Also troubling is that if drugs are only tested on men, it is not clear how these drugs will affect women. This seems unjust, since women's tax dollars support these studies yet women do not get the same benefit from them as men. The NIH, under the leadership of

Bernadine Healy, sought to address this problem, but the progress so far has been discouraging.[25]

People no longer think of all research as a risky burden they want to avoid. Consequently, the rule "women, children, and the sickest last" no longer seems gallant—it seems unfair. Issues about the fair selection of subjects in research have shifted radically, especially in the last few years. Many people with life-threatening illnesses want to participate in trials as a way to gain access to promising investigational new drugs. In addition, poor people may see participating in a clinical trial as their only or best way to get good medical care. Finally, excluding large groups makes it difficult to generalize the findings.

Randomization

The double-blind, placebo-control methodology is often regarded as the gold standard in clinical trials. Randomization eliminates nuisance variables that might confound the results, such as age or nutritional habits, by distributing people with differences in these variables throughout the arms of the studies. This helps ensure that the results of the study are due to the different modalities that patients receive.

Randomization is justifiable when the treatments are equally good. It is unethical to assign patients randomly to clinical trials when the arms are not in clinical equipoise, especially when a disease is fatal or rapidly progressing. The view of investigators and patients about what is equally good, however, may be different. Investigators may view what they regard as an insufficiently tested treatment as no better than a placebo. Patients may not because there are no other treatments and their disease is progressing rapidly. Thus, they do not want to be in a randomized, controlled trial. For example, ganciclovir is an antiviral drug. Investigators wanted to use it to treat cytomegalovirus retinitis, which is an opportunistic infection causing blindness. A randomized, placebo-control trial was planned that would exclude patients taking

AZT, but critics objected that such a randomized clinical trial would be unethical.[26] The views of the critics won the day, but others objected that this drug was released without rigorous testing.

Ending Trials

When AZT was first shown to help some AIDS patients, a double-blind, placebo-controlled, randomized clinical trial was begun. Some patients received AZT, others a sugar pill placebo. After several months of testing the AZT against a placebo, 16 of the 137 patients on the placebo arm died while only 1 of the 145 patients receiving AZT died. The trial was ended, and those having gotten the placebo then received AZT.[27] Arguments about whether this trial should have ended earlier or later are moral arguments about how to balance two important values: the safety of individual patients and the social utility of reliable research. The controversy was not just about what we know and when but about who controls the decision when to end studies or use placebos.

Health care professionals may have a different perspective than investigators. Investigators typically focus on helping future patients and are reluctant to end a study unless they believe the results are conclusive. Doctors and nurses, however, are committed to providing their individual patients good care. Many wanted their patients to get AZT and not the placebo.

Suppose, however, that AZT had been proven harmful. This is a possible outcome, since to justify the clinical trials it should be uncertain whether the patients are better off with the placebo or the experimental treatment. If thalidomide (at one time given for nausea in pregnancy but later found to cause severe birth defects) had been tested against a placebo, those in the placebo group would have done far better. After the thalidomide tragedy, when many of the FDA's regulations were put in place, a dominant concern was to protect the public from untested and potentially dangerous new treatments. If AZT had been not clearly useful but harmful, this attitude might have persisted. But AZT was very successful compared to the placebo—and appeared to be so from the beginning. Although a double-blind format was used in the study, rumors persisted that physicians and nurses knew which patients were getting the AZT and opposed giving placebos to their patients.

RESEARCH AS A COOPERATIVE VENTURE

I have argued here and elsewhere[28] that research should be viewed as a cooperative venture between patient-subjects and investigators. Critics of this view argue that patients do not really understand enough about technical matters to be partners in any meaningful way. Although it is true that not all patients can participate, representatives from affected groups could have a role in planning for the testing and use of promising new therapies.

AIDS activists have focused attention on some longstanding moral disputes over how to conduct trials. They have helped to change how clinical trials are done by speeding up the approval of drugs, getting patients access to therapies being tested, obtaining some information about preliminary trends, and changing how patients are selected for trials. AIDS activists want more of a say in making moral and evaluative choices about when to begin trials, end studies, randomize, use placebos, and select subjects from different groups. Advocates for other diseases also have newsletters, follow new promising treatments, and demand more control.

Even if research becomes more of a cooperative venture, we are still left with some very difficult choices. When it comes to new drugs or medical procedures, how much protection do we want and how much access and freedom? We often limit freedom for protection. The degree of protection we want is a social and moral problem not just a scientific matter. We are in the position of having to decide how much testing we as a society consider appropriate for establishing the safety and efficacy of promising new treatments before allowing them to be made available. Reaching such a decision is not unlike determining how much screening we desire in airports or how much safety inspection of buildings we want. It is only natural that when we think about the drugs that caused great harm, like thalidomide, we want a great deal of protection. But when we think about drugs that turned out to be beneficial, like AZT, we want to have early access to them and are impatient with long trials. We cannot have it both ways.

Research needs to be a cooperative venture where patients or their advocates acknowledge proven research methods and investigators acknowledge patients' views of what is in their interest. It would build trust and a spirit of compromise to acknowledge that research is a cooperative venture; one hopes that it would result in an informed and productive partnership. The primary goal of clinicians, investigators, and patients is to fight disease. Fighting each other by designing studies in which subjects will not enroll or cooperate or by proposing poor testing methods that investigators cannot accept thwarts the common goal of fighting disease. Accordingly, activists need to acknowledge that the rapid progress that has been made in medical research in recent decades has come from using proven research methods. On the other hand, the broad powers that some investigators want are discordant with other values of our country. We live in a country where people can do dangerous and foolish things. They can swim in shark infested waters and camp near active volcanoes if they wish. Accordingly, patients may object when they are prohibited from taking promising new treatments that they believe are their only hope for improved health. If they can assume risks for themselves for sport, why can they not take risks for health? Since neither patients, nor investigators, nor clinicians can succeed in achieving the goal of fighting disease without the others, the best policy is to foster cooperation, mutual trust, and a spirit of compromise.

NOTES

1. M. Zelen, A New Design for Randomized Clinical Trials, *New England Journal of Medicine* 300 (1979):1242–1245; J.S. Tobias, Informed Consent and Controlled Trials, *Lancet* (1988, vol. 2):1194.

2. R. Dresser, Wanted: Single, White Males for Medical Research, *Hastings Center Report* 22, no. 1 (1991):24–29; B. Healy, The Yentl Syndrome, *New England Journal of Medicine* 325 (1991):275; P.A. Pizzo, Pediatric AIDS: Problems within Problems, *Journal of Infectious Diseases* 161 (1990):316–325.

3. D.P. Byar et al., Design Considerations for AIDS Trials, *New England Journal of Medicine* 323 (1990):1343–1348; U.S. Public Health Service, Expanded Availability of Investigational New Drugs through a Parallel Track Mechanism for People with AIDS and HIV-related Disease, *Federal Register*, May 21, 1990, 20856–20860.

4. B. Lo, Ethical Dilemmas in HIV Infection: What Have We Learned? *Law, Medicine and Health Care* 20 (1992):92–103.

5. U.S. Public Health Service, Expanded Availability of Investigational New Drugs.

6. Byar et al., Design Considerations for AIDS Trials.

7. Ibid., 1344.

8. S. Staver, New Antiviral Agent, D4T, Now Available to Treat HIV, *American Medical News,* October 19, 1992, 4.

9. K. Schaffner, Ethical Problems in Clinical Trials, *Journal of Medicine and Philosophy* 11 (1986): 297–315.

10. G.J. Annas. AIDS, Compassion and Drugs, *Hastings Center Report* 21, no. 4 (1991):44–45; J.B. Kadane, Progress toward a More Ethical Method for Clinical Trials, *Journal of Medicine and Philosophy* 11 (1986):385–404; M.J. Lacher, Physicians and Patients as Obstacles to a Randomized Trial, *Clinical Research* 26 (1978):375–379; J. Waldenstrom, The Ethics of Randomization, in *Research Ethics*, edited by K. Bare and K.E. Tranoy (New York: Alan R. Liss, 1983), 243–249; Zelen, A New Design for Randomized Clinical Trials; Tobias, Informed Consent and Controlled Trials.

11. Annas, AIDS, Compassion and Drugs.

12. Zelen, A New Design for Randomized Clinical Trials.

13. D. Wikler, Ethical Considerations in Randomized Clinical Trials, *Seminars in Oncology,* December 8, 1981, 437–441.

14. C. Fried, Medical Experimentation: Personal Integrity and Social Policy, in *Clinical Studies*, vol. 5, edited by A.B. Bearn et al. (New York: Elsevier Press, 1974);

F. Gifford, The Conflict between Randomized Clinical Trials and Therapeutic Obligation, *Journal of Medicine and Philosophy* 11 (1986):347–366; Kadane, Progress toward a More Ethical Method for Clinical Trials; D. Marquis, An Argument That All Prerandomized Clinical Trials Are Unethical, *Journal of Medicine and Philosophy* 11 (1986):367–384; Wikler, Ethical Considerations in Randomized Clinical Trials.

15. B. Freedman, Equipoise and the Ethics of Clinical Research, *New England Journal of Medicine* 317 (1987):141–145.

16. Lo, Ethical Dilemmas in HIV Infection, 94.

17. D. Belanger et al., How American Oncologists Treat Breast Cancer: An Assessment of the Influence of Clinical Trials, *Journal of Clinical Oncology* 9 (1991):7–16.

18. D.F. Hayes, What Would You Do If This Were Your . . . Wife, Sister, Mother, Self? *Journal of Clinical Oncology* 9 (1991):1–3.

19. T.C. Merigan, You Can Teach an Old Dog New Tricks. How AIDS Trials Are Pioneering New Strategies, *New England Journal of Medicine* 323 (1990):1341–1343.

20. S.S. Ellenberg, Randomization Designs in Comparative Clinical Trials, *New England Journal of Medicine* 310 (1984):1404–1404–1408; B. Fisher, The National Surgical Adjuvant Project for Breast and Bowel Cancer, NSABP Protocol B-06, distributed in 1980 to surgeons; K.M. Taylor et al., Physician's Reasons for Not Entering Eligible Patients in a Randomized Clinical Trial of Surgery for Breast Cancer, *New England Journal of Medicine* 310 (1984):1363–1367.

21. T.L. Beauchamp and J.L. Childress, *Principles of Biomedical Ethics,* 3rd ed. (New York: Oxford University Press, 1989); Ellenberg, Randomization Designs in Comparative Clinical Trials; Marquis, An Argument That All Prerandomized Clinical Trials Are Unethical.

22. Lo, Ethical Dilemmas in HIV Infection.

23. L.M. Kopelman, Consent and Randomized Clinical Trials: Are There Moral or Design Problems? *Journal of Medicine and Philosophy* 11 (1986):317–345.

24. Pizzo, Pediatric AIDS.

25. Dresser, Wanted: Single, White Males for Medical Research; Healy, The Yentl Syndrome.

26. Lo, Ethical Dilemmas in HIV Infection.

27. Beauchamp and Childress, *Principles of Biomedical Ethics.*

28. Kopelman, Consent and Randomized Clinical Trials.

Part III

End of Life, Assisted Suicide, and Euthanasia

Advance Directives in the 1990s: Medical Care of the Dying and the Myth of Sisyphus

James F. Bresnahan

Advance directives in the wider sense include any kind of directions, oral or written, by which a person makes known his or her wishes concerning the kinds of medical treatment he or she would want or not want at a time in the future when this person may have become incapable of expressing these wishes. In this wider sense, advance directives have moral power to shape decisions of caregivers concerning treatments to be forgone or administered, but these directives may or may not have legal power to compel caregivers to follow the person's wishes.

In the stricter sense, advance directives are documents made legally valid by statute in which a person gives directions and/or appoints a surrogate decision maker who will act on behalf of the person in order to deal with future questions that may arise about what kinds of medical treatment this person would want or not want, especially at the point this person is no longer capable of expressing his or her wishes. In both the wider and stricter senses, advance directives are particularly important for determining what caregivers ought to do or not do when death approaches for a no longer competent person dying despite high-technology medical treatment.

Growing public interest in advance directives originates from at least two concerns: a more theoretical "academic" preoccupation with patient autonomy and an urgently "practical" countercultural concern with what I call "appropriate care of the dying."[1]

While these two concerns can and often do coincide, they can be very different from one another in regard to the goals to be achieved by the use of advance directives. Which concern comes to predominate in our society will be very important for the future development of the ethos of high-technology medical care provision, especially provision of care for the dying.

THE THEORETICAL CONCERN WITH PATIENT AUTONOMY

The theoretical concern regards an advance directive primarily as an expression of patient autonomy. The advance directive, therefore, is valued first as a counterfoil to traditional Western physician paternalism, which is seen as a negation of the personal freedom of patients to control their living and dying according to their personally held values. Many academics involved in writing and speaking about medical ethics articulate this intellectual preoccupation with autonomy under the rubric of informed consent, which is held to be required for the patient's proper participation in decision making regarding medical treatment. This preoccupation has been cogently challenged most recently by Pellegrino and Thomasma.[2]

The theoretical preference for patient autonomy as the central focus of bioethics has developed to the point that values important to the physician, such as nonmaleficence (do no harm) and beneficence (act in the patient's best interests), are completely subordinated to patient autonomy.[3] Patient autonomy is thus seen as the value that trumps all other competing values when disputes arise between a patient and medical caregivers about what, if any, medical interventions (diagnostic or therapeutic) will be permitted, especially in the care of a dying patient.

Use of advance directives, whether they constrain or authorize the use of cure-oriented high-technology interventions in the care of the dying, is welcomed by the proponents of this academic view more because it rights the imbalance between the impaired power of the patient and the enhanced power of the caregiver than because it ensures more appropriate care of the dying. That is, advance directives are not viewed primarily as a needed constraint on tendencies to abuse the dying prevalent among caregivers and others, including the families of the dying.

Although proponents of patient autonomy as the supreme value may also be concerned about such matters, they tend to assume that what is inappropriate use of high technology in the care of the dying lies beyond consensus in our radically pluralistic society and that decisions about high-technology treatments should be left to individual patients. From this perspective, individual patients best express their autonomous moral preferences in this matter of how to be treated when dying by preparing legally valid advance directives—whether they mandate useless treatment or not.[4]

The development of law (common case law as well as statutory law) parallels and has itself helped shape the development of this theoretical bias toward patient autonomy as the ethical trump card in disputed questions of appropriate medical intervention, especially when death approaches. Law, given its understandable preoccupation with contractual relationships, has made informed consent the root of legal obligations arising from patient-physician interactions, especially in the area of disputes about abating so-called life-prolonging medical interventions in the case of the dying.[5]

Unfortunately, this primarily theoretical approach can result in arguments that make the exercise of autonomy through composition of an advance directive the only important value, regardless of the content of the directive. I believe that this approach has contributed to contemporary demands for decriminalizing physician-assisted suicide and physician-effected active euthanasia—demands that I believe will, if given in to, ultimately reduce the quality of care provided to the dying.[6] (On the other hand, I believe these demands also express a kind of preemptive self-defense against what is widely perceived to be inability of the providers of high-technology care to appropriately restrain use of cure-oriented treatment harmful to the dying.)

THE PRACTICAL CONCERN WITH CONSTRAINING EXCESSIVE PROLONGATION OF DYING

The other, more practical, concern favoring use of advance directives derives from a perception that in our scientifically advanced culture, with its vaunted high-technology medical care, there exists an urgent need to find ways to constrain death-denying, obsessively activist employment of medical technology and pharmacology where these can and should be judged to have become sources of affliction rather than of healing.[7]

I believe that a primarily practical concern about inappropriate care of the dying is principally found among people who have had direct experience of the excessive suffering still too frequently borne by those who die while undergoing high-technology care. Both caregivers and survivors of often torturous technological and pharmacological interventions have welcomed the development of advance directives in order to constrain the use of such interventions in their own cases when they may be incapacitated and so unable to demand it. And they have advised other persons, especially those dear to them, to seek to use advance directives for the same purpose. It is from the point of view of these persons who entertain this very practical concern to use advance directives to constrain what they regard as senseless and hurtful medical interventions that the ancient Greek myth of Sisyphus illuminates the problematic struggle underlying use of advance directives today.

THE MYTH OF SISYPHUS

In Greek mythology, Sisyphus is punished by Zeus for cleverly evading death. Sisyphus is finally condemned to push a great rock perpetually up a mountain side, a rock that keeps rolling back down to the bottom.[8] Never achieving completion of his onerous task, Sisyphus suffers laborious frustration forever in place of death.

Advocates of the use of advance directives, like Sisyphus, encounter perpetual frustration— in their attempt to control the abusive use of cure-oriented treatments merely to prolong dying. In fact, they are faced with the daunting prospect of having to overcome a deeply ingrained propensity within our culture to deny the normality of human dying, to consider death the principal enemy against which medicine must struggle. At the present time, if one wishes to undergo useless and torturous treatment, one need not execute an advance directive. But recent reports indicate not only that advance directives continue to be rarely employed[9] but that the directions they contain limiting cure-oriented treatment are frequently resisted or ignored.[10]

On the level of individuals and intimate groups, advance directives can and usually do serve very important, sensible human purposes, I believe that we also employ advance directives, at least implicitly, to critique widely shared attitudes that we consider inconsistent with sensible and compassionate care of the dying. In other words, we use advance directives as a lever to change the dominant attitudes and practices of our medical care sector and of the larger society, although apparently to no effect.

Our culture persists in acting as if it is always morally problematic not to institute cure-oriented treatments, even in cases in which such treatments will admittedly burden, not benefit, the dying. Our culture persists in regarding hospice care of the dying as a shabby substitute for "real medicine,"[11] and this in spite of excellent directions available to us on how to provide good care of the dying.[12] Our culture persists in denying that relief of suffering of the dying can take moral precedence over medical efforts, to achieve quantitative prolongation of biological existence.[13]

How ironic that in seeking vainly to achieve common-sense acceptance of the normality of death and to deal with dying in a clinically realistic way, a way that most human beings would prefer, we have to experience the perpetual frustration that afflicts Sisyphus because he tried to evade death.

HOW TO USE ADVANCE DIRECTIVES

Though our use of advance directives seems to have done little to change the presently dominant cultural refusal to deal realistically and appropriately with death and dying, we can still profit greatly as individuals from planning and executing them.

First, the intellectual and spiritual effort to prepare an advance directive requires that one share one's understanding of the meaning of death with one's family and close friends. Such sharing about such a basic, yet frightening dimension of human existence leads us back from denial and the self-deluding tactics of denial to fundamentally authentic living in relationship to others. It reminds us that we are not totally in control of our own lives, much less of persons to whom we are personally related. It reminds us, too, that part of being an autonomous person is striving to live out, calmly and courageously, an acceptance of what we do not control. For religious believers, this should involve an explicit spirit of gratitude for what has been given and of hope in eternal life, as well as loving care for those who are left behind after death. These dispositions are not without meaning for many who do not admit to being religious believers.

Second, these forms of sharing can lead to efforts of individuals and basic personal groups to support the development of hospice-type programs at the grass-roots level. Service of those in need, especially the dying and their families, central to the actual historical development of health care in Western civilization, can again become a task in which we can all participate. This, in turn, may provide the additional leverage needed to influence the widely shared cultural avoidance of dealing with death that our use of advance directives alone seems unable to alter.

Perhaps the frustration felt by Sisyphus is caused as much by the loneliness of his task as by his apparent inability to complete it.

NOTES

1. J.F. Bresnahan, Catholic Spirituality and Medical Interventions in Dying, *America* 164 (1991):670–675.

2. E.D. Pellegrino and D.C. Thomasma. *For the Patient's Good: The Restoration of Beneficence in Health Care* (New York: Oxford University Press, 1988).

3. Ibid., 11–36.

4. The response of some commentators to the sad case of Helga Wanglie illustrates this preoccupation with the formal exercise of freedom. See the thoughtful discussion of what happened and the various reactions to it in S.H. Miles, Informed Demand for "Nonbeneficial" Medical Treatment, *New England Journal of Medicine* 325 (1991):512–515; S.H. Miles: Interpersonal Issues in the *Wanglie* Case, *Kennedy Institute of Ethics Journal* 2, no. 1 (1992):61–72.

5. For a fine discussion of the need to reshape the legal view of the problem of allowing the discontinuation of what most dying patients regard as excessively burdensome treatments, see D.S. Davis, Shifting the Burden of Proof, *Second Opinion: Health, Faith, Ethics* 18, no. 3 (1993):31–36. For a sharp critique of the majority's hesitation to acknowledge a fundamental liberty interest in ending useless treatment of the dying in the celebrated Nancy Curzan case, see G.J. Annas, The Insane Root Takes Reason Prisoner: The Supreme Court and the Right to Die, *Health Care, Law and Ethics* 8, no. 1 (1993):21–27.

6. A cogently argued but dead wrong espousal of justified homicide in the name of mercy appears in Physician-assisted Suicide and the Right to Die with Assistance, *Harvard Law Review* 105 (1992):2021–2040. See also J.F. Bresnahan, Getting Beyond Suspicion of Homicide: Reflections on the Struggle for Morally Appropriate Care of the Dying under High Technology Medical Care, *Health Care, Law and Ethics* 8, no. 1 (1993):31–34, 38.

7. Direct testimony regarding the prevalence of excessively burdensome treatment of the dying by caregivers who do, in fact, clinically recognize the approach of inevitable death appears in M.Z. Solomon et al., Decisions near the End of Life: Professional Views on Life-sustaining Treatments, *American Journal of Public Health* 83, no. 1 (1993):14–23. The imposition of excessive suffering on the dying due to the unwillingness of caregivers to stop cure-oriented treatment is discussed in the following articles: S.H. Wanzer et al., The Physician's Responsibility toward Hopelessly Ill Patients, *New England Journal of Medicine* 310 (1984):955–959; S.H. Wanzer et al., The Physician's Responsibility toward Hopelessly Ill Patients: A Second Look, *New England Journal of Medicine* 320 (1989):844–849.

8. For an interesting account of the myth of Sisyphus, see Yves Bennefoy, *Greek and Egyptian Mythologies,* translated under the direction of Wendy Doniger (Chicago: University of Chicago Press, 1992), 106–108.

9. See the evaluation of the use of advance directives and recommendations in J. La Puma et al., Advance Directives on Admission: Clinical Implications and Analysis of the Patient Self-Determination Act of 1990, *JAMA* 266 (1991):402–405; see also M.L. White and J.C. Fletcher, The Patient Self-Determination Act: On Balance, More Help Than Hindrance (editorial), *JAMA* 266 (1991):410–411.

10. Solomon et al., Decisions near the End of Life.

11. R.J. Miller, Hospice Care as an Alternative to Euthanasia, *Law, Medicine and Health Care* 20, nos. 1–2 (1992):127–132.

12. N.H. Cassem, The Dying Patient, in *The Massachusetts General Hospital Handbook of Hospital Psychiatry*, 3rd ed., edited by N.H. Cassem (St. Louis: Mosby Year Book, 1991).

13. For a sustained argument that relief of suffering is a goal of medicine just as primary as prolonging life, see E.J. Cassell, *The Nature of Suffering and the Goals of Medicine* (New York: Oxford University Press, 1991).

Chapter 23

Ethical Issues in the Use of Fluids and Nutrition: When Can They Be Withdrawn?

T. Patrick Hill

The issue of withholding and withdrawing artificial nutrition and hydration from dying and permanently unconscious patients has become a serious ethical problem in the last ten years. It helps to measure the gravity of the problem when we remember that between 10,000 and 60,000 dying or permanently unconscious patients are actually maintained on sustenance supplied artificially by tubes.

In the case of one million recovering patients who annually receive artificial nutrition and hydration, no one doubts that artificial sustenance is a boon. But for those patients who, with or without artificially provided sustenance, have no hope of recovering from their illness, supplying nutrition and hydration may be as inappropriate as maintaining a brain-dead body on a ventilator. "Yet, perhaps because of the uniquely symbolic significance of nourishment in the minds of many, artificial feeding appears to be more difficult to discontinue than any other treatment. And this applies both to patients who are expected to die in a relatively short time, and to permanently unconscious and other patients whose death may not occur for months or years unless sustenance by tube is stopped."[1]

Is there something intuitively sound about this symbolism? If so, does it justify the difficulty we feel when we consider discontinuing artificial feeding? Or is it possible on the basis of rational analysis to come to the conclusion that there are indeed sound ethical reasons why we should withhold or withdraw artificial nutrition and hydration? This essay will attempt to show that in the case of dying and permanently unconscious patients, our intuitive sensitivity to the symbolism of nourishment notwithstanding, there are solid ethical grounds for discontinuing artificial sustenance and permitting death from natural causes to occur.

The ethical questions surrounding the withdrawal of fluids and nutrition from a dying patient are more complicated in one significant respect than the withdrawal of any other life-sustaining treatment, such as antibiotics or cardiopulmonary resuscitation. The basic medical justification for the withdrawal of antibiotics, for example, is that under a particular set of clinical circumstances, they can no longer achieve their clinical purpose. When that happens, the basic ethical justification for withdrawal would come from the absence of any inherent value, again under these particular circumstances, in continuing to provide antibiotics. The ensuing death of the patient is medically acceptable on the grounds that it results from an underlying pathology now no longer considered treatable. The death is ethically acceptable as something that has happened in the natural course of events; in this case, the inevitable progress of a fatal illness over which there is now no human control and for which there is no human responsibility.

Fluids and nutrition used in the care of a dying patient do not fit quite as readily into this line of medical and ethical reasoning. For one thing, they embody the natural instinct to care for the most vulnerable, the dying, when all hope of cure is gone. But they can also serve to draw the distinction between cure and care in the medical setting. There may be a point in the course of illness beyond which medical treatment is useless and can, as a result, be stopped or withheld; it appears counterintuitive to say the same of care. There is no medical justification for ceasing to provide care to a dying patient, and since there is always inherent value in providing care, there is no ethical justification for withholding it either. According to this line of reasoning, as long as fluids and nutrition are seen only as being a means of caring for, not curing, a dying patient, there would be no medical or ethical justification for withholding them in some form or another or in some degree or another.

Consequently, it is of paramount importance to determine if and when fluids and nutrition can be regarded as having a medical purpose in addition to that of providing human care and, beyond that, to determine if and when the provision of fluids and nutrition to a dying patient serves no medical purpose and does not constitute the provision of human care to that patient.

In order to do this, it is necessary to acknowledge the difference between food and drink, on the one hand, and artificial nutrition and hydration, on the other. "The common forms of eating and drinking are not at issue; this is not a matter of denying a person a lunch. At issue here is a range of medical technologies that vary in complexity, sophistication and, at times, danger. To-

tal parenteral feeding is a world apart from dining on fried chicken, and the difference between them is obvious."[2] There is a universal need for food and drink to sustain life. There is no such need for artificial nutrition and hydration to sustain life.

As a universal need, food and drink might best be seen as a means of human care. Artificial nutrition and hydration, however, since they are designed to address a medical condition, such as a temporary or permanent inability to swallow, are better seen as a form of clinical treatment. Consequently, their use and purposes will be determined by the patient's diagnosis and prognosis. Understood this way, according to Devine, artificial nutrition and hydration are an integral part of a larger medical effort to restore someone to health or maintain that person at a certain level of human functioning. But when that effort ceases overall to have a medical purpose, nutrition and hydration, as a constitutive part of the effort, also cease to have any purpose.[3] In other words, just as the purposes of the medical treatment plan for the patient justify the decision to provide nutrition and hydration, so any eventual purposelessness of the same medical treatment plan can justify the cessation of treatment, including nutrition and hydration.

If one is not prepared to accept the clean distinction, as suggested here, between food and drink and nutrition and hydration, one can at least admit that nutrition and hydration may oscillate between being administered for purposes of care and purposes of cure. In that sense, nutrition and hydration can be seen as positioned somewhere on a spectrum that is defined at one end as only a means of curing and at the other end as only a means of caring. As a means of curing, nutrition and hydration are morally neutral in themselves; as a means of caring, they become morally positive in themselves. Consequently, the more they move on this spectrum away from being means of care and toward being means of cure, the more legitimate it can become to withdraw nutrition and hydration when the overall medical plan, of which nutrition and hydration are a part, is suspended on the grounds of medical futility. At that point, alternatives for the purposes of care to deal with the patient's hunger and thirst can be used.

The difference between food and water and nutrition and hydration is then an important consideration when making an ethical decision to withhold the latter. So also is the difference between hunger and thirst and malnutrition and dehydration. A 1987 report by the Hastings Center draws the distinction by describing hunger and thirst as a need felt by the patient and defining malnutrition and dehydration as a chemical condition of the patient's body. "Medical procedures for supplying nutrition and hydration treat malnutrition and dehydration; they may or may not relieve hunger and thirst. Conversely, hunger and thirst can be treated without necessarily using medical nutrition and hydration techniques, and without necessarily correcting dehydration or malnourishment."[4] To support the validity of this distinction, the report observes that dehydrated patients, for example, can find relief from thirst by having their lips and mouths moistened with ice chips or a lubricant.[5] This observation gives additional weight to the argument that hunger and thirst are more appropriately the object of interventions to provide care whereas malnutrition and dehydration are more appropriately the object of interventions to achieve cure.

Once the case has been made for nutrition and hydration as a medical intervention, one can make the assumption that the ethical criteria used in deciding to withdraw other medical life-sustaining treatments are applicable in deciding when to withdraw nutrition and hydration.

The core criterion around which all the others will congregate is the integrity of the patient as a person. Modern medicine operates by isolating symptoms and treating them accordingly. While this discriminating methodology, which undeniably reflects the sophistication of contemporary medical practice, is highly effective, it runs the serious risk of atomizing the patient organ by organ, system by system, particularly as a terminal illness runs its course and the body decompensates as a result. Under these circumstances,

it is all too easy to lose sight of the person who is the patient and discount the personal control over treatment decisions without which it will be impossible for these decisions to be ethical.

This entails, on the part of those providing medical treatment, the utmost respect for the physical integrity of the body on which the patient has a fundamental claim. And central to any recognition of the physical integrity of the body as a necessary condition for ethical medical interventions is the patient's informed consent. Hence the need for the patient's consent to be treated and the need to respect the patient's refusal to begin or continue treatment. In other words, it must be a basic working assumption on the part of those responsible for treatment, in this case nutrition and hydration, that they may not withdraw them without the consent of the patient. Even more important, they must recognize that the only source of final authority in the patient-physician relationship is the patient. "Although physicians must often be authoritative about the options available to patients, all involved must recognize that the actual authority over the patient never resides with the physician. Patients alone, or their legal surrogates, have the right to control what happens to them."[6]

All the requirements for an ethically satisfactory decision to withdraw or withhold nutrition and hydration will not be found in the patient's subjective preferences alone, significant as they are. Without direct reference to the clinical context, namely, the actual medical condition of the patient and its projected course, it would be ethically unacceptable to withhold life-sustaining treatment such as nutrition and hydration. Although it is true that ethical decisions are guided by principles, they are also rooted in the actual circumstances that suggest those particular principles and provide the justification for their use in a given case.

This observation is important for the way it illustrates an essential feature of ethical analysis, which, according to one ethicist, "is an exchange between the moral meaning found in the empirical context and the moral meaning found in the several principles contending for application in this concrete case."[7] The moral meaning of the empirical context will be measured in terms of bodily integrity and the extent to which withholding life-sustaining treatment will enhance or diminish that integrity. And as we have already seen, bodily integrity is something to which the patient has a claim and something which the physician must respect.

The next question then is, what is the strength of this claim? How forcefully can the claim to bodily integrity and its corollary, informed consent, be made to justify the decision to withhold or withdraw nutrition and hydration? In responding to this question, ethicists have resorted to the language of rights, saying that bodily integrity is so central to the patient that it can be claimed as a right.

Rights, according to philosophers like Richard Wasserstrom, are "moral commodities" that automatically create obligations and duties.[8] "In other words, a right is a claim, the force of which derives, not from the physical strength or socioeconomic standing of the right holder but the inherent reasonableness of the right being claimed relative to the circumstances under which it is being claimed."[9] Relative to bodily integrity, that would mean a patient's claim to discretion over his or her body. In the context of deciding to withhold or withdraw nutrition and hydration, the implications of such a claim are troublesome because they create obligations and duties for treatment providers. That could and does result in an adversarial situation as the patient or the physician seeks to control the outcome. In turn, that threatens the moral relationship between the patient and the physician presupposed by the patient's claim and the corresponding responsibilities of the physician.

But this problem has less to do with the concept of rights than it has to do with how we understand their function. Understood as a prerogative of the patient alone to be exercised against the physician, the right to bodily integrity can make it very difficult to achieve "the kind of joint decision-making of all the concerned parties that is required by a full theory of moral responsibility."[10] For this reason, philosophers like John Ladd prefer to understand rights as claims to something rather than claims against somebody. A distinct advantage of this interpretation is that it presupposes cooperation rather than competition. Another is that rather than requiring particular obligations of particular individuals, rights entail collective responsibilities on the part of society at large. Ladd therefore refers to rights as ideal and argues that they "relate to things that a society ought to provide for its members so that they will be able to live a good life, that is, a moral life constituted by moral relationships of responsibility and caring."[11]

If we understand the right to bodily integrity as an ideal right on which the decision to withhold nutrition and hydration can be based, thereby permitting the patient to control the circumstances of his or her death, then the manner of the patient's dying becomes a moral enterprise in the same way that the manner of the patient's life has been a moral enterprise. In which case, the decision to withhold or withdraw life-sustaining treatment, such as nutrition and hydration, may constitute the patient's most profound moral need at that stage in life. "As such it will be a necessary means to pursue whatever moral goals have been directing his life up to this point and should now be directing the circumstances and time of his death, if the two are to be consonant."[12]

But rights have a habit of conflicting with other rights, and it is particularly important to understand what this might mean in the present context. The patient's claim to bodily integrity and its corollary, informed consent, in relation to the withdrawal of nutrition and hydration can and does, for example, conflict with society's right to preserve life as an interest central to the integrity of society itself. This conflict lies in one form or another at the heart of the decision to withdraw nutrition and hydration from the patient. As a decision taken in the interests of bodily integrity and informed consent on the part of one individual that leads inevitably to death, it is, potentially at least, a threat to the communal interests society has in the preservation of life in general.

At the same time, both claims can be justified. As a result, neither claim presumably is absolute. It follows then that one or the other claim can only be made legitimately when in doing so the individual does not essentially compromise society and society does not essentially violate the individual. Therefore, any decision on the part of a patient to withdraw nutrition and hydration, if it is to be ethically acceptable, must not constitute a threat to society's legitimate interests in the preservation of life.

The task then becomes one of establishing a working tension between the two claims so that when they do indeed conflict, there is a way to avoid paralysis and achieve a mutually acceptable way of determining which claim, the individual's or society's, should prevail in a given set of circumstances.

In its seminal decision in the case of Karen Ann Quinlan, the New Jersey Supreme Court was acutely conscious of the conflicting claims and of the need to provide a formula by which to resolve the conflict in a way that does justice to both individual and society at the same time. "We think that the State's interests [in the preservation of life] weakens and the individual's right to privacy grows as the degree of bodily invasion increases and the prognosis dims. Ultimately, there comes a point at which the individual's rights overcome the State interest."[13]

In discussing the ethical criteria to be used in withholding nutrition and hydration, this statement is significant in the way it advances self-determination (or privacy, as the court called it) by protecting the bodily integrity from futile medical treatment in the face of an increasingly dim prognosis. Where there is less and less hope that medical interventions will do anything for the well-being of the patient, there is a greater justification, should the patient wish it, to withhold life-sustaining treatment like nutrition and hydration.

So far, this discussion has attempted to lay the ethical foundation for decisions to withhold or withdraw nutrition and hydration from a patient. When either decision is made, the patient will die eventually, raising the question whether such an outcome is, on the face of it, ethically acceptable. In other words, the assumption is that it is

not. Thus, if death has occurred as a result of the decision to withhold or withdraw nutrition and hydration, it becomes necessary to show that someone has the right to make that decision. If someone does, what is the basis of that right? And assuming there is some basis for such a right, what circumstances and outcomes would justify its exercise?

The discussion, up to this point, has attempted to show that the individual with the rights to bodily integrity and self-determination would logically be able to exercise those rights by making decisions, for example, to withhold or withdraw medical treatment in general and nutrition and hydration in particular. In drawing the distinction between care and cure in order to show that nutrition and hydration have more to do with the latter, it becomes possible to see that under appropriate circumstances nutrition and hydration, like any other medical treatment, could be the object of such a decision. In other words, the individual is vested with moral authority to make decisions of this kind, and nutrition and hydration fall within the legitimate range of this authority. And even though this moral authority or right is not absolute, conflicting with a state interest in the preservation of life, there are circumstances in which the individual right to self-determination can take precedence over the state interest.

It remains now to look at those circumstances as they appear in the clinical setting. Since nutrition and hydration are to be considered as a medical treatment, the decision to withdraw or withhold them will depend in some measure on whether, given the patient's condition, they can provide sufficient benefit without imposing at the same time a burden disproportionate to that benefit. Too frequently in this context, the discussion of benefits and burdens is conducted in relation to clinical outcomes. Accordingly, the argument goes, when benefits to the patient's well-being are less than the burdens he or she has to suffer to obtain those benefits, decisions to forgo such treatment are ethically acceptable, even when they hasten death as a result. This is a cogent argument as presented in terms of outcomes. But the real strength of the argument is derived from the individual's right to bodily integrity and self-determination. Otherwise, what would justify ethically the opposite decision to start or continue treatment even though its burdens outweigh the benefits?

This is a critical point because on it rests the principle of self-determination and the correct relationship between the patient and the physician and the responsibility of the physician to provide for informed consent or refusal on the part of the patient. Independently of the patient, the physician can determine that, given his or her patient's diagnosis and prognosis, all treatment options entail greater burden than benefit. On the face of it then, withholding or withdrawing treatment can medically be the right thing to do. But this would not be the ethically acceptable thing, at least minus any consideration given to the principle of patient bodily integrity and the principle of self-determination. Neither of these principles can be secure in the absence of consent or refusal from the patient, who realistically can only provide one or the other on the basis of an awareness of the treatment options and a clear grasp of their respective benefits and harms. Therefore, what gives ethical sanction to the outcomes of a decision, in this instance to withdraw nutrition and hydration, is not solely the objective calculation that the burdens of treatment outweigh any benefits. However necessary that calculation is, for ethical purposes it is not sufficient to meet the demands of the bodily integrity and self-determination of the patient. That will come from the patient's consent to or refusal of treatment informed by a calculation of its burden proportionate to the benefits.

We have seen that in this question of withdrawing nutrition and hydration there is a real and legitimate tension between the rights of the individual and the communal interests of the state. There is also a parallel tension between the rights of the patient and the legitimate claims to professional integrity on the part of the treating physician. Arguably, this tension is never as clearly drawn as when decisions to withdraw nutrition and hydration are being considered. The fundamental ethical question is whether physicians should be involved at all? What in the patient-physician relationship could justify such a decision? Is there anything in the nature of this relationship that would sanction, for example, an obligation on the part of physicians to accede to a patient's request to withdraw nutrition and hydration over their better professional judgment?

At stake, from their point of view, are professional obligations to treat the patient in order to further his or her well-being and to avoid doing harm. In this situation, the question for the physician is how, clinically, does withdrawing nutrition and hydration benefit a patient and also avoid doing harm?

Far from being an oxymoron, the question is reasonable in itself and has been made answerable in part as a result of the argument that nutrition and hydration can be considered a medical treatment. As such, they are morally neither good nor bad in themselves so that there can be no presumption that they should or should not be administered. Like the withdrawal of other treatments then, such as chemotherapy in the case of a patient in the terminal stages of cancer, the withdrawal of nutrition and hydration should be subjected, as we have already said, to a calculation of its benefits proportionate to its burdens in order to provide objective medical reasons why withdrawal not only benefits the patient but also does not harm him or her.

Is that possible? One answer to this question is empirical and will tell us what physiologically happens to a patient from whom nutrition and hydration have been withdrawn. The other is ethical and tells us what becomes of the moral standing of the patient from whom this treatment has been withdrawn. Let us consider the empirical answer first. According to Paul C. Rousseau, artificial hydration has long been thought to ease the discomfort of terminal illness.[14] He points out, however, that recent studies suggest something very different:

> As death approaches, dehydration occurs naturally from inadequate oral intake, gastrointestinal and renal losses, and the loss of secretions from the skin and lungs. Transitory thirst, dry mouth and changes

in mental status have been found to develop—but the headache, nausea, vomiting or cramps frequently associated with water deprivation rarely occur. The mental changes—while upsetting to relatives—bring relief to patients by lessening their awareness of suffering.[15]

Rousseau adds that while the administration of IV fluids may produce a feeling of well-being, that feeling can be of short duration. "In time, artificial hydration is likely to heighten the discomfort of a terminally ill patient, and often exacerbates underlying symptoms."[16]

There is additional clinical evidence in support of the assertion that nutrition and hydration can be harmful to the dying patient. "Tube feeding itself may produce pain; erosions or hemorrhage of the nasal septum, oesophagus, and gastral mucosa have been reported; and nasogastric feeding as well as gastrostomy feeding has been associated with aspiration pneumonia."[17]

With clinical evidence like this, it is reasonable to conclude that "withholding or withdrawing artificial feeding and hydration from debilitated patients does not result in gruesome, cruel, or violent death."[18] Indeed, Rousseau would go further on the basis of his clinical evidence. "Accompanied by comfort measures and emotional support, dehydration is a humane therapeutic response to terminal illness."[19] The Hastings Center guidelines arrive at a similar conclusion: "Patients in their last days before death may spontaneously reduce their intake of nutrition and hydration without experiencing hunger or thirst."[20] As a result, decisions to withhold such treatment can meet the physician's twin obligation to do what is in the patient's best interests and to do no harm to the patient.

As persuasive as this clinical evidence is, are there ethical reasons as persuasive that would justify a physician withdrawing or withholding nutrition and hydration in order to do what is in the patient's best interests and to do no harm to the patient? Essentially, this question is asking what effect does the withdrawal of nutrition and hydration have on the moral standing of the patient? If, as some assert, "life is 'the first right of

the human person' and 'the condition of all the others,'"[21] what circumstances would justify a decision that would inevitably lead to the death of the patient?

Kevin O'Rourke, a medical ethicist, is addressing the same issue when he asserts that "one of the basic ethical assumptions upon which medicine and efforts to nurse and feed people are based is that life should be prolonged and because living enables us to pursue the purpose of life."[22] Included in the purpose of life are happiness, fulfillment, and human relationships, which, O'Rourke observes, "imply some ability to function at the cognitive-affective, or spiritual, level."[23]

Despite the theological orientation of these two particular assertions, there is nothing in either of them that is not reaffirmed in the traditional presumption in clinical practice, which is to favor life. But implicit in the question under consideration in this chapter is the possibility that now there are clinical circumstances in which the presumption in favor of life is no longer ethically acceptable.

To rephrase the question for purposes of ethical analysis, what becomes of the obligation to prolong life when, despite the continuation of treatment, the patient will remain alive but will not recover sufficiently to be him- or herself physically, mentally, and psychologically? Recover, that is, to resume the central purposes of his or her life knowingly, willingly, and emotionally. That implies at least that, before the obligation to prolong life ceases, there is a level of purposefulness to which the patient ought to be able to lay claim and to obtain which the physician can reasonably continue to treat. But if no such level can be hoped for given the patient's prognosis, we place an impossible burden on the patient by continuing to treat: the expectation of life without, however, the means to appropriate it in any personal sense through mental, volitional, or emotional behavior.

Considered in those terms, there seems ample justification to agree with O'Rourke when he concludes that "if efforts to prolong life are useless or result in a severe burden for the patient insofar as pursuing the purpose of life is concerned, then the ethical obligation to prolong life is no longer present."[24]

This is an ethical argument for withholding or withdrawing nutrition and hydration from the patient and should not be confused with the clinical argument for withholding or withdrawing nutrition and hydration from the patient on the grounds that their use imposes burdens disproportionate to any benefits. But the basis for making this particular ethical argument rests in part on the clinical calculation that the burdens of treatment will outweigh its benefits. The clinical calculation is necessary but not sufficient to make the ethical argument. It is important to draw this distinction if we are to see the real limitations of the arguments based on clinical data alone and at the same time to see how unsatisfactory it is to make principled ethical arguments that are not informed by clinical data.

The distinction illustrates another critical point. Too frequently we consider treatments like nutrition and hydration as though they possessed some moral quotient of their own. It would be more accurate, as suggested earlier, to view them as essentially amoral or ethically neutral. And so, to be realistic, any ethical analysis of nutrition and hydration begins with the consequences of their use rather than with nutrition and hydration themselves. Here, the important point is that modern medical practice, in sustaining life, can and does overreach itself with consequences for which it is directly responsible but concerning which it has no professional ability to determine to be ethically acceptable or unacceptable. Accordingly, from the perspective of the patient receiving such treatment, we can no longer presume that medicine, whatever the intentions of physicians, is a benign exercise, at least as far as its outcomes are concerned. As one commentator has put it, "Doctors now choose from a vast array of interventions that, when combined with effective therapies for underlying conditions, often greatly prolong survival."[25] However, as the evidence of one intensive care unit after another will verify, "the quality of life so skillfully sought can range from marginally tolerable to positively miserable."[26] In other words, the distinction between clinical and ethical reasons for withholding life-sustaining treatment shows that there is a difference between judging a clinical intervention like nutrition and hydration to be medically successful in the quantitative, technical sense and judging it to be personally acceptable in relation to the qualitative needs and preferences of the patient. And because of this difference, it is necessary, when making an ethical argument for withholding nutrition and hydration, to acknowledge that the patient's preferences and underlying values will take precedence.

Any decision, therefore, to withhold life-sustaining treatment, like nutrition and hydration, should be made only after the most careful consideration of the patient's best interests as reflected in their preferences and apart from the clinical outcomes as such (since they do not necessarily coincide, they must always be viewed separately). The natural hesitation we feel in making a decision to withdraw or withhold life-sustaining treatment cannot, however, justify holding the patient hostage to our hesitation on the grounds that its initiation or continuation will be medically successfully. Rather, armed with the principles laid out above, we can conclude not only that it is ethically acceptable to withhold or withdraw nutrition and hydration but that it may be the only ethical thing to do in the circumstances examined here.

NOTES

1. Choice in Dying, Background Paper on Artificial Nutrition and Hydration (Choice in Dying, New York, September 1990), 1.

2. R.J. Devine, The Amicus Curiae Brief: Public Policy versus Personal Freedom, *America*, April 8, 1989, 323–334.

3. Ibid., 324.

4. *Guidelines on the Termination of Life-sustaining Treatment and the Care of the Dying* (Briar Cliff Manor, N.Y.: Hastings Center, 1987), 59–60.

5. Ibid., 60.

6. J.E. Ruark, et al., Initiating and Withdrawing Life Support, *New England Journal of Medicine* 318 (1988):25–30.

7. D.C. Maquire, *Death by Choice* (Garden City, N.Y.: Image Books, 1984), 82.

8. R. Wasserstrom, Rights, Human Rights, and Racial Discrimination, in *Human Rights,* edited by A.I. Melden (Belmont, Calif: Wadsworth, 1970), 99.

9. T.P. Hill, The Right to Die: Legal and Ethical Consideration, *Southern Medical Journal* 85, no. 8 (1992):25–57.

10. J. Ladd, The Definition of Death and the Right to Die, in *Ethical Issues Relating to Life and Death,* edited by J. Ladd (New York: Oxford University Press, 1979), 135.

11. Ibid., 139.

12. Hill, The Right to Die.

13. In re Quinlan, 70 N.J., 10, 355 A2d 647, at 37.

14. P.C. Rousseau, How Fluid Deprivation Affects the Terminally Ill, *R.N.*, January 1991, 73–76.

15. Ibid., 73.

16. Ibid., 74.

17. J.C. Ahronheim and M.R. Gasner, The Sloganism of Starvation, *Lancet* 335 (1990):279.

18. Ibid.

19. Rousseau, How Fluid Deprivation Affects the Terminally Ill, 76.

20. *Guidelines on the Termination of Life-sustaining Treatment,* 60.

21. U.S. Bishops' Committee for Pro-Life Activities, Nutrition and Hydration: Moral and Pastoral Reflections, *Origins* 21, no. 44 (1992):705–712.

22. K. O'Rourke, The AMA Statement on Tube Feeding: An Ethical Analysis, *America,* November 22, 1986, 322.

23. Ibid.

24. Ibid.

25. Ruark et al., Initiating and Withdrawing Life Support, 25.

26. Ibid.

Chapter 24

Withholding CPR As Futile Therapy

Cory Franklin

Should physicians withhold cardiopulmonary resuscitation (CPR) from patients based on the argument that it is futile therapy? The answer to this controversial question has profound implications for the American health care system medicolegally, bioethically, and, not incidentally, financially. In a recent essay, Coogan has made a compelling case that "the long traditions of beneficence and nonmaleficence support the physician . . . in retaining the responsibility for what care will be delivered in the patient's best interests."[1] Certainly his concern that when it is impossible to support the patient's value system the focus should be on ameliorating suffering and not prolonging dying is an estimable one shared by many observers.

The question, however, is of sufficient gravity that it should not be resolved solely on the basis of bioethical theorizing within the academic world. If physicians do withhold CPR (based ultimately on the beneficence model), the full implications of this must be explored in practical clinical terms. It is an unfortunate truism that in the real world of hospital wards and intensive care units (often over-crowded, understaffed, or both) physicians and health caregivers do not always act out of beneficence. Although the ideal model is indeed the long tradition of benefi-

cence, too often decisions are made based on convenience (either that of the family, the physician, or the institution), financial remuneration, or some notion of beneficence that does not withstand closer scrutiny. This is not meant to impugn the motives of all or even most physicians but merely to put into perspective what is commonly involved in decisions to sustain life.

Given this, there are good reasons not to view CPR as simply another medical therapy offered to the patient at the discretion of the physician. For the purposes of this chapter, I will categorize the arguments as either medical, legal, or ethical. These distinctions are obviously somewhat artificial, since there is a considerable degree of overlap.

MEDICAL CONSIDERATIONS

As the American Medical Association (AMA) guidelines state, futility does not express a discrete quantity but a range of probabilities and may be contingent on the specific objectives of medical therapy.[2] It can still be asked, however, whether CPR is medically futile therapy for specific groups of patients. Certainly the medical literature has suggested it may be; for purposes of discussion, patients with malignancies, elderly patients, and patients in a persistent vegetative state (PVS) have been mentioned.[3] Every clinician who has worked in the ICU has encountered patients in these groups whose lives will not be saved by resuscitation and for whom resuscitation could even be considered cruel. Medicine must obviously come to grips with such situations and find ways to deal with these patients (though generally the best way to manage most such patients is through more complete discussion with them and their surrogates rather than through unilateral declarations of futility).[4]

Medical experience alone, however, is not sufficient to determine whether CPR is futile for all of these patients. Furthermore, there are at least two problems with the medical literature on futility. The first, potentially remediable, is that virtually all of the studies are retrospective. In no case (at least that I am aware of) has a researcher asked prospectively, "Do all the patients with this condition [whatever it may be] die despite receiving CPR?" By performing retrospective studies, researchers are susceptible to biases, some subtle, some not so subtle, that allow for overly broad conclusions. The mortality for in-hospital CPR is extremely high (not only for the aforementioned patient groups but for all patients), and consequently few patients in these groups survive. However, even a small number of survivors transforms the question from a purely medical one (is this care futile?) to a question of resource allocation (is the effort worthwhile considering the small number of survivors?).[5]

The clinician's predicament regarding unsalvageable patients is complicated by the fact that virtually all clinicians have been surprised by an unexpected outcome in the ICU.[6] Furthermore, the medical literature is not as likely to publish reports about CPR survivors (in any group of patients) as studies demonstrating prohibitive survival, which increase readership and provoke a greater response. (Such studies are the medical literature's equivalent of "man bites dog.")

Some may claim that this argument is ultimately hair-splitting—that it is simply impossible to prove what we know is true (i.e., these patients are not benefited by CPR). Rather than cavil over what should constitute adequate scientific proof (although one would think that for such an important issue, proof should be rigorous), let me advance a second, stronger medical argument regarding the futility of CPR.

In large measure, the futility of CPR is related to the interpretation of what constitutes cardiopulmonary resuscitation. When CPR is defined as cardiac massage and life-support (intubation, mechanical ventilation, and vasopressor therapy) *instituted at the moment of cardiac arrest,* mortality figures are understandably high because cardiac arrest, which causes myocardial and cerebral anoxia, is an extremely lethal condition. In effect, it is not the therapy per se that is futile but the fact that it is used in a setting of marked deterioration. To use an analogy, if there is fire in all seven rooms of a seven-room house, calling the fire department might be considered futile (even though the fire department is extremely helpful in other situations).

But just as most house fires begin in one room (and could, in theory, be controlled by promptly calling the fire department), most cardiac arrests in hospitalized patients (with or without chronic diseases) are preceded by premonitory symptoms, especially signs of respiratory insufficiency and/or hypotension. Quite often the prompt institution of mechanical ventilation or vasopressor drugs (to restore blood pressure) will forestall or prevent cardiac arrest (and thus prove lifesaving).[7] If CPR is defined as life support *instituted in anticipation of cardiac arrest,* then it is difficult, indeed impossible, to call it medically futile therapy for any large group of patients.

A practical example serves to illustrate the point: Suppose a patient suffering from colon cancer and liver metastasis suffers cardiac standstill on the hospital ward. A plausible argument could be made based on the medical literature (if we set aside the retrospective issue) that CPR (intubation, mechanical ventilation, and cardiac blood pressure medications) will not extend the patient's life, would be futile, and should not be instituted. However, if the same patient was examined one hour before the cardiac arrest and found to be hypotensive and require intubation (a likely scenario), then no one could argue that these interventions would be futile (either based on the literature or on personal experience, since patients do survive after receiving these interventions). Unless it had been discussed with the patient beforehand and the patient elected not to undergo such measures, the appropriate action would be to institute life support (i.e., CPR). Failing to do so would be to invite cardiac standstill, in which case the exact same measures, instituted an hour later, would be considered futile.

This is not a trivial distinction. To use the house fire analogy, if one ignores the fire in one room until it spreads to the whole house, then it may be moot to call the fire department. In the same way, avoiding the issue of life support until the moment of cardiac arrest renders the question of CPR moot. One could make the argument that physicians could (for economic reasons or because they wished to avoid uncomfortable discussions) avoid informing a patient of his or her options simply by ignoring premonitory symptoms, waiting for cardiac arrest, and then citing futility as a reason not to institute life support. If we consciously ignore what happens in the period before cardiac arrest (when life support may be lifesaving), then it is possible, under the futility doctrine, for patients to suffer cardiac arrest and never be offered the option of life support. From the medical standpoint, allowing physicians to invoke futility would provide a disincentive in certain cases to both talking to patients and paying attention to serious medical problems.

This is not to say that life support should automatically be instituted for critically ill patients with chronic diseases (the "do everything" position). That would be inappropriate. Many if not most patients with far advanced diseases will elect not to undergo life support. But the decision should ultimately be a result of informed consent and not medical sophistry, even if life support is used for patients who have very poor odds of survival. The issue is and should be, does the patient (or surrogate) have the neces-

sary information to make an informed decision about whether to undergo life support, including information about the likelihood of survival and a decent quality of life.[8] This question must presume that life support will be instituted, not in a halfhearted way, but promptly and when medically appropriate. Offering it as an afterthought, in a setting of certain or near-certain failure, almost ensures medical futility.

LEGAL CONSIDERATIONS

Several years ago, in a letter to the *New England Journal of Medicine,* I related a story about the question of futile therapy and the attitude of health care lawyers.[9] In two separate meetings, a colleague and I informally asked a group of physicians and a group of lawyers, "Can a physician override the wishes of a conscious, competent patient who requests CPR if the physician feels it is not indicated?" The first group, composed of roughly 20 physicians who worked in ICUs, answered yes by approximately a four to one margin. The second group was composed of an equal number of health care lawyers, and their unanimous answer was no. While not necessarily representative, this illustrates the difference in attitudes between physicians and lawyers on the question of futility.[10]

As Coogan noted, physicians (and this may be especially true of ICU physicians) are likely to operate from a position of beneficent paternalism, which is evident in their response to the question we posed regarding futility and CPR. Interestingly, in the discussion among the ICU physicians who responded to our question, it was evident they were answering from the standpoint of their role as physicians. They did not consider the question from their potential role as patients. We did not ask them (though perhaps we should have) if they believed in the physician's prerogative to override a patient's wishes even in cases where they were patients and it meant letting someone overrule *their* wishes.

In contrast with the physicians, the health care attorneys seemed especially sensitive to the importance of informed consent (autonomy). Many lawyers acknowledged the importance of the physician's input into the decision (and in fact some of them may have actually believed that the clinician's evaluation of futility might be the ultimate deciding factor), but they were unanimous in their belief that the final say in performing CPR had to rest with the patient. The model cited commonly was one of informed consent.[11]

In the informed consent model, physicians have an immense degree of authority in regard to what they tell patients. As Coogan notes, physicians commonly state that true informed consent is impossible because they cannot possibly notify the patient of all the nuances and implications of a diagnosis and proposed treatment.[12] However true this is, physicians often draw different conclusions than attorneys. Physicians who believe educated informed consent is impossible are inclined to minimize the time spent on the informed consent process either by deciding for the patient or by presenting the information in a disinterested manner and letting the patient decide without professional input. Attorneys look to see whether the process was done in the spirit of truly informing the patient and whether the patient was in fact making the decision based on a reasonable degree of information.

How then do the two disciplines regard futile life support? The many medical articles on the subject attest to the acceptance of the concept that even in a shared model it is the physician's professional judgment that is ultimately decisive.[13] The attitude of the health care attorneys is that, while the physician may feel that CPR is futile, it is incumbent upon the physician to notify the patient and let him or her decide. Certainly most patients would decide against CPR (especially after a convincing explanation by the physician), and in those cases where the patient did not wish to follow the proffered advice, the physician, having fulfilled his or her legal and ethical obligation, would be free to sign off the case, providing another physician could be secured for the patient.

From a legal standpoint, the attorney's approach makes more sense, because it relieves the physician of the ultimate responsibility for the CPR decision and ensures that this will not be an area of contested decision making in the courts. (For good or ill, the emphasis that the AMA and other authors place on physician judgment in ascertaining futility is an open invitation to legal challenge in selected cases.) Neither physicians nor attorneys are likely to relish the prospect of future lawsuits over the propriety of withholding resuscitation based on futility where there might be obvious conflicts in expert testimony over "futility" or quality of life. Medicolegally, where the courts are concerned, as long as the patient has had appropriate notification by his or her doctor, that patient retains the ultimate say over whether to receive life support (and must bear the consequences of his or her decision).

Critics will assert that such a policy is resource wasteful—that allowing patients to decide will ultimately bankrupt our system.[14] Without question there will be situations in which life support is used in an expensive and inefficient manner (as some may argue happened in the Wanglie case).[15] However, the amount of money the system saves will be directly dependent on how we define CPR. The amount of money saved when CPR is defined as the procedures instituted at the time of cardiac arrest is far less than that when it is defined as the procedures used in anticipation of cardiac arrest (where futility is less tangible and we are back to the gray area of resource allocation). Moreover, claims that the system will be bankrupted are exercises in hyperbole (there are far better examples of wasteful policies), and in any case it is the purpose of the medicolegal system to protect individual patients rather than seek areas of questionable economy in medical care. (The fact that the legal system is doing a poor job of both protection and economizing may be a commentary on how the system is being manipulated by so many forces.)

Coogan's contention that medicine is not an off-the-rack consumable quantity like retail merchandise is true, but it misses the point.[16] He is correct that the doctor-patient relationship is different from the salesperson–retail buyer relationship and that the patient cannot purchase critical care on demand. The reason is that, whereas the buyer basically knows what kind of coat he or she wants to purchase, the patient has no idea of the type of critical care needed or the point at which it will be needed. This lack of knowledge means that the patient must have a more complete explanation of what is being offered than a shopper.

Here is where the legal system has an obvious stake in minimizing the dire consequences of a poor judgment—much more so than when someone buys a poorly fitting coat. This is why we must support the informed consent model as a means of empowering the patient. Coogan's analogy is erroneous because the patient is not in a roughly equivalent relationship to the physician (as the shopper is with the salesperson). Would those who claim that physicians should be allowed to invoke futility unilaterally (which in effect gives even more power to the dominant party in an unequal relationship) also advocate that a salesperson be able to force a consumer to purchase a coat?

ETHICAL CONSIDERATIONS

The ethical argument against the unilateral invoking of futility is grounded in the unique relationship of trust that exists between patient and physician. Certainly this relationship has no exact counterpart in other professions. Yet one of the curious aspects of biomedical writing is how infrequently trust is cited as the cornerstone of the patient-physician relationship. It is an essential aspect of many of the duties the physician owes the patient, including telling the truth, maintaining confidentiality, and minimizing his or her own interests.

By emphasizing trust, we must acknowledge its ongoing and pervasive nature. Every encounter that a physician has with a patient acts to increase or diminish the trust the patient feels. Particularly momentous acts—a physician performing lifesaving surgery versus being caught lying—will have a tremendous impact on the patient's level of trust. By the same token, the actions of physicians as a group also have important consequences for the collective trust of the community. Consider how the discovery of a cure or the unveiling of a scandal involving research on patients affects the trust felt by society at large.

The ongoing and pervasive aspects of trust are what make the unilateral declaration of futility such a bad policy. When futility is invoked in a beneficent fashion (to ameliorate suffering and not prolong dying), it will promote the trust felt by patients and the community. Unfortunately, in the opposite case, when physicians deny patients life support in an arbitrary fashion, the decrease in trust is precipitous.

As was stated above, futility is difficult to define. As a consequence, futility can be used as an excuse for not instituting life support for any number of reasons. When physicians invoke futility for reasons other than beneficence, such as when they perceive they are acting in the interests of the broader community, the implications for trust will ultimately be devastating, especially considering the momentous nature of these decisions. When done capriciously, the invoking of futility can destroy people's trust in physicians in general.

It is critical to remember Veatch's basic point—that the physician's main role (even if not the only role) is to act as patient advocate. In cases where life support is unlikely to be effective, the physician's role is to advise the patient of this fact, not to unilaterally decide for the patient (unless, of course, that is the patient's wish). By minimizing patient input into life-support decisions (and indeed rendering it meaningless in worst-case situations), physicians risk destroying the notion that their responsibilities include patient advocacy. In the long run, destruction of this notion would lead to far more serious problems than the critical resource allocations problems we face.

Given the serious inequities in our health care system, can advocates of the futility doctrine truly believe that futility would not be invoked capriciously? Invoking futility with an economic rationale in mind (futility and rationing are commonly linked in articles on both subjects) allows the possibility that it would become an instrument of social policy. In this context, we must confront the fact that the futility doctrine might be used in a discriminatory or invidious fashion (e.g., physicians might base life-support discussions on payment status). That is a situation better prevented than remedied after the fact.

How best to prevent it? Unfortunately, there is no rule or law that will ensure futility is used only beneficently. The answer is quite simple: make it clear that decisions about life support ultimately rest with patients (which was advocated by the President's Commission and the Minnesota court in the Wanglie case).[17] The legal point of view that CPR is basically an informed consent issue (indirectly supported by the Wanglie decision) is ethically appropriate, especially in view of the movement in society for more disclosure regarding what physicians do to and for patients.

What about the argument that physicians do not offer heart transplants to every elderly patient dying of heart failure and that this is ultimately because it would be futile therapy? It is a specious argument: Transplantation is not routine therapy (defined as readily available in every hospital), it involves a scarce resource (donor organs), and the time and expense involved are clearly of a different magnitude than in the case of CPR. Moreover, patients understand that offering life support is not the same as offering transplantation. Without question, the range of therapies to offer routinely is open to debate (uncertain cases should be highlighted in ethics committees and medical texts), but noting the absurdity of offering transplantation to a nonagenarian does little to clarify the question.

Even if one accepts the above arguments against unilateral declarations of futility by physicians, a number of serious questions remain (besides the obvious financial ones). What do we do when an incompetent patient with no surrogates requires life support that physicians feel is futile? Is it appropriate to simply withhold care or is an institutional mechanism necessary to ensure there is no abuse of patients unable to look after their own interests? What about offering surgery to patients in cases where the surgeon is reluctant to operate and the outcome is likely to be dismal (e.g., abdominal aortic aneurysm resection in an elderly patient with an acute myocardial infarction)? These cases differ from life-support decisions because the therapy requires much more active involvement by the physicians, and thus routine notification of the patient, while desirable, might not be mandatory. What about performing cardiac massage in ICU situations where full resuscitation (blood pressure medications and mechanical ventilation) is already being carried out, making further measures impossible? What about CPR in situations of obvious cerebral herniation or massive exsanguination?

The point of these examples is that physician judgment cannot and should not be eliminated from these situations. As a matter of practice, physicians must be allowed some discretion in making decisions (one corollary is that physician judgment should be open to review). No doubt better studies and better science will also change our approach to some of these questions in the future. None of this alters the fact that allowing physicians to withhold life support and resuscitation because they feel it is futile, no matter how beneficent their intentions, would be an unwarranted step backwards toward the type of paternalism modern American society has turned away from. If we agree that all professional ethics must, in some way, be responsive to the society that the profession serves, then in medical crises the final decision must generally rest with the patient.

NOTES

1. M. Coogan, Medical Futility in Resuscitation: Value Judgement and Clinical Judgement, *Cambridge Quarterly of Health Care Ethics* 2, no. 2 (1993):197–205.

2. American Medical Association, Council on Ethical and Judicial Affairs, Guidelines for the Appropriate Use of Do-Not-Resuscitate Orders, *JAMA* 265 (1991):1868–

1871; S.J. Youngner, Who Defines Futility? *JAMA* 260 (1988):2094–2095.

3. G.E. Taffet et al., In-hospital Cardiopulmonary Resuscitation, *JAMA* 260 (1988):2069–2072; D.J. Murphy et al., Outcomes of Cardiopulmonary Resuscitation in the Elderly, *Annals of Internal Medicine* 111 (1989):199–205; American Medical Association, Council on Scientific Affairs and Council on Ethical and Judicial Affairs, Persistent Vegetative State and the Decision to Withdraw or Withhold Life Support, *JAMA* 263 (1990):426–430.

4. L.J. Schneiderman and J.D. Arras, Counseling Patients to Counsel Physicians on Future Care in the Event of Patient Incompetence, *Annals of Internal Medicine* 102 (1985):693–698; J.D. Lantos et al., The Illusion of Futility in Clinical Practice, *American Journal of Medicine* 87 (1989):81–84.

5. L.J. Blackhall, Must We Always Use CPR? *New England Journal of Medicine* 317 (1987):1281–1285; D.L. Scheidermayer, The Decision to Forgo CPR in the Elderly Patient, *JAMA* 260 (1988):2097–2098.

6. W. Arts et al., Unexpected Improvement after Prolonged Posttraumatic Vegetative State, *Journal of Neurology, Neurosurgery and Psychiatry* 48 (1985):1300–1303.

7. C.M. Franklin et al., Decreases in Mortality on a Large Urban Medical Service by Facilitating Access to Critical Care: An Alternative to Rationing, *Archives of Internal Medicine* 148 (1988):1403–1405; R. Schein et al., Clinical Antecedents to In-hospital Cardiopulmonary Arrest, *Chest* 8 (1990):1388–1392.

8. G.A. Sachs and C.K. Cassel, The Medical Directive, *JAMA* 263 (1990):1069–1070.

9. C.M. Franklin and E.C. Rackow, Decisions about CPR, *New England Journal of Medicine* 318 (1988):1272.

10. Ibid.

11. W.M. Gild, Informed Consent: A Review, *Anesthesia and Analgesia* 68 (1989):649–653.

12. Coogan, Medical Futility in Resuscitation: Value Judgement and Clinical Judgement.

13. Youngner, Who Defines Futility?; T. Tomlinson and H. Brody, Futility and the Ethics of Resuscitation, *JAMA* 264 (1990):1276–1280.

14. D. Callahan, *Setting Limits: Medical Goals in an Aging Society* (New York: Touchstone Books, 1988).

15. In re Helen Wanglie, Fourth Judicial District (Dist. Ct., Probate Ct. Div.) PX-91-283, Minnesota, Hennepin County; S.H. Miles, Informed Demand for "Non-beneficial" Medical Treatment, *New England Journal of Medicine* 325 (1991):512–515.

16. Coogan, Medical Futility in Resuscitation: Value Judgement and Clinical Judgement.

17. President's Commission for the Study of Ethical Problems in Medicine and Biomedical and Behavioral Research, *Deciding to Forego Life-Sustaining Treatment* (Washington, D.C.: President's Commission, 1983), 240–241; G. Franklin, When and How to Write Do-Not-Resuscitate Orders, *Journal of Critical Illness,* 5 (1990):938–952; M. Angell, The Case of Helen Wanglie: A New Kind of "Right to Die" Case, *New England Journal of Medicine* 325 (1991):511–512.

Chapter 25

Medical Futility

Steven H. Miles

For the purposes of this chapter, a determination of medical futility should be taken to be a *medical* determination that a therapy is of no value to a patient and should not be prescribed.[1] The current debate about medical futility is one of the most important and contentious in medical ethics. Proponents believe that allowing physicians to withhold therapies they consider futile can be done without disturbing the current paradigm of medical ethics, which respects patient autonomy with regard to informed consent and the right to refuse treatment. Others believe that withholding treatment on the basis of futility is simply an unacceptable form of medical paternalism. Some adopt the position that doctors can identify medical futility but that this does not necessarily justify imposing decisions to forgo life-sustaining therapy.[2]

Regardless of any effect on policy, this important debate is leading to a re-examination of the nature of a patient's entitlement to health care and of the ends of medicine. It has two aspects: an examination of the concept of medical futility and its derived clinical criteria and an inquiry into the nature of the authority to act and the procedures for acting on the conclusion that a therapy is futile.

CLINICAL USAGE

Four clinical types of futility have been widely discussed.

First, there are therapies that are *physiologically implausible*.[3] It is futile to use interferon to cure stomach cancer because interferon has no effect on stomach cancer. Here, physiologic effects are assessed against an objective that both the doctor and patient agree on.

Second, there are therapies with important physiologic effects that medical judgment concludes are *nonbeneficial* to the patient as a person. Physicians have argued in court that a respirator, immunosuppressive medications, or dialysis cannot benefit irreversibly unconscious patients despite the preferences of their families for life-prolonging intensive care.[4] Somewhat related are therapies that effect a desired personal benefit at the expense of causing vastly disproportionate iatrogenic harms.[5] For ex-

The work that provided the basis for this chapter was supported by the Health of the Public Program of the Pew Charitable Trust and the Rockefeller Foundation. Dr. Miles is a Henry J. Kaiser Family Foundation faculty scholar in general internal medicine. Grateful acknowledgment is given to Roland Ingram, Jr., M.D., for his careful critique of an early draft.

ample, physicians have maintained that aggressive care for Baby Rena or Child Jane Doe, who are in constant pain and terminally ill, should be stopped as a matter of medical authority.[6]

Third, there are therapies which are *very unlikely* to produce a desired physiologic or personal benefit.[7] For example, a physician could say that it is futile to use a brain scan to rule out brain cancer as a cause of headaches, because of the very tiny chance that a brain cancer is the cause of the headaches (despite the usefulness of brain scans for detecting brain cancer). It may be argued that the hope of success is a type of subjective benefit, but even so, the small chance of success can be scientifically determined and differs from a patient's choice to pursue an unusual benefit.

Fourth, there are *nonvalidated* (but plausible) therapies for which there is no clinical experience to prove the (usually low) probability of benefit. For example, an insurer refused to pay for a bone marrow transplant to treat Ms. Harper's breast cancer, which had metastasized to her eyes and liver, because it was not validated—even though a clinician estimated it might provide a 20 percent chance of years of cancer-free survival.[8]

These four types of futility are not mutually exclusive. Implanting a baboon heart to save a dying baby or freezing one's head for a later cure could be considered implausible, unlikely to work, nonbeneficial, and nonvalidated.

WHAT IS FUTILITY?

There are three major ways of understanding the concept of futility: as a logical ideal, as a professional duty, and as an institution.

Futility As a Logical Ideal

The significance of futility lies in its role in two linked arguments. The *defining* argument proceeds as follows: Non-y therapies are futile therapies. X is a non-y therapy. Therefore, X is a futile therapy. In line with the four types of futility, "non-y" might mean nonplausible, nonbene-

ficial, nonlikely, or nonvalidated. The *duty* argument goes like this: There is no duty to provide futile therapies. X is a futile therapy. Therefore, there is no duty to provide X. Unless there are two separate but linked arguments, futility is merely equivalent to "non-y" or "nondutiful." This suggests that a futile treatment or therapy is one that, because it is non-y, need not be provided. The debate about futility focuses on both the defining argument and its moral implications.

Criticism of the defining argument focuses on the term "non-y." Schneiderman et al. break "non-y" into quantitative and qualitative aspects.[9]

Quantitative futility refers to the high reliability, rather than certainty, of a clinical conclusion.[10] For example, resuscitation might be futile for an 85-year-old man with emphysema and septicemia who suffers a cardiac arrest because he has less than a 2 percent chance of surviving to discharge. The statistical proof of futility poses novel statistical problems for research design.[11] The distinction between futile treatments and "unlikely" treatments that an informed, risk-taking patient might choose must be made phenomenologically rather than logically and depends on value judgments or social agreement.[12]

Qualitative futility raises the issue of who should be authorized to define an outcome as nonbeneficial. Four futile outcomes are widely discussed:

1. permanent loss of consciousness[13]
2. permanent holistic dependence on life support[14]
3. permanent loss of consciousness *and* holistic dependence on life support[15]
4. death in the very near future[16]

The criticisms of quantitative and qualitative futility, though thought provoking, may not decisively overturn the concept. They may simply show that any clinical criteria for futility must be founded upon an underlying phenomenological or social concept rather than a purely logical construction. Thus, if futility is accepted, it will necessarily be probabilistic rather than certain and it will represent a social consensus about the practice of medicine rather than logically derived or self-evident. Those who hold that there is a historical or social consensus defining health care or the role of the physician argue that futility may be defined in relation to medical outcomes.[17] Others point out, for example, that some patients might consider the very small chance of very brief patient survival on life support after CPR to be highly beneficial, not futile.[18] To autonomy-centered critics, such concerns either invalidate the concept of futility or restrict its usage to physiologically implausible treatments.[19]

Regardless of how futility is defined, the moral implications of futility will continue to be debated. Should, for example, physicians be empowered to conclude that life support in some instances is nonbeneficial? Should they be empowered to act on that conclusion even if there is a dissenting patient or proxy? Callahan accepts that futile outcomes can be diagnosed but says that the empowerment of physicians to act unilaterally on a determination of futility by withholding treatment must be based on an explicit, antecedent social agreement.[20] He favors basing such agreement on the concept of a natural life course.[21] Many clinicians would, to some extent, agree. For example, given the interpersonal meaning of feeding to caregivers, few physicians would stop tube-feeding a permanently unconscious patient over the objections of the family even if intensive care had been foreclosed.

Futility As a Professional Duty

It may be argued that acting on a determination of medical futility is an implicit professional duty of the physician. There are several ways to ground such a duty. First, there is the view that a physician expert in prognostication should not prescribe therapies that cannot restore health to a dying person.[22] Yet the determination of futility would have to be based on professional standards of practice rather simply the physician's own conviction.[23] A new Veterans Administra-

tion policy, for example, defines futility in relation to "prevailing medical practice,"[24] which might be further defined in professional treatises.[25] Second, some would ground this decision-making authority in a physician's duty to not cause pain.[26] But many life support–dependent patients are unconscious and feel no pain.[27] Third, the authority of medical futility might be grounded in an appeal to efficiency. For example, futile CPR should not be provided because it is wasteful or not cost-effective.[28] As Weber points out, such appeals tend to be depersonalized.[29] This support for medical futility does not so much override a patient's preference with a stronger professional view of the appropriate end of medicine as it voids preference altogether ("I'm sorry, there is nothing more I can do").

There are several possible moral implications of medical futility. Some hold that once a "diagnosis" of medical futility has been made, the authority to make subsequent decisions belongs solely to the physician.[30] Some further propose that such a diagnosis also nullifies the duty to inform a patient of a potential treatment.[31] Blackhall, for example, wrote that there is no duty to offer CPR to a woman dying of leukemia or to inform her that it was being withheld,[32] a view that others have strenuously disagreed with.[33] Some believe that allowing physicians to withhold demanded therapy would adversely affect the doctor-patient relationship.[34] A patient's choice of a painful and pointless CPR would physically pain the patient rather than the caregivers, however much it distressed them to provide that treatment.

A great deal of work must be done to support any of these claims and create professional consensus. With regard to any treatment, to the degree that other physicians are willing to provide that treatment, the basis for considering it medically futile is legally mooted[35] or ethically weakened.[36] Furthermore, it is one thing to say that a physician does not have a duty to propose a futile treatment and another to say that the physician may refuse a patient's demand for that treatment. In a clinical setting where resources are presumptively available, Lantos et al. did not see a compelling reason to disempower an informed but medically misguided patient and thus concluded that futility was an "illusion."[37]

Futility As an Institution

Futility can also be understood as a type of "institution." An institution is a pattern of behavior by individuals and groups that is supported by laws and mores expressing a view of the relation of the individual to society[38] and of technical abilities to nature.[39] Unlike logical arguments, institutions are necessarily probabilistic and phenomenological. One could define medical futility as an institution that annuls a perceived duty to perform a medical practice based on the outcome of treatment.

Institutions can only be understood within their culture. Our society has a technology-intensive health care system that pools and redistributes resources and that supposedly offers everyone a right to participate in decision making (though not a right to receive any possible medical intervention). Discussing futility in a hypothetical world with infinite medical resources undoubtedly simplifies the discussion but obscures how it may function in our society. For this reason, the relation of futility to the just allocation of health care needs to be examined.

TRAGIC CHOICES AND HUMANE JUSTICE

Medical futility can confront a person with having to make a painful decision: the decision that a life-sustaining treatment should not be employed to try to prolong a precious life. Calabresi and Bobbitt's elegant analysis of social policies for such decisions illuminates the institution of futility.[40] A tragic choice, in their parlance, is a policy for allocating finite resources in such a way as to preserve conflicting values (e.g., life and fairness) that are the moral foundation of social collaboration. Tragic choices have first- and second-order components. First-order policies determine global allo-

cations. Second-order policies distribute those resources to specific individuals or groups. Tragic choices must be rationalized to limit their psychic costs to important, conflicting values. Thus, global allocations must be depicted as lifesaving and relatively adequate and second-order decisions must be decentralized so that the central policies do not explicitly sacrifice life. Calabresi points out that second-order decisions will necessarily deform some ideals about how decisions should be made.

Medical futility fits Calabresi's paradigm if it is understood to be a second-order institution for tragic choices about life-sustaining treatments with poor outcomes. A decision to not use medically futile therapy does not devalue life and may even minimize rationing effective care. Medical futility is a decentralized clinical judgment that distances policy makers from having to explicitly deny life-sustaining treatment. This empowerment of clinicians "deforms" respect for patient autonomy in some decisions to withhold life-sustaining treatment in that a treatment that is available as a matter of global policy might be withheld because of a particular physician's professional judgment.

Calabresi's analysis explains the recent interest in medical futility as the United States accepts the duty to provide universal access to health care. We cannot afford to meet every personal claim for health care.[41] We need new institutions to make second-order tragic choices tolerable. Medical futility allows the doctor to be patient centered, technically competent, and fully equipped to save life.[42] It construes choices to withhold futile care as primarily biomedically realistic and only then as socially responsible. This is not bedside rationing of effective care such as the kind Oregon has been trying to institute.

The empowerment of clinical judgment regarding medical futility potentially conflicts with the American bioethical view of respect for autonomy, according to which nearly any sincere preference is seen as legitimate.[43] On this view, a patient's right to refuse life-sustaining treatment entails that a physician who withholds requested but futile treatment may be seen as devaluing life and autonomy. A path out of this cul-de-sac lies in reconstructing the difference between the negative right to refuse a treatment or choose among therapies that a physician is willing to prescribe and the positive right to demand a treatment that the medical profession is unwilling to prescribe. This distinction could preserve current understandings of autonomy while permitting medical institutions to decide when futile therapies were not part of the right to health care.[44]

It would be especially difficult to apply this institutional concept of medical futility to nonvalidated, plausible therapies. Our society believes that technical progress will solve tragic problems. Entrepreneurs and researchers implicitly or explicitly promise such relief. Many desperately ill persons choose to participate in medical experiments or to undergo treatments before they are fully tested. The recent controversy over government procedures for releasing unproven AIDS treatments for clinical use illustrates the power of the desire for medical cures. Permitting private purchase of nonvalidated therapies (e.g., noninsured immunotherapies for cancers) both undercuts the definition of futility and poses a complex problem for fair access to new therapies.

There is a tension between medical futility, autonomy, and justice. Futility applies to the most marginally effective treatments. Affirming a patient's right to be provided such treatments virtually precludes the possibility of universal, equitable access to less dramatic but statistically more effective life-supporting treatments. Those who claim that autonomy should always override determinations of medical futility seem to have an elitist view of "autonomy" that only makes sense if one assumes the existence of a privileged class of health care consumers.

EMPOWERING PHYSICIANS

The empowerment of physicians to make determinations of medical futility requires a legal foundation and a supporting ethos. The social "value" of being able to offer the hope of rescue to dying persons[45] makes it unlikely that the United States can enact general, first-order policies defining futile care. Ethicists' proposals for explicit central rules for decisions regarding futility are unlikely to be feasible.[46] Italy, Britain, and the United States all modified first-order policies regarding organ allocation, thus leaving bedside allocation to decentralized, second-order decision makers.[47] Even New Jersey's brain death law now accommodates moral dissent.[48]

The legal foundation for futility as a second-order institution is the duty of physicians to prescribe or not prescribe according to reasonable medical judgment. Current statutes alluding to a physician's duty to render appropriate care[49] do not explicitly define a duty or power to withhold inappropriate but requested life-prolonging treatment. Early court rulings are inconclusive on this matter.[50] Recent statements by prestigious medical associations will help define the legal and clinical standard of care in medically futile situations.[51]

I believe that the explicit empowerment of physicians to make determinations of medical futility might best come through the development of professional association practice guidelines (e.g., regarding intensive care for irreversibly comatose persons) and hospital practice guidelines. The scope of such practice guidelines should be restricted to therapies that a vast majority of persons would not accept for themselves so that a medical diagnosis of futility is less likely to be construed as devaluing life by the majority culture.

THE FRAGILITY OF FUTILITY

Some parties will reject medical futility. Some physicians will give "lifesaving" baboon heart transplants to dying babies. Some families will insist on prolonged intensive care for permanently unconscious persons (including persons who are brain dead) or demand therapies that produce only brief prolongation of life.[52] Such dissents expose the latent conflict of values in tragic choices. Sometimes a local or temporary accommodation can be made. Even persons who are brain dead are sometimes supported to allow the family to come to terms with the event. Routinely making such accommodations or putting them in a public policy, such as New Jersey's law permitting sectarian dissent to determinations of brain death, suggests that a treatment is not futile and that sincere patient demands may legitimately claim health resources for instituting or continuing the treatment.

The usefulness of medical futility as a basis for decision making can be destroyed by insisting on complete certainty or social unanimity on its medical criteria and legal standing. We would

be ill served by such demands. Medical futility is a psychologically tolerable way of dealing with the difficult end-of-life decisions that families are forced to confront. It provides a framework within which the value of life, the inevitability of death, professional responsibility, remorse, and social justice can be reconciled. Were discussions of medical futility banned in the name of "truth," determinations of futility would likely be replaced by explicit, politically imposed decisions about which lives are not worth expending resources on. Without futility, medically supported life would be a commodity whose span is meted out on the basis of dollars rather than bounded by natural morality.

NOTES

1. It is useful to restrict the definition of futility to a medical determination rather than a patient's conclusion. There are well-established principles and laws supporting a patient's right to refuse therapies that he or she considers futile, disproportionately burdensome, or morally objectionable with or without the concurrence of his or her physician. The current debate focuses on the situation where a physician concludes that a therapy is futile, either absent a patient's own preference or in the face of a dissenting conclusion by a patient or proxy.

2. D.W. Brock and S.A. Wartman, When Competent Patients Make Irrational Choices, *New England Journal of Medicine* 322 (1990):1595–1599.

3. A.A. Brett and L.B. McCullough, When Patients Request Specific Interventions: Defining the Limits of the Physician's Obligation, *New England Journal of Medicine* 315 (1986):1347–1351; Hastings Center, *Guidelines on the Termination of Life-sustaining Treatment and the Care of the Dying* (Briarcliff Manor, N.Y.: Hastings Center, 1987), 32; T. Tomlinson and H. Brody, Futility and the Ethics of Resuscitation, *JAMA* 264 (1990):1276–1280; S.J. Youngner, Futility in Context, *JAMA* 264 (1989):1295–1296.

4. J.J. Paris et al., Physician's Refusal of Requested Treatment: The Case of Baby L, *New England Journal of Medicine* 322 (1990):1012–1015; S.H. Miles, Informed Demand for "Non-beneficial" Medical Treatment, *New England Journal of Medicine* 325 (1991):512–515; A. Reid, After Transplant, A Fight over Care, *Boston Sunday Globe,* June 23, 1991, A21, A23; L. Ross, Family Says Treatment Withheld, *Florida Times Union,* May 23, 1991, A1, A2.

5. Tomlinson and Brody, Futility and the Ethics of Resuscitation; Paris et al., Physician's Refusal of Requested

Treatment; L. Blackhall, Must We Always Do CPR? *New England Journal of Medicine* 317 (1987):1281–1284; S. Braithwaite and D.C. Thomasma, New Guidelines on Foregoing Life-sustaining Treatment in Incompetent Patients: An Anti-cruelty Policy, *Annals of Internal Medicine* 104 (1986):711–715; C.J. Hackler and F.C. Hiller, Family Consent to Orders Not to Resuscitate, *JAMA* 264 (1990):1281; F.D. Moore, The Desperate Case: CARE (Costs, Applicability, Research, Ethics), *JAMA* 261 (1989):1483–1484.

6. B. Weiser, A Question of Letting Go, *Washington Post,* July 14, 1991, A1, A18, A19; R.D. Smothers, Atlanta Court Bars Efforts to End Life Support for Stricken Girl, 13, *New York Times,* October 18, 1991, A10; In re Doe, Super. Ct., Fulton County, Ga., CAF D-93064.

7. Tomlinson and Brody, Futility and the Ethics of Resuscitation; L.J. Schneiderman et al., Medical Futility: Its Meaning and Ethical Implications, *Annals of Internal Medicine* 112 (1990):949–954.

8. E. Eckholm, Patients and Insurers Clash on Therapy's Outer Limits, *New York Times,* September 19, 1991, A1, A12.

9. Schneiderman et al., Medical Futility.

10. F.A. Chervernak and L.B. McCullough, Justified Limits on Refusing Intervention, *Hastings Center Report* 21, no. 2 (1991):12–17.

11. D.J. Murphy and D.B. Matchar, Life-sustaining Therapy: A Model for Appropriate Use, *JAMA* 264 (1990):2103–2108; W.A. Knaus et al., Short-term Mortality Predictions for Critically Ill Hospitalized Adults: Science and Ethics, *Science* 254 (1991):389–394.

12. Schneiderman et al., Medical Futility; J.D. Lantos et al., Survival after Cardiopulmonary Resuscitation in Babies

of Very Low Birth Weight, *New England Journal of Medicine* 318 (1988):91–95; S.J. Youngner, Who Defines Futility? *JAMA* 260 (1988):2094–2095.

13. American Thoracic Society, Withholding and Withdrawing Life-sustaining Therapy, *Annals of Internal Medicine* 115 (1991):478–486; Society of Critical Care Medicine, Task Force on Ethics, Consensus Report on the Ethics of Foregoing Life-sustaining Treatments in the Critically Ill, *Critical Care Medicine* 18 (1990):1425–1439.

14. D.J. Murphy, Do-Not-Resuscitate Orders: Time for Reappraisal in Long-term Care Institutions, *JAMA* 260 (1988):2098–2101.

15. American Medical Association; Council on Ethical and Judicial Affairs, Guidelines for the Appropriate Use of Do-Not-Resuscitate Orders, *JAMA* 262 (1991):1868–1871; K. Faber-Langendoen, Resuscitation of Patients with Metastatic Cancer: Is Transient Benefit Still Futile? *Archives of Internal Medicine* 151 (1991):235–239.

16. Hackler and Hiller, Family Consent to Orders Not to Resuscitate; Murphy, Do-Not-Resuscitate Orders; American Medical Association, Council on Ethical and Judicial Affairs, Guidelines for the Appropriate Use of Do-Not-Resuscitate Orders; Faber-Langendoen, Resuscitation of Patients with Metastatic Cancer; G.E. Taffett et al., In-hospital Cardiopulmonary Resuscitation, *JAMA* 260 (1988):2069–2072.

17. Tomlinson and Brody, Futility and the Ethics of Resuscitation; Schneiderman et al., Medical Futility; N.S. Jecker, Knowing When to Stop: The Limits of Medicine, *Hastings Center Report* 21, no. 3 (1991):5–8; D.W. Amundsen, The Physician's Obligation to Prolong Life: A Medical Duty without Classical Roots, *Hastings Center Report* 8, no. 2 (1978):23–30; L.R. Kass, *Toward a More Natural Science: Biology and Human Affairs* (New York: The Free Press, 1985).

18. Murphy and Matchar, Life-sustaining Therapy.

19. President's Commission for the Study of Ethical Problems in Medicine and Biomedical and Behavioral Research, *Deciding to Forego Life-sustaining Treatment* (Washington, D.C.: U.S. Government Printing Office, 1983), 240; see also Brock and Wartman, When Competent Patients Make Irrational Choices; S.J. Farber, Ethics of Life-Support and Resuscitation, *New England Journal of Medicine* 318 (1988):1757.

20. D. Callahan, Medical Futility, Medical Necessity: The Problem without a Name, *Hastings Center Report* 21 (1991):30–35.

21. D. Callahan, *Setting Limits: Medical Goals in an Aging Society* (New York: Simon and Schuster, 1987).

22. Tomlinson and Brody, Futility and the Ethics of Resuscitation; Hackler and Hiller, Family Consent to Orders Not to Resuscitate; Lantos et al., Survival after Cardiopulmonary Resuscitation in Babies of Very Low Birth Weight; American Thoracic Society, Withholding and Withdrawing Life-sustaining Therapy; Society of Critical Care Medicine, Task Force on Ethics, Consensus Report on the Ethics of Foregoing Life-sustaining Treatments in the Critically Ill; Taffett et al., In-hospital Cardiopulmonary Resuscitation; G.E. Applebaum et al., The Outcome of CPR Initiated in Nursing Homes, *Journal of the American Geriatrics Society* 38 (1990):197–200; American Medical Association, Council on Ethical and Judicial Affairs, Decisions near the End of Life, *JAMA* 267 (1992):369–372; S.H. Miles et al., CPR in Nursing Homes: Policy and Clinical Realities, *Minnesota Medicine* 74 (1991):31–35.

23. Tomlinson and Brody, Futility and the Ethics of Resuscitation; Chervernak and McCullough, Justified Limits on Refusing Intervention.

24. Department of Veterans Affairs, Withholding and Withdrawal of Life-sustaining Treatment, M-2, part 1, chap. 31.03.b(2).

25. American Medical Association, Council on Ethical and Judicial Affairs, Guidelines for the Appropriate Use of Do-Not-Resuscitate Orders.

26. Taffert et al., In-hospital Cardiopulmonary Resuscitation; Braithwaite and Thomasma, New Guidelines on Foregoing Life-sustaining Treatment in Incompetent Patients.

27. M. Angell, The Case of Helen Wanglie, A New Kind of "Right to Die" Case, *New England Journal of Medicine* 325 (1991):511–512.

28. Hackler and Hiller, Family Consent to Orders Not to Resuscitate; Kass, *Toward a More Natural Science;* Applebaum et al., The Outcome of CPR Initiated in Nursing Homes.

29. M. Weber, The Development of Bureaucracy and Its Relation to Law, in *Weber: Selections in Translation,* edited by W.G. Runciman, translated by E. Mathews (Cambridge: Cambridge University Press, 1978), 351.

30. J.D. Lantos et al., The Illusion of Futility in Clinical Practice, *American Journal of Medicine* 87 (1989):81–84.

31. Hackler and Hiller, Family Consent to Orders Not to Resuscitate.

32. Blackhall, Must We Always Do CPR?

33. Tomlinson and Brody, Futility and the Ethics of Resuscitation; Youngner, Futility in Context; Murphy and Matchar, Life-sustaining Therapy; American Medical Association, Council on Ethical and Judicial Affairs, Guidelines for the Appropriate Use of Do-Not-Resuscitate Orders.

34. Farber, Ethics of Life-Support and Resuscitation; Weber, The Development of Bureaucracy and Its Relation to Law; S.H. Miles, Between a Dream and a Poem: Relational Perspectives on the Wanglie Case, *Kennedy Institute of Ethics Journal* 2 (1992):61–72.

35. Paris et al., Physician's Refusal of Requested Treatment.

36. Miles, Informed Demand for "Non-beneficial" Medical Treatment.

37. Lantos et al., The Illusion of Futility in Clinical Practice.

38. R.N. Bellah et al., Introduction, in *The Good Society* (New York: Knopf, 1991), 10–11.

39. J. Ellul, *The Technological Society* (New York: Vintage, 1964).

40. G. Calabresi and P. Bobbitt, *Tragic Choices* (New York: Norton, 1978).

41. H. Aaron and W.B. Schwartz, Rationing Health Care: The Choice before Us, *Science* 247 (1990):417–422.

42. M. Danis and L. Churchill, Autonomy and the Common Weal, *Hastings Center Report* 21, no. 1 (1991):25–32.

43. R.N. Bellah et al., Culture and Character, in *Habits of the Heart* (Berkeley: University of California Press, 1985).

44. Paris et al., Physician's Refusal of Requested Treatment; Chervernak and McCullough, Justified Limits on Refusing Intervention; I. Berlin, Two Concepts of Liberty, in *Four Essays on Liberty* (Oxford, Oxford University Press, 1969); I. Berlin, Introduction, in *Four Essays on Liberty,* xxxvii–1v.

45. A. Jonsen, Bentham in a Box: Technology Assessment and Health Care Allocations, *Law, Medicine and Health Care* 14 (1986):172–174.

46. Brock and Wartman, When Competent Patients Make Irrational Choices; Murphy and Matchar, Life-sustaining Therapy; Farber, Ethics of Life-Support and Resuscitation; R.M. Veatch, Justice and the Economics of

Terminal Illness, *Hastings Center Report* 18, no. 4 (1988):34–40.

47. Ellul, *The Technological Society.*

48. R.S. Olick, Brain Death, Religious Freedom, and Public Policy: New Jersey's Landmark Legislative Initiative, *Kennedy Institute of Ethics Journal* 1 (1991):275–292.

49. F.H. Marsh and A. Staver, Physician Authority for Unilateral DNR Orders, *Journal of Legal Medicine* 12 (1991):115–165.

50. Paris et al., Physician's Refusal of Requested Treatment; Miles, Informed Demand for "Non-beneficial" Medical Treatment; Reid, After Transplant, A Fight over Care; Ross, Family Says Treatment Withheld; Weiser, A Question of Letting Go; Smothers, Atlanta Court Bars Effort to End Life Support for Stricken Girl, 13; Brophy v. New England Sinai Hospital, 398 Mass. 417; 497 NE 2d 626 (1986).

51. American Medical Association, Council on Ethical and Judicial Affairs, Guidelines for the Appropriate Use of Do-Not-Resuscitate Orders; Faber-Langendoen, Resuscitation of Patients with Metastatic Cancer; Jecker, Knowing When to Stop; American Medical Association, Council on Ethical and Judicial Affairs, Decisions near the End of Life; American Medical Association, Council on Ethical and Judicial Affairs, Decisions to Forego Life-sustaining Treatment for Incompetent Patients (American Medical Association, Chicago, 1991).

52. Paris et al., Physician's Refusal of Requested Treatment; Miles, Informed Demand for "Non-beneficial" Medical Treatment; Hackler and Hiller, Family Consent to Orders Not to Resuscitate; Schneiderman et al., Medical Futility.

Chapter 26

The Problem with Futility

Robert D. Truog, Joel E. Frader, and Allan S. Brett

"Futility" is one of the newest additions to the lexicon of bioethics. Physicians, ethicists, and members of the media are increasingly concerned about patients and families who insist on receiving life-sustaining treatment that others judge to be futile. A clear understanding of futility has proved to be elusive, however. Many clinicians view futility the way one judge viewed pornography: they may not be able to define it, but they know it when they see it.[1]

The notion of futile medical treatment may go back to the time of Hippocrates, who allegedly advised physicians "to refuse to treat those who are overmastered by their diseases, realizing that in such cases medicine is powerless."[2] More recently, the concept has appeared frequently in court decisions and policy statements.[3] The so-called Baby Doe law exempts physicians from providing treatment that would be "virtually futile."[4] The Council on Ethical and Judicial Affairs of the American Medical Association (AMA) recently concluded that physicians have no obligation to obtain consent for a do-not-resuscitate (DNR) order when cardiopulmonary resuscitation (CPR) is deemed futile.[5] The fact that this concept has appeared in law and policy may seem to indicate that it is clearly understood and widely accepted. In reality, however, the notion of futility hides many deep and serious ambiguities that threaten its legitimacy as a rationale for limiting treatment.

PARADIGMS OF FUTILITY

Contemporary discussions of futility have centered primarily on cases involving patients in a persistent vegetative state and those involving the use of CPR. A third type of case, involving organ-replacement technology, has received little attention but is helpful to our understanding of futility.

Futility and the Persistent Vegetative State

The first type of scenario involving the question of futility is represented by the recent Minnesota case of Helga Wanglie.[6] Mrs. Wanglie was an 86-year-old woman who had been dependent on mechanical ventilation and in a persistent vegetative state for more than a year.

Source: Reprinted from *The New England Journal of Medicine*, Vol. 326, No. 23, pp. 1560–1564, with permission of the Massachusetts Medical Society, © 1992.

Her husband insisted that she believed in maintaining life at all cost, and that "when she was ready to go . . . the good Lord would call her."[7] Her physicians, on the other hand, believed that the continued use of mechanical ventilation and intensive care was futile. When attempts to transfer her elsewhere failed, they sought to have a court appoint an independent conservator with responsibility for making medical decisions on her behalf. The judge denied this petition and reaffirmed the authority of her husband as legal surrogate. Three days later, Mrs. Wanglie died.

Cases like that of Mrs. Wanglie seldom reach the courts, but they are probably not rare. A similar case involving a child with severe brain damage was concluded with a settlement favorable to the family before a judicial decision.[8]

Futility in Cases Involving CPR

The second prototypical scenario involves the use of DNR orders. Although the techniques of CPR were originally intended only for use after acute, reversible cardiac arrests, the current practice is to use CPR in all situations unless there is a direct order to the contrary. Since cardiac arrest is the final event in all terminal illness, everyone is eventually a candidate for this medical procedure. DNR orders were developed to spare patients from aggressive attempts at revival when imminent death is anticipated and inevitable. Nevertheless, patients or families sometimes request CPR even when caregivers believe such attempts would be futile. Some have argued that in these circumstances a physician should be able to enact a DNR order without the consent of the patient or family.[9]

Futility and Organ-Replacement Technology

Although the bioethical debate over the question of futility has been most concerned with cases involving CPR and the treatment of patients in a persistent vegetative state, a third type of futility-related judgment has gone essentially unchallenged. It involves the increasingly large number of interventions that could possibly prolong the life of virtually any dying patient. For example, extracorporeal membrane oxygenation can replace heart and lung function for up to several weeks. Physicians now use this intervention when they expect organ systems eventually to recover or while they await organs for transplantation. However, it could prolong the life of almost anyone with cardiorespiratory failure, reversible or not. Patients thus kept alive may remain conscious and capable of communicating. Caregivers do not now offer this therapy to terminally ill patients, presumably because it would be futile. This judgment has gone largely unchallenged, yet it is not obvious why a clinician's unilateral decision not to use "futile" extracorporeal membrane oxygenation is inherently different from a decision not to use "futile" CPR or "futile" intensive care. If all three treatments can be characterized as objectively futile, then unilateral decisions not to offer them should be equally justified.

As it is used in these three cases, the concept of futility obscures many ambiguities and assumptions. These can be usefully grouped into two categories: problems of value and problems of probability.

FUTILITY AND VALUES

It is meaningless simply to say that an intervention is futile; one must always ask, "Futile in relation to what?" The medical literature provides many examples in which the importance of identifying the goals of treatment has not been fully appreciated. The effectiveness of CPR, for example, is often discussed in terms of whether patients who require the procedure can survive long enough to be discharged from the hospital.[10] This definition of success usually implies that short-term survival is a goal not worth pursuing. Patients or family members may value the additional hours of life differently, however. Indeed, physicians and other caregivers have repeatedly been shown to be poor judges of patients' preferences with regard to intensive care.[11]

Schneiderman and colleagues have argued that treatments that merely preserve permanent unconsciousness or that cannot end dependence on intensive medical care should be considered futile.[12] Although society may eventually endorse decisions to override the previously expressed wishes of patients or the desires of surrogates who demand such treatments, it does not follow that the treatments are futile. Mr. Wanglie would have rejected this conclusion, and there is no reason to dismiss his view out of hand. The decision that certain goals are not worth pursuing is best seen as involving a conflict of values rather than a question of futility.

Certainly in this context, the plurality of values in our society makes agreement on the concept of futility difficult if not impossible. Several groups have therefore attempted to arrive at a value-free understanding of the concept.[13] The most promising candidate thus far is the notion of "physiologic futility." As the guidelines on the termination of life-sustaining treatment prepared by the Hastings Center state, if a treatment is "clearly futile in achieving its physiological objective and so offer[s] no physiological benefit to the patient, the professional has no obligation to provide it."[14] For example, the physiologic objective of mechanical ventilation is to maintain adequate ventilation and oxygenation in the presence of respiratory failure, and the physiologic objective of CPR is to maintain adequate cardiac output and respiration in the presence of cardiorespiratory failure. The New York State Task Force on Life and the Law mistakenly concludes that CPR is physiologically futile when it will "be unsuccessful in restoring cardiac and respiratory function or [when] the patient will experience repeated arrest in a short time period before death occurs."[15] CPR is physiologically futile only when it is impossible to perform effective cardiac massage and ventilation (such as in the presence of cardiac rupture or severe outflow obstruction). Saying that CPR is physiologically futile when it will be unsuccessful in restoring cardiac function is like saying that mechanical ventilation is physiologically futile if it cannot restore respiratory function. The immediate physiologic effect of

the intervention differs from the broader and more uncertain question of prognosis.

Physiologic futility, understood in narrow terms, comes close to providing a value-free understanding of futility. Unfortunately, it applies to a very small number of real cases involving CPR. Similarly, since in the case of Mrs. Wanglie mechanical ventilation could maintain adequate oxygenation and ventilation, her treatment could not be considered futile in the physiologic sense. Even the use of extracorporeal membrane oxygenation in terminally ill patients cannot be considered physiologically futile, since it can maintain circulation and ventilation. The concept of physiologic futility therefore falls short of providing guidance in most cases resembling those described above.

FUTILITY AND STATISTICAL UNCERTAINTY

In most medical situations, there is no such thing as never. Futility is almost always a matter of probability. But what statistical cutoff point should be chosen as the threshold for determining futility? The statement from the Council on Ethical and Judicial Affairs of the AMA concludes that physicians have no obligation to provide futile CPR, but it fails to specify any level of statistical certainty at which the judgment is warranted.[16] The AMA statement fails to acknowledge that this is even an issue. Should each physician decide independently what probability of success should be considered to indicate futility?

Even if we could agree on a statistical cutoff point for determining futility, physicians are often highly unreliable in estimating the likelihood of success of a therapeutic intervention. Psychological research[17] has shown that estimates of probability are susceptible to "severe and systematic errors."[18] Empirical studies have corroborated the limitations of clinical assessment in estimating both prognosis[19] and diagnosis.[20] Even in theory, statistical inferences about what might happen to groups of patients do not permit accurate predictions of what will happen

244 HEALTH CARE ETHICS

to the next such patient. In addition, the tendency to remember cases that are unusual or bizarre predisposes physicians to make decisions on the basis of their experiences with "miraculous" cures or unexpected tragedies.

Schneiderman and colleagues recently argued that a treatment should be considered futile when 100 consecutive patients do not respond to it.[21] But how similar must the patients be? In assessing the efficacy of mechanical ventilation to treat pneumonia, for example, is it sufficient simply to recall the 100 most recent patients who received artificial ventilation for pneumonia? Or must this group be stratified according to age, etiologic organism, or coexisting illness? Clearly, many of these factors will make an important difference.

FUTILITY AND RESOURCE ALLOCATION

Although medical practice has increasingly emphasized patients' autonomy, there is growing pressure on physicians to slow the increase in health care costs by foreclosing some options. Thus, we have a tension between the value of autonomy, exercised in the form of consent to use or omit various interventions, and the desirability of a more Spartan approach to the consumption of medical resources. We promote patients' freedom to request whatever the medical menu has to offer, but we also require that interventions be guided by considerations of cost and the likelihood of benefit.[22] Unfortunately, there is no consensus about what constitutes a just method of balancing the preferences of individual patients against the diverse needs of society.

To some, the concept of futility provides at least a partial solution to this dilemma: It offers a reason to limit therapy without the need to define a fair procedure for allocating resources. This approach allows treatments to be denied on the grounds that they are simply not indicated, apart from the matter of cost. Despite its attractions, there are good reasons why we should not use this concept to solve problems of allocation.

First, arguments based on the futility concept conceal many statistical and value-laden assumptions, whereas strategies based on resource allocation force these assumptions to be stated explicitly. Societies may choose to limit the use of therapies that may be of value and have a reasonable likelihood of success in some cases. For example, the much discussed Oregon plan for allocating Medicaid funds[23] seeks to reflect community values in ranking various health care goals (placing preventive care ahead of cosmetic surgery, for example). Since rationing policies make explicit the values and probabilities that futility-based arguments leave implicit, it is clearly preferable to develop and adopt them rather than use futility arguments as a cover for limiting the availability of scarce and expensive resources.

Another problem with invoking the idea of futility in the debate over allocation is that we have no reason to believe that it is applicable in enough cases to make a difference in the scarcity of medical resources. Although it may be true that beds in the intensive care unit (especially those used for extracorporeal membrane oxygenation) are relatively scarce, it seems unlikely that patients similar to Helga Wanglie occupy an important fraction of those beds, let alone account for a major proportion of the cost of medical care in the United States. From a macroeconomic perspective at least, we must remain skeptical that an appeal to the idea of futility will get us very far.

MOVING BEYOND FUTILITY

Our rejection of futility as a useful concept does not imply that we endorse patients' unrestricted demands for interventions such as those described in our prototypical scenarios. On the contrary, when providers oppose such demands they are usually acting from a profound sense that further treatment would be fundamentally wrong. Our task is to take account of that sense of wrongness without resorting to unilateral, provider-initiated declarations of futility.

In many of the situations in which questions of futility arise, providers believe that the treatment in question would not be in the patient's interests, even from the patient's perspective, and that any insistence by the patient (or surrogate) on further interventions is based on faulty reasoning, unrealistic expectations, or psychological factors, such as denial or guilt. In these circumstances, providers are obligated to make every effort to clarify precisely what the patient intends to achieve with continued treatment. If the patient's goals appear to reflect unrealistic expectations about the probable course of the underlying illness or the probable effect of medical interventions, providers should attempt to correct those impressions. Because inadequate or insensitive communication by providers probably accounts for a substantial proportion of unrealistic requests, such discussions will successfully resolve many conflicts.[24] Empirical studies of ethics consultations have demonstrated precisely this point.[25]

Although this appeal to the patient's interests may seem to contain some of the same ambiguities as arguments using the concept of futility, there is a subtle but important distinction between the two. Judgments about what is in the patient's interest are properly grounded in the patient's perspective, whereas judgments cast in the language of futility falsely assume that there is an objective and dispassionate standard for determining benefits and burdens. Nevertheless, even after providers make sustained attempts to clarify patients' preferences, some patients or surrogates will continue to demand life-sustaining interventions when the caregivers feel deeply troubled about providing them. In many such cases, unrestrained deference to the wishes of the patient or surrogate conflicts with two other values that do not require a unilateral judgment of the futility of treatment: professional ideals and social consensus.

The ideals of medical professionals include respect for patients' wishes, to be sure, but they also include other values, such as compassionate action and the minimization of suffering. Consider, for example, a bedridden victim of multiple strokes who has contractures and bedsores and who "communicates" only by moaning or grimacing when she is touched. Physicians asked to perform chest compressions, institute mechanical ventilation, or use other life-sustaining interventions in such a patient may regard these actions as cruel and inhumane.[26] Moreover, physicians and other caregivers have a legitimate interest in seeing that their knowledge and skills are used wisely and effectively. For example, if surgeons were repeatedly pressured to perform operations that they believed to be inappropriate, they would certainly suffer a loss of dignity and sense of purpose. Although appealing to professional ideals can serve as a convenient means of protecting the interests of physicians at the expense of patients' values, these ideals are legitimate factors to weigh against other values. To dismiss this perspective as irrelevant in decision making is to deny an essential part of what it means to practice medicine.

Although we believe that health care professionals should not be required to take part in care that violates their own morals, the law in this area remains uncertain. On the one hand, courts have upheld a state interest in protecting the ethical integrity of the medical profession. This may provide some basis for protecting doctors who wish to refrain from cruel or inhumane treatment, despite the wishes of the patient or surrogate.[27] On the other hand, in the two cases that have led to court decisions (those of Helga Wanglie and of Jane Doe in Atlanta)[28] the judges upheld the surrogates' decision-making authority. Clearly, this area of the law remains to be defined.

Finally, social consensus is yet another expression of the values at stake in some medical decisions. In a pluralistic society, differences in personal values and interests occasionally run so deep that they cannot be resolved by the introduction of additional facts or by further private debate. At certain critical junctures, the resolution of these conflicts may require an explicit public process of social decision making.[29] Social consensus has been sought, for example, to address the issue of fair allocation of resources.[30] The involvement of society is also essential when the most highly charged questions of morality are at stake, as in the increasingly heated debate over euthanasia.[31]

In the prototypical scenarios described at the outset of this article, an ongoing attempt to achieve social consensus is perhaps most conspicuous with regard to the prolongation of life for patients in a persistent vegetative state. From a legal perspective, the relevant decisions began with the case of Karen Quinlan[32] and have extended through that of Nancy Cruzan.[33] These cases have increased awareness of the ethical issues raised by the situation of patients in a persistent vegetative state and have helped to consolidate the view that it is acceptable to withdraw life-sustaining treatment from patients in such a state. Controversy does remain about who has the ultimate authority to make these decisions. Some hold that the choice must remain with the patient or surrogate, whereas others believe that under some circumstances this prerogative may be overridden. For example, the Hastings Center[34] and the Society of Critical Care Medicine[35] have concluded that providing intensive care to patients in a persistent vegetative state is generally a misuse of resources, and the President's Commission stated that such patients should be removed from life support if such action is necessary to benefit another patient who is not in a persistent vegetative state.[36] It is unclear how this debate will conclude, but the confluence of medical, legal, and ethical thinking about the persistent vegetative state is an example of how social consensus may evolve.

In summary, the Wanglie case demonstrates how the resolution of these conflicts must proceed on many levels. Most such cases will benefit from sustained attempts to clarify the patient's values and the likelihood of the various relevant outcomes and to improve communication with patients or their surrogates. When this approach fails, physicians and other caregivers should ask themselves whether the care requested is consistent with their professional ethics and ideals. When these ideals appear to be violated, either alternative venues for such care should be found or the conflict should be addressed in a public forum. This broader review could be provided through institutional mechanisms, such as the hospital's ethics committee, or by the courts. The public scrutiny that attends such cases will further the debate over the appropriate use of medical resources and foster the development of consensus through legislation and public policy.

CONCLUSION

In outlining the perspectives of the principal stakeholders—patients and their surrogates, physicians, and society—we have avoided the construction of a rigid formula for resolving conflicts over interventions frequently regarded as futile. Because of clinical heterogeneity, pluralistic values, and the evolutionary nature of social consensus, most clinical decision making on behalf of critically ill patients defies reduction to universally applicable principles.

The notion of futility generally fails to provide an ethically coherent ground for limiting life-sustaining treatment, except in circumstances in which narrowly defined physiologic futility can be plausibly invoked. Futility has been conceptualized as an objective entity independent of the patient's or surrogate's perspective, but differences in values and the variable probabilities of clinical outcomes undermine its basis. Furthermore, assertions of futility may camouflage judgments of comparative worth that are implicit in debates about the allocation of resources. In short, the problem with futility is that its promise of objectivity can rarely be fulfilled. The rapid advance of the language of futility into the jargon of bioethics should be followed by an equally rapid retreat.

NOTES

1. Jacobellis v. State of Ohio, 84 S. Ct. 1676 (1964).
2. Hippocrates, The Art, in *Ethics in Medicine: Historical* *Perspectives and Contemporary Concerns* (Cambridge, Mass.: MIT Press, 1976), 6–7.

3. A.M. Capron, In re Helga Wanglie, *Hastings Center Report* 21, no. 5 (1991):26–28; J.D. Lantos et al., The Illusion of Futility in Clinical Practice, *American Journal of Medicine* 87 (1989):81–84; Standards for Cardiopulmonary Resuscitation (CPR) and Emergency Cardiac Care (EEC): V. Medicolegal Considerations and Recommendations, *JAMA* 227, suppl. (1974):864–866; Appendix A: The Proposed Legislation, in *Do Not Resuscitate Orders: The Proposed Legislation and Report of the New York State Task Force on Life and the Law*, 2nd ed. (New York: New York State Task Force on Life and the Law, 1986), 83.

4. 1984 Amendments to the Child Abuse Prevention and Treatment Act, Public Law 98-457, 1984.

5. American Medical Association, Council on Ethical and Judicial Affairs, Guidelines for the Appropriate Use of Do-Not-Resuscitate Orders, *JAMA* 265 (1991):1868–1871.

6. S.H. Miles, Informed Demand for "Non-beneficial" Medical Treatment, *New England Journal of Medicine* 325 (1991):512–515.

7. Brain-damaged Woman at Center of Lawsuit over Life-Support Dies, *New York Times,* July 5, 1991, A8.

8. J.J. Paris et al., Physicians' Refusal of Requested Treatment: The Case of Baby L, *New England Journal of Medicine* 322 (1990):1012–1015.

9. L.J. Blackhall, Must We Always Use CPR? *New England Journal of Medicine* 317 (1987):1281–1285; J.C. Hackler and F.C. Hiller, Family Consent to Orders Not to Resuscitate: Reconsidering Hospital Policy, *JAMA* 264 (1990):1281–1283; D.J. Murphy, Do-Not-Resuscitate Orders: Time for Reappraisal in Long-Term-Care Institutions, *JAMA* 260 (1988):2098–2101.

10. S.E. Bedell et al., Survival after Cardiopulmonary Resuscitation in the Hospital, *New England Journal of Medicine* 309 (1983):569–576.

11. M. Danis et al., A Comparison of Patient, Family, and Physician Assessments of the Value of Medical Intensive Care, *Critical Care Medicine* 16 (1988):594–600; M. Denis et al., A Comparison of Patient, Family, and Nurse Evaluations of the Usefulness of Intensive Care, *Critical Care Medicine* 15 (1987):138–143; M. Denis et al., Patients' and Families' Preferences for Medical Intensive Care, *JAMA* 260 (1988):797–802.

12. L.J. Schneiderman, Medical Futility: Its Meaning and Ethical Implications, *Annals of Internal Medicine* 112 (1990):949–954.

13. Hastings Center, *Guidelines on the Termination of Life-sustaining Treatment and the Care of the Dying* (Briarcliff Manor, N.Y.: Hastings Center, 1987), 32; Appendix C: New York Public Health Law Article 29-B—Orders Not to Resuscitate, in *The Proposed Legislation and Report of the New York State Task Force on Life and the Law*, 2nd ed. (New York: New York State Task Force on Life and the Law, 1986), 96.

14. Hastings Center, *Guidelines on the Termination of Life-sustaining Treatment and the Care of the Dying*.

15. Appendix C: New York Public Health Law Article 29-B.

16. American Medical Association, Council on Ethical and Judicial Affairs, Guidelines for the Appropriate Use of Do-Not-Resuscitate Orders.

17. A. Tversky and D. Kahneman, Judgment under Uncertainty: Heuristics and Biases, *Science* 185 (1974):1124–1131; A.S. Elstein, Clinical Judgment: Psychological Research and Medical Practice, *Science* 194 (1976):696–700.

18. Tversky and Kahneman, Judgment under Uncertainty.

19. R.M. Poses et al., The Answer to "What Are My Chances, Doctor?" Depends on Whom the Question Is Asked: Prognostic Disagreement and Inaccuracy for Critically Ill Patients, *Critical Care Medicine* 17 (1989):827–833.

20. R.M. Poses et al., The Accuracy of Experienced Physicians' Probability Estimates for Patients with Sore Throats: Implications for Decision Making, *JAMA* 254 (1985):925–929.

21. Schneiderman et al., Medical Futility.

22. H. Aaron and W.B. Schwartz, Rationing Health Care: The Choice before Us, *Science* 247 (1990):418–422.

23. D.M. Eddy, What is Going on in Oregon? *JAMA* 260 (1991):417–420.

24. Murphy, Do-Not-Resuscitate Orders; S.J. Youngner, Who Defines Utility? *JAMA* 260 (1988):2094–2095.

25. T.A. Brennan, Ethics Committees and Decisions to Limit Care: The Experience at the Massachusetts General Hospital, *JAMA* 260 (1988):803–807; J. La Pluma, Consultations in Clinical Ethics: Issues and Questions in 27 Cases, *Western Journal of Medicine* 146 (1987):633–637.

26. S. Braithwaite and D.C. Thomasma, New Guidelines on Foregoing Life-sustaining Treatment in Incompetent Patients: An Anticruelty Policy, *Annals of Internal Medicine* 104 (1986):711–715.

27. A. Meisel, *The Right to Die* (New York: Wiley, 1989), 104.

28. In re: Doe, Civil Action No. D93064 (Fulton County, Ga., October 17, 1991).

29. D. Callahan, Medical Futility, Medical Necessity: The-Problem-without-a-Name, *Hastings Center Report* 21, no. 4 (1991):30–35.

30. Eddy, What's Going on in Oregon?

31. R.I. Misbin, Physicians' Aid in Dying, *New England Journal of Medicine* 325 (1991):1307–1311.

32. In the Matter of Karen Ann Quinlan, an Alleged Incompetent, 355 A.2d 647; or 70 NJ 10, March 31, 1976.

33. G.J. Annas, Nancy Cruzan and the Right to Die, *New England Journal of Medicine* 323 (1990):670–673.

34. Hastings Center, *Guidelines on the Termination of Life-sustaining Treatment and the Care of the Dying*, 112.

35. Society of Critical Care Medicine, Task Force on Ethics, Consensus Report on the Ethics of Foregoing Life-sustaining Treatments in the Critically Ill, *Critical Care Medicine* 18 (1990):1435–1439.

36. President's Commission for the Study of Ethical Problems in Medicine and Biomedical and Behavioral Research, *Deciding to Forego Life-sustaining Treatment: Ethical, Medical, and Legal Issues in Treatment Decisions* (Washington, D.C.: U.S. Government Printing Office, 1983), 188–189.

Chapter 27

When Patients or Families Demand Too Much

Larry R. Churchill

For over two decades bioethics has championed the rights of patients and their families in medical decision making. Yet the ethical issues of patient care are not confined to advocacy for a more active role for patients and families. They also include the effort to discern the appropriate roles for patients and families in morally ambiguous situations. One such situation is when patients or their families are thought to demand too much. A notable recent case is that of Mrs. Helga Wanglie and her family.[1]

"Too much" can have a technical, professional, or social definition. A technical definition denotes ineffectiveness or futility. Continued tube feeding of Mrs. Wanglie, for example, would not have restored her to a conscious state or reversed her underlying pathology. "Too much" means here therapies with no therapeutic effect. A professional definition of "too much" implies excessive and harmful, contrary to professional ethics or individual conscience. An intervention that merely prolonged dying or increased suffering, for example, would be "too much" in this sense. And a social definition of "too much" implies disproportionate or unfair and is based on a notion of equity and a distribu-

tional ideal for benefits and burdens. Here, "too much" means more than the Wanglie family had the right to expect or demand. All three meanings of "too much" must be addressed, for they are entangled, but it is important to see that they can also be discussed separately.

I begin with the technical aspect and focus on notions of futility. Many judgments of futility are now seen as two distinct judgments: one of fact (which belongs to the physician), the other of value (which belongs to the patient). The *Hastings Center Guidelines on the Termination of Life-sustaining Treatment,* published in 1987, puts it this way:

> In the event that the patient or surrogate requests a treatment that the responsible health care professional regards as clearly futile in achieving its physiological benefit to the patient, the professional has no obligation to provide it. However, the health care professional's value judgment that although a treatment will produce physio-

The research and writing for this essay was supported by the Charles E. Culpeper Foundation through a Scholarship in Medical Humanities.

logical benefit, the benefit is not sufficient to warrant the treatment, should not be used as a basis for determining a treatment to be futile.[2]

This interpretation protects the physician's conscience from patient demands but leaves the definition of futility in nonmedical hands.

Stuart Youngner has emphasized the potential deception when "futility" encompasses both facts and values:

> Physicians are in the best position to know the empirical facts about the many aspects of futility. I would argue, however, that all except for physiological futility and an absolute inability to postpone death, also involve value judgments. . . . Physicians should not offer treatments that are physiologically futile or certain not to prolong life. . . . Beyond that, they run the risk of giving options disguised as data.[3]

The ethical principle at work here is the principle of autonomy and the chief duty of the health care professional is to respect every patient's autonomy. Autonomy means self-rule; its opposite is heteronomy, rule by others. Autonomy as a moral principle is historically rooted in freedom as a political principle, to which John Locke's *Second Treatise of Government* (1690) gave definitive expression. Freedom, Locke asserted, is not license "but a *liberty* to dispose, and order as he lists, his person, actions, possessions, and his whole property, within the allowance of those laws under which he is, and therein not to be subject to the arbitrary rule of another, but freely follow his own."[4] The eighteenth-century monument to autonomy is the work of the German philosopher Immanuel Kant. Whereas Locke was concerned to protect individuals from the power of the state, Kant focused on freedom of the will. His "practical imperative" requires that others be treated as ends in themselves and never only as a means.[5] For Kant this respect for the moral freedom of others was grounded in a recognition of their rational nature. In bioethics, this raises difficult issues of when and to what extent the ra-

tional capacities of patients are compromised, when and to what extent family wishes are rationally (as opposed to emotionally) based, and in which cases autonomy should give way to medical beneficence.

The grounds for respect for autonomy were most powerfully stated by John Stuart Mill. In *On Liberty* (1859), Mill argued that

> the sole end for which mankind are warranted, individually or collectively, in interfering with the liberty of action of any of their number is self-protection. . . . The only purpose for which power can be rightfully exercised over any member of a civilized community, against his will, is to prevent harm to others. . . . In the part which merely concerns himself, his independence is, of right, absolute. Over himself, over his own body and mind, the individual is sovereign.[6]

Champions of patient autonomy believe that many so-called futility judgments tend to be oversimplified, with the value component suppressed. When this value component is *not* suppressed, it becomes clear that, on the basis of the principle of autonomy, the patient's values should be decisive. For example, an article in the August 1989 *Annals of Emergency Medicine*, arguing for futility as a factual determination in CPR decisions, posed the following as key questions to answer: "Will CPR immediately save life? Will it relieve pain and suffering? Will it restore adequate human functioning? Will it promote satisfactory quality of life?"[7] It takes only a moment's reflection to see that "adequate," "human," and "satisfactory quality of life" imply *value* judgments. This was, of course, precisely the argument of the Wanglies. A persistent vegetative state may have looked like a grim existence to the health care team, but to Mrs. Wanglie it was adequate, human, and satisfactory, or so the family thought, and also "the will of God,"[8] according to them. Respirators and feeding tubes were then *not* futile—they achieved their physiologic aim. What was in dispute was the value of the life that Helga Wanglie possessed.

Her family contended that Mrs. Wanglie should decide, that in the absence of her participation they themselves were the proper interpreters of her values, and that her values supported choosing continued treatment.

Several bioethicists who have commented on this case have supported the Wanglie family without agreeing with the Wanglies' decision. Marcia Angell, for example, expressed sympathy with the view of the physicians but felt that any effort by them to "impose" their views on the family would be wrong. Such a position is consistent with that of the *Hastings Center Guidelines* and with Youngner's view, which call for a strict separation between futility judgments in the physiologic sense and value judgments about quality of life. Everything not futile in the strict sense falls under the purview of the patient or family. This position is a bulwark against paternalistic imposition of values from the medical community and is consistent with the dominant trend in bioethics over the past 20 years. Yet it also raises a new set of problems.

First, a strict separation of fact from value threatens to remove professional values from the picture.[9] The medical sense of what is "best," morally speaking, becomes irrelevant. The patient-customer or the surrogate decision maker is always right. This stark distinction between biology and ethics, between medical facts and patient values, threatens to turn the personal wants of patients into medical needs and exacerbates a central problem in our current approach to health care policy. The separation of medical and nursing judgments from values (all of which supposedly belong to the patient) is demeaning to health care professionals and undermines their role as professionals, that is, as persons who render judgments based on knowledge and experience.

Second, leaving futility determinations entirely to the patient or family confuses self-determination as the right to *refuse* treatment with self-determination as the right to *demand* treatment.[10] The right to refuse is basic and essential to autonomy; this is the sovereignty of which Mill spoke. The right to be left alone is fundamental. The right to receive is something different and is contingent on a wide array of factors, including availability, costs, alternative uses, and the conscience of health professionals. It does not follow that simply because patients or their families want treatments, they are justified in having them.

The issue of patient or family demands for questionable interventions is unlikely to go away. Although few families may be as adamant as the Wanglies, there are an estimated 10,000 persons being maintained in a persistent vegetative state in the United States. Some patients or families may be frugal or conservative about medical interventions, but others will want more care than physicians think it beneficial for them to have. And with the advent of the Patient Self-Determination Act, all patients admitted to health care facilities are offered opportunity to express their wishes about care at the end of life. Some will sign living wills forgoing heroic or marginal treatments, but others may take this opportunity to express a desire for everything available, regardless of low probability of benefit and regardless of cost.

Some assistance in thinking about futility can be gleaned from the Latin roots of the term *futile*. Futile means, etymologically, "free flowing" or "pouring forth."[11] The image is a leaky vessel, a useless container for liquid, which will not hold its water or fulfill its purpose. This raises a new the issue of what purposes medical treatments serve.[12]

Schneiderman, Jecker, and Jonsen have made a useful distinction between the *effect* of a treatment and a *benefit* to the person.[13] For example, the respirator for Mrs. Wanglie had the effect of carrying oxygen through her body, but it had no benefit for her since it did not restore her capacity. Schneiderman, Jecker, and Jonsen argue that the purpose of all treatments is ultimately to benefit patients, not just create an effect. In the Wanglie case, we could then say that the respirator was of no benefit. Note that the claim here is not that her case was "hopeless," which is an emotional term, or that her quality of life was too low to preserve, although that judgment is ultimately entailed. It is rather that Mrs. Wanglie was beyond beneficial intervention. Various organ systems could be kept functioning, but they no longer served the person who was initially the subject of treatment. The treatments, then, go nowhere; they cannot achieve their goal. Mrs. Wanglie, permanently unconscious and dying, could not be averted from that course, and the treatments prolonged the trajectory of her dying but could not reverse it.

This mode of reasoning is helpful, though not fully compelling. A family could still argue, as the Wanglies apparently did, that (1) they wanted the dying stretched out over months, potentially years, because they still believed in a miracle and (2) no treatment is ever futile until the patient dies. They might also argue that permanent unconsciousness does not preclude benefit. Perhaps it is also true that the Wanglie family simply could not accept Mrs. Wanglie's death and were in a prolonged state of denial, underwritten by a vitalistic theology. But this is unfair speculation. The basic point is that the concept of futility will carry only a limited amount of the argumentative freight. Sharpening our thinking is necessary but not sufficient, because what is at stake is what people can live with after all the clarifications are made.[14]

Here two points should be noted. First, families with a member who is critically ill need advice and a voice in decisions. But they also need health professionals who appreciate they are coping with loss and tragedy. Although families have both a need and a right to be part of decisions about care, there is no obligation to give them choices that have little or no meaning. Offering a choice for a treatment when there is very low probability of benefit is often confusing to families, who rightly reason that physicians will only suggest therapies they believe will help. I do not mean here that families cannot understand, will choose badly, or will act out of guilt or denial. I rather mean that *choice* is not always a great thing. Sometimes being given choices is more a disservice to families than a service. It is one thing to ask about the range of choices to which patients and families have a right. It is an-

other thing to ask what patients and families can live with and how physicians can help them interpret tragic losses.

There is a large and important place for autonomy in health care. Still, it is not the only or even the supreme value. Futility has not only an empirical, strictly scientific meaning but a psychosocial meaning as well. "Futile" as a term for characterizing "treatments it would be unwise to choose" has a place in medical judgments. Such treatments would include not just absolutely useless treatments but ones with a low probability of benefit. Judgments that certain treatments are futile are needed to shield patients and their families from compounding tragic loss with wrenching decisions about therapies that are pointless to institute. It is well to remember that patients and families can be disenfranchised by being presented with choices as well as enabled by them. Tomlinson and Brody have expressed this point well in relation to decisions about CPR. "It is *for the sake of patient autonomy,* then that physicians must be able to restrict the alternatives made available to patients and must be able to employ value judgments in doing so."[15] The point applies to other therapies with equal force. It will take wise physicians to protect patient autonomy without lapsing into paternalism. And wisdom is sometimes of no avail, as patients or families can continue to demand everything. Still, it is important to remember that patients and their families need not merely choices but meaningful choices, and options that are too plentiful or have no substantial benefits are often confusing and disorienting.

In placing stress on meaningful choices and not just choices per se, I do not suggest that the physicians caring for Mrs. Wanglie can be faulted. Indeed, the Wanglie family expressed appreciation for the care Mrs. Wanglie received. It is likely that the moral tension in this particular case was not ever solvable by more skillful or parsimonious offering of options. Still, the general point is a valid one. There is an important difference between choices that hold real probability of benefit and those that simply symbolize care (and sometimes reinforce denial). Patients and families must continue to rely on physicians to help them know the difference. A physician's obligation to take the lead in sorting out the difference is part of what it means to be a helping professional.

The second point is that the resources we have for health care need to be protected from the zealotry of those like the Wanglies who will stop at nothing. Although some argue that it is unethical to consider cost in caring for a patient, I argue that it is unethical not to consider cost. This is not a proposal for bedside rationing; it is an argument for efficient health care policies. The bill for the care of Mrs. Wanglie exceeded $1 million. While one might argue that her insurance entitled her to everything her family demanded, I believe this is a shortsighted and superficial view. It is hard to believe that other policyholders would agree to coverage for everything that any one policyholder might demand, especially treatments that consistently go counter to medical advice.[16] The larger question of social justice in health care is at issue here. The cost of Mrs. Wanglie's care could have provided truly useful, basic care for over 2,000 children. Here practice guidelines and limits on insurance coverage consistent with these guidelines would be helpful.

In summary, I argue for the presumptive priority of the principle of autonomy in most cases but against the presumption of its priority in all cases. I argue for autonomy as a pragmatic goal in patient care and against it as a contextless, ideological commitment. I recommend a return to the professional value of protecting patients and families from meaningless choices—choices about treatments that have very little probability of benefit. Here we must rely on a common-sense notion of benefit and not take an extreme, vitalistic view as the norm. Such a stance does not diminish autonomy for patients or families, since being offered an array of long-shot interventions on the slim hope that one of them might work is ordinarily more a disservice to patients than a way of respecting their rights. When choices are meaningful, the rights of patients and families to decide for themselves should be vigorously protected.

Demanding "too much" can mean demanding futile treatments. Here I have argued that futility must be referenced to particular psychosocial factors and to policy guidelines, not merely to physiologic effects. Demanding "too much" can mean demanding actions that violate professional conscience, and in such cases respect for professional values must balance respect for patient autonomy in determining the scope of medical obligations. Demanding "too much" can also mean using medical resources in a way that jeopardizes the care of others; and in this kind of situation the demands for a just system must contextualize and occasionally counterbalance patient or family demands for care.

We are experiencing the problems described in the Wanglie case because we have ignored the need for sound health care policies. To extricate ourselves from an endless repetition of these wrenching dilemmas, we will need to develop realistic futility criteria, benefit-burden tests, admissions criteria for ICUs, and a variety of other benchmarks of sound medical and nursing judgment under the umbrella of national health care policies that are economically feasible and morally just.

NOTES

1. S.H. Miles, Informed Demand for "Non-beneficial" Medical Treatment, *New England Journal of Medicine* 325 (1991):512–515.

2. *Guidelines on the Termination of Life-sustaining Treatment and Care of the Dying: A Report of the Hastings Center* (Briarcliff Manor, N.Y.: Hastings Center, 1987), 32.

3. S. Youngner, Who Defines Futility? *JAMA* 260 (1988):2094–2095.

4. J. Locke, *Second Treatise of Government,* edited by C.B. MacPherson (Indianapolis: Hackett, 1980), 32.

5. I. Kant, *Foundations of the Metaphysics of Morals,* translated by L.W. Beck (New York: Macmillan, 1985), 47.

6. J.S. Mill, *On Liberty* (Indianapolis: Hackett, 1978), 9.

7. T. Ramos and J.E. Reagan, "No" When the Family Says "Go": Resisting Families' Requests for Futile CPR, *Annals of Emergency Medicine* 18 (1989):898–899.

8. S.H. Miles, personal communication.

9. A.S. Brett and L.B. McCullough, When Patients Request Specific Interventions, *New England Journal of Medicine* 315 (1986):1347–1351.

10. T. Beauchamp and J. Childress, *Principles of Biomedical Ethics,* 3rd ed. (New York: Oxford University Press, 1989), 59–60.

11. *The Compact Edition of the Oxford English Dictionary,* s.v. "futile."

12. A.R. Jonsen, What Does Life Support? *The Pharos,* Winter 1987, 4–7.

13. L.J. Schneiderman et al., Medical Futility: Its Meaning and Ethical Implications, *Annals of Internal Medicine* 12 (1990):949–954.

14. J.D. Lantos et al., The Illusion of Futility in Clinical Practice, *American Journal of Medicine* 87 (1989):81–84.

15. T. Tomlinson and H. Brody, Futility and the Ethics of Resuscitation, *JAMA* 264 (1990):1279.

16. Miles, Informed Demand for "Non-beneficial" Medical Treatment, 514.

Chapter 28

Care of the Hopelessly Ill: Proposed Clinical Criteria for Physician-Assisted Suicide

Timothy E. Quill, Christine K. Cassel, and Diane E. Meier

One of medicine's most important purposes is to allow hopelessly ill persons to die with as much comfort, control, and dignity as possible. The philosophy and techniques of comfort care provide a humane alternative to more traditional, curative medical approaches in helping patients achieve this end.[1] Yet there remain instances in which incurably ill patients suffer intolerably before death despite comprehensive efforts to provide comfort. Some of these patients would rather die than continue to live under the conditions imposed by their illness, and a few request assistance from their physicians.

The patients who ask us to face such predicaments do not fall into simple diagnostic categories. Until recently, their problems have been relatively unacknowledged and unexplored by the medical profession, so little is objectively known about the spectrum and prevalence of such requests or about the range of physicians' responses.[2] Yet each request can be compelling. Consider the following patients: a former athlete, weighing 80 lb (36 kg) after an eight-year struggle with the acquired immunodeficiency syndrome (AIDS), who is losing his sight and his memory and is terrified of AIDS dementia; a mother of seven children, continually exhausted and bed-bound at home with a gaping, foul-smelling, open wound in her abdomen, who can no longer eat and who no longer wants to fight ovarian cancer; a fiercely independent retired factory worker, quadriplegic from amyotrophic lateral sclerosis, who no longer wants to linger in a helpless, dependent state waiting and hoping for death; a writer with extensive bone metastases from lung cancer that has not responded to chemotherapy or radiation, who cannot accept the daily choice he must make between sedation and severe pain; and a physician colleague, dying of respiratory failure from progressive pulmonary fibrosis, who does not want to be maintained on a ventilator but is equally terrified of suffocation. Like the story of "Diane," which has been told in more detail,[3] there are personal stories of courage and grief for each of these patients that force us to take very seriously their requests for a physician's assistance in dying.

Our purpose is to propose clinical criteria that would allow physicians to respond to requests for assisted suicide from their competent, incurably ill patients. We support the legalization of

Source: Reprinted from *The New England Journal of Medicine*, Vol. 327, No. 19, pp. 1380–1384, with permission of the Massachusetts Medical Society, © 1992.

such suicide, but not of active euthanasia. We believe this position permits the best balance between a humane response to the requests of patients like those described above and the need to protect other vulnerable people. We strongly advocate intensive, unrestrained care intended to provide comfort for all incurably ill persons.[4] When properly applied, such comfort care should result in a tolerable death, with symptoms relatively well controlled, for most patients. Physician-assisted suicide should never be contemplated as a substitute for comprehensive comfort care or for working with patients to resolve the physical, personal, and social challenges posed by the process of dying.[5] Yet it is not idiosyncratic, selfish, or indicative of a psychiatric disorder for people with an incurable illness to want some control over how they die. The idea of a noble, dignified death, with a meaning that is deeply personal and unique, is exalted in great literature, poetry, art, and music.[6] When an incurably ill patient asks for help in achieving such a death, we believe physicians have an obligation to explore the request fully and, under specified circumstances, carefully to consider making an exception to the prohibition against assisting with a suicide.

PHYSICIAN-ASSISTED SUICIDE

For a physician, assisting with suicide entails making a means of suicide (such as a prescription for barbiturates) available to a patient who is otherwise physically capable of suicide and who subsequently acts on his or her own. Physician-assisted suicide is distinguished from voluntary euthanasia, in which the physician not only makes the means available but, at the patient's request, also serves as the actual agent of death. Whereas active euthanasia is illegal throughout the United States, only 36 states have laws explicitly prohibiting assisted suicide.[7] In every situation in which a physician has compassionately helped a terminally ill person to commit suicide, criminal charges have been dismissed or a verdict of not guilty has been brought[8] (and L. Gostin, personal communica-

tion). Although the prospect of successful prosecution may be remote, the risk of an expensive, publicized professional and legal inquiry would be prohibitive for most physicians and would certainly keep the practice covert among those who participate.

It is not known how widespread physician-assisted suicide currently is in the United States, or how frequently patients' requests are turned down by physicians. Approximately 6,000 deaths per day in the United States are said to be in some way planned or indirectly assisted,[9] probably through the "double effect" of pain-relieving medications that may at the same time hasten death[10] or the discontinuation of or failure to start potentially life-prolonging treatments. From 3 to 37 percent of physicians responding to anonymous surveys reported secretly taking active steps to hasten a patient's death, but these survey data were flawed by low response rates and poor design.[11] Every public-opinion survey taken over the past 40 years has shown support by a majority of Americans for the idea of physician-assisted death for the terminally ill.[12] A referendum with loosely defined safeguards that would have legalized both voluntary euthanasia and assisted suicide was narrowly defeated in Washington State in 1991,[13] and more conservatively drawn initiatives are currently on the ballot in California, before the legislature in New Hampshire, and under consideration in Florida and Oregon.

A POLICY PROPOSAL

Although physician-assisted suicide and voluntary euthanasia both involve the active facilitation of a wished-for death, there are several important distinctions between them.[14] In assisted suicide, the final act is solely the patient's, and the risk of subtle coercion from doctors, family members, institutions, or other social forces is greatly reduced.[15] The balance of power between doctor and patient is more nearly equal in physician-assisted suicide than in euthanasia. The physician is counselor and witness and makes the means available, but ultimately the patient must be the one to act or not act. In voluntary euthanasia, the physician both provides the means and carries out the final act, with greatly amplified power over the patient and an increased risk of error, coercion, or abuse.

In view of these distinctions, we conclude that legalization of physician-assisted suicide, but not of voluntary euthanasia, is the policy best able to respond to patients' needs and to protect vulnerable people. From this perspective, physician-assisted suicide forms part of the continuum of options for comfort care, beginning with the forgoing of life-sustaining therapy, including more aggressive symptom-relieving measures, and permitting physician-assisted suicide only if all other alternatives have failed and all criteria have been met. Active voluntary euthanasia is excluded from this continuum because of the risk of abuse it presents. We recognize that this exclusion is made at a cost to competent, incurably ill patients who cannot swallow or move and who therefore cannot be helped to die by assisted suicide. Such persons, who meet agreed-on criteria in other respects, must not be abandoned to their suffering; a combination of decisions to forgo life-sustaining treatments (including food and fluids) with aggressive comfort measures (such as analgesics and sedatives) could be offered, along with a commitment to search for creative alternatives. We acknowledge that this solution is less than ideal, but we also recognize that in the United States access to medical care is currently too inequitable, and many doctor-patient relationships too impersonal, for us to tolerate the risks of permitting active voluntary euthanasia. We must monitor any change in public policy in this domain to evaluate both its benefits and its burdens.

We propose the following clinical guidelines to contribute to serious discussion about physician-assisted suicide. Although we favor a reconsideration of the legal and professional prohibitions in the case of patients who meet carefully defined criteria, we do not wish to promote an easy or impersonal process.[16] If we are to consider allowing incurably ill patients more control over their deaths, it must be as an expression of our compassion and concern about their ultimate fate after all other alternatives have been exhausted. Such patients should not be held hostage to our reluctance or inability to forge policies in this difficult area.

PROPOSED CLINICAL CRITERIA FOR PHYSICIAN-ASSISTED SUICIDE

Because assisted suicide is extraordinary and irreversible treatment, the patient's primary physician must ensure that the following conditions are clearly satisfied before proceeding. First, the patient must have a condition that is incurable and associated with severe, unrelenting suffering. The patient must understand the condition, the prognosis, and the types of comfort care available as alternatives. Although most patients making this request will be near death, we acknowledge the inexactness of such prognostications[17] and do not want to exclude arbitrarily persons with incurable, but not imminently terminal, progressive illnesses, such as amyotrophic lateral sclerosis or multiple sclerosis. When there is considerable uncertainty about the patient's medical condition or prognosis, a second opinion or opinions should be sought and the uncertainty clarified as much as possible before a final decision about the patient's request is made.

Second, the physician must ensure that the patient's suffering and the request are not the result of inadequate comfort care. All reasonable comfort-oriented measures must at least have been considered, and preferably have been tried, before the means for a physician-assisted suicide are provided. Physician-assisted suicide must never be used to circumvent the struggle to provide comprehensive care or find acceptable alternatives. The physician's prospective willingness to provide assisted suicide is a legitimate and important subject to discuss if the patient raises the question, since many patients will probably find the possibility of an escape from suffering more important than the reality.

Third, the patient must clearly and repeatedly, of his or her own free will and initiative, request to die rather than continue suffering. The physician should understand thoroughly what continued life means to the patient and why death appears preferable. A physician's too-ready acceptance of a patient's request could be perceived as encouragement to commit suicide, yet it is important not to force the patient to "beg" for assistance. Understanding the patient's desire to die and being certain that the request is serious are critical steps to evaluating the patient's rationality and ensuring that all alternative means of relieving suffering have been adequately explored. Any sign of ambivalence or uncertainty on the part of the patient should abort the process, because a clear, convincing, and continuous desire for an end of suffering through death is a strict requirement to proceed. Requests for assisted suicide made in an advance directive or by a health care surrogate should not be honored.

Fourth, the physician must be sure that the patient's judgment is not distorted. The patient must be capable of understanding the decision and its implications. The presence of depression is relevant if it is distorting rational decision making and is reversible in a way that would substantially alter the situation. Expert psychiatric evaluation should be sought when the primary physician is inexperienced in the diagnosis and treatment of depression, or when there is uncertainty about the rationality of the request or the presence of a reversible mental disorder the treatment of which would substantially change the patient's perception of his or her condition.[18]

Fifth, physician-assisted suicide should be carried out only in the context of a meaningful doctor-patient relationship. Ideally, the physician should have witnessed the patient's previous illness and suffering. There may not always be a pre-existing relationship, but the physician must get to know the patient personally in order to understand fully the reasons for the request. The physician must understand why the patient considers death to be the best of a limited number of very unfortunate options. The primary physician must personally confirm that each of the criteria has been met. The patient should have no doubt that the physician is committed to finding alternative solutions if at any moment the patient's mind changes. Rather than create a new subspecialty focused on death,[19] assistance in suicide should be given by the same physician who has been struggling with the patient to provide comfort care, and who will stand by the patient and provide care until the time of death, no matter what path is taken.[20]

No physician should be forced to assist a patient in suicide if it violates the physician's fundamental values, although the patient's personal physician should think seriously before turning down such a request. Should a transfer of care be necessary, the personal physician should help the patient find another, more receptive primary physician.

Sixth, consultation with another experienced physician is required to ensure that the patient's request is voluntary and rational, the diagnosis and prognosis accurate, and the exploration of comfort-oriented alternatives thorough. The consulting physician should review the supporting materials and should interview and examine the patient.

Finally, clear documentation to support each condition is required. A system must be developed for reporting, reviewing, and studying such deaths and clearly distinguishing them from other forms of suicide. The patient, the primary physician, and the consultant must each sign a consent form. A physician-assisted suicide must neither invalidate insurance policies nor lead to an investigation by the medical examiner or an unwanted autopsy. The primary physician, the medical consultant, and the family must be assured that if the conditions agreed on are satisfied in good faith, they will be free from criminal prosecution for having assisted the patient to die.

Informing family members is strongly recommended, but whom to involve and inform should be left to the discretion and control of the patient. Similarly, spiritual counseling should be offered, depending on the patient's background and beliefs. Ideally, close family members should be an integral part of the decision-making process and should understand and support the patient's decision. If there is a major dispute between the family and the patient about how to proceed, it may require the involvement of an ethics committee or even of the courts. It is to be hoped, however, that most of these painful decisions can be worked through directly by the patient, the family, and health care providers. Under no circumstances should the family's wishes and requests override those of a competent patient.

THE METHOD

In physician-assisted suicide, a lethal amount of medication is usually prescribed that the patient then ingests. Since this process has been largely covert and unstudied, little is known about which methods are the most humane and effective. If there is a change in policy, there must be an open sharing of information within the profession, and a careful analysis of effectiveness. The methods selected should be reliable and should not add to the patient's suffering. We must also provide support and careful monitoring for the patients, physicians, and families affected, since the emotional and social effects are largely unknown but are undoubtedly far-reaching.

Assistance with suicide is one of the most profound and meaningful requests a patient can make of a physician. If the patient and the physician agree that there are no acceptable alternatives and that all the required conditions have been met, the lethal medication should ideally be taken in the physician's presence. Unless the patient specifically requests it, he or she should not be left alone at the time of death. In addition to the personal physician, other health care providers and family members should be encouraged to be present, as the patient wishes. It is of the utmost importance not to abandon the patient at this critical moment. The time before a controlled death can provide an opportunity for a rich and meaningful goodbye between family members, health care providers, and the patient.

For this reason, we must be sure that any policies and laws enacted to allow assisted suicide do not require that the patient be left alone at the moment of death in order for the assisters to be safe from prosecution.

BALANCING RISKS AND BENEFITS

There is an intensifying debate within and outside the medical profession about the physician's appropriate role in assisting dying.[21] Although most agree that there are exceptional circumstances in which death is preferable to intolerable suffering, the case against both physician-assisted suicide and voluntary euthanasia is based mainly on the implications for public policy and the potential effect on the moral integrity of the medical profession.[22] The "slippery slope" argument asserts that permissive policies would inevitably lead to subtle coercion of the powerless to choose death rather than become burdens to society or their families. Access to health care in the United States is extraordinarily variable, often impersonal, and subject to intense pressures for cost containment. It may be dangerous to license physicians to take life in this unstable environment. It is also suggested that comfort care, skillfully applied, could provide a tolerable and dignified death for most persons and that physicians would have less incentive to become more proficient at providing such care if the option of a quick, controlled death were too readily available. Finally, some believe that physician-assisted death, no matter how noble and pure its intentions, could destroy the identity of the medical profession and its central ethos, protecting the sanctity of life. The question before policy makers, physicians, and voters is whether criteria such as those we have outlined here safeguard patients adequately against these risks.

The risks and burdens of continuing with the current prohibitions have been less clearly articulated in the literature.[23] The most pressing problem is the potential abandonment of competent, incurably ill patients who yearn for death despite comprehensive comfort care. These patients may be disintegrating physically and emotionally, but death is not imminent. They have often fought heroic medical battles only to find themselves in this final condition. Those who have witnessed difficult deaths in hospice programs are not reassured by the glib assertion that we can always make death tolerable, and patients fear that physicians will abandon them if their course becomes difficult or overwhelming in the face of comfort care. In fact, there is no empirical evidence that all physical suffering associated with incurable illness can be effectively relieved. In addition, the most frightening aspect of death for many is not physical pain, but the prospect of losing control and independence and of dying in an undignified, unesthetic, absurd, and existentially unacceptable condition.

Physicians who respond to requests for assisted suicide from such patients do so at substantial professional and legal peril, often acting in secret without the benefit of consultation or support from colleagues. This covert practice discourages open and honest communication among physicians, their colleagues, and their dying patients. Decisions often depend more on the physician's values and willingness to take risks than on the compelling nature of the patient's request. There may be more risk of abuse and idiosyncratic decision making with such secret practices than with a more open,

carefully defined practice. Finally, terminally ill patients who do choose to take their lives often die alone so as not to place their families or caregivers in legal jeopardy.[24]

CONCLUSION

Given current professional and legal prohibitions, physicians find themselves in a difficult position when they receive requests for assisted suicide from suffering patients who have exhausted the usefulness of measures for comfort care. To adhere to the letter of the law, they must turn down their patients' requests even if they find them reasonable and personally acceptable. If they accede to their patients' requests, they must risk violating legal and professional standards, and therefore they act in isolation and in secret collaboration with their patients. We believe that there is more risk for vulnerable patients and for the integrity of the profession in such hidden practices, however well intended, than there would be in a more open process restricted to competent patients who met carefully defined criteria. The medical and legal professions must collaborate if we are to create public policy that fully acknowledges irreversible suffering and offers dying patients a broader range of options to explore with their physicians.

NOTES

1. S.H. Wanzer et al., The Physician's Responsibility toward Hopelessly Ill Patients, *New England Journal of Medicine* 310 (1984):955–959; S.H. Wanzer et al., The Physician's Responsibility toward Hopelessly Ill Patients: A Second Look, *New England Journal of Medicine* 320 (1989):844–849; American Medical Association, Council on Ethical and Judicial Affairs, Decisions near the End of Life, *JAMA* 267 (1992):369–372; J. Rhymes, Hospice Care in America, *JAMA* 264 (1990):369–372; L. Broadfield, Evaluation of Palliative Care: Current Status and Future Directions, *Journal of Palliative Care* 4, no. 3 (1988):21–28; K.A. Wallston et al., Comparing the Quality of Death for Hospice and Non-hospice Cancer Patients, *Medical Care* 26 (1988):177–182.

2. National Hemlock Society, *1987 Survey of California Physicians Regarding Voluntary Active Euthanasia for*

the Terminally Ill (Los Angeles: Hemlock Society, 1988); Center for Health Ethics and Policy, *Withholding and Withdrawing Life-sustaining Treatment: A Survey of Opinions and Experiences of Colorado Physicians* (Denver: University of Colorado Graduate School of Public Affairs, 1988); S. Helig, The SFMS Euthanasia Survey: Results and Analysis, *San Francisco Medicine*, May 1988, 24–26, 34; M. Overmyer, National Survey: Physicians' Views on the Right to Die, *Physicians Manage* 31, no. 7 (1991):40–45.

3. T.E, Quill, Death and Dignity: A Case of Individualized Decision Making, *New England Journal of Medicine* 324 (1991):691–694.

4. Wanzer et al., The Physician's Responsibility toward Hopelessly Ill Patients; Wanzer et al., The Physician's Responsibility toward Hopelessly Ill Patients: A Second Look; American Medical Association, Council on Ethi-

cal and Judicial Affairs, Decisions near the End of Life; Rhymes, Hospice Care in America; Broadfield, Evaluation of Palliative Care; Wallston et al., Comparing the Quality of Death for Hospice and Non-hospice Cancer Patients.

5. D.E. Meier and C.K. Cassel, Euthanasia in Old Age: A Case Study of Ethical Analysis, *Journal of the American Geriatric Society* 31 (1983): 294–298.

6. P. Aries, *The Hour of Our Death* (New York: Vintage, 1982).

7. S.A. Newman, Euthanasia Orchestrating "the Last Syllable of . . . Time," *University of Pittsburgh Law Review* 53 (1991):153–191; L.H. Glantz, Withholding and Withdrawing Treatment: The Role of the Criminal Law, *Law, Medicine and Health Care* 15 (1987–1988):231–241.

8. Newman, Euthanasia Orchestrating "the Last Syllable of . . . Time"; Glantz, Withholding and Withdrawing Treatment.

9. A. Malcolm, Giving Death a Hand: Rending Issue, *New York Times*, June 14, 1990, A6.

10. American Medical Association, Council on Ethical and Judicial Affairs, Decisions near the End of Life; Meier and Cassel, Euthanasia in Old Age.

11. National Hemlock Society, *1987 Survey of California Physicians Regarding Voluntary Active Euthanasia for the Terminally Ill*; Center for Health Ethics and Policy, *Withholding and Withdrawing Life-sustaining Treatment;* Helig, The SFMS Euthanasia Survey; Overmyer, National Survey.

12. Malcolm, Giving Death a Hand; T. Gest, Changing the Rules on Dying, *U.S. News and World Report*, July 9, 1990, 22–24; Hemlock Society, *1990 Roper Poll on Physician Aid-in-Dying, Allowing Nancy Cruzan to Die, and Physicians Obeying the Living Will* (New York: Roper Organization, 1991); Hemlock Society, *1991 Roper Poll of the West Coast on Euthanasia* (New York: Roper Organization, 1991).

13. R.I. Misbin, Physicians' Aid in Dying, *New England Journal of Medicine* 325 (1991):1307–1311.

14. R.F. Weir, The Morality of Physician-assisted Suicide, *Law, Medicine and Health Care* 20 (1992):116–126.

15. J. Glover, *Causing Death and Saving Lives* (New York: Penguin, 1977), 182–189.

16. N.S. Jecker, Giving Death a Hand: When the Dying and the Doctor Stand in a Special Relationship, *Journal of the American Geriatric Society* 39 (1991):831–835.

17. R.M. Poses et al., The Answer to "What Are My Chances, Doctor?" Depend on Whom Is Asked: Prognostic Disagreement and Inaccuracy for Critically Ill Patients, *Critical Care Medicine* 17 (1989):827–833; M.E. Charlson, Studies of Prognosis: Progress and Pitfalls, *Journal of General Internal Medicine* 2 (1987): 359–361; R.S. Schonwetter et al., Estimation of Survival

Time in Terminal Cancer Patients: An Impedance to Hospital Admissions? *Hospice Journal* 6 (1990):65–79.

18. Y. Conwell and E.D. Caine, Rational Suicide and the Right to Die: Reality and Myth, *New England Journal of Medicine* 325 (1991):1100–1103.

19. G.I. Benrubi, Euthanasia: The Need for Procedural Safeguards, *New England Journal of Medicine* 326 (1992):197–199.

20. Jecker, Giving Death a Hand.

21. American Medical Association, Council on Ethical and Judicial Affairs, Decisions near the End of Life; Weir, The Morality of Physician-assisted Suicide; C.K. Cassel and D.E. Meier, Morals and Moralism in the Debate over Euthanasia and Assisted Suicide, *New England Journal of Medicine* 323 (1990):750–752; W. Reichel and A.J. Dyck, Euthanasia: A Contemporary Moral Quandary, *Lancet* (1989, vol. 2):1321–1323; M. Angell, Euthanasia, *New England Journal of Medicine* 319 (1988):1348–1350; J. Rachels, Active and Passive Euthanasia, *New England Journal of Medicine* 292 (1975):78–80; J. Lachs, Humane Treatment and the Treatment of Humans, *New England Journal of Medicine* 294 (1976):838–840; P.J. van der Maas, Euthanasia and Other Medical Decisions Concerning the End of Life, *Lancet* 338 (1991):669–674; P.A. Singer and M. Siegler, Euthanasia: A Critique, *New England Journal of Medicine* 322 (1990):1881–1883; D. Orentlicher, Physician Participation in Assisted Suicide, *JAMA* 262 (1989):1844–1845; S.M. Wolf, Holding the Line on Euthanasia, *Hastings Center Report* 19, no. 1, suppl. (1989):13–15; W. Gaylin et al., "Doctors Must Not Kill," *JAMA* 259 (1988):2139–2140; K.L. Vaux, Debbie's Dying: Mercy Killing and the Good Death, *JAMA* 259 (1988):2140–2141; C.F. Gomez, *Regulating Death: Euthanasia and the Case of the Netherlands* (New York: The Free Press, 1991); D. Brahams, euthanasia in the Netherlands, *Lancet* 335 (1990):591–592; H.J.J. Leenen, Coma Patients in the Netherlands, *British Medical Journal* 300 (1990):69.

22. Singer and Siegler, Euthanasia; Orentlicher, Physician Participation in Assisted Suicide; Wolf, Holding the Line on Euthanasia; Gaylin et al., "Doctors Must Not Kill"; Vaux, Debbie's Dying; Gomez, *Regulating Death*; Brahams, Euthanasia in the Netherlands; Leenen, Coma Patients in the Netherlands.

23. Weir, The Morality of Physician-assisted Suicide; Cassel and Meier, Morals and Moralism in the Debate over Euthanasia and Assisted Suicide; Reichel and Dyck, Euthanasia; Angell, Euthanasia; Rachels, Active and Passive Euthanasia; Lachs, Humane Treatment and the Treatment of Humans; van der Maas et al., Euthanasia and Other Medical Decisions Concerning the End of Life.

24. Quill, Death and Dignity.

Chapter 29

Euthanasia: The Way We Do It, The Way They Do It

Margaret P. Battin

INTRODUCTION

Because we tend to be rather myopic in our discussions of death and dying, especially about the issues of active euthanasia and assisted suicide, it is valuable to place the question of how we go about dying in an international context. We do not always see that our own cultural norms may be quite different from those of other nations and that our background assumptions and actual practices differ dramatically. Thus, I would like to examine the perspectives on end-of-life dilemmas in three countries: The Netherlands, Germany, and the USA.

The Netherlands, Germany and the United States are all advanced industrial democracies. They all have sophisticated medical establishments and life expectancies over 70 years of age; their populations are all characterized by an increasing proportion of older persons. They are all in what has been called the fourth stage of the epidemiologic transition[1]—that stage of societal development in which it is no longer the case that most people die of acute parasitic or infectious diseases. In this stage, most people do not die of diseases with rapid, unpredictable onsets and sharp fatality curves; rather, the majority of the population—as much as perhaps 70–80 percent—die of degenerative diseases, especially delayed degenerative diseases, that are characterized by late, slow onset and extended decline. Most people in highly industrialized countries die from cancer; atherosclerosis; heart disease (by no means always suddenly fatal); chronic obstructive pulmonary disease; liver, kidney, or other organ disease; or degenerative neurological disorders. Thus, all three of these countries are alike in facing a common problem: how to deal with the characteristic new ways in which we die.

DEALING WITH DYING IN THE UNITED STATES

In the United States, we have come to recognize that the maximal extension of life-prolonging treatment in these late-life degenerative conditions is often inappropriate. Although we could keep the machines and tubes—the respirators, intravenous lines, feeding tubes—hooked

Source: Adapted from *The Journal of Pain and Symptom Management*, Vol. 6, No. 5, pp. 298–305, with permission of the U.S. Cancer Pain Relief Committee, © 1991.

up for extended periods, we recognize that this is inhumane, pointless, and financially impossible. Instead, as a society we have developed a number of mechanisms for dealing with these hopeless situations, all of which involve withholding or withdrawing various forms of treatment.

Some mechanisms for withholding or withdrawing treatments are exercised by the patient who is confronted by such a situation or who anticipates it: these include refusal of treatment, the patient-executed DNR order, the living will, and the durable power of attorney. Others are mechanisms for decision by second parties about a patient who is no longer competent or never was competent. The latter are reflected in a long series of court cases, including *Quinlan, Saikewicz, Spring, Eichner, Barber, Bartling, Conroy, Brophy,* the trio *Farrell, Peter,* and *Jobes,* and *Cruzan.* These are cases that attempt to delineate the precise circumstances under which it is appropriate to withhold or withdraw various forms of therapy, including respiratory support, chemotherapy, antibiotics in intercurrent infections, and artificial nutrition and hydration. Thus, during the past 15 years or so, roughly since *Quinlan* (1976), we have developed an impressive body of case law and state statute that protects, permits, and facilitates our characteristic American strategy of dealing with end-of-life situations. These cases provide a framework for withholding or withdrawing treatment when we believe there is no medical or moral point in going on. This is sometimes termed *passive euthanasia;* more often, it is simply called *allowing to die,* and it is ubiquitous in the United States.

For example, a recent study by Miles and Gomez indicates that some 85 percent of deaths in the United States occur in health care institutions, including hospitals, nursing homes, and other facilities, and of these, about 70 percent involve electively withholding some form of life-sustaining treatment.[2] A 1989 study cited in the *Journal of the American Medical Association* claims that 85–90 percent of critical care professionals state that they are withholding and withdrawing life-sustaining treatments from patients who are "deemed to have irreversible disease and are terminally ill."[3] Still another study identified some 115 patients in two intensive-care units from whom care was withheld or withdrawn; 110 were already incompetent by the time the decision to limit care was made. The 89 who died while still in the intensive care unit accounted for 45 percent of all deaths there.[4] It is estimated that 1.3 million American deaths a year follow decisions to withhold life support;[5] this is a majority of the just over 2 million American deaths per year. Withholding and withdrawing treatment is the way we in the USA go about dealing with dying, and indeed "allowing to die" is the only legally protected alternative to maximal treatment recognized in the United States. We do not legally permit ourselves to actively cause death.

DEALING WITH DYING IN THE NETHERLANDS

In the Netherlands, voluntary active euthanasia is also an available response to end-of-life situations. Although active euthanasia remains prohibited by statutory law, it is protected by a series of lower and supreme court decisions and is widely regarded as legal, or, more precisely, *gedoogd,* legally "tolerated." These court decisions have the effect of protecting the physician who performs euthanasia from prosecution, provided the physician meets a rigorous set of guidelines.

These guidelines, variously stated, contain five central provisions:

1. that the patient's request be voluntary
2. that the patient be undergoing intolerable suffering
3. that all alternatives acceptable to the patient for relieving the suffering have been tried
4. that the patient have full information
5. that the physician consult with a second physician whose judgment can be expected to be independent

Of these criteria, it is the first that is central: Euthanasia may be performed only at the voluntary request of the patient. This criterion is also understood to require that the patient's request be a stable, enduring, reflective one—not the product of a transitory impulse. Every attempt is to be made to rule out depression, psychopathology, pressures from family members, unrealistic fears, and other factors compromising voluntariness.

Putting an end to years of inflammatory discussion in which guesses about the frequency of euthanasia had ranged from 2,000 (close to correct) to 20,000 cases a year, a comprehensive study requested by the Dutch government was published in late 1991; an English version appeared in the *Lancet*.[6] Popularly known as the Remmelink Commission report, this study provided the first objective data about the incidence of euthanasia as well as a wider range of medical practices at the end of life: the withholding or withdrawal of treatment; the use of life-shortening doses of opioids for the control of pain; and direct termination, including active euthanasia, physician-assisted suicide, and life-ending procedures not termed euthanasia. This study was supplemented by a second empirical examination, focusing particularly carefully on the characteristics of patients and the nature of their euthanasia requests.[7]

About 130,000 people die in the Netherlands every year, and of these deaths, about 30 percent are acute and unexpected and 70 percent are predictable and foreseen, usually the result of degenerative illnesses comparatively late in life. Of the total deaths in the Netherlands, the Remmelink Commission study found about 17.5 percent involved decisions to withhold or withdraw treatment in situations where continuing treatment would probably have prolonged life; another 17.5 percent involved the use of opioids to relieve pain but in dosages probably sufficient to shorten life. A total of 2.9 percent of all deaths involved euthanasia and related practices.

About 2,300 people, 1.8 percent of the total deaths in the Netherlands, died by euthanasia, understood as the termination of the life of the patient at the patient's explicit and persistent request. Another 400 people, 0.3 percent of the total, chose physician-assisted suicide. About 1,000 additional patients died as the result of "life-terminating procedures" not technically called euthanasia; in virtually all of these cases, euthanasia had been previously discussed with the patient, the patient had expressed in a previous phase of the disease a wish for euthanasia if his or her suffering became unbearable, or the patient was near death and clearly suffering grievously yet verbal contact had become impossible.

Although euthanasia is thus not frequent—a small fraction of the total annual mortality—it is nevertheless a conspicuous option in terminal illness, well known to both physicians and the general public. There has been very widespread public discussion of the issues that arise with respect to euthanasia during the last several years, and surveys of public opinion show that public support for a liberal euthanasia policy has been growing: from 40 percent in 1966 to 81 percent in 1988.[8] Doctors too support the practice, and although there is a vocal opposition group, the opposition is in the clear minority. Some 54 percent of Dutch physicians said that they had performed euthanasia or provided assistance in suicide, including 62 percent of *huisarts* (general practitioners), and an additional 34 percent said that although they had not actually done so, they could conceive of situations in which they would be prepared to do so. Thus, although many who had practiced euthanasia mentioned that they would be most reluctant to do so again and that "only in the face of unbearable suffering and with no alternatives would they be prepared to take such action,"[9] some 88 percent of Dutch physicians appear to accept the practice in some cases. As the Remmelink Commission commented, "a large majority of physicians in the Netherlands see euthanasia as an accepted element of medical practice under certain circumstances."[10]

In general, pain alone is not the basis for deciding upon euthanasia, since pain can, in most cases, be effectively treated. Rather, the "intolerable suffering" mentioned in the second criterion is understood to mean suffering that is intolerable in the patient's (rather than the physician's) view and can include a fear of or unwillingness to endure *entluistering,* that gradual effacement and loss of personal identity that characterizes the end stages of many terminal illnesses. In a year, about 25,000 patients seek reassurance from their physicians that they will be granted euthanasia if their suffering becomes severe; there are about 9,000 explicit requests, and more than two-thirds of these are turned down, usually on the grounds that there is some other way of treating the patient's suffering. In 14 percent of cases, the denial is based on the presence of depression or psychiatric illness.

In the Netherlands, many hospitals now have protocols for the performance of euthanasia; these serve to ensure that the court-established guidelines have been met. However, euthanasia is often practiced in the patient's home, typically by the general practitioner who is the patient's long-term family physician. Euthanasia is usually performed after aggressive hospital treatment has failed to arrest the patient's terminal illness; the patient has come home to die, and the family physician is prepared to ease this passing. Whether practiced at home or in the hospital, it is believed that euthanasia usually takes place in the presence of the family members, perhaps the visiting nurse, and often the patient's pastor or priest. Many doctors say that performing euthanasia is never easy but that it is something they believe a doctor ought to do for his or her patient when nothing else can help.

Thus, in the Netherlands a patient facing the end of life has an option not openly practiced in the United States: to ask the physician to bring his or her life to an end. Although not everyone does so—indeed, about 97 percent of people who die in a given year do not—it is a choice widely understood as available.

FACING DEATH IN GERMANY

In part because of its very painful history of Nazism, Germany appears to believe that doctors should have no role in causing death. Although societal generalizations are always risky, it is fair, I think, to say that there is vigorous and nearly universal opposition in Germany to the notion of active euthanasia. Euthanasia is viewed as always wrong, and the Germans view the Dutch as stepping out on a dangerously slippery slope.

However, it is an artifact of German law that, whereas killing on request (including voluntary euthanasia) is prohibited, assisting suicide is not a violation of the law, provided the person is *tatherrschaftsfähig,* capable of exercising control over his or her actions, and also acting out of *freiverantwortliche Wille,* freely responsible choice. In response to this situation, a private organization, the *Deutsche Gesellschaft für Humanes Sterben* (DGHS), or German Society for Humane Dying, has been providing support to its very extensive membership (over 50,000 persons) in choosing suicide as an alternative to terminal illness.

At least until recently, a person who had been a member of the DGHS for at least a year, provided he or she had not received medical or psychotherapeutic treatment for depression or other psychiatric illness during the last two years, could request a copy of DGHS's booklet *Menschenwürdiges und selbstverantwortliches Sterben* (Dignified and responsible death). This booklet provided a list of about ten drugs available by prescription in Germany, together with the specific dosages necessary for producing a certain, painless death. DGHS recommended that the member approach a physician for a prescription for the drug desired, asking, for example, for a barbiturate to help with sleep or chloroquine for protection against malaria on a trip to India. If necessary, the DGHS would also arrange for someone to obtain drugs from neighboring countries, including France, Italy, Spain, Portugal, and Greece, where they may be available without prescription. In unusual cases, the DGHS would also provide what it calls *Sterbebegleitung* (accompaniment in dying), which involved arranging for a companion to remain with the person during the often extended period that is required for the lethal drug to take full effect. However, the *Sterbebegleiter* was typically a layperson, not someone medically trained, and physicians played no role in assisting in these cases of suicide. To preclude suspicion by providing evidence of the person's intentions, the DGHS also provided a form—printed on a single sheet of distinctive pink paper—to be signed once when joining the organization, expressing the intention to determine the time of one's own death, and again at the time of the suicide and left beside the body.

Because assisting suicide is not illegal in Germany, provided the person is competent and in control of his or her own will, there is no legal risk for family members, the *Sterbebegleiter*, or others in reporting information about the methods and effectiveness of suicide attempts, and the DGHS encouraged its network of regional bureaus (five, in major cities throughout the country) to facilitate feedback. On this basis, it regularly updated and revised the drug information it provided. It has claimed some 2,000–3,000 suicides per year among its members.

However, scandal has engulfed the founder and president of the DGHS, Hans Henning Atrott, arrested for selling cyanide for exorbitant sums to many members, including an attorney hospitalized for mental illness. In May 1992 police raided Atrott's office, where they found capsules of cyanide, barbiturates, and a large amount of cash. What the outcome of the scandal will be remains to be seen, though it is clear that the focus is on Atrott's alleged profiteering and his assisting a mentally ill person rather than on the DGHS's regular practice of assisting competent terminally ill individuals to commit suicide. DGHS has eliminated the booklet and the practice of providing drugs, but it continues to exist.

To be sure, assisted suicide is not the only option open to the terminally ill patient in Germany, nor is there clear evidence concerning its frequency either within the DGHS or in nonreported cases outside it. There is increasing emphasis on help in dying that does not involve direct termination, and organizations like Omega, which offers hospice-style care and an extensive program of companionship, are attracting increasing attention. The DGHS is a conspicuous, widely known organization, and many Germans appear to be aware that assisted suicide is available even if they do not use the services of the DGHS.

OBJECTIONS TO THE THREE MODELS OF DYING

In response to the dilemmas raised by the new circumstances of death, in which the majority of the population in each of the advanced industrial nations dies of degenerative diseases after an extended period of terminal deterioration, different countries develop different practices. The United States legally permits only withholding and withdrawal of treatment, though of course active euthanasia and assisted suicide do occur. The Netherlands also permits voluntary active euthanasia, and although Germany rejects euthanasia, it tolerates assisted suicide. But there are serious moral objections to be made to each of these practices, objections to be considered before resolving the issue of which practices our own culture ought to permit.

Objections to the German Practice

German law does not prohibit assisting suicide, but postwar German culture discourages physicians from taking any active role in death. This gives rise to distinctive moral problems. For one thing, it appears that there is little professional help or review provided for patients' choices about suicide; because the patient makes this choice essentially outside the medical establishment, medical professionals are not in a position to detect or treat impaired judgment on the part of the patient, especially judgment impaired by depression. Similarly, if the patient must commit suicide assisted only by persons outside the medical profession, there are risks that the patient's diagnosis and prognosis are inadequately confirmed, that the means chosen for suicide will be unreliable or inappropriately used, that the means used for suicide will fall into the hands of other persons, and that the patient will fail to recognize or be able to resist intrafamilial pressures and manipulation. Furthermore, as the new DGHS president Dr. Hermann Pohlmeier points out, this does not prevent even the DGHS itself from *promoting* rather than simply supporting choices of suicide, as he believes it had been doing under the scandal-ridden leadership of former president Atrott. It is for this reason that Pohlmeier has discontinued some of DGHS's earlier practices.

Objections to the Dutch Practice

The Dutch practice of physician-performed active voluntary euthanasia also raises a number of ethical issues, many of which have been discussed vigorously both in the Dutch press and in commentary on the Dutch practices from abroad. For one thing, it is sometimes said that the availability of physician-performed euthanasia creates a disincentive for providing good terminal care. There is no evidence that this is the case; on the contrary, Peter Admiraal, the anesthesiologist who is perhaps the Netherlands' most vocal proponent of voluntary active euthanasia, insists that pain should rarely or never be the occasion for euthanasia, as pain (in contrast to suffering) is comparatively easily treated.[11] Instead, it is a refusal to endure the final stages of deterioration, both mental and physical, that motivates requests.

It is also sometimes said that active euthanasia violates the Hippocratic oath. Indeed, it is true that the original Greek version of the oath prohibits the physician from giving a deadly drug, even when asked for it; but the original version also prohibits performing surgery and taking fees for teaching medicine, neither of which prohibition has survived into contemporary medical practice. Dutch physicians often say that they see performing euthanasia—where it is genuinely requested by the patient and nothing else can be done to relieve the patient's condition—as part of their duty to the patient, not as a violation of it.

The Dutch are also often said to be at risk of starting down the slippery slope, that is, that the practice of voluntary active euthanasia for patients who meet the criteria will erode into practicing less-than-voluntary euthanasia on patients whose problems are not irremediable and perhaps by gradual degrees will develop into terminating the lives of people who are elderly, chronically ill, handicapped, mentally retarded, or otherwise regarded as undesirable. This risk is often expressed in vivid claims of widespread fear and wholesale slaughter, claims based on misinterpretation of the 1,000 cases of "life-ending treatment" mentioned earlier. However, the Dutch are now beginning to agonize over the problems of the incompetent patient, the mentally ill patient, the newborn with serious deficits, and other patients who cannot make voluntary choices, though these are largely understood as issues about withholding or withdrawing treatment, not about direct termination.[12]

What is not often understood is that this new and acutely painful area of reflection for the Dutch—withholding and withdrawing treatment from incompetent patients—has already led in the United States to the development of a vast, highly developed body of law: namely, that series of cases just cited, beginning with *Quinlan* and culminating in *Cruzan*. Americans have been discussing these issues for a long time and have developed a broad set of practices that are regarded as routine in withholding and withdrawing treatment. The Dutch see Americans as much further out on the slippery slope than they are, because Americans have already become accustomed to second-party choices about other people. Issues involving second-party choices are painful to the Dutch in a way they are not to us precisely because *voluntariness* is so central in the Dutch understanding of choices about dying. Concomitantly, the Dutch see the Americans' squeamishness about first-party choices—voluntary euthanasia, assisted suicide—as evidence that we are not genuinely committed to recognizing voluntary choice after all. For this reason, many Dutch commentators believe that the Americans are at a much greater risk of sliding down the slippery slope into involuntary killing than they are. I fear, I must add, that they are right about this.

Objections to the American Practice

There may be the moral problems raised by the German and the Dutch practices, but there are also moral problems raised by the American practice of relying on withholding and withdrawal of treatment in end-of-life situations. The German, Dutch, and American practices all occur within similar conditions—in industrialized nations with highly developed medical systems where a majority of the population die of illnesses exhibiting characteristically extended downhill courses—but the issues raised by our own response to this situation may be even more disturbing than those of the Dutch or the Germans. We often assume that our approach is "safer" because it involves only letting someone die, not killing him or her; but it too raises very troubling questions.

The first of these issues is a function of the fact that withdrawing and especially withholding treatment are typically less conspicuous, less pronounced, less evident kinds of actions than direct killing, even though they can equally well lead to death. Decisions about nontreatment have an invisibility that decisions about directly causing death do not have, even though they may have the same result, and hence there is a much wider range of occasions in which such decisions can be made. One can decline to treat a patient in many different ways, at many different times—by not providing oxygen, by not instituting dialysis, by not correcting electrolyte imbalances, and so on—all of which will cause the patient's death; open medical killing also brings about death but is much more overt and conspicuous. Consequently, letting die also invites many fewer protections. In contrast to the standard slippery slope argument, which sees killing as riskier than letting die, the more realistic slippery slope argument warns that because our culture relies primarily on decisions about

nontreatment, grave decisions about living or dying are not as open to scrutiny as they are under more direct life-terminating practices and hence are more open to abuse.

Second, reliance on withholding and withdrawal of treatment invites rationing in an extremely strong way, in part because of the comparative invisibility of these decisions. When a health care provider does not offer a specific sort of care, it is not always possible to discern the motivation; the line between believing that it would not provide benefit to the patient and that it would not provide benefit worth the investment of resources in the patient can be very thin. This is a particular problem where health care financing is highly decentralized, as in the United States, and where rationing decisions without benefit of principle are not always available for easy review.

Third, relying on withholding and withdrawal of treatment can often be cruel. It requires that the patient who is dying from one of the diseases that exhibits a characteristic extended, downhill course (as the majority of patients in the Netherlands, Germany, and the United States do) must in effect wait to die until the absence of a certain treatment will cause death. For instance, the cancer patient who forgoes chemotherapy or surgery does not simply die from this choice; he or she continues to endure the downhill course of the cancer until the tumor finally destroys some crucial bodily function or organ. The patient with amyotrophic lateral sclerosis who decides in advance to decline respiratory support does not die at the time this choice is made but continues to endure increasing paralysis until breathing is impaired and suffocation occurs. We often try to ameliorate these situations by administering pain medication or symptom control at the same time we are withholding treatment, but these are all ways of disguising the fact that we are letting the disease kill the patient rather than directly bringing about death. But the ways diseases kill people are far more cruel than the ways physicians kill patients when performing euthanasia or assisting in suicide.

THE PROBLEM: A CHOICE OF CULTURES

Thus we see three similar cultures and countries and three similar sets of circumstances but three quite different basic options in approaching death. All three of these practices generate moral problems; none of them, nor any others we might devise, is free of moral difficulty. But the question that faces us is this: Which of these options is best?

It is not possible to answer this question in a less-than-ideal world without some attention to the specific characteristics and deficiencies of the society in question. In asking which of these practices is best, we must ask which is best *for us.* That we currently employ one set of these options rather than others does not prove that it is best for us; the question is, would practices developed in other cultures or those not yet widespread in any be better for our own culture than that which has developed here? Thus, it is necessary to consider the differences between our own society and these European cultures that have real bearing on which model of approach to dying we ought to adopt.

First, notice that different cultures exhibit different degrees of closeness between physicians and patients—different patterns of contact and involvement. The German physician is sometimes said to be more distant and more authoritarian than the American physician; on the other hand, the Dutch physician is sometimes said to be closer to his or her patients than either the American or the German is. In the Netherlands, basic primary care is provided by the general practitioner or family physician, who typically lives in the neighborhood, makes house calls frequently, and maintains an office in his or her own home. This physician usually also provides care for the other members of the patient's family and will remain the family's physician throughout his or her practice. Thus, the patient for whom euthanasia becomes an issue—say, the terminal cancer patient who has been hospitalized in the past but who has returned home to die—will be cared for by the trusted family physician on a regular basis. Indeed, for a patient in severe distress, the physician, supported by the visiting nurse, may make house calls as often as once a day, twice a day, or even more frequently (after all, the physician's office is right in the neighborhood) and is in continuous contact with the family. In contrast, the traditional American institution of the family doctor who makes house calls is rapidly becoming a thing of the past, and although some patients who die at home have access to hospice services and receive house calls from their long-term physician, many have no such long-term care and receive most of it from staff at a clinic or from house staff rotating through the services of a hospital. The degree of continuing contact the patient can have with a familiar, trusted physician clearly influences the nature of his or her dying and also plays a role in whether physician-performed active euthanasia, assisted suicide, and/or withholding and withdrawing treatment is appropriate.

Second, the United States has a much more volatile legal climate than either the Netherlands or Germany; our medical system is increasingly litigious, much more so than that of any other country in the world. Fears of malpractice actions or criminal prosecution color much of what physicians do in managing the dying of their patients. We also tend to develop public policy through court decisions and to assume that the existence of a policy puts an end to any moral issue. A delicate legal and moral balance over the issue of euthanasia, as is the case in the Netherlands, would not be possible here.

Third, we in the United States have a very different financial climate in which to do our dying. Both the Netherlands and Germany, as well as every other industrialized nation except South Africa, have systems of national health insurance or national health care. Thus the patient is not directly responsible for the costs of treatment, and consequently the patient's choices about terminal care and/or euthanasia need not take personal financial considerations into account. Even for the patient who does have health insurance in the United States, many kinds of services are not covered, whereas the national health care or health insurance programs of many other countries variously provide many sorts of relevant services, including at-home physician care, home nursing care, home respite care, care in a nursing home or other long-term facility, dietitian care, rehabilitation care, physical therapy, psychological counseling, and so on. The patient in the United States needs to attend to the financial aspects of dying in a way that patients in many other countries do not, and in this country both the patient's choices and the recommendations of the physician are very often shaped by financial considerations.

There are many other differences between the USA on the one hand and the Netherlands and Germany, with their different options for dying, on the other. There are differences in degrees of paternalism in the medical establishment and in racism, sexism, and ageism in the general culture, as well as awareness of a problematic historical past, especially Nazism. All of these and the previous factors influence the appropriateness or inappropriateness of practices such as active euthanasia and assisted suicide. For instance, the Netherlands' tradition of close physician-patient contact, its absence of malpractice-motivated medicine, and its provision of comprehensive health insurance, together with its comparative lack of racism and ageism and its experience in resistance to Nazism, suggest that this culture is able to permit the practice of voluntary active euthanasia, performed by physicians, without risking abuse. On the other hand, it is sometimes said that Germany still does not trust its physicians, remembering the example of Nazi experimentation, and given a comparatively authoritarian medical climate in which the contact between physician and patient is quite distanced, the population could not be comfortable with the practice of active euthanasia. There, only a wholly patient-controlled response to terminal situations, as in non-physician-assisted suicide, is a reasonable and prudent practice.

But what about the United States? This is a country where (1) sustained contact with a personal physician is decreasing, (2) the risk of malpractice action is increasing, (3) much medical care is not insured, (4) many medical decisions are financial decisions as well, (5) racism is on the rise, and (6) the public has not experienced direct contact with Nazism or similar totalitarian movements. Thus, the United States is in many respects an untrustworthy candidate for practicing active euthanasia. Given the pressures on individuals in an often atomized society, encouraging solo suicide, assisted if at all only by nonprofessionals, might well be open to considerable abuse too.

However, there are several additional differences between the United States and both the Netherlands and Germany that may seem relevant here. First, although the United States is indeed afflicted by a great deal of racism and sexism, it is also developing an increasingly strong tradition of independence in women. In many other countries, especially in the Far East and the Islamic countries, the role of women still involves much greater disempowerment and expectations of subservience; in contrast, the United States is particularly advanced—though, of course, it has a long way to go. The United States may even be ahead of the Netherlands and perhaps Germany in this respect. Whatever the case, this issue is of particular importance with respect to euthanasia, especially among elderly persons, because it is women whose life expectancies are longer than those of men and hence are more likely to be confronted with late-life degenerative terminal conditions.

Second, American culture is more confrontational than many others, including Dutch culture. While the Netherlands prides itself rightly on a long tradition of rational discussion of public issues and on toleration of others' views and practices, the United States (and to some degree also Germany) tends to develop highly partisan, moralizing oppositional groups. In general, this is a disadvantage, but in the case of euthanasia it may serve to alert a public to issues and possibilities it might not otherwise consider, especially to the risks of abuse.

Third, though this may at first seem to be a trivial difference, it is Americans who are particularly given to personal self-analysis. This tendency is evident not only in America's high rate of utilization of counseling services, including religious counseling, psychological counseling and psychiatry, but is even more clearly evident in its popular culture: its diet of soap operas, situation comedies, and pop psychology books. It is here that the ordinary American absorbs models for analyzing his or her own personal relationships and individual psychological characteristics. While of course things are changing and our cultural tastes are widely exported, the fact remains that the ordinary American's cultural diet contains more in the way of professional and do-it-yourself amateur psychology and self-analysis than anyone else's. This long tradition of self-analysis may put us in a better position for certain kinds of end-of-life practices than many other cultures: despite whatever other deficiencies we have, we live in a culture that encourages us to inspect our own motives, anticipate the impact of our actions on others, and scrutinize our own relationships with others, including our physicians. This disposition is of importance in euthanasia contexts because euthanasia is the kind of fundamental choice about which one may have somewhat mixed motives, be subject to various interpersonal and situational pressures, and so on. If the voluntary character of these choices is to be protected, it may be a good thing to inhabit a culture in which self-inspection of one's own mental habits and motives is encouraged.

Finally, the U.S. population is characterized by a kind of "do-it-yourself" ethic, an ethic that devalues reliance on others and encourages individual initiative and responsibility. (To be sure, this ethic has been somewhat eclipsed in recent years and is little in evidence in the series of court cases cited earlier, but it is still part, I think, of the American character.) This ethic seems to be coupled with a sort of resistance to authority that perhaps also is basic to the American temperament. If this is really the case, Americans might be especially well served by end-of-life practices that emphasize self-reliance and resistance to authority.

These, of course, are mere conjectures about features of American culture that would support appropriate use of euthanasia or assisted suicide. These are the features that one would want to reinforce should these practices become general, in part to minimize the effects of the negative features. But of course these positive features will differ from one country and culture to another, just as the negative features do. In each country, a different architecture of antecedent assumptions and cultural features develops around end-of-life issues, and in each country the practice of euthanasia, if it is to be free from abuse, must be adapted to the culture in which it takes place.

What, then, is appropriate for our own cultural situation? Physician-performed euthanasia, though not in itself morally wrong, is morally jeopardized where legal, time, and especially financial pressures on both patients and physicians are severe; thus, it is morally problematic in our culture in a way that it is not in the Netherlands. Solo suicide outside the institution of medicine (as in Germany) may be problematic in a country (like the United States) that has an increasingly alienated population, offers deteriorating and uneven social services, is increasingly racist, and in other ways imposes unusual pressures on individuals, despite opportunities for self-analysis. Reliance only on withholding and withdrawing treatment (as in the United States) can be cruel, and its comparative invisibility invites erosion under cost-containment and other pressures. These are the three principal alternatives we have considered, but none of them seems wholly suited to our actual situation for dealing with the new fact that most of us die of extended-decline, deteriorative diseases. However, permitting physicians to supply patients with the means for ending their own lives still grants physicians some control over the circumstances in which this can happen—only, for example, when the prognosis is genuinely grim and the alternatives for symptom control are poor—but leaves the fundamental decision about whether to use these means to the patient alone. It is up to the patient then—the independent, confrontational, self-analyzing, do-it-yourself authority-resisting patient—and his or her advisors, including family members, clergy, the physician, and other health care providers, to be clear about whether he or she really wants to use these means or not.

Thus, the physician is involved but not directly, and it is the patient's decision, although the patient is not making it alone. We live in an imperfect world, but of the alternatives for facing death—which we all eventually must—I think that the practice of permitting physician-assisted suicide is the one most nearly suited to the current state of our own flawed society. This is a model not yet central in any of the three countries examined here—the Netherlands, Germany, or the United States—but it is the one, I think, that suits us best.

NOTES

1. S.J. Olshansky and A.B. Ault, The Fourth Stage of the Epidemiological Transition: The Age of Delayed Degenerative Diseases, *Milbank Memorial Fund Quarterly/Health and Society* 64 (1986):355–391.

2. S. Miles and C. Gomez, *Protocols for Elective Use of Life-sustaining Treatment* (New York: Springer-Verlag, 1988).

3. C.L. Sprung, Changing Attitudes and Practices in Foregoing Life-sustaining Treatments, *JAMA* 262 (1990):2213.

4. N.G. Smedira et al., Withholding and Withdrawal of Life Support from the Critically Ill, *New England Journal of Medicine* 322 (1990):309–315.

5. *New York Times*, July 23, 1990, A13.

6. P.J. van der Maas et al., Euthanasia and Other Medical Decisions Concerning the End of Life, *Lancet* 338 (1991):669–674.

7. G. van der Wal et al., Euthanasie en hulp bij zelfdoding door artsen in de thuissituatie, parts 1 and 2, *Nederlands Tijdschrift voor Geneesekunde* 135 (1991):1593–1598, 1600–1603.

8. E. Borst-Eilers, paper delivered at Controversies in the Care of Dying Patients, University of Florida, Orlando, February 14–16, 1991.

9. Van der Maas et al., Euthanasia and Other Medical Decisions Concerning the End of Life, 673.

10. Ibid., 671.

11. P. Admiraal, Euthanasia in a General Hospital, address to the Eighth World Congress of the International Federation of Right-to-Die Societies, Maastricht, Holland, June 8, 1990.

12. H. ten Have, Coma: Controversy and Consensus, *Newsletter of the European Society for Philosophy of Medicine and Health Care,* May 1990, 19–20.

Chapter 30

"Doing the Good Thing"? Psychological Reflections on Self-Determination and Dying

Jurrit Bergsma

"Will these men survive" the sergeant asked, looking at the severely wounded and burned soldiers. "Surely not," the doctor replied. The sergeant took out his knife to cut the throat of the soldiers. Astonished, the doctor asked, "Why?" And the sergeant replied: "Doctor, if I am ever in this horrible condition, I hope someone with mercy will do a good thing, take his knife and do the same for me."[1]

This discussion of euthanasia from a psychological standpoint begins with historical reflections on suffering and active euthanasia, followed by a narrative about life and death. Next, the theme of identity and autonomy as related to self-determination will be explored. The fourth section contains arguments regarding the pros and cons of euthanasia. The chapter concludes with comments on the relationship between concepts about euthanasia and practical circumstances. This relationship is important because any discrepancy between concept and practical application presents difficulties for patients and health professionals. These difficulties underscore inconsistencies in the relationship between society's principles and personal actions and form the basis for profound confusion in the discussion on the values concerning euthanasia.

SUFFERING AND ACTIVE EUTHANASIA

Suffering is a typical human state made possible by the human capacity to reflect. We use this capacity to watch the image of ourselves in a variety of states, from intense happiness through severe pain. This subjective observation of the self-image allows us to make evaluative comparisons, comparisons of the current state with former states in our lifetime or with personal ideals formulated during reflective moments in our lives. Suffering, then, can be understood as an outcome of processing experiential comparisons with these other states or conditions. As we experience suffering, we can question the sense, reason, or meaning of the experienced discrepancies and assign a positive or negative value to each period. Because of this questioning, we have been able to develop philosophical and religious systems, creations resulting from the meaningful organization of ideas and reflections about life and its events, burdens, and delights.

Suffering in general is an outcome of a comparison with other more favorable conditions within the context of such an organization. Suffering is a substantial aspect of human life, encompassing experiences such as physical pain, psychological unfulfillment, and social disillusion. Sometimes people are able to attribute a value to their suffering, but when an acceptable evaluation is lacking, suffering becomes a sometimes intolerable burden or at least changes the color of existence and engenders depression.

Here we come to another unique characteristic of human beings, the inclination to incorporate personal phenomena in one's (historical) existence by the attribution of an evaluative meaning or by ascribing a place in the experienced structure of one's life.[2] To satisfactorily incorporate suffering into human life, history has seen many attempts to give positive attributes to this evaluative outcome. Within the complexity of the many different systems of reasoning or belief, suffering has been perceived as the ultimate challenge in the attempt to perfect one's spirit or character. Philosophers who perceived suffering as without meaning were perhaps too easily categorized as advocates of the view that *life* is meaningless. From the beginning of Western civilization, generations grew up with the conviction that it is a sin to qualify suffering as a senseless human experience.

The Oedipus trilogy, one of the most enlightening stories at the foundation of our civilization, offers intriguing examples of suffering. Even today these examples are brilliant metaphors explaining essential and basic human conflicts.[3] The way Antigone questions the problem of suffering in case of unjust premises (when Haemon, Creon's son, kills himself because of the wrong judgments his father made) helps us understand that suffering is also an interhuman experience, requiring empathy with other humans. This means suffering related to love, compassion, or disillusion: suffering in consort with fellow human beings. The Greek tragedies represent these archetypes of human and interhuman suffering just as Christ's dying on the cross became an archetype of human suffering for the good of all.

Whether in history, religion, philosophy, or art, suffering has been identified as one of the most valuable or detestable experiences of human existence, and a direct relation to death and dying has been indicated. Physical suffering in the process of dying was often perceived as a gateway to a guaranteed and brilliant eternal future—a means of achieving a better afterlife. If immediate death should not occur, suffering might still lead to a better and brighter life, in turn being a preparation for a better afterlife. In some religious metaphors, suffering and its acceptance may even lead to a "new" satisfactory individual life.

When, in human history, suffering did *not* receive these positive attributions, dying was perceived as the legitimate and welcome escape from a senseless way of existing. Involuntary states of intense suffering created by disease, dissolution, separation, or torture may therefore lead to craving for death if it becomes impossible to attribute any positive meaning to this suffering. Greek tragedies often offer suicide or assassination as a possible answer in cases of uncomprehended mental suffering.

In this historical context, invited killing can be understood as a next step. Mercy killing is already mentioned in the Middle Ages, as is suicide, and it certainly does not figure only in heroic stories and mythology.[4] Even so, the artificial creation of suffering as a means of personal purification or as punishment became a favored way of dealing with the (supposed) enemy. For centuries, torture was a religiously acceptable way to treat (supposed) nonbelievers or sinners. From the crusades through Calvin, there is a broad array of embarrassing examples.[5]

It is important to remember that in some historical visions, human suffering was considered a phenomenon with an important function, and in other visions, it was viewed as a senseless occurrence. These differences of opinion concerning suffering are still crucial in contemporary discussions of mercy killing.

During the sixteenth century, nonreligious people began to be able to read. Suffering and its relation to death became an important topic of general interest, the more so because plagues, religious conflict, and extreme poverty often forced direct and concrete confrontation with the realities of suffering.

By the seventeenth century, expressions like *euthanasia* (interpreted as a "decent way of dying" or "easy passage") became familiar.[6] Francis Bacon relates the "easy passage" to the task of the physician by saying, "the task of a physician includes also the reduction of pain even when it may serve to make a fair and easy passage." The reduction of (senseless) suffering may lead to the patient's dying but that is preferable to severe pain. *The Holy State and the Profane State* by Fuller, published in 1642 and sometimes considered the first book on medical ethics, states, "If the physician is not able to keep the body alive, let him create the opportunity for life to leave the body in an easy way." This implies an active role for the physician, although, in Fuller's opinion, the physician always "tries to escape" the confrontation with dying patients.

According to Zedler's lexicon (1734), the meaning of *euthanasia* includes "using means" to soften a patient's suffering. In 1735, two dissertations were published on the topic of euthanasia: *De Euthanasia Medica* (Schulz) and *De Dythanasia Medica* (Hernig). In these books, the term *euthanasia* is related only to the art of alleviating suffering during the dying process, managing or manipulating dying itself. Yet assisting the patient to make an easy passage requires initiative and active intervention on the part of the doctor.

We may conclude that insofar as people were opposed to senseless suffering (pain), the option of an active medical intervention to reduce the suffering was recognized as acceptable. How widespread these ideas were is difficult to determine. Certainly they were present in the professional medical as well as in the nonprofessional world.

LIFE AND DEATH

The discussion on euthanasia acquired a more general and also a different character during the nineteenth century. It is interesting that chloroform and opium, drugs already known for centuries, only at that time started to be used as anesthetics. This development is related to the increasing attention paid to the individual person during the nineteenth century, including recognition of the wounded soldier as an individual sufferer. This was also the era in which discussion of the meaning of personal suffering became widespread.[7] Medicine starts to apply anesthetics for pain in operations on patients, and at the same time literature, religion, science, and politics start to focus on physical, mental, and social suffering.

The wounded soldiers on the battlefield, the victims of industrial development, and the victims of aggressive violence or psychological interaction within families engaged people's conscience: why these types of suffering occurred remained incomprehensible. From this viewpoint, the application of anesthesia and the use of ether and morphine for pain relief are cousins of Marx's philosophy to liberate people from an industrial dictatorship and Freud's desire to liberate patients from their neurotic obsessions. These ideas allow new, nonreligious visions of suffering, life, and death. Individuality, personal responsibility, compassion, and political engagement (democracy as responsibility for one's own world) gradually become more visible dimensions of human existence. The phrases originating in the French revolution become concrete.

Nevertheless, it is surprising to see how it is only in 1843 that Dr. Reiman discovers the causal relation between pain relief and early death.[8] Earlier intuitions like Bacon's did not have an impact. Because the "viaticum" was expected to be given while the patient was conscious, the hastened death could be dangerous to the soul. The use of opium or ether as a relief for suffering was a recognized practice, although not always accepted, but its causal relation with an earlier death was now explicit within this religious context.

Discussion of euthanasia acquired yet another character between 1830 and 1860 because of the possibility of being able to manipulate the moment of dying. *Euthanasia* increasingly was used to mean assistance in dying. An early illustration of the problem is the study *Zur Psychologie und Euthanasia*, published in 1832 by Schalle. He agrees with the idea of reduction of pain but believes this reduction has to have a function in the liberation of the soul. He does not yet present a full-blown discussion of the connection between pain relief and easy passage. Instead he focuses on an acceptable level of consciousness, a level that allows the patient to receive Holy Communion. In this regard, the question of whether there should be pain or not is still an open one, but there is recognition that too much pain as well as too much medication may impede the last Communion. The issues of choice and intervention in the natural course of living and dying have been raised. Reiman's mentioning of the causal relationship between medication and passing away fits this historical change in thinking.

Schalle's contribution indicates that discussions of peaceful dying or easy passing away simply did not exist in clerical circles. The clergy had not even entered the arena at this point. According to their tenets, any artificial assistance in the process of dying was unacceptable and consequently denied as an option. The debate that started at the time of Reiman's statement was among doctors, philosophers, legislators, and lay people and involved lay as well as theological arguments.

As the meaning of *euthanasia* shifted, the role of the physician became more visible. The new discussions point up the manipulative aspects of assisted dying and underscore (1) the doctor's role in dealing with the patient's suffering and dying and (2) the doctor's active role in the process of passing away.

From 1850 on, the discussion becomes even more general and open. In 1873, the British journal *Spectator* published a series of letters about active medical intervention in cases of nonacceptable suffering. Again the discussion was mainly between those who had a direct and practical relationship to the issue. Bishops and other clergy remained reluctant to enter the debate, and they tended to restrict themselves to thinking about general principles concerning suffering, death, and dying. Such principles were able to serve as guidelines for those who worked in the field and who were confronted with individuals who preferred to die in a merciful way, but they were not even formulated with that aim.

Suffering, dying, and dying with dignity, perceived for centuries as exclusively religious topics, became the focus of secular discussion. The crystallizing during the nineteenth century of the individual as a unique identity supported active secular participation in the consideration of life and death issues.

IDENTITY AND AUTONOMY

Increasing interest in the individual and autonomous person was manifested in the development of psychology as an independent science. Freud's theories about personal development and identity also reflected this interest being a compromise between biological roots and the social (normative) environment of the individual person. The basic connections are evident in becoming a person. A person is an individual able to reflect on his or her existence and consciousness independently, which is a precondition for self-analysis and the plumbing of one's deepest biological and social conflicts. Concepts such as intimacy and validation of existence are impossible without reflection. Although many variations on the concept of identity have since been developed, the basic idea of identity as an integrated triad remains a part of psychological thinking.

The current picture of identity encompasses (1) a physical facet, the body, its organs and systems, but also its exterior, motor abilities and expressive facilities; (2) a social facet, which contains psychological potentials like thinking, emotions, feelings, and perceptions but also the social capacities of relating and communicating; and (3) the moral facet, representing personal values and norms, the ethical and religious considerations as related to transcendental options of religion and culture.[9]

Within this general scheme of identity, more specific refinements have been generated by modern scientists, physiologists, neuropsychologists, sociologists and social psychologists, philosophers, and theologians. These refinements are related to scientific interest and (scientific) views on mankind. The main risk in this scheme, theoretical as well as practical, is overestimating one of the facets of personal identity. Dissolution and disintegration are apt to occur in cases of scientific overspecializing without consideration of appropriate connections. During the last few decades, then, some holistic movements in scientific thinking try to address the implicit risks of such overspecialization, but they still seem to be mainly visions without real practical consequences.

What is interesting from several perspectives are the developments in personality theory since the early 1900s that are grafted on but not congruent with Freud's principles. Freud's ideas about identity are based on a biologically deterministic model à la Descartes. The causalities are clearly defined, and the behavioral types are directly related to circumscribed obstructions during (sexual) development in childhood. More recent psychiatric and psychological theories oppose the deterministic vision of humankind. In between are former students of Freud such as Eric Fromm or Karin Horney. Even more influential are representatives of the humanistic movement such as Carl Rogers and his followers. They highlight individual freedom and self-determination and consider full personality development and autonomy as the optimum. They reject Freud's biological determinism in principle and have helped to create a climate in which a person's independence or autonomy becomes more important than just the concept of health.

Because of general confusion about the concept of autonomy, the *psychological* view of autonomy as a personality construct needs examining. One of the main aspects of personality growth, whatever the theoretical vision may be, is confrontation with "problems" and finding solutions. Problem solving is one of the most important activities for becoming an adult. The theory of problem solving developed by Hettema shows how tactics used to solve ad hoc problems in early life may develop into a strategy, a type of problem solution related to a certain kind of problem by a specific person.[10] Certain strategies become characteristic for a person. The more strategies one has developed, the more problems one is supposed to be able to handle in an effective way. The psychological concept of efficacy is related to the use of strategies.

Some strategies allow fast adaptation to challenging situations (effective analysis of the problem) or right delegation ("this is not something I know how to solve"). Autonomy depends on the existence of strategies for independent and effective problem solving. Its prerequisites include (1) clear *future* goals (what is desired?), (2) *anticipation* (which obstructions may occur?), (3) awareness of *personal instruments* (knowledge, intuition, experience), (4) awareness of *means*, and (5) *flexibility of adjustment* to the original goal. In fact, (3) and (4) are subcategories of anticipation (what can happen? what can be done in response?).

From a psychological standpoint, autonomy is a characteristic of a mature adult identity. There can be significant differences in autonomous behavior.[11] Many people have grown up in situations where they did not meet the variety of challenges needed for optimal development of personal strategies; other people lack the genetic potential for optimal development.

Using autonomy as an ultimate ethical norm risks psychological overquestioning; withholding this norm may reduce significant human challenge. The psychological approach gives insight into the differences between people who bring different strategies and genetic potential to their autonomous development. Self-determination and autonomy (which are nearly identical) are not absolute norms, but they are significant characteristics for a person and consequently have a specific impact on the person's interaction with his or her environment. Self-consciousness and the capacity for

self-reflection consequently are two basic conditions for autonomy and self-determination.

This brings us back to the first main section of
this chapter. Self-reflection is the basis for the
intimate validation of personal circumstances
and the self-image and experienced discrepancies within that context. Suffering can be the
outcome of a personal evaluation of one's situation on the basis of personal comparisons.

ARGUMENTS

Within a relatively short time, countries in the
Western World became highly differentiated
both politically and technologically, yet they
share a certain degree of technological dependence as well as "intense democratic awareness"
and an emphasis on "individual development
and independence." The consequences of this
development, which accelerated during the nineteenth and twentieth centuries, include a significant secularization, a relatively high level of
education, a relatively high degree of affluence,
and a personal craving for freedom in behavior
and self-expression.

The two world wars were shocking collective
experiences and increased people's desire for freedom, self-expression, and self-determination.
Health and independence became highly valued
conditions for self-development and self-determination; in Fromm's terminology, they represent
freedom from obstructions and thereby optimize
freedom to express oneself.[12]

Given this background, suffering can perhaps
be better understood but it still remains the outcome of evaluative comparisons. Today's societal context provides other and new values to be
included in the evaluative process. The goals
people set for their individual lives are completely different from those set only one century
ago. The increasing awareness of individuality
and personal roles contrasts with the typical expectations associated with membership in a
group or social class at the turn of the nineteenth
century. This shift in values has created a need
for a new behavioral and technological instru-

mentarium for relieving suffering and new
means to adjust to individual's preferred situations.

Except in cases of so-called pathology, suffering has ceased to be an aspiration or aim in life.
Suffering is now an unacceptable obstruction of
self-expression and gradually has lost its purify-
ing religious goal. The goal of the contemporary
autonomous individual is the creation of a situation in which obstructions like suffering play a
minor role. And even if death approaches early
and a person is aware of the impossibility of adjustment to original or acceptable alternative life
goals, the decision to end the suffering (or to
temporarily continue this condition in favor of
some important short-term goals) is likely to be
part of the strategy considered by the person.

A new facet within this context is that the idea
of a "terminal condition" is now expanded from
just a physical level to a social and maybe even
cultural level. The loss of security-providing
group structures—conditions for empathy and
compassionate relationships within the neighborhood, family, or church—entails that social
isolation and loneliness can also be experienced
as meaningless. A personal evaluation of the
consequences of what we could call a "terminal
social state" could result in a wish for easy passage from this alienated environment. Educated
Westerners typically have sufficient knowledge
of ways and means to bring about a termination
of life. Obstructing a strategy to commit suicide
could be construed as an invasion of the highly
valued freedom to determine the course of one's
individual life.

Quite often suffering is not the harbinger of
death. In such cases, the autonomous person will
consider gains and losses. If the autonomous individual considers lifelong suffering (a severe
handicap or chronic illness) an unacceptable
burden he or she can invite a friend or someone
else to assist him or her in committing suicide.

If life goals are less clear and the need for self-
determination is not predominant, decisions can
be handed over to relatives, friends, or professionals. Some people feel incapable of bearing
the responsibility for their last decisions alone

and want to share these decisions or even delegate them to others.

PRACTICAL CIRCUMSTANCES

Imagine a patient with an upper lesion of the spine who has lost nearly all motor ability but is still able to consider his situation and how it relates to his life goals. The person is fully competent to consider all the consequences of possible treatments. Perhaps he is completely able to redirect the route of his life and adjust to the new situation. The only problem is that physically he has become completely dependent on others and has lost the ability to use his own body as a physical instrument. Whatever he decides, he depends on somebody else to realize his wishes.

Immense confusion in health care arises because of the idea that a person like this has lost his or her autonomy.[13] This idea stems from a perception of personal identity as a triad of separate identities. Physical dependency results from the loss of an instrument, not the loss of the capacity to reflect on one's suffering and achieve self-determination. Physical dependency does not entail the loss of insight into strategies for realizing defined life goals; it is simply a specific kind of dependency that requires understanding, empathy, and compassion from others.

Medical technology occupies itself mainly with the physical facet of identity. Medicine increasingly views the body of a person as a system of organs and physical relationships, each providing a field of restricted interest for some medical specialist. If the suffering patient mentions the unacceptability of his or her situation, the hematologist may reply with figures about the concentration of white blood cells. The division of the human identity as a consequence of specialization creates misjudgments regarding autonomy. For example, a diabetic person will be able to restructure his or her life to deal with the condition; the diabetes does not destroy the person as an autonomous entity.[14] The segmentation of human identity creates a new way of suffering never known before. This suffering includes losing one's freedom to decide about

one's personal life and death simply because of physical dependency. Yet a person's physical ability is only an instrument of autonomy, not autonomy itself. Autonomy belongs to the whole person. It is a characteristic of a whole person—a whole, not segmented identity. Artificial segmentation creates the risk that freedom may be taken from a person who is fully capable of making his or her own decisions but depends on the assistance of others to execute these decisions.

If someone blocks this type of assistance, the ability of the person to carry out plans for easy passage is impeded, even though the blockage may be morally correct for the individual causing it. If another relative, friend, or professional is willing to carry out the wishes of the dependent person, that helper should be supported by society. Such support would demonstrate that society really does view individual freedom and independence as the most important values.

Active euthanasia presents us with a paradox. Personal development and responsibility are valued more highly than ever before in human history. Society stimulates us to be free individuals with a healthy physical body, a highly developed intelligence, good social abilities, and high personal standards. But as soon as a patient suffers, whether from pain or from the loss of instrumental capacities, society is ready to deny that person's freedom and use medical technology as a dictator to restrain the person from exercising the most basic rights ever developed. More than two thousand years of philosophical discussion, reflection, and evaluation are often discarded in favor of misguided paternalism.[15]

Why does the person who loses use of his or her limbs or suffers some other serious physical disability have to be made a prisoner by taking away "freedom from" and "freedom to"? We do, indeed, create a prisoner out of such a person when we take away such freedoms in the name of caring. Even in Greek society, suffering was the outcome of personal reflection on one's total condition within the context of personal relations. In that era, freedom to decide and to accept the consequences of any decision was respected by society. As a result of false moral standards in our society, we are obstructing people's freedom to accept the consequences of actions they wish to initiate after reflectively evaluating their unbearable and unacceptable suffering.

Democratic societies have an obligation to protect their members from many kinds of harm.

Democratic societies do not have an obligation to restrict their members' freedom to choose to end their suffering. By denying free and autonomous individuals the right to decide their fate, we repudiate centuries of development of the philosophy that supports our civilization.

That is not the good thing to do.

NOTES

1. Paraphrase of a passage derived from Ambroise Paré (1536) and found in the dissertation of theologian Dick Meerman, Goed doen door dood te maken (Doing the good thing by killing) (Nijmegen University, The Netherlands, 1991).

2. Research on the construction of narratives patients use as a legitimation of their cancer or heart disease was done in my institute by Dr. H. ten Kroode, whose dissertation is called Het verhaal van de kankerpatient, (Utrecht University, The Netherlands, 1990). The first time attention was given to this phenomenon was in my book Health Care: Its Psychosocial Dimensions, translated by D. Thomasma (Pittsburgh: Duquesne University Press, 1982).

3. Sophocles, The Theban Plays, translated by E.F. Watling (London: Penguin, 1988).

4. Examples can be found in R.L. Fox, Pagans and Christians (London: Penguin, 1988); and P. Brown, Body and Society (New York: Columbia University Press, 1988).

5. See, for example, P. Johnson, History of Christianity (New York: Atheneum, 1976).

6. Many of these historical notes on mercy killing and euthanasia have been derived from Meerman, Goed doen door dood te maken.

7. J.H. van den Berg, Koude Rillingen over de rug van Charles Darwin (Nijkerk, The Netherlands: Callenbach,

1984). This is a critical study of Darwin's work and Darwinism.

8. Meerman, Good doen door dood te maken.

9. My book Identiteit, lichamelijke verstoring en autonomie (Lochem, The Netherlands: De Tijdstroom, 1988) describes the relation between disturbances of the human body, their effect on identity, and the consequences for autonomy.

10. P.J. Hettema, Personality and Adaptation (Amsterdam: North Holland, 1979).

11. B.P. Baltes and O.G. Brimm, Lifespan Development and Behavior (New York: Academic Press, 1986).

12. E. Fromm, Escape from Freedom (New York: Rinehart, 1963).

13. Van den Berg, Koude Rillingen over de rug van Charles Darwin.

14. A study on autonomy in diabetes patients was done by Dr. T. Kuypers. Her dissertation, Complicaties bij diabetes (Utrecht University, The Netherlands, 1990), shows there is an understandable relation between higher scores on autonomy questionnaires and lesser complications in diabetes.

15. A good illustration of this indirect pressure is given by H. Brody, The Healer's Power (New Haven: Yale University Press, 1992).

Part IV

National Issues in Health Care

Practicing Medicine, Fiduciary Trust Privacy, and Public Moral Interloping after *Cruzan*

Michael A. Rie

Our postmodern society lacks a cohesive moral framework in law to accommodate conflicting individual interpretations of the good life and good death.[1] The *Cruzan* opinion is a wakeup call to all citizens and their physicians from an "original intent" judicial majority underscoring the Judeo-Christian foundations of the common law.[2] These religious proscriptions against suicide were incorporated by the common laws of England and the United States. Though suicide had been largely decriminalized in the United States,[3] the Missouri Supreme court, Chief Justice Rehnquist, and Justice Scalia conclude that the state has the power to define the limits of individual privacy if the state has expressed a public policy strongly favoring the preservation of human life. Those who interpret the Constitution as a precise text of eighteenth-century authors point out that privacy rights are not mentioned. The concept of a right to personal privacy is a recent event developed in *Griswold vs Connecticut* in which Justice Douglas found a marital right to privacy implicit but unstated in the Constitution and went on to state that "specific guarantees in the Bill of Rights have penumbras formed by emanation . . . that give them life and substance." In the subsequent case of *Eisenstadt vs Baird*, again concerning state intrusion into personal choices of procreation and contraception, Justice Brennan writing for a 6–1 majority stated, "It is the right of the individual married or single, to be free from unwarranted governmental intrusions into matters so fundamentally affecting a person as to whether to bear or begat a child." These "created rights" of privacy became the legal foundations in *Roe vs Wade* as well as the seminal decision *In re Quinlan*.

Between *Quinlan* and the judicial proceedings in *Cruzan*, Americans and their physicians became aware of the problem of external criticism of an individual's decision to hasten death by requesting withdrawal of modern technologic care that prolonged the dying process while raising the spector of physician-assisted suicide. In *Cruzan* the Supreme Court has reaffirmed federalism and the power of states[4] to set procedural standards for due process regarding an individual's exercise of his or her liberty interest. This essay accepts the judicial reality that effecting autonomous decisions to refuse treatment when one becomes incompetent requires an affirmative articulation via an advance directive if a citizen wishes to be permitted by the state to exer-

Source: Reprinted from *The Journal of Medicine and Philosophy*, Vol. 17, pp.647–664, with permission of Kluwer Academic Publishers, Inc., © 1992.

cise his or her common-law liberty interest to be left alone when medical care is no longer desired.

The lack of a fundamental constitutional right to privacy and judicial deference to the individual states in *Cruzan* has had a decidedly positive effect. Those states like Massachusetts that embrace substituted judgment standards are unaffected while the principle of clear and convincing evidentiary standards in Missouri and New York are permitted to stand. Judicial deference has had the additional positive legislative action (in theory) by Congressional passage of the Patient Self-Determination Act (PSDA) within six months of *Cruzan*.[5]

For the physician good medical practice begins and ends[6] with the creation and maintenance of a fiduciary trust relationship with the patient. This is the case in all jurisdictions. As physicians we have become sensitized to the issue that strict documentation of autonomy by the patient is necessary in decisions regarding withdrawal of technologic life support, as there is a large segment of society that regards the exercise of such decisions by a physician as assisted suicide. There is a heightened defensiveness among physicians that results in prolongation of medical care when it may not be desired by the patient, as the physician may fear external criticism. Though this be an everyday problem well known by the public and health care professionals, several surveys show that only a small percentage of Americans create advance directives that delegate the decision-making authority to another person should the patient become incompetent in the persistent vegetative state.[7] The positive effect of *Cruzan* has been to heighten public awareness that the exercise of a citizen's liberty in these decisions legally requires an explicit antecedent articulation by the patient in writing.

The PSDA is a legislative response to *Cruzan* in which Congress mandated that federally reimbursed hospitals had an affirmative duty to inform patients of state laws regarding the citizen's right to create and use written advance directives. This is a requirement of hospitals as one basis for receiving federal funds for the care of patients. A general corollary to this principal should be that if a patient clearly sets forth the circumstances for withdrawal of previously desired and customary medical care, then the patient is entitled under common law to mandate that further care be stopped even if it hastens death. Should providers fail to heed the request after proper notice by the patient or his or her proxy, then one could infer that Congress intended for Medicare recipients to have the option of asking the federal government to terminate reimbursement to providers for ongoing treatment that was now declared by the patient or his or her surrogate to constitute the crime of battery. The articulation of battery would lend clarity to those who questioned the patient's articulation and would be consistent with the old tradition in common law that medical care when not desired constitutes a nonconsensual criminal invasion of a person.[8]

This chapter will argue that the *Cruzan* opinion has been a tremendously important and positive event for individual liberty in a country that does not grant a constitutional right to privacy within the strict definition of the Constitution. While many have been surprised and chagrined by the opinion,[9] this opinion was nothing more than could be expected of a strict interpretation Supreme Court that celebrates the Federalist Papers. This opinion has been helpful to the individual liberty of those who do not hold the Judeo-Christian penchants of the common law as well as physicians who care for such individuals because it has established individual responsibility for articulating the morality that one holds in preserving individual liberty. If one lives in Missouri and New York State in 1994, then the exercise of liberty in health care requires that one give careful thought to these matters long before one is incompetent, sick, or dying. While the possibility exists that one might change one's mind, numerous public surveys show repeatedly that nearly 85 percent of the American public would not want to be sustained by gastrointestinal feedings in the persistent vegetative state.[10] To bring clarity and definition to the exercise of liberty in a society where many individual and institutional moral interlopers would like to obstruct the exercise of personal morality in health care decisions, it would appear that the best solution would be to make these rights clearly those of the individual and to have that individual clearly understand that he or she should delegate to his or her surrogate the full force of legal enforcement visited upon those extraneous interlopers to the patient-doctor relationship that sought to obstruct the patient's liberty.

We are then left with the realization that the exercise of liberty in health care under *Cruzan* requires that individual states permit the existence of advance directives to be effected when a patient becomes incompetent. *Cruzan* resulted in the swift passage in Massachusetts of a comprehensive durable power of attorney for health care statute that otherwise would not have been enacted. *Cruzan* galvanized the people in Massachusetts and elsewhere to realize that their liberty was at risk unless they took steps legislatively and personally to take responsibility for the circumstances surrounding the conclusion of their lives in a world of moral interlopers. This was an essential political ingredient that was necessary to effectuate the legislation in Massachusetts and other states where there was strong political opposition to this type of legislation prior to *Cruzan*. In so doing, there has been extremely purposeful dialogue across institutions of society that are often at odds with each other on this issue. In Massachusetts, the passage of the durable power status came about in part through the unique political alliance of the American Association of Retired Persons, the Massachusetts Medical Society, the Massachusetts Bar Association, and the nursing profession, with ultimate acceptance of the legislation by the Catholic Archdiocese of Boston. Only one year before, such political consensus would have been impossible. It is apparent that by suggesting that liberty was not to be taken lightly, but must be cherished and asserted vigorously by citizens, the Supreme Court of the United States caused the populous to understand fully

the importance of cherishing their right and articulating with clarity their interest in its maintenance.

It is central to the *Cruzan* opinion that Chief Justice Rehnquist found that had there been a clear and convincing statement by Nancy Cruzan that she wanted withholding of gastrostomy feedings then that would have been embraced within the liberty interests of the common law. Given this ruling it is unlikely that states will continue to be able to write or amend natural death statutes to include limitations on this form of choice within the construct of an advance directive. Though the evidentiary standards will exist, they can be met by the use of what will be described here as a "fully enforceable protective advance directive." Advance directive legislation now exists in almost all the states, and the Patient Self-Determination Act requires all Medicare-reimbursed hospitals and institutions to appraise patients of their rights to self-determination under the applicable statutes in their states. This should result in more patients writing enforceable advance directives with purposeful clinical content. Indeed in recent years there has been an outpouring of research and interest in refining the medical directive[11] and the advance directive so that they would have more useful content for physicians dealing with patients in the clinical setting. Physicians who are faced with an advance directive that clearly specifies the surrogate and clearly specifies the delegation of authority to the surrogate for particular items or general areas of authority, and as well circumscribes the limits at which the physician's behavior will be considered to constitute a battery upon the patient, are likely to accede to the directive. Characteristically physicians are afraid that there will be complaints about the withdrawal of life support from others than the surrogate. The beauty of surrogate status, which is sanctioned in law, is that it assures that interlopers have no legal standing when patients become incompetent. If the patient's directive also creates the definition of medical battery and financial sanctions to be applied in the face of medical battery, then it is quite likely that physicians will take these directives seriously and will be likely to act on them, as there will now be a risk to the physician for not carrying out the directives whereas historically there was no such risk but there was risk of approbation from interlopers.

As clearly stated by Justice Rehnquist, the right to refuse treatment is a corollary to the general right to consent to treatment and not to have treatments forced upon one against one's will. *Cruzan* upholds this general common-law principle. To ensure that one's rights are respected one would hope that patients have the general right to find mechanisms of enforcement of their wishes that will not require appeals to the courts or other cumbersome administrative procedures that will not result in the desired clinical actions within a reasonable time frame. Patients should be allowed the right (via their advance directive) to signal those circumstances under which they no longer wish to pay health care institutions or providers for care that is no longer desired. By granting patients the capacity to have their health insurers stop payments and even retroactively deny payments for care that was given against their will, it will allow providers to test the full moral capacity of their beliefs should they find themselves morally constrained not to honor the patient's wishes.

Described in Appendix 31-A is a protective model advance directive with enforcement provisions and written for the specific needs of Missouri and New York State residents. It is offered as a way to advance patient rights within the clear and convincing standard guidelines set up by Missouri and New York and upheld by the United States Supreme Court. Though this be a lengthy document, its creation requires a high level of communication between the subject writing the document and close family members or other chosen surrogates, with subsequent transmission of this document to health care providers and institutions prior to the delivery of health services. Such communication breaks the usual Judeo-Christian taboos relating to the circumstances of individual death and brings out beliefs of possible surrogates that might not be in synchrony with the writer of an advance directive. As the document makes demands upon providers that form an antecedent contingency for entering into a health care relationship, it is a pre-emptive advance directive that clearly sets the nature and the tenor of discussion on the table. This is a healthy event in medicine, as physicians and patients in our culture are generally reticent to discuss matters of death and the need for such discussion is great under *Cruzan*. The construction of such an advance directive in concert with *Cruzan* is likely to advance further the openness of discussion and candor that is required between family members and the subject and the physician and other caregivers in an attempt to improve the overall communications surrounding cultural taboos, personal uncertainties, and prevarication before, during, and after the development of serious illness. If there is anything that drives physicians to distraction and despair about this subject, it is prevarication or uncertain wishes being expressed on behalf of the patient.

For practicing physicians such a document is helpful because it defines (in terms developed by the patient) circumstances that may require termination of care, even when a physician may not consider the patient to be terminally ill but the circumstances of life are unbearable for the subject and the use of technology is intrusive upon the subject's quality of life and constitutes a desecration of personhood. In clinical practice such events are not uncommon. Individuals may have achieved a very low level of life in an intensive care unit with full ventilatory and circulatory support in which survival is precedented in the medical literature but the circumstances are those in which the subject or the surrogate no longer wishes care to be received. In such circumstances patients' wishes are not heeded and medical paternalism reigns supreme in almost all circumstances. The benefit of the advance directive recommended in this chapter is that both legal and economic sanctions can then be brought to bear against the institution and the individual providers that require a certain risk taking on the part of those providers to continue to provide services for which they would otherwise be remunerated. If there are real moral views that the hospital or physicians would hold that would impede the exercise of liberty interests of the patient, then the institution by definition would have an affirmative obligation to seek other kinds of care of other health care institutions, and the duty would be an affirmative one belonging to the institution and not to the patient, as is usually the case in these matters.

There are many who will object to a complex advance directive as advocated in this chapter. Indeed the approach taken in Massachusetts and elsewhere is to try to develop extremely simplified documents that require very simple checkoffs or determinations by the subject. This chapter argues against the simplified advance directives because the physician usually requires much more information to be confident that the patient's views concerning complex ethical issues in various health care scenarios have been detailed. Though the medical directive advocated by Emanuel and Emanuel is complex, it discloses a range of views that people have in our society that are not homogenous and predictable even if they wish to have an advance directive to assure respect for their personhood as death approaches.[12] Buttressing individual liberty in a society that does not permit privacy requires the clear articulation of that liberty. For those who practice medicine, the clearer the message being articulated by the patient, the easier it is to understand the intents of the patient and to respect them without fear of innuendo, moral interloping by outsiders, or, even worse, moral interloping by family members who did not share the patient's values or have agendas of a nonmoral nature that could affect the care of the patient.

These protective advance directives allow for quality-of-life decisions to be made and for the greatest latitude to be extended to the liberty interests under the common law. If patients want to decline further invasive therapy in the exercise of their liberty interests when death is not certain but life is intolerable, then the unconsenting physician will need to go to court to pre-clude criminal charges and financial sanctions. The court would then need to rule that the state's interest in the preservation of life is so strong that the clear and convincing standard for articulating the liberty interest notwithstanding, the state will override that liberty interest and establish judicially mandated state health care requirements for the care of individuals who have become the property of the state. Were we to arrive at such circumstances, it is apparent that the Supreme Court of the United States would be forced to recognize that there is not an economic right but an economic imperative for patients to be the property of the state and for the state to disperse public funds for the care of individuals whose liberty interests had been clearly overridden by the state's interest in the preservation of life.

Though this is a hard circumstance to contemplate, the *Cruzan* court came as close as it could to setting the standard for preservation of life by state mandate in a case where the patient was already under the care of the state. Nancy Cruzan was a patient in a state hospital. Her health care was being paid for by the state of Missouri, and no attention was paid to whether she had been deprived of a fiduciary trust relationship with an individual physician as opposed to agents of the state. Under the circumstances in *Cruzan* we must assume that individuals who reside in state hospitals in Missouri have less access to the exercise of liberty interests than those who might have resided in a state hospital in Massachusetts, where the substituted judgment doctrine prevails. This raises troubling questions about how Medicare and Medicaid funds are used by state mandates and about subordination of federal legislative mandates directing the use of those funds. In such circumstances more federal funds would be dispersed to physicians (but not DRG-reimbursed hospitals) in Missouri than in Massachusetts, creating unequal economic entitlements to federal funds in different states.

One should not expect that either the circumstances surrounding one's demise or the geography of one's demise will be predictable. Therefore, even individuals who live in states that have less rigid standards than that which is clear and convincing evidence should consider writing advance directives that allow for all contingencies that would relate to travel or changes in geography if one wanted to have some sense of assurance about these matters in the United States.

In conclusion, the *Cruzan* opinion will lead to the development of more specific, meaningful, and contentfull advance directives that are now almost universally acknowledged in the United States as well as acknowledged in the Patient Self-Determination Act. Specific advance directives and thoughtful discussion between the subject and surrogates who would become the decision makers when the patient becomes incompetent are absolutely essential. Physicians need to have confidence in the meaning and individual nuances of care involving patients. Better advance directives with more forethought and careful discussion about the subject of death, which is often a taboo for the patient, the family, and the physician until matters are too far gone, will be a major cultural health care challenge for the American people. Enhancing individual responsibility enhances individual liberty. Though this may be a culturally and emotionally charged and painful subject for many, the advance directives that will exist after *Cruzan* will make for a better practice of medicine and a more responsible society of humans in which to practice medicine.

NOTES

1. H.T. Engelhardt, Jr., *The Foundations of Bioethics* (New York: Oxford University Press, 1986).

2. M. Battin, *Ethical Issues in Suicide* (Englewood Cliffs, N.J.: Prentice-Hall, 1982); M.A. Rie, A Social Responsibility to Die? Freedom, Aging and AIDS, *Journal of Clinical Anesthesia* 1 (1989):222–227.

3. H.T. Engelhardt and M. Malloy, Suicide and Assisting Suicide: A Critique of Legal Sanctions, *Southwestern Law Journal* 36 (1982):1003–1037.

4. S. Wachtler, A Judge's Perspective: The New York Rulings, *Law, Medicine and Health Care* 19, nos. 1–2 (1991):60–62.

5. E. McCloskey, Between Isolation and Intrusion: The Patient Self-Determination Act, *Law, Medicine and Health Care* 19, nos. 1–2 (1991):80–82.

6. M.A. Rie, Helga Wanglie's Ventilator: The Limits of a Wish, *Hastings Center Report* 21, no. 4 (1991):23–35.

7. C.H. Baron, Why Withdrawal of Life Support for PVS Patients Is Not a Family Decision, *Law, Medicine and Health Care* 19, nos. 1–2 (1991):73–75.

8. M.A. Rie and H.T. Engelhardt, Jr., The Financial Enforcement of Living Wills: Putting Teeth into Natural Death Statutes, in *Advance Directives in Medicine*, edited by C. Hackler et al. (New York: Praeger, 1989), 85–92.

9. G. Annas, The Long Dying of Nancy Cruzan, *Law, Medicine and Health Care* 19, nos. 1–2 (1991):52–59.

10. Baron, Why Withdrawal of Life Support for PVS Patients Is Not a Family Decision.

11. L. Emanuel and E. Emanuel, The Medical Directive: A New Comprehensive Advanced Care Document, *JAMA* 261 (1989):3288–3293.

12. Ibid.

Durable Power of Attorney for Health Care Decisions

1. DEFINITIONS

1.1 *"ATTORNEY-IN-FACT"* means _____.

1.2 *"Incapacity to Make Medical Treatment Decisions"* means the inability to understand the consequences of making Medical Treatment decisions and to communicate those decisions.

1.3 *"Irreversible Mental or Physical Disability"* includes, but is not limited to: permanent unconsciousness (i.e., a persistent vegetative state or irreversible coma, in which purposeful interaction with the environment, awareness of pain or pleasure, and any cognitive awareness are permanently absent), stroke, Alzheimer's or other dementia, Lou Gehrig's disease, locked-in syndrome, and brain damage due to head trauma.

1.4 *"Medical Treatment"* means any care, treatment, service, or procedure to maintain, diagnose, or treat my mental or physical condition, including but not limited to: antibiotics, artificially supplied nutrition and hydration, blood transfusions, chemotherapy, cardiac resuscitation, cardioversion, dialysis, medication, respiratory support (including tracheostomies), surgery (including amputation of gangrenous limbs).

1.5 *"PRINCIPAL"* means _____.

2. GENERAL APPOINTMENT

I, _____ ("Principal"), hereby appoint my _____ ("ATTORNEY-IN-FACT") as my ATTORNEY-IN-FACT to express and implement, to the full extent permitted by law, my specific and general instructions and desires concerning all Medical Treatment decisions in the event I am unable (even temporarily) to do so myself. I delegate this authority because I trust my ATTORNEY-IN-FACT to make the decisions I would have made if I had been able to choose, and to do so in timely fashion. If my ATTORNEY-IN-FACT cannot determine what my wishes would have been, I direct that he/she determines my best interest.

3. NOMINATION OF COURT-APPOINTED FIDUCIARY

If any type of court-appointed fiduciary (e.g., committee of the person, conservator, or guardian) must be appointed to make decisions concerning my health care in the event I am unable to do so, I hereby nominate my ATTORNEY-IN-FACT to serve in that position.

4. STATEMENT OF DESIRES

4.1 *General Statement.* If I should have an Irreversible Mental or Physical Disability from which my attending physician (or any other physician(s) my ATTORNEY-IN-FACT selects) determines that there is "no reasonable expectation of my significant improvement" (as defined by my ATTORNEY-IN-FACT), I authorize my ATTORNEY-IN-FACT to direct the individuals or institutions responsible for my care to withhold or withdraw Medical Treatment that primarily prolongs my dying and is not necessary for comfort care as described in paragraph 4.2. Because I fear having an Irreversible Mental or Physical Disability more than death itself, I do not want Medical Treatment that prolongs my life (except as described in paragraphs 4.2 and 4.3) if I have such disability, even if it is inexpensive, easy to administer, and may bring me back to my full mental and physical capabilities for a certain period, but will not cure the Irreversible Mental or Physical Disability from which I suffer. If my ATTOR-NEY-IN-FACT is unable to implement this document, I direct that this document nevertheless be honored by all those concerned with my care to the full extent permitted by law. I also direct that my attending physician make a copy of this document part of my medical record as soon as he/she becomes aware of it.

4.2 *Comfort Care.* I direct that I be given any Medical Treatment to keep me comfortable and relieve pain, even if it is addictive and/or shortens my life. Unless my ATTORNEY-IN-FACT so directs, however, I do *not* want any Medical Treatment, even comfort care, and particularly prolonged intravenous or enteric hydration and nutrition, if it prolongs my life when I have an Irreversible Mental or Physical Disability.

4.3 *Medical Treatment Prior to a Determination of Irreversible Mental or Physical Disability.* I *do* want Medical Treatment prior to it being determined by my attending physician (or any other physician(s) my ATTORNEY-IN-FACT selects) that I have no expectation of significant improvement in accordance with paragraph 4.1. In the event that such determination is not made within a period of a week from the time I become incapable of making Medical Treatment decisions and a physician my ATTORNEY-IN-FACT selects examines me, I want Medical Treatment not necessary for my comfort withheld or withdrawn, subject to my ATTORNEY-IN-FACT's discretion to lengthen the period.

4.4 *Place of Care.* I do not want to be transferred to a hospital from a nursing home (or other location) for the purpose of receiving Medical Treatment in contravention of this document or my ATTOR-NEY-IN-FACT's instructions.

5. SCOPE OF ATTORNEY-IN-FACT'S POWERS

I direct that my ATTORNEY-IN-FACT have the broadest possible scope of authority to make any decisions concerning my health care. These powers include but are not limited to: (a) providing, withholding, or withdrawing consent to specific Medical Treatment (including those that primarily prolong my dying); (b) granting releases to medical personnel; (c) employing and discharging medical personnel; (d) determining, based on consultation with my attending physician (or any other mental health professional(s) my ATTORNEY-IN-FACT selects), my capacity to make health care decisions; (e) discussing my medical condition and prognosis with physicians; (f) expending or withholding my funds necessary to implement treatment or to enforce the instructions in this document; (g) interpreting any ambiguities in this document; (h) overriding any provisions in this document; (i) making health care decisions on my behalf, based on the ATTORNEY-IN-FACT's good faith determination of my wishes had I been able to choose for myself, or if unable to determine them, to make the decision which the ATTORNEY-IN-FACT determines to be in my best interest; (j) making decisions concerning donations of my organs; (k) communicating any treatment decisions I made, either orally or in writing; (l) having primary visitation rights; and (m) seeking judicial intervention, if necessary, to implement a treatment plan, to request civil damages (described further in paragraph 8) for not honoring the instructions as expressed by me, this document, or my ATTORNEY-IN-FACT.

6. PROPERTY ISSUES

I hereby authorize and direct whoever shall be responsible for my estate or have power over any property of mine to reimburse my ATTORNEY-IN-FACT for any costs (including legal fees) reasonably incurred in or as a result of acting pursuant to this document. I also prohibit whoever shall have power over any of my property from disbursing funds for my health care *not* authorized by my ATTORNEY-IN-FACT.

7. EFFECTIVENESS

I intend this document to become effective upon my incapacity to make Medical Treatment decisions (as determined by my treating physician or any other mental health professional(s) my ATTORNEY-IN-FACT selects). I intend that the authority conferred on my ATTORNEY-IN-FACT is exercisable notwithstanding my disability or incompetence. This document will remain in effect unless I willfully and voluntarily amend or revoke it. By "revocation," I mean written or oral revocation in the presence of two witnesses of sound mind over the age of 18. I direct my attending physician to enter any revocation in my medical record as soon as he/she becomes aware of such revocation.

8. WAIVER OF LIABILITY/ENFORCEMENT OF DOCUMENT

8.1 *Waiver.* I hereby release from liability, indemnify, and hold harmless my ATTORNEY-IN-FACT for any action taken in good faith pursuant to this document. I also hereby indemnify, hold harmless, and release from liability any physicians, hospital administrators, or any other individuals who, absent actual knowledge of my revocation of this document, rely in good faith on this document or my ATTORNEY-IN-FACT's instructions.

8.2 *Enforcement.* I consider any Medical Treatment in violation of this document or my ATTORNEY-IN-FACT's instructions to be a nonconsensual touching and Medical Treatment without my informed consent. I therefore direct my ATTORNEY-IN-FACT (or any other person(s) legally authorized to do so if my ATTORNEY-IN-FACT is unable to do so) to take any legal measures to protect these rights, including but not limited to seeking: declaratory or injunctive relief, compensatory and punitive damages, attorneys fees, costs, and guardian ad litem fees.

9. INTERPRETIVE RULES

I direct my ATTORNEY-IN-FACT to use my directions as set forth in this document as a guide for making medical decisions on my behalf, but authorize him or her to override them if he/she determines such action to be more consistent with my preferences as otherwise known to him/her or in my best interest. My ATTORNEY-IN-FACT's decisions are to be final, binding, and conclusive, and should not be questioned absent a showing based strictly on the most clear and convincing evidence that he/she has deliberately acted in violation of my directions. The decisions of my ATTORNEY-IN-FACT shall control notwithstanding any decisions by any other individual(s), including but not limited to _____. Any ambiguities in this document should be interpreted by my AT-TORNEY-IN-FACT to confer the broadest powers on him/her to make health care decisions to the full extent permitted by law. I waive the attorney-client privilege or physician-patient privilege if discussions between me and my attorneys or physicians can help interpret any ambiguities in this document. I intend this document to be a clear and convincing expression of my desire to control my Medical Treatment to the full extent permitted by law in the state of _____ and any other jurisdiction in which I may be treated.

10. SEVERABILITY

If for any reason any provision of this document is determined not to be legally binding, I ask that it be deemed severable and that all other provisions be deemed binding to the greatest extent possible.

11. PARAGRAPH HEADINGS

The paragraph headings are inserted herein only as a matter of convenience and in no way define, modify, or restrict the scope of intent of any provision herein.

12. DISTRIBUTION OF DOCUMENT

The following people will be given a copy of this document, all copies of which shall be deemed originals:

_____(ATTORNEY-IN-FACT)

Address

_____(Attorney)

Address

_____(Attorney)

Address

13. ACCEPTANCE BY ATTORNEY-IN-FACT

As ATTORNEY-IN-FACT I, _____, understand that acceptance of this appointment means that if my father/mother/spouse, etc. _____ becomes incapable of making Medical Treatment decisions for himself/herself, I have a duty to act in good faith and to implement any medical decisions he/she has communicated to me orally or in writing, to make medical decisions for him/her that I think he/she would have made for himself/herself if he/she had been able to choose, or if I cannot determine these decisions, to make the decisions which I consider to be in his/her best interest. I also understand that, before this document becomes effective, I must, pursuant to N.Y. Gen. Obl. Law § 5-1602, declare in writing that my father/mother/spouse has become incapable of making medical decisions for himself/herself. I am of sound mind, over 18 years of age, and am not _____ attending physician.

_____

Typed name of individual

Address and Phone

SIGNATURE OF PRINCIPAL

IN WITNESS WHEREOF, I declare that I am of sound mind, and fully capable of understanding the nature and consequences of executing this document, and I willfully and voluntarily have set my hand this _____ day of _____, 19_____.

_____

Typed name of individual

Address and Phone

WITNESS ACKNOWLEDGMENT

I declare that_____, who appears to me of sound mind and to understand the nature and consequences of executing this document, has voluntarily signed this document in my presence. I am of sound mind and over the age of 18 years. I am not the person appointed as ATTORNEY-IN-FACT and am not the attending physician of _____.

_____   _____

(Signature)   (Address)

                                         _____

_____   _____

(Signature)   (Address)

                                         _____

STATE OF NEW YORK) SS:

      COUNTY OF)

On this _____ day of _____, 19_____ before me personally came _____, to me known to be the individual described in and who
executed the foregoing instrument, and he/she duly acknowledged to me and executed the same.

_____
(Notary Public)

On the _____ day of _____, 19_____, before me
personally came _____, a subscribing witness to the foregoing instrument,
with whom I am personally acquainted, who, being by me duly sworn, did depose and say that he/she
resides at _____; that he/she knows to be the individual described in and who
executed the foregoing instrument; and that he/she, said subscribing witness, was present and saw
_____ execute the same; and that he/she, said witness, at the same time subscribed his/her name as witness thereto.

_____
(Notary Public)

Chapter 32

Distributive Justice: Must We Say Yes When Society Says No?

Susan S. Braithwaite

In the United States we suffer a pressing need for reform to ensure universal access to health care and affordability of cost. The efficacy of modern-day medical interventions makes access a greater moral issue than ever before, but health care providers have retreated from their historical position of offering charity care to the poor, probably because of the cost of medical care and the profitability of the health care industry, which have led to the commercialization of medicine.[1] The author believes that justice requires a societal solution to ensure access but here addresses the question of what the provider should do while waiting for society to make an effective response.

In the context of discussing allocation of health care resources, *justice* suggests different meanings to different people. A person who restricts use of the term to one of its senses may thus reveal his or her alignment on certain social and economic policies. The term *justice* in this essay will encompass only the limited concept of distributive justice associated with an egalitarian philosophy, as elaborated below. The discussion concerns microallocation decisions in health care (choices to provide or not provide specific services to individual patients) and will not treat macroallocation decisions (e.g., the commitment of public funds to dialysis or transplant programs or to research on cancer).

(Several closely related topics lie beyond the scope of the essay. For example, does the concept of social equality imply a claim upon society for health care?[2] More broadly, is health care a right?[3] To the problems of inadequate access and unaffordable cost, what responses should society make? Do institutions and corporations share responsibility with physicians for upholding professional values? Does the profit motive signify an erosion of values in medicine or does competition among health care providers enhance quality and ultimately benefit society?[4])

ACCESS

We owe much of the present-day impetus for reform to articulate critics from within the medical profession.[5] Despite the argument that free market principles have provided Americans with the best health care in the world,[6] we in fact deliver excellent health care only to those who are already "in the system," leaving at risk between 31.1 and 37.0 million uninsured Americans and many additional underinsured Americans, as well.[7]

Insurance status impacts on the willingness of health care providers to accept a patient into their systems, and both health and employment status impact on the ability of a patient to receive insurance at a reasonable rate.[8] While hospitals now must accept those uninsured patients who present with emergencies,[9] they cover the cost of the care of the uninsured through a chaotic system of cross-subsidization using a portion of the payments of insured patients (some call this a system of taxation without representation that, despite its beneficent intent, fails to guarantee equity for the poor).

Public assistance programs do not relieve the problem of maldistribution of services to the poor. In order to qualify for Medicaid coverage, the income of a potential recipient must fall below the federal poverty level. Because Medicaid payment scales do not compete favorably with those of private insurers, many providers reject patients with public aid coverage.

The risks to the uninsured include not only the obvious financial risk of incurring an unrepayable debt but also objective risks to health. The uninsured receive less preventive medicine, fewer high-cost interventions, and fewer hospitalizations; their condition on arrival to hospitals is worse; and death occurs 1.2 to 3.2 times more often. The adverse outcomes include an increased frequency of death from asthma, lesser frequency of appropriate cardiac bypass surgery, increased case mortality rate from ectopic pregnancy, and increased risk of low-birth-weight infants.[10]

COSTS

Unbridled payment of medical fees by Medicare and by third-party payers during the previous three decades and the high cost of administering our multipayer system have resulted in skyrocketing expenditures on health care in this country.[11] Under an unchecked, fully insured fee-for-service system, the self-interest of the physician may lead to the provision of more

evaluation and treatment than the patient needs; no incentive interrupts the cycle of rising costs, development and naive consumption of technology, and increasingly sophisticated patient expectations.

DISTRIBUTIVE JUSTICE

Discourse on the definition of justice often pits libertarianism[12] against egalitarianism.[13]

This chapter will use the term *justice* in the Rawlsian sense of fair equality of opportunity. When extended to the health care arena,[14] *justice* refers to distribution of resources so as to correct unfair restrictions of opportunity dealt by ill health. The egalitarian would argue that we owe each citizen some level of access to health care, just as we owe him or her nondiscriminatory access to jobs and to the legal system, education, and other entitlements. The egalitarian usually does not define health itself as an entitlement and does not claim that justice requires equality of medical outcome. Egalitarian thought accepts the possibility of government intervention toward attainment of the goal of distributive justice. Among egalitarians, controversy arises on acceptability of a two-tiered system of health care delivery and services, stratified according to the ability to pay.[15]

The libertarian definition of justice asks us to distinguish unjust outcomes (harms resulting from unconsented-to actions of others) from outcomes that are simply unfortunate. The libertarian challenges the egalitarian position that unfortunate outcomes of the lotteries of nature and society constitute a claim upon others for restitution.[16] Under a libertarian definition of justice, society should protect individual control of property and should not coerce unwilling individuals to subsidize all demands for care by the needy. Libertarians by definition subscribe to a multi-tiered system and characteristically recognize a role both for charity and for societal support of a minimal acceptable level of care.

In American medicine, a dominantly libertarian system protects physician employment choices, provides incentives for technological and pharmaceutical development and for excellence of practice patterns, offers less costly coordinated care alternatives for employers and government agencies, and allows the well-to-do or insured patient to become a discerning consumer and to prioritize how much he or she wants to spend individually on health care. The market system may force society to plan deliberately for the care of the poor[17] and to decide where to rank health care in comparison to other goods.[18]

However, the free market system has cost us money and other advantages, including other liberties. The libertarian, arguing against government regulation and taxation for health care, must confront the present-day fact that individual providers "tax" him or her through a chaotic and involuntary system, using his or her payments to subsidize whatever care they do give the indigent.[19] Free market principles may drive physicians out of needed primary care specialties into more remunerative career choices,[20] and they may result in prejudice and exclusion of physicians of other national origin from practice in this country.[21] In the $50,000 plus income bracket, the fear of losing health care insurance has prevented up to 36% of Americans from changing jobs at some time.[22] Finally, the free market system, as it presently exists, offers little freedom of choice to the indigent except for emergency care.

THE PROSPECTS FOR SOCIETAL INTERVENTION TO ACHIEVE JUSTICE

Some of the proposed solutions to the problems of access and cost address our reimbursement system[23] whereas others do not apply uniquely to any particular reimbursement plan, although implementation is likeliest to occur first within governmentally influenced programs.[24]

Proposed solutions that address the problem of cost containment necessarily require some compromise and to a greater or lesser degree infringe the interests of physician and patient.[25] However, the health of the indigent probably would improve under a system of publicly funded medical care.[26] Justice requires society to ensure a minimum acceptable level of care for all, but society will postpone implementing a full solution perhaps for years. How will and should providers behave in the meantime?

HOW PROVIDERS SAY NO

In discussing the duties of providers, one must address the question of individual versus corporate responsibility. Even if we could agree that bioethical principles prohibit the individual physician from seeking self-aggrandizement, could we agree on applying that prohibition to health care institutions and corporations? A health care institution holds further financial obligations to employees and to patients and their carriers and employers; therefore, subject to appropriate public safeguards,[27] perhaps it should compete like other businesses.[28]

Nevertheless, at eleemosynary institutions the responsibility of executives is not primarily to make profit but to render certain services.[29] Furthermore, professional and individual ethics apply to persons who work for groups, institutions, and corporations. If an employer does not permit employees to act in accordance with their moral code, they might feel obligated to leave or seek reform.[30] On this basis, guidelines on distributive justice that apply to individual providers also apply to the groups for which they work, at least to the extent that a group must not impede the expression of the ethical code of each individual.

Entrepreneurism in medicine may oppose the principle of justice and undermine the virtue and trustworthiness of the profession.[31] A few examples follow.

1. *Some providers dismiss established patients because of change in socioeconomic status.*

2. *Some individuals, groups, institutions, and corporations court paying patients.* Some providers engage in marketing or channeling of program development to favored socioeconomic groups, preferential treatment of paying pa-

tients, pandering to paying patients, or coercion of physicians to recruit and retain paying patients.

Most commentators on the issue of advertising either support advertising on the basis of free market principles or oppose it on the grounds that patients will be misled into accepting unnecessary interventions.[32] One might hypothesize that advertising and marketing could further alienate the medically indigent from the particular provider who advertised, from the intervention that the advertising promoted, or from the health care system in general. As the uninsured will understand all too well, the advertiser does not want their business.

No instance of preferential treatment compels our attention more than the application by a physician or group of differential standards of medical care with regard to two patients whose health status, in terms of severity of illness and prognosis, is similar but whose insurance status differs. For example, an endocrinologist may refer two patients for consultation for diabetic gastroparesis resistant to conventional management. The gastroenterology group may keep the insured patient in its practice for periodic adjustment of medication or for investigational therapy but return the uninsured patient back to the referring physician with a judgment that nothing more can be done, that nothing is indicated, or that the problem is partly psychogenic. The endocrinologist may strongly suspect that the insurance status accounted for the difference in advice, but the impression will remain anecdotal, since no two patients are truly matched in all relevant respects.

Systematic differences in practice patterns may occur when a physician or group practices at different sites. Differences in institutional funding, staffing, available services, acuity of patient illness, chronicity of patient admissions, environment, socioeconomic aspects of the patient population, and other factors always will force different hospitals to provide different standards of care. Inadequate resources at some sites make it harder for physicians to do their jobs and necessarily impact on the level of care.

Nevertheless, some aspects of care fall largely within the control of the practitioner, group, service, or department. At all sites where he or she practices, a given physician should exhibit comparable habits with respect to record-keeping, supervision of trainees, timeliness of consultations, availability for continuity care, preoperative evaluation and counseling, frequency of inpatient visits, graciousness to referring and consulting services, and so on. Nevertheless, with respect to these habits, a comparison of sites where physicians are salaried and indemnified against malpractice claims by their employer (public and government-run hospitals) with sites where they charge fees for service (private nonprofit or for-profit hospitals and clinics) may disclose differential treatment rendered by the same physicians.

To train new physicians, we must permit evolution of autonomy within the time frame of the training program, and we must be reconciled to occasional mistakes, but justice requires that physicians-in-training should not differentially be granted autonomy according to the patient's insurance status or, within a given training program, according to the site of caregiving. To examine the commitment of a medical school or training program to distributive justice, an analysis might correlate the insurance and socioeconomic status of patients with the presence of students and residents and with the level of involvement of attending physicians.

A higher percentage of primary care physicians would improve access and reduce cost of care in this country. The author can think of no better formula for sabotaging the primary care initiative[33] than to permit de facto segregation of patients according to insurance status. The mechanisms by which such segregation occurs include

- favoring public hospitals or charitable facilities as training sites
- at private hospitals, sending self-referred "no-docs" and emergency room patients to residents' primary care clinics
- impeding referrals of emergency room patients to specialty clinics

- funneling paying patients into specialty clinics (requiring physician referral to these clinics)
- in residents' clinics, restricting the faculty supervisory role to underpaid and non-tenure-track primary care physicians or eliminating supervision altogether
- excluding residents and students from specialty clinics and satellites where paying patients are seen

3. The indebtedness of graduating medical students and the dependency of medical school solvency upon patient payments may contribute to perpetuation of the profit motive in medicine. The average medical student debt in 1990 was $46,224.[34] This indebtedness may well influence the choices of specialty and attitudes of our new graduates toward access and cost.

Revenues from the clinical practice of faculty members now have become the single largest source of support for medical schools.[35] Therefore, academic medical centers may present as role models a faculty whose main function is "maintaining an institutional black bottom line,"[36] a faculty complicitous in restricting access, a faculty teaching but not delivering distributive justice. At academic medical centers, one can hear comments like the following from the professors and their staff: "The doctor does not accept public aid." "We have to improve our payer mix." "We have to capture that market." Furthermore, it may be deceptive for an institution to present practitioners to the public as academic faculty, who do no teaching or research, and who engage in services remunerative to the institution at higher-than-average cost to the payer, with worse-than-average amenities for the patient, and without explicit patient or carrier understanding of payment distribution.

4. Many providers refuse to do a fair share of care for the uninsured and underinsured. Many providers adopt a system to control the volume of underreimbursed care that, if it were implemented by all private providers, would prevent regional societal needs from being met.

HOW PROVIDERS SAY YES

Many physicians, groups, institutions, and corporations eschew marketplace tactics and additionally provide some nonemergency care to the underserved.[37] They do so without a good operational definition of fair share, without reassurance that others will follow suit, and with full knowledge that their isolated action will not ensure even regional equity of distribution of health care services. Such activities demonstrate a willingness to extend the principle of beneficence to patients who are not yet established with the caregiver and to commit resources to distributive justice at the microallocation level despite economic disincentives.

For the individual, examples of attempting to provide a fair share include charitable donations, employment at a noncompetitive salary in a facility for the underserved, or rendering nonbilled services either in a private practice or at local sites that are designated for charitable health care delivery.[38] Time of life and other commitments may determine the degree of commitment to charitable work and the form the charity takes. For managed care organizations, fair share options include emergency room service and the acceptance of Medicare and Medicaid patients; for hospitals, the establishment of a catchment area from which the indigent must be accepted;[39] and for a consortium of incorporated hospitals,[40] the practice of supporting some inner-city hospitals that operate at a loss through the profits of suburban hospitals. Religious and charitable organizations may administer plans for matching needy patients with willing physicians.[41] The Catholic Health Association of the United States and the Lewin/ICF division of Health and Sciences Research recognize the following community benefits to be institutional services for the poor and the broader community: traditional charity care, unpaid cost of public programs, nonbilled services, cash and in-kind donations made by the facility, education and training of health professionals, research activities, and services generating low or negative margins.[42]

How much is a fair share? For nonprofit organizations, should we use the amount of the tax exemption to define a minimum fair share?[43] This rule seems arbitrary, since there is no assurance that a dollar amount equal to all charitable tax exemptions would meet societal needs. A utilitarian analysis of needs, means, and the effects of fair share proposals on all affected parties might permit us to state dollar amounts and/or rules from which dollar amounts could be derived. Under a voluntary system, however, one must expect widespread nonparticipation in fair share action guidelines. The advice to do "a fair share" therefore usually reduces to the advice to "do some." Many now speak in terms of regional needs and sense of community.[44] Certain academic medical centers, probably those with special strength in primary care, have taken the lead in prioritizing community services (according to need) for their students.[45]

VIRTUE ETHICS, CARE ETHICS, AND THE FAIR SHARE OBLIGATION

It remains to be argued whether a provider is morally obligated to renounce marketplace practices and/or to provide a fair share of under-reimbursed nonemergency care. Of course a provider must remain solvent in order to do any good at all. We recognize that physicians can earn their living and health care organizations can provide employment to individuals only through collection of patient and third-party payments. The legitimacy of establishing reasonable restrictions to limit the volume of under-reimbursed care is not being disputed here.

Does any type of bioethical justification support the notion that there is an obligation to do a fair share—or, indeed, that there is any defense for doing a fair share? Although physicians need to strike a balance between charity and self-preservation, self-preservation does not require self-aggrandizement. By categorically excluding nonpaying nonemergency patients (failing to do a fair share), a physician abandons the precepts and some of the virutes of the profession (benevolence, distributive justice) for the sake of excessive gain. The individual who abandons a moral precept or a virtue because he or she is grasping or who fails to seek the mean or moderate position between suffering injustice and committing it fails an ancient definition of the just person.[46] Therefore, we can reject frank avarice in medicine, but we still must ask the question of whether there is a fair share obligation.

In general, it is difficult to make a strong moral argument that charity is obligatory.[47] Refusal to do a fair share may signify a perception of futility or fear of annihilation in the competitive marketplace,[48] or it may signify a libertarian perspective in justice. The question of whether one must do a fair share is not readily resolved by identifying oneself as a libertarian or egalitarian, however, since advocacy for a fair share can be argued from either position.

Deontologic reasoning and utilitarian reasoning are almost indistinguishable on the issue of whether doing a fair share is obligatory. Deontologic reasoning (a duty-driven ethic) does not constitute the dominant motivation for most practitioners who try to offer a fair share. Even if it did, we still would recognize that many duties in medicine relate to the attainment of measurable objective goals. Assessment of distributive justice by measurable parameters would lead inexorably to utilitarian moral reasoning.

But the answer to the utilitarian question of what would yield the greatest good seems unknowable or is at least not agreed upon. Private charitable endeavor will not adequately address the health care deprivation of rural or inner-city patients. Will "dabbling in charity" produce significant net good at all? Might charity create injustice to those who were "taxed" involuntarily as a way of cross-subsidizing the needy? Will charity demean patients or lead to patient noncompliance with medical recommendations? Will those who offer no charity gain a competitive edge and destroy the charity givers? Might a modest improvement of access forestall the day when society will address distributive justice effectively?

If we could show that charity achieved justice, then we could invoke the bioethical principle of justice to support the notion that there is a fair share obligation. The defense of the fair share obligation would stand or fall on utilitarian grounds. Because we cannot accurately infer the broad consequences of reliance upon or resort to charity, nor can we construct appropriate controlled trials, by default we must use a different justification.

Rather than claim certainty about what we hope to accomplish with charity, it might be more fruitful to ask who we want to be. The author in fact believes the fair share obligation is best defended by a virtue ethic[49] or care ethic.[50] Although a sense of justice may motivate a provider to offer a fair share, the action he or she takes can correct societal injustice only slightly if at all. Furthermore, several motivations other than a sense of justice may impel caregivers to do a fair share. Virtue ethics recognize justice as only one among many virtues, and the care ethic specifically contrasts the justice perspective with the care perspective.

Community-based service deserves a special comment. Most theories of equity underscore the principle of impartiality. Why should geographic proximity determine a patient's candidacy for charity from a particular provider? Why should not the concerned physician move to an underserved area, or organize care for the third world, or work overtime at his or her regular job in order to subsidize remote health care in this country for the most needy or for those most likely to benefit?

One might argue, on utilitarian grounds, that by working near home we eliminate overhead costs of transferring funds through charitable organizations. The more important argument, however, is that the caregiver actually sees patients and does not simply fund caregiving by someone else. This care ethic, in contrast to most theories of justice, permits partiality and emphasizes the importance of direct relationships in the moral life of individuals. Therefore, the care ethic may justify preferential concern for the immediate community of a provider and restriction of charitable activity to relationships with specific patients.

CONCLUSION

Justice requires a societal solution to the problem of access to health care. This chapter discusses ideal provider behavior for the interim, censures competitive market business practices in medicine, and supports the concept of a fair share obligation. However, in the absence of data on efficacy, the strongest justification for these guidelines would derive from utilitarian reasoning on their probable contribution toward the achievement of distributive justice. Unfortunately, the author acknowledges that such reasoning could lead either to support of the guidelines or of their opposites. Although collective adherence to the injunction to provide charitable care cannot meet the requirements of distributive justice even regionally, nevertheless either a virtue ethic or a care ethic might motivate individual providers to renounce marketplace behavior and to provide a fair share of care to the underserved.

NOTES

1. P.H. Werhane, The Ethics of Health Care as a Business, *Business and Professional Ethics Journal* 9, nos. 3–4 (1990):7–20.
2. M. Kaus, *The End of Equality* (New York: Basic Books, 1992), 89–95.
3. M. Siegler, A Physician's Perspective on a Right to Health Care, *JAMA* 244 (1980):1591–1596.
4. J. Kupersmith et al., For-Profit Management of a University Hospital, *New England Journal of Medicine* 318

(1988):1402–1403; G. Graham, The Doctor, the Rich, and the Indigent, *Journal of Medicine and Philosophy* 12, no. 1 (1987):51–61; G.W. Rainbolt, Competition and the Patient-centered Ethic, *Journal of Medicine and Philosophy* 12, no. 1 (1987):85–99; P.T. Menzel, Morality, Autonomy and Efficiency: What Health Care System Should We Have? *Journal of Medicine and Philosophy* 17 (1992):33–57; M. Friedman, Gammon's Law Points to Health-Care Solution, *Wall Street Jour-*

nal, November 12, 1991, A20; R.E. Herzlinger, A Third Approach to the Medical-Insurance Crisis: Healthy Competition, *Atlantic Monthly,* August 1991, 69–81.

5. A.S. Relman, American Medicine at the Crossroads: Signs from Canada, *New England Journal of Medicine* 320 (1989):590–591; J.A. Ginsburg and D.M. Prout, Access to Health Care (position paper), *Annals of Internal Medicine* 112 (1990):641–661; G.D. Lundberg, National Health Care Reform: An Aura of Inevitability Is upon Us, *JAMA* 265 (1991):2566–2567.

6. M.L. Sprang, Government-run Universal Health Insurance Equals Universal Mediocrity, *Chicago Medicine* 94, no. 14 (1991):4–5.

7. D.U. Himmelstein et al., The Vanishing Health Care Safety Net: New Data on Uninsured Americans (Cambridge, Mass.: Center for National Health Program Studies; Cambridge, Mass.: Physicians for a National Health Program; Washington, D.C.: The Public Citizen Health Research Group; Joint Report, 1992); Ginsburg and Prout, Access to Health Care; P.J. Farley, *Who Are the Underinsured? National Health Care Expenditures Study* (Hyattsville, Md.: National Center for Health Services Research, 1984): T. Bodenheimer, Underinsurance in America, *New England Journal of Medicine* 327 (1992):274–278.

8. J.K. Igelhart, Medical Care of the Poor—A Growing Problem, *New England Journal of Medicine* 313 (1985):59–63; M. Freudenheim, Doctors Dropping Medicare Patients, *New York Times,* A1, A13; G. Kolata, New Insurance Practice: Dividing Sick from Well, *New York Times,* 1992, A1, A7.

9. Comprehensive Omnibus Budget Reconciliation Act, Public Law 99-272 (April 7, 1986), sec. 9121.

10. R.L. Schiff et al., Transfers to Public Hospitals: A Prospective Study of 467 Patients, *New England Journal of Medicine* 314 (1986):552–557; M. Ingwerson, Cracks in the Health-Care Safety Net, *Christian Science Monitor,* November 19, 1991; W. Carr et al., Variations in Asthma Hospitalizations and Deaths in New York City, *American Journal of Public Health* 82, no. 1 (1992):59–65; K.P. Nederlof et al., Ectopic Pregnancy Surveillance, United States, 1970–1987, *Morbidity and Mortality Weekly Report CDC Surveillance Summary* 39, no. 4 (1990):9–17; K.C. Goldberg et al., Racial and Community Factors Influencing Coronary Artery Bypass Graft Surgery Rates for All 1986 Medicare Patients, *JAMA* 267 (1992):1473–1477; A. Kempe et al., Clinical Determinants of the Racial Disparity in Very Low Birth Weight, *New England Journal of Medicine* 327 (1992):969–973.

11. Ginsburg and Prout, Access to Health Care; S. Woolhandler and D.U. Himmelstein, The Deteriorating Administrative Efficiency of the U.S. Health Care System, *New England Journal of Medicine* 324 (1991):1253–1258; L. Belsie, From Business, Urgent Cries for Reform, *Christian Science Monitor,* November 21, 1991; F. Barringer, Hospital Executives' Pay Rose Sharply in Decade, *The New York Times,* September 30, 1992, A8.

12. R. Nozick, *Anarchy, State, and Utopia* (New York: Basic Books, 1974).

13. J. Rawls, *A Theory of Justice* (Cambridge, Mass: Harvard University Press, 1971).

14. N. Daniels, *Just Health Care* (Cambridge: Cambridge University Press, 1985), 28–58.

15. T.L. Beauchamp and J.F. Childress, *Principles of Biomedical Ethics,* 3rd ed. (New York: Oxford University Press, 1989), 278–280.

16. H.T. Engelhardt, Rights to Health Care, in *The Foundations of Bioethics* (Oxford: Oxford University Press, 1986), 336–374.

17. "In the absence of skimming, those who can pay are subject to an informal tax, a shifting of costs, to provide care to those who cannot pay. . . . Skimming compels individuals, communities, and governments to confront the question of the level of care they wish to provide for the indigent. . . . If one holds that at the very least taxes should be publicly discussed and democratically enacted, then one will be constrained, however reluctantly, to acknowledge the virtues of skimming" (H.T. Engelhardt and M. Rie, Morality for the Medical-Industrial Complex: A Code of Ethics for the Mass Marketing of Health Care, *New England Journal of Medicine* 319 [1989]:1088).

18. "A major point of competition policy is to force consumers, insurers and providers to take serious stock of how the value of health care, bought with a given marginal dollar, compares to the value of the other things that a dollar can buy" (P.T. Menzel, Economic Competition in Health Care: A Moral Assessment, *Journal of Medicine and Philosophy* 12, no. 1 [1987]:77).

19. "Cross subsidization can be viewed as an inefficient uncoordinated welfare system hidden from public view and unaccountable to the public or to its representatives in government . . . the demise of cross subsidization should be welcomed, not lamented. . . . perhaps the strongest argument for cross-subsidization is the claim that it does—though admittedly in a haphazard and inefficient way—what is not likely to be done through more explicit social policies" (D.W. Brock and A.E. Buchanan, The Profit Motive in Medicine, *Journal of Medical Philosophy* 12, no. 1 [1987]:15–16).

20. M.D. Schwartz et al., Medical Student Interest in Internal Medicine, *Annals of Internal Medicine* 114, (1991):6–15; J.M. Colwill, Where Have All the Primary Care Applicants Gone? *New England Journal of Medicine* 326 (1992):387–393; R.G. Petersdorf, Primary Care Applicants—They Get No Respect, *New England Journal of Medicine* 326 (1992):408–409.

21. E. Gahr, Keeping out Real M.D.s, *Insight on the News* 8, no. 11 (1992):12–13, 38; A. Varki, Of Pride, Prejudice, and Discrimination, *Annals of Internal Medicine* 116 (1992):762–764.

22. E. Eckholm, Health Benefits Found to Deter Switches in Jobs, *New York Times*, September 26, 1991, A1.

23. B.A. Brody, Justice and Competitive Markets, *Journal of Medicine and Philosophy* 12, no. 1 (1987):37–50; A. Enthoven and R. Kronick, A Consumer-Choice Health Plan for the 1990's, parts 1, 2, *New England Journal of Medicine* 320 (1989): 29–37, 94–101; A.S. Relman, Reforming the Health Care System, *New England Journal of Medicine* 323 (1991):991–992; S.H. Miles et al., Health Care Reform in Minnesota, *New England Journal of Medicine* 327 (1992):1092–1095; A.L. Caplan and P.A. Ogren, Do the Right Thing: Minnesota's HealthRight Program, *Hastings Center Report* 22, no. 5 (1992):4–6; M.S. Dukakis, The States and Health Care Reform, *New England Journal of Medicine* 327 (1992):1090–1095; H.D. Scott and H.B. Shapiro (American College of Physicians, Health and Public Policy Committee), Universal Insurance for American Health Care: A Proposal of the American College of Physicians, *Annals of Internal Medicine* 117 (1992): 511–519; W.C. Maddrey et al., Health Care Reform: An American Imperative, *Annals of Internal Medicine* 117 (1992):528–529; D.U. Himmelstein et al., A National Health Program for the United States: A Physicians' Proposal, *New England Journal of Medicine* 320 (1989):102–108; S. Woolhandler and D.U. Himmelstein, A National Health Program: Northern Light at the End of the Tunnel, *JAMA* 262 (1989):2136–2137; K. Grumbach et al., Liberal Benefits, Conservative Spending: The Physicians for a National Health Program Proposal, *JAMA* 265 (1991):2549–2554.

24. A.L. Caplan, Money, Medicine and Morality, in *If I Were a Rich Man, Could I Buy a Pancreas?* (Bloomington and Indianapolis: Indiana University Press, 1992), 283–335; D.M. Fox and H.M. Leichter, Rationing Care in Oregon: The New Accountability, *Health Affairs* 10, no. 2 (1991):7–27; H.G. Welch, Health Care Tickets for the Uninsured: First Class, Coach, or Standby? *New England Journal of Medicine* 321 (1989):1261–1264; R. Steinbrook and B. Lo, The Oregon Medicaid Demonstration Project—Will it Provide Adequate Medical Care? *New England Journal of Medicine* 326 (1992):340–344; D. Callahan, Rationing Medical Progress: The Way to Affordable Health Care, *New England Journal of Medicine* 322 (1990):1810–1813.

25. G.W. Grumet, Health Care Rationing through Inconvenience: The Third Party's Secret Weapon, *New England Journal of Medicine* 321 (1989):607–611; N. Daniels, Why Saying No to Patients in the United States Is So Hard: Cost Containment, Justice, and Provider Autonomy, *New England Journal of Medicine* 314

(1986):1380–1383; D.P. Sulmasy, Physicians, Cost Control, and Ethics, *Annals of Internal Medicine*, 116 (1992):920–926.

26. R.G. Beck and J.M. Horne, Study of User Charges in Saskatchewan, 1968–1971, in *User Charges for Health Services: A Report of the Ontario Council of Health* (Toronto: Ontario Council of Health, 1979), 133–162; W.G. Manning et al., Health Insurance and the Demand for Medical Care: Evidence from a Randomized Experiment, *American Economic Review* 77 (1987):251–277; R.H. Brook et al., Does Free Care Improve Adults' Health? Results from a Randomized Controlled Trial, *New England Journal of Medicine* 309 (1983):1426–1434; E.B. Keeler et al., How Free Care Reduced Hypertension in the Health Insurance Experiment, *JAMA* 254 (1985):1926–1931.

27. D.F. Thompson, Hospital Ethics, *Cambridge Quarterly of Healthcare Ethics* 1 (1992):203–210; P.B. Hofmann, Commentary, *Cambridge Quarterly of Healthcare Ethics* 1 (1992):210–212; D.T. Ozar, Commentary, *Cambridge Quarterly of Healthcare Ethics* 1 (1992):213–215.

28. E.W. Hoy et al., Change and Growth in Managed Care, *Health Affairs* 10, no. 4 (1991):18–36; M.H. Waymack, The Ethics of Selectively Marketing the Health Maintenance Organization, *Theoretical Medicine* 11 (1990):301–309.

29. "A corporate executive is an employee of the owners of the business.... He has ... responsibility ... to conduct the business in accordance with their desires, which generally will be to make as much money as possible.... Of course, in some cases his employers may have a different objective.... A group of persons might establish a corporation for an eleemosynary purpose—for example, a hospital or a school. The manager of such a corporation will not have money profit as his objective but the rendering of certain services" (M. Friedman, The Social Responsibility of Business Is to Increase Its Profits, in *Ethics, Leadership and the Bottom Line*, edited by C.A. Nelson and R.D. Cavey [Croton-on-Hudson, N.Y.: North River Press, 1991], 246).

30. J.D. Stoeckle and S.J. Reiser, The Corporate Organization of Hospital Work: Balancing Professional and Administrative Responsibilities, *Annals of Internal Medicine* 116 (1992):407–413.

31. D. Hemenway et al., Physicians' Responses to Financial Incentives: Evidence from a For-Profit Ambulatory Care Center, *New England Journal of Medicine* 322 (1990):1059–1063; A.S. Relman, Practicing Medicine in the New Business Climate, *New England Journal of Medicine* 316 (1987):1150–1151; A.S. Relman, The Health Care Industry: Where Is It Taking Us? *New England Journal of Medicine* 325 (1991):854–859; L.S. Lewin et al., Setting the Record Straight: The Provisions of Uncompensated Care by Not-for-Profit Hospitals,

New England Journal of Medicine 318 (1988):1212–
1215; R. Pear, U.S. Says Hospitals Demand Physicians
Pay for Referrals, *The New York Times*, September 28,
1992, A1, A9; E.D. Pellegrino, Trust and Distrust in
Professional Ethics, in *Ethics, Trust, and the Profes-
sions: Philosophical and Cultural Aspects*, edited by
E.D. Pellegrino et al. (Washington, D.C.: Georgetown
University Press, 1991), 69–89; S. Braithwaite, The
Courtship of the Paying Patient, *Journal of Clinical Eth-
ics* 4, no. 2 (1993):124–133.

32. A.R. Dyer, Ethics, Advertising and the Definition of a
    Profession, *Journal of Medical Ethics* 11, no. 2
    (1985):72–78; R.W. Geist, Advertising in Medicine: A
    Physician's Perspective, *New England Journal of Medi-
    cine* 229 (1978):483–486; J.M. Reade and R.M. Ratzan,
    Yellow Professionalism: Advertising by Physicians in
    the Yellow Pages, *New England Journal of Medicine*
    316 (1987):1315–1319; A.S. Brett, The Case against
    Persuasive Advertising by Health Maintenance Organi-
    zations, *New England Journal of Medicine* 326
    (1992):1353–1357.

33. General Internal Medicine and the General Internists:
    Recognizing a National Need (position paper), *Annals
    of Internal Medicine* 117 (1992):778–779.

34. R.G. Hughes et al., Are We Mortgaging the Medical
    Profession? *New England Journal of Medicine* 325
    (1991):404–407.

35. E.J. Stemmler, The Medical School: Where Does It Go
    from Here? *Academic Medicine* 64 (April 1989):182–
    185.

36. A. Sadeghi-Nejad, Academic Physicians: Today's Di-
    nosaurs? *American Journal of Medicine* 90 (1991):371–
    373.

37. S. Braithwaite and J. Bresnahan, Access to Health Care
    II, in *Program Notes of the First Chicago Conference on
    Ethics in Healthcare Institutions* (Chicago: Chicago
    Clinical Ethics Programs, 1992).

38. For example, the Maywood Primary Care Clinic in
    Maywood, Illinois, a new venture in primary care for
    which the Cook County Department of Public Health
    provides nursing staff and which is further staffed
    through Loyola University by volunteer students and
    physicians, some of whom have continued on after go-
    ing into private practice; by volunteer clerks from the
    community; and by a volunteer dietitian from Rosary
    College and Loyola University.

39. For example, the Foster G. McGaw Hospital of Loyola
    University Chicago, located in Maywood, Illinois.

40. For example, the Evangelical Health Systems of the
    Evangelical Hospital Corporation, located in Oakbrook,
    Illinois.

41. For example, the Catholic Charities of the Archdiocese
    of Chicago, Physician Referral Service, located in Roll-
    ing Meadows, Illinois.

42. *Social Accountability Budget for Not-for-Profit
    Healthcare Organizations* (St. Louis: Catholic Health
    Association of the United States; Washington, D.C.:
    Lewin/ICF, a Division of Health and Sciences Research,
    1990), xviii.

43. Ibid., xvii. In 1987, in Utah, four hospitals lost their not-
    for-profit property tax exemption because their chari-
    table care cost less than the exemption.

44. R.Q. Marston, The Robert Wood Johnson Foundation
    Commission on Medical Education, *JAMA* 268
    (1992):1144–1145; A.R. Kovner and P.A. Hattis, Ben-
    efiting Communities, *Health Marketing Quarterly* no. 4
    (1990): 6–10; *Social Accountability Budget for Not-for-
    Profit Healthcare Organizations;* S. Braithwaite, To-
    ward Justice in Microallocation: A Fair Share of Under-
    reimbursed Services, submitted to *Proceedings of the
    Institute of Medicine of Chicago.*

45. J. Showstack et al., Health of the Public: The Academic
    Response, *JAMA* 267 (1992):2497–2502.

46. Aristotle, Nichomachean Ethics, Book V, in *The Com-
    plete Works of Aristotle*, vol. 2, edited by J. Barnes
    (Princeton, N.J.: Princeton University Press, 1984),
    1781–1797.

47. Beauchamp and Childress, *Principles of Biomedical
    Ethics*, 200–203, 371–372.

48. "What is needed is an effective mechanism for enforc-
    ing a coordinated scheme for distributing the costs of
    providing some minimal level of care for all without
    imposing unreasonable competitive disadvantages on
    particular institutions" (Brock and Buchanan, the Profit
    Motive in Medicine, 14).

49. T.L. Beauchamp, Aristotle and Virtue Theories, in
    *Philosophical Ethics: An Introduction to Moral Phi-
    losophy* (New York: McGraw-Hill, 1991), 209–252; A.
    MacIntyre, The Return to Virtue Ethics, in *The Twenty-
    Fifth Anniversary of Vatican II: A Look Back and a Look
    Ahead,* edited by R.E. Smith (Braintree, Mass.: Pope
    John XXIII Medical-Moral Research and Education
    Center, 1990), 241–249.

50. A.C. Baier, The Need for More Than Justice, *Canadian
    Journal of Philosophy*, suppl. 13 (1987):41–56; A.L.
    Carse, The "Voice of Care": Implications for Bioethical
    Education, *Journal of Medicine and Philosophy* 16
    (1991):5–28; C. Gilligan, Moral Orientation and Moral
    Development, in *Women and Moral Theory*, edited by
    E.F. Kittay and D.T. Meyers (Savage, Md.: Rowman
    and Littlefield, 1987), 19–33.

Chapter 33

Equality and Inequality in American Health Care

Charles J. Dougherty

INEQUALITIES, BORN AND MADE

Among the most profound inequalities of life is the fact of illness. Some of us are born healthy. Others are sickly from the start. Some inherit sound bodies. Others are heir to genetic mishaps and tragedies. Some enter early environments that preserve health and foster growth. Others have surroundings that undermine health and stunt growth. Some enter relationships that educate, nurture, and balance the mind. Others' early relationships deprive, abuse, and distort mental development. For some, physical and mental health at the outset make success and happiness in life distinct possibilities, even likelihoods. For others, childhood illness makes lifetime success and happiness remote possibilities, even impossibilities.

It is part of the human condition that these inequalities of health and illness continue throughout adult life. Genetics and early development account for some of the differences, perhaps a great many. Some adult variation is shaped by individual choice, the most familiar and least understood human experience. Often the distribution of health and illness cannot be accounted for at all, or accounted for only by those placeholders for explanation—accident, luck, and fate.

But in the particular human condition of contemporary America, there are social realities that help to account for a great deal of the disparities of health and illness. Chief among these conditions are socioeconomic status and race. Americans living in or near poverty and members of minority groups, and especially those who are in both categories, have uniformly worse health status than other Americans. They are far more likely not to survive infancy, to be debilitated by disease and injury, and to die prematurely.[1]

Some features of the general human condition may play a role in these marked differences. It is not impossible that genetics plays some role in the very marked racial differences in American infant mortality rates, for example, even though there are plausible social explanations.[2] Poor and minority Americans are individuals, too. They make their own choices, even if the range of options they face are shaped by their cultures and circumstances. Their lives are also en-

Source: Reprinted courtesy of the Kettering Foundation from *Freedom and Equality: Humanities Perspectives on Health Care, Crime, and the U.S. Economy,* ©1992.

tangled with the unfathomables of accident, luck, and fate; though poverty and minority membership plainly affect the rate of accidents, life's mixture of good and bad luck, and the fates of individuals.

A central role in determining states of health and illness is played by two fundamental American realities, one inherently malign, the other a positive and important value in its proper place but disabling in its presently hypertrophic expression. The first reality is racism. In spite of considerable strides in the legal arena, de facto racism remains a characteristic feature of the American scene. It skews the distribution of illness through the inequality of living and working conditions that it breeds; through the violence that has become part of the fabric of many minority neighborhoods; through the poor education, unemployment, and absence of the two-parent family that marks much of the minority experience; and, most importantly, through the barriers to health care created by lack of health insurance and primary care in the inner cities.

The value that helps to explain the health experience of many poor minority Americans is the disproportionate emphasis placed on individual freedom in American society. Individual freedom is a genuinely important value; its rebirth in formerly Communist nations is one of the triumphs of the age. But excessive individual freedom in the health care domain has left the United States alone among major industrial nations in failing to create a national health care system that ensures basic care for all citizens. Instead of the community service it is elsewhere, health care in America is largely a commodity produced and marketed for profit.[3] Instead of making access to the basics a matter of right as it is elsewhere, health care in America is generally available to those who can pay and to the insured.

These facts are linked to the value of freedom in three ways. First, American providers and payers have succeeded in their insistence on professional and marketplace freedoms—the claim of a right to treat health care as a matter of commerce. Doctors, hospitals, insurers, drug compa-

nies, and producers of medical goods all demand and have secured wide entrepreneurial freedom. Secondly, consumers have refused to relinquish the freedom to choose their own package of insurance coverage, individually and through employment groups. Specters of waiting lists, lowered quality, and bureaucratic incompetence are invoked at the mere mention of a national health care plan, in spite of the generally favorable experience with such arrangements in the industrial democracies of Europe, Canada, East Asia, and Australia. Finally, citizens have refused to pay the taxes that a system of universal coverage would entail because higher taxes mean less discretionary wealth and that in turn means less individual freedom.

Unfortunately, racism and an exaggerated emphasis on freedom work together in the United States to reinforce the inequalities of health and illness. An inevitable implication of freedom is inequality of outcomes. When the value of freedom dominates, some choose well and win; some choose poorly and lose. Some businesses prosper; some go bankrupt. When the value of freedom dominates health care, some individuals have a regular source of health care; some don't. And this inevitable implication of freedom is socially acceptable to majority Americans so long as the some who don't have access to care are largely members of racial minorities, whose lot in life apparently matters less.[4]

BUILDING EQUALITY

Both racism and an exaggerated conception of freedom can be confronted by efforts to increase equality in American life generally. For a number of reasons, greater equality is especially important in health care.

Matters of Fact

In fact, humans are fundamentally equal in several ways essential to health care. The human body, though differing in its many expressions, operates on the same general principles, knowledge of which makes health care itself possible. Every body has the same biological structure, the same range of functions, and the same general needs. Each is subject to the same set of diseases and disabilities. Bodies differ, of course, in gender and age, relative strength, and resistance to disease. But these differences are minor compared to the similarities, the equalities, of human bodies from a health care perspective.

A similar point can be made about the human mind. In daily encounters attention is drawn to the diversities of culture and personality and how they create differences in worldview and behavior. Yet from a health care perspective, these differences must be set against the context of the larger similarities of the human mind. Though circumstances and experiences shape people in distinctive ways, humans share, by and large, a common mental experience. The same set of desires—for affection, honor, and productive activity, for example—and the same list of fears—of failure, abandonment, injury, and death, for example—are part of the human scene across time and place. This is what makes great literature possible: It transcends the limits of time and place to speak with authority about the constants of human experience. Even extreme cases of mental illness—autism, depression, multiple personality disorder—are thought by mental health professionals to be exaggerated expressions of mental experiences common to all or to be dysfunctions in the brain, part of our common bodily inheritance. Thus in spite of the diversity that appears, at a more reflective level the equality of mind is a fact.

The final and most critical equality central to health care is the fact of death and anticipation of it. Alone among species, humans are capable of understanding their personal mortality and of conceiving life as a temporal trajectory with a beginning and an end. Health care deals intimately with death, fear of death, and the myriad conditions that cause death and provoke fear of it. Though the nature and circumstances of individuals' deaths vary greatly, one universal fact, one ultimately equalizing fact, remains: We each know that we must die.

In addition to these facts about human equality, there are two other considerations that argue for greater equality in health care. Both are grounded in the negative consequences of inequality—one at the personal level of health care, the other at the social level.

Equalizing Advocacy

At the personal core of health care is the doctor-patient relationship. In the Hippocratic oath, the doctor-patient relationship became the occasion for the first explicit discussion in the West of the ethical dimensions of a professional role.[5] The reason for this ethical focus is clear. The relationship between a doctor and a patient is one of marked inequality. The typical patient enters a therapeutic encounter with anxiety and often with pain and dysfunction. He or she relies on the doctor to address these forms of suffering with competence and compassion. Except for subjective experience and personal history, the doctor knows more about the patient's body and mind than the patient does—more about the present state of his or her illness and health, more about various strategies for confronting illness and preserving health, and more about likely outcomes. Because of this inequality in knowledge, doctors have tremendous authority. Even in this age of mandatory second opinions, the medical advice of a doctor with whom there is a personal relationship is irresistible to most Americans. Moreover, doctors have legal authority to control access to contemporary medical resources to a large degree. About 70 percent of all tests and treatments in American health care require a doctor's order.[6]

There are equalizing strategies to redress this imbalance in the doctor-patient relationship. On the side of the doctor, a moral duty is recognized to put the interests of patients first and to protect them from harm. This fiduciary obligation is meant to protect patients from the exploitation possible by virtue of the disparity of knowledge and power in therapeutic relationships. On the side of the patient, the requirement that providers obtain informed consent before all major tests and treatments represents a major equalizing innovation in the second half of the twentieth century. This right protects patient autonomy and checks doctors' tendency toward paternalism.[7]

But there are reasons why both doctors' fiduciary responsibility and patients' right to informed consent may fail to re-establish the human equality routinely lost in the doctor-patient relationship. Multiple new conflicts of interest have developed in the entrepreneurial climate that has pervaded American medicine for the last two decades.[8] An aggressive "let the buyer beware" attitude now competes with the traditional professional mandate to "first, do no harm" to patients. At the same time, in many care settings informed consent is an empty formality of signing legal documents. It does not reach its moral goal of ensuring that patients are genuine partners in therapy.

A third equalizing strategy can both strengthen doctors' commitment to their fiduciary responsibility and secure the moral meaning of patients' right to informed consent. That strategy is to ensure that every American has access to a primary health care provider—a family practice doctor or nurse practitioner, for example—who can serve as a personal point of entry into the health care system and as a professional advocate for the patient throughout his or her care. It is precisely here, in the widely absent primary care network, that the American health care delivery system shows one of its most conspicuous failures.[9] Millions of Americans—largely the poor and members of minority groups—have no primary health care provider. They avoid and delay needed care and rely when they must on the nearest hospital emergency room. Every inner-city emergency room is filled with patients who could have been seen for their conditions in the office of a primary care provider. Not only is office care by a primary provider likely to be more comprehensive, continuous, and personal than that available in the ER, but it is also significantly cheaper. The tertiary care provided to those without primary care is often superb from a technological perspective.

There is access through the emergency rooms of major urban teaching hospitals to some of the best medical technology in the world. But without the equalizing influence of a primary care advocate, this social arrangement yields comparatively poor outcomes overall and offers therapeutic encounters that many of the least well off Americans find deeply alienating.[10]

National Self-Interest

The social consideration that underscores the need for greater equality in the health care system is national self-interest. Great Britain's history of health care reform is illustrative by way of counterexample. Britain began a national health insurance program in 1911 in order to maintain a healthier and more productive workforce and army. Lloyd George crystallized the issue: "You can not maintain an A-1 empire with a C-3 population."[11] During World War II, when Britain faced the bleakest of prospects, a national health service was promised as a way of defining a community of aspiration in the midst of a national calamity.[12] In both cases, equalizing health care reforms were rooted in national self-interest.

For its own national interest, the United States needs a workforce that can produce the wealth needed to support an affluent culture. The United States also needs a health care financing system that allows the nation to compete effectively with other economies around the world. But there are many indications that the present health care system's inequalities are working against achievement of these two requisites of a robust society.

By all estimations the future workforce of the United States will be composed increasingly of minority Americans. Yet these are just the individuals that have the hardest time accessing the health care system appropriately. They are disproportionately represented among the uninsured and underinsured.[13] Moreover, they have worse health status not only in terms of infant mortality and average lifespan but also in terms of morbidity. They experience, for example, more bed disability days, more chronic illnesses, and a self-reported health status lower than the nonpoor majority population.[14] As U.S. industry comes to be more and more dependent on minority Americans, the workforce will also be less and less healthy. This trend will make the United States less competitive with other advanced democracies whose working people are all covered by some form of national health care plan.

In addition to this general cost of inequality in the health care arena, there are other specific burdens produced by the way Americans finance and deliver care. First, it is becoming clear that one of the factors accounting for the emergence of costly and demoralizing patterns of welfare dependency over the last 20 years is lack of universal health coverage.[15] A single mother contemplating leaving welfare to return to work, for example, must weigh not only the prospect of netting less money from the private sector than from welfare. She must also weigh the prospect of losing health insurance for herself and her children since welfare and Medicaid eligibility are linked in most states and many low-wage jobs, especially in the small business sector, offer no health insurance fringe benefits. Illness or likelihood of illness on the part of parent or children becomes an almost unassailable argument for staying on welfare.

Second, one of the hallmarks of a successful modern service economy is the ability to accommodate rapid change, to bring new kinds of services and products into the market quickly. This in turn requires a mobile workforce, one filled with individuals willing to change jobs with some frequency over a working lifetime. But the American choice to link health insurance status to employment—rather than to citizenship or residency, for example—is beginning to work against American business by creating structural barriers to job mobility.[16] Competition in the private health insurance industry has generated a socially perverse incentive: the need to avoid covering those who are ill or who are at high risk of becoming ill. Therefore many insurers have adopted pre-existing illness exclusions for new employees. These exclusions from coverage in

turn provide a strong disincentive against changing jobs for working people who have had serious illnesses themselves or in their families. A new job may mean the loss of insurance coverage for just the condition that will most likely require treatment. This self-destructive consequence of the health insurance system is taking its toll not only on the poor and minorities. Many working Americans of all descriptions simply cannot afford to change jobs.

Finally, the inequalities in the U.S. health care system have made the problem of escalating health care costs virtually intractable. In spite of the fact that millions are uninsured and underinsured and in spite of mediocre achievement on key vital statistics, the United States spends more on health care than any other nation in the world—more in absolute dollars, more per capita, and more as a percentage of GNP. The U.S. Department of Commerce projects that the nation will devote 14 percent of GNP to health care in 1992.[17] There is a deep irony here. American stress on freedom and suspicion of government has prevented development of a national health care program. But comparative international experience suggests that the way to contain overall health care costs is by global governmental budgeting through a national health care program. Refusal to establish such a program has meant that American health care has become more and more a corporate enterprise, a matter of business. But this has fed the cost spiral and hurt business generally. Costly measures to protect and increase market shares of insured patients have been implemented by hospitals, nursing homes, and doctors' groups. Health care advertising has exploded in the last decade, for example, creating an entirely new set of costs wholly unrelated to the care of patients. While inner-city and rural hospitals and clinics have closed, overcapacity has been constructed in America's suburbs, duplicating expensive technology and feeding patterns of overutilization. In the absence of the discipline of an overall budget, expensive and intrusive administrative measures have been relied on to "micromanage" the behavior of providers. As a result many U.S. businesses are fighting unman-ageable cost increases in their employee benefits packages. At the same time, these businesses are competing against foreign companies whose governments have national health care programs that allow them to contain health care costs bet-ter and to spread them more equally than in the United States.[18]

Greater equality is therefore an appropriate prescription for some of what ails American health care. It fits with the broader equalities of human experience, equalities touched intimately by health care. It can also help to address the negative consequences of inequality in thera-peutic relationships and some of the system's failures that most jeopardize the nation's self-interest.

JUSTICE, PRUDENCE, AND EQUALITY

How much equality is appropriate for the American health care system? It is impossible to achieve equality in health status or in the out-come of health care interventions since the causes of health and illness are so varied and in-dividual circumstances so complex. But greater equality in access to health care is a reasonable goal.

Strict Equality of Treatment

The simplest, most egalitarian formulation for health care access is to mandate the same treat-ment for all conditions that are substantially similar. The obvious way to embody this for-mula in a system of care is through construction of a national health service that provides equal treatment to all, treating everyone the same who has the same medical condition, without regard to other considerations such as wealth or race.

But there is a serious value problem with the strict equality of such a national health service. While the exaggerated expression of freedom deserves rejection, there is a legitimate and im-portant range to this value. Recognition of the importance of freedom entails the acceptance of

some measure of inequality. If freedom is al-lowed in the health care system, then some simi-lar conditions will be treated differently. This can occur because some have greater wealth to purchase more or better care and insurance for it, or because those with even moderate wealth pri-oritize the purchase of health care and insurance higher than their neighbors do. It would cer-tainly be curious, if not wrong, were Americans permitted the inequalities of freedom every-where in the economy except in health care. Moreover, the practical measures that would be necessary to prevent Americans from buying services outside an egalitarian national health service would be Draconian.

Thus achievement of more equality in health care is an important goal, but strict equality of status and outcome is unattainable and strict equality of treatment undesirable. How much equality then is an appropriate goal for Ameri-can health care? A response to this question can be focused around two considerations: the amount of equality that is required by justice and the amount of equality that is politically prudent.

Justice and the Social Contract

A theory of social or distributive justice pro-vides an account of the minimal arrangements required by morality. Alternately put, a theory of justice provides a framework for articulating the social rights of individuals, in this case, the health care that individuals deserve as a matter of right.

There are many competing accounts of social or distributive justice, but one of the most per-suasive is the social contract theory. In its vari-ous forms, this theory can be found in the writ-ings of Plato and on the pages of contemporary writing in philosophy and jurisprudence.[19] The core insight of the tradition is that justice is grounded in an implicit contract or promise indi-viduals make to one another by virtue of living together in society. Since no such promise has ever been made explicitly by all members of any society, the central conceptual challenge of social contract theory has been to give an intelligible interpretation to the notion of a morally binding promise never actually made.

One contemporary version of social contract theory, that of John Rawls, holds that the character of the social contract can be defined by imagining what would be promised by individuals about to enter a new society together if those original people were conceived to be reasonable and free of biases.[20] These hypothetical people can be conceived to be reasonable by assuming that they are able to understand what is in their own interest generally and able to select appropriate means to attain it. They can be conceived to be free of biases by assuming they are denied knowledge of their own particular interests, the knowledge that draws real people toward selfishness.

A Supernatural Lottery

The mechanics of this Rawlsian scheme are complex, but the main insight can be clarified through the use of a simple if fanciful scenario. Imagine that God, an all-powerful being, calls together a group of angels, that is, a group of intelligent spiritual beings without bodies. Because the angels have no bodies, they are not differentiated by gender, race, or ethnicity. There are no stronger or weaker angels, no healthier or sicker, no older or younger. Without bodies the angels also have no differing social and economic circumstances; angels are not richer or poorer. God informs the assembled angels that they will all become humans and be placed on earth to live together. Each will be given a specific human body in a random process God calls the "natural lottery." Thus they will be assigned genders and separated into different racial and ethnic groups by lot. The bodies they receive in the natural lottery will make some of them strong, others weak; some healthy, some sick and dying; some young, some old. Because their bodies will be situated in differing social and economic circumstances, some angels will be

wealthy and well placed, others poor and marginalized.

But God is also all-merciful. Before the natural lottery begins, the angels are allowed to agree among themselves on the social arrangements that will structure their human lives together. God assures them that whatever social arrangements they agree to will be made binding elements of justice on earth. In essence, God creates the conditions for a social contract: reasonable and nonbiased agents agreeing on the kind of society they will accept.

How would angels deliberate about society in anticipation of the natural lottery? Not knowing their gender, race, or ethnic group, they will reject sexism, racism, and discrimination. Each angel knows that he or she has a chance of suffering considerably under such arrangements. Similarly they will reject differential treatment of the young and old, strong and weak, rich and poor whenever those differences are likely to make their lot in life worse than it otherwise would be. On the other hand, they will allow differences that work to everyone's advantage regardless of what lot he or she draws. The negotiating strategy each angel will adopt is straightforward: Agree only to social arrangements that will make my future human life the best life it can be, even if my draw in the natural lottery gives me one of the worst lives.

When the angels reach the health care question, their strategy will remain the same. Knowing the health-related inequalities of human life, they realize that they may be among those who have severe medical needs. Moreover, they know that virtually all people need health care sometime. Consequently, they will insist on universal access to health care. Unless all are covered, each risks being among those who are left out. Presuming that they also know that a society's medical demands can become financially endless, they will agree to put some limits on the care to which all have a right. No society can afford to provide all health care services to everyone, as this would be incompatible with the enjoyment of other economic goods. Thus they will agree that everyone should be guaranteed a right to a basic package of health care. They will not agree to providing everything that health care might offer, but they will agree to establishing a decent minimal level of care for all.

What is the ethical implication of this fanciful tale? It shows that when we imagine ourselves to be reasonable and free of biases we see that the social contract must include a health care system that covers everyone for a basic package of care. But justice is a normative concept. It requires that we be as reasonable and as free of biases as possible. Therefore justice requires a health care system equal enough to provide everyone with the basics.

This scenario also illustrates an important point about moral psychology. Real lives are lived after the natural lottery, so to speak. We each know our own situation. By definition, most of us are members of the majority. Most Americans are white and nonpoor. Most of us are insured for a basic package of health care. Knowledge of their own situations thus blinds the majority of Americans to the injustice worked by the inequalities of the present health system. But when a hypothetical situation creates the possibility that anyone may be among the millions of uninsured and underserved Americans, the injustice of the situation becomes transparent. Thus the thought experiment of a supernatural lottery accomplishes a movement fundamental to moral psychology. It requires that present social arrangements be assessed from others' points of view. It accomplishes the reciprocity of perspective central to the Golden Rule. It thereby describes the moral minimum that justice demands.

Playing, Paying, and National Health Insurance

This requirement of justice could be satisfied by any number of different health care arrangements. Since this is a minimal ethical requirement, the easiest way for Americans to satisfy it would be to make the fewest necessary changes in the present U.S. health care system. Most nonelderly Americans now receive their health care coverage as a fringe benefit through their employment. A program already exists—Medicaid—that is designed to provide financial assistance to (some of) those who are not otherwise insured and cannot pay for their own health care. Thus the easiest practical way to satisfy the moral demands of justice is by spreading employment-based coverage as far as possible and then covering those who remain uncovered by an expanded Medicaid program. Generally speaking, this is the "play-or-pay" approach to health care reform: Mandate that all employers cover all their employees with health insurance or pay a tax (generally about 7 percent of payroll) into a pool to fund government coverage in an expanded Medicaid program.[21]

If successful, play-or-pay would erase the extreme inequality created by a system that allows millions to go completely uncovered and to face financial barriers to care. It would, however, leave in place the inequalities of a clearly two-tiered health care system of relatively comprehensive coverage for those insured at work (though wide variations may be expected) and a minimal package of basic coverage for those in the government program.

Play-or-pay would achieve moral decency. But just as it is often prudent for individuals to go beyond what is required by respect for another's rights, it can also be prudent for a society to do more than what justice demands. Considerations of justice define the ethical floor below which society should not fall, but a successful social structure needs more than a floor. Another reform alternative goes further than play-or-pay in the direction of equality and can contribute to building a more successful American society: a national health insurance program with a single payer, funded by progressive taxation and designed to cover the vast majority of Americans.[22] Although this direction for reform creates more equality than justice alone demands, there are several prudential considerations that make this alternative preferable to play-or-pay.

First, there are technical problems with play-or-pay that are avoided by national health insurance. Imposition on small businesses of an insurance mandate (play) or a new tax (pay) will create a severe economic burden that will drive many businesses out of business. This will create more unemployment, swelling the numbers of those dependent on Medicaid and triggering an increase in the tax rate imposed under the pay option. At the same time, many large businesses that have been playing (insuring their employees) may opt to pay the tax instead, either because it is cheaper or because it frees them from the labor friction produced by the management of health care benefits. This will also put more Americans into the Medicaid program and lead to additional pressure on the pay option tax rate.

This double movement of small and large businesses to the pay side of play-or-pay may indirectly create a form of national health insurance for many, perhaps most, Americans. But there will be an important difference. If the United States "backs into" national health insurance this way, the insurance pool that results from the expanding pay option of play-or-pay will not be supported financially by companies that continue to play. These will include companies with insurance costs lower than the tax mandated under the pay option—generally companies with younger, healthier, low-risk workforces. But this will entail a system with private insurance for the cheap to insure, public insurance for the expensive to insure. This is a policy formula bound to create financial disaster for the public program.

Play-or-pay also holds little promise for serious cost control. Most specific play-or-pay proposals try to restrain spending with measures intended to micromanage providers' behavior, a strategy that has failed over the last decade. The one approach with an international track record of restraining costs is global budgeting, just what a national health insurance program would have to do.

A play-or-pay arrangement would not of itself be capable of addressing the main evidence of de facto racism in the American system: the evacuation of health care providers and resources from the minority-dominated inner cities. By contrast, a national health insurance program would have available many strategies to attract health care providers and resources to these underserved populations and help ensure that they have the primary care advocates they need. For example, a national health insurance program could enhance fee-for-service payments to providers in designated low-income areas or pay risk-adjusted capitated rates to organized provider networks to draw services to populations with greater needs.

Serious political problems will result from the two-tiered structure of the play-or-pay approach. Admittedly, even a national health insurance program would leave room for a second tier. Americans could buy health care services outside the national package because such freedom is an important value and the practical implications of forbidding it are too ominous. But the two tiers of a national health insurance program would be fundamentally different than those generated by play-or-pay. Under a national health insurance program, disincentives could be put in place (no tax benefits, for example) to keep individual purchases of noncovered services to a minimum. When new services are demanded by a large segment of the public, these services could be folded into the national program. Thus recourse to care outside the national plan could be made a marginal activity, perhaps accounting for less than 10 percent of total health care spending. By contrast, play-or-pay will create a substantial two-tiered system. Depending on how many employers elect the pay option, the percentage covered under the Medicaid tier might range from 20 percent to more than half the population. Moreover, while the small second tier outside a national health insurance program would likely be composed of very wealthy Americans, the substantial second tier of play-or-pay would be composed disproportionately of poor and minority Americans.

The significance of this speculation about the size and character of a second tier of health care is political: Programs for the poor tend to become poor programs, underfunded and low in quality. On the other hand, if the middle class is served by a national health insurance program, it will be adequately funded and will sustain high quality. This point is clear in the history and present condition of Medicare, the program for all elderly Americans, and Medicaid, the program for the poor. Medicare, in spite of its many problems, works effectively and is defended vigorously by politicians. Medicaid is a public policy disaster and a political orphan.

Equality and Community

This observation about politics leads to the last prudential consideration that supports establishment of greater equality in health care than justice alone requires. Politics is not only about the power to create programs and to ensure that they are adequately funded and well run. It is also about symbols. Politics is one of the arenas in which Americans symbolize the balance the nation strikes between self-interested and other-regarding motives, between the forces of individualism and those of the common good. It is where the solidarity of citizens is fragmented or reinforced. In politics, the national identity is reshaped through the public assignment of priorities to the competing values of freedom and equality.

Different arguments can be made about how much emphasis these opposing forces should be given in various endeavors of public and private life. But whatever balance is struck elsewhere, in health care there should be more emphasis on other-regarding motives, more stress on the common good, greater social solidarity, and a higher priority on equality. In health care, life and death and the quality of the experience in between are literally at stake. It is an arena in which altruistic care for those in need is not exceptional behavior but the rule. In health care, the well-being of the public is an explicit responsibility. Through health care, serious efforts are made to correct some of the worst inequalities of the natural lottery and to adjust more favorably the unfathomables of accident, luck, and fate. Because of these features, the health care policies of a nation can define a sense of community capable of transcending divisions of race and socioeconomic status. Through the health care system, it is possible to assert in the most concrete of terms that every American life is worthy, that every American is equally valuable.

Because of America's racism and exaggerated emphasis on the value of freedom, the nation stands in need of a renewed sense of community. Health care is a symbolically important place to strive for it. Commitment to greater equality than justice itself requires through construction of a national health insurance program is one way to attain it. At this time in the nation's life, it may be one of the few practical opportunities available for the reconstruction of a sense of American community.

NOTES

1. C.J. Dougherty, *American Health Care: Realities, Rights, and Reforms* (New York: Oxford University Press, 1988), 3–19.

2. P. Wise and D. Pursley, Infant Mortality as a Social Mirror, *New England Journal of Medicine* 326 (1992): 1558–1559.

3. C.J. Dougherty, The Cost of Commercial Medicine, *Theoretical Medicine* 11 (1990):275–286.

4. On the racial dimensions of national health policy, see J. Califano, The Challenge to the Health Care System, in *Health Care for the Poor and Elderly: Meeting the Challenge*, edited by D. Yaggy (Durham, N.C.: Duke University Press, 1984), 45–57. On racism and medical

education, see J. Holloman, Jr., Access to Health Care, in *Securing Access to Health Care*, vol. 2, President's Commission for the Study of Ethical Problems in Medicine and Biomedical and Behavioral Research (Washington, D.C.: U.S. Government Printing Office, 1983), 79–106.

5. Hippocrates, *Hippocratic Writings*, edited by G.E.R. Lloyd (New York: Penguin, 1986).

6. A. Relman, The New Medical-Industrial Complex, *New England Journal of Medicine* 303 (1980):963–965.

7. T. Beauchamp and J. Childress, *Principles of Biomedical Ethics*, 3rd ed. (New York: Oxford University Press, 1991), 307–365.

8. R.M. Green, Medical Joint-Venturing: An Ethical Perspective, *Hastings Center Report* (1990):22–26.

9. G. Moore, Let's Provide Primary Care to All Americans—Now! *JAMA* 265 (1991):2108–2109.

10. D. Brooks et al., Medical Apartheid, *JAMA* 266 (1991):2447–2449.

11. P. Starr, *The Social Transformation of American Medicine* (New York: Basic Books, 1982), 239.

12. H. Aaron and W. Schwartz, *The Painful Prescription* (Washington, D.C.: Brookings Institution, 1984), 13.

13. Dougherty, *American Health Care*, 11–12; T. Bodenheimer, Underinsurance in America, *New England Journal of Medicine* 327 (1992):274–277.

14. American Medical Association, Council on Ethical and Judicial Affairs, Black-White Disparities in Health Care, *JAMA* 263 (1990):2344–2346; Dougherty, *American Health Care*, 4–8.

15. E. Eckholm, Solutions on Welfare: They All Cost Money, *New York Times*, July 26, 1992, 1ff.

16. Bodenheimer, Underinsurance in America, 275.

17. U.S. Department of Commerce, *U.S. Industrial Outlook, 1992*, GPO #S/N 003-009-005-97-3, (Washington, D.C.: U.S. Department of Commerce, 1992).

18. U.S. General Accounting Office, *Health Care Spending Control: France, Germany, and Japan*, GAO/HRD-92-9, (Washington, D.C.: U.S. General Accounting Office, 1991); A. McGuire et al., *Providing Health Care: The Economics of Alternative Systems of Finance and Delivery* (New York: Oxford University Press, 1991).

19. Plato, *Crito*, in *Plato: The Collected Works,* edited by E. Hamilton and H. Cairns (Princeton, N.J.: Princeton University Press, 1969), 35–39; see also, for example, P. McCormick, *Social Contract and Political Obligation* (New York: Garland, 1987).

20. J. Rawls, *A Theory of Justice* (Cambridge, Mass.: Harvard University Press, 1971).

21. Play-or-pay proposals include John D. Rockefeller IV, The Pepper Commission Report on Comprehensive Health Care, *New England Journal of Medicine* 323 (1990):1005–1007; Excellent Health Care for All Americans and at Reasonable Cost, in *Report of the National Leadership Coalition on Health Care Reform* (Washington, D.C.: National Leadership Coalition on Health Care Reform, 1991).

22. On national health insurance, see D. Himmelstein and S. Woolhandler, A National Health Program for the United States: A Physicians' Proposal, *New England Journal of Medicine* 320 (1989):102–108; Catholic Health Association, *Setting Relationships Right: A Working Proposal for Systemic Healthcare Reform* (St. Louis: Catholic Health Association, 1992); E.R. Brown, Health USA: A National Health Care Program for the United States, *JAMA* 267 (1992):552–558; C.J. Dougherty, An Axiology for National Health Insurance, *Law, Medicine and Health Care,* Spring-Summer, 1992, 82–91.

Chapter 34

Tarasoff and the Moral Duty To Protect the Vulnerable

John W. Douard and William J. Winslade

We begin this chapter by considering whether any moral duties arise out of our special relationships with other persons. We argue that we sometimes incur moral obligations to aid certain persons who are dependent on and vulnerable to us. In some situations, our simple obligations are obvious, but in others our complex duties conflict. Moral maturity is gained in part through reflection about moral conflicts.

In the second section of this chapter, we examine some key moral conflicts embedded in, but obscured by, the legal controversy engendered by the *Tarasoff* case. We try to show that the California Supreme Court was sensitive to underlying moral issues and sought to resolve them by the *Tarasoff* rule.

However, the limited guidance of common-law rules, even morally sensitive and sensible ones, are illustrated by the *Tarasoff* rule. We argue in the third section of this chapter that the moral issues posed by the *Tarasoff* facts demand a legislative, rather than a judicial, resolution.

SPECIAL RELATIONSHIPS AND SPECIAL DUTIES

One distinction often drawn by moral philosophers is this: There are obligations and duties that flow from our special relationships to particular others, and obligations and duties that flow from our membership in the moral community of persons as a whole. Most philosophers will agree that some such distinction is necessary to capture the moral experience, including some of the moral conflicts, of people who live in modern Western societies. But beyond this agreement, there is a great deal of disagreement over the relative strength of special and general obligations.

This is not merely a sterile academic dispute. Most of us are inclined to treat people with whom we are in special relationships according to special rules. Indeed, we are apt to judge deviations from what might be called "moral partiality" as deviations from an important social norm—fidelity to those to whom we are most closely bound by ties of affection and mutuality. Hume expressed a widely held view when he noted that

> in the original frame of our mind, our strongest attention is confined to ourselves; our next is extended to our rela-

Source: Reprinted from *Review of Clinical Psychiatry and the Law,* Vol. 1, by R.I. Simon, ed., pp. 163–176, with permission of American Psychiatric Press, Inc., © 1990.

tions and acquaintance; and 'tis only the weakest which reaches to strangers and indifferent persons. This partiality, then, and unequal affection . . . makes us regard any remarkable transgression of such a degree of partiality, either by too great an enlargement, or contraction of the affections, as vicious and immoral.[1]

Too much affection for ourselves and too much affection for strangers, both at the expense of our family and friends, seem to many people as equally morally myopic.

This eminently reasonable sensibility, however, is sometimes transformed into something very different, about which there is a great deal of disagreement. It is sometimes held, and not just by philosophers, that special obligations *always* override general social obligations when there is conflict. And perhaps, what is even more disturbing, giving priority to special obligations can exhaust our sense of duty altogether. As Goodin put this point,

> It is our *particular obligations* that all too often blind us to our social responsibilities. Whatever claim the world at large may have upon us, it inevitably takes second place behind the claims of particular others; our families, friends, colleagues, clients, compatriots, and so on. These rights, duties, and obligations arising out of those special relationships always seem to take priority. Duty, even more than charity, begins at home. Strangers ordinarily get, and are ordinarily thought to deserve, only what (if anything) is left over.[2]

It does indeed seem that we are "all too often blind" to our larger social responsibilities. But we sometimes express moral disapproval of the person who refuses to warn, protect, or otherwise come to the aid of another to whom he or she is not specially related and who is clearly at risk of being harmed. We praise as heroes people who, at great risk to themselves, step in to protect a stranger, e.g., a child in danger. And we feel moral outrage when someone refuses to warn or protect an innocent stranger from harm

when the person who refuses is not him- or herself at risk.

The phrase "I don't want to get involved" became a cause of concern to journalists and social critics in 1962, when Kitty Genovese was attacked in an alley and eyewitnesses did not come to her aid or even call the police. On the face of it, this would seem to be the sort of situation about which Goodin is warning us; presumably the people who did not aid Kitty Genovese would have acted differently if she had been a close relative or friend. With no bonds of affection or mutuality, is there a moral imperative that the witnesses violated and that enjoys relatively widespread acceptance? Although the witnesses themselves might be inclined to justify their action (or inaction) by claiming there is no such imperative, the fact that many people found that behavior unacceptable suggests that mutual aid is at least taken to be a social ideal. We may not want it embodied in a legal prescription, but it is an ideal nonetheless.

From another point of view, however, it would appear that many people in our society consider it their right *not* to warn, protect, or otherwise provide aid to others, except to those to whom they are specially bound. Liberty is also undeniably a social ideal, and liberty is often construed as either (1) freedom from interference by others or (2) freedom to choose a course of action independently of the needs and desires of unrelated others. The law reflects both of these negative conceptions of liberty by placing constraints on justified interference and refraining from making mutual aid at an individual level a legal duty. One might say that mutual aid is a matter of voluntary charity or benevolence. Benevolence, especially toward strangers, is often taken to be supererogatory, that is, praiseworthy but above and beyond the call of duty. From this point of view, one can criticize the witnesses to Kitty Genovese's plight, not because they had a duty to warn or protect her, but because they failed to act from a praiseworthy disposition of benevolence.

We believe there is a moral duty, generally acknowledged in our society, to warn or protect others that rests on a claim that others have on us when they are *dependent* on and *vulnerable* to us. In certain situations, if our inaction is likely to result in a significant amount of harm to others, we may be obligated to act.

That duty emerges most forcefully, perhaps, in situations in which people are related to one another by certain filial or fiduciary bonds. Moral theories that give pre-eminence to impartiality, such as utilitarianism or social contract theory, are hard pressed to ground the very strong sense of duty people have to those who are dependent on them. On utilitarian grounds, for example, there should be no special relationships at all, from a moral point of view—every person's utility should count as no more and no less than every other person's utility. But this view is in flagrant violation of ordinary moral canons, as even utilitarians, such as Henry Sidgwick, are quick to point out: "Common sense . . . seems . . . to regard it as immediately certain . . . that we owe special duties of kindness to those who stand in special relations to us."[3]

The fact of the matter is that people who stand in special relations to us are often, as a result of those relationships, specially dependent on us. Certainly our children, friends, and professional clients have a compelling claim on us, not because they are voluntarily related to us, as some philosophers would have it, but because we are their primary source of help when they need it. Such mutual dependencies may not always be the result of voluntary commitments, but even when they are, e.g., in contractual associations, their morally important feature is that they are contexts in which people are vulnerable to one another. The moral force of a promise or contract is moot when the parties to the promise or contract have absolutely equal standing. According to the social contract tradition of political theory, the raison d'être of a contract is to protect contracting parties from domination. Protection from harm is an even more salient feature of filial relationships than for contractual relationships.

But, in a sense, all human association, including civil association itself, leaves people exposed to the willingness of others to aid and protect in order to prevent serious harm (when there are no strong overriding considerations—a point to which we will return later). Only the strongest form of egoism—according to which only an agent's own interests ought morally to be of any concern to him or her—will deny that all members of a society have some responsibilities to some people in some circumstances. But the clearest cases of such responsibilities—responsibilities to particular people with whom an agent has a special relationship—are cases in which one agent can intervene to prevent a significant harm to another. As we have suggested above, such responsibilities are fixed by virtue of the interdependencies characteristic of such relationships. Now, because all social relationships involve interdependence to some extent, it is always possible that situations can arise in which one person depends on another for aid, even among strangers. Clearly, someone who is in a position to warn a blind man that he is about to step into a stream of traffic has an obligation to do so. The person in danger is vulnerable not just to the drivers of the oncoming cars, but also to witnesses in a position to warn. In a sense, the man's vulnerability establishes a special relationship to certain other agents.

Both the situation of Kitty Genovese and that of the blind man are clear-cut cases because they involve, by hypothesis, no conflicting obligations that might pull in contrary directions. However, the circumstances that make up our lives together are usually more complex. We have multiple responsibilities that often result in conflicting obligations and, indeed, tragic conflicts at that. A stable social order, to some degree, requires institutional methods for relieving us of some of our social responsibilities. For instance, a just social order will distribute primary goods to citizens who need them. A secure social order will designate agencies, such as fire and police departments, that bear a special responsibility to protect its members. Neighbors are not always prepared adequately, or even reliably concerned enough, to help their neighbors; in many modern societies, the distribution of social responsibilities becomes a responsibility of good society. Nonetheless, individuals are still very often, as a result of either voluntary commitments or unforeseeable circumstances, called on to satisfy conflicting obligations.

But even in situations of moral conflict, there are cases over which there would be little disagreement from any moral point of view (excluding the pure egoist). A physician on the way to meet friends for dinner is morally required to forgo the promise made to the friends if witness to an accident and no other physician is present at the scene. Nor is that obligation only a result of the physician's professional role (although it is that, as well). Anyone who is specially placed to aid someone in dire trouble has a prima facie responsibility to do so, because the person in need is vulnerable to the witness. To put this point another way, we are vulnerable to those who are in a special position to help us when we are in serious danger, because if they do not exercise their capacity to come to our aid, we may suffer harm. The only morally legitimate excuse not to provide aid in such circumstances is that someone else may thereby be subjected to even more serious harm (in the limit, that may be oneself).

We suggest that it is an important part of learning how to live well in civil association to (1) properly order one's conflicting responsibilities and (2) develop the capacity to make correct judgments about how to act relative to that ordering in specific, and often unforeseen, circumstances. We are not born with these capacities, and their proper development takes time, thoughtfulness, experience, moral education, and a willingness to engage in moral inquiry. This conception of moral reasoning was best expressed by Dewey and Tufts:

> The struggle is not between a good which is clear [to a person] and something else which attracts him but which he knows to be wrong. It is between values each of which is an undoubted good in its place but which now get in each other's way. He is forced to reflect in order to come to a decision. Moral theory is a generalized exten-

sion of the kind of thinking in which he now engages.[4]

VULNERABILITY AND THE RIGHT TO EQUALITY

In 1976, the California Supreme Court issued the now familiar *Tarasoff* principle:

> When a psychotherapist determines, or pursuant to the standards of his profession should determine, that his patient presents a serious danger of violence to another, he incurs an obligation to use reasonable care to protect the intended victim against such danger. The discharge of such duty, depending on the nature of the case, may call for the therapist to warn the intended victim or others likely to apprise the victim of the danger, to notify the police, or to take whatever other steps are reasonably necessary under the circumstances.[5]

The *Tarasoff* principle has been controversial, especially in the psychotherapeutic community, since its formulation, and the controversy has continued for more than a decade. We believe that fundamental questions about the moral basis of a general duty to warn/protect others, and the moral status of special relationships with respect to this general duty, have not been adequately addressed.

We argue that the *Tarasoff* decision can be grounded in the moral duty to protect the vulnerable, which cannot be overridden merely by the principle of confidentiality. The principle of confidentiality arises out of certain contractual arrangements, which may be suspended when they significantly increase the vulnerability of persons affected by such arrangements. This is because, in certain circumstances, people who are particularly vulnerable are owed protection, not out of benevolence, but on the basis of their right to equality of concern and respect. In a word, the duty to protect is a matter of justice and is to that extent an issue of political morality.

In a previous discussion, one of us (W.J.W.) argued that

one can sympathize with the court in its efforts to arrive at results and articulate rules that do justice to the vast array of competing interests. But some human problems subjected to the legal process produce at best only enigmatic justice that, even if it is not blind, is ambiguous, obscure, and perplexing.[6]

The interests at stake in the types of situations to which the *Tarasoff* principle may be thought to apply are those of the potential victim of a violent patient, the patient, the patient's psychotherapist, the therapeutic community, and the society as a whole. The task of the California Supreme Court was to strike the right balance among these interests and to formulate a principle that would adjudicate them fairly. What this amounts to in practice is establishing the legal scope of the various rights, that is, the legally protected interests.

A great deal has already been written about the social context in which the court arrived at its decision, so we will not say much about that context here. It is important to keep in mind, however, two elements of that context that exerted pressure on the court in two different directions. On the one hand, the patients' rights movement and the libertarian attacks on the medical model of mental illness had been effective in constraining the procedure for the involuntary commitment of psychiatric patients judged by their therapists to be dangerous. On the other hand, there was (and is) a great deal of anxiety in society at large about law and order, and people were (and are) understandably frightened at the prospect of potentially homicidal individuals being outside the reach of institutional control. It was against this background that the court made its decision.

What is important about this background for our purposes is that both the claim that patients have civil rights and the claim that citizens have a right to protection from violence are made by, or on behalf of, people who perceive themselves to be vulnerable. In general, recognition of rights will help protect the vulnerable from unjust treatment. We shall argue later that an analysis of the *Tarasoff* principle must have at its center the responsibility social institutions have toward those who are vulnerable. And because we are all vulnerable, we all have an interest in making sure that responsibility is discharged.

First, however, we need to provide a somewhat more detailed analysis of what it means to say that rights protect the vulnerable from injustice. It has become fairly common over the last 20 years for a group or individual to claim a *right* to a good (e.g., liberty) when all that can be justified is an *interest* of some degree of strength in obtaining that good. This focus of political morality on rights was no doubt stimulated by the civil rights movement of the 1950s and 1960s. But what is often lost from view in rights-centered ethical theories is that the fundamental political right, which is at the heart of the civil rights movement, is the right to equality. As Dworkin argued, a just political order "must not only treat people with concern and respect, but with equal concern and respect. It must not distribute goods and opportunities unequally on the ground that some citizens are entitled to more because they are worthy of more concern."[7] (A somewhat more cynical view would be that for governments to be perceived as just, they must be perceived to be so arranged as to ensure equal concern and respect.)[8] All other rights presuppose the right to equality in this sense. The fundamental reason for the priority of a right to equality (and not, we should point out, equality of rights) is, of course, that it is a necessary condition of justice. (Some say that justice is the "first virtue" of a social order.)[9]

When citizens of a social order are vulnerable either to the state or to other citizens, the right to protection from those on whom they are dependent is underwritten by the right to equality of concern and respect. When people are vulnerable or at risk, they are in that respect constrained from fully exercising their capabilities. It is for this reason that a right to health care is often claimed; to be sick is to be especially vulnerable to the vicissitudes of life, and in a just society all should have equal access to the care they need.

People are vulnerable in different ways and to different degrees. The mentally ill are vulnerable, and, depending on the nature of their illness, they may be severely constrained in realizing their life plans (or even having a reasonable life plan). Furthermore, they experience suffering, anxiety, and alienation. On the basis of their right to equal concern and respect alone, they have a right to the best treatment society can afford to offer.

Because confidentiality is a cornerstone of psychotherapy, it is sometimes claimed to be a right. But that is not the case if what is meant is a fundamental political right. It is certainly in the interest of patients that the information they divulge to their therapists be kept confidential. The principle of confidentiality serves their right to equality, because it protects them from abuses to which they are vulnerable and is clinically important to successful therapy.

But the principle of confidentiality arises in the context of therapy as the result of an implicit (or explicit) contract between therapist and patient. The vulnerability that is the result of information divulged in therapy entitles patients only to as much confidentiality as is reasonable and responsible for therapists to promise as part of their side of the bargain. According to Menninger, although

> it is true that the physician has loyalty to his patient, . . . [n]o patient has a right to exploit the confidential relationship offered by the physician *a particeps criminus*. The physician cannot condone moral and legal irresponsibility on the part of the patient, and to do so may be actually harmful to the patient.[10]

Even before the *Tarasoff* decision, psychotherapists were expected to accept such constraints on the scope of confidentiality. If there is good reason to believe a patient intends to harm him- or herself or a third party, and he or she cannot be involuntarily committed, the limited entitlements that arise from a promise are suspended and the therapist has a moral duty to protect.

This is not merely a legal point, and before *Tarasoff* there was no legal duty to protect. But there was a moral duty. If a third party is in danger of being harmed, the person is vulnerable, and that vulnerability is increased by lack of information about the danger. The person's right to equal concern and respect entitles him or her to that information, and the therapist, as holder of the information, has a moral obligation to provide it.

The contention of the California court, however, is that therapeutic discretion alone cannot protect third parties in *Tarasoff*-like cases. Society has a responsibility to provide a legal framework that will establish incentives intended to motivate psychotherapists to protect potential victims of their violent patients' plans. The court based its decision partly on an article by Fleming and Maximov in which they argued,

> There now seems to be sufficient authority to support the conclusion that by entering into a doctor-patient relationship the therapist becomes sufficiently involved to assume some responsibility for the safety, not only of the patient himself, but also of any third person whom the doctor knows to be threatened by the patient.[11]

Later we shall argue that the common-law courts may not be the appropriate device for providing that legal framework, although legal constraints on therapeutic discretion, we believe, are in order. Before turning to this critical issue, it is necessary to examine two cases the California supreme court held fall under the *Tarasoff* principle. They illustrate an ambiguity of the *Tarasoff* principle that has caused concern among therapists.

LEGAL RESOLUTION OF MORAL ISSUES

One of the difficulties of the *Tarasoff* principle raised by psychotherapists is that a common-law court decision is interpreted at every application. The original *Tarasoff* case involved a patient, a readily identifiable victim, and a psychotherapist, but extensions of *Tarasoff* have been argued since 1976.

In 1983, the California Supreme Court ruled, in *Hedlund v. Superior Court of Orange County*, that the *Tarasoff* principle can be extended to include some individuals "not explicitly targeted by the patient":

> A psychotherapy patient shot and injured his lover, La Nita, in the immediate presence of her young son, Darryl. At the time of the shooting, Darryl was sitting next to his mother. La Nita threw herself over the boy, effectively protecting him from physical injury. She brought action against the psychotherapists, claiming that they breached a duty to warn her that she was in danger from this patient. According to the court summary, the patient had told therapists that he intended to severely harm this woman. The violence was considered foreseeable. And the primary victim was identifiable [conditions similar to those in the original *Tarasoff* case] . . . Most significant in this case, the court held that the duty to warn also extended to the young boy. Because Darryl was very close to his mother, emotional injury to the boy was thought to be as foreseeable as the physical injury to his mother.[12]

The first thing to note about this case is the degree of responsibility the psychotherapist is expected to bear. He or she is held to be obligated to warn/protect not just the woman who was the object of the patient's threat, but her son also. On what ground does this obligation rest, and how is it to be justified in the face of the therapist's obligation to the patient? To answer the second part of this question first, a dissenting opinion in the *Tarasoff* case (by Justice Mosk) refers to the inability of therapists to accurately predict violence, and not to any overriding contractual obligation to the patient. Mosk, in effect, is asserting that the therapist has an excuse for not breaching confidentiality, but that does not entail that the rule of confidentiality cannot be overridden by a deeper moral principle, such as the duty to protect the vulnerable, when the excusing condition does not hold. Psychotherapists

may have good reasons to believe their patients will act in certain ways, even if rigorous canons of scientific predictability are inappropriate, and their reasonable expectations may (and often are) the result of their special relationship to patients.

The moral obligation rests on the duty to protect the vulnerable. That this is indeed the court's view of the matter is supported by the claim that the child is owed an obligation even though he is not threatened explicitly by the patient in the context of therapy. The patient harmed the child; if it was reasonable to believe the mother was in danger, a foreseeable and vulnerable witness to the patient's attack on the mother is also owed protection. In this case, the child is a foreseeable victim because of the likelihood of his close proximity to the mother.

Earlier, we argued that a duty to protect the vulnerable, which the *Tarasoff* principle ascribes to psychotherapists, is supported by the fundamental value of a democracy—specifically, the right to equal concern and respect. The *Hedlund* case suggests that vulnerability is indeed the moral context of the *Tarasoff* principle. But a right to equality is a principle of political morality, and a duty to protect the vulnerable is a civic duty of all persons. Why did the California Supreme Court create a public policy (for California) establishing the liability of psychotherapists, even though no such legal sanction has been thought justifiable as an incentive to motivate a general civic duty to warn/protect the vulnerable?

We can only suggest an outline to that question here. Psychotherapy is a profession that enjoys considerable legal and social status in our society. As in the case of its parent profession, medicine, it is charged with multiple public responsibilities in exchange for the status, including a special responsibility to society. That responsibility was acknowledged before *Tarasoff*, as we have observed in the passage quoted from Menninger. If that responsibility is being shirked, society has a right to establish a policy that circumscribes the area in which therapeutic discretion is deemed appropriate.

What had changed by 1976 were (1) state civil commitment laws that narrowed the grounds for commitment (and a concomitant emphasis on the constraining role of federal constitutional rights),[13] (2) the public perception of the social responsibilities of psychotherapists, and (3) the interpenetration of psychotherapy and the criminal justice system. A conundrum of the increasing stringency of civil commitment procedures to ensure the protection of the rights of the mentally ill is that public security may be perceived to be at risk. But policy that requires psychotherapists to widen their "gaze" beyond the boundaries of the clinical relationship is not just in the public's interest, it is also a matter of legal and moral principle. Psychotherapy plays a role in the criminal justice system in the United States, which is charged to protect the vulnerable in our society. It is this role in ensuring equal justice that entails professional responsibilities, such as the duty to warn/protect, that go beyond ordinary civic duties and require constraint on therapeutic discretion. As Fleming and Maximov put it, "[T]he ultimate question of resolving the tension between the conflicting interests of patient and potential victim is one of social policy, not professional expertise."[14]

But even if we agree that psychotherapists have a duty to warn or protect, a policy that specifies such a duty is problematic when it is asserted by common-law courts. *Tarasoff* and its successors have to be interpreted whenever a case is litigated, and each litigation can alter the ground rules. For example, in *Lipari v. Sears Roebuck and Co.*, the U.S. District Court for the District of Nebraska (1980) claimed that a doctor need only "reasonably foresee that the risk engendered by his patient's condition would endanger other persons."[15] It is not necessary, according to this ruling, that the therapist be able to identify a potential victim. The important point for our purpose is not that the duty has been extended in Nebraska from the *Tarasoff* baseline, but that psychotherapists have no clear guidelines for determining when

they have a duty to warn/protect and how to discharge that responsibility.

Common-law courts have in the past been more or less successful in establishing precedents in the service of fairness and equality. But the reasonable extent and limits of the social responsibility of psychotherapists are quite as much a matter of public debate and legislative prerogative as the civil rights of patients were in the 1960s and 1970s. In a constitutional democracy they are, in fact, two sides of the same coin: the reconciliation of liberty and justice.

When they resolve conflicts of legal-right claims, common-law courts, at their best, try to treat competing interests fairly. But the problems posed by *Tarasoff* situations need to be addressed by a legislative policy, accompanied by society-wide debate that will clarify the limits of therapeutic discretion, the legitimate claims of society to protection from violent outpatients, and the civil liberties of all patients in the mental health system. The aftermath of the *Tarasoff* decision has been salutary because it has focused attention on the social responsibilities of psychotherapists (and, by extension, of all professionals). It has been harmful because it has led to confusion about, and fear of, legal culpability on the part of therapists when they are asked to treat potentially violent patients.

The clarification and scope of the *Tarasoff* principle seem at this point to be of primary importance. The *Tarasoff* principle itself seems to be accepted generally: "It appears that the therapists around the country already act as though *Tarasoff* applies to them," as a recent book on mental health law points out.[16] But the variety of cases that may fall under *Tarasoff* is wide, and uncertainty about their legal culpability is hardly fair to therapists. Even granting that the *Tarasoff* principle is reasonable or is founded on a reasonable public expectation regarding their safety, common-law court decisions may not be the appropriate instrument for such a policy. According to Calabresi,

> Courts are not suited to do many things because they do not have the data necessary to know what should be done; be-

cause action in some areas requires detailed regulatory language; because not all the issues a legislative reconsideration would reveal to be at stake can be made apparent in an adversary setting; because judicial action in some areas has to be retroactive and hence may defeat justified expectations or fail to give needed warnings; or because judicial intervention fosters legislative abrogation of responsibility.[17]

Legislatures, e.g., in California, are now either adopting or considering adoptions of laws that express, clarify, and limit the *Tarasoff* principle. Such statutes may not coincide exactly with the *Tarasoff* principle, but if they are written well they may at least spell out the therapists' responsibilities to society in greater detail and provide a more reliable guide than the courts are equipped to do.

We have argued that there is a moral basis for the *Tarasoff* principle: equality of concern and respect. We have argued, further, that the value of equality is embedded in a political morality, and that the institutional role of psychotherapy renders it susceptible to policy constraints. Those policy constraints are most appropriately imposed, in the context of public debate about professional responsibilities, by the representatives of the public—the legislature.[18]

NOTES

1. D. Hume, *A Treatise of Human Nature*, edited by L.A. Selby Bigge (Oxford: Clarendon Press, 1949), 488.

2. R. Goodin, *Protecting the Vulnerable* (Chicago: University of Chicago Press, 1985), 2.

3. H. Sidgwick, *The Methods of Ethics*, 7th ed. (London: MacMillan, 1974), 242.

4. I. Levi, *Hard Choices* (Cambridge: Cambridge University Press, 1986), 2.

5. Tarasoff v Regents of University of California, 17 Cal3d 425, 131 Cal Rptr 14, 551 P2d 334. 20. 34 (1979).

6. W.J. Winslade, Psychotherapeutic Discretion and Judicial Decisions: A Case of Enigmatic Justice, in *The Law-Medical Relation: A Philosophical Exploration*, edited by S.T. Spicker et al. (Boston: Reidel, 1981), 155.

7. R. Dworkin, *Taking Rights Seriously* (Cambridge, Mass.: Harvard University Press, 1977), 272–273.

8. G. Calabresi and P. Bobbitt, *Tragic Choices* (New York: Norton, 1978), 17–28.

9. J. Rawls, *A Theory of Justice* (Cambridge, Mass.: Harvard University Press, 1971), 3.

10. R. Slovenko, Psychotherapy, Confidentiality, and Privileged Communication (Springfield, Ill.: Charles C Thomas, 1966), 56.

11. J.G. Fleming and B. Maximov, The Patient or His Victim: The Therapist's Dilemma, *California Law Review* 62 (1974):1025–1068.

12. A.R. Felthous, *The Psychotherapist's Duty to Warn or Protect* (Springfield, Ill.: Charles C Thomas, 1989), 12.

13. S.R. Smith and R.G. Meyer, *Law, Behavior, and Mental Health: Policy and Practice* (New York: New York University Press, 1987), 588–595.

14. Fleming and Maximov, The patient or His Victim: The Therapist's Dilemma.

15. Lipari v Sears Roebuck and Co., 497 F Supp 185 (D Neb 1980).

16. Smith and Meyer, *Law, Behavior, and Mental Health*.

17. G. Calabresi, *A Common Law for the Age of Statutes* (Cambridge, Mass.: Harvard University Press, 1982), 146.

18. It is worth pointing out that similar arguments can be advanced for a duty to protect with respect to other professionals, e.g., teachers and (with, we suspect, careful qualifications) lawyers. We cannot, however, advance such arguments within the scope of this chapter.

Chapter 35

Beneficence, Scientific Autonomy, and Self-Interest: Ethical Dilemmas in Clinical Research

Edmund D. Pellegrino

The ethics of clinical research may be viewed from three different perspectives: first, the process of acquiring new knowledge; second, the moral use of the knowledge acquired; and, third, the ethics of the investigator seeking this knowledge.

The ethics of the *process* of human investigation has been the focus of attention ever since the Nuremberg trials exposed the atrocities perpetrated by Nazi physicians on their experimental subjects. The ethics of process emphasizes informed consent, institutional review boards, and legal regulation of human experimentation. The moral *use* of the knowledge gained by clinical investigation has also received wide discussion on subjects such as fetal tissue transplantation, reproductive technology, the artificial heart, and human gene therapy. Much less attention has been given to the third perspective, which is concerned with the personal morality of the clinical investigator. Yet it is the clinical investigator who is the ultimate safeguard of the safety of the experimental human subject. It is the investigator who designs the experiment, prepares the protocol for peer review, obtains the necessary consent, interprets the results, and monitors the safety of the experiment.

It is from this third perspective that I wish to examine the ethics of clinical research in this chapter: first, because this perspective is so often neglected; second, because it is so central to the moral quality of human investigations; and third, because it is of such special significance in, for example, pediatric research, where the vulnerability of the infant or child imposes graver responsibilities on the investigator than is the case with adults, who can give informed consent or refusal.

The essence of the moral dilemma faced by all clinical investigators is the potential conflict between the investigator's roles as scientist, as physician, and as private individual. Each role is dominated by a different value: for science, it is truth; for medicine, it is beneficence toward the patient; and for the investigator as an individual, it is self-interest. Each value, along with its subsidiary set of standards and procedures, is legitimate in its own right. But when these values come into competition, as they may in clinical research, serious moral dilemmas result.

Source: Reprinted from *Georgetown Medicine*, Vol. 1, No. 1, pp. 21–28, with permission of Georgetown Center for the Advanced Study of Ethics, © 1991.

How investigators deal with these value conflicts ultimately determines the safety of the patient. This, in turn, determines the degree to which society will permit or restrict the scientific autonomy necessary for valid research. But no matter how rigidly human experimentation is regulated, the ethical sensitivity of the investigator remains an ineradicable factor in the moral equation.

It is the moral sensitivity I wish to examine under three headings: first, the covenantal nature of clinical investigation; second, the difference in the value systems of the investigator's concurrent roles as scientist, physician, and individual; and third, the resolution of potential conflicts through application of the ordering principle of "autonomy-in-trust."

THE COVENANTAL NATURE OF CLINICAL RESEARCH

We must recognize from the outset that clinical research is an invasion of the integrity and privacy of the person who is the research subject. This invasion necessarily places the person at some risk for a result that, by the very nature of research, must be problematic. Nothing in the nature of science or its internal need for freedom and autonomy constitutes an autonomous moral right to engage in human experimentation. Rather, clinical research is a privilege accorded the investigator by social consensus. Society permits experimentation with humans because of the benefits that the whole society, as well as the experimental subject, may gain from new medical knowledge. The clinical investigator thus enters a covenant with society when he or she accepts the privilege of experimentation involving his or her fellow human beings.

In addition, the investigator is also party to a covenant with the experimental subject. For the potential good of others, of medical science in general, or of the subject him- or herself, physicians persuade a patient to become simultaneously a patient and a subject. By that act, the good of the patient, which should be primary in the purely therapeutic encounter, is now compromised by another good—the knowledge to be gained by experimental manipulation of the patient's care. The patient is, therefore, knowingly put at some risk for the sake of an uncertain good. By consenting to participate in a research protocol, the subject trustingly yields up some personal moral claims to safety in return for a potential good for him- or herself or others. The patient-subject thus has a moral claim on the investigator's fidelity to respect the implied promise that the investigator will judiciously balance the patient's interests and those of the scientific protocol.

These two covenants—one with society and one with the experimental subject—form the basis for the moral obligations specific to clinical investigation. Although these covenants arise in a trust relationship that institutional review boards and research regulations can help to safeguard, their subtler nuances cannot be spelled out in such regulations. Rather, like the therapeutic relationship, these covenants rest ultimately on the character and moral integrity of the investigator.

Society permits human experimentation under carefully circumscribed conditions because it is the only way medical knowledge can be verified for use in the amelioration and cure of human disease. In vitro studies, animal models, and computer simulations can go only so far. Ultimately, the new drug or surgical procedure must be tested in human subjects. To be faithful to both covenants—with the patient and with society—these tests must, in the first instance, be scientifically sound. To proceed with a research plan that lacks scientific integrity places human subjects at risk needlessly and irresponsibly. It does violence to society's and the subject's legitimate expectations of science and scientists.

Even as we acknowledge the importance of the canons of good science, however, we must also appreciate that clinical medicine is not itself a science. It possesses a set of values that differ from those of science in fundamental ways. Let us look at some of these differences.

THE VALUES OF SCIENCE

The end of scientific endeavor is truth, that is, knowledge as a good for its own sake. This is the ordering value in science. To achieve this end, science must be free to examine any question and use any method appropriate to the questions it poses. It must design those questions rigorously and examine them experimentally for their verifiability and falsifiability. Observations must be accurate, honestly reported, objectively interpreted, subjected to peer review, and shared openly with colleagues and the world at large.

These values and standards imply a certain degree of objectivization of the subject under study. But in clinical investigations, the "object" of study remains a human being—either a healthy volunteer or a sick person. Here, and in the case of higher animals in general, the canons of science may conflict with another set of values—those that define the endeavor of medicine.

THE VALUES OF MEDICINE

In contradistinction to science, whose ordering value is truth, the ordering value of medicine is beneficence. Medical knowledge is sought for a specific end: the healing, helping, and curing of human beings. The good of the patient is the primary end of medicine. To achieve this end, medical knowledge must be particularized to meet the needs of *this* patient in *this* clinical situation. Its aim is not, like the aim of science, the discovery of generalized concepts, theories, or laws about human physiology or disease.

In addition, medical knowledge must be applied compassionately and sensitively to the uniqueness of the predicament of illness in *this* person, a predicament that is not wholly penetrable by the physician. Truth-telling and confidentiality are mandatory if fidelity to the trust that patients must place in doctors is to be preserved. In those critical moments when a clinical decision is made, the character of the physician remains the patient's ultimate safeguard, for which no contract, however carefully con-

structed, can fully substitute. Whatever agreement is made with the patient must inevitably be channelled through and carried out by another person—the physician.

Medicine is, therefore, not primarily science, though it uses science. In medicine, truth must be sought and applied for the good of the patient. It is not an end in itself. Medical truth, unlike scientific truth, is in service to the value of beneficence. It is this inescapable fact that not only gives a moral complexity to the activity of the physician who engages in clinical investigations but also limits the scientific autonomy of clinical investigators.

THE INVESTIGATOR'S SELF-INTEREST

In addition to the inherent tension between the values of science and medicine, there is a third set of values that further complicates the ethics of clinical research. These values derive from motives and impulses of self-interest that are normal to human beings but may, under the special circumstances of clinical research, present moral hazards.

Like other humans, the clinical scientist desires to advance his or her own career, improve his or her income, and experience the satisfaction of peer approval and public recognition. These motives may result in an excessive drive to compete, to be the "first" to report results, to win the Nobel Prize, or simply to enjoy the personal satisfaction of an elegant experimental design elegantly carried out. Whatever its source, unrestrained self-interest can blunt moral sensitivity. It can lead to conscious or unconscious violations of the covenants between physician and society and between physician and research subject that permit clinical research in the first place.

For example, self-interest may erode the high standard of moral sensitivity that should guide experiments with especially vulnerable groups: the aged, the hopelessly ill, the retarded, the infant with multiple defects, the fetus, the patient with HIV infection, the embryo or that new fictive entity, the "pre-embryo." In addition, a researcher may justify his or her compromise of informed consent by citing the benefits to society or other patients or the eventual cure of a serious disease. When does the investigator step over the line between a truly informed consent and telling just enough to keep the subject from being scared off? No formula can spell this out in advance. No set of regulations can fully protect even the well-educated, fully competent subject. How much more vulnerable are the poorly educated, the sick, or the parents of a desperately or hopelessly ill child or infant?

For the physician-scientist, the moral obligations of the investigator are much heavier than the legal. A legally adequate consent form may not be morally valid. A morally valid consent aims at true "con-sent," an agreeing together in which both parties enter a relationship based on mutual trust and the expectations of fidelity to that trust. Obviously, there must be written consent forms, and they must be examined and approved by peers and institutional review boards. However, it is the moral integrity of the investigator who obtains the consent that assures the moral validity of the consent procedure. It is the investigator who decides how much to tell the patient or family, which facts to emphasize, which to withhold, and how to present them.

Institutional pride or hubris is a further corrosive influence. The institution's drive to be "first" is a mixed motive; it can be effective in raising institutional morale and productivity, but it is also capable of submerging moral imperatives on grounds of exigency and "survival." In competition with other hospitals or universities, institutional pride can desensitize an institutional review board to certain dubious projects. It can lead to unrealistic reliance on the character of a staff member who is nationally prominent or politically powerful.

The intellectual hubris of the investigator plays its part too. It tempts the academic physician-investigator to arrogate the privilege of scientific autonomy to him- or herself. The public, it is argued, cannot possibly comprehend the importance of scientific research or judge the details of a particular experiment. In the long run, it is further argued, the good of all will be better served if we place our trust in the integrity of the scientist's judgment.

Even if we grant that the majority of clinical investigators are honorable people, the dangers of this line of reasoning are obvious. Experience sadly teaches that there is no necessary correlation between academic prestige or intellectual acuity and moral behavior. In a matter as complex and finely balanced as clinical research, the general public may be more perceptive of the moral dilemmas than the most "enlightened" scientist.

Personal profit has, in recent years, come to rival prestige and career advancement as a motivating factor in scientific investigation. Pharmaceutical companies are understandably eager to have their products evaluated in humans by the most renowned institutions and investigators. This is understandable and even legitimate since new therapeutic agents should be evaluated by experienced and responsible investigators. To this end, for-profit companies have expanded the ways in which they can provide financial incentives. They may assume a portion of the investigator's salary, provide certain "fringe" benefits like travel and accommodations at deluxe resorts for "research" meetings, offer consulting fees, give gifts of various kinds, or promise a share in the profits from the products one is testing.

The matter is further complicated when the health care industry enters long-term contractual arrangements with a university to support research. The usual proviso is that a company will support research facilities and personnel in return for privileged access and a share in the patenting rights to the products developed. These industry-university compacts are especially attractive today when governmental and philanthropic sources of research funding are insufficient. Some of our most prestigious universities have entered into what may well turn out to be Faustian compacts. Eventually, many of them will be forced to pay their part of the bargain, especially if corporate profits fall to unacceptable levels or the "investment" in research turns out to be insufficiently productive financially.

Freedom of access and the sharing of research results have, traditionally, been values of science. In many of the contractual arrangements between investigators and pharmaceutical companies, there are provisos that recognize the investigator's right to publish in peer-reviewed journals. Still, it is a fact of business that one does not alert one's competitors to a new product before it is ready for marketing. It is difficult to say just how strongly such negative incentives to data sharing actually operate. It is not unfair to suppose that investigators, for fear of losing long-term research support, might consciously or unconsciously withhold information about new discoveries until the time to release it is commercially propitious.

These are a few examples of the kinds of conflicts of interest that pose a potential danger to experimental subjects. They can compromise beneficence, the central value in medicine. They can also pose a threat to the values of science. The objectivity, accuracy, and reliability of observations and data interpretation that science requires can subtly be destroyed by financial incentives as well as institutional and personal pride. The brute fact of the matter is that if investigations do not produce papers in quantity, if their results are not definitive or are contrary to the interests of those who support them, the emoluments and rewards will stop. Thus, both scientific probity and subject safety may become victims of self-interest.

PHYSICIAN AND SCIENTIST—CAN ONE BE BOTH?

The unique personal conflict in clinical research, and the one least soluble by simple measures is the conflict of identity the investigator must inevitably experience between his or her role as scientist, interested in fact and data collection, and his or her role as physician, interested in care and cure. The physician-investigator must perforce be committed simultaneously to the values of science and the values

of medicine. Even if he or she can avoid the temptation of self-interest noted above, he or she faces a difficult task of balancing and ordering the values of truth and beneficence against each other.

This problem was recognized several decades ago by Otto Guttentag, who considered it serious enough to suggest that the physician caring for the patient might be other than the physician conducting the experiment. The issue Guttentag raised is far from settled. It can manifest itself at almost every point in any clinical experiment and especially in randomized clinical trials. It has never been squarely faced.

One example of this conflict is in getting consent for a patient's entry into a study. The patient's major concern is understandably for the most effective treatment of his or her disease. If the patient suffers from a chronic or fatal disease for which there is no treatment or only a dubious one, he or she is vulnerable to any promise of help. Under these circumstances, an experimental protocol raises expectations that all is not lost.

It becomes very difficult for patients to separate the physician-scientist role from that of physician-healer. For patients, these roles are personified in all the physicians taking care of them. The physician can easily obtain consent to an experimental protocol simply by emphasizing the hope of cure and downplaying the risk and experimental nature of the treatment. Even the built-in uncertainties of the randomized clinical trial can escape the patient's consciousness under these circumstances. Selective hearing is a powerful device that helps the patient sustain hope when the illness is incurable. The investigator must guard against taking advantage of this normal tendency in such people.

After consent has been obtained, the physician-investigator's role can become even more ambiguous. As the patient's physician, he or she would be impelled to intervene at the first sign of danger by modifying or discontinuing the protocol. As scientist, he or she would be bound to persist in the protocol until the statistical evidence for harm or benefit was conclusive. If the investigator discontinues the experiment too soon, he or she frustrates his or her scientific obligations. If the investigator waits too long, he or she frustrates his or her obligations as the patient's doctor.

When the study involves a double-blind procedure, there are further problems. If the physician does not know whether his or her patient is on a placebo or a potent, impotent, or toxic medication, he or she will have difficulty interpreting whether changes in the clinical course are a result of the disease or a therapeutic or toxic effect of the agent being tested. As the investigator, he or she must remain "blind" until it is statistically clear that the patient is suffering from an aberrant or beneficial effect of the treatment. As the subject's personal physician, he or she would need to break the code at the first suspicion of harm.

Another difficulty arises when the treatment under study is an improvement over an accepted and reasonably effective standard treatment, e.g., testing the efficacy of a new drug for rheumatoid arthritis, angina pectoris, or hypertension. Here the experimental design might include a control group, a group on standard medication, and a group on the new medication. If assignment to these groups is randomized, a patient might, for a time, be deprived of standard treatment and placed on a new, untried, and possibly ineffective treatment or on a placebo. Again, the physician-as-scientist must adhere to the protocol. On the other hand, the physician-as-caregiver who gives priority to beneficence over scientific truth might not think the associated risks of a procedure justifiable for a particular patient.

There are many other circumstances that put the physician's roles as caregiver and as scientist into conflict. These role conflicts need more careful scrutiny. They do not constitute absolute impediments to clinical research; they underscore the need for the investigator to be self-critical and to recognize when the values he or she must observe as a physician are in conflict with the canons of science or self-interest.

The moral dangers inherent in clinical research can never be removed entirely. Human experimentation is a necessity if new treatments are to be discovered and validated. The regulatory measures already in force have done much to place legal, social, and institutional constraints on clinical research. But not enough emphasis has been placed on the special nature of the freedom and autonomy the clinical investigator enjoys. One way the needs of good science can be balanced against the needs of the patient-as-subject is through a consideration of the concept of "autonomy-in-trust"—the recognition of a moral order of priority that will resolve conflicts as they arise.

SCIENTIFIC "AUTONOMY-IN-TRUST"

The intellectual autonomy of the scientist is autonomy held in trust. By "autonomy-in-trust" I mean the conscious acknowledgement by the investigator that he or she is allowed freedom to pursue rigorous scientific goals in human experimentation only if the welfare of the patient is always respected as primary and superior to the values of science and self-interest. This concept implies that the scientist-physician will always regard beneficence as the guiding principle even to the point of effacing his or her own self-interest or nullifying the scientific validity of his or her work. The autonomy necessary to good science is morally tenable if it is seen as held in trust for the good of the patient.

No quantitative formula can set forth explicitly the limits within which autonomy-in-trust should operate. Instead, the investigator must develop a sensitivity to the privilege he or she is permitted in doing research involving humans. That privilege is fragile and deserves constant awareness not only of the intersections among the three value systems I have been describing, but of the priority of the well-being of the experimental subject whenever there is even the potential for conflict.

Freedom is afforded the scientist to pursue problems that interest him or her because society believes that knowledge is a good in itself or because of its applicability to human problems.

Society recognizes that valid knowledge cannot be obtained without freedom of inquiry. For this reason, we allow freedom in the scientist's selection of problems, methods, and forms of reporting data. Society expects, in return, that the scientist be worthy of the freedom he or she is privileged to enjoy.

On the strength of this expectation, the scientist is thus allowed a certain latitude or "discretionary space" in the pursuit of knowledge. The dimensions of that space vary with the nature of the subjects and objects under study and with the potential effects of the study on human society. The precise dimensions within which autonomy-in-trust can be exercised are manifestly difficult to set. Should research on the atomic bomb have been pursued? Is experimentation on the human fetus or embryo permissible? Are studies of the genetic or racial variations in intelligence warranted? Are there limits to the risks a human subject is permitted to undertake—even voluntarily—in the interests of gaining medical knowledge or helping others?

In the specific instance of clinical research, the dimensions of discretionary space must be narrowly defined. Respect for persons and the imperative of beneficence take precedence over scientific curiosity. If the investigator chooses to be physician and caregiver as well, then he or she must realize at the outset that the needs of the experimental protocol must be subservient to the needs of his or her patient. The multiplicity of possibilities for conflict between the values of science, medicine, and self-interest forces us to reconsider whether it is morally licit for one person to be scientist and physician simultaneously.

Arguments can be marshalled on both sides of this question. Those who favor unification of roles of investigator and caregiver place their trust in the binding power of the traditional ethics of medicine, the trustworthiness of the majority of investigators, and the avoidance of interphysician conflict when one physician is clearly in charge. Those who would separate these roles hold that there is a clear advantage when one physician is unequivocally the advocate for the patient's welfare and another for the probity of the experiment. Further, the skills, attitudes, and motivations required for physician-caregiver and physician-investigator roles are different. Different kinds of people are attracted to each role. It is unusual for one person to possess the traits of both.

There is probably no general rule that can cover all investigational situations. It is clear that better surveillance over the possibility of conflicts is in order. In some cases a separation of roles seems advisable. For example, when the investigator receives most of his or her support from a pharmaceutical firm, owns stock in that company, or receives financial emoluments, separation of roles seems the only morally prudent alternative. This is particularly true if the purpose of the experiment is to evaluate an improvement in an already effective treatment. The same is true when the research is clearly nontherapeutic and of no therapeutic benefit to the patient. Protection of the patient's interest should be in the hands of a physician other than the investigator, one whose prime obligation is to the patient and not the experiment.

On the other hand, when the intent of the research is to try a new agent in a patient with a serious or fatal disease and the outcome for the patient-subject is the prime focus of the research, then it seems better for the physician giving care and the physician-investigator to be the same person. Here the relationship between scientific knowledge and the good of the patient is so intimate that it is preferable to have one physician who can discuss and weigh both with the patient.

Clearly, a reassessment of the usually accepted fusion of roles in the physician-investigator is in order. Much depends on the contexts, purposes, and expectations of the research protocol. Autonomy-in-trust demands a renewed emphasis on care and precision in identifying and resolving the moral dilemmas inherent in different types of clinical investigations.

The safe rule in every case is to favor beneficence over scientific rigor when the two seem to be in conflict or when in doubt. The possible loss of knowledge cannot outweigh the possibility of harm to the subject even if the utilitarian calculus indicates great benefit to many and harm to only a few. This is the case particularly with the mentally retarded, the very young, the terminally ill, and the senile. Whenever valid consent is impossible and the experiment risky, only therapeutic research aimed at benefit to the subject seems morally defensible. It is especially dangerous to hold, as some ethicists do, that infants and the retarded, for example, own an obligation to society or to other infants to be subjects of research. No one can presume on the willingness of another to run the risk of experimentation: We cannot presume to attribute activism to those who cannot possibly express their own views on the matter.

This applies to parents as well as guardians of infants and children below the age of competence. Parents do not have absolute rights over their children. Someone must be an advocate for the infant and the child, and this may have to be the physician. He or she may have to protect the child against even well-intended parents who might permit dubious forms of experimentation in hope that it might help others. This is another reason why it is particularly important to distinguish the role of the investigator from that of the caregiver.

Not all experimental procedures in infants and children are ruled out. Therapeutic investigations that could benefit the subject would be licit, provided all other safeguards are scrupulously observed. Nontraumatic studies of a nontherapeutic type—like examinations of body fluids, excretions, or secretions or noninvasive procedures or observations of various sorts—would be licit if they were done in association with other procedures needed in the care of the subject.

Experimentation on fetuses or embryos, spontaneously or intentionally aborted, is a special subject with its own moral complexities. It deserves more than the superficial treatment I can give here. Suffice it to say that everything depends upon what we consider to be the ontological status of the fetus and embryo. In my view, they are deserving of the same respect as the infant or child. Their vulnerability is extreme, and the rule of beneficence is particularly stringent upon those who have the unborn in their care.

But even if the subject is capable of making his or her own choices and is willing to run risks, there are limits on what ought to be permissible. A particularly dangerous recent example is so-called "pay-as-you-go" research. This is another manifestation of the growing belief that untrammeled competition will redound to the benefit of patients by providing incentives to investigators to try nonstandard treatments.

In this kind of research a commercial laboratory enters into a contract with a person to try out a new treatment. For example, monoclonal antibodies can be developed from the patient's own tumor cells bonded to an antitumor agent and then used as treatment. The patient pays all the expenses of the research, plus a profit to the laboratory. In this way, it is argued, bold new treatments will be developed that might otherwise founder in the complex review processes.

The dangers of such research are obvious. All the usual safeguards that surround human experiments are compromised. There is no peer review, no institutional review board or ethics committee, no statistically controlled trial, no monitoring of the results and the dangers. Sharing of information is seriously impeded since investigators are in competition with one another for the market. Finally, there is the serious conflict between the financial interest of the investigator, the interests of good science, and the good of the patient. A more perilous misapplication of the privilege of clinical research can hardly be imagined.

CONCLUSION

I have cited some examples of the ways in which the physician's role as investigator-scientist may be in conflict with his or her role as caregiver. These examples underscore the need for a more careful scrutiny of the value conflicts possible even in so well-intentioned an enterprise as therapeutic research. They are not reasons for Draconian measures to regulate such research. However, they are reasons for a much greater sensitivity on the part of institutions and investigators to the fact that clinical research places restraints on the autonomy of science and self-interest.

The conflicts between the values of science, medical care, and self-interest have implications for the preparation, selection, and supervision of clinical investigations. Many unfortunate occurrences have resulted from the laxity of senior investigators who are involved in the supervision of too many projects and who are overeager to expand their own publication lists. Some training in ethics should be mandatory for all investigators who are to be involved with human subjects. Some code or explicit set of moral commitments should be developed and subscribed to by all investigators.

Given the emphasis in Western society on autonomy, the rights of patients, and the wariness about abuses of power by science and technology, clinical investigators must recognize the value conflict inherent in their work. Their best guarantee of freedom in the pursuit of medical knowledge and the good of patients lies in research that is scientifically valid and ethically responsible. To compromise either is, on the one hand, to endanger patients and, on the other, to lose the privilege of freedom without which science cannot thrive.

Chapter 36

The Ethics of Health Care As a Business

Patricia H. Werhane

The crisis in health care about which we read and worry is real. Fully 12 percent of our gross national product is spent on health care, and costs are rising. Even so we are not providing even minimum access to health care for at least 37 million citizens. Yet few Americans want to relinquish their ability to choose their health care specialist and place of treatment. With improved technology the vague claim to a right to health care has been translated into the demand for good health care. Indeed, a demand for the best available treatment is considered by many to be an entitlement. Along with these increased costs and development of rights claims, malpractice suits proliferate by those who find their rights have been abrogated.

The blame for the crisis in health care often falls to the alleged exploitation and commodification of health care by the market. In what follows I am going to suggest that this is too simple a description of the problem. I shall argue that we have misread the market model as the self-regulating glorification of economic egoism and that therefore the market paradigm adopted by health care is a faulty one. Further, I shall argue, no one model or paradigm can deal with the complexity of health care nor its difficulties.

However, I shall claim that a careful rereading of Adam Smith, the eighteenth-century economist and philosopher to whom is often erroneously attributed an egoistic market model, might be helpful in setting out a framework for dealing with many of these issues.

According to Charles Dougherty,

> general features of the pervasive hold of commercialism in medicine include an increase in competition and decline in professionalism among physicians, a view of health care as a commodity and patients as consumers, and a general depersonalization of doctor-patient relationship including dilution of the tradition of physician as patient advocate.[1]

According to this view, a form of economic egoism has corrupted the health care system, replacing the caring and professional models with that of competing self-interests, encouraging greed, confusing professional interests with profit, depersonalizing patient relationships, diluting benevolence and charity with a concern

Source: Reprinted from *Business & Professional Ethics Journal*, Vol. 9, Nos. 3 & 4, pp. 7–20, University of Florida, Center for Applied Philosophy, with permission of Patricia H. Werhane, © 1991.

for economic viability, and thus excluding those who cannot afford health care from the system.

These serious accusations, and many of the problems Dougherty and others cite have arisen because of the commodification of health care. Without contesting that, I shall argue that the fault for these difficulties lies not in commodification per se but in the kind of market model we have projected on the health care system and in our assumption that such a complex system or set of systems can be subsumed under one paradigm.

To begin, let us review briefly the theory of the market that is said to dominate health care. Such a view is often attributed to Adam Smith, and it defends a sort of nineteenth-century radical individualism, linking it with self-interest. Summarily put, the model seems to presuppose that

> economic man, self-interested and fundamentally asocial, motivated by an insatiable desire to improve his material condition, is the model that explains human motivation and action.[2]

In his well-known book, the *Wealth of Nations*, Adam Smith is read as having promulgated this egoistic picture of human motivation and as having solved the problem of the dichotomy between one's alleged natural selfish passions and the public interests. When human beings are granted what Smith calls the "natural liberty" to pursue their own interests, Smith is then interpreted as having concluded that self-interested economic actors in competition with each other create a market through which its famous invisible hand functions both to regulate self-interests and to produce economic growth and well-being such that no individual or group of individuals is allowed to take advantage or to take advantage for very long.[3] So, more crudely put, in the marketplace, at least, under optimal competitive conditions the relentless pursuit of self-interest or at least disinterest in the well-being of others (within specified conditions such as the law) is both self-regulating and contributes to the public good.

Given this sort of moral psychology and philosophy of economics, it is no wonder that when this paradigm becomes the modus operandi for health care, or even for business, there are difficulties. How is it we have allowed ourselves to become enamored with this paradigm, and what else is at issue?

As background to answer these sorts of questions I want to suggest, all too briefly, an obvious point. It is this. "Our conceptual scheme mediates even our most basic perceptual experiences."[4] To state the point simply, we each operate our own "camera" of the world, projecting intentions, interests, desires, points of view, and biases that work as selective filters or censors on experience.[5]

This phenomenon accounts for our pluralism—the variety of ways we conceive the world and the variety of disparate social structures we create. The latter, noticed by Michael Walzer, explains the fact that sometimes individuals, social groups, institutions, or even whole societies are able to organize their concerns, institutions, and social goods into overlapping but distinct spheres of analysis and interest. Walzer focuses on what he calls "spheres of justice," arguing that each social sphere generates its own set of social goods, and each set of social goods commands distinct principles of distribution. These spheres may conflict or even contradict each other, but our ability to run several projectors on our experience at the same time and to distinguish and compartmentalize our foci allows these spheres to function simultaneously. Conversely, the projectival organization of experience also explains another phenomenon noticed and criticized by Walzer, namely, the disconcerting fact that sometimes individuals, groups, institutions, or even whole societies attempt to bring all their concerns, activities, organizations, social structures, and social goods under the framework of one paradigm, or one theory, or one principle of distribution. Specifically, Walzer contends that the dominance of the market model, or what he calls "market imperialism," skews the distribution of a variety of social goods, obstructs distributions based on need and desert, and commodifies political power.[6] In health care, we shall see how this alleged market imperialism has led to such difficulties. But, I shall argue, these difficulties arise as much from an unjustifiable conception of the market as from the misapplication of that conception in regard to the health care system.

How does the fact that we either project a number of different paradigms on the world or try to unify experience under one framework apply to health care? Until recently, I would suggest, there were at least six overlapping health care scenarios operating in our society, each of which had its distinct domain of influence. Because they overlapped, in some cases they were contrary to each other, but somehow these conflicts did not always precipitate serious dilemmas.

First there was an ideal of the profession, the notion that health care providers and specialists are autonomous, self-regulating individuals whose primary professional commitment is to medicine, and more specifically to the health care and healing of patients. Second, part of that ideal included the view that these professionals are caring, benevolent, even self-sacrificing in pursuit of their professional goals—a sort of Albert Schweitzer or Mother Teresa picture of medical professionals.

Third, hospitals and nursing homes were by and large nonprofit institutions. It was thought that their first concern, too, was the care and healing of patients. Fourth, for those who could not pay, there were thought to be benevolent health care specialists, organizations, and institutions, in particular, local community hospitals, who would provide for their needs.

Fifth and sixth, two other social phenomena existed as adjuncts to the health care system, the judicial system to protect constitutional rights, and the market, which provided material goods and services. These two spheres were thought to be peripheral to the health care system. By and large, issues of health care, e.g., malpractice, poor provision of nursing care, etc., were seldom brought to the attention of the courts. And while there certainly was commercialization of health care, that is, for-profit institutions and physi-

cians and other health care specialists who made money as well as treated patients, these phenomena were thought to be relatively secondary to the motivation of health care specialists and to the operation of health care institutions.

These scenarios each captured some of what in fact was true while highlighting some concerns and neglecting other data. These spheres seemed to operate simultaneously without causing much friction despite obvious problems, e.g., that some physicians were involved in entrepreneurial ventures that conflicted with patients' interests, that not all hospitals or nursing homes were unprofitable nor was their care always adequate, that malpractice was going on, that not every indigent patient was treated or treated adequately, and that not everyone in our society had access even to minimum health care.

Part of the present crisis in health care originates in the fact that at one time we imagined these scenarios represented reality, and because they overlapped, altogether by and large they did. But seldom did we try to make sense of all six spheres in terms of one paradigm, nor did we subject these spheres to one set of evaluative criteria. More recently, however, we have created or were led by changing circumstances to new models. At the same time we have sometimes imagined that there is *a* system of health care, conflating these distinct spheres of operation and thereby subjected the whole system to one evaluative perspective, attempting to apply a single set of principles for evaluation or distribution for quite different social phenomena.

At least three models now dominate our way of thinking about health care. First, and not on my previous list of paradigms, the technology model. There have been enormous advances in medical technology and with them a sort of "invincible" or Robocop notion that technology will make possible widespread advances in healing coupled with a sort of *Cocoon* view of immortality. Second, along with technological growth the escalating costs partly due to the use of technology, we have developed an "entitlement theory" of rights. Briefly put, this is the thesis that as citizens of a constitutional democracy under our Bill or Rights, each one of us has extended basic entitlements: rights to minimum basic health care, rights to good health care or even a right to the best technology can provide, rights to choose our provider, and rights to be protected from malpractice, poor treatment, or neglect. We have tried to empower our legislatures to grant these entitlements and the courts to protect them without regard to costs nor with attention to reciprocal duties to ensure equal entitlements for everyone.

Third, in the last 20 years commercialization of medicine has become a dominant trend in health care. Physicians have become entrepreneurs; for-profit hospitals, nursing homes, and HMOs have proliferated; insurance policies have quantified treatment with DRGs; health care specialists and health care organizations have begun advertising; and there is a trend toward the commodification of blood, organs, and, if Richard Posner has his way, even babies.

Accompanying this rising market orientation of health care is another confusing phenomenon. Where formerly there were overlapping but distinct spheres of concern in health care, we now sometimes superimpose one model or one methodology for analysis on another. For example, using the methodology from economics, one sometimes analyzes crucial dilemmas in medicine only in terms of markets, costs, and benefits, sometimes imagining that markets will both create benefits and regulate abuses. Or we conflate all cases under a rights model and wonder why we have problems with cost containment or even with providing equal minimum care. Or, appealing to the advances of technology, we treat patients as objects of experimentation rather than as human beings.

At the same time, we are reminded of "the good old days" of the caring model and try to keep it alive. One remembers the country doctors and the visiting nurses, benevolent, kindly, caring souls, and one wonders why our present health care specialists no longer emulate these ideals.

We have, then, mixed up our paradigms. We are at best unclear as to how to analyze conflicting claims, resorting often to the temptation to conflate issues and paradigms in an attempt to come up with solutions to growing health care dilemmas. Worse, having allowed an egoistic market paradigm to play a central role, we then blame the commercialization of medicine for the crisis in health care.

How, then, are we to deal with these issues? I do not have a solution for the problems in health care. But I want to argue that the kinds of paradigms one uses as frameworks for dealing with these issues both create dilemmas *and* determine the kinds of solutions available to solve these dilemmas. Since part of the crisis in health care is the adoption of an egoistic market model as I have depicted it, to get at the roots of the issues, let us re-examine that model. To do so I shall return to the philosophy of Adam Smith. Interestingly, this egoistic model is not an accurate reflection of the philosophy of Adam Smith. More importantly, Smith's moral psychology and the kind of framework Smith actually sets out for a viable political economy are useful not merely to bring into question economic egoism, but can serve as a metaframework for the analysis of complex social, ethical, and economic issues such as those introduced by health care. Let me outline briefly some salient features of Smith's moral psychology and then turn to his philosophy of economics to see why this is the case.

In his book on moral psychology, *Theory of Moral Sentiments*, Smith attacks radical individualism, recognizing that each of us is dependent on each other and on society. At the same time he defends the value of autonomy, advancing a more moderate individualism that claims that each of us is best able to care for ourself. But Smith does not identify individualism with egoism. While he clearly states that acting in one's own self-interest is not always bad, and indeed may produce benefits, Smith also carefully differentiates prudence from greed and avarice. More importantly, Smith argues that each of us is motivated by a variety of selfish, social, and unsocial passions of equal strength, each of which develops its particular interests and thus its virtues and vices. Self-interest or self-love is derived from the selfish passions, but self-love is not identified with selfishness, because self-love, like the other interests, can be virtuous (the virtue of prudence) or evil (greed or avarice).[7] Our interests in others, including empathy, the desire for approval, and the desire to emulate what society finds to be virtuous are motivated by the social passions that have equal weight with the selfish ones. Again these interests can be virtuous (the virtues of benevolence and justice) or evil.

Smith uses his moral psychology as a groundwork for his philosophy of economics in the *Wealth of Nations*. There Smith argues that self-interest is not the sole motivating force even in economic activities and that the social passions play three essential roles in economic activities. First, part of our pursuit of wealth, Smith notices, is not greed but is due to the desire for the approval of others. Second, economic exchanges are not based merely on competition but on mutual cooperation and coordination in which such competition takes place. Smith writes that "it is not from the benevolence of the butcher, the brewer, or the baker, that we expect our dinner, but from their regard to their own interest"[8] to illustrate the point that while our self-interests appear to dominate in the economy, co-operation is both natural and essential. None of these tradespeople acts benevolently, yet each depends on our approval for his or her self-interest. Moreover, in the small-town atmosphere implied in the example, these tradespeople depend on mutual cooperation to stay in business. Although the butcher, brewer, and baker are not necessarily benevolent, they not only are *not* malevolent but in the "corner grocery store" economy Smith depicts these shopkeepers cannot function without mutual cooperation. The fact that we "never talk to them of our own necessities but of their advantages" illustrates that some sort of fellow-understanding underpins economic relationships and in particular competition. Third, the virtue of justice, the "consciousness of ill-desert,"[9] is externalized in the legal system of jurisprudence that is an essential part of any societal framework and a necessary condition for the functioning of any viable economy. Indeed, in defending economic

liberty Smith argues that every man, *as long as he does not violate the laws of justice*, is left perfectly free to pursue his own interest"[10] (emphasis added).

It is true that Smith argued that "nobody but a beggar chooses to depend chiefly upon the benevolence of his fellow-citizens."[11] Despite this, Smith clearly distinguishes between acting in one's self-interest and greed and argues that avarice prevents good economic performance.[12] Thus, whereas benevolence may not play a role in economic exchanges, greed is antithetical to a well-run system and is to be prevented or discouraged. Moreover, neither prudent self-interest nor benevolence is the most basic virtue in economic affairs, justice is. Although both benevolence and justice derive from the social passions, Smith distinguishes them. Benevolence is not universally applicable nor enforceable, because one is not obliged to be benevolent. Justice, on the other hand, is limited to the protection of citizens from harms, safeguarding basic rights, and the guarantee of contracts and other forms of fair play. So defined, justice embraces only those principles that are always immoral to violate. Since, Smith continues, one has perfect duties not to cause harm, to protect rights, and, as consciousness of ill-desert, to safeguard fair play, those duties are universally applicable or enforceable.[13] This is the reason why benevolence or charity should not play a role in economic exchanges. Fair play in competition can be enforced; benevolence cannot. So, while the beggar cannot expect kindness, he or she *can* expect and require justice.

But what about the market itself, the famous invisible hand? Here Smith is most cautious and least understood. First, he argues, the market is most efficient and most fair when there is competition between similarly matched parties—a level playing field.[14] Second, the famous invisible hand, the market itself, is not an independent or autonomous regulator of economic behavior. Rather, the character of the market is created by economic activities. How and to what extent the market regulates economic behavior is a direct outcome of the kind of behaviors that create various market conditions. So greed, unfair competition, lack of enforcement of justice, and/or the absence of economic cooperation produce different market conditions and thus give the market a different personality than when those factors are not operative. The market, then, is a complex set of outcomes created by and changing as a result of economic activities. So it functions as a regulator only to the extent that economic actors are self-restrained, that there is not unfair competition, in a climate of judicial enforcement.

Finally, an ideal political economy is one that emulates justice as well as utility. A free market for commerce is the best sort of economy, but Smith limits the scope of economic activities to those appropriate for commerce and competition. Markets deal with goods and services, not with persons. Nor is it ever the case that any economic consideration overrides those of rights and justice. Smith is critical of economic regulations, and he is worried that most of us do not have the capability of understanding what is good for society. But government does have positive functions, specifically to provide universal education and public works, those works that are in no one's particular interest to provide.

Smith's analysis, then, far from defending an egoistic laissez-faire model for economic behavior, develops a highly qualified version of economic liberty in which economic liberty can function effectively and beneficially only where one is also prudent and cooperative in a system of law and justice and a climate of equal economic opportunity.

Despite Smith's arguments, however, we have by and large adopted the paradigm of economic egoism, assuming, wrongly, that the supposed invisible hand of the market will adjust our imprudent behavior despite our efforts to the contrary. How, then, is Smith's analysis helpful? Smith would argue that what is wrong with the market model in health care is the exploitation of the market on the basis of self-interest, and the extension of the market paradigm to inappropriate areas of concern. So Smith would question many of the "customs" currently operating that

have developed from the commercialization of health care. The misreading of economic liberty as license to maximize one's interests, the misguided reliance on the market as an alleged autonomous regulator of greed, skews prudence, self-restraint, and coordination of market activities. Moreover, the misappropriation of economic egoism in areas where it is inappropriate, in particular, in dealing with human beings and their needs and rights, has led to many of the difficulties and dilemmas in health care we now face. Smith's five criteria for viable competition: economic liberty, prudence, cooperation, justice, and equal economic opportunity should set guidelines for evaluating market-driven phenomena.

In addition to questioning the egoistic model of markets, Smith would place other important caveats on the commercialization of health care. First, the market is a limited sphere applying only to those goods and services that can be commidified. Economic models, and thus commercialization, can never include commodification of persons, their bodies, or their rights. Second, Smith would admire technology but be wary of the technology mode, a Robocop caricature of human beings, because technology, like industrialization, is a means to well-being, not an end to itself. Third, the rights model has been both overextended and misconceived. Smith limits basic or natural rights to rights to life, to reputation, and to personal liberty, and rights are not entitlements. Rather they are equal claims for which there are concomitant and reciprocal duties. Any claim to a right to health care, then, is an entitlement only to the extent that others have realizable equal entitlements, where one has concomitant responsibilities first for the care of oneself and secondly to honor equally the rights claims of others. The realization of these entitlements equally, Smith would admit, does in part depend on the economic well-being of a particular society. Interestingly, Smith argues that universal mandatory public education must be provided by government in any society, for without that most of us "become as stupid and ignorant as it is possible for a human being to become."[15] Given this view and Smith's theory of rights, if medicine had been in a more advanced state in Smith's day, one wonders if he might have made the same arguments for universal basic health care as part of government's duty to prevent harms to one's rights to life and liberty.

Nevertheless Smith would be critical of the caring model. Smith would argue that caring is a virtue just as benevolence is. But as a model for dealing with problems in health care, it is not comprehensive for a number of reasons. First, one need not be benevolent, caring, or charitable, and being benevolent does not preclude being arbitrary or unfair to those one does not include in the circle of benevolence. Therefore the impartial norms of justice should underlie this model. Second, caring does not preclude noncooperation or greed. Third, however, the notion of caring can be accommodated with Smith's notion of justice. What justice demands is not the absence of caring, but its equal application. What a just caring model demands, and also what the rights model demands, in the context of Smith's idea of public works, is a provision for equal minimum basic health care needs for all of society.

Smith writes little about professionalism, but it is obvious that the spheres of commerce, technology, and rights do not encompass a fourth sphere, that of the health care specialist as a professional. Each of these is a different social sphere with particular and distinct goals. While any professional is expected to be prudent, cooperative, and just, the moral guidelines for a professional are not identical with the guidelines for those engaged in commerce. However, profitability does not exclude nor preclude the ideals of a profession that set standards for the behavior of health care specialists. The confusion lies either in the conflating of commerce with professionalism, which can lead to a commodification of patient-specialist relationships, or in the absolute division of professionalism and commerce such that a professional imagines that his or her entrepreneurial endeavors in the health care field have no spillover effect on his or her patients or professional ideals.[16] But again, it is the misinterpretation of the market model, the dominance of any Ayn Rand version of egoism, and a confusion of professional and commercial interests, not commerce itself, that has led to the decline of professionalism in health care.

Given Smith's caveats or provisos, there is no reason to condemn commercialization of certain aspects of health care when they meet Smith's five criteria (economic liberty, prudence, cooperation, justice, and a level playing field). What needs to be changed, then, is the *Wall Street* movie of markets and the trend toward market imperialism that illicitly extends the scope of its application. Moreover, a limited and revised market model is not antithetical to a more equal distribution of health care benefits. There is one interesting idea to be gleaned from the market model, an idea traceable to Milton Friedman.[17] Some years ago, during one of its public education crises, the City of Chicago proposed a voucher system for public education wherein schools would be privatized and parents would be given vouchers for the education of their children, vouchers to be redeemable at the school of their choice. A form of this system had been adopted by Milwaukee and is in the process of being instituted in that school system. Similarly, one could reallocate the distribution of health care benefits by issuing vouchers for each person in an amount necessary to cover annual basic health care needs. Smith would likely approve of this model since it minimizes paternalism and places the responsibility for one's health on the individual while attempting to equalize the protection of some of our most basic rights. Like mandatory universal education, however, Smith might include mandatory minimal provisions so that one could not use one's vouchers totally frivolously. Again, however, even if this idea is worth considering, it is only one step in the direction of taking care of our society's health care, since it does not address problems of increased costs, technology, or the decline of professionalism.

Finally, Smith's precepts of justice, while limited to preventing harms, safeguarding basic rights, and ensuring fair play, are useful in setting minimum criteria for developing and evaluating health care policies, particularly those proposals that attempt to apply a single set of rules, benefits, or distributative criteria to all health care phenomena. For surely it is the case that at a minimum (1) no policy should improve the situation of some if it worsens the situation of others or in general increases harms; (2) no policy should be unfair either to individuals, groups of individuals, or to those who would be affected by similar decisions, or minimally it should not contribute to increasing biases, unequal opportunities, or favoritism; and (3) no policy should be adopted or enforced that violates basic rights, those rights to which every person unquestionably has claim, or again, at the least, it should not violate more rights than the status quo.[18]

What is to be learned from Smith is that it is not commercialization that is evil but its exploitation. Yet without being a misanthrope, one must be cautious about the virtues of caring and benevolence. Commodification of some aspects of health care, the abandonment of the caring model, and the development of national health care policies do not imply either the end of good health care nor exclude provisions for the poor provided that justice, not self-interest, prevails.[19]

NOTES

1. C. Dougherty, The Costs of Commercial Medicine, *Theoretical Medicine* 11 (1991).

2. C. Venning, The World of Adam Smith Revisited, *Studies in Burke and His Time* 19 (197):61. It should be noted that Professor Venning disputes this reading of Smith in her article.

3. For versions of this interpretation of Smith, see, for example, G. Shack, Self-Interest and Social Value, *Journal of Value Inquiry* 18 (1984):123–137; A.O. Hirschman, *The Passions and the Interests* (Princeton, N.J.: Princeton University Press, 1977); R.H. Frank, *Passions within Reason* (New York: Norton; 1988); A. Etzioni, *The Moral Dimension* (New York: The Free Press, 1988); M. Myers, *The Soul of Modern Economic Man* (Chicago: University of Chicago Press, 1983).

4. P. Railton, Moral Realism, *Philosophical Review*, 95 (1986):172.

5. See P.H. Werhane, Introducing Morality to Thrift Decision Making, *Stanford Law and Policy Review* 2 (1990):126.

6. See M. Walzer, *Spheres of Justice* (New York: Basic Books, 1983), esp. chaps. 1, 4.

7. Smith notes, "How selfish soever man may be supposed, there are evidently some principles in his nature, which interest him in the fortune of others, and render their happiness necessary to him, though he derives nothing from it except the pleasure of seeing it. . . . The greatest ruffian, the most hardened violator of the laws of society, is not altogether without it" (A. Smith, *The Theory of Moral Sentiments*, edited by L. Macfie and D.D. Raphael [Indianapolis: Liberty Classics, 1976], I.i.1.1).

8. A. Smith, *The Wealth of Nations*, edited by R.H. Campbell and A.S. Skinner (Oxford: Oxford University Press, 1976), I.ii.2.

9. Smith, *The Theory of Moral Sentiments*, II.ii.3.4.

10. Smith, *The Wealth of Nations*, IV.ix.51.

11. Ibid., I.ii.2

12. Ibid., II.iii.25–26.

13. A. Smith, *Lectures on Jurisprudence*, edited by R.L. Meek et al. (Indianapolis: Liberty Classics, 1978), i.14, v.142.

14. This is because, Smith argues, "the whole of the advantages and disadvantages of the different employments of labour and stock . . . be either perfectly equal or continually tending to equality" (*The Wealth of Nations*, I.x.a.1).

15. Ibid., V.i.f.50.

16. See R. Green, Physicians as Businesspeople and the Problem of Conflict of Interest, *Theoretical Medicine* 11 (February 1991).

17. See M. Friedman, *Capitalism and Freedom* (Chicago: University of Chicago Press, 1962).

18. See Smith, *The Theory of Moral Sentiments*, II.ii; Smith, *Lectures on Jurisprudence,* i.9–15.

19. See G. Agich, Medicine As Business and Profession, *Theoretical Medicine* 11 (February 1991).

Chapter 37

The Ethics of Medical Entrepreneurship

David C. Thomasma

As shrinking revenues from the health care system began to hit physicians themselves and efforts were made to control physicians' income from public sources, physicians have increasingly sought ways to protect their own income. In the past, the public could expect that physicians would put patient needs first and place their own interests second. Only rarely did physicians become blatant entrepreneurs concerned mainly with how to make money.[1]

The alarms have sounded in society upon learning of the extent to which some physicians have responded through entrepreneurship to cost-cutting measures in health care. Evidence exists that physician self-referral leads to excessive costs, since such physicians tend to refer to the institutions in which they have an interest from three to five times as often as other physicians treating similar patients. Given these data, in 1988–1989, Rep. Fourtney Stark (D-Calif.) proposed a bill (HR939) to control entrepreneurship among physicians, thus setting in motion a national and state-level discussion about physician self-interest and the duty to protect patients and society from unnecessary tests and the attendant costs of such tests. The bill was seen

by some as inconsistent with good old American values and by others as a noble effort to resurrect the ancient ethical commitments of medicine to the best interests of patients.

After sketching the arguments on both sides, this chapter proposes a series of compromises that would allow physicians to conduct joint ventures and otherwise profit from patients not their own without harming the interests of patients and society in general. At root, the compromises require physicians to discuss their economic interests with their patients. The profit from joint ventures would be "taxed" so that marginal inner-city practices of other physicians might be subsidized and the medical schools from which the parties of the joint venture graduated would be able to receive capitalization grants.

PROPOSED LEGISLATION

The bill that Representative Stark introduced into the 1988–1989 legislative season would have barred Medicare payments to joint ventures such as hospitals and diagnostic facilities in which the referring physician has a substantial financial interest. Civil penalties would also have been included. Critics of the bill included legislators themselves. But physicians involved in the joint ventures have also complained bitterly, arguing, for example, that the joint ventures themselves have come about as a result of Congressional policies that have limited reimbursement to hospitals, policies such as the implementation of DRGs. Others argue, like David Giles, that the bill reflects a kind of "Stalinist approach," since its thrust would be to execute the whole crowd rather than attempting to find the criminal.[2] The implication of Giles' view is that Congress is interested in cracking down on Medicare abuse. But he seems to miss the point. Congress is indeed obligated to monitor taxpayers' funding of the health care system through Medicare and Medicaid, yet it is also interested in cracking down on excessive entrepreneurism in medicine as well.

Stark, in proposing the bill suggested "that a physician would compromise the physician-patient relationship" to profit from a free-standing medical business to which he or she can refer patients.[3] Not only Congress, but also Medicare regulators, state licensing agencies, and the courts are concerned about the ethics of physician profit-making. There is also a danger perceived by those responsible for the public good: increased costs to the states and patients as a result of reduced competition for services. Individual states began to consider proposals to limit physician self-referral shortly after the Stark bill began to be discussed in 1990. Although most of these bills have little chance of enactment, it is broadly agreed that the states should set some limits on physician self-referrals.[4]

The American Medical Association itself proposed, through its judicial council, that self-referrals would be proscribed. But at the 1992 annual AMA meeting, the delegates did not agree and forced a withdrawal of the proposed policy. The judicial council countered by noting that delegates cannot rule out judicial council judgments.[5] The deep divisions regarding this issue within the profession and within the community continue to haunt us.

THE ETHICAL ISSUES

The ethical issues raised by medical entrepreneurship are complex. Arnold Relman, editor-in-chief of the *New England Journal of Medicine*, sketched the ethical challenges of practicing medicine in the new business climate.[6] These challenges shape the responses of individual physicians and professional societies to proposed legislation. Elizabeth McMillan, former senior associate of the Theology, Mission and Ethics division of the Catholic Health Association, has pointed out that the most common response is to act personally affronted. This response lies on the personal level of ethics, how individuals treat one another. But, as she rightly indicates, there are two other levels of analysis: social ethics ("how public policy and social attitudes affect people") and corporate ethics ("how institutions affect people").[7] Let us examine physician entrepreneurism from these three points of view.

Personal Ethics

Until recently, medicine was governed by a code of ethics that emphasized personal virtues such as probity, truthfulness, trustworthiness, promise keeping, and the like. In retrospect, there was something "clubby" and "gentlemanly" about this code. The American Medical Association code has gradually eroded until now it resembles nothing more than a set of legalistic injunctions.

Nonetheless, many physicians and surgeons today still recall "the old days." They reflect with dismay on the changes in modern health care and long to return to the days when patients and physicians trusted one another. Sometimes this vision of the past acquires a romantic aura that does not accurately reflect conflicts within the doctor-patient relationship during the past. Perhaps it is wiser to accept this kind of thinking as a form of wish that the doctor-patient relationship be nonconfrontational.

Major changes in the delivery of health care have also had an impact on this somewhat idyllic view of the doctor-patient relationship. For one thing, medicine is now delivered in large institutions, with an increasingly impressive array of technology, and through strangers, some of whom, such as specialists running the machinery, are not even trained in medicine itself. So the patient is confronted by white-robed caregivers who do not necessarily share the primary ethic of medicine, even as articulated in the past. A new ethic governing the relation of strangers to one another is required. I will say more about this in the final section of this chapter.

For now, however, it is sufficient to note that the more physicians object to bills like the one proposed by Stark, the greater the potential for negative public reaction. Robert L. Phillips, president of Health Business Development Associates, a consulting firm, addressed this point at the annual meeting of the American Hospital Association in 1989. He said in this regard, "Physicians are likely to be added to the critical list" of trusted professionals whose integrity is questioned.[8]

Today there is a tremendous opportunity for physicians to profit from services they themselves do not perform. There is a trend toward outpatient services and organized medical groups that are capitally funded by physicians. These services are currently reimbursed by Medicare, and at the same time hospitals are being forced to limit admissions. Physician income may decline as a result. There is a perception on the part of many physicians that if they do not join such ventures, they will be left "out in the cold," suffering a precipitous decline in patients and income. The desire for profit seems almost limitless. At present, joint ventures are being scouted for buy-outs by newly established publicly traded companies formed to take advantage of any curtailing of physician involvement in such ventures.

At the same time, one does not have to look far to perceive public reaction to this state of affairs. An Ann Landers column contained many letters about the crisis in nursing and in health care in general. One, from San Francisco, presumably from a nurse, said, "Our hospital is a beautiful shell. The building is magnificent, but patient care stinks. Hospitals lose money, but suppliers get rich. It's like the Pentagon scandals. The taxpayers get ripped off, but some huge companies made zillions. The administrators should be held accountable."[9] Other letters betrayed the same level of bitterness and burnout that has an impact on the quality of care in our institutions and on the public perception of all health care providers. Profit and care clash directly in this perception.

Social Ethics

H. Tristram Engelhardt, Jr., and Michael Rie have argued that there is nothing inherently wrong with entrepreneurship in health care. In fact, they conclude that it is "virtuous."[10] This conclusion rests on their view of social ethics. On this view, a libertarian notion of social good, there is absolutely nothing wrong with individual and group entrepreneurship in health care. Not only is there nothing wrong, but competitive institutions "skimming and dumping" patients are actually virtuous because they take the paying patients and dump those who cannot pay off on public institutions. In this way, society itself is forced to come to grips with the amount of health care it wishes to provide for the poor and the uninsured.

According to Engelhardt and Rie, individuals are free of obligations to one another unless they take on an obligation voluntarily. In the past, they argue, health care was provided to the poor without willing consent. We were paying for their care through inflated fees. Popular ideas of justice may even make this type of system appear to violate the rights of others.

While some of Engelhardt and Rie's claims are true, some are not. Non-profit hospitals do not make profit in the manner that for-profit hospitals do. For one thing, their "excess of revenue over expenditures" does not go into the pockets of the hospital trustees or distant investors. It all goes into capital improvement or expansion for other activities related to the improvement of patient care. This is very different from the primary orientation of a corporate entity, which is to provide a return to investors. That return is a moral obligation, too. It is the fact that the obligation to maximize the investors' money and the obligation to the sick conflict that constitutes the major objection to for-profit medicine.

According to a different view of society, individuals owe each other care for needs they themselves cannot provide. Erich Loewy, for example, argues that the morally significant feature of any being is its capacity to suffer. As that capacity increases, so too does our obligation to care for that being should it encounter an illness, accident, or other impediment to fulfillment, especially if it cannot provide the means for its own care. The greater the potential to suffer, the greater the value of the lives of those beings.[11] Countering libertarianism is a growing movement called communitarianism that proposes responsibilities to the community exist as adjuncts of rights.[12]

When people become seriously ill and know that treatments are available to others who can pay for them, they will not quietly accept a social system that forever condemns them as outsiders. Health care eludes 37 million people in the United States who are uninsured or underinsured. A "thirst for justice" among health care professionals is desperately needed.[13] A number of proposals have been made for covering everyone, but only a few call for a national health plan. The new administration has promised some sort of national health plan, and some states have developed their own plans. Nevertheless, we are acutely aware that we have only limited resources for health care for all citizens.

Yet in the realm of social justice, a person "called" to the profession of health care would accept an obligation to participate in designing and operating institutions and policies that would result in a just and equitable distribution of health care as well as other socially important services. Such involvement is required of individual health care professionals, health care professions as corporate entities, and the entire community. The provision of just and merciful health care to all is thus a shared responsibility.

Advocacy for the sick, in all its dimensions, is also a responsibility, especially today, when our social mores tend to accept inequality and two levels of medical care.[14]

Based on the communitarian view of society, quite different from the libertarian view, a new ethic of health care for the twenty-first century can be developed. It is really the old ethic of "helping, but doing no harm," but it has to be filtered through the realities of modern health care delivery.

We may start this analysis by citing the principle of vulnerability. In a previous work on the philosophy of medicine, Pellegrino and I derived an axiom regarding vulnerability from the nature of medicine itself. We argued that, in order to attain the goal of medicine, healing, several ethical axioms were required.[15] Vulnerability was one of these axioms. It is essential to respect the vulnerability of patients, who are at a twofold disadvantage with regard to caregivers. First, patients are in a state of need; they depend on the caregivers to provide treatment (even if the work of healing is done by the patients). Second, patients have much less power than the caregivers.

A secular principle of justice cannot easily supply any special moral obligations to care for certain segments of the population, even if they are so obviously suffering. Some more recent efforts to argue for altruism purely from the point of view of philosophy have been made by Robert Veatch[16] and Robert E. Goodin.[17]

Goodin, in his *Protecting the Vulnerable*, analyzes important cases regarding the vulnerable in contracts, in business relations, in family relations, among friends, and with respect to benefactors. He builds a case that society bears specific responsibilities toward those who, in any particular relationship, are especially vulnerable to exploitation or harm. The heart of his argument is that we usually suppose that the basis for special responsibilities to protect the vulnerable from harm comes from self-assumed duties and obligations, often self-assumed through contracts, implicit or explicit. A good example of the former might be the obligation of parents to provide for their children first[18] or the obligation of a health care professional to take care of his or her own patients.[19]

This supposition is probably wrong, according to Goodin. Rather than obligations grounded in contracts by which we voluntarily commit ourselves to a limited range of persons (as the libertarians would have it), the obligation is grounded in the vulnerability of the persons themselves: "Examining several cases closely, however, suggests it is the *vulnerability* of the beneficiary rather than any voluntary commitment per se on the part of the benefactor which generates these special responsibilities"[20] (emphasis added). The beauty of this argument is that it rests on real cases that have been adjudicated in American courts. Thus, the conclusion reached by Goodin is based upon how we actually behave, how our deepest values expressed in our social thought and jurisprudential theory are brought to bear on individual persons in conflict. Furthermore, if vulnerability is indeed the basis of responsibilities, then we have responsibilities toward many more people than we might have imagined.

The problem with the argument is that many people in society have "limited benevolence," as Hume put it. We are all too familiar with the "me too" generation, the social narcissism that infects our society, and the stringent calls for autonomy and individualism on the part of the libertarians.[21] For them, there is no duty that is not explicitly and freely accepted by individuals. That people are vulnerable or poor or downtrodden or disvalued is unfortunate but not unjust. Persons who have not directly caused such problems are not responsible for their solution, unless they voluntarily assume the responsibility. Indeed, Rawls's arguments for social duties in justice are based on a theory of self-interest. Behind a veil of ignorance about our own eventual social standing, we would be impelled to altruism to protect our own needs and interests.

That is why David Ozar argues that it is insufficient, in terms of social justice, to concentrate merely on the rules governing good contracts. At the base of any contract or covenant between persons is a duty to correct any imbalance within the contract or covenant.[22]

But where does this claim come from? Can it be sustained philosophically? The only way is by social agreement about the nature of human society itself. Originally, Western society was infused by a religious vision of the interrelationship of individuals. But as the religious foundation eroded, the principle of vulnerability found itself embodied in philosophical theories of social justice. Rawls, for example, argues that we must protect peoples' "needs," "primary goods," or "vital interests."[23] This duty applies despite differing social judgments regarding those needs and vital interests.

To explore this duty further, let us now look at institutional ethics.

Institutional Ethics

A big question for institutional ethics in health care is not whether business practices are ethical. They can be. In fact they may be "virtuous" in the Engelhardt and Rie sense, but only if they contribute to the health of the institution and its ability to remain competitive in terms of quality of care. In this way, the institution lasts as a community of healers, with all that entails (not least the continued employment of its members in a common enterprise focused on bringing about the good).

The real question is whether specific marketing practices can be accepted in institutions that deliver an essential service for the common good. By this I mean that the conflict between business practices and the goal of service to the sick must be resolved.

The ethics of business as it is presently understood cannot therefore be relied upon to guarantee that extra measure of solicitude that a dedication to the sick requires. The physician functioning in an institution or group venture has a positive responsibility to resist and even to refuse to participate in actions that endanger a patient out of motives of fiscal necessity. The "economic transfer," for example, of the patient whose insurance is insufficient to pay for care in a private institution is increasingly causing ethical dilemmas for conscientious physicians.

Equally to be condemned is the practice of asking whether a patient is insured adequately before seeing him or her. Likewise, excessive fees, overutilization of diagnostic or therapeutic services, exuberant advertising, maneuvers to "dominate" the market, and a whole host of morally questionable business practices should be eschewed by any physician who claims authenticity for his or her care for the sick. The physician's "right" to treat whom he or she pleases should be voluntarily limited.

It is important, therefore, to reassert the vocation, the calling, of health care providers working in institutions and group ventures. Today, hospitals everywhere are tempted by fiscal exigencies to retreat from the care of the poor, to sell out to for-profit corporations, or to compromise with the commercialization and monetary practices adopted by their "competitors." Yet, it is precisely the ubiquity and the noncompassionate nature of many of today's fiscal exigencies that create an ever-greater need for continued involvement in setting the goals of our social institutions. Healing has always been essential to the good of the community. The focus on healing must not be lost in favor of monetary policies that destroy not only the common good but also institutional integrity. Our belief in healing must make a difference in institutional behavior.

TOWARD A DISTINCTIVE ETHICS FOR MEDICINE

Larry Churchill has perceptively called for a more distinctive ethics for medicine.[24] Too much of modern medical ethics represents a retreat from earlier traditions of dedication to the sick. Churchill argues further that it is difficult for Americans to think about rationing health care not only because such rationing seems, on the face of it, repugnant but also because we "do not have a robust tradition of social ethics in America."[25]

It is obvious that theorizing about health care is fruitless unless it is informed by reality. The doctor and the patient, the hospital and the nurs-

ing home, and Medicare and Medicaid all exist within the context of political pressures to cut care and a social environment obsessed with power and the powerful. This is the source of the mixed message: Yes, persons are important. Yes, there is a value of human life. But no, this particular person is "too far gone" to worry about. No, this old person should no longer receive care.

One way that persons have been protected in the past has been through the development of a secular medical ethics. The enormous burst of energy that characterizes biomedical ethics of the last two decades has resulted in the exposure of a vast array of complex and largely unresolved problems. The predominant mode of ethical discourse has been philosophical and analytical. Since little or no agreement on principle is possible, the emphasis has been on procedural rather than normative ethics.[26]

This focus on the procedural reflects the fact that we live in a pluralistic society. Since the Enlightenment we have progressively lost consensus on the most fundamental moral issues.[27] This is especially true of issues regarding the respect we should pay to human life, especially to vulnerable human life.

Valuable as this approach has been in encouraging discourse among those with differing belief systems, it suffers from the lack of a coherent moral philosophy of medicine upon which to ground principles, duties, rules, and virtues. It does achieve the limited aim of consensus on certain points, but it submerges, without eradicating, the deeper moral sources, religious and secular, of the entire rational superstructure of medical ethics. Policy ethics is the most abstract of all medical ethics.

It is difficult to construct a modern ethic of health care without some considerations of policies that protect the principle of vulnerability already mentioned. A policy ethic that does protect that principle with regard to entrepreneurship might have features such as the following. First, the ethic needs to govern the relationship of strangers to one another and to aid in the removal of barriers that "estrangement" creates.

Second, all implicit covenants should be laid bare. For example, there is nothing wrong with a physician owning all or part of a medical joint venture, but his or her interests should be explained to the patient, along with details about alternatives, and the patient should be allowed to make the final choice.

Third, it is not intrinsically wrong to make a living from one's expertise. What seems offensive is the lack of a sense of limits for compensation. Fees do contain some excess of revenue over expenditure. Presumably that is the charge for the physician's time and effort—what the physician receives after he or she has paid practice expenses. The question morally is, how much compensation is legitimate? There is no doubt that many fees are not morally defensible and that some investments are morally unconscionable. Most of the jokes and cartoons about doctors and money touch on the issue of limits. What makes the jokes poignant is that the profits are derived from substantial payments made by individuals, some of whom can ill afford to transfer so much money.

Fourth, since the American system of health care delivery includes a major capitalistic component (for-profit institutions), we have already accepted the view that one may make a profit from the illnesses of others (something worth debating ethically in any event). Nonetheless, it is an infringement of the rights of physicians as a class to limit or bar their investment in health care enterprises. Rather than curtail such investment altogether, perhaps the model of a "blind trust" might be helpful—the individual physicians could have investments in health care ventures but would not know which ones. In a "double-blind" system, neither physicians nor their patients would know where the investments lay.

Fifth, restrictions on investment might adversely affect individual and group initiative. Perhaps this possibility is what concerns most individuals about the Stark bill and other similar measures, including the efforts of the AMA to outlaw physician referrals. It is quite possible that group health corporations and services will not eliminate competition and increase costs but might in fact do the opposite by bringing ingenuity and know-how to the health care marketplace. The American Hospital Association itself supports joint ventures on grounds such as these and holds that such ventures should be legitimate business ventures and participation should not be limited to past and/or future referrals.[28] Yet surely this response fails to meet the instinctive concern of Representative Stark and many others regarding the erosion of trust between doctor and patient. Is this not too high a price to pay?

CONCLUSION

Perhaps the best compromise might be to curtail excessive profit made from the illnesses of others by requirements to donate time for the poor, build operations in the inner city, and return funding (a new kind of capitalization) to the medical school where one was trained.

Another idea might be to "tax" income made by physicians when they refer patients to enterprises they own or have a financial interest in. The resulting funds could then be used to assist the poor in getting the medical care they need. The danger of the two-tiered system is thereby avoided as far as possible, as is the whiff of evil in the capitalism of health care.

At a time when most of the world is altering its view of Marxist-Leninist socialism and turning to capitalism, it is important to stress that neither system is inherently evil. Only what we make of it by our communal sense of justice can turn the economic system we use into a force for good or ill. We are now at an important juncture in the development of our health care system, and our choices now will determine whether that system is a force for good in the near and intermediate future.

NOTES

1. E.D. Pellegrino, and D.C. Thomasma, *For the Patient's Good: The Restoration of Beneficence in Health Care* (New York: Oxford University Press, 1988).

2. The Stark Bill: Just One More Battle, *Catholic Health World* 5, no. 14 (1989):2.

3. S. Morris, Physician Self-Referrals Spark Debate, *Chicago Tribune*, August 2, 1989, sec. 3, p. 3.

4. Cure Physician "Self-Referral," *Chicago Tribune*, June 9, 1992, sec. 1, p. 19.

5. AMA Moves to Curb Physician Self-Referrals, *Chicago Tribune,* May 7, 1992, sec. 1, p. 31.

6. A. Relman, Practicing Medicine in the New Business Climate, *New England Journal of Medicine* 316 (1987):1150–1151.

7. As quoted in The Stark Bill.

8. Morris, Physician Self-Referrals Spark Debate.

9. A. Landers, Nurse Situation Still Critical, RNs Report, *Chicago Tribune*, August 13, 1989, sec. 5, p. 3.

10. H.T. Engelhardt, Jr., and M. Rie, Morality for the Medical-Industrial Complex, *New England Journal of Medicine* 319 (1988):1086–1089.

11. E.H. Loewy, Obligations, Community and Suffering: Problems of Community Seen in a New Light, *Bridges* 2 (1990):1–16.

12. E.H. Loewy, *Suffering and the Beneficent Community: Beyond Libertarianism* (Albany, N.Y.: State University of New York Press, 1991).

13. J. Drane, *Becoming a Good Doctor: The Place of Character and Virtue in Medical Ethics* (Kansas City, Mo.: Sheed and Ward, 1988), 153–163; E.D. Pellegrino and D.C. Thomasma, *The Virtues in Medical Practice* (New York: Oxford University Press, in press).

14. R. Worthington, Many States Wary of Rigid National Health-Care Plan, *Chicago Tribune*, January 10, 1993, sec. 1, p. 1.

15. E.D. Pellegrino and D.C. Thomasma, *A Philosophical Basis of Medical Practice* (New York: Oxford University Press, 1981), 155–169.

16. R. Veatch, *The Foundations of Justice* (New York: Oxford University Press, 1986).

17. R.E. Goodin, *Protecting the Vulnerable* (Chicago: University of Chicago Press, 1985).

18. Ibid; R.L. Trivers, The Evolution of Reciprocal Altruism, *Quarterly Review of Biology* 46 (1971):35–57; M. Ridley and R. Dawkins, The Natural Selection of Altruism, in *Altruism and Helping Behavior*, edited by J. Rushton and R. Sorrentino (Hillsdale, N.J.: Lawrence Erlbaum, 1981), 19–39; P. Singer, *The Expanding Circle* (Oxford: Clarendon Press, 1981).

19. R. Veatch, *A Theory of Medical Ethics* (New York: Basic Books, 1981), 386.

20. Goodin, *Protecting the Vulnerable*, xi; see also pp. 42–108.

21. H.T. Engelhardt, Jr., *The Foundations of Bioethics* (New York: Oxford University Press, 1986).

22. D. Ozar, The Social Obligations of Health Professionals, in *Medical Ethics: A Guide for Health Professionals*, edited by J.M. Monagle and D.C. Thomasma (Gaithersburg, Md.: Aspen Publishers, 1988), 271–283.

23. J. Rawls, *A Theory of Justice* (Cambridge, Mass.: Harvard University Press, 1971).

24. L. Churchill, *Rationing Health Care in America: Perceptions and Principles of Justice* (Notre Dame, Ind.: University of Notre Dame Press, 1987), 20–42.

25. Ibid., 20.

26. D.C. Thomasma, The Possibility of a Normative Medical Ethics, *Journal of Medicine and Philosophy* 5 (1980):249–260.

27. A. MacIntyre, *After Virtue* (Notre Dame, Ind.: University of Notre Dame Press, 1984).

28. Morris, Physician Self-Referrals Spark Debate.

Part V

Institutional and Relationship Issues

Chapter 38

Educating Ethics Committee Members: Programs and Networking

Ray Moseley and Mary Harward

Increasingly, hospitals, nursing homes, and other health care institutions have established or plan to establish ethics committees. The purpose of such committees varies considerably among institutions. Some committees have diverse functions, such as discussing general ethical topics, reviewing and formulating hospital policy, educating hospital staff, and providing ethics case consultation. Some committees limit their activities to one or more of these functions. The quality of the ethics committee's performance in any activity, though, directly relates to the expertise of its membership.

Some health care providers believe that the only prerequisites for ethics committee membership is "good morals" and a willingness to express an opinion. We believe that this approach to committee membership is inadequate. For an ethics committee to perform effectively, especially when offering ethics case consultation, the members must be educated in ethical theory and practice. The members also must be educated as to their roles and functions within the committee.

In this chapter we identify the essentials of clinical ethics that are needed by ethics committee members and discuss the possible roles of members. Most committee members have not had training in clinical ethics during their professional education; therefore, we identify several methods for educating members.

THE ESSENTIALS OF CLINICAL ETHICS

A prospective ethics committee member should clearly understand the crucial elements of clinical ethics. This does not mean that the member must be able to knowledgeably discuss a specialized area of ethical theory, such as Immanuel Kant's arguments for a rule against lying. Instead, the member should understand how to (1) accurately identify ethical conflicts; (2) relate ethical practices to current case law and state and federal statutes; (3) discuss ethical issues appropriately using the vocabulary of ethics; (4) logically and objectively approach ethical analysis; and (5) openly discuss, debate, and resolve ethical issues brought before the ethics committee.

Identifying Ethical Conflicts

An ethics committee member should be able to identify, analyze, and resolve ethical problems. A committee member should clearly distinguish between ethical and "problem patient" dilemmas. For example, cases might be referred for an ethics consultation that involve communication problems or personality conflicts between physicians. An ethics committee may choose to participate in analysis and resolution of these cases but should understand that they involve disputes between physicians and not ethical problems.

Relating Law and Ethics

The relationship between the law and ethics also should be clear to all committee members. Ethics committees may fall into the trap of utilizing legal consultation as *the method* to resolve ethical problems. Of course, the ethics committee members should be familiar with pertinent case and state law since many laws and legal cases regarding medical care are rooted in ethical analysis. Despite this connection, it is naive to believe that the law will unambiguously resolve ethical dilemmas for ethics committees. In many cases in which ethical dilemmas arise, the applicable law is not clear or is subject to several interpretations (and misinterpretations).

Using the Language of Ethics

Members of ethics committees should be conversant in the language of clinical ethics. Most health care areas use specialized language to clarify life and death issues; thus, diseases, symptoms, medicines, and procedures are discussed in highly technical language to ensure precise, focused communication. However, the use of precise vocabulary is frequently absent when ethical issues are discussed. Members of ethics committees should understand the precise meaning and ethical ramifications of terms such as *terminal, futile, extraordinary, informed consent, autonomy,* and *competence.*

Analyzing Ethical Dilemmas

Ethical analysis is more complex than a "matter of opinion." Many physicians base their ethical thinking on what they "feel" is the right thing

to do. Any disagreement with the decision is dismissed because they think "there is no right answer" to ethical problems. These contentions persist largely because of misinterpretation of the principle that different views and opinions should be tolerated in a free society. A "principle of tolerance" does not imply that *all* views or positions are ethically indistinguishable; it merely states that persons have the right to espouse and believe these different views.

Two additional points about ethical analysis should be understood by committee members. First, ethical theory and case analysis can be used to evaluate the validity of an argument in supporting a position. Specifically, one should analyze the logic, consistency, and accuracy of any argument. If the case is discussed using the method of analogy, the appropriateness of the analogy should be reviewed. Second, many ethical problems, especially those found in medicine, are extremely complex. Ethical analysis will raise questions about the medical indications of any recommended therapy; patient preferences; quality-of-life issues; and contextual factors such as the personal opinions of patients, family members, and health care providers, institutional policies, economic factors, and societal influences.[1] Frequently, the answers to these questions are not clearly known, and often decisions must be made without all of the facts. Because of these difficulties and the complexities of analyzing values, it should be no surprise that frequently a *single, crystal-clear* ethical answer will not present itself. This problem should not discourage but rather stimulate a committee to search for facts and to carefully and expertly analyze the identified ethical issues. After all, many medical problems (e.g., the diagnosis and treatment of a fever of unknown origin) are also difficult to resolve. In spite of the difficulty, the best decision possible must still be made, given the inherent uncertainty.

Discussing Ethical Issues Openly

Ethics committee members also must be receptive to open discussion and disagreement.[2] A fundamental practice of clinical ethics is acceptance and encouragement of open debate regarding an ethical problem, as long as that debate is based on logical, consistent, and accurate reasoning. This principle is surprisingly difficult for health care professionals to accept, probably because of the relatively rigorous decision-making hierarchy among health care professionals and the formal ways they usually disagree on medical issues. Health care disagreements rarely take the form of an open, straightforward verbal debate over the merits of proposed courses of action. Most disagreements are discussed through chart notes or indirect verbal innuendoes using relatively innocuous code words such as "I'm not comfortable with that." On the contrary, ethical debates should try to sharpen and clearly verbalize the exact points of disagreement.

Along with acknowledging the occurrence of disagreements, members of ethics committees should strive to be open-minded and objective. Objectivity is also surprisingly difficult to achieve. Many clinical ethical problems touch on deep-seated prejudices that relate more to one's life experiences than to professional education. These prejudices are extremely difficult to overcome. However, there are a number of educational techniques that may aid in the goal of developing ethical committee members into a knowledgeable, functional, and productive unit.

THE ROLES OF ETHICS COMMITTEE MEMBERS

Members of an ethics committee need to clearly understand the committee's functions and their role in its process. One point that can create confusion is determining whether a member of an ethics committee is serving on the committee as a representative of a department or profession or as an individual with health care expertise and sound, objective ethical judgment. We believe that members should be seen as the latter. The ethically optimal resolution is not always achieved by basing one's actions on the prevalent opinions of one's colleagues. Ethics is not perspective oriented but reason oriented. Ethically, there is not a nursing perspective or a

physician perspective; there is, though, an *ethically correct* perspective. Certainly, however, information or insight that a nurse or a physician might bring from his or her profession may be useful. The ethically correct course of action is the one that is best supported through the logical, accurate, and objective discourse outlined above.

If an ethics committee elects to provide ethics consultation, special issues related to this area need to be explicitly understood.[3] A committee will not usually provide consultation until the committee members are well educated in the ethics areas defined above and the committee has gained the confidence and support of the hospital staff.

Ethics consultation involves specific skills in communication and case analysis. A committee may decide that only a few members will become "expert" in these skills. Once formed, the ethics consult has several procedural issues to address. For example, how will consults be brought to the committee, who can request an ethics consult, will the committee's recommendations be documented in the chart, and how will patient and physician confidentiality be protected? Also ethics consults can serve as forums for discussion while a case is active or for review after the events have occurred.

EDUCATIONAL TECHNIQUES

Most hospital staff and ethics committee members will have no formal background or education in ethical theories, case analysis, and practices. One of the primary functions of the committee is to ensure appropriate education for the members and the staff, including physicians, nurses, other clinical staff, and administrators. Several venues for adult education are available to accomplish these goals.

Readings

The ethics committee can maintain a pertinent library on ethical issues that is readily available to committee members and hospital staff. The readings should be current and chosen carefully for content and readability. Journal articles also are useful but should be carefully selected. Busy staff members are unlikely to read a 75-page discourse on the finer points of ethical theories that may be extremely interesting to experts in the field but will have little practical application for the clinician. The American College of Physicians publishes an ethics manual that provides an excellent reading list.[4] Many articles related to ethics are now published in the clinical journals such as the *New England Journal of Medicine, JAMA, Annals of Internal Medicine,* the *Journal of General Internal Medicine,* and the *Journal of Family Practice.*

Discussions

During the development and growth of an ethics committee, discussions about the future role of the committee will be an open forum for education. As pointed out above, committees at different hospitals may have very different functions. The educational process for a given committee will directly reflect its particular functions. Select committee members may want to focus on a particular area of expertise, review that area, then educate the other members about the topic. Such topics could include hospital policy; current state legislation and case law regarding ethical issues, especially refusal and withdrawal of treatments; the Patient Self-Determination Act and its implications; the process of ethics case consultation; management of the dying patient; and informed consent.

Once established, the ethics committee can begin to educate hospital staff. Hospital staff meetings are excellent forums for this. Sometimes the committee's participation will be as brief as updating staff on recent hospital policies related to ethics. If the committee is involved in consultation, a case-oriented conference also will be instructive. Such conferences should not be limited to physicians only. Nursing; occupation, respiratory, and physical therapy; social work and chaplain services; and the administration all need to be involved. "Grand rounds" and in-service discussions in the various specialties

also can be devoted to ethical issues on a regular basis.

Conferences

Many medical schools sponsor one- or two-day conferences on practice aspects of medical ethics that are useful for committee members. Many ethics committees find a monthly or bi-monthly conference on ethical topics within the hospital to be a useful forum for educating staff.

Visiting Experts

Most medical schools have medical ethics or medical humanities departments. Many of the faculty are available to provide conferences and/or workshops at local hospitals and can be of assistance in getting an ethics committee started.

Networking

In many cases, ethics committees are joining together to form regional or statewide networks. For example, in Florida, a bioethics network has been established to link professionals at all levels who have an interest in bioethics. The specifics of the organization of this network may aid others in establishment of similar networks.

The mission of the Florida Bioethics Network (FBN) is "to enhance and promote members' awareness of and knowledge about bioethical issues, further preparing them to serve their respective institutions, other health professionals, and all health care consumers, and influence constructively practice standards and policy development in the delivery of health care." The FBN has adopted four major objectives:

1. to provide channels of communication to identify emerging concerns in the field; discuss current topics; debate controversial issues; and highlight ethical, legal, social, and political developments and reference resources for continuing education

2. to assist in the formation, development, and functioning of institutional bioethics committees

3. to serve as a statewide center for Florida health care organizations

4. to conduct educational programs

These objectives are met in several ways. The most visible is a quarterly newsletter distributed to all FBN members and to the CEO of every Florida Hospital Association hospital. The major FBN meeting is an annual business and educational conference that focuses on one or two topics of special interest to ethics committees or on a topic of general interest. Other states with large numbers of professionals interested in ethics may wish to establish similar networks.

NOTES

1. A.R. Jonsen et al., *Clinical Ethics,* 3rd ed. (New York: McGraw-Hill, 1992).

2. B. Lo, Behind Closed Doors: Promises and Pitfalls of Ethics Committees, *New England Journal of Medicine* 317 (1987):46–50.

3. G.J. Agich and S.J. Youngner, For Experts Only? Access to Hospital Ethics Committees, *Hastings Center Report* 21, no. 5 (1991):17–48; K.S. Simpson, The Development of a Clinical Ethics Consultation Service in a Community Hospital, *Journal of Clinical Ethics* 3 (1992):124–130; J.C. Fletcher et al., eds. *Ethics Consultation in Health Care* (Ann Arbor, Mich.: Health Administration Press, 1989).

4. American College of Physicians, American College of Physicians Ethics Manual, 3rd ed., *Annals of Internal Medicine* 117 (1992):947–960.

Chapter 39

Health Care Institutional Ethics: Broader than Clinical Ethics

Dennis Brodeur

Bioethical problems have dominated the ethical concerns of hospitals and other health care institutions for the past two decades. The termination of treatment, autonomy, informed consent, advance directives, and issues of reproduction have occupied center stage. However, there are many other ethical issues that health care institutions must address.

Today, health care centers are complex, interdependent systems of patients, families, professionals, payers, processes, communities, and businesses. These multiple players interact in intricate ways. Their daily activities, an institution's mission, and its impact on the community are sources of ethical concern. The bioethical principles of autonomy, beneficence, nonmalificence, and justice are not sufficient to address the issues that arise.

There is, of course, still a need to address bioethical issues. Because patients and their needs are the focus of much of an institution's activity, clinical ethical issues will arise and require attention. Other chapters in this book analyze these issues. This chapter focuses on the ethical issues that administrators (and sometimes trustees) need to address from a personal, institutional, and communal perspective. These include issues of justice (social, distributive, and commutative), the promotion of the common good, the meaning of work, the definition of health, the role of government, and the allocation of resources, to name a few. This chapter will not outline a comprehensive theory of justice, argue for a process of allocating or rationing resources, define the concept of health, or argue for a particular philosophical understanding of work. But it will attempt to sketch areas of concern in the value or ethical conflicts that arise in health care institutions.

Health care institutions play a significant public role in their communities. They provide medical services and education and are often major employers. The trustees and the managers of a health care institution confront ethical issues that involve clinical matters, the institution's structure, its strategic direction, personal and personnel commitments, and the public nature of the institution.

CLINICAL CONCERNS

Institutions are increasingly asked to play a role in clinical and patient/family ethical issues. A few examples are the Patient Self-Determination Act, required community education for Medicaid recipients, organ donation request laws, and regulations for medical experimentation involving human subjects. The Joint Commission on Accreditation of Healthcare Organizations, in the patient rights section of its accreditation manual for hospitals, requires that "the patient or the patient's designated representative participate in the consideration of ethical issues that arise in the care of the patient."[1] Institutions must develop processes to allow the patient or the patient's designee access to ethics consultants, an ethics committee, or a defined process to address ethical questions.

These clinical issues are typically dealt with using traditional ethical principles such as autonomy, beneficence, and justice.[2] The limits of these principles (e.g., the limits of an institution's or professional's obligation to treat a patient who requests "everything") force health care institutions into other arenas of ethical concern than those represented by the clinical setting. Clinical issues often wind up involving questions of community need,[3] government regulation,[4] and organizational structure.[5]

Trustees and managers must ensure that mechanisms are established to address clinical ethical concerns. New clinical ethical issues will arise as medicine and technology continue to develop. It is more likely that consensus will be achieved in response to some of these clinical concerns than in the case of issues involving the institution's worklife, its sense of justice, the concept of health, or the definition of a socially accountable health care institution.

HUMAN RESOURCES

Usually agreement exists about the organization's ethical commitments to human resources and personnel issues. Most people would state that an organization's greatest resources are its human resources and that the inappropriate or unethical treatment of the work force leads to a collapse of the institution's mission and ability to serve the public. A list of ethical principles and rules could be developed that,

prima facie, seem to be normative: Treat people as an end not as a means, pay personnel justly, do not lie to or manipulate individuals in the work force, institute mechanisms for participatory decision making, ensure that personnel policies are just and do not discriminate, treat all with dignity and respect, ensure fair disciplinary policies, and do not allow physical or sexual harassment in the workplace.

Surveys of human resource professionals reveal that there are issues underneath this normative agreement about what is ethical in the workplace. A recent survey of human resource management personnel indicates that the ten most serious ethical situations are as follows:[6]

1. hiring, training, or promotion based on favoritism
2. allowing differences in pay, discipline, promotion, and so on, because of friendships with top management
3. sexual harassment
4. sexual discrimination in promotion
5. using discipline for managerial and nonmanagerial personnel inconsistently
6. not maintaining confidentiality
7. sex discrimination in compensation
8. using nonperformance factors in appraisals
9. arrangements with vendors or consulting agencies leading to personal gain
10. sex discrimination in recruitment and hiring

For example, 22.6 percent of the personnel managers who responded indicated that sex discrimination in recruitment and hiring was an ethical issue they confronted in 1991, and nearly 31 percent indicated that the hiring, training, or promotion of personnel based on favoritism was an issue.

Clearly, the prima facie agreement on normative ethical principles among human resource managers does not ensure that all people in the workplace act in accordance with ethical standards. The temptation might be to dismiss unethical practices as aberrant behaviors of unethical managers. Yet one suspects that most managers would identify themselves as behaving ethically in most if not all situations. The root cause of some of these ethical problems lies in the culture of the organization.

Boards of trustees who establish ethical parameters for personnel policies and managers who implement these policies in the workplace must be attentive to the policies, practices, processes, and other factors that contribute to unethical behavior. For example, they need to give careful consideration to the writing of policy manuals, the designing of disciplinary procedures, and other activities that reflect the ethical commitment of the organization. This attention to ethical matters in personnel policies has to be deliberate, ongoing, and public.

WORK AND HUMAN RESOURCES

There are philosophical and ethical assumptions about work and the nature of the workplace that undergird the human resource commitments of all institutions. Primary among them is an understanding of the nature of work. Philosophical,[7] religious,[8] and management science[9] writings explore these issues.

What is the relationship between work processes, products or goods, and human life? Is work a drudgery for human beings, something to be done for a shift or workweek or to scrape out a living? Are the products and services developed the most important focus, taking precedence over the people who produce them? Or is the worker the primary focus?

Work is a means through which human beings express significant aspects of personal life, support the development of family, build community, and create a culture. Human beings are not made for work; rather work is the expression of the dignity, specialness, and creativity of human beings. The ethical demand is to create a work environment in which all people are allowed to express their personal dignity and realize their creative possibilities. Health care institutions employ a great number of individuals who view their work as a vocation, a calling, or a ministry.

Even those workers who perform more routine tasks, when discussing their job, often characterize their activity and work processes as contributing to a greater end—the care of those in need. The ethical challenge to managers is to create a work environment that is expressive of human dignity, filled with "joy," and personally fulfilling.

Authors who focus on the question of work, including management science authors, describe a number of other "normative" principles that help create a meaningful work environment. First, there is the principle of subsidiarity, which entails that decisions should be made at the level where they have the greatest impact and that the owners of work processes should be involved in the decision-making process.

The second principle is that decisions should be based on a consensus. This does not preclude decisiveness or quick decision-making in certain settings but suggests that groups who work together, examine the root causes of problems, and seek departmental and cross-departmental solutions are more likely to find effective solutions and to create a work environment that is respectful of all individuals. Failure to develop these types of strategies can demoralize employees, create an institutional dynamic that is disrespectful of human dignity, and give the impression that the most important things about work are the products or services and not the people doing the work.

Third, organizational assistance must be provided to workers to ensure they are able to assert their rights. The means of such assistance can take different forms: unions as understood in the National Labor Relations Act; unions as understood in European social, political, and economic life; associations of workers and employees; and councils or governing bodies of workers within an institution.

The creation of labor law in the United States was spurred on by the discrepancy in power between the owners of capital and the workers. Although legal experts, philosophers, and theologians would acknowledge this historical fact, their exploration of the meaning of worker rights will not result in the same conceptual framework. For example, worker and manager groups could be developed that protect workers rights without any third-party intervention. But this might be judged "illegal" from a labor law perspective, which sees unions as a "third party" with a distinct purpose and set of rights. Witness the concern of unions about quality management teams of workers and managers as a mechanism that threatens to undercut union rights, even if such arrangements respect and promote the dignity and rights of the workers.[10]

Managers and trustees, sometimes quick to seek an "operations" solution to these issues, need to think about the rights of workers and the power and responsibilities of ownership and must deal with all of these issues when organizing the workplace. They need to make a commitment to the assurance of employee rights and to inclusion of workers in the process of creating, nurturing, and sustaining the work environment.

Finally, although perhaps not purely an ethical commitment, managers need to ask what management style, technique, or process best helps to build the work environment that respects the dignity of each worker. Management style will have a direct impact on the type of managers recruited and hired. Ultimately, management style is a means to achieve an ethical end—a workplace where employees are not subordinated to goods and services and where their human dignity is given due regard.

ORGANIZATIONAL IDENTITY AND STRATEGIC DIRECTION

Another area for ethical reflection for trustees and managers is the mission of the health care institution and the means it uses to accomplish this mission. The latter part of the 1980s and the early part of the 1990s saw issues related to organizational mission come to the forefront, because many health care institutions saw their nonprofit tax status challenged in state and federal courts.[11]

What are the ethical commitments that an institution has to the community it serves? In part, the ethical commitments of health care institutions arise out of the value commitments of the community, the community's identified needs, and the institution's resources available to meet these needs. Managers are required to lead health care institutions in their analysis of community needs and in strategic directions designed to meet these needs.

For the purpose of this discussion, the focus will be on nonprofit health care institutions. Nonprofit institutions must be financially sound, act as appropriate stewards of resources, and generate excess revenues over expenses. Concerns about how an institution manages its business activities as a responsible steward of resources and how it acts justly in the "business community" are particular questions of business ethics. Ethical business practices are the subject matter of a particular line of ethical inquiry. The more specific question to be addressed here is, what are the organizational ethical concerns of nonprofit health care institutions as they provide goods and services for the community?

Paul Starr and Rosemary Stevens both trace the growth of the voluntary health care sector.[12] According to Stevens' analysis, this growth also involved a shift from voluntary hospitals whose purpose was to mobilize resources at the local level to a range of disparate institutions that successfully fought government intervention and organized medicine. By the late 1930s, voluntary hospitals exemplified (in ideal cases) "public responsibility without government compulsion" and "private initiatives untainted by selfish gain."[13]

Today, voluntary or nonprofit institutions have lost touch with the principles of that earlier era. Medicine is increasingly more organized, health care institutions depend on federal and state government for a large part of their revenues, and the government has an increasingly larger role in designing both health care financing and health care delivery systems. Health care institutions have adjusted their practices to survive and grow in this environment. As a result, some people looking at health care today do not see public charitable corporations but rather big business.

Communities pressed for tax dollars to maintain services ask questions about the appropriateness of the tax status of health care institutions in light of their "charity" care and their community benefit. But there is a schizophrenic attitude in American society regarding its health care institutions. On the one hand, communities expect that health care institutions will be close to home; be filled with the latest high technology; abound in expertise; be efficient, quality, full-service providers; take care of the poor; not be worried about insurance or payment arrangements; and not be very expensive. The costs of providing these services should be mostly covered by income derived from the overall activities of the institutions, which should not overly depend on public monies from towns, cities, counties, or states. And while health care institutions do all of the things demanded of them, questions of global health care budgets or the rationing of resources should not be necessary. On the other hand, health care institutions should not be involved in projects that raise money through non-health-related activities (except for philanthropic fund raising), should be careful about joint ventures and other business practices, and should compete openly in the marketplace while not looking like a business. Obviously there needs to be some resolution of these conflicting requirements.

This is not to suggest that there are not appropriate limits to a nonprofit institution's excess revenue, capitalization of proprietary projects, inurement, or executive compensation. However, at the root of these issues are questions about whether health care services are public or private goods, whether competition and the marketplace help or hinder the provision of these goods, and how many tiers of health care services society really wants.

There is no clear policy that will resolve every issue. In the absence of a national health plan, and even when a national health plan is enacted, managers and trustees of voluntary institutions must do their best to create institutions that re-

spond to the needs of the communities they serve. This will not be easy, and strategies may differ depending upon regulations, court decisions, and laws. Managers and trustees need to develop strategic directions that guide their institutions through this maze while meeting the needs of as many as possible. This is not only sound business strategy, it is at root an ethical imperative.

The ethical components of strategy are definitional and procedural (stated differently, they involve both ends and means). Definitional concerns include the defining of health. What is health? Is it the optimal functioning of the whole person? Is the definition, from a health care institution's perspective, individual focused or does it need to include a broader community perspective? What end is the institution aiming for? Which services are for patients individually and which are for the community's health benefit? Increasingly, "health benefit" is measured in terms of both community gain and individual gain. Consequently, preventive services, community education programs, primary health care, advocacy programs, and other activities become part of the institution's mission in the community.[14]

The means used require managers to define the process of the allocation and rationing of health care resources. No global budget for health care in the United States exists at this time. Yet each health care institution has a general sense of an "annual total budget" available to it through its strategic and financial planning process, its cash reserves, its charitable funds, and its debt capacity. After determining the health needs of the community, managers must match the human and fiscal resources necessary to meet these needs. If all health needs cannot be met, the institution must ration services based on the revenues it has.

The institution must devise a definition of rationing—the denial of certain possibly beneficial resources to some or all people—that is publicly defensible, socially accountable, quantitative, and clear.[15] Often this is not done. Rationing is surreptitious and secret, leveled only against the poor and not publicly recognized. Or in certain circumstances an institution will fall into fiscal difficulty because rationing was not done and services were provided without appropriate reimbursement.

Not all people agree that rationing is necessary, and some believe that the elimination of inefficiencies and waste could go a long way toward ensuring universal access to cost-effective and quality health care services. The ethical challenge for those who believe that rationing is not necessary is to define appropriate outcomes and cost-efficient practices and then build a system that allows sound stewardship of available resources.

Procedural concerns include ensuring that managers exhibit integrity and behave ethically. For example, financial managers must be honest and must establish financial mechanisms that are not illegal or unscrupulous, are respectful of persons, and so on. Planners must honestly assess the needs of the community when developing health care services and match available financial resources with the institution's commitment to serve those in need. Operations personnel must make decisions about services and personnel that are aligned with these strategic directions, and the chief executive officer must integrate these activities within the institution and revise them accordingly as he or she interacts with the external environment.

THE PUBLIC NATURE OF THE CORPORATION

A health care institution's commitment to service is a kind of public statement. Such a statement has ethical importance because it can contribute to the building of a community.

Trustees must ask a basic question: How will this institution make a difference to the community served in the future? The fiduciary responsibility of trustees can cause them to look backwards: What *was* the financial performance of the institution last month (or last year)? How many goals *were* achieved last year? How well *did* the institution manage debt? But their ethical responsibility is mainly a forward-looking responsibility: How *will* this institution make a difference in the world tomorrow? Planning how the moral obligations of the institution will be met is the work of the board.[16]

Creating tomorrow's vision demands ethical sensitivity to the public nature and service orientation of the organization. Generally, this includes a special concern for the sick and vulnerable but also a special concern for the disenfranchised and the poor. Both types of concern will influence the trustees and the managers in deciding upon and establishing the services that will be provided. The trustees and managers will also need to respond to community, state, or national demands for a more just social order; to address factors that contribute to poor health; and to use their considerable financial and institutional power to shape the community's future. These ethical concerns are often addressed through networking; building partnerships among business people, educators, and payers; and working with public and elected officials to achieve improvements in the health status of the community.

The preferential tax treatment of most health care institutions, their public trust, and their mission to serve obligate trustees and managers to work for the public good, creating a social order that allows for the fuller development of all members of their communities. At times, this requires an institution to challenge the medicalization of social problems—to point to, for example, the causes of lead poisoning; the prevalence of malnutrition; the abusive treatment of children, the vulnerable, and the elderly; the lack of vaccinations; and the inaccessibility of health services. If these issues are not addressed in the community, in part through health care institution leadership, costs will rise, people will be further harmed, and the health status of the community will deteriorate.

Very often, health care institutions in smaller communities and groups of health care institutions in suburban and urban communities constitute a leading economic and political force. Structuring an institution's powerful economic position for community gain and not just self-interest is an ethical requirement flowing from the mission of the institution. Moral persuasion may be the tool most often employed in these situations, but a community's trust in and dependence upon an institution or a conglomerate of institutions can give tremendous ethical power to trustees and managers.

The ethical commitment to the common good has implications for other institutional practices as well. Why would a health care institution not be sensitive to environmental issues? In the wake of the increasing costs of cure and care, can institutions be indifferent to returning people to a polluted or harmful environment? Environmental awareness will lead institutions to consider more closely the appropriate disposal of its wastes and toxins and the use of environmentally harmful products. Addressing environmental issues impacts daily operations and public policy stances.

Institutions also need to develop a self-critical perspective. They need to ask how their location, clinics, and policies affect access to care for the poor. Suburban institutions that share a community concern may ask where to place the newest clinic or professional office building or where to advertise. How do institutions contribute to the geographical isolation of the sick? What policies or regulations should institutions advocate for to increase access, equitable reimbursement, and community support? There is a tendency in health care institutions only to advocate for policies that will ensure their own continued existence. The ethical question of tomorrow is whether health care institutions can advocate for changes that are consonant with increased outpatient services, lower reimbursement, and different delivery structures; a rearrangement of public dollar commitments to address preventive health needs and decrease dependence on institutions; and an improvement of those social structures that tend to prevent illness and increase the health status of the community. There will always be a need for health care institutions, but perhaps the most equitable health care structure for tomorrow will consist of a new and different alignment of today's institutions and those that are yet to be developed.

CONCLUSION

Institutions are powerful forces in public and political life. Health care institutions are no exception. The ethical concerns of health care institutions are broader than and stretch beyond the practice of clinical medicine. Managers and trustees of a health care institution, if faithful to their mission, identity, and public stature, must systematically address the institution's role in promoting the welfare of the public it serves, and of its employees, creating a better environment for healthy living, influencing the politics and economics of its community, and developing a just public order. Trustees and managers should focus on distinct but complementary objectives to achieve these general goals. Neither group will be able to accomplish much, however, if there is not a deliberate and systematic approach to address the ethical commitments of the institution.

NOTES

1. Joint Commission on Accreditation of Healthcare Organizations, *1993 Accreditation Manual for Hospitals,* vol. 1 (Oakbrook Terrace, Ill: Joint Commission on Accreditation of Healthcare Organizations, 1993), 106.

2. See T. Beauchamp and J. Childress, *Principles of Biomedical Ethics* (New York: Oxford University Press, 1983), 59–220.

3. See D. Seay and R. Sigmond, The Future of Tax Exempt Status for Hospitals, *Frontiers of Health Services Management* 5, no. 3 (1989):3–39.

4. C. Mackelvie and B. Sandborn, Mooring in Safe Harbors, *Health Progress* 70 (1989):32–36; J. Iglehart, The Recommendations of the Physician Payment Review Committee, *New England Journal of Medicine* 320 (1989):1156–1160; D. Kinzer, The Decline and Fall of Deregulation, *New England Journal of Medicine* 318 (1988):112–116.

5. See, for example, A. Enthoven and R. Kronick, A Consumer-Choice Health Plan for the 1990s, *New England Journal of Medicine* 320 (1989):29–37; U. Reinhardt,

Wither Private Health Insurance? Self Destruction or Rebirth? *Frontiers of Health Services Management* 9, no. 1 (1992):5–31.

6. Human Resources Management: 1991 SRHM-CCH Survey (Commerce Clearing House, Chicago, June 26, 1991), 1–12.

7. See, for example, H. Arendt, *The Human Condition* (Chicago: University of Chicago Press, 1958), 79–174.

8. J. Coleman, ed., *100 Years of Catholic Social Thought: Celebration and Challenge* (Marynoll, N.Y.: Orbis Books, 1991), 201–269.

9. E. Marszalek-Gaucher and R. Coffey, *Transforming Health Care Organizations: How to Achieve and Sustain Organizational Excellence* (San Francisco: Jossey-Bass, 1990), 148–171; L. Dobyns and C. Crawford-Mason, *Quality or Else: The Revolution and World Business* (Boston: Houghton-Mifflin, 1991), 52–126.

10. K. Jenero and C. Lyons, Employee Participation Programs: Prudent or Prohibited? *Employee Relations Labor Journal* 17 (1992):535–566.

11. Seay and Sigmond, The Future of Tax Exempt Status for Hospitals; D. Pellegrini, Hospital Tax Exemption: A Municipal Perspective, *Frontiers of Health Services Management* 5, no. 2 (1989):44–46.

12. P. Starr, *The Social Transformation of American Medicine* (New York: Basic Books, 1982); R. Stevens, *In Sickness and in Wealth: American Hospitals in the Twentieth Century* (New York: Basic Books, 1989).

13. Stevens, *In Sickness and in Wealth,* 141.

14. See *AHA Community Benefit and Tax Exempt Status: A Self-Assessment Guide for Hospitals* (Chicago: American Hospital Association, 1988); *Social Accountability Budget: A Process for Planning and Reporting Community Service in a Time of Fiscal Constraint* (St. Louis: Catholic Health Association, 1989).

15. One suggested approach is presented in *With Justice for All? The Ethics of Health Care Rationing* (St. Louis: Catholic Health Association, 1991).

16. See J. Carver, *Boards that Make a Difference: A New Design for Leadership in Non-Profit and Public Organizations* (San Francisco: Jossey-Bass, 1991), 1–23; 40–55.

Chapter 40

Relationships in Health Care Revisited

Roberta Springer Loewy

INTRODUCTION

During the last few years there has been an explosion of publications on topics in the field of health care ethics, including work on the nature of the relationship between providers and recipients of health care. This chapter will concentrate on providing a deeper, more critical ethical analysis of the nature of that relationship.

Much effort has been expended in trying to find a relationship model that can adequately capture both how provider-recipient relationships do, in fact, operate and how they ought, ideally, to be conceived. Each proposed model makes certain assumptions about principles, means, intentions, consequences, and "virtuous" behavior on the part of the participants. Nevertheless, the implications that can be drawn from those assumptions have already been colored by the methodological perspective used in the process of evaluation. For this reason, prudence dictates that the particular method of inquiry be clearly elucidated at the outset of any such discussion. Therefore, what are considered to be the three traditional methodological perspectives need briefly to be reviewed, and some of their assumptions clarified, before they are rejected in favor of an alternative approach.

TRADITIONAL METHODOLOGICAL PERSPECTIVES

The first traditional approach assumes a principle (or principles) and then concentrates on discovering the best means available to preserve that principle (or those principles) irrespective of any actual ends or consequences. This perspective is generally known as deontologism. On this sort of account, values or ends are stipulated as "right" or "wrong" as a matter of principle.

The second traditional approach assumes certain shared ends or values and then concentrates on discovering the appropriate means by which those ends or values might be acquired or preserved. This perspective is generally referred to as consequentialism. Yet, central to its operation is, in fact, a hidden (though no less compelling) appeal to a general principle: the principle of utility.

The third traditional approach assumes that the character of the agents involved within any given activity is of primary importance. In other words, within this traditional perspective, judgments of value and choices of ends and principles are made on the basis of their influence on the development of the agent's character. This approach is generally referred to as virtue ethics. Often cast in a theological context because of its contingent but frequent connection with conventional religions, its primary concern is to promulgate what it considers to be accepted standards of function or excellence irrespective of the particular rationale for their adoption. On this sort of account—perhaps because of its contingent, historical identification with religion—there is already an implicit appeal to some pre-established, fixed ideal or form by which human nature, human ends or values, and human goods are evaluated.

AN ALTERNATIVE METHODOLOGICAL PERSPECTIVE: JUSTIFICATION AND DESCRIPTION

Certainly each of these alternatives has its attractions. The problem common to these traditional approaches, however, is the need to take as axiomatic at least one principle, end, or ideal. The idea that something be taken as axiomatic implies a certain independent standing and/or meaning that, in turn, gives the impression that some special ontological status accrues to it. Such a notion should be resisted for a number of reasons. Foremost among those reasons is that the adoption of a fixed, independent meaning for any "thing"—be it idea or object—creates an unavoidable logical gulf when decisions between what is and what ought to be the case must be made. To be sure, it is a gulf that we have ourselves created. Nonetheless, once in existence, it will influence our thinking.

For this reason alone, the traditional alternatives should be questioned, if not rejected out of hand. This is not to deny the legitimacy of the classical "is/ought" distinction; rather, it is to admit that such a distinction is always made within some particular inquiry into some very specific problematic situation. "Oughts" are a result—not simply the logical condition—of complex, reflective inquiry. They are born in the careful examination and accumulation of past successful experiences. They survive and de-

velop to the degree that they succeed in helping us to anticipate and to control future experiences.

Hence, the methodological perspective defended here treats theories, principles, ends, and ideals merely as pliant, potential tools in the activity of reflective inquiry.[1] Though collectively such tools are necessary to the enterprise, no particular tool can acquire any special ontological standing. As a matter of fact, the tentative nature of such tools—conceived merely as the distilled wisdom of past successful inquiries—is finally recognized for what it is: a cumulative guide and not a predetermined straitjacket.

For example, to advert to the topic of this chapter, only in the process of examining a variety of relationships—identifying what is found to be both functional and dysfunctional in each—can distinctions between what is and what ought to be the case be considered. But this occurs only in light of the fact that such conclusions are always potentially subject to re-evaluation and reconstruction. So, to anticipate some critics, I contend that philosophizing about ethical issues requires, but is not exhausted by, such things as "philosophical anthropology" and "philosophical psychology," since, whatever else philosophy is, it is the complex, progressive, and uniquely human process of reflective inquiry.

Parenthetically, such a methodological perspective not only relieves us of the alleged ontological gulf between is and ought but liberates us from other similar, equally rigid dualistic characterizations that have heavily influenced the way we think about things: descriptive/normative, practical/theoretical, substantial/formal, real/ideal, emotive/cognitive, and individual/social, to name some of the most familiar. To reiterate, it is not the purpose of this chapter to challenge the legitimacy per se of such distinctions. Of course they exist and they are essential—but they are not fixed, independently existing essences. In other words, my point is to criticize the separation, polarization, reification, and subsequent inevitable distortion of things that, of themselves, have no ontological significance. Their sole importance lies in their possible use in improving our existence in the world and our relationships with one another.

A CRITICAL REVIEW OF TRADITIONAL RELATIONSHIP MODELS

Any number of health care relationship models have been suggested and analyzed during the rise of health care ethics as a profession. Although Robert M. Veatch's 1972 article describing four distinctive models of medical practice is considered an early classic in the literature,[2] ethical analysis of the relationship between patients and physicians can be found at least as early as 1956.[3] Recent literature painstakingly distinguishes between as many as six different models.[4] It is beyond the scope of this chapter to redescribe and contrast these various models in all of their complexity—that has already been accomplished by the authors themselves. I am more interested in a critical analysis of what it is these models have in common that drives or conditions their basic presuppositions.

In a previous paper, I claimed that, whether they realize it or not, all the proposed models share one fundamental assumption: that because individual persons are respected as the prime units of moral reference, "autonomy" is, at bottom, a fundamental commonality.[5] This assumption is so strong that autonomy becomes the identifying feature of personhood (i.e., that class of sentient rational beings whose membership includes, but is not necessarily restricted to, humans).

At any rate, how broadly or narrowly the notion of autonomy is used and, in turn, the ways in which its legitimacy is respected and safeguarded differ significantly between actual models. I claimed that current models fall roughly into two camps: (1) those that construe unsolicited concern and involvement of others as a direct threat to what they consider autonomy to be and (2) those that consider such unsolicited concern and involvement to be integral to the development and sustenance of what they identify as autonomy.

Because of historical precedent in the literature, I labelled the first set of models "autonomy based" and included in it such archetypes as the "collegial," "commercial," "contracted clinician," and "engineering" models. The second set I entitled "beneficence based" and included in it such examples as the "guild," "priestly," "paternal" and "maternal" models. In retrospect, this choice of labels was unfortunate, as it inadvertently perpetuates the myth that autonomy and beneficence are fundamentally antagonistic notions—an idea that I (and several others, though perhaps for different reasons) have expressly been at pains to deny.[6] However, the validity of my criticisms of these two sets of models remains unaffected, labels notwithstanding.

In brief, I claimed that those who explain relationships in terms of the autonomy-based perspective want to advocate marketplace competition between individuals uncritically presumed to be equals as the surest method for preserving the autonomy of all parties. I argued that, on the contrary, many of our most cherished or significant relationships—like those in health care—are between persons who are unequal in the sense of having contrasting strengths and weaknesses. For these relationships, the competitive atmosphere of the marketplace is actually destructive. Of more consequence is the ambiguity of the phrase "individuals uncritically presumed to be equals."

To be more specific, a "buyer" in the health care marketplace is ignorant of the very commodity at issue: the alternatives of expertise "for sale." Because of competition between these experts, the marketplace itself undermines the conditions necessary for the relationship between buyers and sellers of health care to endure. Such unfettered competition between experts effectively prevents the development of (or actively destroys) those internal attributes and motivations (such as loyalty and trust) required to sustain the vital and personal relationship between provider and recipient of health care. In short, there is nothing in the marketplace models to prevent the development of the autonomy of the experts at the expense of the recipients of that expertise.

On the other hand, I claimed that those who explain relationships chiefly in terms of beneficence emphasize the necessity for mutual cooperation between individuals as the most successful way of complementing the unique, inherent strengths and weaknesses of each individual party to a relationship. Yet I argued that using the criterion of beneficence exposes weaker members of the relationship to various forms of coercion. So, like the first view, this one fails to provide us with ways of distinguishing adequately between "autonomous" behavior that is ethically tolerable and "autonomous" behavior that is not.

I concluded that neither view articulates a method that can identify and adequately guard against what amounts to unjustified coercion of some by others. I then sketched the broad outline of a different prototype, the "consensus model," and suggested elements that it would have to incorporate to make it a more viable alternative. But in retrospect, it appears to be not so much a model as a method that attempts to reconcile the strengths of those models already in existence.

Using such a Deweyan methodology, I claimed that only in the course of democratic dialectical engagement can relationships avoid the kinds of autonomous behavior we want to characterize as unjust or unethical, whether the resulting power is based on "coercion" or "benevolence." Engagement of this kind involves a cooperative but critical discourse between all of those relevantly affected by any judgments or decisions made on the basis of such discourse. Moreover, democratic dialectical engagement not only tolerates a multiplicity of perspectives, it celebrates them as essential to understanding the relevant aspects of any problematic situation. For the remainder of this chapter, I will investigate more carefully both the general presuppositions of this claim and the particular ramifications that it has for health care relationships.

AUTONOMY AS EMPOWERMENT: A DEVELOPMENTAL BIOPSYCHOSOCIAL PROCESS

I claimed earlier that all of the traditional relationship models implicitly appeal to some arbitrarily limited notion of autonomy. As the basis for a deeper, more critical analysis, here are the four definitions of autonomy found in *Webster's Third New International Dictionary*:

1. the quality or state of being independent, free and self-directing

2. the degree of self-determination or political control possessed by a minority group, territorial division or political unit in its relations to the state or political community of which it forms a part

3. the sovereignty of reason in the sphere of morals; possession of moral freedom or self-determination; power of the individual to be self-legislating in the realm of morals

4. independence from the organism as a whole in the capacity of a part for growth, reactivity or responsiveness

From the standpoint of our Western tradition, autonomy has been differentiated into two kinds: (1) "autonomy of the will" or self-determination (as in Kant's freedom of a rational will to self-legislate) and (2) "autonomy of action" or independence from external constraint or regulation. Built into such a division, of course, are certain assumed, simplistic dichotomies that, to borrow a phrase from Wittgenstein, have held us captive.[7] In this instance, besides the obvious internal/external duality, mental/physical, formal/material, and individual/social dualisms predominate. One of the resulting distortions is what Jonathan Moreno has recently referred to as "the myth of the asocial individual."[8] This myth is really nothing more than the popular notion of rugged individualism embraced without benefit of disciplined, logical thought. It is as though we have forgotten to turn off our specialized "tunnel vision" that permits us to ignore a background in order to analyze some conventionally stipulated foreground.

From a Deweyan perspective, however, autonomy is much more complex. It is something we point to or identify as a living possibility in some very explicit dynamic situation or experience. By this I mean that we do not merely "apply" some sort of external definition or logic to a problematic situation, which then "clears things up." Rather, we attempt to make a whole indeterminate situation or experience progressively more clear. That is, we work to uncover the internal logic of the present experience with the tentative tools we have either acquired from others or fashioned from the analysis of our own past experiences, "failures" as well as "successes."

In so doing, we discover in the context of the situation just what constitutes the maximum possible autonomy of all those concerned—and at what cost. Instead of using some external standard or ideal, we mine the potentials of the situation using accumulated principles, ends, and ideals of past experience as tentative, pliable guides. By the way, from this perspective, competition can be recognized as a central feature of our reflective inquiry into problems—competition of ideas, that is, not of persons.

Using this perspective in place of the more traditional approaches, let us reconsider *Webster's* various definitions of autonomy. All four definitions point to a common thread: Autonomy is characterized as a quality, state, capacity, and/or power belonging to an entity. That entity may be anything from a very simple, but specialized part of a whole, living organism (fourth definition) to a sentient rational organism (first definition). It may even be a group of sentient rational organisms (second definition).

The fourth definition of autonomy would be considered a purely biological description, as it does not require rational sentience, the hallmark of personhood. The first definition is essentially a psychological description, insofar as it presupposes the sort of rational reflection necessary for self-direction. On the other hand, the second definition of autonomy is primarily a social description, in that it recognizes that any sentient being's potential for autonomy is at least partially determined by existing social and political conditions. The third definition, of course, is the most subtle. It is the moral definition of autonomy. There are several aspects of this definition that need clarification.

First, the "sovereignty of reason" would seem to imply that moral autonomy, in particular, requires the ability to understand and reflectively consider the extent of both the natural and the conventional constraints posed by the other three definitions. That is, the biological, the psychological, and the social definitions of autonomy are each *material conditions* for the possibility of moral autonomy.[9] (This is *not* equivalent to saying that moral autonomy is somehow reducible to any of its material conditions.)

Second, the "power of the individual to be self-legislating" would seem to imply that moral autonomy requires the conscious adoption of some sort of agenda or routine, as in "following a rule"—not blindly but with a real understanding of the mechanics and implications of means/ends deliberation. Of course, built into self-legislative choice are the unavoidable possibilities of error—whether in choice of ends or pursuit of means—and "fate," the catch-all term for all of those unexpected things "beyond reasonable control." The whole point of means/ends deliberation, however, is not to eliminate error and fate. Rather, it is to identify and minimize them (or maximize the control of their consequences) through careful, reflective inquiry. As Dewey painstakingly argued concerning the mediate nature of experience, "Inquiry is the controlled or directed transformation of an indeterminate situation into one that is so determinate in its constituent distinctions and relations as to convert the elements of the original situation into a unified whole."[10] In short, because it identifies how we best succeed at conceiving, evaluating, and wielding power, a habit of reflective inquiry itself is our most important and powerful tool for confronting experience. Moreover, because it is a methodology, it adapts itself to the peculiar context of each unique, problematic situation as presented to us.

So, where does this leave us with respect to the notion of autonomy? What I have tried to develop is the notion that what we consider to be "foundational concepts"—ideas such as autonomy, for example—are neither fixed nor basic (if by "basic" is meant either simple or straightforward). Rather, they are richly complex, subtle, and flexible tools, having manifold aspects which help us evaluate particular things, persons, and situations. As such—at least in the language of traditional Western ethical thought—they are instrumental goods. What autonomy will "mean," therefore, is necessarily specific to the problematic situation in which it actually functions. I would argue that such concepts develop and evolve so as to preserve a dynamic biopsychosocial homeostasis that parallels the function of the dynamic homeostasis characteristic of organic life in general.[11]

How are the two types of homeostasis similar? Certainly both biopsychosocial homeostasis (the way I have described it) and organic homeostasis share a similar function: the preservation of "power" within some system. However, as any physicist knows, configuration or organization of that power is the crucial point. That is, the way in which any system's power is constantly redistributed and balanced is what stabilizes that system. Remember, what we are talking about here are dynamic systems—systems characterized by, and understood in terms of, change.

How do they differ? In biopsychosocial homeostasis, the habit of reflective inquiry is one of the central controlling factors of the system. This makes us, as sentient, rational beings, responsible in ways we are not and cannot be from the standpoint of organic homeostasis alone. We are not the creators of our biopsychosocial system yet we are not simply its pawns. Because we do "have a hand in it," biopsychosocial homeostasis describes a moral system.

RAMIFICATIONS FOR HEALTH CARE: CONCLUDING ILLUSTRATIONS

The best way to examine such a methodology at work is to use it to analyze a typical problem in health care. The case I have chosen concerns a 68-year-old mother of eight who came from Italy as a small child and still speaks little English. She married quite young, and her husband, in keeping with their cultural traditions, has never involved her in major family decisions. She entered the hospital for a biopsy of the colon, which revealed the existence of an adenocarcinoma. Liver function tests indicated a strong likelihood of metastasis. When the surgeon, accompanied by a translator, visited her for the purpose of outlining the various treatment alternatives, she refused to enter into a discussion and referred him directly to her husband, saying, "He makes all the decisions in the family. He will know what to do."

The surgeon spoke to the husband and children, who all spoke fluent English. They all insistently agreed that the patient must not be told that she has cancer, nor anything about her prognosis. The surgeon, along with other members of the health care team, felt strongly that she should be actively involved in decisions about her care. Therefore, the health care team agreed to say nothing to the patient for 24 hours in order to give the family a chance to re-evaluate their position.

The family became agitated, and the husband insisted that his wife had never been "bothered" by such decisions before. He appealed to cultural traditions in which it is considered necessary to "protect loved ones" from knowledge of diseases that could result in death. The surgeon and the rest of the health care team remained adamant that it is necessary to discuss with all competent patients their respective diagnoses and prognoses as well as the potential benefits and burdens of each alternative treatment option in order that they may make informed decisions about their own care.

Which perspective would offer the greatest chance of safeguarding this patient's "autonomy"? If we appeal to the traditional methods of evaluating a case like this one, resorting to the application of axiomatic principles, ends, or ideals, it seems we are doomed to choose between one form of abandonment or another. Why? Well, either she is abandoned to the choices her husband and family decide for her or she is abandoned to the health care team's definition of autonomy for her. Moreover, we are forced to preserve one group's set of values by trampling on the other group's set of values.

By using the kind of method I have been espousing, the health care team's prime responsibilities will be

- to confirm whether this patient's single remark to the surgeon—to the effect that she wants her husband to make all of the decisions about her care—is truly consistent with her attitudes toward and responses to similar situations in the past
- to investigate just how adamant she is in refusing even to discuss her diagnosis, her prognosis, and alternative treatment modalities
- to provide a medically acceptable care plan consistent with her interests as she conceives them

That is, only by understanding the historical evolution of this patient's experience can we begin to determine her genuine voice in the dialogue. If she knowingly and responsibly chooses at the outset of the dialogue to empower another to make those decisions, then that too can be an authentic decision for that family constellation—even though we might personally be uncomfortable with it. We may even genuinely believe that her life style does not allow her to maximally exercise her voice in the dialogue but our personal preferences give us no mandate to coerce her to change an accustomed life style that she has tacitly or explicitly chosen and that directly affects no one else adversely.

CONCLUSION

As children growing up within a community, we are at the mercy of our adult role models, who imbue us with the tacit perspectives, customs, and social practices of our particular culture. Along with the maturation process comes the responsibility of testing and re-evaluating those relatively passively acquired beliefs and habits. Re-evaluation of old and acquisition of new beliefs and habits occur at every level of consciousness, sometimes willy-nilly, sometimes with the distinct intention of making our "worldview" internally coherent. The frequency and depth of such activity depends on each individual's sensitivity and commitment to the need to order experience. That sensitivity, in turn, depends on a whole range of external and internal factors. The willingness to accept the personal consequences of our choices is but one of the signs of genuine autonomous behavior.

Knowledge is infinitely more vast than any one individual's capacity to amass it. Besides, our finite lives involve so much more for us than reflective inquiry. After all, reflective inquiry and its product, knowledge, are only means to the end of living. With the increasing specialization of knowledge, each individual becomes a potential mine of unique and valuable insights and information. Some individuals simply choose to trust others—sooner and more often than the rest of us might—to make some of their informed choices in their stead. Whether we agree or not, this too can represent autonomy.

NOTES

1. The theory I am espousing, of course, is hardly new; it had its most systematic development and expression in John Dewey's experimental theory of knowing—and it is precisely how Dewey did all of his philosophizing. A typical example that readily comes to mind can be found in Dewey's *Quest for Certainty*, edited by J.A.

Boydston, vol. 4 of *The Later Works, 1925–1953* (Carbondale: Southern Illinois University Press, 1988), esp. chap. 7. However, its most extensive development can be found in Dewey's *Logic: The Theory of Inquiry*, edited by J.A. Boydston, vol. 12 of *The Later Works*.

2. R.M. Veatch, Models for Ethical Medicine in a Revolutionary Age, *Hastings Center Report* 2, no. 3 (1972): 5–7.

3. T.S. Szasz and M.H. Hollender, A Contribution to the Philosophy of Medicine: The Basic Models of the Doctor-Patient Relationship, *Archives of Internal Medicine* 97 (1956):585–592.

4. G.C. Graber and D.C. Thomasma, *Theory and Practice in Medical Ethics* (New York: Continuum, 1989).

5. R.S. Loewy, A Critique of Traditional Relationship Models, *Cambridge Quarterly of Healthcare Ethics* 3, no. 1, in press.

6. In the evolution of his sustained argument that suffering is the precondition for the possibility of what we recognize as "ethics," E.H. Loewy now also denies the traditional opposition of autonomy and beneficence. To see the transition in his thinking, compare the structure of his first position in *Suffering and the Beneficent Community: Beyond Libertarianism* (New York: State University of New York Press, 1991) with the structure of his more recent argument in *Freedom and Community: The Ethics of Interdependence* (Albany: State University of New York Publishers, 1993). Thomasma and Graber, in *Theory and Practice in Medical Ethics*, also deny the traditional opposition, but they, unlike Loewy or me, argue that beneficence always has prima facie precedence over autonomy or any other principle.

7. L. Wittgenstein, *Philosophical Investigations*, translated by G.E.M. Anscombe (New York: Macmillan, 1958), pt. 1, sec. 115.

8. J.D. Moreno, The Social Individual in Clinical Ethics, *Journal of Clinical Ethics* 3, no. 1 (1992):53–55.

9. This sort of explanation is what might be called an argument from "material transcendence." Dewey first discusses it as early as 1905 while responding to critics—of pragmatism in general and his philosophy of experience in particular. See J. Dewey, The Knowledge Experience and Its Relationships, edited by J.A. Boydston, vol. 3 of *The Middle Works, 1899–1924* (Carbondale: Southern Illinois University Press, 1977), 171–177.

10. J. Dewey, *Logic: The Theory of Inquiry*, edited by J.A. Boydston, vol. 12 of *The Later Works, 1925–1953* (Carbondale: Southern Illinois University Press, 1988), 108.

11. For a thorough description and a more extensive analysis of homeostasis, see E.H. Loewy, *Freedom and Community*, 46–49. The way in which I use the notion, however, differs somewhat from his.

Chapter 41

Technology, Older Persons, and the Doctor-Patient Relationship

Myles N. Sheehan

An 84-year-old man with an independent life style begins to have bouts of chest pain and shortness of breath that restrict his activity. Gradually the pains increase in frequency and severity, and the man consults his physician, who makes the diagnosis of unstable angina and admits him to the hospital. Aggressive efforts to relieve the recurring episodes of chest pain are not effective. Where does the doctor go from here? One response, depending on the patient's wishes, is to proceed with coronary catheterization and angiography and, depending on the results of the angiogram, follow with angioplasty or coronary bypass surgery.

Many individuals might be deeply disturbed at the notion of an elderly man undergoing catheterization, bypass surgery, the concomitant intensive care, and the associated rehabilitation process. Why all this high technology to solve a problem? Where is the caring in this approach? How can our nation afford to use its resources on an old man when infant mortality rates are too high, our public educational system is the subject of much concern, and the infrastructure of the country needs extensive repair? After all, we want to live good lives of high quality, not be kept alive forever.

The patient's physician, likewise, may have qualms about which course to recommend. There are a number of possible adverse outcomes no matter what is done or not done. Could this case turn into one of those horrible disasters where someone is kept on machines when there is no hope for functional recovery? Maybe it is this man's time to die. What if the family becomes impossible and unrealistic, threatening and hostile if the results are less than perfect? Would a transfer to the university hospital be the best course, because it has more specialists and more sophisticated technology than the local hospital? Health care costs are out of control; should a physician recommend such an expensive approach for this old man? Does a doctor have to offer every possible therapy to every person, regardless of the likely benefits and risks?

Appropriate provision of medical care and use of technology is becoming a burdensome issue in American medicine. With the fastest growing segment of the population consisting of those 85 years and older, and demographic projections anticipating 21 percent of the population will be over 65 years of age in 2030 (rather than the 1980 figure of 11 percent), the need for some clarity in making decisions about technology in medicine is urgent.[1] As the case example illustrates, a variety of questions may be raised in attempts to come to such decisions. Disparate pressures are building that make it very hard to define the issues, much less answer the questions. In a country where some individuals insist on maximal medical care and the utmost in aggressive technological intervention, others are demanding the right to receive physician assistance in the committing of suicide. The moral arguments appear too confused, too varied, and too emotional for any individual health care professional to practice in a rational and coherent manner.

Alasdair MacIntyre, in his book *After Virtue,* notes the difficulty of reaching agreement on moral arguments in our society.[2] MacIntyre has a number of reasons that he offers as to why this is the case. Among them is what he terms the "conceptual incommensurability" of alternate positions in moral debate. Competing premises can be followed through to conclusions that are valid, yet we are unable to discern the truth of the arguments or logically choose one argument as better than another. The purpose of this chapter is to clarify issues in the debate concerning health care technology, especially in the medical care of the elderly, with the goal of assisting health care professionals in evaluating the use of technology in their own practice. Beginning with MacIntyre is appropriate for several reasons. The arguments surrounding technology use display the kind of conceptual incommensurability that he describes as characteristic of contemporary moral argument. Appeals to emotion often lurk beneath the surface of what appears to be highly logical argumentation. MacIntyre suggests that the rational basis for moral decision making (and coherent moral society) lies in determining the consistency of various positions within a shared vision of our common purpose or ends. Although complete agreement on

shared purpose is unlikely, I will argue that physicians and the elderly for whom they care can frequently recognize common ends and make reasonable decisions about the use of technology.

TECHNOLOGY AND HUMAN RELATIONSHIPS

There is a clear sense of dissatisfaction with American medicine—a feeling that doctors use too much technology and are not responsive to the needs and desires of those whom they should help. There is much that is accurate in this sense of dissatisfaction. It is, however, too facile in its criticism of technology. Physicians are not the sole culprit in the way technology is used in medical care, and a critique of technology that considers only what is new, expensive, and mechanical is naive. Such criticism neglects the pervasive use of all sorts of technology throughout our lives and the ways technology influences human relationships, including those between doctors and patients. Greater clarity about individual decisions regarding technological application requires considerations of our societal responsibilities and relationships.[3] A personal narrative may help to make this point.

In late August 1991, Hurricane Bob brushed the eastern coast of the United States before crashing into Rhode Island, southeastern Massachusetts, and Cape Cod. My parents' year-round home is on Cape Cod. I was on vacation that week and had planned to take my mother and father away for a few days up to northern New Hampshire. We left early on the morning that Hurricane Bob hit New England. The traffic leaving the Cape was bad, and long delays led us to be caught in the approaching storm. The ride was terrible—blinding rains, strong winds, flooding on the roadways. Doggedly, I kept on driving and we arrived after a seven-hour drive, two and a half hours more than normal. The day after the storm, my parents, watching the morning television news programs and seeing the pictures of damage, were horrified and decided that we must return to the Cape to see if their home had survived. Thankfully, the damage to the house itself was minor, but the devastation to the area was tremendous. Several trees littered our lawn. A portion of the garage had been removed by a falling tree. Power and telephone lines were knocked down. We were without electricity for four days.

Life changed. We went to bed by nine or ten, the flickering light of the candles not enough to allow reading. We awoke early with the return of the sun. The electric stove would not work. Food had to be eaten fresh and prepared over a fire. There was no phone to call friends and relatives. There was no television to distract us. The feeling of isolation was profound. My parents and I had to interact in a different way than was our custom. The daylight became our good time together, working outside repairing damage and removing debris. The evenings were difficult, with a hurried meal in a darkening house. As night wore on, we were without the distractions of television and forced to sit quietly together in the candlelight, with long pauses in our conversation. Without a phone to speak to family and friends, nor television to tell us what was happening, we felt cut off from the world. We were pushed in on ourselves, separated from others, and made to feel our dependence on nature.

The experience of my family and the effects of Hurricane Bob may seem unrelated to the topic of technology and its application to life-threatening crises. There are, however, two points that are germane. First, the effects of the storm emphasized the pervasive nature of technology in the lives of modern Americans. Life was radically changed without power or communications. Second, the storm revealed how technology mediates relationships between people in our society. The lack of television or other distractions forced my parents and me to converse and interact in a way that is not our habit. The evenings became a time to tell stories, sit quietly, and maybe try to read by candlelight. We interacted directly with each other, without the mediating influence of the television or some other device.

An appreciation of how our lives are intertwined with technology and how technology mediates personal relationships leads to a crucial insight. A critique of technology in medicine is deficient if it treats medicine in isolation from the technological style of the larger culture in which the practice of medicine is embedded. The way medicine is practiced in our culture is part of the way our society lives. The hurricane highlighted the fact that technology need not be complex, new, or expensive. A telephone, a stove, and a refrigerator are all common appliances that are examples of technology. Likewise, technology in medicine is not simply gleaming magnetic resonance imaging scanners and the sophisticated hardware of an intensive care unit. Technology has many forms, and the variety of forms technology takes in medicine must be acknowledged before an analysis of its use in the treatment of the seriously ill can be considered.

In medicine, as in every aspect of our lives, technology mediates relationships between individuals. A patient's visit to a physician involves a direct, personal encounter. The doctor speaks with the patient, learning the reason for the visit and asking questions to clarify the patient's complaint. There is a physical examination, with the doctor touching and probing the patient. The visit concludes with more conversation and with the doctor suggesting a course of action to be followed. But the encounter with the physician is rarely one of simply conversation and the touch of a physical examination. Instead, blood pressure is taken with a sphygmomanometer, eyes are inspected with an ophthalmoscope, ears examined with an otoscope, and heart and lungs auscultated with a stethoscope. An electrocardiogram may be done, and chances are the physician will have a sample of blood drawn for analysis. There may be X-rays taken or some other diagnostic imaging study performed. Frequently, the patient will receive a prescription to alleviate symptoms or cure the problem. The relationship between two people, doctor and patient, occurs not just through conversation and touch but through the mediation of diagnostic and therapeutic equipment of various kinds and the provision of a pharmaceutical preparation.

It may seem strange to refer to a simple office visit as a technological encounter. Recognition of the technological nature of even this basic interaction, however, may make it easier to be more discerning when considering the uses of the more complex and expensive machinery commonly mentioned in discussions of medical technology.[4] Technology changes the medical encounter. Listening to a patient's heart with a stethoscope is far different from pressing an ear against a patient's chest. A simple visit to the doctor for a routine complaint is filled with technology, even if it is familiar and not very flashy. Similarly, the use of so-called high-tech devices and procedures like ventilators or cardiac catheterizations still occurs within the context of a relationship between a doctor and a patient. To blame technology for the difficult problems we face in its application to the seriously ill misses the point. Technological interaction is the stuff of our society. What happened in the hurricane is only a rudimentary example of how our lives in this country are mediated by technology. The recognition of how pervasive technology is throughout medicine suggests that some of the dissatisfaction felt with medical care is not so much the fault of technology as of the quality of the relationship between doctor and patient.

Unfortunately, the use of technology can so dominate the encounter that it becomes the technical rather than the human that seems essential in the interaction. Again, this is not the exclusive problem of medicine. The hurricane forced me to relate to my parents on a different level because of the absence of distractions. There was no television to be our companion, and so we were forced to focus on each other. From the example of the hurricane, one can consider two types of relational styles. One could be called the personal, where people interact with each other. In the other type, the focus is on technology and the personal relationship serves only as an entree to the technological. It is not only in medicine

that relationships meant to be personal and intimate are somehow changed for the worse by technology. In the evenings, families may sit together in front of the television. For some families, the TV serves as the focus to draw them together and provide common entertainment. In others, the TV itself is the focus of interaction, and individual family members exist together watching the screen but not conversing or speaking in any meaningful way with each other.

Likewise, in medicine, the use of technology can eliminate the personal. Going back to the example of the 84-year-old man with chest pains, his condition might evoke two different responses from his physician. The physician might begin by taking a careful history and performing a physical examination, judiciously supplemented by diagnostic and therapeutic interventions. The other response would be to truncate the history and physical examination and launch a diagnostic cascade: an electrocardiogram, a cardiac catheterization, and, depending on the result of these tests, an angioplasty or coronary bypass surgery. In any adequate evaluation of chest pain, much of the interaction involves technology. The use of these tests and therapeutic measures saves lives and lowers morbidity in certain instances. A diagnostic and treatment plan that uses technology as part of an ongoing interaction and conversation between physician and patient, however, is different from diagnosis and treatment based on tests and technical interventions. In the former, the individual is treated whereas in the latter one is treating the results of tests. In any given case, the end result may be the same but the doctor-patient relationship is fundamentally different: It changes from an encounter mediated by technology to an encounter that is primarily technological. The patient and physician do not interact so much as the patient becomes a kind of raw material for the technology to process.

The human outcome of these two types of encounters differs and reveals two possibilities for the place of technology in doctor-patient relationships: Technology can be used at the service of a doctor-patient relationship or technology can direct the encounter between doctor and patient. When a doctor interacts with a patient with care and attention for the individual, the two people are involved in a relationship that has as its goal the patient's well-being and health. (*Well-being* and *health* are admittedly vague terms, but I will not further define them.) The interaction between doctor and patient where the approach is not personal but a routine application of tests and treatments does not preclude taking the patient's well-being and health as a goal. It is, however, a relationship primarily directed toward producing a result—health—through the application of technological means. The patient may be made better by the application of technology, but the consequences are not always so benign. The physician has related not to the patient but rather to a symptom complex that, despite possibly superb and timely interventions, may remain problematic. The result is unsatisfactory. In a patient-oriented interaction, the nature of the relationship, which is geared toward well-being and improving function, provides the opportunity for a variety of personal responses by the two individuals despite an outcome that is not the one desired. In the interaction that relies on technology rather than personal relationship, a failure to cure means a failure in the relationship.

The replacement of personal encounter with technology is not solely the fault of physicians. Many patients labor under an illusion that the application of sophisticated diagnostic tests means they are being well cared for by their physician. Others feel that all medical problems require an aggressive technological approach and demand such care. Frequent and often vehement requests by a patient with chronic headaches for a CT scan to rule out a brain tumor, in the absence of clinical signs or historical details associated with brain neoplasms, is an example familiar to most practicing physicians. A suggestion that the headache may be related to difficulties at home or work may cause such a patient to "fire" the doctor if he or she will not perform the diagnostic study demanded. Patients, perhaps as much as physicians, are reluctant to enter into a personal relationship. Given that technology serves to distance people even within families, this reluctance to establish a personal relationship with a stranger is not surprising. Many assume that technology will clarify diagnosis and therapy, whereas careful history taking and suggestions about changes in one's life style are perceived as a waste of time and an affront to privacy. There may be little appreciation that diagnostic testing, although providing more information, need not clarify treatment or prognosis. Diagnostic testing can, ironically, actually add to ambiguity by providing results that not only do little to change therapeutic options but actually confuse the clinical picture.

The strength of a personal type of doctor-patient relationship lies in its potential to deal with ambiguity and failure. The skillful application of technology does not guarantee a happy outcome. When one confronts care at the end of life, ambiguity frequently becomes an important element of the doctor-patient relationship no matter how skilled the physician. It may not be clear when someone will die, why they are doing poorly, what the results of sophisticated diagnostic tests mean prognostically, nor what treatment option, if any, is the best. The lack of a clear indication as to what is "the right thing to do" is a not uncommon event.

Physicians now practice medicine in a climate where decisions to institute, withhold, or withdraw life-sustaining technology are not limited to the patient-doctor relationship but are part of larger disputes within society. Many see medical technology as the culprit in current problems with the health care system. Our confusion about what to do with the use of technology in medicine, our difficulty in establishing priorities in health care, increasing demands for assisted suicide and euthanasia reflect underlying societal issues. In the past, physicians' decisions occurred within a framework of a relatively narrow group of treatment options that gave some promise of benefit. For many conditions, however, there was nothing that could be done and death could not be forestalled. We are now in the position of being able, in many cases, to hold death in abeyance even though our abilities to alter the underlying disease process or restore function to the sick person are limited.

The heart of the critique of the technological nature of American medicine lies in our fears as to what will happen to us when we become sick. More frightening than death is the contemplation of serious illness. Americans are afraid that technology will be used indiscriminately in their care rather than as a tool in the doctor-patient relationship. All of us are uneasy with the possibility of suffering alone without hope for the future. Most of us worry about being artificially maintained without any prospect of recovery. We fear that our physical pain will not be adequately treated. We are anxious over the possibility of decline and isolation. There is a mistrust of American medicine—of its commitment to limit suffering and not abandon the chronically sick to illness and death. Limiting the suffering of an individual and not abandoning him or her to illness cannot be accomplished merely by technological means. It requires the personal commitment of one person to another. Technology will inevitably be brought to bear in the encounter between doctor and patient but suffering and isolation can only be relieved by compassion and personal contact.

Despite the best of medical care, we will all die. Our deaths may occur suddenly or after a brief period of illness, but for some there will be a long period of sickness, a chronic decline, and a gradual loss of function. Suffering can be of many kinds. The most obvious is related to physical pain. Less obvious but not less pernicious is the kind of suffering caused by the loss of independence, or the diminished ability to see and hear, or a combination of illness and frailty that results in isolation and loneliness. The varieties of suffering are multiple. Technology has a role in the treatment of suffering but only an instrumental role. Recall the example of the hurricane. Those in its wake were forced to confront each other. There was no longer a reassuring television to relate to. Instead, there were other

people and dark nights and no telephones. One was thrown back on one's creatureliness: Notions of independence and the sense of removal from the natural world were radically challenged. Likewise, the experience of suffering strips an individual and forces reliance on others. A medical relationship based on technological interaction provides little succor in situations where cure is not possible, chronic illness results, and the experience of suffering becomes the major issue in the patient's life. A personal relationship with a physician provides the opportunity for relief of suffering through human interaction as well as the use of technology.

Relationship or not, when facing serious illness and the end of life, we are facing a situation laden with ambiguity. We all face decline and death but we do not know how or when or under what circumstances. The medical treatment we receive may cause us to live longer and in relative comfort or it may leave us simply lingering. We hope for care that is truly caring, attentive to our needs, our pain, and our loneliness. But we fear being left alone, either abandoned to illness without adequate medical attention or the recipient of medical care that is highly technical, depersonalized, and dehumanizing. We recognize that even with the best doctors and nurses there is no guarantee of good outcome. There remains the numbing and often suppressed knowledge that death cannot be denied. This seems to be our peculiar condition at the end of the twentieth century: We fear death and we fear what may be done to keep us living. Medical technology can extend our lives but sometimes it prolongs our lives beyond bearing. Death, to paraphrase Samuel Johnson, remarkably focuses our attention. Who will care for us and how will they show that care as we age and face the limits of our own mortality?

TECHNOLOGY, RELATIONSHIPS, AND CARING FOR THE ELDERLY

A crucial question is the meaning of caring in the use of technology. *Caring* is a word that can be much abused. It can be used to refer to sentimentality and to warm feelings that have little substance. Caring that is substantial and non-trivial is more hard nosed: It is an attitude that lets caregivers face the patients who come their way, both successful agers and end-stage Alzheimer's patients, with a combination of technical excellence and compassion. Daniel Callahan's *Setting Limits* and *What Kind of Life?* have received much attention and acclaim for their proposals regarding health care, technology, medical expenditures, and care of the elderly.[5] According to Callahan, health expenditures should be directed toward the prevention of premature death and palliative care for those with chronic illness. After a reasonable life span, resources should not be directed to life extension or the curing of illness but to caring and limiting pain. Callahan, however, is mistaken in his views that caring is an inherently more limited venture than efforts aimed directly at care.

The medical care of older persons is both challenging and poignant because of the unavoidable backdrop of mortality. There are instances where death is seen as a blessing, but it is also an occasion of apprehension and sorrow. Caring for those who, because of advancing years or progressive illness, are approaching the end of their lives requires a sensitivity to the fear that dying may provoke.[6] There is frequent unease caused by the recognition that one's time on this earth is coming to an end. Some elderly people fear that they will be abandoned to their fate and left to die alone. Physicians can be compassionate companions of the patients who struggle with these fears but they cannot cure them. The existential terror that such a recognition may trigger is not one that can be resolved by drugs, or technology, or resources other than those within the individual and those people and things that give meaning to the individual's life.

The clinician's obligation to limit suffering and not abandon patients may be best seen against the backdrop of these fears. Doctors can limit the suffering caused by confrontation with our existential finitude but cannot end it, unless they so drug their patients that self-consciousness is abolished. However, doctors can not only show compassion in the face of existential suffering but also use their skills and resources to control physical pain and not leave a patient abandoned. Abandonment can take a variety of forms. The most obvious would be neglecting an individual and leaving him or her alone to suffer. Abandonment can also be more subtle. A physician may well be physically present but not responsive to a patient's suffering. In the case of an older patient, this may take the form of easy assumptions about conditions not being treatable in the elderly, and consequent neglect of therapies that might have a chance of maintaining or restoring function. Conversely, a type of abandonment may occur when some physicians resort to a relentless high-technology diagnostic and therapeutic onslaught rather than carefully assessing the patient's wishes and best interests given the probable outcomes. The physician's commitment to limit suffering and not abandon is twofold. First, prior to the use of specifically medical knowledge, there must be sympathy for the patient as a person who is likely frightened and in pain. Second, medical skill and use of various therapeutic options ought to be directed toward the provision of care that relieves symptoms, restores function to the extent possible, and is consistent with the desires of the patient.

Callahan does an excellent job in establishing the attitude of caring that is prior to the distribution of resources. There is no doubt of his abundant compassion and good will in wishing that pain and suffering be limited: "At the center of caring should be a commitment never to avert its eyes from, or wash its hands of, someone who is in pain or is suffering, who is disabled or incompetent, who is retarded or demented; that is the most fundamental demand made upon us."[7] Callahan's thesis is that medical care has gone awry in a hunt for progress that emphasizes technological achievement rather than attending to personal caring. Our society is threatened by the growing burdens of health care cost, a burden fueled by unwholesome and unrealistic expectations that medicine can keep us young, restore health, and make us whole and vital regardless of age or illness.

Callahan's vision of health care for the elderly rests on his belief that aging individuals have life goals and sources of meaning that are specific to them as the elders of society. The elderly have a role in society that gives them meaning and respect:

> It should be the special role of the elderly to be the moral conservators of that which has been and the most active proponents of that which will be after they are no longer here. Their indispensable role as conservators is what generates what I believe ought to be the *primary* aspiration of the old, which is to serve the young and the future. Just as they were once the heirs of a society built by others, who passed on to them what they needed to keep it going, so are they likewise obliged to do the same for those who will follow them.[8]

The elderly deserve care. But older persons need to depart the stage of this life gracefully and not be caught up in an unseemly struggle to maintain their lives without regard for the society around them. Medicine must scale back its technological repertoire, not seek new cures and technologies and limit access to some therapies based on age.

Unfortunately, Callahan's discussion of caring is laced with unfair indictments of medicine and physicians: "Caring is just not the trait that is emphasized for physicians the way medical knowledge is. The technical skills they deploy are impersonal, directed to organ and system failures, not to the particularities of individual suffering."[9] Callahan overlooks the integral nature of the technical skills and resources used in caring for the particularities of individual suffering. Being a caring, competent doctor frequently requires the use of technology in ways that will limit a patient's suffering and not leave him or her abandoned to the experience of illness and ultimately death. Caring involves a willingness to listen to the patient's fears and suffering and be willing to develop a response that will help that patient as a person who is requesting care. Sometimes that response will be emotional support; at other times it will involve medications and treatments for the underlying illnesses that create suffering and limit function. Sometimes it will involve aggressive therapy using invasive high technology because the alternative is a lingering and unhappy death. The technical side of caring requires considerable ingenuity; it is a response to the seemingly infinite variety of suffering that afflicts individuals. Callahan misses the point. For him "the individual need for cure is infinite in its possibilities, the need for caring is much more finite—there is always something we can do for each other. The possibilities of caring are, in that respect, far more self-contained than the possibilities of curing."[10] This statement is incoherent. If "there is always something we can do for each other," does that not imply an infinity of possibilities?

Callahan falsely believes that caring (without a curative intent) is a relatively circumscribed clinical exercise whereas treatment with curative intent means an infinite variety of expensive, aggressive, and often futile measures. Callahan reduces all doctor-patient relationships to a technological mode of encounter and ignores that the personal relationship can still employ high technology in delivering care. Part of acting rightly as a physician is to listen to what patients say about what hurts them and makes their life hard.

When the 84-year-old man in the example at the beginning of the chapter first went to see his physician, the physician was undoubtedly able to hear the suffering and fear that his relentless chest pain caused. Suffering in this instance has a face on it, the face of this old man. He knows the risk of myocardial infarction, and he may well state that he does not want to be in pain nor short of breath but that he is not afraid of dying. The physician knows that the myocardial infarction may not kill this man but may leave him debilitated and limit his ability to be independent. This is not the "greedy geezer" of ageist mythology who is somehow sapping the lifeblood of the young and living the high life on his Social Security check. How might the physician try to limit his suffering and not abandon him to myocardial ischemia and the specter of ongoing pain, infarction, and congestive heart failure? She could use her personal skill and knowledge and available social resources and recommend that the man proceed with cardiac catheterization and angioplasty or bypass grafting, depending on the results of the catheterization. Is this curing or caring? The man will die in a matter of years even if the operation is successful, so there should be no illusion that the physician is robbing the grim reaper. The physician should also realize, however, that unstable angina, recurrent myocardial infarction, and congestive heart failure are probably grimmer than death. Precipitous decline and loss of function with an unpleasant lingering period at death's door are hard to deal with, both emotionally and financially. Caring means the physician can sympathize with this man in his humanity, recognize the suffering caused by his illness, and be aware that unless aggressive treatment is offered the patient will be abandoned to a fate he finds intolerable and very few would want.

All the elderly who are sent to surgery for coronary bypass grafting, vascular reconstruction, prosthetic heart valves, and artificial joints will die one day. Myocardial ischemia, peripheral vascular disease, congestive heart failure, hip fractures, and degenerative joint disease are common sources of suffering in older patients. This inevitable fact of mortality does not imply that the appropriate response is to hold patients' hands and give analgesics while they experience myocardial infarction, suffer the pain of ischemic ulcers and gangrene, struggle with pulmonary edema, or become bedbound and crippled. Effective caring attempts to aid individuals by letting them know that resources and support are available for care, rehabilitation, and aggressive therapy if such provide some promise of relieving physical distress. There is no sharp dichotomy between caring and curing, nor is caring an inevitably more limited venture. Callahan's comment that the technical skills of physicians are often impersonally directed to organ systems rather than "the particularities of individual suffering" neglects the truth that the relief of suffering by physicians requires technical skills and resources to be directed toward the treatment of malfunctioning organs in an effort to render the whole person well.

CONCLUSION

The responsible use of technology in the care of the elderly is linked to our ability to emphasize the personal in doctor-patient relationships. Neither a reflexive use of high-technology equipment nor an automatic rejection of it on the basis of age is an appropriate response. This conclusion seemingly begs the question of the limits of technology use. Does a personal relationship between doctor and patient justify anything and everything in health care? No, but it sets the framework for what will be used by allowing decision making to be a shared process. Physicians need to cultivate the ability to speak with their patients about their wishes regarding life-sustaining technology. They should not reduce decision making to a process of mechanically fulfilling patient wishes but must supply the information that can make those wishes truly informed. Technology is not a list of items on a medical menu that are chosen at will. Rather, technology serves as a means to assist the doctor and patient in recognizing the patient's values and goals in health care. Within the context of the care of the elderly, physicians must determine two things: what nonabandonment and limiting suffering means for each patient and the appropriate ways, personal and technological, to provide personal, attentive care.

This does not mean that there will be an end to societal conflict or that individual decision making will become easy. Some physicians will not be able to communicate with their patients and ascertain their goals and values. Other doctors will lack the prudence to choose wisely from the available technologies, the ones that provide real promise for assisting the elderly. Some older people will adopt an attitude that demands the aggressive use of all sorts of high-technology equipment regardless of the cost to themselves in terms of pain or suffering or the cost to other members of society because of the associated high price tag. One can describe a number of possible shortcomings. The underlying theme, however, of this chapter is that personal relationships and meaningful communication between individuals remain a possibility. In the context of those relationships and attempts to communicate, patients can talk to their doctors about what it is like to grow old, what they want from life, what they fear, and how they want to be cared for when their life is threatened by illness. Although there will remain questions, obscurity, and ambiguity, clarifying these basic questions will go a long way toward putting technology in its appropriate place in the relationship between the doctor and the older patient: as a tool for limiting suffering and providing the type of care the patient desires.

NOTES

1. B.J. Soldo and K.G. Manton, Demography: Characteristics and Implications of an Aging Population, *Geriatric Medicine,* 2nd ed., edited by J.W. Rowe and R.W. Besdine (Boston: Little, Brown, 1988).

2. A. MacIntyre, *After Virtue,* 2nd ed. (Notre Dame, Ind: University of Notre Dame Press, 1984).

3. P.R. Wolpe, Medicine, Technology, and Lived Relations, *Perspectives in Biology and Medicine* 28 (1985):314–322. Although I take a very different approach in this chapter and develop themes independently, I am indebted to Wolpe for his observations regarding the links between society, technology, medicine, and the physician-patient relationship.

4. M. MacGregor, Technology and the Allocation of Resources, *New England Journal of Medicine* 320 (1989):118–120.

5. D. Callahan, *Setting Limits* (New York: Simon and Schuster, 1987); D. Callahan, *What Kind of Life?* (New York: Simon and Schuster, 1990).

6. E.P. Seravalli, The Dying Patient, The Physician, and the Fear of Death, *New England Journal of Medicine* 319 (1988):1728–1730.

7. Callahan, *What Kind of Life?* 145.

8. Callahan, *Setting Limits,* 43.

9. Callahan, *What Kind of Life?* 148.

10. Ibid., 145.

Part VI

Methodology: Old and New Approaches

Chapter 42

Getting Down to Cases: The Revival of Casuistry in Bioethics

John D. Arras

THE REVIVAL OF CASUISTRY

Developed in the early Middle Ages as a method of bringing abstract and universal ethico-religious precepts to bear on particular moral situations, casuistry has had a checkered history.[1] In the hands of expert practitioners during its salad days in the sixteenth and seventeenth centuries, casuistry generated a rich and morally sensitive literature devoted to numerous real-life ethical problems, such as truth-telling, usury, and the limits of revenge. By the late seventeenth century, however, casuistical reasoning had degenerated into a notoriously sordid form of logic-chopping in the service of personal expediency.[2] To this day, the very term "casuistry" conjures up pejorative images of disingenuous argument and moral laxity.

In spite of its tarnished reputation, some philosophers have claimed that casuistry, shorn of its unfortunate excesses, has much to teach us about the resolution of moral problems in medicine. Indeed, through the work of Albert Jonsen[3] and Stephen Toulmin,[4] this "new casuistry" has emerged as a definite alternative to the hegemony of the so-called "applied ethics" method of moral analysis that has dominated most bioet-

hical scholarship and teaching since the early 1970s.[5] In stark contrast to methods that begin from "on high" with the working out of a moral theory and culminate in the deductivistic application of norms to particular factual situations, this new casuistry works from the "bottom up," emphasizing practical problem-solving by means of nuanced interpretations of individual cases.

This chapter will assess the promise of this reborn casuistry for bioethics education. In order to do that, however, it will be necessary to say quite a bit in general about the nature of this form of moral analysis and its strengths and weaknesses as a method of practical thinking. Indeed, a general catalogue of the promise and potential pitfalls of the casuistical method

Source: Reprinted from *The Journal of Medicine and Philosophy*, Vol. 16, No. 1, pp. 29–51, with permission of Kluwer Academic Publishers, © 1991.

This article is based upon a presentation at a conference on "Bioethics as an Intellectual Field," sponsored by the University of Texas Medical Branch, Galveston, Texas. The author would like to thank Ronald Carson and Thomas Murray for their encouragement.

should be directly applicable to the assessment of casuistry in educational settings.

Before we can exhibit the salient features of this rival bioethical methodology, we must first confront an initial ambiguity in the definition of casuistry. As Jonsen describes it, "casuistry" is the art or skill of applying abstract or general principles to particular cases.[6] In this context, Jonsen notes that the major monotheistic religions were likely sources for casuistic ethics, since they all combined a strong sense of duty with a definite set of moral precepts couched in universal terms. The pre-eminent task for devout Christians, Jews, and Muslims was thus to learn how to apply these universal precepts to particular situations, where their stringency or applicability might well be affected by particular factual conditions.

Defined as the art of applying abstract principles to particular cases, the new casuistry could appropriately be viewed, not so much as a rival to the applied ethics model, but rather as a necessary complement to any and all moral theories that would guide our conduct in specific situations. So long as we take some general principles or maxims to be ethically binding, no matter what their source, we must learn through the casuist's art to fit them to particular cases. But on this gloss of "casuistry," even the most hidebound adherent of the applied ethics model, someone who held that answers to particular moral dilemmas can be deduced from universal theories and principles, would have to count as a casuist. So defined, casuistry might appear to be little more than the handmaiden of applied ethics.

There is, however, another interpretation of casuistry in the writings of Jonsen and Toulmin that provides a distinct alternative to the applied ethics model. Instead of focusing on the need to fit principles to cases, this interpretation stresses the particular nature, derivation, and function of the principles manipulated by the new casuists. Through this alternative theory of principles, we begin to discern a morality that develops, not from the top down, as in most interpretations of Roman law, but rather from case to case (or from

the bottom up), as in the common law. What differentiates the new casuistry from applied ethics, then, is not the mere recognition that principles must eventually be applied, but rather a particular account of the logic and derivation of the principles that we deploy in moral discourse.

A "CASE-DRIVEN" METHOD

Contrary to "theory-driven" methodologies, which approach particular situations already equipped with a full complement of moral principles, the new casuistry insists that our moral knowledge must develop incrementally through the analysis of concrete cases. From this perspective, the very notion of "applied ethics" embodies a redundancy, while the correlative notion of "theoretical ethics" conveys an illusory and counterproductive ideal for ethical thought.

If ethics is done properly, the new casuists imply, it will already have been immersed in concrete cases from the very start. To be sure, one can always apply the results of previous ethical inquiries to fresh problems, but to the casuists good ethics is always "applied" in the sense that it grows out of the analysis of individual cases. It's not as though one could or should first develop a pristine ethical theory planing above the world of moral particulars and then, having put the finishing touches on the theory, point it in the direction of particular cases. Rejecting the idea that there are such things as "essences" in the domain of ethics, Toulmin,[7] citing Aristotle and Dewey, argues that this pursuit of rigorous theory is unhinged from the realities of the moral life and animated by an illusory quest for moral certainty. Thus, whereas many academic philosophers scorn "applied ethics" as a pale shadow of the real thing (i.e., ethical theory), the new casuists insist that good ethics is always immersed in the messy reality of cases and that the philosophers' penchant for abstract and rigorous theory is a misleading fetish.

According to both Jonsen and Toulmin, the work of the National Commission for the Protection of Human Subjects of Biomedical and Behavioral Research provides an excellent example of this case-driven method in bioethics.[8] Although the various commissioners represented different academic, religious, and philosophical perspectives, Jonsen and Toulmin (who served, respectively, as commissioner and consultant to the commission) attest that the commissioners could still reach consensus by discussing the issues "taxonomically." Bracketing their differences on "matters of principle," the commissioners would begin with an analysis of paradigmatic cases of harm, cruelty, fairness, and generosity and then branch out to more complex and difficult cases posed by biomedical research. The commissioners thus "triangulate[d] their way across the complex terrain of moral life,"[9] gradually extending their analysis of relatively straightforward problems to issues requiring a much more delicate balancing of competing values.

Thus, instead of looking for ethical progress in the theoretical equivalent of the Second Coming—i.e., the establishment of *the* correct ethical theory—Jonsen and Toulmin contend that a more realistic and attainable notion of progress is afforded by this notion of moral "triangulation," an incremental approach to problems whose model can be found in the history of our common law. Just as English-speaking peoples have developed highly complex and sophisticated legal frameworks for thinking about tort liability and criminal guilt without the benefit of pre-established legal principles, so (Jonsen and Toulmin argue) ought we to develop a "common morality" or "morisprudence" on the basis of case analysis—without recourse to some pre-established moral theory or moral principles.

THE ROLE OF PRINCIPLES IN THE NEW CASUISTRY

Contrary to common interpretations of Roman law and to deductivist ethical theories, wherein principles are said to pre-exist the actual cases to which they apply, the new casuistry

contends that ethical principles are "discovered" in the cases themselves, just as common law legal principles are developed in and through judicial decisions on particular legal cases.[10] To be sure, common law and "common law morality" (or "morisprudence") contain a body of principles too, but the way these principles are derived, articulated, used, and taught is very different from the Roman law and deductivist ethical approach.[11]

The Derivation and Meaning of Principles

Jonsen and Toulmin have sent mixed messages regarding their views of the derivation of moral maxims and principles. In some places they appear to incline toward a weaker interpretation of casuistry as the art of applying whatever moral maxims happen to be lying around at hand in one's culture. At other places, however, Jonsen and Toulmin suggest a much stronger and more controversial view, according to which moral principles of "common law morality" are entirely derived from (or abstracted out of) particular cases. Rather than stemming originally from some ethical theory, such as utilitarianism or Rawls's theory of justice, these principles are said to emerge gradually from reflection upon our responses to particular cases.

Whichever view of the derivation of principles modern casuistry ultimately embraces, both are fully compatible with the casuistical thesis that the full articulation of those principles cannot be determined in isolation from particular factual contexts. In order to fully understand any principle or maxim, one has to ask, through a process of interpretation, how it might apply to a variety of situations. Thus, whereas "privacy" might simply mean an undifferentiated interest in "liberty" to a theorist unfamiliar with the cases, to the casuist the meaning and scope of personal privacy is delimited and shaped by the features of the cases that have called for a public response. Thus, whether or not consensual sodomy is protected by a moral right of privacy will depend upon how the casuist interprets the features of previous controversial cases dealing with such issues as family life, contraception, and abortion.

The Priority of Practice

In the applied ethics model, principles not only "come before" our practices in the sense of being antecedently derived from theory before being applied to cases, they also have priority over practices in the sense that their function is to justify (or criticize) practices. Indeed, it is precisely through this logical priority of principles over practice that the applied ethics model derives its critical edge. It is just the reverse for the new casuists, who sometimes imply that ethical principles are nothing more than mere *summaries* of meanings already embedded in our actual practices.[12] Rather than serving as a justification for certain practices, principles within the new casuistry often merely seem to *report* in summary fashion what we have already decided.

This logical priority of practice to principles is clearly evident in Jonsen's and Toulmin's ruminations on the experience of the National Commission for the Protection of Human Subjects. In attempting to carry out the mandate of Congress to develop principles for the ethical conduct of research on humans, the commissioners could have straightforwardly drafted a set of principles and then applied them to problematic cases. Instead, note Jonsen and Toulmin, the commissioners acted like good casuists, plunging immediately into nuanced discussions of cases. Progress in these discussions was achieved, not by applying agreed-upon principles, but rather by seeking agreement on responses to particular cases. Indeed, according to this account, the *Belmont Report*, which articulated the commission's moral principles and serves to this day as a major source of the "applied ethics" approach to moral reasoning, was written at the end of the commission's deliberations, long after its members had already reached consensus on the issues.[13]

The Open Texture of Principles

In contrast to the deductivist method, whose principles glide unsullied over the facts, the principles of the new casuistry are always subject to further revision and articulation in light of new cases. This is true not only because casuistical principles are inextricably enmeshed in their factual surroundings, but also because the determination of the decisive or morally relevant features of this factual web is often a highly uncertain and controversial business.

By way of example, consider the question of withdrawing artificial feeding as presented in the case of Claire Conroy.[14] One of the crucial precedents for this case, both legally and morally, was the *Quinlan* decision.[15] What were the morally relevant features of Karen Quinlan's situation, and what might they teach us about our responsibilities to Claire Conroy? Was it crucial that Ms. Quinlan was described as being in a persistent vegetative state? Or that she was being maintained by a mechanical respirator? If so, then one might well conclude that Claire Conroy's situation—i.e., that of a patient with severe dementia being maintained by a plastic, nasogastric feeding tube—is sufficiently disanalogous to Quinlan's to compel continued treatment. On the other hand, a rereading of *Quinlan* might reveal other features of that case that tell in favor of withdrawing Conroy's feeding tube, such as the unlikelihood of Karen ever recovering sapient life, the bleakness of her prognosis, and the questionable proportion of benefits to burdens derived from the treatment.

Although the *Quinlan* case may have begun by standing for the patient's right to refuse treatment, subsequent readings of that case in light of later cases have fastened on other aspects of the case, thereby giving rise to modifications of the original principle, or perhaps even to the wholesale substitution of new principles for the old. The principles of casuistic analysis might thus be said to exhibit an "open texture."[16] Somewhat in the manner of Thomas Kuhn's "paradigms" of scientific research,[17] each significant case in bioethics stands as an object for further articulation and specification under new or more complex conditions. Viewed this way, casuistical analysis might be summarized as a form of reasoning by means of examples that always point beyond themselves. Both the examples and the principles derived from them are always subject to reinterpretation and gradual modification in light of subsequent examples.

Teaching and Learning

In contrast to legal systems derived from Roman law, where jurors are governed by a systematic legal code, common-law systems derive from the particular judicial decisions of particular judges. As a result of these radically differing approaches to the nature and derivation of law, common law and Roman law are taught and learned in correspondingly different ways. Students of Roman law need only refer to the code itself, and perhaps to the scholarly literature explicating the meaning of the code's various provisions, whereas students of common law must refer directly to prior judicial opinions. Consequently, the so-called "case method" of legal study is naturally suited to common-law jurisdictions, for it is only through a study of the cases that one can learn the concrete meaning of legal principles and learn to apply them correctly to future cases.[18]

What is true of the common law is equally true of "common-law morality." According to the casuists, bioethical principles are best learned by the case method, not by appeals to abstract theoretical notions. Indeed, anyone at all experienced in teaching bioethics in clinical settings must know (often by means of painful experience) that physicians, nurses, and other health care providers learn best by means of case discussions. (The best way to put them to sleep, in fact, is to begin one's talk with a recitation of the "principles of bioethics.") This is explained not simply by the fact that case presentations are intrinsically more gripping than abstract discussions of the moral philosophies of Mill, Kant, and Rawls; they are, in addition, the best vehicle for conveying the concrete meaning and scope of whatever principles and maxims one wishes to teach. Contrary to ethical deductivism and Roman law, whose principles could conceivably be taught in a practical vacuum, casuistry demands a case-driven method of instruction. For casuists, cases are much more than mere illustrated rules or handy mnemonic devices for the "abstracting impaired." They are, as Jonsen and Toulmin argue, the very locus of moral meaning and moral certainty.

Although Jonsen and Toulmin have yet to consider the concrete pedagogical implications of their casuistical method, we can venture a few suggestions. First, it would appear that a casuistical approach would encourage the use, whenever possible, of real as opposed to hypothetical cases. This is because hypothetical cases, so beloved of academic philosophers, tend to be theory driven; that is, they are usually designed to advance some explicitly theoretical point. Real cases, on the other hand, are more likely to display the sort of moral complexity and untidiness that demand the (nondeductive) weighing and balancing of competing moral considerations and the casuistical virtues of discernment and practical judgment (*phronesis*).

Second, a casuistical pedagogy would call for lengthy and richly detailed case studies. If the purpose of moral education is to prepare one for action in the real world, the cases discussed should reflect the degree of complexity, uncertainty, and ambiguity encountered there. If for casuistry moral truth resides "in the details," if the meaning and scope of moral principles is determined contextually through an interpretation of factual situations in their relationship to paradigm cases, then cases must be presented in rich detail. It won't do, as is so often done in our textbooks and anthologies, to cram the rich moral fabric of cases into a couple of paragraphs.

Third, a casuistical pedagogy would encourage the use, not simply of the occasional isolated case study, but rather of whole sequences of cases bearing on a related principle or theme.

Thus, instead of simply "illustrating" the debate over the termination of life-sustaining treatments with, say, the single case of Karen Quinlan, teachers and students should read and interpret a sequence of cases (including, e.g., the cases of Quinlan, Saikewicz, Spring, Conroy, and Cruzan) in order to see just how reasoning by paradigm and analogy takes place and how the so-called "principles of bioethics" are actually shaped in their effective meaning by the details of successive cases.

Fourth, a casuistically driven pedagogy will give much more emphasis than currently allotted to what might be called the problem of "moral diagnosis." Given any particular controversy, exactly what kind of issues does it raise? What, in other words, is the case really about? As opposed to the anthologies, where each case comes neatly labelled under a discrete rubric, real life does not announce the nature of problems in advance. It requires interpretation, imagination, and discernment to figure out what is going on, especially when (as is usually the case) a number of discussable issues are usually extractable from any given controversy.

PROBLEMS WITH THE CASUISTICAL METHOD

Since the new casuistry attempts to define itself by turning applied ethics on its head, working from cases to principles rather than vice versa, it should come as no surprise to find that its strengths correlate perfectly with the weaknesses of applied ethics. Thus, whereas applied ethics, and especially deductivism, are often criticized for their remoteness from clinical realities and for their consequent irrelevance,[19] casuistry prides itself on its concreteness and on its ability to render useful advice to caregivers in the medical trenches. Likewise, if the applied ethics model appears rather narrow in its single-minded emphasis on the application of principles and in its corresponding neglect of moral interpretation and practical discernment, the new casuistry can be viewed as a defense of the Aristotelian virtue of *phronesis* (or sound practice judgment).

Conversely, it should not be surprising to find certain problems with the casuistical method that correspond to strengths of the applied ethics model. I shall devote the second half of this essay to an inventory of some of these problems. It should be stressed, however, that not all of these problems are unique to casuistry, nor does applied ethics fare much better with regard to some of them.

What Is "a Case"?

For all of their emphasis upon the interpretation of particular cases, casuists have not said much, if anything, about how to select problems for moral interpretation. What, in other words, gets placed on the "moral agenda" in the first place, and why? This is a problem because it is quite possible that the current method of selecting agenda items, whatever that may be, systematically ignores genuine issues equally worthy of discussion and debate.[20]

I think it safe to say that problems currently make it onto the bioethical agenda largely because health practitioners and policy makers put them there. While there is usually nothing problematic in this, and while it always pays to be scrupulously attentive to the expressed concerns of people working in the trenches, practitioners may be bound to conventional ways of thinking and of conceiving problems that tend to filter out other, equally valid experiences and problems. As feminists have recently argued, for example, much of the current bioethics agenda reflects an excessively narrow, professionally driven, and male outlook on the nature of ethics.[21] As a result, a whole range of important ethical problems—including the unequal treatment of women in health care settings, sexist occupational roles, personal relationships, and strategies of *avoiding* crisis situations—have been either downplayed or ignored completely.[22] It is not enough, then, for casuistry to tell us *how* to interpret cases; rather than simply carrying out the agenda dictated by health professionals, all of us (casuists and ethicists alike) must begin to think more about the problem of *which* cases ought to be selected for moral scrutiny.

An additional problem, which I can only flag here, concerns not the identification of "a case"—i.e., what gets placed on the public agenda—but rather the specification of "the case"—i.e., what description of a case shall count as an adequate and sufficiently complete account of the issues, the participants, and the context. One of the problems with many case presentations, especially in the clinical context, is their relative neglect of alternative perspectives on the case held by other participants. Quite often, we get the attending's (or the house officer's) point of view on what constitutes "the case" while missing out on the perspectives of nurses, social workers, and others. Since most cases are complicated and enriched by such alternative medical, psychological, and social interpretations, our casuistical analyses will remain incomplete without them. Thus, in addition to being long, the cases that we employ should reflect the usually complementary (but often conflicting) perspectives of all the involved participants.

Is Casuistry Really Theory Free?

The casuists claim that they make moral progress by moving from one class of cases to another without the benefit of any ethical principles or theoretical apparatus. Solutions generated for obvious or easy categories of cases adumbrate solutions for the more difficult cases. In a manner somewhat reminiscent of pre-Kuhnian philosophers of science clinging to the possibility of "theory free" factual observations, to a belief in a kind of epistemological "immaculate perception," the casuists appear to be claiming that the cases simply speak for themselves.

As we have seen, one problem with this suggestion is that it does not acknowledge or account for the way in which different theoretical preconceptions help determine which cases and problems get selected for study in the first place.

Another problem is that it does not explain what allows us to group different cases into distinct categories or to proceed from one category to another. In other words, the casuists' account of case analysis fails to supply us with principles of relevance that explain what binds the cases together and how the meaning of one case points beyond itself toward the resolution of subsequent cases. The casuists obviously cannot do without such principles of relevance; they are a necessary condition of any kind of moral taxonomy. Without principles of relevance, the cases would fly apart in all directions, rendering coherent speech, thought, and action about them impossible.

But if the casuists rise to this challenge and convert their implicit principles of relevance into explicit principles, it is certainly reasonable to expect that these will be heavily "theory laden." Take, for example, the novel suggestion that anencephalic infants should be used as organ donors for children born with fatal heart defects. What is the relevant line of cases in our developed "morisprudence" for analyzing this problem? To the proponents of this suggestion, the brain death debates provide the appropriate context of discussion. According to this line of argument, anencephalic infants most closely resemble the brain dead; and since we already harvest vital organs from the latter category, we have a moral warrant for harvesting organs from anencephalics.[23] But to some of those opposed to any change in the status quo, the most relevant line of cases is provided by the literature on fetal experimentation. Our treatment of the anencephalic newborn should, they claim, reflect our practices regarding nonviable fetuses. If we agree with the judgment of the National Commission that research that would shorten the already doomed child's life should not be permitted, then we should oppose the use of equally doomed anencephalic infants as heart donors.[24]

How ought the casuist to triangulate the moral problem of the anencephalic newborn as organ donor? What principles of relevance will lead him or her to opt for one line of cases instead of another? Whatever principles he or she might eventually articulate, they will undoubtedly have something definite to say about such matters as the concept of death, the moral status of fetuses, the meaning and scope of respect, the nature of personhood, and the relative importance of achieving good consequences in the world versus treating other human beings as ends in themselves. Although one's position on such issues perhaps need not implicate any full-blown ethical theory in the strictest sense of the term, they are sufficiently theory laden to cast grave doubt on the new casuists' ability to move from case to case without recourse to mediating ethical principles or other theoretical notions.

Although the early work of Jonsen and Toulmin can easily be read as advocating a theory-free methodology comprised of mere "summary principles," their recent work appears to acknowledge the point of the above criticism. Indeed, it would be fair to say that they now seek to articulate a method that is, if not "theory free," then at least "theory modest." Drawing on the approach of the classical casuists, they now concede an indisputably normative role for principles and maxims drawn from a variety of sources, including theology, common law, historical tradition, and ethical theories. Rather than viewing ethical theories as mutually exclusive, reductionistic attempts to provide an apodictic *foundation* for ethical thought, Jonsen and Toulmin now view theories as limited and complementary *perspectives* that might enrich a more pragmatic and pluralistic approach to the ethical life.[25] They thus appear reconciled to the usefulness, both in research and education, of a severely chastened conception of moral principles and theories.

One lesson of all this for bioethics education is that casuistry, for all its usefulness as a method, is nothing more (and nothing less) than an "engine of thought" that must receive *direction* from values, concepts, and theories outside of itself. Given the important role such "external" sources of moral direction must play even in the most casebound approaches, teachers and students need to be self-conscious about which traditions and theories are in effect driving their

casuistical interpretations. This means that they need to devote time and energy to studying and criticizing the values, concepts, and rank orderings implicitly or explicitly conveyed by the various traditions and theories from which they derive their overall direction and tools of moral analysis. In short, it means that adopting the casuistical method will not absolve teachers and students from studying and evaluating either ethical theories or the history of ethics.

Indeterminacy and Consensus

One need not believe in the existence of uniquely correct answers to all moral questions to be concerned about the casuistical method's capacity to yield determinate answers to problematical moral questions. Indeed, anyone familiar with Alastair MacIntyre's disturbing diagnosis of our contemporary moral culture[26] might well tend to greet the casuists' announcement of moral consensus with a good deal of skepticism. According to MacIntyre, our moral culture is in a grave state of disorder: Lacking any comprehensive and coherent understanding of morality and human nature, we subsist on scattered shards and remnants of past moral frameworks. It is no wonder, then, according to MacIntyre, that our moral debates and disagreements are often marked by the clash of incommensurable premises derived from disparate moral cultures. Nor is it any wonder that our debates over highly controversial issues such as abortion and affirmative action take the form of a tedious, interminable cycle of assertion and counterassertion. In this disordered and contentious moral setting, which MacIntyre claims is *our* moral predicament, the casuists' goal of consensus based upon intuitive responses to cases might well appear to be a Panglossian dream.

One need not endorse MacIntyre's pessimistic diagnosis in its entirety to notice that many of our moral practices and policies bear a multiplicity of meanings; they often embody a variety of different, and sometimes conflicting, values. An ethical methodology based exclusively on the casuistical analysis of these practices can reasonably be expected to express these different values in the form of conflicting ethical conclusions.

Political theorist Michael Walzer's remarks on health care in the United States provide an illuminating case in point. Although Walzer might not recognize himself as a modern day casuist, his vigorous antitheoretical stance and reliance upon established social meanings and norms certainly make him an ally of the methodological approach espoused by Jonsen and Toulmin.[27] According to Walzer, if we look carefully at our current values and practices regarding health care and its distribution—if we look, in other words, at the choices we as a people have already made, at the programs we have already put into place, etc.—we will conclude that health care services are a crucially important social good, that they should be allocated solely on the basis of need, and that they must be made equally available to all citizens, presumably through something like a national health service.[28]

One could argue, however, that current disparities—both in access to care and in quality of care—between the poor, the middle class, and the rich reflect equally "deep" (or even deeper) political choices that we have made regarding the relative importance of individual freedom, social security, and the health needs of the "nondeserving" poor. In this vein, one could claim that our collective decisions bearing on Medicaid, Medicare, and access to emergency rooms—the same decisions that Walzer uses to argue for a national health service—are more accurately interpreted as grudging aberrations from our free market ideology. According to this opposing view, our stratified health care system pretty well reflects our values and commitments in this area: a "decent minimum" (read "understaffed, ill-equipped, impersonal urban clinics") for the medically indigent, decent health insurance and HMOs for the working middle-class, and first-cabin care for the well-to-do.[29]

Viewed in the light of Walzer's democratic socialist commitments, which I happen to share,

this arrangement may indeed look like an "indefensible triage," but placed in the context of American history and culture, it could just as easily be viewed as business as usual. Thus, on one reading our current practices point toward the establishment of a thoroughly egalitarian health care system; viewed from a different angle, however, these same "choices we have already made" justify pervasive inequalities in access to care and quality of care. The problem for the casuistical method is that, barring any and all appeals to abstract principles of justice, it cannot decisively adjudicate between such competing interpretations of our common practices.[30] When these do not convey a univocal message, or when they carry conflicting messages of more or less equal plausibility, casuistry cannot help us to develop a uniquely correct interpretation upon which a widespread social consensus might be based. Contrary to the assurances of Jonsen and Toulmin, the new casuistry is an unlikely instrument for generating consensus in a moral world fractured by conflicting values and intuitions.

In Jonsen and Toulmin's defense, it should be noted that abstract theories of justice divorced from the conventions of our society are equally unlikely sources of uniquely correct answers. If philosophers cannot agree among themselves upon the true nature of abstract justice—indeed, if criticizing our foremost theoretician of justice, John Rawls, has become something of a philosophical national pastime[31]—it is unclear how their theorizing could decisively resolve the ongoing debate among competing interpretations of our common social practices.

It might also be noted in passing that even Rawls has become increasingly loathe in his recent writings to appeal to an abstract, timeless, and deracinated notion of justice as the ultimate court of appeal from conflicting social interpretations. Eschewing any pretense of having established a theory of justice "sub specie aeternitatis," Rawls now claims that his theory of "justice as fairness" is only applicable in modern democracies like our own.[32] He claims, moreover, that the justification of his theory is derived, not from neutral data, but from its "congruence with our deeper understanding of ourselves and our aspirations, and our realization that, given our history and the traditions embedded in our public life, it is the most reasonable doctrine for us."[33] Notwithstanding the many differences that distinguish their respective views, it thus appears that Rawls, Walzer, and Jonsen and Toulmin could all agree that there is no escape from the task of interpreting the meanings embedded in our social practices, institutions, and history. Given the complexity and tensions that characterize this moral "data," the search for uniquely correct interpretations must be seen as misguided. The best we can do, it seems, is to argue for our own determinate but contestable interpretations of who we are as a people and who we want to become. Neither theory nor casuistry is a guarantor of consensus.

Conventionalism and Critique

The stronger, more controversial version of casuistry and its "summary view" of ethical principles gives rise to worries about the nature of moral truth and justification. Eschewing any theoretical derivation of principles and insisting that the locus of moral certainty is the particular, the casuist asks, "What principles best organize and account for what we have already decided?" Viewed from this angle, the casuistic project amounts to nothing more than an elaborate refinement of our intuitions regarding cases. As such, it begins to resemble the kind of relativistic conventionalism recently articulated by Richard Rorty.[34]

Obviously, one problem with this is that our intuitions have often been shown to be wildly wrong, if not downright prejudicial and superstitious. To the extent that this is true of *our own* intuitions about ethical matters, then casuistry will merely refine our prejudices. Any casuistry that modestly restricts itself to interpreting and cataloguing the flickering shadows on the cave wall can easily be accused of lacking a critical edge. If applied ethics might rightly be said to have purchased critical leverage at the expense of the concrete moral situation, then casuistry

might be charged with having purchased concreteness and relevance at the expense of philosophical criticism. This charge might take either of two forms. First, one could claim that the casuist is a mere expositor of *established* social meanings and thus lacks the requisite critical distance to formulate telling critiques of regnant social understandings. Second, casuistry could be accused of ignoring the power relations that shape and inform the social meanings that its practitioners interpret.

In response to the issue of critical distance, Jonsen and Toulmin could point out that the social world of established meanings is by no means monolithic and usually harbors alternative values that offer plenty of critical leverage against the regnant social consensus. As Michael Walzer has recently argued, even such thundering social critics as the prophet Amos have usually been fully committed to their societies rather than "objective" and detached, and the values to which they appeal are often fundamental to the self-understanding of a people or group.[35] (How else could they accuse their fellows of hypocrisy?) The lesson for casuists here is not to become so identified with the point of view of health care professionals that they lose sight of other important values in our culture.

The second claim, while not necessarily fatal to the casuistical enterprise, is harder to rebut. As Habermas has contended in his longstanding debate with Gadamer, interpretive approaches to ethics (such as casuistry) can articulate our shared social meanings but ignore the economic and power relations that shape social consensus. His point is that the very conversation through which cases, social practices, and institutions are interpreted is itself subject to what he calls "systematically distorted communication."[36] In order to avoid merely legitimizing social understandings conditioned on power and domination—for example, our conception of the appropriate relationship between nurses and physicians—casuistry will have to supplement its interpretations with a critical theory of social relationships, or with what Paul Ricoeur has called a "hermeneutics of suspicion."[37]

Reinforcing the Individualism of Bioethics

Analytical philosophers working as applied ethicists have often been criticized for the ahistorical, reductionist, and excessively individualistic character of their work in bioethics.[38] While the casuistical method cannot thus be justly accused of importing a short-sighted individualism into the field of bioethics—that honor already belonging to analytical philosophy—it cannot be said either that casuistry offers anything like a promising remedy for this deficiency. On the contrary, it seems that the casuists' method of reasoning by analogy only promises to exacerbate the individualism and reductionism already characteristic of much bioethical scholarship.

Consider, for example, how a casuist might address the problem of heart transplants. He or she might reason like this: Our society is already deeply committed to paying for all kinds of "half-way technologies" for those in need. We already pay for renal dialysis and transplantation, chronic ventilatory support for children and adults, expensive open-heart surgery, and many other "high-tech" therapies, some of which might well be even more expensive than heart transplants. Therefore, so long as heart transplants qualify medically as a proven therapy, there is no reason why Medicaid and Medicare should not fund them.[39]

Notwithstanding the evident fruitfulness of such analogical reasoning in many contexts of bioethics, and notwithstanding the possibility that these particular examples of it might well prevail against the competing arguments on heart transplantation, it remains true that such contested practices raise troubling questions that tend not to be asked, let alone illuminated, by casuistical reasoning by analogy. The extent of our willingness to fund heart transplantation has great bearing on the kind of society in which we wish to live and on our priorities for spending within (and without) the health care budget. Even if we already fund many high-technology procedures that cost as much or more than heart transplants, it is possible that this new round of

transplantation could threaten other forms of care that provide greater benefits to more people, and we might therefore wish to draw the line here.[40]

The point is that, no matter where we stand on the particular issue of heart transplants, we *might* think it important to raise such "big questions," depending on the nature of the problem at hand. We might want to ask, to borrow from a recent title, "What kind of life?"[41] But the kind of reasoning by analogy championed by the new casuists tends to reduce our field of ethical vision down to the proximate moral precedents and thereby suppresses the important global questions bearing on who we are and what kind of society we want. The result is likely to be a method of moral reasoning that graciously accommodates us to any and all technological innovations, no matter what their potential long-term threat to fundamental and cherished institutions and values.

CONCLUSION

The revival of casuistry, both in practice and in Jonsen and Toulmin's recent defense,[42] is a welcome development in the field of bioethics. Its account of moral reasoning (emphasizing the pivotal role of paradigms, analogical thinking, and the prudential weighing of competing factors) is far superior, both as a description of how we actually think and as a prescription of how we ought to think, to the tiresome invocation of the applied ethics mantra (i.e., the principles of respect for autonomy, beneficence, and justice). By insisting on a *modest* role for ethical theory in a pragmatic, nondeductivist approach to ethical interpretation, Jonsen and Toulmin join an important chorus of contemporary thinkers troubled by the reductionism inherent in most analytical ethics.[43]

As for its role in bioethics education, no one needs to tell teachers about the importance of cases in the classroom. It's pretty obvious that discussing cases is fun, interesting, and certainly more memorable than any philosophical theory, which for the average student usually has a half-life of about two weeks. Moreover, a casuistical education gives students the methodological tools they are most likely to need when they later encounter bioethical problems in the "real world," whether as health care professionals, clergy, lawyers, journalists, or informed citizens. For all of the obviousness of these points, however, it remains true that all of us, as teachers, could profit from sound advice on how better to use cases, and some such advice can be extrapolated from the work of Jonsen and Toulmin.

For all its virtues vis-à-vis the sclerotic invocation of "bioethical principles," the casuistical method is not, however, without problems of its own. First, we found that the very principles of relevance that drive the casuistical method need to be made explicit, and we surmised that, once unveiled, these principles will turn out to be heavily theory laden. Second, we showed that the casuistical method is an unlikely source of uniquely correct interpretations of social meanings and therefore an unlikely source of societal consensus. Third, we have seen that, because of the casuists' view of ethical principles as mere summaries of our intuitive responses to paradigmatic cases, their method might suffer from ideological distortions and lack a critical edge. Moreover, relying so heavily on the perceptions and agenda of health care professionals, casuists might tend to ignore the existence of important issues that could be revealed by other theoretical perspectives, such as feminism. Finally, we saw that casuistry, focusing as it does on analogical resemblances, might tend to ignore certain difficult but inescapable "big questions" (e.g., "What kind of society do we want?") and thereby reinforce the individualistic tendencies already at work in contemporary bioethics.

It remains to be seen whether casuistry, as a program in practical ethics, will be able to marshal sufficient internal resources to respond to these criticisms. Whatever the outcome of that attempt, however, an equally promising approach might be to incorporate the insights and tools of casuistry into the methodological approach known as "reflective equilibrium."[44] According to this method, the casuistical interpretation of cases, on the one hand, and moral theories, principles, and maxims, on the other, exist in a symbiotic relationship. Our intuitions on cases will thus be guided, and perhaps criticized, by theory, while our theories and moral principles will themselves be shaped, and perhaps reformulated, by our responses to paradigmatic moral situations. Whether we attempt to flesh out this method of reflective equilibrium or further develop the casuistical program, it should be clear by now that the methodological issue between theory and cases is not a dichotomous "either/or" but rather an encompassing "both-and."

In closing I would like to gather together my various recommendations for the use of casuistry in bioethics education:

1. Use real cases rather than hypotheticals whenever possible.

2. Avoid schematic case presentations. Make them long, richly detailed, messy, and comprehensive. Make sure that the perspectives of all the major players (including nurses and social workers) are represented.

3. Present complex sequences of cases that sharpen students' analogical reasoning skills.

4. Engage students in the process of "moral diagnosis."

5. Be mindful of the limits of casuistical analysis. As a mere engine of moral argument, casuistry must be supplemented and guided by appeals to ethical theory, the history of ethics, and moral norms embedded in our traditions and social practices. It must also be supplemented by critical social analyses that unmask the power behind much social consensus and raise larger questions about the kind of society we want and the kind of people we want to be.

NOTES

1. A.R. Jonsen and S. Toulmin, *The Abuse of Casuistry* (Berkeley: University of California Press, 1988).

2. B. Pascal, *Lettres Écrites à un Provincial*, edited by A. Adam (Paris: Flammarion, 1981).

3. A.R. Jonsen, Can an Ethicist Be a Consultant? in *Frontiers in Medical Ethics*, edited by V. Abernethy (Cambridge, Mass.: Ballinger, 1980); A.R. Jonsen, Casuistry and Clinical Ethics, *Theoretical Medicine* 7 (1986):65–74; A.R. Jonsen, Casuistry, in *Westminster Dictionary of Christian Ethics*, edited by J.F. Childress and J. Macgvarrie (Philadelphia: Westminster Press, 1986), 78–80.

4. S. Toulmin, The Tyranny of Principles, *Hastings Center Report* 11 (1981):31–39; Jonsen and Toulmin, *The Abuse of Casuistry*.

5. T.L. Beauchamp and J.F. Childress, *Principles of Biomedical Ethics*, 3rd ed. (New York: Oxford University Press, 1989).

6. Jonsen, Casuistry.

7. Toulmin, The Tyranny of Principles.

8. Jonsen and Toulmin, *The Abuse of Casuistry*, 16–19, 264, 305, 338.

9. Toulmin, The Tyranny of Principles.

10. Jonsen, Casuistry and Clinical Ethics.

11. H. Pitkin, *Wittgenstein and Justice* (Berkeley: University of California Press, 1972).

12. Toulmin, The Tyranny of Principles.

13. Jonsen, Casuistry and Clinical Ethics, 71.

14. Matter of Claire C. Conroy, Supreme Court of New Jersey, 486 A.2d 1209 (1985).

15. Matter of Quinlan, Supreme Court of New Jersey, 355 A.2d 647 (1976).

16. H.L.A. Hart, *The Concept of Law* (Oxford: Oxford University Press, 1961), 120ff.

17. T. Kuhn, *The Structure of Scientific Revolutions*, 2nd ed. (Chicago: University of Chicago Press, 1970).

18. E.W. Patterson, The Case Method in American Legal Education: Its Origins and Objectives, *Journal of Legal Education* 4 (1951):1–24.

19. R.C. Fox and J.P. Swazey, Medical Morality Is Not Bioethics: Medical Ethics in China and the United States, *Perspectives in Biology and Medicine* 27 (1984):336–360; C. Noble, Ethics and Experts, *Hastings Center Report* 12 (1982):7–9.

20. O. O'Neill, How Can We Individuate Moral Problems? in *Applied Ethics and Ethical Theory*, edited by D.M. Rosenthal and F. Shehadi (Salt Lake City: University of Utah Press, 1988), 84–99.

21. A.L. Carse, The "Voice of Care": Implications for Bioethics Education, *Journal of Philosophy and Medicine* 16 (1991):5–28.

22. V. Warren, Feminist Directions in Medical Ethics, *Hypatia* 4 (1989):77–82.

23. M.R. Harrison, The Anencephalic Newborn as Organ Donor (commentary), *Hastings Center Report* 16 (1986):21–22.

24. G. Meilaender, The Anencephalic Newborn as Organ Donor (commentary), *Hastings Center Report* 16 (1986):22–23.

25. Jonsen and Toulmin, *The Abuse of Casuistry*, chap. 15.

26. A. MacIntyre, *After Virtue* (Notre Dame, Ind.: Notre Dame University Press, 1981).

27. M. Walzer, *Spheres of Justice* (New York: Basic Books, 1983); M. Walzer, *Interpretation and Social Criticism* (Cambridge, Mass.: Harvard University Press, 1987).

28. Walzer, *Spheres of Justice*, 86ff.

29. R. Dworkin, *Spheres of Justice*: An Exchange, *New York Review of Books* 30, no. 12 (1983):44; G. Warnke, Social Interpretation and Political Theory: Walzer and His Critics, *Philosophical Forum* 21 (1989–1990):204–206.

30. Dworkin, *Spheres of Justice*: An Exchange.

31. N. Daniels, *Reading Rawls*, 2nd ed. (Stanford, Calif.: Stanford University Press, 1989); R.J. Arneson, ed., Symposium on Rawlsian Theory of Justice: Recent Developments, *Ethics* 99 (1989):695–944.

32. J. Rawls, Kantian Constructivism in Moral Theory: The Dewey Lectures, 1980, *Journal of Philosophy* 77 (1980):518.

33. Ibid., 519; see also J. Rawls, Justice as Fairness: Political Not Metaphysical, *Philosophy and Public Affairs* 14 (1985):228.

34. R. Rorty, *Contingency, Irony, and Solidarity* (Cambridge: Cambridge University Press, 1989).

35. Walzer, *Interpretation and Social Criticism*.

36. J. Habermas, The Hermeneutic Claim to Universality, in *Contemporary Hermeneutics*, edited by J. Bleicher (London: Routledge and Kegan Paul, 1980), 181–211.

37. P. Ricoeur, Hermeneutics and the Critique of Ideology, in *Hermeneutics and Modern Philosophy*, edited by B.R. Wachterhauser (Albany: State University of New York Press, 1986), 300–339.

38. Fox and Swazey, Medical Morality Is Not Bioethics; Noble, Ethics and Experts; MacIntyre, *After Virtue*.

39. D. Overcast et al., Technology Assessment, Public Policy and Transplantation, *Law, Medicine and Health Care* 13, no. 3 (1985):106–111.

40. Report of the Massachusetts Task Force on Organ Transplantation (Massachusetts Task Force on Organ Transplantation, Boston 1984); G. Annas, Regulating Heart and Liver Transplants in Massachusetts, *Law, Medicine and Health Care* 13, no. 1 (1985):4–7.

41. D. Callahan, *What Kind of Life?* (New York: Simon and Schuster, 1990).

42. Jonsen and Toulmin, *The Abuse of Casuistry.*

43. B. Williams, *Ethics and the Limits of Philosophy* (Cambridge, Mass.: Harvard University Press, 1985); S. Hampshire, *Morality and Conflict* (Cambridge, Mass.: Harvard University Press, 1983); C. Taylor, The Diversity of Goods, in *Utilitarianism and Beyond*, edited by A. Sen and B. Williams (Cambridge: Cambridge University Press, 1982), 129–144.

44. J. Rawls, *A Theory of Justice* (Cambridge, Mass.: Harvard University Press, 1971); N. Daniels, Wide Reflective Equilibrium and Theory Acceptance in Ethics, *Journal of Philosophy* 76 (1979):256–282.

Chapter 43

Discovering Challenges to Ethical Theory in Experience-Based Narratives of Nurses' Everyday Ethical Comportment

Patricia Benner

Surprising distances and dogmas appear when contrasting formal ethical theory and everyday skillful ethical comportment. For example, from Kant on, we have linked moral agency exclusively to the ability to make autonomous choices. However, in a study of critical care nursing practice, nurses talk about patient agency, their desires, bodily tendencies, and following the body's lead when caring for nonverbal patients. This form of moral agency called "following the body's lead" and associated with bodily intentionality (bodily tendencies, characteristics, and preferences)[1] cannot have the same ethical clarity as fully conscious deliberate choice. However, this subtler form of agency is recognized and guides the use of technology in the practice of expert critical care nurses.

Central to the caring practices of nurses are recognition practices and an ethic of responsiveness (i.e., responding to the concerns, needs, preferences, and tendencies of their patients). This practical form of knowledge—a knowing how rather than knowing that—is conveyed through observation of nurses' practice and through their narrative accounts of their practice. This chapter will illustrate some of the practical gaps between formal procedural ethical theory and everyday ethical comportment by examining the caring and recognition practices of expert nurses.

Public dialogue about stories from practice augment and extend a socially embedded understanding of notions of the good and concrete visions of how skillful ethical comportment is lived out in a practice. Experienced-based narratives of practice provide access to practical reasoning, skill acquisition, notions of the good, and ethical problems and dilemmas. This practicalist approach to the study of everyday skilled ethical comportment requires an exploration of a particular practice with its own boundaries and self-understanding.[2] By definition, such an approach focuses on particular concerns, actions, and human relationships within a community of practitioners.[3]

The socially embedded practical knowledge of everyday skilled ethical comportment exceeds what can be captured by ethical theories

The writing of this chapter was sponsored in part by a grant from the Helene Fuld Foundation. The contributions of the National Endowment for the Humanities Faculty Enrichment Institute "Ethics: Principles or Practices?" University of California, Santa Cruz, July 6, 1992 to August 7, 1992, directed by Hubert L. Dreyfus and David Hoy, are gratefully acknowledged.

because the particular relationship, context, historical understanding, skilled know-how, and perceptual and recognition skills as well as skilled responsive readings of the situation encompass more than prescriptive or descriptive theories can accommodate. This view of the everyday ethical knowledge embedded in practice need not stand in opposition to ethical theory. Nor does it fall outside of the rationality of practical reasoning. Rather it can be understood as a dialogical relationship between theory, stories of practice, and engagement in practice.[4] For example, nurses at different skill levels were found to have different levels of perceptual recognition ability and thus different forms of moral agency, depending upon their level of expertise.[5]

Sara Ruddick's understanding of practice as socially embedded knowledge and skill and the writings of Dreyfus, MacIntyre, and Taylor about practice as a living tradition, a community of practice that has a narrative and dialogical structure, have guided this practicalist approach.[6] This perspective might be contrasted with a technological or scientific view of practice according to which the practitioner is merely applying the latest scientific research and technology or the most current set of principles and rules for moral conduct. The technological view overlooks the distinction between knowing that and knowing how and thus the moral imagination and skilled perceptual acuity that must develop over time through engaging in practice.[7] Inherent in the technological view is the assumption that the practical world is capricious and chaotic and only ordered by theory and science. This view also unwittingly assumes that theory and science are the source of innovation and must be imported into practice with as little interpretation and change as possible. It overlooks skill as knowledge and practice as a source for innovation and theory.[8] In contrast, a practicalist view holds that practice has far more complexity than theory or science can capture. Patterns and meanings are apparent to the skilled practitioner engaged in practice. Theory both constitutes and is constituted by a background of skills, habits,

practices, and meanings.[9] The beginning practitioner draws on rules and principles, but increasingly the practitioner is able to perceive a given situation in terms of past concrete whole cases.[10] This view corrects the radical separation of the knower and the known characteristic of a Platonic and Cartesian view of theory.

Six areas of practical knowledge have been identified from the study of nursing practice: (1) graded qualitative distinctions; (2) common meanings; (3) background assumptions, expectations, and sets; (4) paradigm cases and personal knowledge; (5) maxims; and (6) unplanned practices.[11] Since these areas of practical knowledge are encountered in the actual practice process, they are best captured by observation and by narrative accounts by the practitioners (accounts that contain as much chronology, conversation, immediacy, and fidelity to the actual situation as possible). In telling their stories, nurses often hear their own concerns, moral conflicts, and visions of the good. In other words, stories are heard in their own terms and not just as illustrations of theory.

For the past 17 years, I and my colleagues have been studying the practice of nurses, listening to their stories. The plot and theme of these stories typically fall into four broad categories: (1) constitutive and sustaining narratives, (2) narratives of learning, (3) narratives of objectification and distance, and (4) loss of story or description of tasks.[12] In constitutive and sustaining narratives, nurses present stories that depict their best understanding of the practice, the vision of their practice that sustains them. In narratives of learning, the point is to convey experiential learning, to describe a situation that taught something new and altered clinical understanding or self-understanding as a practitioner. In a narrative of objectification and distance, the storyteller is more of an observer than an engaged participant. The story happens in front of the storyteller's gaze so that the storyteller does not convey a sense of agency and engagement in the situation. When understanding breaks down and caring practices deteriorate, stories of rejection, exclusion, dominance, control, and power struggles are heard. The stance is one of objectification and disengagement and fits the descriptions of "burnout" or loss of human caring.[13] The narrative does not take the form of transformation or learning. The final category consists of descriptions of tasks and events without a storyline. In a study of clinical nursing expertise, some nurses could not remember particular patients or families and literally could not tell any stories from their practice.[14] As one nurse explained, "I cannot tell you what I do in particular; I can tell you what I do in general." When pressed for an account of the current day, these disengaged nurses offered descriptions of what they had done rather than stories of care of particular patients or families. They had become technicians doing tasks rather than practitioners engaged in therapeutic interventions of care and restoration. It is not hard to understand why practice would deteriorate to this "job description" level given the overwork and institutional press for efficiency and the societal taboos against getting "too involved." Remarkably, these nurses are not exemplary according to their peers. They do not live up to the socially embedded expectations of excellent nursing practice. These disengaged nurses were not chosen to be preceptors for other nurses by their peers and supervisors though they had been working for five or more years. The goal of the larger project, which is not addressed here, is to examine the structural and social impediments that cause objectifying disengaged practice while identifying excellent practice as a basis for creating organizational designs that facilitate excellent practice.

DEVELOPING AN ETHIC OF RESPONSIVENESS: "FOLLOWING THE BODY'S LEAD"

The following interpretations are drawn from an interview and observational study of the practice of nursing in critical care units. The data used here come from narrative accounts of practice from beginning nurses, intermediate nurses (those who have two years of work experience),

expert nurses (those who have at least five years of work experience and are recognized by peers and supervisors as expert practitioners), and experienced, competent nurses (those who have five or more years of experience but are not selected as preceptors or considered experts by their peers).

The sample consists of 130 nurses in intensive care units in eight different hospitals in three different regions of the United States. All nurses were interviewed in small groups three times. In small-group interviews, nurses gave narrative accounts of their clinical practice. The members of each group were asked to do active listening, question the storyteller for any needed clarification, and offer similar or contrasting incidents.[15] Recognition practices (i.e., recognition of changes in patients and recognition of patient concerns, characteristics, and bodily tendencies) were a pervasive theme in the nurses' narratives. These practices were often characterized as "knowing a patient" or "following the body's lead." Knowing a patient and following the body's lead, especially in the case of nonverbal adult or infant patients, prevented nurses from misusing technology and doing harm while intending to do good.[16] This theme is illustrated in the following nurse's description of a premature infant:

> I think she was between 700 and 800 grams. And she was clearly declaring herself ready [to be weaned from the ventilator] and I was sure that was what would happen. . . . So I went directly to the attending [physician] with the blood gasses [showing oxygen saturation] and I said, "I think she's trying to tell us something. I don't see how you can keep ventilating this kid." Except that I knew that he didn't usually do things like this and that something was just wrong. And I needed to be satisfied why this small gestational-age baby couldn't be extubated. In my own mind, I needed to be satisfied. And so I did push it one more time. Risk wrath and all this stuff [from the physician], because I wasn't settled with it.

Her knowledge of the infant prompts her to take a stand for good practice, a stand that she knows that the physician would take if he had not thought that this baby was at a younger gestational age than was the case. She finally clears up the confusion and the infant is successfully extubated. She concludes with an ethical maxim: "Like I say, if you're not helping you're doing harm with ventilating. . . . It's a little thing but if that kid wasn't extubated that day then there's always chances of things going wrong and all this trauma." Her ethic of attentiveness and care guides her use of technology. Her expert caring practices enable her to attend to the infant's particular needs and not blindly follow the doctor's orders. The background question in this and other similar episodes seems to be, "What if I usurp the patient's own best capacities for healing?" To count as caring, the nurse's practice must serve the patient's own growth, recovery, concerns, and intentionality. This intentionality shows up as embodied intentionality, a reading of bodily responses, characteristics, and dispositions.[17] Intensive care nursery nurses repeatedly describe making astute observations of the embodied tendencies and characteristics of babies. The babies are given a distinct social space and otherness—a way to declare themselves in relation to what others would do to or for them. One might argue theoretically that the babies have moral worth without making the stronger claim for member-participant agency. It is possible to assert that this is pure projection, but the descriptions of the babies' characteristics are definitive and realistic and attain consensual validation from other caretakers. This recognition expertise is fallible and not omniscient, but the nursing care of premature infants depends on its general reliability. The nurses' discourse indicates that they relate to the infants as human beings with desires and capacities, and through their knowledge and relationship, the infants are given member-participant status. The infants are perceived as becoming stronger and more independent. Clearly the traditional notion of moral agency, based on autonomous choice,

does not apply, but through the nurses' relationship and attentive practice, the infants can show tendencies, capacities, suffering, and comfort. The nurses do not take an oppositional, all-or-none position of deciding for a passive individual. Through relationship and noticing, the infants are given human status and visibility and thus a way to make claims on other human beings. The infants do not have to have the characteristics necessary for total autonomy to make demands for ethical responses from their families, nurses, and physicians.

Nurses sometimes call this knowledge of the preferences and capacities "following the body's lead."[18] the careful practical reasoning and trial and error detection that accompany learning about a particular patient's desires and capacities demonstrate that they are not projections. For example, the following nurse describes how she painstakingly learned to feed a critically ill premature infant:

> Nurse 1: This kid just started throwing up a lot whenever we tried to feed him, so it was just trying different things. First off, feeding him more slowly, burping him better, which didn't really seem to matter. Feeding him more slowly, trying to catch him at a time before he started crying really hard, and having a bottle at the bedside ready to go as soon as he indicated that he was hungry just so he wouldn't get worked up, because then he seemed more likely to throw up. . . . He liked a certain nipple best, a certain speed. He liked the formula warmed to the exact right degree and just the whole combination of things that helped him eat better.
>
> Nurse 2: That is amazing, they have little individual personalities even when they're young. We had a baby who wouldn't eat anything warmed. Everything had to be cold. We had to write this down for everyone.

The practice dictates a response-based ethic that depends on knowing the particular infant.[19] An ethic of care and responsiveness necessarily requires experiential learning about particular infants and families and communities. This relational, experiential knowledge requires narrative in order to keep the meanings, concerns, and notions of good tied to the context and particular caring relationship:

I: You were all talking a little bit about knowing a kid. I don't know if you could each talk a little bit about what is it to know a kid? Especially, a 600-gram kid. Do you know a 600-gram kid?

Nurse 1: Absolutely, if you don't you're dead. (Laughter)

I: This is a question that I thought about. What about getting attached to a kid too. I wondered in the early period when you first were in ICN and working with these really young kids who from my point of view seemed kind of undifferentiated. Did you get attached to kids then or did it take a while before you really felt like these little ones have personalities and are different?

Nurse 2: I think it took a little while to really get attached to the very small ones. It's as they get a little bit older. When they're two days' old they don't really have any personality and they do all look alike. They're not quite human. They've got really translucent skin and they are red and squirmy. But after they get older, a little bit older, when they're a month old or so and they're sort of into the chronic stage that they start developing their idiosyncrasies and you know whether they're going to tolerate suctioning well or twit out for half an hour. Things like that. Whether feeding them makes them feel better or feel worse.

Nurse 1: Yeah, what comfort measures work and what don't. Do they like to be bundled? Do they like to suck their fingers or does that make them have bradycardia. That sort of thing. You learn about each kid. I think you learn it really quickly though. I can go in and take a chronic preemie that I don't know and by the end of the 12 hours I know exactly what works.

Nurse 2: Yeah, because you know what to try.

Nurse 1: Yeah. What's the most likely thing to learn and you go down the list until you find something that does [comfort].

Nurse 2: It took a while, it took years probably to get to that point. That I could get in there, try all my little tricks, figure out what works and what doesn't, and get the kid squared away. Although sometimes they don't and sometimes nothing works.

These nurses are describing a skilled ethical comportment of attentiveness, responsiveness, and comfort that is learned over time by working with many premature infants. It is the same kind of attentiveness and skill that enabled the nurse to recognize when the child could safely be extubated and be removed from artificial ventilation. The nurses are quick to point out that their knowledge does not reduce the other to total recognition—the other remains other and sometimes "nothing works." This practice of knowing the patient includes verbal patients and families but it is most striking when discussed in relation to the nonverbal infant or adult:

Nurse: I got to know her in a semisedated level and paralyzed, on a level you get to know a lot of patients in ICU. You still feel like you know them, but I got to really know her family very well, her mother, her husband, her father, and her brothers. . . .

I: You talked about that you can know a patient when they are sedated, just talk about what you mean by that for the sedated patient.

Nurse: It's something, I think, that's hard to describe, but I feel like I get to know them differently than when they're normal, I'm sure. But there's some sense of who this person is. It's like when you touch them, or when you say something to them, what happens on their monitors. Or maybe just to see what the effect of what you're doing shows up in what's happening to the patient, how they look, even when they're paralyzed just whether their features look a little different, something looks different about them, if they seem to be comfortable when you are there. You get to know them through talking to their family, who they are. They give you all these stories. When I contacted nurses that had taken care of her when she was a pediatric patient because she had a lot of episodes down on Peds to find out how they'd handled the parents and what she was like. I don't know, you just get to really know them. I felt like I really knew her. I felt like she was a little baby, almost, like an eight-year-old or a ten-year-old, that needed a lot of special attention and that she probably throws tantrums if she doesn't get her way. And that gets in the way of how she's going to recover because she couldn't afford to do that.

Knowing each particular patient is central to caring for the patient and fostering recovery. The patient is accorded member-participant status—status as someone who can be known in human terms even when he or she is not fully conscious. Recognition practices and understanding are imprecise moral arts that cannot guarantee success. Sometimes the other remains a misunderstood other. The lack of certainty and perfection, however, do not diminish the important of the skill or practice. Recognition practices and understanding are essential to constituting others and allowing others to be understood. The informal nursing discourse of knowing a patient points up the distinctions between mere explanation and the moral art of engaged reasoning and action.

THE DIALOGUE BETWEEN EXPLANATION AND UNDERSTANDING: A MORAL ART

The moral art of understanding and attentiveness is illustrated in a narrative by nurse Linda Sawyer in which she begins working with Ellen, a woman with diabetes.[20] Ellen's disease had been explained by medical science, but the problems of living with her disease had not been understood, nor had the attentiveness and ethical responsiveness required for treatment begun:

The joy of Home Health nursing for me is the ability to spend more time with a patient and to really be able to make an impact on the person's health status and quality of life. The case of Ellen is an example of such care. Ellen was diagnosed with juvenile diabetes at age 5 and soon after that also developed a seizure disorder. I first met Ellen when she was being seen by our agency for stasis ulcers of her heels. . . . On this admission, I became the case manager. She was 38 years old and described as intellectually slow. She lived with a very loving family who were knowledgeable about her condition. She and her family belonged to a very supportive church. On this admission Ellen had a stasis ulcer of her left heel and cellulitis of her foot with an open wound the length of the bottom of her foot. Ellen had frequent grand mal seizures and was on two anticonvulsant medications, and also had frequent hypoglycemic reactions. The family, patient, and physicians described these problems as "to be expected" and "that's Ellen."

I always have difficulty accepting that things couldn't be better and see part of my role as one of a detective. Ellen's mother told me that Ellen always had several episodes of hypoglycemia a week, often causing her to be admitted to the hospital or go to the emergency room. Often her mother would get phone calls at work from various emergency rooms telling her that Ellen had been riding the bus or shopping and had become unconscious.

Her mother could recognize hypoglycemia at night from subtle changes in her breathing. Ellen was not doing blood glucose monitoring, and I taught her and her mother to check her blood sugar level four times a day. Her record showed wide ranges from 40 to above 400 even in the same day. I discussed this with her physician, who then referred Ellen to a diabetic specialist. The specialist worked out a sliding scale of short- and long-acting insulin to decrease hypoglycemia at night. Her mother and I then did some fine-tuning of the regimen to stabilize Ellen at home [adjusting the dosages in response to the patient's responses].

Meanwhile diabetic complications were increasing. [In the narrative, the nurse gives a detailed list of the complications and her responses to them. Her goal was to make adjustments that would give Ellen as much independence and control as possible.]

Ellen had been wheelchairbound, only walking to the bathroom with a walker, for over two years. As Ellen's stasis ulcer healed, I noticed that Ellen walked with her weight distributed on the sides of her feet and heels. I asked for a physical therapy consult to have a special shoe made for her, and she was retrained to walk with a four-pronged cane. Imagine Ellen's and all of our excitement when Ellen walked into church and to her doctor's appointments with her "beautiful" black shoes and cane. Everyone was thrilled. Although Ellen's heel has broken down again several times since, it was superficial, easily healed, and her mother and I feel confident that we can deal with problems and better prevent their recurrence. I referred Ellen for nutrition counseling to see if weight reduction would decrease the stress on her feet as well as improve her diabetic control.

After a recent vacation, I returned to find Ellen's blood sugars out of control. I could find no pattern in her sugars and no obvious reason for this change. This felt different than Ellen's previous erratic glucose results. I called her physician and told her that I was worried that something else was going on. The doctor ordered blood tests and found that Ellen had become hypothyroid. She was started on thyroid supplements and improved.

I'm lucky in my job that I can continue to see Ellen long term since she has an unstable condition and the health care plan understands that my care keeps her from being hospitalized or requiring more expensive care. Ellen has not been admitted to the hospital in over three years and has only been to the emergency room twice. Her mother says that Ellen has never been so stable with her diabetes and seizures, and how relieved they are to not go through constant emergencies. . . . Ellen jokes with me on our visits and says, "Give me a chance, Linda. Just give me a chance." A chance is what I try to give Ellen everyday—a chance to be able to walk on her two feet for as long as possible, a chance to live with her chronic illness.

Even the shortened narrative reveals moral engagement and practical reasoning. Explanation had become a way of coping with the troubling problems in Ellen's life: "It was to be expected; after all, these are the typical complications of diabetes. But scientific explanation and disengaged observation do not ensure that Ellen, her family, or her health care practitioners will engage in the daily treatments and recognize and respond to changes, patterns, and suffering. Self-care and other care requires an engaged relationship of practical reasoning and understanding. Skilled ethical comportment requires attentiveness and responsiveness and finally the ability to recognize changing patterns of responses. Of course, it would be far better for Ellen to be able to recognize the changing patterns, and this increased independence is Linda Sawyer's goal in teaching Ellen and her mother blood glucose monitoring. Here day-to-day practice must inform the quest to make the patient autonomous rather than as "independent as possible."

It is especially difficult to recognize a changed pattern when one is living the change slowly over time. In this case, Linda Sawyer's distance and professional knowledge helped her to recognize a problem had arisen and to react appropriately. She noticed that Ellen's blood sugar patterns had changed, and she began to do detective work rather than dismiss the problem as unresolvable. This process of recognition and response requires the practitioner to know the particular patient and establish a relationship characterized by attentiveness and a skilled engagement. Knowing a patient makes attunement and responsiveness possible.

THE ROLE OF EMOTIONAL RESPONSES IN LEARNING ETHICAL COMPORTMENT

Engagement refers to a quality of emotional connection. Engaged reasoning and ethical responsiveness are skillful emotional responses that are experientially learned. A nurse reflects on the emotional responses that guided her ethical comportment while caring for a critically ill one-year-old with a life-shortening metabolic disorder:

> Nurse: I just remember very specifically the variety of emotions that I went through taking care of her, from feeling like a good nurse, feeling like a bad nurse and feeling like I was doing something to feeling like I wasn't doing anything.
>
> I: Can you remember times when you felt like a really good nurse?
>
> Nurse: When I was able to make L. get through the eight hours and be able to explain everything that was going on to the parents to the point where they understood it, I felt like a really good nurse. An when L. wouldn't do well and [blood] pressures were bottoming out, and when I had to do blood draws [she refers to the pain created by the blood draws and the parents' revulsion of seeing blood drawn from the scalp veins], that was when I'd come out crying and I couldn't believe I had to poke her again.

This nurse's emotional response guided her experiential learning and ethical sense of the situation. This illustrates Taylor's link between emotional responses and ethical understanding:

> What I know is also grounded in certain feelings. It is just that I understand these feelings to incorporate a deeper, more adequate sense of our moral predicament. If feeling is an affective awareness of situation, I see these feelings as reflecting my moral situation as it truly is; the imports they attribute truly apply.[21]

Taylor points up the role of sentience in recognizing "distinctions of worth" and whether or not one has a grasp of the situation. The links between emotional response, recognition, and ethical comportment are evident in Linda Sawyer's narrative of attentiveness and noticing, and they are also evident in the development of ethical expertise:

> Central to this view of skill acquisition as gaining an increasingly differentiated world of judgment, perception, and distinctions of worth or goods is the role of emotion in experiential learning. The concrete experience of the practitioner learning about better and poorer outcomes, learning distinct patient/family concerns, and learning from contrasts and similarities between various clinical situations helps to shape an emotionally imbued world of possibilities, concerns, risks and dangers. Experiential learning is tied to emotional responses to actual situations. Initially the advanced beginner may be flooded with anxiety and fear of making a mistake and may have to dampen emotional responses. But already at the competent stage, a sense of discomfort or dread may signal the nurse to re-examine his or her interpretation of the situation. Anxiety is now more situationally attuned. At the proficient stage, attunement increases to the point that emotional responses signal the nurse to notice changing relevance because increasingly loss of a good grasp of the situation is felt by the nurse. With expertise, emotional responses, the skill of seeing and associated actions are increasingly tied together.[22]

Taylor's view of agency guided our understanding of the nurses' changing forms of agency illustrated in the narratives:

> Agents are beings for whom things matter, who are the subjects of significance. This is what gives them a point of view in the world. What distinguishes persons from other agents is not strategic power, that is the capacity to deal with the same matter of concern more effectively. . . . What springs to view is that persons have qualitatively different concerns. . . . The centre

is no longer the power to plan, but rather the openness to certain matters of significance.[23]

This openness to matters of significance allows the skilled practitioner to have a sense of salience that facilitates pattern recognition.[24] Engaged reasoning creates different powers and vulnerabilities than disengaged reasoning. Both skilled engaged reasoning and critical reflection are needed, even for an ethic of care, so that distortion, self-deception, and patterns of oppression do not cloud one's perceptions. Nurses' understanding of the clinical situations when moving from competence to proficiency increase their ability to respond to matters of significance—often in the form of emotional responsiveness. The proficient nurses' stories describe changing preconceptions, plans, and predictions in response to the particular situation. Emotional responses are also linked to being open or closed to the situation's demands. Nurses use maxims that point to experientially gained wisdom that help them to stay open to the situation. For example, one nurse states, "Take care of these patients and get fooled a million times." Staying open to being possibly fooled curbs tunnel vision and projection. Another nurse talks about the ethics of vigilance, watching to make sure that excessive or no longer needed tests or treatments are not carelessly continued:

> Nurse 1: It's even minor stuff . . . "Why are you going to sanguinate this kid when it's like sitting up watching TV eating?". . . It's just little stuff like that. And when they [new nurses] get a little more experienced they and their assessment skills get better, they can notice that maybe they're wheezing a little bit or that they're a little cold. They're a little blue or something. But it's like cleaning up. [Reference to remembering and noticing what needs to be done.] And you can avoid such trauma if you are more aware of what's going on.
>
> Nurse 2: You get caught with your pants down. And then you never ever do that same mistake again.

> Nurse 3: But you also remember what has happened to you. I mean I have worked with nurses who never learn. [Gives an example of a nurse not changing and not remembering.]

Remembering, as these nurses talk about it, covers a lot of learning. It is closely linked to experience and is a well-developed practice of attentiveness. Attentiveness and noticing are qualitatively different caring practices. Attentiveness is required for catching the multiple details that can be missed in health care. It is based on a deliberate set of habits and practices. Noticing is less deliberate than attentiveness and is dependent on expert engagement and a sense of salience that guides recognition of the unusual or unexpected pattern. Noticing is part of an ethic of responsiveness, giving the other moral worth as other.

CONCLUSION

Being in the situation with the best theoretical and educational guidance for noticing qualitative distinctions develops ethical comportment. Ethical learning and skillful ethical comportment are based upon a continued focus on what works and what does not work in specific situations. The notions of good represented by norms and moral principles cannot be extended and enriched without this focus. Furthermore, the practice itself offers new possibilities for theorizing. Family, close others, and health care workers extend the moral agency of the patient through their recognition practices. A theoretical system that can only accommodate fully deliberate conscious statements as moral agency misses this rich moral source of agency and understanding in everyday ethical comportment through recognition practices for the nonverbal person. Abstract principles are necessary for orienting and alerting the learner to the appropriate regions of concern and for clarifying the public discourse, but they cannot ensure that one will recognize in practice when these norms might be relevant, nor can they guarantee that the ideal can be actualized. Explanation does not always engender understanding or ethical response.

Stories of actual practice can uncover moral concerns and notions of good central to everyday ethical comportment. A story is not a purely subjective construction, though one can only tell about what one sees and knows. Thus, stories are both given and constructed. The storyteller reports thoughts, feelings, and experiential knowledge of an event. In the story, the actual skillful ethical comportment of practitioners can be examined and developed. In a health care system driven by economic pressures, the press for efficiency can crowd out the understanding and engaged reasoning that create stories. Telling the stories of practice can help us recognize moral concerns and notions of good that have been covered over in our ethical theories or are invisible and devalued because they do not show up well in the objectified institutional reports of services rendered. Creating a public space for narratives of practice gives voice to our moral concerns, notions of good, and moral conflicts. Ethical consultants called to assist with moral dilemmas, breakdown, and conflict offer most when they are able to elicit the stories of the various participants in a situation. Engaged and disengaged reasoning are both required. But analysis of ethical breakdowns designed for adjudicating disputes and determining rights constitutes only a small portion of our ethical lives. We need to listen to our stories of practice to examine distinctions of worth, competing goods, and the relational ethics of care, responsiveness, and responsibility.[25]

NOTES

1. M. Merleau-Ponty, *Phenomenology of Perception* (London: Routledge and Kegan Paul, 1962); P. Benner and J. Wrubel, Skilled Clinical Knowledge: The Value of Perceptual Awareness, *Nurse Educator* 7, no. 3 (1982):11–17; S. Gadow, Clinical Subjectivity: Advocacy with Silent Patients, *Nursing Clinics of North America* 24 (1989):535–541.

2. S. Ruddick, Maternal Thinking, *Feminist Studies* 6 (1980):342–367; S. Ruddick, *Maternal Thinking: Toward a Politics of Peace* (Boston: Beacon, 1989); A. MacIntyre, *After Virtue* (Notre Dame, Ind.: University of Notre Dame Press, 1991); C. Taylor, *Sources of the Self* (Cambridge, Mass.: Harvard University Press, 1989); C. Taylor, *The Ethics of Authenticity* (Cambridge, Mass.: Harvard University Press, 1992).

3. J. Lave, *Cognition in Practice* (New York: Cambridge University Press, 1988); J. Lave and E. Wenger, *Situated Learning: Legitimate Peripheral Participation* (Cambridge: Cambridge University Press, 1991); L.A. Suchman, The Problem of Human Machine Interaction, in *Plans and Situated Actions* (Cambridge: Cambridge University Press, 1987); P. Benner, *From Novice to Expert: Excellence and Power in Clinical Nursing Practice* (Menlo Park, Calif: Addison-Wesley, 1984); P. Benner and J. Wrubel, *The Primacy of Caring, Stress and Coping in Health and Illness* (Menlo Park, Calif.: Addison-Wesley, 1989); P. Benner, The role of Experience, Narrative and Community in Skilled Ethical Comportment, *Advances in Nursing Science* 14, no. 2 (1991):1–21.

4. H.L. Dreyfus and S.E. Dreyfus, with T. Athanasiou, *Mind over Machine: The Power of Human Intuition and Expertise in The Era of the Computer* (New York: The Free Press, 1986); P. Benner, The Role of Experience, Narrative, and Community in Skilled Ethical Comportment, *Advances in Nursing Science* 14, no. 2 (1991):1–21.

5. P. Benner et al., From Beginner to Expert: Gaining a Differentiated Clinical World in Critical Care Nursing, *Advances in Nursing Science* 14, no. 3 (1992): 13–28.

6. Ruddick, *Maternal Thinking: Toward a Politics of Peace*; H.L. Dreyfus, *What Computers Can't Do: The Limits of Artificial Intelligence*, rev. ed. (New York: Harper and Row, 1979); H.L. Dreyfus, *Being-in-the-World: A Commentary on Being and Time Division I* (Cambridge: Cambridge University Press, 1990); MacIntyre, *After Virtue*; C. Taylor, *Philosophical Papers*, vols. 1, 2 (Cambridge: University of Cambridge Press, 1985); Taylor, *The Ethics of Authenticity*.

7. Benner and Wrubel, Skilled Clinical Knowledge.

8. Taylor, *Philosophical Papers*, vols. 1, 2.

9. M. Heidegger, *Being and Time*, translated by J. Macquarrie and E. Robinson (New York: Harper and Row, 1962); Dreyfus, *Being-in-the-World*.

10. Benner, *From Novice to Expert*; Dreyfus et al., *Mind over Machine*; Benner et al., From Beginner to Expert.

11. Benner, *From Novice to Expert*.

12. Benner, The Role of Experience, Narrative, and Community in Skilled Ethical Comportment.

13. C. Maslach, *Burnout: The Cost of Caring* (Englewood Cliffs, N.J.: Prentice-Hall, 1982).

14. P. Benner et al., *Expertise in Nursing Practice: Clinical Judgement and Skillful Ethical Comportment* (New York: Springer, in press).

15. Benner et al., From Beginner to Expert; Benner et al., *Expertise in Nursing Practice.*

16. Benner et al., The Nature of Clinical Expertise in Nursing Practice.

17. Merleau-Ponty, *Phenomenology of Perception*; Gadow, Clinical Subjectivity; Benner and Wrubel, *The Primacy of Caring*; P. Benner, The Role of Articulation in Understanding Practice and Experience as Sources of Knowledge, in *Philosophy in a Time of Pluralism: Perspectives on the Philosophy of Charles Taylor*, edited by J. Tulley and D.M. Weinstock (Cambridge: Cambridge University Press, in press).

18. Ibid.

19. C. Tanner et al., The Phenomenology of Knowing a Patient, *Image, the Journal of Nursing Scholarship* (in press).

20. This narrative was originally presented by Linda Sawyer, R.N., M.S., at the California Nurses' Association conference entitled "The Nurse as Clinical Expert: Nurses Who Have Made a Difference," San Francisco, California, May 17, 1991. Used with permission.

21. Taylor, *Philosophical Papers*, vol. 1, p. 61.

22. Tanner et al., From Beginner to Expert.

23. Taylor, *Philosophical Papers*, vol. 1, p. 104.

24. P. Benner and C. Tanner, Clinical Judgment: How Expert Nurses Use Intuition, *American Journal of Nursing* 87 (1987):23–31.

25. C. Taylor, *Recognition Practices and the Politics of Multiculturalism* (Cambridge: Cambridge University Press, 1992).

Chapter 44

Ethical Issues in Pharmacy: Questions without Answers

Bruce David White

The separation that once existed between "theory" and "practice" in nursing, medical, pharmacy, and other health professional educational programs is difficult to defend today. Not too long ago, the first half of the professional curriculum for pharmacists was devoted to confirming the scientific underpinning (theory) of practice. The latter half of the curriculum allowed educators to teach and demonstrate the practical aspects of pharmacy through on-the-job training under watchful supervisors. Today's pharmacy educational foundations rest on this model, but the distinctive educational line between theory and practice has become so blurred that the gray zone may cover much of a student's formal undergraduate training. Educators are attempting to bring the practical relevance of educational foci into the curriculum as early as possible (perhaps largely to keep students excited about their professional training and to help eliminate redundant information). This shift is valid because practical clinical applications are important to students as they learn the theoretical bases of pharmacy practice.

Similarly, it is difficult to discuss pharmacy ethics in terms of theory and practice. The two are not separable. One can readily find chapters about "pharmacy ethics" that include descriptive explanations of the formal codes of ethics developed by pharmacy trade associations.[1] But having read these professional standards, the pharmacist still faces difficulty in applying these formal codes to hard cases in practice.

Medical ethics (or, more broadly, bioethics, health care ethics, clinical ethics) encounters the same near-impossible task: helping clinicians apply often vague, aspirational moral standards in specific patient care contexts so they can come to terms with identified deeply troublesome moral dilemmas and feel "comfortable"[2] with the result (i.e., as momentarily settled about the decision as possible).[3]

In order to focus on the individual pharmacist's needs in dealing with ethical dilemmas, one might consider (1) the few models proposed for ethical decision making and (2) how these models might be helpful in dealing with specific cases. Models are difficult to apply; often they do not fit a particular situation at all. However,

The author gratefully acknowledges the thoughtful review of Stuart D. Finder, Ph.D., Assistant Professor of Medicine (Medical Ethics) and Associate Director, Center for Clinical and Research Ethics, Vanderbilt University Medical Center, Nashville, Tennessee.

they are valuable in systematically determining priorities in assessing values that are important to individuals.

ETHICAL ANALYSIS MODELS

Ethical problems highlight moral conflicts that occur in practice. Moral conflicts arise between perceived ethical duties or moral principles or between individuals that have to make decisions or render professional judgments. And since patient care dilemmas must be resolved, any conflicts involved must also be settled in some reasonable fashion for the moment, even though some conflicts may never really come to an end.[4]

To meet their responsibilities, pharmacists must apply professional codes and standards (or their own individual beliefs or interpretations of collective opinions) to solve immediate problems. How do they do this? They might adopt one of several models: a professional responsibility or "duty" model, a "principles" model, or a modified "shared decision making" model. It is important to note, however, that models are usually only of value for starting discussions; deeper reflective analysis depends less on models and more on thinking about personal values and options in particular situations.

The "Duty" Model

This might be described as an agreed list of "shoulds" promulgated by pharmacists with the tacit authority to speak for fellow pharmacists. A model of this type appeared in 1921 in the *Journal of the American Pharmaceutical Association:*

- *Pharmacists' Duties to Patrons*
  - They should safeguard the delivery of medicines to patrons.
  - They should meet the standards of the *United States Pharmacopeia* and the *National Formulary.*
  - They should hold the health and safety of their patrons to be their first consideration.

- *Pharmacists' Duties to Physicians*
  - Pharmacists should not, under any circumstances, substitute one article for another.
  - Pharmacists should follow the physician's directions explicitly in the manner of filling and refilling prescriptions.
  - Pharmacists should never discuss the therapeutic effect of a physician's prescription with a patron.

- *Pharmacists' Duties to Fellow Pharmacists*
  - Pharmacists should courteously aid a fellow pharmacist who in an emergency needs supplies.
  - Pharmacists should not undersell a fellow pharmacist for the sake of commercial advantage.
  - Pharmacists should never request a copy of a prescription from a fellow pharmacist.[5]

Even with professional codes such as this, some stated goals appear inconsistent with others ("hold the health and safety of their patrons to be their first consideration" versus "never discuss the therapeutic effect of a physician's prescription with a patron").

The apparent advantage of this model is that a statement can theoretically be developed on every issue. The disadvantages are that statements cannot be written for every conceivable problem and that over time the consensus changes within the profession.

The "Principles" Model

One might assert that ethical problems only arise when conflicts between personal and professional principles (general guidelines or rules worthy of deep respect in life and practice) appear. When pharmacists act professionally, they should do so with deferential regard to deepseated principles: that whatever is done in practice should be done for the patient's good (the principle of beneficence), that whatever is done in practice should be done in such a way as to cause as little harm to the patient as possible (the principle of nonmaleficence), that patients should be involved in making their own health decisions (the principle of self-determination or respect for the individual), that the end result should seem "useful" to the individual and society (the principle of utility), and that fairness in the system should be promoted (the principle of justice).[6]

Consider the following case: A pharmacist is asked to deliver an experimental chemotherapeutic agent when it is not clear that the patient has agreed to participate in the drug trial. Would the pharmacist be doing the right thing in supplying the drug to the patient without the patient's informed consent (trust might be compromised if it is perceived that the pharmacist has participated in keeping the truth from the patient)? Would the pharmacist cause more harm by bringing the issue up (nonmaleficence)? In particular, would the pharmacist jeopardize the overall benefits to society that might result from learning more about the drug, since the patient might refuse to participate in the trial (utility and justice)? Again, it is difficult to apply principles and the value given to principles in hard cases independently of the other persons involved.

The "Shared Decision Making" Model

Bioethics authors use various names to refer to this particular model, which allows for shared decision making between practitioners and patients and others involved in the caregiving process.[7] The version of this model presented in *Clinical Ethics*[8] exemplifies the type and is easily adapted for pharmacy purposes (Figure 44–1). The physician and the pharmacist determine the medical or pharmacy indications for intervention; they then, in conjunction with the patient, agree on a course of action. Each participant of the decision process is allowed an opportunity to express preferences and note concerns regarding various options. The three par-

ticipants are left to settle ethical conflicts among themselves; trust is promoted through shared decision making. If one participant wants to delegate individual decision-making responsibility to another and that person is willing to accept this additional role (e.g., the patient accepts the physician's therapy recommendation without question or the physician is willing to accept the pharmacist's therapy recommendation with no objection), conflicts will still exist (e.g., does the surrogate decision maker decide the issue based on what is in the other's best interest or according to the latest scientific data?) but some decision can be made.

One should note that this model is based on what many would call an inappropriate assumption: that all three—patient, physician, pharmacist—are equally empowered in the decision-making process. It seems obvious that the physician has essential control, although that was perhaps more true in the past than it is now. In today's health care environment, decision-making power and authority often rests outside

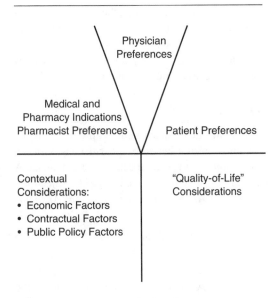

Source: Adapted from *Clinical Ethics*, 3rd ed., by A.R. Jonsen, M. Siegler, and W.J. Winslade, with permission of McGraw-Hill, Inc., © 1992.

Figure 44–1 Shared Decision Making Model.

the traditional physician, patient, and pharmacist triad: Other factors—economic, contractual, and public policy—operate to influence the process and outcome. This model takes into account the influence of these "outside" forces on the relationship. One need only consider the contractual arrangements with third-party payer health plans and pharmacists, physicians, and patients to recall the influence of economics and public policy. Individual preferences, whether the pharmacist's, physicians', or patient's, may now take second place when health care decisions are made in this context.

Furthermore, the physician, patient, and pharmacist relationship does not exist in a vacuum. Competent adult patients use their own quality-of-life criteria in making health care decisions (self-determination), but what about nonautonomous adults (incompetents or elders) or children—who will make the necessary decisions for them?

ETHICAL CONCERNS IN SPECIFIC SITUATIONS

Conversations, just like passages and phrases in written materials, must be viewed in their own unique setting. Many clinical ethics textbooks, casebooks, conferences, and discussions begin with specific fact situations to properly set the stage for an explanation and analysis of a particular dilemma. In these problem cases, there are usually an endless number of independent variables that defy easy characterization and generalization. If one accepts that ethical concerns often emerge from conflicts (conflicts within one individual or between several persons, whether over duties or principles, or in patient care negotiations), it is relatively easy to list or catalog a number of issues that arise in common situations in pharmacy practice.

Conflicts in Supplying Products

Pharmacists deliver goods and services—prescription and nonprescription drugs and information about these drugs—to patients and less

directly to physicians and other health care professionals.

Prescription Drug Products

The pharmacist recognizes that the analgesic dose of the ordered drug (e.g., morphine) for a cancer patient is tantamount to a lethal dose. How should the pharmacist question the dose? Should the discussion deal openly with the issue of active euthanasia? How should the pharmacist proceed if the physician states that he realizes that the patient's death may result directly from the administration of the drug?

May a pharmacist dispense drugs to the state correctional facility to be used as a lethal injection to execute a condemned criminal? Does the fact that it is delivered upon a signed prescription matter? Since the pharmacist is providing a lethal dose to an individual, might this not be interpreted as participating in active euthanasia? Or does the fact that it is a legally condoned execution permit participation? If physician-assisted suicide was allowed by law, would it then be morally permissible for the pharmacist to dispense the drug?

The pharmacist is asked to supply an abortifacient (either a "morning-after drug" or a suppository). How will the pharmacist deal with the possibility of the abortion personally? Must the pharmacist know the circumstances behind the possible abortion (because morning-after pills might be prescribed when the patient is the victim of rape or incest) or does it really matter?

The pharmacist is questioned by a lady who uses birth control pills. She is violently opposed to abortion of any kind. She has heard that the pill is not 100 percent effective in suppressing ovulation and that occasionally a fertilized egg might implant, in which case, because of the hormonal regulation from the pill, the uterine lining might slough anyway. She asks, "Then I might be aborting?" How should the pharmacist respond?

What responsibility does a pharmacist have to alert a patient and his or her physician about the possibility that a prescribed drug (e.g., a mild tranquilizer) is being used more often than is usually indicated or in what appears to be excessive amounts? Does this responsibility change if the pharmacist notices that a number of providers are prescribing the same drug to the same patient?

The hospital pharmacist is asked to deliver an experimental drug or a product that appears to be used in a manner inconsistent with present prescribing practice (an "unapproved use" or "innovative use"). How satisfied must the pharmacist be that the patient has been given adequate information? Is the pharmacist obliged to ensure "informed consent"? Should the pharmacist investigate the matter at all?

The pharmacist is asked to dispense a placebo. How should the pharmacist respond to direct questions from the patient about the drug and its use and possible side effects? How should the pharmacist respond to questions about trust and truth-telling if the patient learns about the "deception"?

A long-term care pharmacist, recently employed to provide quality assurance review of facility medication utilization, tells the director of nursing that one practitioner has authorized continuous use of a major tranquilizer for every one of her patients. The nursing director confirms that the drug is prescribed principally to "keep the patients quiet." How might the pharmacist raise the issue of using psychotropic drugs for patients who might not need them continuously? (A number of malpractice claims could be made if the patients suffer injurious side effects, and the argument that the pharmacist might have prevented these side effects through appropriate intervention might be valid. Of course, the same type of argument might be made to support nursing malpractice claims.)

There are several pharmaceutical manufacturers that are developing "genetic-modifying" drugs. Undoubtedly, pharmacists will be asked to dispense these drugs, which have the potential to change not just the patient's genome but perhaps the genomes of future generations. Drugs will be used without assessing complete impact. Should pharmacists be involved in calculating individual and societal benefits and risks?

Other Products

Should pharmacists participate in supplying products that are known to be harmful when used in excess and have a high potential for abuse? Should pharmacists offer to sell tobacco products and alcoholic beverages in their pharmacies? Should warning statements be placed conspicuously about the premises if these products are sold?

Should high-dose vitamin and food supplements and herbs with uncertain health benefits be sold in pharmacies?

Should nonprescription products or chemicals with an unapproved or questionable medicinal use (e.g., DMSO for arthritis) be supplied by pharmacists?

Information

May pharmacists provide drug-specific information leaflets (e.g., leaflets based on *United States Pharmacopeia Dispensing Information*) to patients when prescriptions are dispensed? May this be done without prescriber authorization? May pharmacists answer detailed and precise questions from patients about prescription drug indications, contraindications, and adverse effects? May pharmacists respond to questions from patients about practitioner prescribing habits and specific products?

How extensively may pharmacists counsel patients about prescription and nonprescription drug use? Is the pharmacist's obligation independent of the prescriber's responsibility to provide similar information? Should physicians be notified of this counseling at all?

How much information about a patient's drug use (information that might be contained in the patient's pharmacy profile) should be disclosed to other health care professionals without the patient's authorization? Is it permissible to release this information merely upon a request from the patient's physician?

Economic Conflicts

Pharmacists perhaps more than any other health care professionals are seen by patients as "small businesspersons." Patrons understand that many pharmacists operate their pharmacies much like other small business owners and managers run hardware stores, dry cleaners, electrical shops, and restaurants. Pharmacists more than most other health care providers are just as accessible as other small businesspersons, and patrons can more readily evaluate the cost of pharmaceutical goods and services than the costs associated with physicians and hospitals. Patrons also understand that if a pharmacist is not able to "make a living" from gross receipts, just like any other person running a small business, the pharmacy will close. But the public sees the pharmacist in another light too, because pharmacists cater to patients' health needs and drugs are often a "matter of life and death."

Questionable Prescriptions

Should pharmacists fill "legal" prescriptions that might be questionable (e.g., for excessive amounts of narcotics or for patients that are obtaining controlled substances from numerous prescribers)? Does it matter that "the pharmacist down the street would fill it without thinking twice"?

Technician Responsibilities

A pharmacist might utilize a nonpharmacist assistant (a pharmacy technician) in receiving drug orders, dispensing prescriptions, and counseling patients. But what are the extremes of professional responsibility? Should the technician type labels, reconstitute preparations, or caution a patient about side effects upon delivery?

Employee Relations

Is it permissible to ask employees to submit to occasional lie detector examinations or periodic random drug urinalysis? Does it matter that the managing pharmacist feels that this is an unwarranted intrusion into junior employees' privacy and would not want to submit to such tests personally?

Advertising

Would it be proper to advertise the cost of prescription drugs? What would it matter if the state required the pharmacy to post the cost of the standardized amounts of the "top 20" prescription drugs dispensed?

Mail-Order Pharmacies

May a pharmacist work for a mail-order pharmacy and fill prescriptions for patients who never have an opportunity to discuss the prescription face to face? How might this differ from filling prescriptions at a Veterans Administration medical center or on Public Health Service reservations, where pharmacists usually do not see patients or have occasion to hand-deliver prescriptions? Does it matter that the mail-order pharmacy does not keep patient profiles to allow for simple cross-referencing of possible drug-drug interactions?

Medicaid or Health Care Plan Boycotts

Would it be proper for a pharmacist not to participate in the state's Medicaid program or a particular contractual, prepaid health care plan (health maintenance organization or preferred provider organization) because the reimbursement fee was arguably too meager? Would it matter that the dispensing fee was truly less than the cost of filling the prescription for the pharmacy?

Drug Policy Conflicts

Pharmacists serve individual patients, but they also have duties to society as a whole. Most pharmacy schools are public-supported institutions of higher learning; the state tax structure has in fact subsidized pharmacists' training. Public policy encourages all health care providers to promote equity in health care delivery. Practitioners have a utilitarian obligation to practice their professions effectively and effi-

ciently. To the extent practitioners waste resources or defraud payers, all patients suffer. But
in the United States, most "public policies" are
not clear. Pharmacists and other health care professionals are often left to interpret mixed sig-
nals from policy makers.

Voluntary Destructive Behaviors

Should pharmacists support higher care premiums for smokers? Should pharmacists work
for institutions that will not offer liver transplants to alcoholics with cirrhosis? Must the illnesses result from self-destructive behavior before their costs are considered?

Uninsured Patients

Is it permissible for pharmacists to charge
paying patrons more for their prescriptions in
order to subsidize assistance and uninsured patients? Should pharmacists provide prescription
drugs at cost or below cost to those patients who
are not covered by assistance programs and have
no other means of obtaining the products?

"Drug Lag"

Should pharmacists cooperate with pharmaceutical manufacturers to identify patients suffering from terminal illnesses (e.g., cancer or
AIDS) to enroll them in experimental drug programs? Would it matter that these patients are
eager to participate and appear very willing to
work with manufacturers to test the products?

RESOLVING CONFLICTS IN PRACTICE

As the issues listed above indicate, pharmacists face many unique ethical dilemmas. Learning ethical analysis models and trying to apply
them to sets of facts to reach "good" decisions
often does not help in their resolution. The personalities and values of the players in each instance must be taken into account. The fact situations are too varied to apply even previously
good solutions to new cases. The key appears to
be thinking and acting reflectively when confronting morally troublesome dilemmas.

Pharmacists and all health care professionals
face remarkable moral uncertainties in practice.
Chances are these uncertainties will only increase with time. Ethical issues are an integral
part of the theory and practice of pharmacy, and
pharmacists must confront and resolve them as
best they can every day. For this reason, pharmacists must be prepared to deal with anticipated
concerns and have a framework to handle the dilemmas of the future.

NOTES

1. M.J. Myers and M. Montagne, Ethics, *Remington's
   Pharmaceutical Sciences,* 18th ed., edited by A.R.
   Gennaro (Easton, Pa.: Mack Publishing Company,
   1990), 20–27; W.W. Travis, A Code of Ethics for Pharmacy, *American Journal of Pharmacy* 135 (1963):252–
   256; American Pharmaceutical Association Code of
   Ethics, in *Pharmacy Ethics,* edited by M. Smith et al.,
   (New York: Pharmaceutical Products Press, 1991), 74–
   75; Code of Ethics of the American Society of Consultant Pharmacists, in Smith et al., *Pharmacy Ethics,* 76–
   78.

2. Not necessarily convinced that the result is ethically
   good, but rather comfortable that the resolution, of all
   possible ones, has been the least disconcerting to those
   involved. Medical malpractice lawyers are often upset
   about the way a particular case is settled but yet are satisfied that the issue was resolved in the most satisfactory
   manner available to the parties.

3. A.R. Jonsen et al., *Clinical Ethics,* 3rd ed. (New York:
   McGraw-Hill, 1992).

4. Just as, in some cases, a lawsuit must be settled despite
   the fact that the parties never really end their dispute.
   See D.B. Brushwood and J.C. Vivian, *Ethics Perspec-
   tives: Guidelines for Dealing with Ethics in Pharmacy
   Practice,* instructor's manual to videotape (Kalamazoo,
   Mich.: The Upjohn Co., 1988), 2–4.

5. C.H. Lawell, Pharmaceutical Ethics, in Smith et al.,
   Pharmacy Ethics, 76–78.

6. T.L. Beauchamp and J.F. Childress, *Principles of Biomedical Ethics,* 3rd ed. (London: Oxford University
   Press, 1989).

7. T. Scully and C. Scully, *Making Medical Decisions*
   (New York: Fireside Paperbacks, 1987).

8. Jonsen et al., *Clinical Ethics.*

Chapter 45

Bioethics As Social Problem Solving

Paul T. Durbin

Although situational or act-oriented theories recognize rules, they treat them as summary rules or rules of thumb that are expendable. Their hypothesis is that moral rules summarize the wisdom of the past by expressing better and worse ways to handle recurring problems. Such rules assist deliberation but can be set aside at any time according to the demands of the situation. . . . We have argued against this interpretation of moral rules.

— Tom L. Beauchamp and
James F. Childress

What I offer here are some philosophical reflections on bioethics[1] roughly in the last quarter of the twentieth century. I offer the reflections in the spirit of American pragmatism—not the recent version of Richard Rorty[2] but the older, progressive tradition of John Dewey[3] and George Herbert Mead[4] and the still older views of William James.[5]

BIOETHICS PHILOSOPHICALLY CONSTRUED

Robert Veatch quotes a representative of the American Medical Association as saying it is not up to philosophers but to the medical profession to set its moral rules:

> So long as a preponderance of the providers of medical service—particularly physicians—feel that the weight of the evidence favors the concept that the public may be better served—that the greatest good may be best accomplished—by a profession exercising its own responsibility to the state or to someone else, then the medical profession has an ethical responsibility to exert itself in making apparent the superiorities of [this] system.[6]

Veatch cites this claim in a book that places it in a broader context, within a framework of "different systems or traditions of medical ethics . . .

including the Hippocratic tradition, various Western religions, ethical systems derived from secular philosophical thought, and ethics grounded in philosophical and religious systems of non-Western cultures"[7] (e.g., China and India, but also the old Soviet Union and Islamic countries). Nonetheless, Veatch takes it to be obvious that any such profession-related or parochial or denominational system of medical or health care ethics requires "critical thinking" about "how an ethic for medicine should be grounded."[8]

Far and away the most popular summation of this foundational approach is provided in Tom Beauchamp and James Childress's *Principles of Biomedical Ethics*.[9] According to Albert Jonsen, a critic of this approach, the first edition of the *Principles* filled a vacuum in the early years of the bioethics movement; it "provided the emerging field of bioethics with a methodology" that was in line with "the currently accepted approaches of moral philosophy" and thus could be readily taught and employed by practitioners.[10]

Jonsen goes on to provide a neat summary: "That method consisted of an exposition of the two major 'ethical theories,' deontology and teleology, and a treatment of four principles, autonomy, nonmaleficence, beneficence, and justice, in the light of those theories."[11] Jonsen adds that "the four principles have become the mantra of bioethics, invoked constantly in discussions of cases and analyses of issues."[12]

While Jonsen is critical of the Beauchamp-Childress approach, he recognizes that it is reflective of "currently accepted approaches in moral philosophy." As witness to this, two other popular textbooks, although broader in scope than *Principles*, can be cited.

Michael Bayles, in *Professional Ethics*,[13] provides what is probably the most widely used single-author textbook for professional ethics generally. Like Beauchamp, Bayles is a utilitarian, but his approach can be adapted easily to any other ethical theory. Bayles endorses a general rule: "When in doubt, the guide suggested here is to ask what norms reasonable persons [generally, not just in the professions] would accept for a society in which they expected to live."[14] He goes on, however, with this summary of the view he elaborates later in the book:

> There are several levels of justification. An ethical theory is used to justify social values. These values can be used to justify norms. The norms can be either universal (applying to everyone) or role related (applying only to persons in the roles). Roles are defined by norms indicating the qualifications for persons occupying them and the type of acts they may do, such as represent clients in court. Norms can then be used to justify conduct.[15]

This exactly parallels the model used by Beauchamp and Childress.[16]

Joan Callahan's *Ethical Issues in Professional Life*,[17] while perhaps not as popular as Bayles's textbook, is also widely used. It is perhaps most notable for its dependence on the notion of "wide reflective equilibrium." As her sources, Callahan cites John Rawls, Norman Daniels, and Kai Nielsen, but she could as easily have cited dozens of other philosophers espousing one version or another of what Kurt Baier calls the "moral point of view." Here is how Callahan's summary of the approach begins:

> Things are much the same in ethics [as in science]. We begin with our "moral data" (i.e., our strongest convictions of what is right or wrong in clear-cut cases) and move from here to generate principles for behavior that we can use for decision making in cases where what should be done is less clear.[18]

This lays out the top-down, theory-to-decision approach. Then Callahan says,

> But, as in science, we sometimes have to reject our initial intuitions about what is right or wrong since they violate moral principles we have come to believe are surely correct. Thus, we realize we must dismiss the initial judgment as being the product of mere prejudice or conditioning rather than a judgment that can be supported by morally acceptable principles.[19]

This is the application part, but Callahan immediately adds the other pole in the dynamic equilibrium: "On the other hand, sometimes we are so certain that a given action would be wrong (or right) that we see we must modify our moral principles to accommodate that judgment."[20]

This exactly reflects the view of Beauchamp and Childress as stated in this passage:

> Moral experience and moral theories are dialectically related: We develop theories to illuminate experience and to determine what we ought to do, but we also use experience to test, corroborate, and revise theories. If a theory yields conclusions at odds with our ordinary judgments—for example, if it allows human subjects to be used merely as means to the ends of scientific research—we have reason to be suspicious of the theory and to modify it or seek an alternative theory.[21]

Jonsen believes that the term *theory* here is being used very loosely,[22] but if we employ different terms and talk simply about different approaches to ethics, it is clear that some authors have opted for other approaches to bioethics that they think are more congruent with their experiences. A notable example is the team of Edmund Pellegrino and David Thomasma, who say they base their approach on Aristotle and phenomenology—but mostly on good clinical practice.[23]

In one of their books devoted to the foundations of bioethics, Pellegrino and Thomasma summarize their approach:

> Our moral choices are more difficult, more subtle, and more controversial than those of [an earlier] time. We must make them without the heritage of shared values that could unify the medical ethics of [that] era. Our task is not to abandon hope in medical ethics, but to undertake what Camus called "the most difficult task of all: to reconsider everything from the ground up, so as to shape a living society inside a dying society." That task is not the demolition of the edifice of medical morality, but its reconstruction along three lines we have delineated: (1) replacement of a monolithic with a modular structure for medical eth-

ics, with special emphasis on the ethics of making moral choices in clinical decisions; (2) clarification of what we mean when we speak of the good of the patient, and setting some priority among the several senses in which that term may be taken; and (3) refurbishing the ideal of a profession as a true "consecration."[24]

The Pellegrino and Thomasma approach has much in common with the virtue ethic of Alasdair MacIntyre.[25] And the more recent of the two Pellegrino and Thomasma books on foundations culminates in what they call "a physician's commitment to promoting the patient's good." This updated Hippocratic-type oath has an overarching principle—devotion to the good of the patient—and thirteen obligations that are said to flow from it. These range from putting the patient's good above the physician's self-interest through respecting colleagues in other health professions and accepting patients' beliefs and decisions to embodying the principles in professional life.[26] While admitting that such an oath is not likely to meet with general acceptance "given the lack of consensus on moral principles" today, Pellegrino and Thomasma end with this plea: "We invite our readers to consider this amplification of our professional commitment as a means of meriting the trust patients must place in us and as a recognition of the centrality of the patient in all clinical decisions."[27]

The Pellegrino and Thomasma reference to the current lack of a consensus on moral principles hints at a fundamental problem for bioethics. What are decision makers to do if, as seems almost inevitable, defenders of conflicting approaches to bioethics cannot reach agreement? If those attempting to justify particular ethical decisions cannot themselves reach a decision, are we unjustified in the meantime in the decisions that we do make? Beauchamp and Childress attempt to play down this issue, at least as regards utilitarian and deontological theories: "The fact that no currently available theory, whether rule utilitarian or rule deontological, adequately resolves all moral conflicts points to their incompleteness."[28] Admitting that there are many forms of consequentialism, utilitarianism, and deontology, as well as approaches that emphasize virtues or rights, they conclude by defending a *process*—which they say "is consistent with both a rule-utilitarian and a rule-deontology theory"—rather than providing an absolute theoretical justification.[29]

Not all bioethicists are satisfied with this treatment of theoretical disagreement. H. Tristram Engelhardt in particular has devoted much time and energy to arriving at a more satisfying solution.[30] He begins his daunting effort to provide a true foundation for bioethics with a framework: "Controversies regarding which lines of conduct are proper can be resolved on the basis of (1) force, (2) conversion of one party to the other's viewpoint, (3) sound argument, and (4) agreed-to procedures."[31] Engelhardt then demolishes the first three as legitimate foundations for the resolution of ethical disagreement, beginning with the easiest: "Brute force is simply brute force. A goal of ethics is to determine when force can be justified. Force by itself carries no moral authority."[32]

Engelhardt then attacks any assumed religious foundation for the resolution of moral controversy, calling "the failure of Christendom's hope" to provide such a foundation, either in the Middle Ages or after the Reformation, a major failure. He then adds, "This failure suggests that it is hopeless to suppose that a general moral consensus will develop regarding any of the major issues in bioethics."[33]

Engelhardt then turns to properly philosophical hopes: "The third possibility is that of achieving moral authority through successful rational arguments to establish a particular view of the good moral life."[34] But he adds immediately, "This Enlightenment attempt to provide a rationally justified, concrete view of the good life, and thus a secular surrogate for the moral claims of Christianity, has not succeeded."[35] The evidence for this Engelhardt supplied earlier—and it parallels the obvious disagreements among schools of thought referred to by Beauchamp and Childress.

This leaves only the fourth possibility: "The only mode of resolution is by agreement. . . . One will need to discover an inescapable procedural basis for ethics."[36] This may sound like Beauchamp and Childress's retreat to process, but Engelhardt wants to make more of it than that:

> This [procedural] basis, if it is to be found at all, will need to be disclosable in the very nature of ethics itself. . . . Such a basis appears to be available in the minimum notion of ethics. . . . If one is interested in resolving moral controversies without recourse to force as the fundamental basis of agreement, then one will have to accept peaceable negotiation among members of the controversy as the process for attaining the resolution of concrete moral controversies.[37]

This, Engelhardt says, should "be recognized as a disclosure, to borrow a Kantian metaphor, of a transcendental condition . . . of the minimum grammar involved in speaking rationally of blame and praise, and in establishing any particular set of moral commitments."[38]

The generally poor reception that Engelhardt's foundational efforts have received[39] as opposed to the wide recognition he has received for particular contributions to the discussion of concrete controversies, might suggest that there is something fundamentally wrong about the search for ultimate ethical justification in bioethics.

This suggestion leads to the final group of authors to be mentioned in these reflections on philosophical bioethics. Albert Jonsen, mentioned earlier as a critic of the Beauchamp-Childress approach, says this:

> In light of the diversity of views about the meaning and role of ethical theory in moral philosophy, we need not be surprised at the confusion in that branch of moral philosophy called "practical" or (with a bias toward one view of theory) "applied ethics." . . . Authors who begin their works with erudite expositions of te-

leology and deontology hardly mention them again when they plunge into a case . . . . It is this that the clinical ethicists notice and that leads some of them to answer the theory-practice question by wondering whether it is the right question and whether the connection between these classic antonyms is not just loose or tight, but even possible or relevant.[40]

Two of the authors Jonsen is referring to are himself and Stephen Toulmin, who, in *The Abuse of Casuistry*, argue for an approach in which bioethicists should "wrestle with cases of conscience . . . [where they will] find theory a clumsy and rather otiose obstacle in the way of the prudential resolution of cases."[41] Jonsen likens this to deconstruction in literary studies and the critical legal studies approach in philosophy of law; he is also explicit, in another place, about the rhetorical nature of the casuistic approach.[42] Without saddling these other authors with casuistry as *the* approach, Jonsen also puts his and Toulmin's critique of applied ethics within the recent movement of antitheorists headed by Richard Rorty and Bernard Williams.[43] (In a review of *The Abuse of Casuistry*, John Arras adds Stuart Hampshire and Annette Baier.)[44]

In short, recent bioethics, philosophically construed, is a confusing battleground, with contributions from absolute foundationalists to case-focused rejectors of theory and a variety of approaches in between (or all around).

BIOETHICS MORE BROADLY CONSTRUED

It should be remembered—for purposes of this chapter and more generally—that bioethics has never been exclusively or even primarily a philosopher's affair. Indeed, it could be claimed that philosophers are and ought to be outsiders to the real communities making the important bioethical decisions.[45]

One of the earliest calls for the post–World War II medical research community to police itself ethically came from a physician, Henry K. Beecher, writing in 1966 in the *Journal of the American Medical Association* and the *New England Journal of Medicine*—both regular sources of bioethics commentary right down to the present.[46]

Beecher's call for reform was followed up by sociologists (e.g., Bernard Barber et al., *Research on Human Subjects: Problems of Social Control in Medical Experimentation* [1973], and Renée Fox, *Experiment Perilous: Physicians Facing the Unknown* [1974]).[47] Historians also became interested (e.g., James Jones, *Bad Blood: The Tuskegee Syphilis Experiment* [1981]).[48]

Celebrated cases also did a great deal to coalesce the field, from Karen Quinlan and Elizabeth Bouvia to Jack Kevorkian, from Baby Doe to Baby M., from celebrated heart transplant cases to proposals for mandatory testing for the AIDS virus.[49] What even the briefest reflection on these cases reminds us is how bioethics involves patients, families, hospital administrators, lawyers and judges, government officials, and even the public at large.

And public involvement reminds us, further, that significant numbers of commissions have been involved, at the local level (e.g., the New York State Task Force on Life and the Law), at the national level (e.g., the National Commission for the Protection of Human Subjects of Biomedical and Behavioral Research; the President's Commission for the Study of Ethical Problems in Medicine and Biomedical and Behavioral Research), and at the international level (e.g., the European Forum of Medical Associations).

Philosophers have, obviously, been involved in setting up prestigious bioethics institutes. But the institutes themselves are important parts of the bioethics community, with impressive numbers of nonphilosophers on their mailing lists. And physicians (e.g., Willard Gaylin at the Hastings Center, along with many others) and lay people (the Kennedy family, who support the Kennedy Institute) have also played major roles.

For me, the proper locus of bioethics decision making is in typically small groups of physicians, nurses, administrators, lawyers, and local public officials—together with patients and their families—wrestling with specific cases and issues within their own communities. This type of group decision making is exemplified in *Moral Problems in Medicine*, one of the earliest bioethics textbooks (1976), which had six coeditors and at least another half dozen people directly involved.[50] And it continues right down to the present, most notably in the incredible diversity of ethics committees and other groups that have sprung up in hospitals and all sorts of health care institutions since the promulgation of the Reagan Administration's Baby Doe regulations and the enactment of the Patient Self-Determination Act in 1991.[51] Philosophical bioethicists, it seems to me, do some of their best work in these groups, as they work collectively to solve local cases and issues and to formulate policies for their own institutions.

PRAGMATIC REFLECTIONS ON PHILOSOPHICAL BIOETHICS

William James, faced at the end of the nineteenth century with the same sort of disagreement about the foundations of ethics that exists a hundred years later regarding the foundations of bioethics, summed up the situation this way:

> Various essences of good have thus been found and proposed as bases of the ethical system. Thus, to be a mean between two extremes; to be recognized by a special intuitive faculty; to make the agent happy for the moment; to make others as well as him happy in the long run; to add to his perfection or dignity; to harm no one; to follow from reason or universal law; to be in accordance with the will of God; to promote the survival of the human species.[52]

But, James says, none of these has satisfied everyone. So what he thinks we must do is treat them all as having some moral force and go about satisfying as many of the claims as we can while knowing we can never satisfy all of them at once. "The guiding principle for ethical philosophy," James concludes, must be "simply to satisfy at all times *as many demands as we can*."[53] And, following this rule, society has historically striven from generation to generation "to find the more and more inclusive [moral] order"—and has, James thinks, done so successfully, gradually eliminating slavery and other evils tolerated in earlier eras.[54]

In many ways this sounds like Engelhardt's condition of the possibility of ethical discourse, but James would never accept Engelhardt's characterization of the approach as Kantian-transcendental. James is simply advocating a procedural rule to be used by particular communities of ethical truthseekers attempting to find a satisfactory concrete solution for particular problems—in a process that must inevitably go on and on without end. Concrete ethical solutions are not dictated by an abstract commitment to the conditions of ethics but must be worked out arduously through the competition of different ideals.

John Dewey was as opposed to transcendental foundations as James. He would probably have been bemused—and also angry—at the persistent academic search for an ultimate foundation for our practical decisions in bioethics.[55] He would also have attempted, however, to see how the "principled" approach (e.g., of Beauchamp and Childress) is "in effect, if not in profession connected with human affairs."[56] In *Reconstruction in Philosophy*, Dewey continues his attack on ethical theory as "hypnotized by the notion that its business is to discover some . . . ultimate and supreme law"; instead, he proposed that ethics be reconstructed so that we may "advance to a belief in a plurality of changing, moving, individualized goods and ends, and to a belief that principles, criteria, laws are intellectual instruments for analyzing individual or unique situations."[57] In *A Common Faith*, Dewey adds that community efforts to solve social problems progressively can generate an attitude akin to religious faith that makes social problem solving a meaningful venture.[58] And in *Liberalism and Social Action*, Dewey tries to lead the way in applying his approach to the "confusion, uncertainty, and conflict" that marked his times,[59] just as the bioethics community is attempting to do today with respect to the confusion, uncertainty, and conflict plaguing health care today.

George Herbert Mead, an opponent of both utilitarian and Kantian approaches to ethics,[60] offers in place of those a positive formulation of what ethics should mean:

> The order of the universe that we live in *is* the moral order. It has become the moral order by becoming the self-conscious method of the members of a human society. . . . The world that comes to us from the past possesses and controls us. We possess and control the world that we discover and invent. And this is the world of the moral order.[61]

Then Mead adds, "It is a splendid adventure if we can rise to it."[62]

If we pay attention to these American pragmatists, I think what we can say about bioethics in the last quarter of the twentieth century is that philosophers contribute most when they contribute to the progressive social problem solving of particular communities (e.g., policy formulation, case resolution, etc.). Some do this, admittedly, at the national or even international level, but even in those cases they do so as members of groups that include physicians, lawyers, and other concerned citizens. And most do so at the local level—where, in Mead's words, they are only being truly ethical if they are contributing to the social problem solving of some particular group in which they represent only one voice, and a small one at that.

SOME LESSONS

Does the awareness on the part of philosophers of their limited role in bioethics suggest any lessons for us?

The most obvious lesson is humility. Philosophers can and do help to clarify issues (sometimes even provide answers), but the real moral decisions in bioethics, for the most part, are made by others.

Another lesson has to do with the urgency of the real-world problems that bioethics faces, which are, after all, what got philosophers involved in the first place. Medicine and the health care system generally—including those parts of it that operate in open or covert opposition to the entrenched power of physicians and hospitals—face enormous problems today, from rampant inflation and calls for rationing to the questioning of the very legitimacy of high-technology medicine. All the while, doctors, nurses, and other providers must continue to face life-and-death issues every day, not to mention the daunting task of treating the ordinary ills of ordinary people who, with increasing frequency, cannot pay for their medical care.

It is probably inevitable, given the structure of philosophy today as an academic institution, that philosophical bioethicists will continue narrow technical debates among themselves about ultimate justifications of bioethical decisions. But academicism and careerism in bioethics should be recognized for what they are—distractions (however necessary, for some purposes) from the *real* focus of bioethics.

Beyond these lessons for philosophers, does American pragmatism have any lessons to teach the bioethics community more generally? Probably only this: that we should all heed James's call for tolerance and openness to minority views. Bioethics has come a long way in just 25 or so years. Significant consensus has been achieved on issues from informed consent to be a research subject to the importance of asking patients what they want done, if anything, in their last weeks and days and hours. But equally significant issues remain, as they always will in a society open to change. And all of us, from the smallest local bioethics group to the international community, ought to remain open to change. As William James said,

> Every now and then . . . someone is born with the right to be original, and his revolutionary thought or action may bear prosperous fruit. He may replace old "laws of nature" by better ones; he may, by break-

ing old moral rules in a certain place, bring in a total condition of things more ideal

than would have followed had the rules been kept.[63]

NOTES

1. A brief survey of the numerous textbooks in the field suggests that *bioethics*, although not the only label, is probably the most common one.

2. See R. Rorty, *Philosophy and the Mirror of Nature* (Princeton, N.J.: Princeton University Press, 1979); R. Rorty, *Consequences of Pragmatism* (Minneapolis: University of Minnesota Press, 1982); R. Rorty, *Objectivity, Relativism, and Truth* (New York: Cambridge University Press, 1991).

3. The works in the Dewey corpus that I will refer to are *The Quest for Certainty* (New York: Putnam's, 1929); *Reconstruction in Philosophy*, 2nd ed. (Boston: Beacon Press, 1948); *A Common Faith* (New Haven, Conn.: Yale University Press, 1934); and *Liberalism and Social Action* (New York: Putnam's, 1935).

4. See especially G.H. Mead, Scientific Method and the Moral Sciences, in *Selected Writings: George Herbert Mead*, edited by A. Reck (Indianapolis, Ind.: Bobbs-Merrill, 1964), 248–266.

5. The article I refer to is W. James, The Moral Philosopher and the Moral Life, in *The Will to Believe, and Other Essays in Popular Philosophy* (New York: Holt, 1897), reprinted in *The Writings of William James*, edited by J. McDermott (New York: Random House, 1967), 610–629.

6. R.B. Roth, Medicine's Ethical Responsibilities, *JAMA* 215 (1971):1956–1958, reprinted in *Cross Cultural Perspectives in Medical Ethics: Readings*, edited by R.M. Veatch (Boston: Jones and Bartlett, 1989), 155.

7. Veatch, *Cross Cultural Perspectives*, 146.

8. Ibid.

9. T.L. Beauchamp and J.F. Childress, *Principles of Biomedical Ethics*, 3rd ed. (New York: Oxford University Press, 1989).

10. A.R. Jonsen, Practice versus Theory, *Hastings Center Report* 20, no. 4 (1990):32.

11. Ibid.

12. Ibid.

13. M. Bayles, *Professional Ethics*, 2nd ed. (Belmont, Calif.: Wadsworth, 1989).

14. Ibid., 28.

15. Ibid.

16. Beauchamp and Childress, *Principles of Biomedical Ethics*.

17. J.C. Callahan, ed., *Ethical Issues in Professional Life* (New York: Oxford University Press, 1988).

18. Ibid., 10.

19. Ibid.

20. Ibid.

21. Beauchamp and Childress, *Principles of Biomedical Ethics*, 15–16.

22. Jonsen, Practice versus Theory, 34.

23. E.D. Pellegrino and D.C. Thomasma, *A Philosophical Basis of Medical Practice* (New York: Oxford University Press, 1981), xi.

24. E.D. Pellegrino and D.C. Thomasma, *For the Patient's Good: The Restoration of Beneficence in Health Care* (New York: Oxford University Press, 1988), 134.

25. A. MacIntyre, *After Virtue* (London: Duckworth, 1981); A. MacIntyre, *Whose Justice, Which Rationality?* (Notre Dame, Ind.: University of Notre Dame Press, 1988).

26. Pellegrino and Thomasma, *For the Patient's Good*, 205–206.

27. Ibid., 206.

28. Beauchamp and Childress, *Principles of Biomedical Ethics*, 46.

29. Ibid., 62.

30. H.T. Engelhardt, *Foundations of Bioethics* (New York: Oxford University Press, 1986); H.T. Engelhardt, *Bioethics and Secular Humanism: The Search for a Common Morality* (London: SCM Press; Philadelphia: Trinity Press, 1991).

31. Engelhardt, *Foundations of Bioethics*, 30.

32. Ibid., 40.

33. Ibid.

34. Ibid.

35. Ibid.

36. Ibid., 41.

37. Ibid.

38. Ibid., 42.

39. See, for example, J.D. Moreno, Ethics by Committee: The Moral Authority of Consensus, *Journal of Medicine and Philosophy* 13 (1988):411–432, esp. 425ff.; K.E. Tranoy, The Search for a Common Morality, *Medical Humanities Review* 6, no. 2 (1992):22–25.

40. Jonsen, Practice versus Theory, 34.

41. Ibid. The work being described is A.R. Jonsen and S. Toulmin, *The Abuse of Casuistry: A History of Moral Reasoning* (Berkeley: University of California Press, 1988).

42. A.R. Jonsen, Casuistry as Methodology in Clinical Ethics, *Theoretical Medicine* 12 (1991):295–307.

43. Rorty, *Philosophy and The Mirror of Nature*; Rorty, *Consequences of Pragmatism*; Rorty, *Objectivity, Relativism, and Truth*; B. Williams, *Ethics and the Limits of Philosophy* (Cambridge, Mass.: Harvard University Press, 1985).

44. J.D. Arras, Common Law Morality, *Hastings Center Report* 20, no. 4 (1990):36; S. Hampshire, *Innocence and Experience* (Cambridge, Mass.: Harvard University Press, 1986); A. Baier, Some Thoughts on How We Moral Philosophers Live Now, *Monist* 67 (1984):490–497.

45. L.R. Churchill, The Role of the Stranger: The Ethicist in Professional Education, *Hastings Center Report* 8, no. 6 (1978):13–15.

46. H.K. Beecher, Consent in Clinical Experimentation: Myth and Reality, *JAMA* 195 (1966):34–35; H.K. Beecher, Ethics and Clinical Research, *New England Journal of Medicine* 274 (1966):1354–1360.

47. B. Barber et al., *Research on Human Subjects: Problems of Social Control in Medical Experimentation* (New York: Russell Sage Foundation, 1973); R. Fox, *Experiment Perilous: Physicians Facing the Unknown* (Philadelphia: University of Pennsylvania Press, 1974).

48. J.H. Jones, *Bad Blood: The Tuskegee Syphilis Experiment* (New York: The Free Press, 1981).

49. Some of the best examples are discussed in G.E. Pence, *Classic Cases in Medical Ethics* (New York: McGraw-Hill, 1990).

50. S. Gorovitz et al., *Moral Principles in Medicine* (Englewood Cliffs, N.J.: Prentice-Hall, 1976).

51. The growing literature on bioethics committees is reviewed in P.M. McCarrick, Ethics Committees in Hospitals, *Kennedy Institute of Ethics Journal* 2 (1992):285–305.

52. James, Moral Philosopher and Moral Life, in *The Writings of William James*, 620.

53. Ibid., 620.

54. Ibid., 623.

55. Dewey, *The Quest for Certainty*.

56. Dewey, *Reconstruction in Philosophy*, xi.

57. Ibid., 162–163. This does not make Dewey an act utilitarian in the sense opposed by Beauchamp and Childress. Dewey, along with the other traditional pragmatists referred to here, would not have agreed with a theory/act dichotomy. Mead, for one, explicitly states that the *social praxis* of a community is the matrix within which both theories and acts emerge—and they emerge *ethically* if the social problems calling them forth are addressed in a progressive fashion (Scientific Method and the Moral Sciences).

58. Dewey, *A Common Faith*, 27.

59. Dewey, *Liberalism and Social Action*, 92.

60. See H. Joas, *G.H. Mead: A Contemporary Re-examination of His Thought* (Cambridge, Mass.: MIT Press, 1985), 124.

61. Mead, Scientific Method and the Moral Sciences, 266.

62. Ibid.

63. James, Moral Philosopher and Moral Life, in *The Writings of William James*, 625.

Chapter 46

Ethically Responsible Creativity: Friendship of an Understanding Heart: A Cognitively Affective Model for Bioethical Decision Making

John F. Monagle

Ethically Responsible Creativity: Friendship of an Understanding Heart is offered as a contemporary caring and helpful bioethical decision-making model. At this time in the evolution of models, theories, methods, paradigms, and matrices, old and new methodologies are either deficient (lacking an essential component), defective (the meanings of terms have been weakened by ambiguity), or too embryonic to be decisively applied to contemporary bioethical experiences.[1]

Furthermore, the increase of and advancement in medical knowledge and the rapid development of biotechnologies whose applications are anxiously awaited have led to bioethical dilemmas. Medical science is able to maintain lives for years where death would previously have come quickly. Decisions to maintain life have caused serious intellectual and emotional controversies and lawsuits—with differing bioethical and legal results.[2]

Two contrasting cases are presented below: those of Nancy Beth Cruzan and Helga Wanglie and their families.[3] These two cases demonstrate the need for the Ethically Responsible Creativity (ERC) model.

The most important question to be answered in these two cases is, Who will be empowered to be the controlling agent in the making of the ethical decision? The answer to this question is even more important than *what* the controlling agent decides.

The need to correct our models because of such contrasting cases as Cruzan and Wanglie is recognized by most bioethical pioneers. We realize the prescriptive directions, duties, rights, and obligations embedded in principles[4] as well as cookbook recipes for doing bioethics fail when they are enclosed in the ethical heat of the oven: they prove to be deficient, defective, or embryonic when applied to similar patients in similar experiences.

Some suggest applying the virtues in conjunction with the four basic principles in an attempt to account for the text and context of the physician-patient relationship.[5] The hope is that, if the virtues are recognized, cherished, and practiced, physicians will become more sensitized to the individual appropriateness of all treatments and procedures and all medical decisions, including bioethical ones.

Others are beginning the awesome adventure of inquiry, by way of narrative ethics, into the exciting world of bioethics beyond the clinical setting—an inquiry into "what is going on around me and what response is required of me to what is going on around me?"[6] They call for an experiential, inductive paradigm that is concerned with the integration of experienced values.[7] The model or paradigm is embryonic but imaginative and innovative; the quest is praiseworthy and hopefully will yield practical results when focused on bioethical decision making (a small part of the total narrative endeavor).

However, not only are the models presently inadequate to resolve critical ethical issues, but also the meaning of terms, phrases, and principles inherent in the presentations are ambiguous, too widely connotative, and perhaps in some presentations equivocal. All health care professionals involved in ordinary and critical decision making are struggling to define precisely the terms, phrases, and principles applied presently with such generally unexamined facility. Because the terms, phrases, and principles lack precise and universally accepted meanings, they lead to intellectual and emotional disagreements between physicians, patients, and their families as well as health care institutions, the community, and society at large.

The controversial terms, phrases, and principles at the top of the list include *medical necessity, competency,*[8] *appropriateness, hopelessness, futility,*[9] *autonomy, nonmalfeasance, beneficence,* and *justice.* The vagueness in meaning has forced some health care professionals to coin their own phrases in the hospice movement, some of which are paradoxical, such as "hopeless hope" and "futile nonfutility."

However, how do we *fix* (denote precisely) these terms, phrases, and principles? And until the meanings are settled, how can we properly discuss and finalize bioethical decisions? Until they are fixed by strict denotation through societal, medical, ethical, and legal agreement, we must deal with the problem of ambiguity.

Nevertheless, in the Bergsonian meantime we need to make use of some model that will allow us to arrive at bioethical decisions. ERC, which combines the inputting of clinical and ethical data, the application of the four basic ethical principles, and the application of the philosophy of "friendship of an understanding heart" is one such model. Through ERC, *comfortable* bioethical decisions can be reached.[10]

DESCRIPTIVE DEFINITION OF ETHICALLY RESPONSIBLE CREATIVITY

Ethics is the pattern of values and norms that is "taken for granted" in a given culture or professional or institutional setting. The ERC model is intended to be used in situations in which responses to questions of a *societal* nature are required. It is not designed for responding to "moral" questions, that is, individual cases of conscience. (The communication media and some ethicists use the terms *ethics* and *morality* interchangeably, which brings confusion, in my opinion, to the issues in need of resolution.)

The individuals involved in the bioethical decision-making process should be willing to work with the physician, the patient, the family, the health care organization, and the community at large in implementing the bioethical decision (even though the attending physician will have to take ultimate legal responsibility).[11]

Collectively these individuals are responsible for

- the model and methodology used in the decision-making process
- the medical data and ethical considerations offered for discussion and evaluation
- the persons or advisors to be consulted in the decision-making process (e.g., the patient, the family, significant others, the attending physician, consultants, representatives appointed by the health care institution, a clergyperson and/or bioethicist, and representatives of the community at large)
- the priority and significance (weight) given to the values, preferences, wishes, desires and opinions of the patient, the family, significant others, and the attending physician
- the consequences of the decision
- the documentation of the bioethical decision

The term *creativity* is used in the tradition of Plato, Leibniz, Bergson and Whitehead, in the sense of "becoming" or "process." In other words, the components of the ERC model are subject to dynamic medical-ethical evolution. The dynamic process of development of the model allows for change over time. As medical and biotechnical knowledge increases, as society gains greater understanding of the use and limitations of health care discoveries, and as the community develops a consensus on fundamental issues, bioethical decisions hopefully will increasingly be similar in similar cases.

Social demands, public consensus, ethical-legal definitions, court decisions, and state and federal legislation will alter the range of allowable treatments and procedures. Not all will agree with the results of the evolutionary process. Nevertheless, expensive or experimental interventions will be examined and will be permitted or denied based on a patient's diagnosis and prognosis as well as society's willingness to pay. Personal values and preferences will sometimes be overridden by state and federal legislation.[12] Whether we as a nation adopt an egalitarian, federally funded universal health care plan or an egalitarian, competitive managed care plan made accessible and available to all, we can expect that a prioritized list of allowed and denied benefits will evolve. National restrictions, no doubt, will limit individual autonomy. "This does not imply that autonomy has been superseded by other values, but that autonomy must be understood in a larger context which includes, for example, justice, allocation of resources, futility."[13]

Thankfully, we have not reached that point when money as a value has superseded life or quality of life. ERC, therefore, remains a viable model, and hopefully it will be able to adapt to the future.

THE CASES OF NANCY BETH CRUZAN AND HELGA WANGLIE

Although bioethical decision-making models have been refined methodologically and can sometimes be used to achieve the resolution of cases of minor conflict, they are not sufficiently useful in major conflicts related to complex biotechnical situations like those of Cruzan and Wanglie. A certain degree of consternation and frustration gripped me when I studied the contrastingly (seemingly contradictory) positions taken by professionals and families in each case as well as the legal judgments rendered by the courts to resolve these cases. A bioethical decision outside of the court could not be made because of the deficient, defective, or embryonic models being used.

Both women, although separated by age and locality, were basically in similar persistent vegetative states. Unless there were "justifiable" reasons for contrasting (contradictory) opinions, the ethical-legal decisions should have been similar in the two cases. Similar, more harmonious, mutually agreed decisions could have been reached through the use of an adequate decision-making model, such as the ERC model.

Nancy Beth Cruzan, age 37 at death,[14] resident of Jasper County, Missouri, and patient in a Missouri state hospital, was clinically judged to be in a persistent vegetative state (PVS) and to evince no significant cognitive function. She was maintained by artificial nutrition and hydration through a gastronomy tube implanted surgically into her stomach through an incision in her abdominal wall.

The prognosis was that she could remain in this irreversible state for as long as 30 years and that her brain would progressively deteriorate until death. Her parents, Lester and Joyce Cruzan, requested the health care administrator and the attending physician to allow the withdrawal of the intubation, which was only artificially prolonging a life that was virtually meaningless and holding Nancy Cruzan a passive prisoner of inappropriate technology.[15] The Cruzans considered Nancy's condition to be "hopeless" relative to any meaningful recovery and viewed present and future interventions as "futile." However, the attending physician refused to withdraw the artificial nutrition and hydration. His medical reasons were not altogether clear, but from a legal perspective his motivation was quite clear: Both he and the administrator were state employees. They thought that a modicum of defensive medicine was prudent. The law in Missouri was not sufficiently developed to handle this case, so they thought. They feared that they would become subjects of criminal and civil actions. A possible bioethical decision gave way to a decision based on the legal risk of criminal homicide, malpractice (negligence), or both.[16]

Nancy Cruzan's parents had to seek a court resolution. The case went through the Circuit Court of Jasper County (which granted the request of Lester and Joyce Cruzan) to the Missouri Supreme Court (which reversed the decision) to the U.S. Supreme Court (which affirmed the reversal of the Missouri Supreme Court). The U.S. Supreme Court sent the case back to the Jasper County District Court, requiring that "clear and convincing evidence" of Nancy Cruzan's wishes would have to be brought forward before the Jasper County Court could grant the parents' request.[17] The testimony of Lester and Joyce Cruzan, loving parents and closest friends, and the testimony of Nancy's sister and an acquaintance were not accepted by the U.S. Supreme Court as "clear and convincing evidence." The testimony of the Cruzans, according to the dissenting Justices, was disregarded.[18]

Lester and Joyce Cruzan searched and found two additional "acquaintances" who testified that Nancy had expressed to them her desire not to be maintained by artificial means if ever she was in a condition where there was no hope of recovery or even in a condition where she would find herself helpless. The Jasper County District Court had its clear and convincing evidence. The court ruled in favor of the Cruzan's request. Again, the testimony of Nancy's parents as best and closest friends, loving and caring for her, and best suited to knowing and understanding her did not constitute clear and convincing evidence in the view of the U.S. Supreme Court. The U.S. Supreme Court, as "strangers" in the case, had spoken.

Helga Wanglie, age 86, resident of Minneapolis also was in PVS and was maintained by respirator and artificial nutrition and hydration.[19] The health care administrator and attending physician had decided that Mrs. Wanglie, despite the fact that she was fully insured, was a burden to the institution and to the attending physician, who could make more valuable use of his time since he considered all future interventions as "inappropriate."

According to the attending physician, Helga Wanglie's situation was "hopeless," "futile," and irreversible. The attending physician, therefore, sought the consent of Oliver Wanglie, her best friend and loving husband for more than 50 years, to remove the respirator and to withdraw the intubation supplying nutrition and hydration. Oliver Wanglie refused to consent because he stated (and later testified in court) that Helga Wanglie expressly had requested that she would want to be maintained by artificial life support until God decided to take her. The hospital went to court.[20]

The Honorable Patricia L. Belois, of the Fourth District Court, Hennepin County, Minnesota, heard the case and ruled on July 1, 1992, just three days before Helga Wanglie's death, in favor of Oliver Wanglie's request to maintain his wife on artificial life support. Oliver Wanglie, by substituted judgment, could decide as best he saw fit. To Judge Belois, the question of *who* would be the decision-maker was more important than *what* the decision would be.

Although the judgment seemed to be in opposition to other court opinions, because it allowed continued treatment for a patient who was in an irreversible persistent vegetative state and for whom, according to the clinical judgment of a competent physician, all interventions were futile and inappropriate, nevertheless Judge Belois ruled in favor of the autonomy of an incompetent patient as rightly exercised by the substituted judgment of her husband, Oliver Wanglie.[21] Although I personally do not think that the continued treatment was medically appropriate or beneficial, nevertheless I agree with the court's decision in favor of autonomy and in favor of giving the power of substituted judgment to Helga Wanglie's husband. The decision by Judge Belois confirms my conviction that the ERC model is adequate to resolve similar cases. Her Honor stated in effect that no one was better able to know, understand, appreciate, and implement the wishes of Helga Wanglie than her best friend and loving husband of over 50 years. The judge was *amicus familiae*.

THE ERC MODEL

The ERC model (Figure 46–1) is an educational framework that I have used in my pioneering past and continue to expand creatively. Other professional ethicists and more recent settlers have developed or adopted their own diagrammatic decision-making models. All models, no doubt, have been helpful in dealing with the necessary components that are essential in reaching a bioethical decision—at least until recently.

However, the Nancy Cruzan and the Helga Wanglie cases, because of their diverse conclusions, convince me that all other models are deficient in at least one essential component and are therefore incapable of leading to acceptable bioethical decisions.

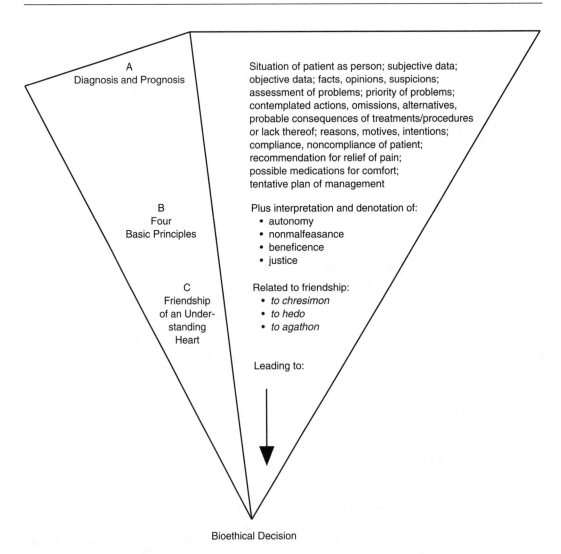

Figure 46–1 Ethically Responsible Creativity: Friendship of an Understanding Heart (a cognitively affective model for bioethical decision making).

Medical-Ethical Data

In the top level of Figure 46–1 are the medical and nonprincipled ethical components that lead to a tentative, *non-infallible*, clinical diagnosis and prognosis. Each patient is recognized as unique. All subjective data that can be gleaned from the patient, the family, and significant others are included. The patient's past medical history, symptoms, and complaints are also considered. Objective data resulting from all necessary or useful treatments and technologies are scrutinized (the ruling-out process). Problems are analyzed to determine their acuity and chronicity. From an ethical perspective, all reasonable actions (omissions) are considered together with their probable consequences. Reasons, motives, and intentions are articulated and documented for review by the ethical advisory group or committee involved in making bioethical decisions.[22] Means of providing maximum comfort and relief of pain are prescribed based on the characteristics of the patient and the patient's situation. A tentative medical-ethical plan of management is outlined based on all pertinent information. The tentative plan at the same time is processed though the middle (second) level.

The Four Basic Principles

In the middle level, the four basic ethical principles of autonomy, nonmalfeasance, beneficence, and justice are applied. When their meanings are properly spelled out, these principles have a limited usefulness as tools in bioethical decision making. It is likely they were applied in both the Cruzan and Wanglie cases. However, their meanings have gone through an evolution, and, in fact, the principles are subject to diverse interpretations.

In past philosophical history and legal jurisprudence, the etymological, ethical, and legal meanings had *fixed* denotations. As language, medical knowledge, and biotechnology evolved, and as ethical-legal cases became more complex, the interpretation, priority, and "weight-value" of their meanings have become more diverse: denotations have given way to broader connotations.

Autonomy

Auto = self, one's own; *nomos* = law. Self-law is self-rule, self-determination; the meaning over time has expanded to include freedom, free choice, free decision making. Autonomy became the core of personhood, the center of moral responsibility for self in the case of both actions and consequences.

The meaning of autonomy has expanded even further to include personal values and preferences. When the patient is judged by others to be incompetent, autonomy then resides in the values, preferences, and choices of the physician (paternalistic model); in the values, preferences, and choices of the family (familial model); or in the values, preferences, and choices of the health care facility (institutional model).

Who determines the meaning of autonomy in a bioethical decision-making situation?

Nonmalfeasance

Non = not, no; *male* = bad, evil, harm; *facere* = to do. *Nonmalfeasance* means to do no harm. The principle of nonmalfeasance requires health care providers to do no harm to the patient.

The meaning of nonmalfeasance expanded from never intentionally doing harm to never unintentionally doing harm. But what is *harm*? Is there malfeasance by commission, omission, activity, or passivity? Metaethically, does malfeasance connote physical, psychological, and spiritual harm?

When the patient is competent, is nonmalfeasance or malfeasance defined by the patient's reaction or response? Does malfeasance include performing acts of "futility" in "hopeless" cases? Does malfeasance include "inappropriate" interventions?

When the patient is clinically judged to be incompetent, is malfeasance determined by the family, by the legal system, or through malpractice suits?[23] In the emergency department, does aggressive medical treatment count as nonmalfeasance? Does defensive medicine count as malfeasance?

Who determines the meaning of nonmalfeasance in a bioethical decision-making situation?

Beneficence

Bene = well; *facere* = to do. The principle of beneficence requires health care providers to act in the best interests of the patient. But what are the patient's best interests? Does the physician act in the best interests of the patient by withdrawal of treatment in futile situations? Does the physician act in the best interests of a terminally ill patient by inducing death or assisting in suicide? Is death in the best *interests* of anyone? By whom is beneficence assessed and defined—by the patient, the physician, the family, the health care facility, the community, society at large?

Who determines the meaning of beneficence in a bioethical decision-making situation?

Justice

Justitia = giving each person his or her due. But does justice mean equity? Does it require equalizing wealth by taking from the rich and giving to the poor? Is justice best served by providing everyone with exactly the same access to treatment? Or does justice merely require that all exchanges occur voluntarily, no matter what the ultimate distribution of wealth and power?

Who determines the meaning of justice in a bioethical decision-making situation?

This critique of principlism[24] is not intended to denigrate the usefulness of principles as tools, but it is intended to show that the principles do not reign supreme and that societal agreement as to which principle has priority in an individual case is lacking. The question remains: Who determines the meaning and application of ethical principles in a bioethical decision-making situation?

In the Cruzan case, the administrator and attending physician *refused to withdraw* nutrition and hydration, the court required *clear and convincing evidence*, and the family's knowledge of the patient's wishes was *not sufficient*. How was autonomy, nonmalfeasance, beneficence, and justice interpreted and by whom?

In the Wanglie case, the administrator and attending physician *insisted on the withdrawal* of life support. They went to court *against* Oliver Wanglie's wishes. The court ruled against the hospital and physician *in favor of* Oliver Wanglie and designated him as the person who should make the ultimate decision. How and by whom were the principles interpreted?

FRIENDSHIP OF AN UNDERSTANDING HEART

Aristotle describes three types of friendship: (1) friendship *to chresimon*, (2) friendship *to hedo*, and (3) friendship *to agathon* (Figure 46–2).[25] (Aristotle's terms can be translated as useful friendship, social friendship, and truly virtuous friendship.)

Before applying these types of friendships to individuals involved in bioethical decision making, we must go back in time to prepare for the future. The relationship in medicine between physician, patient, and family has historically been one of virtual strangers. In ancient Greek society, the relationship was literally between the stranger who treats and the stranger who suffers, waits, and is treated. The historical narrative of physicians as strangers is imbedded in the Hippocratic oath. Part of the oath demands that the physician keep the secrets and mysteries of medicine and pass them on only to his sons (no doubt, one of the roots of medical male chauvinism). It is only in very recent history that the relationship of stranger to stranger began to change to a still ill-defined relationship of physician to patient and family.

Perhaps early in this century, when country doctors were common providers of medical care, there was some semblance of friendship in the relationship. However, friendship was not formally encouraged and probably, when present, was overly romanticized (e.g., in the works of Normal Rockwell).

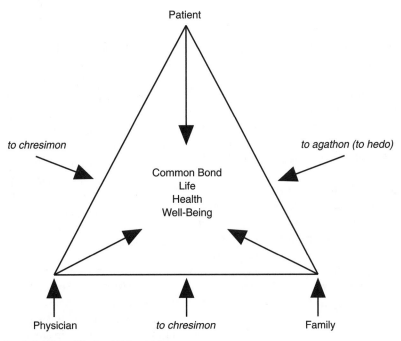

Figure 46–2 Aristotle's Three Kinds of Friendship.

The more realistic relationship of stranger to stranger has been the prevailing one, although it hardly qualifies as a relationship at all. Aristotle states that such connections are those of "acquaintances," and he does not find a place for acquaintances in his presentation of the three kinds of friendship. He does, however, recognize that acquaintances should express themselves in language and gestures of *friendliness* to maintain a peaceful society.

It is only in the recent past, the late 1960s and early 1970s, that we began to read in the bioethical literature of the need to establish better relationships between physicians and patients and families. Paul Ramsey, in his classic work *Patient as Person*, awakened pioneering bioethicists to the need to educate physicians to treat patients as persons, not as objects or target organs.[26] The practice of treating patients as objects or target organs and their families as invaders into the private turf of medicine continued

for a short time after Ramsey's book was published.

In my opinion, real progress toward better relationships occurred during the "malpractice crisis" between 1973 and 1978. The big issue became educated informed consent. Because of the overwhelming number and costs of malpractice suits, physicians in general recognized that patients could no longer be viewed as strangers, objects, or target organs. The principles of autonomy, nonmalfeasance, beneficence, and justice were accepted by physicians and other health care professionals, and presentations by bioethicists of "ethical-legal considerations regarding informed consent" were welcomed.

Nevertheless, we do not to this day have a relationship between the physician and the patient and family that is embedded in a philosophical foundation outside of medicine itself. There is such a foundation in the relationship of friend to friend. This is a caring, noncasuistic, fidelity bond. Family must be included in the bond if we are to put the proper controlling spin on uniform, comfortable bioethical decision making.

A relationship of friendship, as envisioned and practiced in Aristotle's society and down through the centuries by others, is appropriate and realistic if practiced by the physician and the patient and family and will serve as a teleological foundation for the ends of medicine. Aristotle labels this kind of relationship friendship *to chresimon*.[27]

Friendship *to chresimon* is consistent with the philosophy expressed by Democritus and embraced by Aristotle: "Friends hold *in common* what they hold." Physicians, patients, and families hold in common the life, health, and well-being of all persons in the relationship.

Friendship *to chresimon* in contemporary practice requires the physician to do the following:

- See the patient and family at the scheduled time (without more than fifteen minutes delay).
- Take the time to explain to the patient what should be explained and to answer any questions. "The issuance of a diagnosis," states E.D. Pellegrino, "and a standardized explanation may be convenient for the physician or all that his time will permit. Yet, this can be the first step in making the patient an object and not a person."[28] The patient is a person, *not* a client.
- Hear, not just listen. The physician should get to know the patient and family in a relaxed situation so as to devote full attention to what is said.
- Learn the attitudes, values, preferences, and choices of the patient and family.[29]
- Show compassion and accept the patient for who he or she is.[30] This is a component of respectful friendship.
- Give complete, honest answers to questions from the patient and family.[31] Each patient wants answers to all health ques-

tions put in the context of his or her life. Offer hope to the extent that it is realistic.

- Make house calls in necessary but non-emergency situations for patients too sick to travel rather than telling them to take a taxi or call an ambulance.
- Delete from physician bills labels such as "Pay within 10 days or this debt will be turned over to a collection agency." It would be an act of friendship to have the office staff telephone the patient or family to inquire about their ability to pay; arrange for periodic, partial payments if necessary; and eliminate any finance charge for late payments.[32]

Although friendship *to chresimon* is the lowest of Aristotle's types of friendship, nevertheless he emphasizes that it is to be cherished. This type of friendship will disappear when the benefits of the relationship are no longer needed.[33]

Aristotle describes two higher levels of friendship: friendship *to hedo* is best exemplified in relationships among family members and significant others.[34] Friendship *to hedo* also occurs among golf or tennis partners—among people who enjoy socializing with each other. This type of friendship does not usually occur between the physician and the patient and family, but it sometimes does.

Friendship to agathon is the highest type of friendship, according to Aristotle.[35] It usually requires a long time to develop. It is best exemplified by family members and friends who feel close to each other—who accept each other "as is" and for their true and virtuous worth and intrinsic goodness of character.

Aristotle expands this notion of friendship to include love that endures. Love, according to Aristotle, is a superabundance or excess of friendship *to agathon*. Loving friendship is best exemplified by the relationship between husband and wife, parents and children.

This friendship is the friendship of an *understanding heart*.[36] Whatever clinical data and ethical considerations are offered to a patient's family, for example, these will be received according to their mental capacity and ability to understand. They will be considered with an understanding heart.

The physician, on the other hand, may have a different understanding of the data because of his or her medical and biotechnical knowledge.

Confronted with ambiguous terminology and widely connotative principles, and even though the medical facts, opinions, and clinical judgment of the physician are to be respected, nevertheless, the family, relying on the known wishes of the patient (when the patient is incompetent), should make the final decisions regarding treatment based on friendship *to agathon* of an understanding heart. Even if the family's decision is considered to be clinically erroneous by the physician, it should prevail—not because it is good or bad, right or wrong, but because it is a *comfortable* decision and one based on the friendship of an understanding heart. The physician who has become a friend *to chresimon* does not relinquish professional autonomy when he or she defers to the family with regard to ultimate decisions.[37] Unless there are reasons that demonstrate that the family is unfit mentally to make such decisions, they should be allowed to decide what they think is in the best interests of their loved one (i.e., what the loved one would request if he or she were able to express his or her wishes). This is the compassionate, comfortable decision in the light (darkness) of ambiguous terminology (e.g., the meaning of "futility") and widely connotative principles (e.g., the meaning of autonomy and beneficence).

In the cases of Nancy Beth Cruzan and Helga Wanglie, if there had been friendship *to chresimon* between the physician and family, the family would have been given the right to make the final decision. There would have been no compromise of the ethical integrity of the medical profession, nor of any bioethical "norms or standards." Furthermore, there would have been no violation of proper allocation of scarce resources (since proper allocation of scarce resources is a controversial bioethical issue itself).

The physician as friend *to chresimon* is not a gatekeeper responsible for implementing distributive justice.

CONCLUSION

I cannot praise the ruling of the U.S. Supreme Court that forced Lester and Joyce Cruzan to sacrifice the expression of their loving friendship *to agathon* for their daughter Nancy by not allowing them the right to make the final bioethical decision. They were forced to seek clear and convincing evidence of Nancy's wishes from acquaintances. The U.S. Supreme Court Justices in effect designated Nancy's parents as "strangers" in the case.

In the case of Helga Wanglie, I praise the decision of Judge Patricia Belois. She exercised sensitive objectivity by ruling in favor of Oliver Wanglie and by specifying him as the appropriate one to make the bioethical decision for his wife. Judge Patricia Belois put the proper control spin into effect by ruling that *who* should make the decision is more important than *what* decision should be made. She agreed that a loving husband of more than 50 years should be recognized as the one who would know best from his understanding heart what his wife would wish, and in doing so she affirmed that the rightful exercise of autonomy by substituted judgment should be exercised by the person closest (in loving friendship) to the patient. In effect, she judged in favor of the loving friendship of an understanding heart. She allowed Oliver Wanglie to make the comfortable decision.

I am convinced that Ethically Responsible Creativity: Friendship of an Understanding Heart is an adequate model for contemporary bioethical decision making. It includes the consideration of relevant medical-ethical data, the application of the four basic principles, controlled as to denotation and the interpretation of ambiguous terminology by the appropriate decision maker.

When the patient is conscious, he or she, if competent, should be the ultimate decision maker.

When the patient is unconscious or in a persistent vegetative state, the physician, as friend *to chresimon*, yields the right to the family, as friends *to agathon* to make the final bioethical decision.

The control of the interpretation of clinical-ethical data as well as the denotation of all principles together with the individualized understanding of ambiguous terminology is placed in the substituted judgment of friends *to agathon*.

This model also entails that gays and lesbians who are friends of an understanding heart should be allowed to make bioethical decisions for loved ones who are no longer able to make decisions for themselves.

Friendship of an understanding heart is the core element of ethically responsible creativity and should prevail in determining who makes what bioethical decision.

NOTES

1. T.S. Szasz and M.H. Hollender, A Contribution to the Philosophy of Medicine: The Basic Models of the Doctor-Patient Relationship, *Archives of Internal Medicine* 97 (1956):585–592; G.C. Graber and D.C. Thomasma, *Theory and Practice in Medical Ethics* (New York: Continuum, 1969); R.M. Veatch, Models for Ethical Medicine in a Revolutionary Age, *Hastings Center Report* (1972); W.T. Reich, Narrative Bioethics: Some Comments for the SHHV Panel on Literature and Medicine, paper delivered at the SHHV Meeting, Memphis, Tennessee, November 20, 1992; P. Benner, Discovering Challenges to Ethical Theory in Experienced-Based Narratives of Nurses' Everyday Ethical Comportment, Chapter 43 above.

2. M.N. Sheehan, Technology, Older Persons and the Doctor-Patient Relationship, Chapter 41 above.

3. Cruzan v. Harmon, Jasper County, State of Missouri Circuit Court Probate Division, 1989; Cruzan v. Department of Health et al., 760-SW 2nd 408 (1990); Cruzan v. Director, Missouri Department of Health et al., 11o S Ct. 2841, 2855-56 (1990); Cruzan v. Harmon, final decision in favor of Cruzans (December 14, 1990); In Re Helga Wanglie, Fourth Judicial District Court, Probate Court Division, PX-91-283, Hennepin County, Minnesota; A.M. Capron, In Re Helga Wanglie, *Hastings Center Report* (1991):26–28.

4. K.D. Clouser and B. Gert, A Critique of Principlism, *Journal of Medicine and Philosophy* 15 (1990):219–236.

5. E.D. Pellegrino and D.C. Thomasma, *The Virtues in Medicine Practice* (New York: Oxford University Press, 1993). Perhaps in the ultimate analysis ERC is a virtue model.

6. Reich, Narrative Bioethics.

7. In my courses for medical and nursing students, I describe values as important physical, intellectual, spiritual, moral/ethical social considerations necessary in the framework of human existence. The list of values is open-ended, and the students have offered the following: life itself; personal quality of life; environmental, social, and global quality of life; evolving self; family; friends; society; government (structure and persons); internationalism; money; sex and sexuality; professional occupation; leisure; power (authority); religion (as permeating all values and preferences); education; democracy; patriotism; human freedom; principles of autonomy, nonmalfeasance, beneficence, benevolence, justice; law and order; ethnicity; race; cultural pluralism; love.

8. B. Chell, Competency: What It Is, What It Isn't and Why It Matters, *Medical Ethics: A Guide for Health Professionals*, edited by J.F. Monagle and D.C. Thomasma (Gaithersburg, Md.: Aspen Publishers, 1988), 99–108.

9. S.H. Miles, Medical Futility, Chapter 25 above; R. Truog et al., The Problem with Futility, Chapter 26 above.

10. The term *comfortable* refers to those decisions that cannot be said to be good or bad, right or wrong. This is not intended to establish an emotional tenderness that leads to mayhem; rather it brings to a resolution the conflict when both sides are *right and wrong* at the same time in the same case; R.S. Loewy, Relationships in Health Care Revisited, Chapter 40 above.

11. J.F. Monagle, *Risk Management: A Guide For Health Care Professionals*, (Gaithersburg, Md.: Aspen Publishers, 1985); A. Gruber, Social Systems and Professional Responsibility, Chapter 16 above. Gruber calls for more professionals and citizens to become participants in bioethical decision making.

12. For example, the Oregon Plan (disallowed by former President George Bush as discriminatory against the disabled and approved by President Bill Clinton provided that the discrimination is eliminated).

13. W.A. Atchley, Beyond Autonomy: New International Perspectives for Bioethics, taken from the brochure announcing the Third Annual Congress, International Bioethics Institute, April 16–18, 1993, San Francisco, California.

14. Nancy Beth Cruzan was age 30 when she suffered her

injuries in an automobile accident; she was married; Paul, her husband had the marriage dissolved within the first year after the accident. She was not totally brain dead; there was limited response to painful stimuli. See *U.S. Law Week*, June 26, 1990.

15. *U.S. Law Week*, June 26, 1990.

16. Monagle, *Risk Management*.

17. Cruzan v. Harmon.

18. Justices Brennan, Marshall, and Blackmun dissented. In their dissenting opinion, they wrote that "the parents interest is fundamental . . . the court failed to consider statements Nancy had made to family members and a close friend" (*U.S. Law Week*, June 26, 1990, 436).

19. L.R. Churchill, When Patients or Families Demand Too Much, Chapter 27 above.

20. M. Angell, The Case of Helga Wanglie: A New Kind of Right to Die Case, *New England Journal of Medicine*, 325 (1991):92–93.

21. In the *Cruzan* case, the U.S. Supreme Court questioned the right of autonomy of an incompetent patient: "This does not mean that an incompetent person should possess the same right (of autonomy) since such a person is unable to make an informed and voluntary choice to exercise that right or any other right" (*U.S. Law Week*, June 26, 1990, 419, footnote B).

22. Thomasma and Monagle, Hospital Ethics Committees, 397–407, note 8.

23. Monagle, *Risk Management*.

24. Clouser and Gert, A Critique of Principlism.

25. Aristotle, *Nicomachean Ethics*, translated by Martin Ostwold (New York: Bobbs-Merrill, 1962). I find an extraordinarily satisfying sense of completeness in Aristotle's treatment of the nature of friendship.

    BK VIII, 1156A, 10—to chresimon.

    BK VIII, 1156A, 12—to hedo.

    BK VIII, 1156, 6—to agathon.

    BK VIII, 1156, 13–17—"the other is worthy of affection because of the other's goodness in an unqualified sense" —friendship *to agathon*.

    BK IX, 1171A, 11—Love is an hyperbole of friendship.

    BK VIII, 1159B, 29–32—"friends hold in common what they have (hold)".

    BK IV, 1126B, 19–20: acquaintances and friendliness.

    BK VIII, 1156A, 15–21: no longer a useful friendship.

    BK VIII, 1155A, 2–5: friendship as excellence or virtue.

    BK VIII, 1155A, 14: friendship as virtue.

26. P. Ramsey, *The Patient as Person* (New Haven, Conn.: Yale University Press, 1970).

27. Aristotle, *Nicomachean Ethics*, note 25.

28. E.D. Pellegrino, Educating the Humanist Physician: An Ancient Ideal Reconsidered, *JAMA* 227 (1974):1290. This article is sensitive, scholarly, and insightful. It explains the two basic components: their meanings and importance in medical education. One component is cognitive; the other is affective. I am emphasizing the affective component in this chapter.

29. "We now live in an era in which the ancient and long-standing image of the physician as a benign authoritarian is intolerable to most educated people. Patients have the right to make choices among alternative modes of management in keeping with the values they conceive to be most important to them. The physician must understand the basis of the patient's value choices, respect them and work within their confines much more sensitively than ever before. In a matter so personal as health, the imposition of one person's values over another's— even of the physician's over the patient's—is a moral injustice" (Pellegrino, Educating the Humanist Physician, 1293).

30. Compassion as *philanthropia* "Compassion means co-suffering, the capacity and the willingness of the physician *somehow* to share in the pain and anguish of those who seek help from him/her . . . to see the situation as the patient does . . . to 'feel' along with the patient. When it is genuine, compassion is unmistakenly sensed by the patient and it cannot be feigned" (Pellegrino, Educating the Humanist Physician, 1290); M.N. Sheehan, Technology, Older Patients, and the Doctor-Patient Relationship, Chapter 41 above.

31. Pellegrino, Educating the Humanist Physician, 1290.

32. The lack of payment by the patient or family may be an expression of ethical or legal dissatisfaction with the physician's behavior, knowledge, or skill.

33. Aristotle, *Nicomachean Ethics*, D.C. Thomasma, The Ethics of Medical Entrepreneurship, Chapter 37 above.

34. Aristotle, *Nicomachean Ethics*, note 25.

35. Ibid.

36. Friendship of an understanding heart—the wisdom of Solomon. In "Narrative Bioethics," Warren Reich reflects on the parable of the Good Samaritan, a religious narrative that has also had an impact on secular culture. I hope that the wisdom of Solomon might be able to influence the behavior of health care professionals. Medicine is an inexact, fallible science, and no one has all the answers: "Oh Lord, my God, you have made me your servant, king to succeed my father David: but I am a mere youth, not knowing at all how to act. I serve you in the midst of the people whom you have chosen, a people so vast that it cannot be numbered or counted. Give your servant, therefore *an understanding heart* to judge your people and to distinguish right from wrong. For who is able to govern this vast people of yours?" (1 Kings 3:7–9).

37. C. Sabatino, Surrogate Decision-Making in Healthcare, *Real Property, Probate and Trust Law*, June 1992, 74–82; J.A. Menikoff et al., Beyond Advance Directives: Health Care Surrogate, *New England Journal of Medicine*, 327 (1992):1165–1169.

Index